Resourcing and Talent Management

Fifth edition

Stephen Taylor

The Chartered Institute of Personnel and Development is the leading publisher
of books and reports for personnel and training professionals, students,
and all those concerned with the effective management and development
of people at work. For details of all our titles, please contact the publishing
department:
tel: 020 8612 6204
e-mail: publish@cipd.co.uk
The catalogue of all CIPD titles can be viewed on the CIPD website:
www.cipd.co.uk/bookstore

Resourcing and Talent Management

Fifth edition

Stephen Taylor

Chartered Institute of Personnel and Development

Published by the Chartered Institute of Personnel and Development,
151, The Broadway, London, SW19 1JQ

This edition first published 2010
© Chartered Institute of Personnel and Development, 2010

Typeset by 4Word Ltd, Bristol

Printed by The Charlesworth Group

British Library Cataloguing in Publication Data
A catalogue of this publication is available from the British Library

ISBN 9781843982517

Chartered Institute of Personnel and Development, CIPD House, 151, The Broadway, London, SW19 1JQ

Tel: 020 8612 6200

E-mail: cipd@cipd.co.uk Website: www.cipd.co.uk

Incorporated by Royal Charter. Registered Charity No. 1079797

Contents

List of Figures and Tables

Resourcing and Talent Management

The content of this CIPD module is covered as follows:

Resourcing and Talent Management Learning Outcome	Resourcing and Talent Management Chapters
Analyse and evaluate the major features of national and international employment markets from which organisations source staff and ways in which these markets evolve or change.	Chapter 2: Employment Markets and Regulations Chapter 19: Resourcing Strategy Chapter 20: The Future of Work
Play a leading role in the development and evaluation of resourcing and talent management strategies, diversity management and flexible working initiatives.	Chapter 1: Introducing Resourcing and Talent Management Chapter 3: Flexibility Chapter 4: Fairness and Diversity Chapter 19: Resourcing Strategy
Manage recruitment, selection and induction activities effectively, efficiently, lawfully and professionally.	Chapter 6: Job Analysis and Job Design Chapter 7: Recruitment Advertising Chapter 8: Alternative Recruitment Methods Chapter 9: Employer Branding Chapter 10: Selection: The Classic Trio Chapter 11: Advanced Methods of Employee Selection Chapter 12: The New Employee
Undertake and evaluate long- and short-term talent planning and succession planning exercises with a view to building long-term organisational performance.	Chapter 5: Human Resource Planning Chapter 13: Succession Planning
Gather, analyse and use information on employee turnover as the basis for developing robust staff retention strategies.	Chapter 14 Measuring and Analysing Employee Turnover Chapter 15: Improving Employee Retention
Manage retirement, redundancy and dismissal practices fairly, efficiently and in accordance with the expectations of the law, ethical and professional practice.	Chapter 16: Retirement Chapter 17: Dismissals Chapter 18: Redundancy

Walkthrough of textbook features and online resources

LEARNING OUTCOMES

By the end of this chapter, readers should be able to:

● distinguish between tight and loose labour markets and advise about their implications for resourcing and talent planning

● develop appropriate policies and strategies to match labour market conditions

● advise on the attraction and retention of Generation Y workers

● advise on the legal principles governing activities in the fields of resourcing and talent management

● appreciate the relatively rapid evolution of employment legislation and its consequences for employing organisations

● participate in debates and consultation exercises concerning the future direction of employment regulation.

In addition, readers should be able to understand and explain:

● long-term developments in the UK employment market and prospects for the future

LEARNING OUTCOMES

At the beginning of each chapter a bulleted set of learning outcomes summarises what you can expect to learn from the chapter, helping you to track your progress.

KEY ARTICLE

'Regulating labour management in small firms' by Susan Marlow. *Human Resource Management Journal*, Vol. 12, No.3. pages 25–44 (2002)

This article reports the results of a qualitative survey involving interviews with the owners and employees of small businesses. They were asked about the likely future impact of what was at that time a good deal of new legislation. The findings are interesting because of what they have to say about the attitudes of small business owners to labour market regulation. The views of the employees are also interesting and somewhat surprising in respects.

Questions:

1 Why were the managers interviewed as part of this research unconcerned about new employment regulation?

2 In what ways did the managers say that the new regulation might have the effect of working against the interests of employees?

3 Why did the employees who were interviewed say that the new regulation would have little impact on them?

KEY ARTICLES

Current and thought-provoking academic articles from a range of sources, with accompanying questions, encourage in-depth analysis and critical thinking.

 IMPROVING BASIC SKILLS

EXERCISE 2.1

Read the article by Lucie Carrington entitled 'The Skills Equation' featured in *People Management* (23 August 2007, pages 24–28). This can be downloaded from the *People Management* archive on the CIPD's website (www.cipd.co.uk).

In 2006 the Leitch Report looking at the skills-base of the UK population was published. It concluded that far too great a proportion of the population lacked the basic literacy and numeracy skills required to sustain a career in the contemporary business world. The government responded with a White Paper in July 2007 entitled 'World Class Skills: Implementing the Leitch Review of Skills in England', separate responses being issued by

basic skills training to employees who have left school without a defined level of qualification. Some of the costs are shouldered by employers because time must be made available to employees for training purposes. This article looks at organisations which are committed to providing basic skills training of this kind.

Questions:

1 What methods are available to help employers move towards formal provision of basic skills training for employees?

2 Apart from improved skills, what other benefits accrue to employees who participate in these schemes?

EXERCISES

Take your understanding of a topic to the next level by tackling these in-chapter exercises, focused around articles from the CIPD magazine, People Management.

REFLECTIVE QUESTION

What do you think of these findings on new attitudes to work and the workplace among younger people? To what extent are they demonstrating an idealism that can be expected to fall away as they encounter career pressures later in life?

REFLECTIVE QUESTIONS

A number of questions in each chapter prompt you to reflect on what you have read, testing your understanding of important concepts and issues.

CASE SUMMARY

THE RBS GROUP

A good example of an industry that has recently been hit by a major discontinuity is the UK's banking industry. Take the example of the Royal Bank of Scotland (RBS). In 2005 it was the second largest banking group in Europe and one of the largest companies in the world. Until 2009 it was the second largest shareholder in the Bank of China, owning several other subsidiary companies across the banking and insurance sectors. It won many awards for its activities and was generally regarded

institution which soon proved to have been massively overvalued. The bank had also been heavily involved in trading sub-prime securities which caused it to lose a huge amount of money when their value collapsed.

In October 2008 RBS announced a loss of £28 billion, the largest ever recorded in UK corporate history, leading to a drop in its shares of 97 per cent (66 per cent in a single day).

CASE SUMMARIES

Case summaries throughout the text illustrate how key ideas and theories are operating in practice.

EXPLORE FURTHER

- Major developments in the UK employment market are covered in publications regularly published on the National Statistics website. Recent and future trends are discussed by Leitch (2006) in his report and by UKCES in regular publications on their website www.ukces.org.uk.

- There are several good introductions to employment law available. But because they tend to become out of date quickly, it is important to ensure that you read the latest edition. Lewis and Sargeant (2009) is published by CIPD. Lockton (2006), Willey (2009) and Taylor and Emir (2009) have also written good student-friendly introductions.

- Debates about employment law are rarely summarised succinctly in one place. Perspectives on labour law by Anne Davies (2009) provides the best general summary available. The major arguments against employment regulation are effectively advocated by the CBI (2000) and those in favour by the Institute of Employment Rights (2000).

EXPLORE FURTHER

Explore further boxes contain suggestions for further reading and useful websites, encouraging you to delve further into areas of particular interest.

ONLINE RESOURCES FOR STUDENTS

- Annotated weblinks – click through to a wealth of information online including examples of organisations with particularly innovative approaches

- Annual updates – keep up to date with the latest developments in resourcing and talent management

Visit www.cipd.co.uk/tss

ONLINE RESOURCES FOR TUTORS

- Lecturer's Guide – practical advice on teaching this text including feedback on the cases and questions

- PowerPoint slides – build your course around these ready-made lectures

- Key articles – additional articles with accompanying questions, for use in seminars and lectures

Visit www.cipd.co.uk/tss

CHAPTER 1

Introduction

LEARNING OUTCOMES

By the end of this chapter readers should be able to:

- define the terms 'resourcing' and 'talent management'
- distinguish between different kinds of organisational objectives which are met, in part, through resourcing and talent management activities
- establish criteria against which to evaluate decision-making in the resourcing and talent management field
- point out the different ways in which a resourcing or talent management specialist can 'add value' on behalf of an organisation
- outline different ways of thinking about strategy in the field of resourcing and talent planning.

In addition, readers should be able to understand and explain:

- the purpose of the resourcing and talent management function and the contribution it makes to the achievement of organisational goals
- the importance of administrative excellence as the basis for HR credibility and influence within an organisation
- the contribution effective resourcing and talent management can make to long-term organisation success.

 EXERCISE BOX: EXAMPLE

EXERCISE

Throughout each chapter of the book a number of exercises have been included in boxes such as this one. For the most part these are based on articles published in the CIPD's fortnightly journal *People Management*. If you are a student member of CIPD you will be able to access these articles directly through the Institute's website www.cipd.co.uk. You just need to follow the links provided to the *People Management* archive and use the search facility to locate the relevant article. If you are not a member of CIPD you can subscribe to *People Management* and gain access to the archive in the process, but you may well find that your college library subscribes and has both web-access and hard copies of recent editions.

EXAMPLE

A second feature that runs through the book is the inclusion at the end of each chapter of an activity based on recent, seminal or particularly thought-provoking articles published in academic journals. Many of these take a critical view of HRM practices. Wherever possible these articles have been selected from those that can be accessed via the online journals service operated by CIPD through its website (www.cipd.co.uk/onlineinfodocuments/journals), through the CIPD's 'virtual learning environment' or which are readily available electronically through most university libraries. In each case the article is briefly described and questions or an exercise are provided for you to complete while you are reading it. You will find exercises based on further articles on the website associated with this book.

RESOURCING AND TALENT MANAGEMENT

The CIPD through its 'professional map' and educational syllabus delineates resourcing and talent management as a distinct and coherent area of HRM. This book is intended to act as a guide to these management activities. Its aim is to introduce, explore and critically analyse them, in the process drawing readers' attention to the most relevant published research and opinion.

The CIPD's module outline for resourcing and talent planning sums up very concisely how this field is defined for the purposes of the Institute's Level 7 qualifications framework. This is the definition that we will use as the basis for the material covered in this book:

A major and fundamental objective of the HR function is the mobilisation of a workforce. Organisations can only function if they are able to assemble together teams of people with the necessary skills, attitudes and experience to meet their objectives. A further objective is then to retain effective performers for as long as possible. From time to time it is also necessary to dismiss people from organisations.

This module focuses on these activities, focusing not just on the practical aspects of recruitment, selection, employee retention and dismissal, but also on the strategic aspects. Skills can be sourced by hiring employees, but also through other means such as the employment of agency workers, subcontractors and consultants, or through outsourcing arrangements with other organisations. In order to mobilise an effective workforce organisations hire people from employment markets, which obliges them to compete for talent with other employers whenever demand for skills is greater than the available supply. Effective organisations thus develop a strategic approach to the attraction and retention of staff, analysing their key employment markets and gaining an understanding of their dynamics so as to enable them to compete more effectively both now and in the future. Indeed, planning to enable an organisation to meet its future demand for skills is an increasingly important HR role and is central to this module. As the skills that employers seek become more specialised, employment markets have tightened, leading to increased sophistication in the area of resourcing and talent planning. This is reflected in the increased use of proactive diversity management, employer branding, work-life balance initiatives and innovative approaches to job design which are covered in this module.

The module outline goes on to set out its key aims and principal learning outcomes as follows:

Module aims:

1 To equip learners with the knowledge and skills required to undertake core resourcing and talent management activities to a high standard. These include human resource planning, job design, recruitment, selection, induction, succession planning and dismissal.

2 To enable learners to analyse the employment markets from which their organisations source people with a view to developing attraction and retention strategies which are effective, efficient and fair.

3 To encourage learners to appreciate the need to promote flexible working and the diverse possible ways of meeting an organisation's demand for people.

4 To provide learners with knowledge and understanding about long-term developments in the UK's employment markets and demography with a view to planning to meet their organisations' likely future demand for people.

5 To provide learners with knowledge and understanding of major contemporary developments in the field of resourcing and talent management.

Learning outcomes:

On completion of this module learners will be able to:

1 Analyse the major features of the employment markets from which their organisations source their staff and ways in which these markets are evolving or changing.

2 Play a leading role in the development and evaluation of resourcing and talent management strategies, diversity management and flexible working initiatives.

3 Manage recruitment, selection and induction activities effectively, efficiently, lawfully and professionally.

4 Undertake long- and short-term talent planning and succession planning exercises with a view to building long-term organisational performance.

5 Gather and analyse information on employee turnover as the basis for developing robust staff retention strategies.

6 Manage retirement, redundancy and dismissal practices fairly, efficiently and in accordance with the expectations of the law and ethical and professional practice.

Resourcing and talent management activities form a major part of the generalist HR role. They are activities of relevance to all organisations which employ people because they aim to help meet some central, basic objectives:

STAFFING

Staffing objectives are concerned with ensuring that an organisation is able to call on the services of sufficient numbers of staff to meet its objectives. These people may be employed in a variety of different ways, but one way or another they must be able to carry out the tasks and duties needed for the organisation to function effectively. This is often summed up in the phrase 'Securing the services of the right people, in the right place, at the right time'. To achieve this, there is a need to recruit new employees, to retain existing employees and, on occasions, to dismiss others. In recent years the term 'talent management' has become widely used to describe the way that organisations increasingly manage these activities, along with the development of their people, in a coherent fashion. As a result, it is not unusual nowadays to read about the organisations pursuing defined 'talent management strategies'. Meeting staffing objectives is the core purpose of resourcing and talent management activity in organisations.

PERFORMANCE

Performance objectives pick up from the point at which the staffing objectives have been achieved. The aim here is to ensure that, once assembled, the workforce is absent as little as possible, and is well motivated and willing to perform to the best of its ability. To achieve this, there is a need first to monitor individual and group performance and then to develop means by which it can be improved. There are always two distinct areas of performance management activity. The first concerns the identification of sub-standard performance and measures taken to improve it. This can be focused either on groups of employees or on individuals. The second concerns policies and practices which have as their aim the maximisation of performance in a more general sense. In recent years the emphasis here has tended to be on managing people in such a way as to encourage them to demonstrate 'discretionary effort'. The most successful organisations are those whose people are sufficiently committed that they are prepared to work beyond the strict requirements of their contracts in order to help achieve the organisation's aims.

While resourcing and talent management, as defined in the CIPD professional map, does not encompass the detailed day to day management of employee performance, one of its aims is to support the achievement of superior performance on the part of individuals, teams and whole organisations. This is achieved by recruiting and selecting staff who have the capacity to perform well, by retaining them and through the effective management of procedures for dismissing poor performers. In a more general sense many resourcing activities, when managed well, serve to lift morale and commitment on the part of employees and hence contribute positively to the achievement of superior performance.

ADMINISTRATION

Administration objectives are concerned with ensuring that the employment relationships formed are managed efficiently, as well as in accordance with the law, professional ethics and natural justice. In order to achieve these aims consistently, it is necessary to write HR policies, to develop accepted procedures and to draw up other documents relating to the employment of individuals (eg: job descriptions, offer letters, contracts, and disciplinary warnings). Effective job and organisation design can also be cited as significant administrative activities. It is often argued that these kinds of activities represent a cost to organisations, amount to bureaucratic requirements and do not add value. While this is true of over-elaborate and unnecessarily unwieldy practices, it is not the case in more general terms. The truth is that the management of every organisation includes an administrative element. Carrying out those tasks more effectively and efficiently than others is, therefore, one way in which the HRM function contributes to the achievement of competitive advantage.

CHANGE MANAGEMENT

A fourth type of objective draws on elements of the first three but is usefully treated as being distinct in nature. This ensures that proper recognition is given to the significance of change in organisations and its effective management. Increasingly it is argued that we operate in a business environment which is subject to continual change. For many businesses it is no longer a question of managing a discrete episode during which change occurs, but managing processes through which organisations progressively evolve in terms of both their structure and culture. The resourcing function can act as an important 'change agent' through the mechanisms whereby it attracts, retains and motivates staff. Charles Darwin famously argued that the biological species that survive most effectively are not those which are strongest or most intelligent, but those which are best at adapting to change. The more volatile, competitive and unpredictable our business environment becomes, the more relevant this idea is to the world of employment. The organisations which develop the best capacity for flexibility are those which are best placed to seize opportunities as they arise.

DECISION-MAKING AND EVALUATION

If resourcing and talent management activities are to make a real, long-term contribution to the success of an organisation, it is insufficient simply to set out to achieve the above tasks and objectives. Because the environment is continually changing and developing, and because there are always other organisations with which it is necessary to compete, there is always a need to look for ways of improving the methods used to achieve fundamental resourcing objectives. In other words, there is a need regularly to review the policies and practices used in order to maximise the contribution of the resourcing and talent management function to organisational success. It is thus necessary to adjust or rethink the approaches used from time to time, with a view to meeting the requirements of new business circumstances. The objectives do not change, but over time the tools used to achieve them may do so, and to a considerable degree. Decision-making in this area is thus of long-term significance.

Organisations must also evaluate their activities, periodically if not continually, in order to establish whether or not improvements could or should be made to their policies and practices. Key skills thus include the development of a capacity for constructive criticism, as well as a knowledge and understanding of the various possible courses of action that could be taken in any given situation.

It is helpful, when formally evaluating specific resourcing policies and practices, to think about them with three basic questions in mind:

- Are we achieving our objectives as effectively as we could?

- Are we achieving them as efficiently as we could?

- Are we achieving them as fairly as we could?

These three broad criteria (effectiveness, efficiency and fairness) underpin much of the evaluative material included in this book. Where the literature indicates that a variety of different approaches is or can be used to tackle a particular set of resourcing objectives or problems, each of the major options is assessed and its merits considered against the backdrop of different environmental circumstances and with these three basic considerations in mind. Courses of action are thus evaluated not in isolation but in comparison with other possible approaches. This reflects what has to happen in practice. Perfection is rarely possible: what is important is that the best approach is taken when compared with other options. It is also often necessary to compare taking action in a particular field with the results of not taking action, or with the approaches used by competitor organisations.

 REFLECTIVE QUESTION

Which resourcing activities does your organisation formally evaluate on a regular basis? What are the main criteria used?

ADDING VALUE

It is always important to remember that many organisations, including some which are large and successful, find it possible to manage quite happily without employing HR specialists. In many others the function is responsible purely for the accomplishment of basic administrative tasks or is outsourced altogether and devoid of any meaningful influence on the direction of organisational policy. Although we may consider ourselves and our function to carry out indispensable work, other managers often see things rather differently. Unless we are perceived clearly to add value to the organisations we serve, no future existence can be assured and we rapidly find ourselves to be disrespected and lacking in credibility. Much of this book is thus concerned with pointing out the ways in which professionally qualified HR specialists, working through resourcing and talent management activities, can add value for their organisations. The alternative is a function which represents little more than a 'cost' on an organisation's balance sheet.

'Adding value' is a term which is used more often than it is clearly understood. What does it actually mean in practice? The answer lies in three separate types of contribution: delivering business objectives, providing an excellent administrative service and acting as a champion for effective people management.

DELIVERING BUSINESS OBJECTIVES

The most important way in which resourcing and talent management activities add value is by playing a significant role in the achievement of strategic objectives. Key business objectives change over time, often for reasons wholly outside the control of managers. An organisation which is expanding one year may find itself needing to contract substantially in the next. Indeed many organisations nowadays find that they are both contracting and expanding at the same time as one part or area of activity prospers while another flounders. Either way, resourcing activity is central to maximising the extent to which the objectives are met effectively, efficiently and fairly. Expansion requires proficient recruitment and selection of new employees. It also requires the development of staff retention practices that minimise avoidable turnover of valuable people. It also usually requires attention to be given to job analysis and the organisation of work so as to maximise the efficiency with which staff are deployed once recruited. Resourcing practice is also central when an organisation, or part of an organisation, contracts. The aim here is to shed staff in as professional and inexpensive a way as possible, while minimising the damage done to long-term business prospects. Badly handled downsizing programmes not only cost a great deal more than is necessary (often at a time when the financial situation is tight), they also have a knock-on effect on the morale, commitment and performance of surviving staff and can have a profoundly damaging effect on an organisation's image in the wider world.

Organisational performance is another key component of many business strategies. The aim is continually to improve the quality of products and services or to maintain standards which have already been achieved. Frequently this has to be strived for in the face of stiff competition from other organisations and despite tightening cost constraints. Here too the resourcing function can play an important role. Cost-effective recruitment and selection of people who are able to meet performance expectations is a way in which value is added. Once hired, the need is to ensure that the individuals concerned are managed appropriately so that they are willing, as well as able, to perform to expected levels. In tight labour markets particularly, where individuals can leave with relative ease, a sophisticated approach to the management of performance is required. Here HR specialists work together with line managers to develop approaches which maximise the chances of success.

Effective change management is frequently required in order to ensure that business aims are met. However, it is often carried out incompetently by managers who are inclined to give people management considerations a low priority. Whether the change sought is essentially structural or cultural in nature (or both), the chances are that objectives will be met less effectively or not met at all without the contribution of HR professionals focused on employment implications. Managing people's expectations is important here as is proper employee involvement. Above all there is a need to manage the process sensitively with an eye to the long-term future. The alternative is a demoralised workforce which has little trust in those appointed to lead it and is inclined to look for jobs with competitor organisations should the opportunity arise. The result for the organisation is a failure to realise the advantages planned for the change, or more commonly, avoidable expenditure.

ADMINISTRATIVE EXCELLENCE

The idea of HR functions supporting the achievement of business objectives has received such prominence in recent years that readers might be forgiven for considering it to be the only way in which the profession can add value. This is not the case. Helping to achieve business objectives is an essential part of the role, but it is insufficient on its own. Resourcing and talent management specialists also have tasks to achieve which may be less glamorous and more mundane, but which are equally important.

Whether we like it or not, it is important to recognise that all organisations need to be managed. They do not and cannot run themselves. The larger and more complex the organisation, the more administrative activities of one kind or another are necessary. Moreover, because organisations compete with others (or in the case of the public sector are answerable to taxpayers), there is an imperative to achieve these necessary administrative activities as effectively as possible and at the lowest possible cost. Because much administrative activity is the responsibility of HR people, carrying it out with maximum effectiveness and efficiency becomes a potential source of competitive advantage for the organisation. The HR function thus adds value by ensuring that these tasks are achieved to a higher standard and more cost-effectively than competitors.

There is a great deal of resourcing and talent management activity which falls into this category, the major examples being the following:

- human resource planning
- job analysis
- developing competency frameworks
- undertaking supply and demand forecasting
- drawing up job descriptions, person specifications and accountability profiles
- administering recruitment and selection procedures
- training managers to recruit and select effectively

- drawing up contracts of employment
- managing induction processes
- issuing statements of terms and conditions of employment
- maintaining succession plans
- advising line managers and senior managers on matters relating to employment law
- managing dismissal processes effectively, fairly and lawfully
- carrying out exit interviews with leavers
- processing documentation when someone leaves
- managing redundancy programmes
- handling retirements properly
- drawing up and reviewing policy across all these areas of activity.

There is also another reason for striving towards administrative excellence. It is essential that this work is carried out professionally and competently if the function, and its managers, are to gain and maintain credibility within the organisation. If this is not achieved they will not be listened to by other managers and stand no chance whatever of gaining sufficient influence to participate in the direction of wider organisational decision-making. Administrative excellence is a prerequisite for more ambitious aims such as those described above in the context of the achievement of strategic objectives, and those discussed below.

ACTING AS A CHAMPION FOR PEOPLE MANAGEMENT

In recent years a great deal of robust research evidence has been published showing the existence of clear links between effective people management practices and business success. Writers disagree about the precise nature of these links and their magnitude in terms of statistical significance, but most now agree with the claim that organisations which are good at managing their staff increase their chances of achieving long-term competitive advantage in their industries (see Boselie *et al* 2005 for a review of this literature). However, despite the published evidence and the inherent logic underlying the proposition, it remains the case that many managers are unconvinced about its validity. Their scepticism is often hidden behind a general adherence to statements about the importance of people to organisations, but is nonetheless demonstrated in their actions. Again and again HR specialists find that their priorities are not shared by their bosses who are more inclined to focus on short-term financial objectives and on devising means of enhancing effective management control over their organisations. This does not occur because chief executives and other senior directors are incompetent or unscrupulous, but because they are required to answer first and foremost to shareholders and government ministers whose interest is often short-term financial gain or the achievement of savings. These are matters with which HR specialists must be concerned, but they also have a particular responsibility to argue for the very real contribution effective people management can make to the achievement of financial success over the longer term.

This is not to say that all organisations, whatever their financial or labour market position, must put in place 'gold-plated' resourcing and talent management policies and practices. It does not make good business sense for all organisations to seek to be 'employers of choice' or to invest more than all their competitors in the most expensive human resource systems that the market has to offer. However, there remains a need for HR people continually to explain and demonstrate the worth of effective people management practices to a somewhat sceptical audience. If they don't no one else will, and the result is likely to be lost opportunities and, over time, loss of competitive advantage. It is really a question of playing the role of advocate for people management and seeking to ensure that staffing considerations are taken into account when business decisions are being taken. Value is only added if HR professionals are able to remind other managers of the potential impact their actions can have on employee satisfaction, staff turnover rates, performance levels, the incidence of absence and the organisation's reputation in its key labour markets.

REFLECTIVE QUESTION

To what extent do you think the P&D function in your organisation 'adds value'? How would you go about demonstrating that this was the case?

EXERCISE BOX: MAKING A DIFFERENCE

EXERCISE 1.1

Read the article entitled 'survival strategy' featured in *People Management* (28 October 2004, pages 46 and 47). This can be downloaded from the *People Management* archive on the CIPD's website (www.cipd.co.uk).

This article consists of an exchange of letters or e-mails between two senior HR professionals, Neil Hayward of Serco, a large private sector company, and Hilary Douglas, who is responsible for HR at the Treasury. They are discussing the future of the HR function in their different sectors, with a particular focus on the ways in which the function can 'make a difference' in organisations.

Questions:

1 Which of the four main areas of resourcing activity identified above are cited in the article as being of particular importance now and in the future? Why do you think this is the case?

2 In what ways do you think people resourcing activities need to be organised and managed in order to achieve Hilary Douglas's vision of 'falling costs and rising value – a winning combination'.

3 Write a short list of the key points on which the two authors agree and those where there is some disagreement or difference of emphasis. To what extent can their differences be explained by the fact that they work in different sectors?

OPERATIONS AND STRATEGY

A substantial portion of the resourcing and talent management field is concerned with necessary operational matters. It is about achieving the day to day, nuts and bolts basics of HRM as effectively as possible. This is reflected throughout this book, many chapters dealing with operational issues. You will read, for example, about how to develop formal human resource and succession plans, about how to analyse and re-design jobs, about the different methods of recruiting and selecting people, how to analyse and measure employee turnover, how to improve employee retention rates and about fair and effective methods of handling dismissals, redundancies and retirements. These are core professional activities which organisations always expect HR people to carry out efficiently, effectively and lawfully. They are, in many organisations, the prime reason that an HR function exists.

However, the book also gives attention to the development of resourcing and talent management strategy. We deal with this issue directly and fully in Chapter 19, drawing together ideas that have been developed earlier in the book and setting out some of the theories that have been advanced about strategy-making in this field. However, it is necessary at the start to introduce this subject so that you can develop your thinking about it as you study. This also allows an opportunity to introduce our first major area of debate, because there is no general agreement about what exactly constitutes 'a resourcing strategy', 'a talent management strategy' or even 'a resourcing and talent management strategy'. There are different perspectives on this and different ways of defining the terms. Broadly it is possible to identify four distinct viewpoints:

1) A military-type perspective

At the most basic level we can define 'resourcing and talent management strategy' as simply meaning that a broadly strategic approach is taken to the management of the core activities outlined above. It is helpful here to use a military metaphor and to think about a battle. In order to win, an army needs to employ effective tactics, reacting to events in an appropriate way, deploying its resources effectively and generally ensuring that each soldier is both willing and able to play their designated role. These are operational matters. In addition though, to win a battle there needs to be an effective underpinning strategy. Senior officers are charged with developing this, establishing from the start what the core aims of the exercise are, how success or failure will be measured and how the best outcome can be achieved. In developing strategy there will be major fundamental choices to be made, such as where to position different divisions, where best to attack and at what time and how to make the best use of weather and topographical conditions. Sometimes the choices about these matters will be difficult and finely balanced. In making such decisions, as far as possible, army generals step back and look at the battlefield with a cool head and from a distance. The term 'taking a helicopter view' is often used in this context.

A similar type of perspective can be taken about resourcing and talent planning activities, particularly when a defined project or initiative is to be planned and executed. While a 'muddling through' kind of approach can be adopted where there is little overall direction and no clear aim or benchmark against which to evaluate, it is preferable to take a strategic perspective. Hence if an organisation is expanding and is embarking on a recruitment drive, the most effective approach is to start by thinking through the aims. What kind of people do we want to recruit? How should they be different from those we have recruited in the past? What attributes are essential and desirable for the people we recruit to have? How much money is available to spend? Having decided on the aims, the next step is to survey the range of possible recruitment tools that are available and make a decision about which will best help to meet those aims. A planned approach is then taken to implementing the strategy, involving the allocation of tasks to team members and ensuring that they have the equipment, resources and training required to play the allocated role. There also needs to be formal evaluation after the event so that lessons can be learned for the future.

In the same way, a strategic approach can be taken to an HR planning exercise, an employee retention initiative or the management of a redundancy programme. However, more generally and irrespective of whether or not a discrete project is identified, organisations are likely to improve their performance and achieve greater efficiency if a broadly strategic approach is taken to the management of resourcing and talent generally. It should be possible to articulate a clear recruitment strategy, for example, an employee retention strategy and a strategy on retirement matters. The same process of addressing fundamental questions is used. What are the aims? What are the constraints? What are the different options available within our budget? What are the advantages and disadvantages associated with each? Operational decisions then flow from these.

2) An alignment-focused perspective

A second way of defining 'strategy' in respect of resourcing and talent management is to use as a starting point the organisation's overall business strategy. This is the way that most academic researchers and consultants have tended to view HR strategy in recent years, the core idea being that it should be derived from, support and clearly align with the strategic aims of the organisation. The term 'business model' is sometimes used nowadays to describe the overall strategic direction an organisation takes and which differentiates it from its competitors.

So, for example, an organisation's strategy might be to provide low cost services to its customers at a basic level of quality. It makes only a very limited amount of profit on each sale, but has a strong financial position because of its large sales volume. This is the business model followed by fast food chains, by the low cost airlines and by online retailers. Their appeal to the consumer is value for money. What does a resourcing and talent management strategy look like if it is aligned to such a business strategy? First and foremost there needs to be a firm lid kept on costs, so wage budgets are kept under tight control. Pay and conditions are set at the minimum level practicable in order to attract and retain competent staff. There are, in addition, centralised bureaucratic systems established allowing little local discretion for managers in terms of how people are managed. Standard policies are followed across the organisation so that economies of scale are maximised as far as administration is concerned. An alternative is an organisation which aims to compete, primarily on the basis of the quality of its services. Margins are larger, but so are customer expectations. Such a strategy requires, above all, the maintenance of high levels of customer satisfaction. So discretion is given to local managers, and to staff too, so that they are in a position to respond quickly to individual customer demands. As far as staffing is concerned the requirement is to attract and retain people of superior ability, which means following 'best practice' approaches to the recruitment and selection process. A range of sophisticated approaches will also typically be used to try to retain and motivate good, experienced performers. It would be appropriate if such a strategy was followed for the organisation to try to achieve 'employer of choice' status, by which is meant an organisation which people want to work for because it is so well managed from an HR perspective.

In Chapter 19 the concept of strategic alignment is explored in greater depth, examples being examined of some of the key strategic tools and models that have been developed with a view to assisting managers to get the best out of people.

3) A future-oriented perspective

A third way of thinking strategically about resourcing and talent planning is to focus on the environment in which organisations operate and, particularly, on the more predictable long-term trends which have an impact on resourcing activity. This involves looking ahead and taking action in plenty of time so that your organisation is as well-placed as possible to source the required skills and the number and quality of people it requires in the future.

A lot of the material in this book takes this kind of perspective, particularly chapters 2, 5, 13 and 20. These concern long-term trends in the labour market, human resource planning, succession planning and more general debates about the likely future evolution of workplaces and HRM. Inevitably when a future focus is taken it is impossible to be certain about what will happen. As is pointed out in Chapter 5, the unexpected has a habit of occurring and destabilising what were previously confident expectations. But this need not stop organisations from making plans. In fact, the more uncertain the environment the more important it is to think about the future and to engage in sound, evidence-based strategic planning. The key is to think in terms of multiple scenarios and to undertake 'what if?' analyses based on what we know could happen and what we think probably will happen. Future planning can also be flexible, so that as time progresses plans can be adapted and redefined as necessary.

In Chapter 2 you will read about long-term labour market trends. Some aspects are predictable with some confidence, particularly demographic trends. There is no question, for example, that the UK population is ageing at a rapid rate and that we will soon face a situation in which more people are retiring each year, while fewer are coming into the labour market in their late teens and early twenties. The overall population of the country is not falling, and short of some major unforeseen geo-political shock occurring, the world economy is going to continue growing (along with its population) for some time to come as developing countries industrialise. There is thus every reason to anticipate growing demand for labour on the part of organisations. We can therefore predict with some confidence that, all else being equal, many labour markets in the UK are going to tighten considerably over the next twenty years. This will have a serious impact on the ability of organisations to recruit and retain staff and will inevitably affect the methods they employ to do so. The tightening is likely to be made worse as a result of another predictable environmental trend, namely the rapid increase in demand for skilled staff in general and for people with specialised skills and experience in particular. The growing professions are mainly of this type, and yet the rate at which the working population is acquiring these skills is already too slow to enable supply to meet demand. The need to cut public expenditure in order to pay off the debts built up by the government in the first 10 years of the twenty-first century makes it less likely that upskilling can proceed at the same sort of rate that has been achieved in recent years. This second very predictable trend in the resourcing environment compounds the first.

At the same time as employment markets tighten, it is plausible to predict that the next 10 or 20 years will also see increased globalisation of economic activity and an acceleration of technological innovation. That has happened strongly over the past 50 years and there are no reasons to expect any change of direction over the long-term. The result is increased competition for all organisations in the private sector and many in the public sector too. Consumers will become more demanding, the more choice that becomes available to them.

The result, from a resourcing and talent management perspective, is likely to be reduced budgets and a need for managers working in the field to be able to demonstrate that their activities are adding value.

EXERCISE BOX: WILLIAM HILL

EXERCISE 1.2

Read the article by Steve Smethurst entitled 'Onto a Winner' featured in People Management (29 January 2004, pages 35 and 36). This can be downloaded from the People Management archive on the CIPD's website (www.cipd.co.uk).

The article describes the major environmental pressures that drive and constrain the P&D function at the William Hill chain of betting shops.

Questions:

1 What are the major environmental developments which are determining the change in direction of William Hill's business strategy?

2 What are the major implications for resourcing and talent management activities?

3 In what ways is the company's freedom for manoeuvre constrained by other developments in its business environment?

4) An employment market perspective

The fourth and final way that we can conceptualise a resourcing and talent management strategy is to focus very much on an organisation's particular employment markets and on its capacity to recruit and retain the staff it needs. In other words we can focus entirely on the capacity of an organisation to recruit and retain effectively. In Chapter 19 you will read about this type of activity in greater detail and about models that can be used as tools to help develop strategies for competing in employment markets. For now it is just necessary to flag up this kind of thinking and to introduce it as a theme that runs through the book.

The focus here is on tight labour markets. Where there are no skills shortages of any consequence and where recruiting and retaining people is unproblematic, there is no compelling need for organisations to think strategically about how to compete for staff. It becomes an issue when the market is tight and many employers are competing with one another to attract and then to hold on to good performers, in critical roles, whose skills are relatively rare. In such circumstances resourcing and talent planning activities become central to an organisation's ability to meet its objectives, and hence a need develops to formulate and execute strategies designed to compete for people more effectively than other organisations.

The key point to appreciate is that achieving and maintaining this successfully requires sustained activity over a long period of time. The need is to build up steadily an organisation's reputation as an employer, and this is not something that can be done overnight. Furthermore, it requires an organisation to differentiate itself from its labour market competitors in clear ways, so that would-be employees have a clear idea about what it offers them over and above the offerings of others. This means that decisions about terms and conditions of employment, job design, management style and, especially, recruitment practices take on a strategic quality. They have to be managed carefully, over a period of years, in such a way as to bolster the organisation's reputation as an employer in positive ways. In Chapter 9 you will read about employer branding and about other ways that resourcing and talent management specialists can borrow techniques and ideas long used in the marketing function and apply them to the business of competing effectively for staff.

INTEGRATION WITH OTHER P&D ACTIVITIES

It is important to remember that the term 'resourcing and talent management' is an invention of the CIPD. Its purpose is to serve as a means of delineating the management activities described above from those covered by the other CIPD elective subjects that make up its qualifications scheme and professional map such as employee relations, reward management, performance management and training and development. In practice there is no real barrier between these different areas of activity and none should be created, even where each is the responsibility of a different manager. Activity in the resourcing and talent management field often has an impact on that in the other areas and vice versa. Moreover, solutions to problems are frequently to be found through the agency of 'joint actions' drawing on thinking and practice from more than one specialist area. Some examples are as follows:

- A skills shortage can be eased through resourcing activities (eg: better recruitment, more effective retention, better deployment of skilled staff), but also hugely benefits from intervention on the training and development front.

- Activities in the development, reward and relations fields are significant in their ability to underpin job satisfaction. They thus play a major role in reducing staff turnover and making an employer a more attractive proposition for potential employees.

- The effective introduction and utilisation of talent management initiatives are also matters which affect collective employment relationships and are thus a concern of employee relations specialists.

- Poorly introduced initiatives in the resourcing field (eg: changed contractual terms or redundancy programmes) often have very profound employee relations implications.

- The effectiveness of the training and development function has important implications for human resource planning and succession activity and is central to the effective induction of new employees.

Many other examples could also be cited to illustrate the futility, and indeed danger, of seeing resourcing activity as discrete or being undertaken in a theatre which is in some way distinct from the other major HR functions. In practice the lines between each is blurred. It is important to remember this when analysing the likely effectiveness of a future resourcing intervention and when evaluating existing organisational practice.

EXAMPLE

'Strategic Choice and Organisational Context in HRM in the UK Hotel Sector' by Nick Wilton (2006). *The Service Industries Journal*, Vol. 28, No. 8. 903-919

In this article Nick Wilton discusses approaches to the management of people in the hotel industry in the South West of England. He reports the results of an extensive questionnaire survey and follow-up interviews with managers in hotels of different shapes and sizes. He concludes that for the smaller hotels there is little choice available about the HR strategy that they pursue. They are obliged through circumstances to follow a low cost approach and to accept high staff turnover and recruitment problems result from this. Larger hotels, however, do have a choice. Some follow the low cost road, but others have sought to develop longer-term strategies that seek to recruit good people and retain them over time.

Questions:

1 Why is the hotel industry so prone to suffer from high staff turnover and skills shortages?

2 What stops managers in most hotels from addressing these problems strategically by adopting more sophisticated resourcing and talent management practices?

3 What factors in the business environment have made it possible and desirable for some hotels to take a different approach and to develop longer-term resourcing strategies?

KEY ARTICLE BOX

CHAPTER 2

Employment markets and regulation

LEARNING OUTCOMES

By the end of this chapter, readers should be able to:

- distinguish between tight and loose labour markets and advise about their implications for resourcing and talent planning

- develop appropriate policies and strategies to match labour market conditions

- advise on the attraction and retention of Generation Y workers

- advise on the legal principles governing activities in the fields of resourcing and talent management

- appreciate the relatively rapid evolution of employment legislation and its consequences for employing organisations

- participate in debates and consultation exercises concerning the future direction of employment regulation.

In addition, readers should be able to understand and explain:

- long-term developments in the UK employment market and prospects for the future

- major developments in attitudes to work and their implications for resourcing and talent management

- the reasons for the development of employment regulation in the UK

- the major areas of law that impact on resourcing activities and their consequences

- the major strands of the arguments for and against further employment regulation.

EMPLOYMENT MARKET CONDITIONS

Resourcing and talent management, like other HR activities, must focus on supporting the organisation in achieving its core product market objectives. However, this can only be accomplished through successful competition in its labour markets. The use of employees as a means of achieving particular organisational goals is no more than an aspiration if it is not possible, in practice, to find people of the required skills and attitudes who are prepared to work at the rates and in the conditions which the organisation is able to provide. Resourcing specialists thus have to be as interested in what is happening in their labour market environment as they are in the wider commercial environment.

The geographical extent of an employment market can vary considerably. For most jobs and for most of the time the scope is limited to a local area. Economists focus on 'travel to work areas' by which they mean the people living within a commutable distance of the workplace. This marks the boundary for most jobs simply because they are not as well paid or exciting in career terms so as to attract people from further afield. When a workplace is located in the middle of a large city, the travel to work area will include within it hundreds of thousands of potential staff. In more remote rural areas the figures are much smaller. Generally speaking, the higher paid a job is and the greater its prospects, the further people will be prepared to commute, and hence the larger the travel to work area/employment market for that type of position. In the case of more highly paid jobs, the labour market is national in its scope. These are roles which are sufficiently remunerated and prestigious enough to attract applications from all over the country. The more senior jobs in larger organisations fall into this category as do many better-paid professional roles. But some less well-paid positions are also commonly filled from a national market. Graduate recruitment rounds, for example, operate nationally as a rule, along with other jobs that are predominantly filled by younger staff who are more mobile, have fewer domestic ties and are thus able to move around the country in search of good career opportunities. In the case of the highest paid jobs of all, employment markets are international, jobs being advertised all over the world. This is true of the top positions in the financial services industry, in medicine and in sport. There are, however, some international labour markets in areas of work which are relatively low paid. Hotels and restaurants are one example, academia is another. These are industries which employ large numbers of overseas staff who are interested as a means of improving their earning power, building up their work experience or seeking to experience living in the UK for a period

Labour market conditions vary considerably over time and across different types of employment. A 'tight' labour market is one in which employers are obliged to compete fiercely to secure the services of the people they need. This state of affairs arises when there are fewer people looking for jobs than there are jobs available; in other words, when demand for labour outpaces supply. Some labour markets are always tight, whatever the prevailing economic conditions, because the skills required are relatively scarce. In recent years the major examples have been in the IT and sales professions, where really effective people have tended to be in short supply. By contrast, when people are in plentiful supply, labour markets are characterised as being 'loose'. Such situations are a great deal easier to manage from a resourcing perspective. Vacancies are easy and cheap to fill quickly, while managers have to tread less carefully in the way they treat staff because there are fewer alternative job opportunities for dissatisfied employees to take up. This is not to say that staff can be treated badly, as doing so will tend to demotivate them and lead to poorer performance, but there is less of an imperative to ensure that individuals are satisfied with their employment. How tight or loose a labour market is thus determines how much money needs to be spent on wages and benefits, on recruitment budgets and on employee development. The tighter the market, the more money needs to be spent on recruitment and on wages in order to attract sufficient numbers of good applications when vacancies arise. It is also more costly to retain staff, hence the need to provide development opportunities in order to encourage good people to stay.

However, it is not just a question of money, important though that is. Other things matter to staff and would-be staff too. They want to find their work rewarding in the widest sense of the word, they usually want to be involved in decision-making, to be treated courteously and to have a good work-life balance. The tighter the labour market, the more alternative job opportunities there are for people and the greater the need for an employer to work on improving these other aspects of the employment relationship and the quality of the workplace experience.

In practical terms, when tight labour market conditions prevail for a period the result is skills shortages. The tighter the labour market, the more acute the skills shortages. In such circumstances employees enjoy a degree of market power. If they are unhappy in their jobs they can readily find another. Their employers know this and so take steps to ensure that as far as possible they enjoy job satisfaction.

By contrast in loose labour markets there is a surplus of people with the skills required to do the jobs which are available. This means that large numbers of people apply for the jobs that are advertised and that the employer enjoys much greater power. Employees have to accept developments they do not like, because they have no alternative and also, potentially, fear the consequences of resisting.

COMPETING IN A TIGHT LABOUR MARKET

What are the practical consequences for organisations of tightening labour markets? The answer is a reduction in the number of people with the required attributes looking to work in the jobs which are available. This means that it becomes progressively harder to find new recruits and that good people, who have the skills which are most in demand, are more likely to leave their current employment in order to work for another organisation or to set up their own businesses. Because it also alters, however subtly, the power balance within organisations, people who are hard to replace are less easily controlled by management. They are in a position to demand greater autonomy over their own areas of work, more flexibility, better working conditions and more developmental opportunities, in addition to competitive rates of pay. This has an impact on the means used to achieve performance and change management objectives, as well as those related to staffing. Resourcing policies and practices have to reflect employee interests as well as those of the employer, while more care has to be taken over the manner in which people are treated by their managers. People who can, if they wish, resign and find another job elsewhere, are less likely to put up with arbitrary and iniquitous treatment than is the case when alternative career opportunities are few and far between. There is, therefore, a general effect on the whole portfolio of resourcing activity – consequences that need to be taken on board if organisations are going to compete effectively for key staff. However, the major immediate impact of tightening labour market conditions is in the staffing arena. Here several alternative approaches need to be developed and pursued:

- Recruitment initiatives. Employers can allocate a greater budget for recruiting staff by designing more sophisticated advertising and seeking to ensure that it has greater reach. They can also look to recruit people from outside their customary sources. Some of the best known recent examples have been in the NHS, where recruiters have looked overseas in a bid to meet their specialist staffing needs. Efforts have also been made to lure back into work people who have previously left for family reasons or to take early retirement.

- Retention initiatives. When labour markets tighten employers can work harder at retaining the staff that they already employ. The key here is understanding why people leave and then acting accordingly. The main approaches used are described in Chapter 12. They include attitude surveys, exit interviews and surveys of former employees. People resign from jobs for a wide variety of reasons, so employers are foolish to make any rash assumptions.

- Reorganisations. A third response to skills shortages is to reorganise job tasks among existing staff in such a way as to reduce the extent of dependence on hard-to-recruit groups. The term 'skill mix review' is used frequently to describe this process. The aim here is to ensure that people who are in greatest demand (normally those with the rarest skills or qualifications) spend 100 per cent of their time doing what only they are qualified to do. Other activities (eg managerial or administrative) should be carried out by support staff who are easier to recruit.

- Development initiatives. The fourth response involves developing home-grown talent rather than seeking to buy it in 'ready made'. This takes rather longer to achieve and can be the most expensive approach, but should form part of a longer-term strategy for tackling skills shortages. The approach simply involves employing people who do not have the requisite skills and experience, and then giving them the opportunity to gain them.

MANAGING PEOPLE IN LOOSE LABOUR MARKET CONDITIONS

From an HRM perspective managing staff in loose labour market conditions is much less problematic. Recruiting and retaining strong performers is not a problem, because there is surplus labour in the market looking for job opportunities. This means that HR can be carried out safely without employing too many sophisticated approaches. People can, in short, be told what to do, rather than having to be persuaded. It means that organisations can be run very efficiently and that steps can be taken over time to extract greater productivity by pushing people harder.

These types of management responses are common when labour market conditions loosen, but it can be persuasively argued that they are short-sighted.

This is particularly true when an employment market is loose temporarily and may well tighten in the future. Treating people in a way they perceive to be poor or unfair can then backfire when market conditions change, leading good, experienced performers to leave as soon as they get the opportunity. More generally though, treating people less well than they expect to be treated by an employer has other, more immediate negative consequences. Staff will tend to be less engaged, less enthusiastic about their work and less inclined to put effort in. They may minimise their contribution, perform to the minimum acceptable standard or even sabotage management initiatives. Low trust, adversarial employment relations also tend to develop.

 EXERCISE BOX: IMPROVING BASIC SKILLS

EXERCISE 2.1

Read the article by Lucie Carrington entitled 'The Skills Equation' featured in *People Management* (23 August 2007, pages 24–28). This can be downloaded from the *People Management* archive on the CIPD's website (www.cipd.co.uk).

In 2006 the Leitch Report looking at the skills-base of the UK population was published. It concluded that far too great a proportion of the population lacked the basic literacy and numeracy skills required to sustain a career in the contemporary business world. The government responded with a White Paper in July 2007 entitled 'World Class Skills: Implementing the Leitch Review of Skills in England', separate responses being issued by devolved governments elsewhere in the UK. Several of the initiatives suggested involve employers working with government agencies and funding bodies to provide

basic skills training to employees who have left school without a defined level of qualification. Some of the costs are shouldered by employers because time must be made available to employees for training purposes. This article looks at organisations which are committed to providing basic skills training of this kind.

Questions:

1 What methods are available to help employers move towards formal provision of basic skills training for employees?

2 Apart from improved skills, what other benefits accrue to employees who participate in these schemes?

3 What are the major advantages for employers?

THE UK EMPLOYMENT MARKET

Conditions in the UK labour market overall vary depending on the position of the economy, the number of people with the skills that people are looking for and levels of unemployment. The years following the end of the 1989–92 recession saw a steady, year on year tightening of labour markets in the UK as unemployment fell to the lowest levels for a generation. Economic confidence grew and there was an increase in the variety of career opportunities open to individuals. Labour market conditions still varied considerably with different lines of work, and there remained areas of the country in which unemployment was high and job opportunities few, but by and large the late 1990s and first years of the twenty-first century were good for employees with skills that were in demand, and consequently tougher for employers wanting to recruit the best available people.

The position changed when the UK economy, like most others in the western industrialised world, went into recession again in 2008 and 2009. Unemployment rose as businesses retrenched and closed operations, while business confidence fell leading to the creation of fewer new jobs. At the time of writing (2010) the economy is growing again, but the level of the national debt is high. The expectation is that the next few years will see a slow recovery and a steady fall in unemployment as the public sector cuts back on jobs and freezes recruitment, while private sector organisations slowly start to expand again. Despite relatively high levels of unemployment, particularly among younger people, there remain skills shortages in some areas of work. UKCES (2010) estimate that around 20 per cent of employers are still finding it very difficult to fill skills gaps.

Over the longer term, looking five to ten years ahead it is likely that the number of skills gaps will grow as employment markets tighten. It is also likely that we will see the development of a greater divide between the markets for skilled and less skilled workers. The case for anticipating such a scenario can be developed by looking at the long-term underlying trends in the employment market – those which continue despite the short-term ups and downs of the economy.

DEMAND FOR LABOUR

The long-term trend in the UK is towards increased demand for labour. As the economy has grown over the past 60 years, so has the number of jobs and workers. Table 2.1 shows the statistics for people of working age, defined as being men aged 16 to 65 and women aged 16 to 60.

Table 2.1 People in work in the UK 1971–2010

	Employed	Economically active
1971	24.6 million	25.6 million
1976	24.8 million	26.1 million
1981	24.7 million	27.0 million
1986	24.7 million	27.8 million
1991	26.7 million	28.9 million
1996	26.0 million	28.4 million
2001	27.6 million	29.1 million
2006	28.7 million	30.3 million
2008	29.3 million	31.5 million
2010	28.9 million	29.8 million

From these figures it can be seen that the number of people working dips during recessionary periods (early 1980s, 1990s and 2008–10) but that over the long term the trend is upwards. There are some four million more jobs in the UK economy than in the early 1970s and around five million more economically active people of working age. This is a significant trend which has occurred despite millions of job losses during recessions, the introduction of labour saving technologies across most industries, the exporting overseas of many jobs and the wholesale restructuring of the UK economy. There is thus every reason to think that the next 10 years will see further growth in demand for labour too, and that is what the major research reports commissioned by the government suggest will happen (eg: Leitch 2006, UKCES 2010).

But what type of jobs will these be? Here too there is widespread agreement, although some debate over terminology. The long-term trends point strongly towards an increase in the proportion of jobs which are higher-skilled. Table 2.2 shows how the type of work that we do has changed since 2001. Here we see a continuation of trends that go right back to the 1950s, namely growth in the proportion of people employed to do higher-skilled jobs and falls in the proportion employed to do relatively low-skilled work. Between 2001 and 2008 the number of managerial, professional and technical jobs grew by some two million, while the number of jobs in the administrative, skilled trades, operative and elementary categories fell by around one million.

Table 2.2 Occupational groups in the UK 2001–2008

Occupation	% in 2001	% in 2008
Managers & senior officials	12.9	15.2
Professional occupations	11.7	12.9
Associate professional & technical occupations	13.2	14.6
Administrative & secretarial	14.9	12.6
Skilled trades	9.5	8.2
Personal services	7.5	8.6
Sales & customer services	8.6	8.5
Process, plant & machine operatives	8.7	6.9
Elementary occupations	13.2	12.4

UKCES (2010:7–9) examines the 20 fastest growing and 20 fastest contracting professional groups in the UK between 2001 and 2009. Their analysis includes an estimation of 'the predominant qualification level' (PQL) held by people working in these professions. It is notable that of the 20 fastest growing professions over half have a PQL at degree level. By contrast only one of the fastest contracting professions (quality assurance technicians) is dominated by people with degrees. All the others require a more elementary education. Research carried out on behalf of the Leitch review of skills in the UK (Beavan *et al* 2005) projects forward the likely scenarios to 2020. The median projection concluded that UK employment levels in 2020 would be 2.3 million higher than in 2004, and that all the net growth would be at the higher skilled level. In other words, they projected an overall decline in lower skilled jobs. Leitch (2006) himself in his final report estimated that around 40 per cent of all jobs in the UK after 2020 will require holders to have a degree level education.

On the question of likely future demand for labour we can thus conclude with some confidence that more people will be required by employers and that the growth in employment opportunities will very much be focused on people with higher level skills and education. This is not surprising when the changing structure of the economy is considered. The growth industries are finance, business services, health, education and some private services. Sectors such as mining, ship building, agriculture and lower-technology manufacturing are all in long-term decline. Jobs in these sectors have effectively been exported to other countries where labour is readily available at much cheaper rates. We are thus increasingly becoming a knowledge economy, in which people make their living by making use of knowledge and expertise. As Coats (2009:109) concludes:

> There will be relatively few jobs that require brawn alone; workers will need to live by their wits.

SUPPLY OF LABOUR

Looking at longer term trends in the supply of labour it becomes clear that employment markets, at least as far as the more skilled jobs are concerned, are very likely to tighten as the next decade unfolds. There are a number of good reasons for making this prediction. Three separate factors are all contributing to an overall fall in the number of people who will be willing and able to take up such jobs in the future. First is the retirement of the so called 'baby boom generation'. This term refers to people born in the 20 years following the end of the second world war, a generation that is considerably larger than those that precede and proceed it. Between 1945 and 1964 a total of 17.6 million babies were born in the UK, an average of 880,000 each year. This group have been in our labour market over the past 40 years, but are now starting to retire. Labour supply is likely to tighten, however, because there are considerably fewer people in the following generations. There were 16.1 million births between 1965 and 1984 and only 14.8 million between 1985 and 2004.

Another trend that points to tighter markets is female participation, defined as the proportion of women who are economically active. This currently stands at 75 per cent which is high by historic standards. Back in the 1950s fewer than half of women were in paid employment. The number increased rapidly through the 1970s and 1980s, but has since stagnated. This major source of labour that has helped supply to meet demand in labour markets over the past few decades thus appears to have gone almost as far as it can go. Participation rates among men are only just over 80 per cent. Between 2010 and 2020 the state pension age for women will rise to 65 in stages. This will increase the number of women who are classed as being of working age, but it will only have a limited impact on the total number of women in the labour market. This is because many women who are over 60 are in employment in any event, while others will be able to afford to retire at 60 irrespective of whether the state pension is available to them. In any event, the raising of the education leaving age to 18 in 2015 will remove from the working age population more people than join it as a result of the raising of the female state pension age.

The third trend is less clear. This is overseas immigration which has largely been responsible for allowing the supply of labour to meet demand, thus easing skills shortages, over recent years. A majority of the jobs that have been created over the past two decades have been filled by people who were born overseas and have moved to the UK. There are serious question marks over whether these kinds of rates of net immigration will continue in the future. The issue has become politically problematic, leading the government to introduce new rules from 2008 limiting the ability of UK employers to recruit from outside the European Union. Doing so is now a great deal more costly and administratively cumbersome than it was. We can thus conclude that the number of skilled workers from outside the EU is likely to decline or at least stabilise in future years. Government regulations cannot prevent people coming to work in the UK from within the EU, although it is likely that temporary restrictions will be placed in the future on people from new member states. However, there are good grounds for anticipating a reduction in this source of labour supply too. The reason is demographic trends in most of the countries from which UK employers have recruited in the past – Spain, Italy and Eastern European countries in particular. Here birth rates are very low. Couples are now having fewer than 1.3 babies, pointing to a substantial population fall over the next 20 years. As a result in the near future there are going to be many fewer European citizens available to work.

There are also good reasons to doubt that the stock of skills available in the UK labour market will be high enough to meet demand over the coming two decades. The Leitch Report (2006) branded the UK's educational performance as 'mediocre' by international standards. Around 25 per cent of our population is currently educated to degree level or above. This is a reasonable number compared with other industrialised countries, but it falls well short of the 40 per cent that Leitch believes will be sought by employers in 2020. More and more young people are going to university each year, but not in sufficient numbers to allow this looming skills gap to be filled. The real problems though lie at lower levels of educational attainment. The UK compares badly with other countries here, leaving us with a rather greater proportion of poorly educated people than is the case elsewhere. Leitch (2006) points out that five million adults of working age in the UK (16 per cent) lack basic literacy skills, while 21 per cent lack basic numeracy skills. Employers also report problems recruiting people with the social skills they need to undertake the growing number of jobs which involve face to face dealings with customers. There are thus very real potential problems ahead as far as skills are concerned. They may be eased as a result of new government programmes aimed at raising skill levels among adults, but it is difficult not to foresee major skills gaps evolving in the near future.

WHAT WILL THIS MEAN FOR RESOURCING AND TALENT MANAGEMENT?

The major implication of these long-term developments will depend on the type of labour market an organisation is competing in. The analysis appears to point to a situation in which markets for higher-skilled people and for 'knowledge workers' in particular get a great deal tighter, while markets for lower-skilled staff get considerably looser. This is because at the higher level there are likely to be more jobs available than there are people to fill them (ie: skills gaps) while at the lower level there are going to be many more people looking for work than there are jobs available. We are thus likely to see increased variation between different types of organisation in terms of how they approach resourcing and talent management activities.

Where organisations are primarily seeking lower-skilled staff there will be little need for a sophisticated approach to be taken. Recruitment costs will be low and there will be little or no need positively to 'sell' jobs and no big problem retaining effective workers provided they are treated fairly in broad terms. The main problem is likely to be deciding how to deal with large numbers of applications from people seeking opportunities when jobs are advertised. On the other hand, where higher skills are sought, which will be the case for more and more organisations the opposite will be the case. Employment markets are likely to tighten considerably, while more and bigger skills gaps will open up. This will mean that recruitment and retention activities rise right to the top of the HR agenda and that the resourcing and talent management function gains greater significance and a higher profile. It will mean that HR managers who wish to specialise in these areas of work will be in demand and will play a bigger role than they currently do. They may also be able to command higher salaries. But their job will be harder than it is currently because it is going to become tougher to recruit and retain the staff that are needed. The problem will be compounded by the likely increase in the degree of competitive intensity across most sectors (see Chapter 1) which will restrict the extent to which skills shortages can be addressed by raising wages. The upshot is that more sophisticated approaches to resourcing and talent planning are likely to be adopted. Examples are discussed at length later in the book, but it is reasonable to predict that employer branding (Chapter 9), succession planning (Chapter 13) and advanced selection methods (Chapter 11) will be used more than they are at present. Formal resourcing strategies are also likely to be adopted (see Chapter 19) along with policies aimed explicitly at retaining high performers (Chapters 14 and 15). Another major development will be a widening of the recruitment pool for many organisations. They are increasingly going to have to fish for their talent in waters that they do not commonly visit at present. Because the average age of the working population will increase over time, there will be fewer opportunities to employ young people with a view to training them and securing many years' return on that investment. Employers will be obliged either to compete a great deal harder to secure the services of young workers, or accept that they need to resource their organisations from other sources. HR policies will have to be adjusted in order to attract people of an older generation into jobs that have traditionally been filled by school leavers or graduate recruits (see Chapter 16), while we can anticipate more overseas recruitment and the development, at quite senior levels, of teams made up of people from a variety of cultural backgrounds (Chapter 4). Providing people with high quality, well-designed jobs and flexible working conditions will become increasingly necessary in order to recruit and retain successfully.

EXERCISE BOX: MAKING A DIFFERENCE

EXERCISE 2.2

Read the article by Katie Hope entitled 'Scots Missed' featured in *People Management* (13 October 2005, pages 16 and 17). This can be downloaded from the *People Management* archive on the CIPD's website (www.cipd.co.uk).

Across the UK as a whole the population is now rising rapidly, principally as a result of increased migration from overseas. However, the increases are heavily concentrated in south-east England. Other parts of the country continue to see alarming falls in population levels, not least because so many people are drawn towards

London early on in their careers. This article focuses on the response to this issue of the devolved government in Scotland.

Questions:

1 How are Scottish employers tending to address the issue of skills shortages at present?

2 Why is this approach unlikely to provide a viable long-term solution?

3 What longer-term approaches is it argued should be considered?

ATTITUDES TO WORK

Another factor for resourcing specialists to take into account is the possibility that the attitudes of future generations towards work, careers and employment will evolve and be different from those of past and current generations. It is impossible to predict what will happen here with any degree of accuracy, because generational attitudes are to a large extent shaped by the life experiences that members of each generation face. As yet we cannot know what the major factors shaping the views of today's children will turn out to be. We cannot be certain if they will in fact be markedly different in any way from those of their parents and grandparents. Nonetheless it is possible to put forward an informed opinion and to speculate with some degree of confidence about likely developments. For example, we can draw on the limited evidence that is available of prevailing attitudes among those coming up through schools and universities, and who have graduated relatively recently (see Zemke et al 2000, Pollock & Cooper 2000, Sparrow & Cooper 2003, Brown *et al* 2007 and Twenge & Campbell 2008). It is important to be wary of generalisations and important to accept that no one set of beliefs or perspectives is shared by an entire generation. Nonetheless it would seem that the members of 'Generation Y' or the 'nexters' as they are variously called (people born after 1980) tend to share some views in common which are relevant to the workplace and differ to an extent from those of other generations. Some of the most frequently made points are as follows:

- ease with and acceptance of ongoing technological change
- strong intolerance of intolerance in respect of minority groups
- a wish to achieve a greater work-life balance than their parents managed
- a commitment to ethical practices (eg environmental concerns) and an attraction to ethical organisations
- a global perspective (ie not European)
- a resistance to tight systems of control and bureaucratically imposed rules
- greater ease with insecurity than previous generations
- a consumer-like perspective on work which expects satisfaction and 'shops around' for a new job when dissatisfied.

If these findings are correct, and the attitudes do not change as this generation ages and takes on domestic responsibilities, there are important messages for organisations seeking to recruit and retain its members. First we can predict that employees in the future will be less accepting of management prerogative than has been the case in recent decades. There is a possibility that this will herald renewed interest in trade unionism, but the strong individualistic streak picked up by researchers working in this field suggests that a more common form of protest will be to resign and look for work elsewhere. Employers will thus have to get used to a world in which employees are less predisposed to be loyal and less easily bought with pay and perks. Bad management will lead to recruitment and retention problems, and it will be progressively harder to shed an unethical reputation once gained. Hand in hand with less loyalty, goes less respect for management and a greater tendency to question. This suggests that the organisations that are most successful in resourcing terms in the future will be those with flat hierarchies, decentralised power structures and democratic cultures. Tolerance of alternative lifestyles and needs arising outside the workplace are also likely to be essential features of successful future organisations.

While employers will probably have to take greater care than they have to date in promoting an acceptable workplace culture, they are likely to have fewer problems in the future securing acceptance of structural and technological change. Generation Y appear to be a great deal more relaxed about this than their parents were and still are. It will be easier for organisations to reinvent themselves, to merge with others and to restructure as and when required by their business environments. Ongoing change is seen as part of life by the younger generation and is thus less likely to be greeted with suspicion. On the other hand of course, there are disadvantages for employers as the same 'relaxed attitude' to change will mean that employees in the future are more likely to switch jobs or even careers than their predecessors. The price to pay for greater acceptance of organisational change is thus higher staff turnover and an inability to rely on traditional mechanisms of staff control. In short, people in years to come are likely to be less attached to their jobs and workplaces, as well as less concerned about their likely future prospects in any one organisation.

REFLECTIVE QUESTION

What do you think of these findings on new attitudes to work and the workplace among younger people? To what extent are they demonstrating an idealism that can be expected to fall away as they encounter career pressures later in life?

EXERCISE 2.3

EXERCISE BOX: TARGETING THE OLDER GENERATION

Read the article by Roger Trapp entitled 'Older and Wiser' featured in *People Management* (23 December 2004, pages 40 and 41). This can be downloaded from the *People Management* archive on the CIPD's website (www.cipd.co.uk).

This article focuses on the experiences of two companies operating in different sectors (B&Q and Barclays Bank) who have helped to resolve staff shortages by employing older people.

Questions:

1 Aside from skills shortages, what other factors might lead employers to target older workers in their recruitment campaigns?

2 What evidence is presented of the business advantages associated with employing older people?

3 The article debunks some common myths about the employment of older workers, suggesting that they are often better employees than younger colleagues. How far do you agree with this view? What genuine disadvantages could you cite?

INTRODUCING EMPLOYMENT REGULATION

There can be no question that one of the most significant current developments in the HR business environment is the growing volume of regulation which governs employment markets and the employment relationship in the UK. Much of the most significant recent law (eg on working time, data protection and age discrimination) originates in European Union institutions and thus applies across all 25 member states, but a good deal more has a UK origin (eg the national minimum wage and family-friendly measures). Employment law has moved in 20 years from being perceived by lawyers as something of a 'poor relation' to a major area of practice attracting top legal brains. Over 80 different types of case can now be heard by Employment Tribunals (Shackleton 2005) to which must be added the various claims that are brought to the county courts in the fields of health and safety and breach of contract. As more opportunities are given to people to pursue legal actions against their employers, more choose to take them up. While the figures vary somewhat from year to year, it is clear that the total number of claims processed annually by the Employment Tribunal Service is now three, or even four times what it was 10 years ago, and that these are tending to be more complex and to cover more issues than used to be the case (Employment Tribunal Service 2009).

Employment law is a relatively recent development as far as the UK is concerned. Until the 1960s, with the exception of regulations outlawing the exploitation of children, some basic health and safety rules and the limited protection provided by the common law, employers were able to manage their organisations without the limitations that are now imposed through statute. Managers could dismiss staff as and when they pleased, could require them to work whatever hours were deemed necessary, and were in no way restrained by the law if they wished to discriminate against women or members of the ethnic minorities. Indeed it was common to have separate pay scales for male and female employees.

For many employees this unregulated world of work meant a life of insecurity and, in some cases, thorough exploitation. But for the majority this was not the case because trade union membership was high and a good majority of staff worked in unionised environments. They were thus covered by national-level collective agreements which operated across whole industrial sectors, and to which all organisations in those industries signed up. The same approach remains in place to an extent in the public sector today, most staff still being employed on nationally-agreed terms and conditions which cover everyone in particular professional groups.

Protection from abuse of power on the part of employers was thus effectively provided through non-legal mechanisms. This voluntarist system of industrial relations had evolved over decades and appears to have suited both employers and trade unions reasonably well, but it was very different from the traditions of active state involvement that were being developed in other European countries at the same time. Whereas in the UK the way that workplaces operated vis-à-vis employees was almost exclusively determined with reference to contracts of employment, negotiated collective agreements and informal arrangements developed through custom and practice, elsewhere on the continent labour codes created and enforced by government agencies had become the norm.

Over the past 40 years the UK's situation has changed to a very considerable extent. The first major reform came in 1965 with the introduction of statutory redundancy payments and a fledgling industrial tribunal service to enforce the new law. Henceforth staff could not be laid off without a minimum level of compensation being paid by their employers at a level determined by Parliament. The 1970s then saw the introduction of unfair dismissal law, equal pay legislation, and protection from discrimination at work on grounds of sex and race. Health and safety regulation was also greatly extended at this time and protection introduced for employees whose organisations were taken over by or merged with others. During the 1980s the pace of law making in the employment field slowed down as the Thatcher government sought to fight off the demands of those who argued for greater levels of protective regulation. Recessionary conditions and high unemployment would remain, it argued, if additional costs and regulatory burdens were placed on businesses. What was required were incentives for organisations to employ people and to attract investment into the UK from foreign firms. Instead attention was given to reforming the trade unions through the development of a regulatory regime that they had to comply with and by taking steps which reduced their ability to organise lawful industrial action.

The past 15 years have seen a reversal of this position. The trade union laws have largely stayed in place, but we have also seen a substantial increase in the extent to which the individual employment relationship is subject to state-imposed regulation. 1995 saw the introduction of disability discrimination law, and 1998 the establishment of a national minimum wage, working time regulations and comprehensive data protection law. In subsequent years we have seen protection introduced for part-time workers, people employed on fixed term contracts and measures outlawing discrimination on grounds of sexual orientation, religion and age. Maternity rights have been vastly extended and rights for fathers, parents of young children and carers of disabled adults introduced for the first time. There are now circumstances set out in law in which an employer must recognise a trade union, and others in which employers are required to consult with workforce representatives about a broad range of management issues. In short, we have moved a very great distance from a voluntarist regime towards one which has a great deal more in common with the 'codified' approaches of our continental neighbours.

There are no straightforward answers to the question of why the UK has seen such a transformation in the nature and extent of employment regulation in a single generation. The process has not been a planned one and progress continues to be made in a piecemeal, step-by-step fashion. No grand overarching strategy on the part of any government can clearly be identified. However, it is interesting to note how rarely a piece of regulation has been repealed by an incoming government with different priorities from its predecessor. Once in place, employment law appears to be very difficult to displace, suggesting that there is a broad level of agreement among the electorate in favour of the regulatory structure that has been steadily erected. Despite the lack of any single dominant explanation, it is possible to identify a number of factors that have contributed significantly to this transformation:

- UK membership of the European Economic Community (EEC) and now the European Union (EU) has clearly played a major role. A great deal of the employment legislation originates in Europe and would probably not be on our statute books were it not for our membership of the EU.

- The decline in trade union membership and activism the country has witnessed over 25 years has also played an important part. As collective bargaining structures have been dismantled and the numbers joining unions have fallen, new institutional arrangements have had to be put in place to

EXERCISE 2.4

EXERCISE BOX: HISTORICAL ROYAL PLACES

Read the article by Elizabeth Davidson entitled 'A break with tradition' featured in *People Management* (10 July 2003, pages 38–40). This can be downloaded from the *People Management* archive on the CIPD's website (www.cipd.co.uk).

The article begins by describing the action taken by managers of some of London's major historical tourist attractions to ensure that their organisation complied with new and existing employment law. It goes on to report more generally about the rapid growth of consultancies and training arms of law firms whose role is to brief managers about the evolving law.

Questions:

1　What combination of circumstances caused Historical Royal Palaces to alter their established approach to ensuring legal compliance?

2　Why do you think that this organisation has a particular incentive to ensure that it does not breach employment legislation?

3　To what extent do you agree with the final comment in the article: 'There is a whole new generation of employees who know their rights. They know what they can do and what they are entitled to. That can only be a good thing.'

ensure that people are protected against unfair treatment and undue health risks while they are at work. In many important respects employment law thus now fills this gap. Indeed, one of the major reasons for the introduction of unfair dismissal law was the aim of reducing the number of strikes that were precipitated when employers were perceived to have fired someone unjustly (Davies and Freedland 1993: 199–200).

- Government economic policy has also played an important role in helping to shape employment regulation through the decades and continues to do so. In the 1980s the focus was on using legislation to tame trade union power so as to boost UK productivity and the capacity of the economy to change in response to emerging global industrial trends. By contrast, in the past two decades a major driving force behind employment regulation has been the government's desire to encourage people to 'come off welfare and into work'. To that end various regulatory changes have been made which remove barriers which act to deter people from entering or (in the case of mothers with small children) from returning to the workforce.

- The growth of employment regulation can also be viewed in a far wider perspective – as just one of the many areas of national life which have become regulated or which have seen an expansion of their regulatory regimes in recent years. It is not only the employment relationship that has seen its traditional 'voluntarist' nature dismantled in recent decades. The same kind of processes have occurred in the professions, in the City of London (see Moran 2003), in the world of pensions, and more generally across most industry sectors. Everywhere informal, locally established ways of running institutions have been replaced since the 1970s with new formalised structures which impose standard rules on everyone, and help ensure that institutions are accountable for their actions and open to far greater public scrutiny.

- Finally, it is very reasonable to assert that plain political expediency has also played a part. Much of the regulation that has been introduced has been politically popular either in a general sense or among particular constituencies which governments have needed to court in order to gain electoral advantage. This was true of the anti-union measures introduced by the Thatcher governments, of the Disability Discrimination Act introduced by the Major government, and is true of much of the employment protection legislation brought onto the statute books by the Blair and Brown governments.

REGULATION AND RESOURCING AND TALENT MANAGEMENT

Employment law plays an increasing role in influencing resourcing and talent management policies and practices. In some respects it restricts what employers can do without risking legal action being taken against them. Unfair dismissal law is a good example, its purpose being to help ensure that employees are not dismissed for a good reason or in an unfair manner. Other regulations serve to raise employment standards, their purpose being to promote good practice and hence to encourage employers who want to maintain a good reputation to push standards up even higher. This is true, for example of the many new family-friendly statutes that have been passed in recent years.

Two important areas of employment law are discussed at length later in this book. Discrimination law is outlined in Chapters 4 and 16, and dismissal law in chapters 17 and 18. There is thus no need to say more about them at this stage except to flag up their general significance for resourcing and talent management activities. Other areas of relevance are not covered extensively elsewhere, so these need to be introduced here.

THE LAW OF CONTRACT

The law of contract forms part of the common law. It is thus largely judge-made and has not been created through Acts of Parliament. It is, however, no less important for that and must be taken account of in decision-making on resourcing matters. The key points are as follows:

- Employers need to be aware that a contract of employment is only established when there has been a clear, unambiguous and unconditional offer made and a clear, unambiguous and unconditional acceptance received. In addition there must be an intention to create legal relations and some form of consideration (eg wages) made to bring it into existence.

- In principle contracts cannot be changed unilaterally by one party. An employer wishing to make significant changes must first secure the agreement of the employees concerned. Where this is not forthcoming they need to consider making the change financially attractive or, where there is no alternative, dismissing and rehiring on new terms. The latter course leaves open the possibility of an unfair dismissal claim. It is thus best to include in all contracts of employment one or more flexibility clauses giving the employer the right to make reasonable changes from time to time.

- Once a contract of employment is established it confers duties on both parties. Both henceforward owe a duty of mutual trust and confidence to one another. In addition the employer owes a duty of care along with several others, while the employee owes a duty of fidelity and the duty to exercise reasonable skill and care. If either side breaches one of these implied terms of contract, it can lead to breach of contract proceedings or can form the basis of a constructive dismissal claim.

There are a number of practical consequences for employers. First, care must be taken to ensure that the employees' understanding of what constitutes the key terms of their contracts matches what the employer believes their contracts to contain. This is best achieved through the existence of written statements of terms and conditions which are given to new employees before they commence their jobs. It is not necessary to issue everyone with a formal, written contract of employment extending to many pages. A simple offer letter accompanied by a basic summary of the key terms is all that is required. This helps to create certainty and should ensure that accusations of breaches of contract do not occur.

Secondly, it is essential that employers explicitly build into the contracts that they offer employees a degree of flexibility. In other words, one of the terms of the contract needs to give the employer the right to make reasonable changes to terms and conditions from time to time in order to meet business requirements.

Thirdly, it is important that everyone who undertakes a supervisory role is provided with basic training on the law of contract, and in particular on the issue of implied terms. The majority of managers in the UK remain blissfully unaware of the existence of such law and its potential significance, and it is this ignorance which leads to situations in which employees (and more commonly ex-employees) find themselves with a strong legal claim to pursue.

FAMILY-FRIENDLY STATUTES

Recent years have seen the introduction of a range of new rights designed to make it easier for people with family responsibilities to combine these with a career. In addition, we have seen the extension of existing rights, notably the provisions for statutory maternity leave and pay. It is beyond the scope of this book to describe or evaluate these in any detail, but it is important that readers appreciate the extent of the rights that now exist and will exist in the near future. They are significant from a resourcing point of view because they provide rights for employees to be away from the workplace for much longer than has been the case historically. Aside from the need to administer such matters professionally, resourcing specialists also need to build assumptions about take-up of these rights into their human resource planning activities. The upshot is a need to hire more people to work on a temporary or casual basis (to cover absences), to increase staffing generally and to think more openly than has been the tendency to date about job-sharing arrangements and the possibility of allowing much more flexible working. The key areas of law that fall into this category are the following:

- the right to maternity leave/right to return
- the right to maternity pay
- the right to unpaid parental leave
- the right to time off to care for dependants
- the right to paid paternity leave
- the right to request flexible working.

This is an area of law in which employees' rights have improved very considerably over time in incremental steps. New rights and extensions of existing rights are introduced every two or three years. At the time of writing (2010) the government is proposing to extend the period of ordinary maternity leave (ie the period of paid leave to which all employed mothers are entitled) from nine months to 12 months, and to permit part of this to be taken by fathers instead should that be the preference of the couple concerned.

 REFLECTIVE QUESTION

How far do you agree with these proposals for the extension of family-friendly law? From an employer's perspective what would be the major advantages and disadvantages?

WORKING TIME

The Working Time Regulations were introduced in 1998 and have been amended twice since then. The regulations are complex and have been heavily criticised for lacking clarity. The major rights they include are as follows:

- a working week limited to a maximum of 48 hours (averaged over 17 weeks)
- four weeks paid annual leave per year (in addition to bank holidays)
- a limitation on night working to eight hours in any one 24 hour period
- 11 hours rest in any one 24 hour period
- an uninterrupted break of 24 hours in any one seven day period
- a 20-minute rest break in any shift of six hours or more
- regular free health assessments to establish fitness for night working.

There is currently a right for employees to opt out of the 48-hour week, and it remains lawful for employers to require that such a step is taken as a condition of a job offer. However, less known is the existence of a right to opt back in again without suffering any kind of detriment. There is a considerable question mark over whether the right of employees to 'opt out' of their rights under these regulations will survive into the long-term future.

Working time is clearly central to human resource planning and to the organisation of work generally. Hitherto, because of the opt-outs, the lack of clarity about some terminology and the lack of an effective policing regime, many employers have found themselves to be affected by these regulations only to a limited degree. This could well change in the future if the UK is required by the EU to accept forms of regulation that have long been standard in many other European countries.

CONFIDENTIALITY ISSUES

A range of new regulations have been introduced in recent years that affect the use of information in the workplace. The Public Interest Disclosure Act 1998 and The Telecommunications (Lawful Business Practice) (Interception of Communications) Regulations 2000 deal respectively with the rights of 'whistle-blowers' and of employers to snoop on their employees' phone calls and e-mails. A third piece of legislation, The Data Protection Act 1998, is of greater direct relevance to resourcing activities. This is because it sets out to prescribe what kinds of information can be held on employee files and for how long. It also gives employees rights of access to information held on them. The Act covers paper records and information which is held electronically, so it should determine how an organisation uses data held in a computerised personnel information system. The Act requires organisations to appoint a 'data controller' to take responsibility for this area of activity. Typically this person will be a P&D specialist. It is best understood in terms of eight 'data protection principles' which data controllers are obliged to observe:

i personal data should be processed fairly and lawfully

ii it should be collected for specified purposes and used accordingly

ii it should be adequate, relevant and not excessive for the purpose proposed

iv it should be accurate and up to date

v it should not be kept longer than is necessary

vi it must be processed in accordance with the rights of employees

vii it must be safeguarded against unlawful processing, accidental loss, damage or destruction

viii it must not be transferred to a country outside the European Economic area – unless that country has equivalent rights.

The Act gives workers the right to see any files kept on them, to receive copies of the data held and to correct inaccurate information. Employers are required only to process personal data which is 'necessary' and 'justifiable' and must only keep it for as long as is strictly necessary. Adequate security measures must also be taken. Stricter rules apply to 'sensitive data', such as information that relates to people's ethnic origins, religious beliefs, health records or past criminal convictions. This cannot be kept or processed without the employee's express consent. Fines of up to £5,000 can be levied for breaches of the Act.

In 2003 in the case of *Durrant v Financial Services Authority* the Court of Appeal appeared to cut down the scope of the data protection legislation by a large measure. In considering what classes of information could be described as being 'personal data' and thus disclosable under the Act the Lords of Appeal concluded that data is not 'personal' unless it *focuses* on the person concerned. This clearly narrows the number of documents that can be defined as comprising 'personal data' very considerably. Time will tell exactly what types of personnel data are and are not covered by this ruling, but it would appear to restrict it to documents/records which have an individual as their focus.

DEBATES ABOUT EMPLOYMENT REGULATION

MICRO-DEBATES

It is not at all difficult to find fault with many individual pieces of employment legislation. Those representing employee interests or those who come to the debate from a social democratic or marxist perspective tend to argue that measures 'do not go far enough', while employer associations and those who take a liberal or conservative perspective are typically to be found arguing that business is now over-regulated and that individual statutes 'go too far'. Hence, for example, unfair dismissal law is criticised both for favouring employers and for making it too difficult to dismiss under-performing employees. Data protection legislation can be criticised for being backed by inadequate sanctions and thus being too easy for employers to ignore, but also for being a wholly unnecessary set of regulations that create red tape and give employees rights they have no real interest in having. The law of indirect discrimination can penalise employers who have absolutely no intention whatsoever of discriminating unfairly against an individual, but can also be criticised for providing a defence which allows employers to justify practices which have the effect of perpetuating sexual and racial inequality. However, there are some areas of employment regulation that are generally agreed to function badly and several types of criticisms that are made by protagonists from all sides of the debate:

- It is argued that some employment law fails to meet its own objectives in practice. It is thus both burdensome from an employer point of view and ineffective when seen from the perspective of the employee. Equal pay law is a good example. Despite its being on the statute books for over 30 years now, women's hourly rates of pay remain only 82 per cent of those enjoyed by men. Female part-time workers earn only 63 per cent of the male full-time rate – a figure which has hardly narrowed at all since 1970 and is also widening.

- Some employment law is very badly drafted leaving much uncertainty about whether or to what extent it applies in particular situations. Too often, it is argued, governments have passed legislation or issued statutory regulations which lack clarity. It then takes several years for the courts to establish what employers actually have to do in practice through the establishment of precedents in individual cases. The best examples are the Working Time Regulations and the Transfer of Undertakings Regulations. The latter apply in some (but not all) cases in which a business or part of an organisation is taken over or merged with another. The volume of case law in this field is immense yet, after 25 years and major reform in 2006, there are still many grey areas.

- Unnecessary complexity is another general criticism of much UK employment law. Again, this creates uncertainty and makes it hard for employers to act within the law when carrying out their activities even when they wish to. The best example is the law on employment status. Many statutes give rights only to 'employees' (eg unfair dismissal and parental leave) whereas others apply to all 'workers' (eg discrimination law and the national minimum wage). Yet these terms are not fully defined. So over the years the courts have had to devise tests to establish who is an 'employee', who is a 'worker' and who is neither. The law in this area has become far too complex and subject to change, leaving major groups such as agency workers unclear about what rights they have, if any.

 EXERCISE BOX: EUROPEAN LABOUR LAW

EXERCISE 2.5

Read the following two articles featured in *People Management*. They can be downloaded from the *People Management* archive on the CIPD's website (www.cipd.co.uk):

- 'Double Trouble' by Anna Czerny (24 February 2005)
- 'Flexicurity Knocks' by James Brockett (19 April 2007)

Both articles concern proposals put forward by the European Union to form part of a possible new regulatory agenda for the coming 10 years.

Questions:

1 To what extent is it possible to articulate a clear sense of direction for the future of EU employment regulation from these proposals?

2 Why do you think proposals from the EU appear to point in different directions at the same time?

3 How would you like to see the EU's agenda develop in this field and why?

MACRO-DEBATES

At a broader level a further set of debates are carried out which focus on the full range of employment regulation. The question about which the protagonists disagree can basically be summed up as follows:

> Is increased employment regulation beneficial or harmful to the UK's economy and people?

Those who tend as a rule to argue that it has harmful effects include the Confederation of British Industry (2000), the Institute of Directors (see Lea

2001) and pro-business research organisations such as the Institute of Economic Affairs (2001). At the heart of their argument is the claim that much employment regulation serves to place substantial additional costs on employers and that this has the effect of making UK businesses less competitive in international markets than they would otherwise be. While it is accepted that most Western European countries impose even greater costs on their employers, this is not true of the rest of the world. Hence, in an increasingly global economy regulation reduces the capacity of organisations to match the prices of goods and services originating in other countries. Small firms in particular are hit hard because they do not have the flexibility, profit margins or expertise to work within the requirements of the ever-growing volume of employment regulation. According to the CBI the cost to businesses of implementing just the national minimum wage and the working time regulations amounted to over £10 billion (Confederation of British Industry 2000:9). The costs can be categorised under several headings.

- First, there are the direct costs that employers assume as a result of employment regulation. Examples are the costs associated with the payment of Statutory Sick Pay, maternity pay, increased numbers of paid holidays and complying with the expectations of disability discrimination law.

- Secondly there are knock-on costs that arise as a result of employees exercising their rights. A good example is the recruitment of temporary workers to cover when someone exercises their right to time off to care for a dependent relative or takes a period of paternity leave.

- Thirdly, there are costs that derive from lost opportunities. Instead of spending their time running competitive businesses or providing efficient public services, management time is spent finding out how to comply with regulations, making changes to ensure that they act within the expectations of the law and showing regulatory bodies that they are complying in practice.

- Finally there are the costs associated with litigation itself. Employers and their representatives often complain that even those who act entirely lawfully are often called upon to defend their actions in the employment tribunal. Ex-employees can bring cases at no risk to themselves and even if they lose, cause considerable expense on the part of the responding employer in legal fees and management time.

The total impact of these costs is to reduce competitiveness and hence slow down the growth of jobs. Moreover, where budgets and profit margins are tight, the net effect is to cause employers to shed labour and thus create unemployment. Over the longer term employment regulation serves to give organisations a preference for expansion based on capital expenditure (buildings, machinery etc) rather than expanding the number of employees. It also tends to encourage investment overseas in Eastern European and developing countries where employing people is a great deal less restrictive and costly. The net impact is fewer job opportunities for the UK workers whose interests the law is intended to serve.

This argument about employment law being counter-productive is often extended to focus on particular groups of workers. The most significant example is the position of women with young children or when an employer suspects that they probably will start a family in the near future:

> It is clear that many business people are very supportive of maternity benefits and rights (nearly a fifth of members provided more than the statutory maternity benefits in terms of leave or pay). but there is a clear warning from our survey. Already 45% of our members feel that such rights are a disincentive to hiring women of prime child-rearing age. If the regulations are made even more burdensome then employers will be even more reluctant to employ these women (Lea 2001:57).

According to critics, another way that employees suffer as a result of increased regulation arises from its tendency to impose on organisations single, standard ways of doing things. As a result local flexibility is reduced. Whereas once individual workplaces or even departments within larger organisations could devise their own informal workplace rules which met the needs of employer and employee alike, everyone now has to comply with a single centralised and often bureaucratic approach often imposed by a strengthened corporate HR function. Local management discretion over pay, benefits and terms and conditions, for example, has had to be curtailed in order to ensure that equal pay claims can be defended. All manner of informal practices have had to be ditched thanks to data protection law. Not because any employee complained or ever would complain in practice, but because the law expects all organisations to standardise arrangements in ways approved of by the Information Commissioner. Too often, the changes introduced in response to such regulations serve to reduce the quality of working life enjoyed by employees rather than raise it. In particular it mitigates against local, team-based decision-making and enhances the power and reach of administrators.

 REFLECTIVE QUESTION

It is sometimes argued that smaller firms should be exempted from much employment law. What are the arguments for and against this proposition? To what extent do you agree with the idea that employment law should only fully apply to larger organisations?

According to Davies (2009) there are two types of argument that are commonly deployed against the critics of increased employment regulation. The first type revolves around notions of human rights and social justice, the second around its economic impact. The social justice arguments are the most straightforward to grasp. There may well be costs that have to be borne by employing organisations as a result of greater regulation, it is claimed, but these are justified because without it employees would suffer unreasonably as a result of the actions of employers. Employment law is necessary to protect vulnerable people who might otherwise be unjustly exploited by far more powerful employers. In the absence of effective trade unions, the state must step in to provide such protection. Much employment law is intended to give employees a degree of power to resist unjust treatment and hence to help reduce social injustice generally:

- Discrimination law is necessary because without it the position at work and in the labour market of women and certain minority groups would be a great deal worse. This is true of ethnic minorities who suffer from racial and religious discrimination, of gay and lesbian people, of trade union activists, older workers and ex-offenders, all of whom had fewer opportunities and suffered greater prejudice at work in the days before they were protected by the law.

- Dismissal law serves to protect employees from being fired by their employers for no good reason or without first being given a reasonable opportunity to put right whatever fault the employer finds with their work. The alternative is a world of insecure employment where no employee, however effective and long-serving, can be sure that their job is safe from the whims or prejudices of maverick managers.

The economic arguments in favour of employment regulation are harder to summarise briefly and include several distinct strands. Further information is provided by Davies (2009) and in many publications of the Institute of Employment Rights (eg Deakin and Wilkinson 1996, Institute of Employment Rights 2000). However, the broad conclusion reached by their proponents is that *over the long term* the UK economy, as well as employing organisations, stands to benefit rather than to suffer from the regulation of labour markets. There are costs to be borne over the short term, but the overall effect is positive. An important part of this case concerns one of the topics we discussed above – tight labour markets. According to many influential economists the major threat to the future growth of the UK economy is a lack of qualified people to carry out jobs and chronic skills shortages in particular industries. A further recession may be precipitated simply because the UK finds itself without the human resources needed to keep the UK's economic engine running at full speed. This is a far greater threat to our international competitiveness than the costs associated with employment regulation. It is therefore in our economic interests for our government to force employers to provide workplaces in which people want to work and terms and conditions which attract them into employment. Too many people do not work for one reason or another. Some take early retirement, others take time out to care for young children or elderly relatives, some are constantly leaving one job and taking time out while they search for something more satisfactory, while a third group find that they are better off overall by claiming state benefits of one kind or another. Some of these people have skills which are not currently being placed at the disposal of the economy, while others have potential to gain these skills. Without employment regulation, it is argued, the numbers of such people would be higher because working in UK organisations would often be less attractive than it is now. Moreover, further regulation which serves to improve the experience of work, by making workplaces equitable and forcing organisations to employ people on decent terms and conditions, will encourage more people back into work and discourage others from leaving. Importantly, by the same token, employment protection legislation can help the UK to attract skilled workers from overseas to fill vacancies. The better the deal offered by UK employers, the more likely it is that talented people will want to come to live and work here.

A rather different economic argument is also commonly deployed by advocates of employment regulation. Here the focus is on the appropriate long-term strategy for the UK economy as a whole. It starts with an acceptance of the proposition that the UK is not, and will not be for the foreseeable future, able to compete internationally on the basis of low labour costs. However little employment regulation we have, developing countries will always be able to undercut us when it comes to the costs associated with employing people. It follows that some other basis has to be found on which to base our competitive future in a global economy. The only realistic choice is to focus on the development of high-tech and knowledge-intensive industries which compete through their capacity to innovate and to produce high quality products and services. Where we can compete on a cost reduction basis, it will only be through the development of machinery which reduces the need to employ people. It follows that employment law must play its part in pushing sometimes reluctant employers in this direction. If low quality jobs, low pay and sweatshop-type conditions are effectively outlawed, the only alternative is for employers to pay well and to create higher-skilled jobs which enable them to compete on grounds other than price. In turn this requires them to invest in training and hence gives them a strong incentive to retain people they have trained. Hence, employment regulation along with complementary measures taken in fields such as education and research funding is helping UK industry over time to transform itself so as to enable it to compete effectively in the modern global economy.

The third principal economic argument concerns productivity. To a great extent the government accepts the arguments long advanced by researchers in the employment field that good HRM practice is linked to improved business performance. If you treat people well in the workplace they will respond with greater loyalty and with a willingness to work with greater effort. Moreover, they will choose to remain employed and will not continually be looking out for a job move. Beyond this general point is a strong belief on the part of ministers that partnership approaches to the relationship between management and staff are far more likely to bring about business success than autocratic styles or adversarial employee relations climates. Employment regulation can promote the establishment and maintenance of fruitful partnerships between staff (and their representatives) and management. This is partly achieved through requirements to recognise trade unions where that is the will of most staff and partly through various requirements in the legislation to inform and consult with the workforce. More generally employment legislation serves to make it harder for employers to treat their staff in an inequitable or repressive manner. In so doing it plays a role in helping to create workplaces which are managed well and hence stand the best chance of achieving competitive advantage.

KEY ARTICLE BOX

EXAMPLE

'Regulating labour management in small firms' by Susan Marlow. *Human Resource Management Journal*, Vol. 12, No. 3. 25–44 (2002)

This article reports the results of a qualitative survey involving interviews with the owners and employees of small businesses. They were asked about the likely future impact of what was at that time a good deal of new legislation. The findings are interesting because of what they have to say about the attitudes of small business owners to labour market regulation. The views of the employees are also interesting and somewhat surprising in respects.

Questions:

1 Why were the managers interviewed as part of this research unconcerned about new employment regulation?

2 In what ways did the managers say that the new regulation might have the effect of working against the interests of employees?

3 Why did the employees who were interviewed say that the new regulation would have little impact on them?

EXPLORE FURTHER

- Major developments in the UK employment market are covered in publications regularly published on the National Statistics website. Recent and future trends are discussed by Leitch (2006) in his report and by UKCES in regular publications on their website www.ukces.org.uk.

- There are several good introductions to employment law available. But because they tend to become out of date quickly, it is important to ensure that you read the latest edition. Lewis and Sargeant (2009) is published by CIPD. Lockton (2006), Willey (2009) and Taylor and Emir (2009) have also written good student-friendly introductions.

- Debates about employment law are rarely summarised succinctly in one place. Perspectives on labour law by Anne Davies (2009) provides the best general summary available. The major arguments against employment regulation are effectively advocated by the CBI (2000) and those in favour by the Institute of Employment Rights (2000).

CHAPTER 3

Flexibility

LEARNING OUTCOMES

By the end of this chapter, readers should be able to:

- distinguish between tight and loose labour markets and advise about their implications for distinguishing between the concepts of functional, numerical and temporal flexibility

- lead/contribute to a programme of increased functional flexibility or multi-skilling

- advise on the main advantages and disadvantages of employing people on part-time, or fixed-term contracts

- advise on the merits of using subcontractors or homeworkers to carry out organisational activities

- determine the extent to which different forms of temporal flexibility are appropriate to use in particular circumstances

- assess the advantages and disadvantages of outsourcing functions, including those traditionally within the remit of P&D managers.

In addition, readers should be able to understand and explain:

- the content and underpinning rationale of flexible resourcing practices

- contextual factors underlying increased interest in flexible working practices

- key UK trends in the field of flexibility

- the major arguments against increased flexible working practices.

DEFINING FLEXIBILITY

In recent years flexibility issues have become a major preoccupation of managers and commentators interested in resourcing and talent management practice. These issues have come to the fore for many different reasons, but underlying all is the belief that organisations which gain a capacity for greater flexibility can develop sustained competitive advantage. This occurs for three distinct, but equally important reasons:

i an organisation which is flexible is able to deploy its people and make use of their talents more effectively and efficiently than one which is not ii the more flexible an organisation becomes, the better able it is to respond to and embrace change

iii flexibility, particularly in terms of hours of work, is valued by employees and can thus help to recruit and retain strong performers.

The term 'flexibility' covers a broad range of different areas of activity. It is useful to categorise these under two general headings; namely structural flexibility and cultural flexibility. The first refers to the types of contract under which people work and the architecture of the organisation. An organisation which is structurally inflexible could be characterised as one which employs everyone on the same basic set of terms and conditions, which is made up of fairly narrowly defined 'jobs' into which people are required to fit themselves, and which is managed via a traditional hierarchical structure. A flexible organisation, by contrast, deploys people as and when they are needed using a variety of contractual arrangements, and expects its people to work in a variety of different roles as and when required. These characteristics mean that it is better placed to respond quickly to changed circumstances and evolving customer expectations. Cultural flexibility is the other side of the same coin, being concerned with beliefs, attitudes and values. It is little use having an organisation which is structurally flexible if its people do not share a flexible mindset. Willingness to respond to change is as important a capacity to develop as the ability to do so, but it is harder to develop. Ultimately it can only be achieved by gaining the commitment of staff by promoting a working environment characterised by high trust, partnership and mutual respect.

Any survey of flexibility does well to start with a description of the work of John Atkinson and, in particular, his proposed model of the 'flexible firm'. For the purposes of this chapter, this model will be used as the basic definition of the term 'flexibility'. Published in 1984, Atkinson's model has been highly influential and has led to the development of a vigorous academic debate about its merits as a tool of description, prescription and prediction. Its main feature is the suggestion that a flexible firm (by which Atkinson means any organisation which is effective and competitive in the modern business environment) is composed of three basic groups of employees: core workers, peripheral workers and a third group who are employed only on some kind of subcontracted basis. The basic model is illustrated in Figure 3.1.

Central to the model are two distinct types of flexibility: functional and numerical. The former is applied specifically to the core workers – that is, people who are employed on standard, permanent, full-time contracts and who undertake the tasks that are central to the success of the organisation. They are functionally flexible, in that they do not work to rigid job descriptions but carry out a broad range of duties. Moreover, they do not restrict their activities to work of a particular level. Instead, they carry out complex tasks associated with managerial or professional jobs as well as more mundane activities, depending on the day-to-day needs of the organisation.

The peripheral group can also be functionally flexible, but in the model is more strongly associated with the term 'numerical flexibility'. Atkinson divided

Figure 3.1 The Flexible Firm

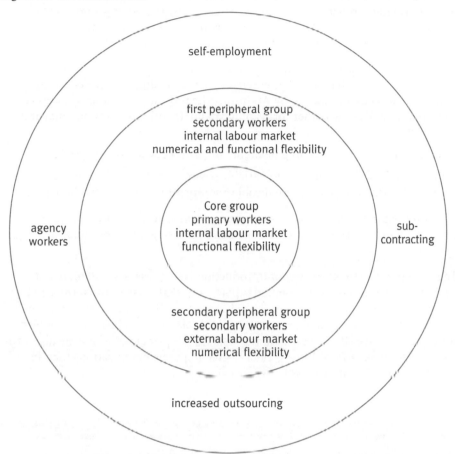

peripheral workers into primary and secondary categories, the first forming part of the firm's internal labour market. These people are mainly full-time and have a certain degree of permanence, but tend to have lower skills than colleagues who enjoy the status of core employees. As individuals they are less central to the organisation's success because their skills are more widely available in the labour market. They therefore enjoy lower job security than the core workers and will be among the first to have their hours cut or to be laid off when business downturns are experienced. The secondary peripheral group are in an even more precarious position, because they are brought in mainly to help cover peaks in business or short-term needs resulting from the absence of other staff. They are employed on either a part-time or temporary basis.

The final group, located beyond the periphery, consists of people who are not employees of the organisation but who are hired on a subcontracted basis to undertake a particular task or set of tasks. In the vast majority of cases this will be temporary, and hence insecure, although it is possible for a series of fixed-term contracts to follow one after another. Some may be professionally qualified people working on a self-employed basis; others may work for an agency or some other service provider. In both cases they are perceived by the other groups as being external to the organisation and thus readily replaceable by a competitor should their work prove to be unsatisfactory or more cheaply provided elsewhere.

Over the years others have proposed similar models (eg Loveridge and Mok 1979, Handy 1989), but none has entered managerial language or generated as much debate as that proposed by Atkinson. The most useful addition to his core concepts have been two other forms of flexibility (ie other than functional and numerical):

● temporal flexibility (meaning flexibility in terms of when people work)

● financial flexibility (referring to variable payment systems which increase the extent to which wage costs are flexible and mirror an organisation's income).

The latter is primarily a concern for remuneration specialists and is covered extensively in books on reward management, including a number published by CIPD.

The final point to make by way of introduction is to stress that the model of flexibility advanced by Atkinson and others, despite the use of the term 'firm', is not intended to be restricted to the private sector. The principles of efficiency and responsiveness to change are just as applicable in the public sector. Indeed, some studies have shown that in many respects the principles of the 'flexible firm model' have been adopted to a greater degree in public organisations than in private companies (Bryson 1999:69).

REASONS FOR INCREASED FLEXIBLE WORKING

Organisations have always sought to achieve a degree of flexibility. For centuries workers have been laid off (either permanently or temporarily) when business levels dip and offered premium overtime rates to work additional hours during periods of peak demand. Moreover, as Pollert (1987 and 1988) has shown, they have always shed subcontractors and peripheral workers first. What is new is the propagation of flexibility in the form of a model intended to guide management actions. In other words, it is the idea that organisations should deliberately develop core and peripheral structures as part of a considered strategy that represents a relatively recent departure from past practice.

People have different ideas about why interest in this subject should have grown so greatly over the past two decades. In truth, the reasons are many and varied, encompassing several of the major contextual developments outlined in Chapters 1 and 2. The following list of factors draws on the analyses of Blyton (1998), Bryson (1999), Heery & Salmon (2000) and Reilly (2001):

i   In response to increased volatility in product markets. Globalisation and e-commerce mean that businesses are required to expand and contract more frequently in order to compete in markets which become more unpredictable every year.

ii   New technologies have provided more scope for businesses to act opportunistically in response to customer demands. Smaller production runs are possible, as is the production of bespoke goods and services, meaning that flexibility is becoming more central to the achievement of competitive advantage.

iii   Ongoing interest in established Japanese management techniques has also fuelled interest in flexibility. The Japanese have long used approaches which are similar to that advocated in Atkinson's model. Functional flexibility for core workers employed on a long-term basis is a particular feature of the traditional Japanese approach.

iv   The decline in the size and influence of trade unions over the past 20 years has made it easier for managers to introduce a greater degree of flexibility. There is less resistance to change and fewer demarcation disputes.

v   Increased female participation in the labour market, together with greater interest in work-life balance issues has meant that a greater proportion of potential employees are looking for atypical working arrangements.

vi   Encouragement from successive governments seeking to create 'flexible labour markets' is a further factor. All recent administrations have sought to minimise unemployment by encouraging economic dynamism. Responsiveness to change and a high degree of efficiency are central components, along with encouragement of 'lifelong learning' and measures to remove barriers preventing people from participating in the workforce.

vii   A tendency towards short-term thinking in financial markets is demonstrated through an increased emphasis on maximising shareholder value. This, it is argued, leads managers to think in terms of short-term horizons. Long-term commitment to individuals is thus less necessary than it used to be in order to develop a financially successful organisation.

viii The growth of private service sector employment as a proportion of the total, together with the evolution of a '24 hour society' are also cited as factors. This kind of employment, by its nature cannot be of the traditional 9–5 variety. Customers need to be satisfied when they want to be satisfied. This requires far greater flexibility on the part of suppliers of services.

In recent years there is evidence to suggest that the major impetus for moves towards greater flexibility has come from employees rather than employers. People are increasingly seeking jobs which will provide them with a good work-life balance and employers are responding by providing greater opportunities for people to work flexibly if they want to. It is interesting to see that academic researchers, who have tended historically to be quite hostile to the idea that developments in this field are employee-driven, are now increasingly researching the field from that perspective (eg Lewis and Roper 2008). There is also survey evidence to suggest that moves towards greater flexibility on the part of organisations are motivated to a substantial degree by a wish to increase retention, promote equal opportunities, enhance an employer's brand and to widen recruitment pools (Wolff 2009a). In other words employers are going down this route partly to improve their efficiency, but also in order to attract and retain good performers.

Another major impetus for more flexible working is regulatory change. In the UK we have had since 2003 a right for some employees to make formal requests to their employers to work flexibly in some way. Initially this right was restricted to parents of young children, but it has since been substantially extended to employees with caring responsibilities for disabled adults (from 2007) and subsequently to parents of all children under the age of 17 (from 2009). The right is restricted so that a formal request can only be made once a year and, if agreed by the employer, this will result in a one-off, permanent change to the contract of employment. Eight reasons are set out in the regulations for employers to turn down requests if they want to, there being no direct mechanism provided whereby such a decision can be challenged in a court.

When this law was first introduced many commentators, as well as trade unions and other groups representing employees, were sceptical that it would have much practical impact. The assumption was that requests would be turned down routinely because employers would see them as creating awkward or inefficient outcomes. In practice these predictions have not materialised. A good majority of requests are in fact accepted by employers, many having decided to extend their schemes to all employees and not just those provided for in the legislation (Wolff 2009a). We have also seen the evolution of a legal argument rooted in the law of indirect sex discrimination (see Chapter 4) which in practice requires employers to justify any decision to turn a request down made by a female employee. According to the latest IRS research (Wolff 2009b) a good majority of employers regularly receive formal requests, around 2 per cent of all employees making such a request in any one year. 75 per cent of organisations agreed to all requests received, only 4 per cent turning all down. This accords with the findings of government research which suggest that as many as 95 per cent of all requests are granted. Moreover, the IRS survey found that in practice most requests to work flexibly are made without recourse to the regulations at all. They are simply agreed with managers at a departmental level.

The ovrall result of the regulations, the desire to improve recruitment and retention and the wish to become more productive is a very substantial increase in flexible working arrangements in the UK over recent years. This was the major finding of the last Workplace Employment Relations Survey (WERS) (Kersley *et al* 2006) and is confirmed by more recent research, such as that carried out by the IRS, for the years since.

FUNCTIONAL FLEXIBILITY

Most writers on functional flexibility focus on developments in manufacturing, where change in this field has been most pronounced, but the principles are equally applicable on all industrial sectors. A programme aimed at increasing an organisation's functional flexibility is essentially one which promotes multi-

EXERCISE BOX: PRODUCTIVITY AND FLEXIBILITY

Read the article by Lynda Gratton entitled 'Feel the burnout' featured in *People Management* (15 July 2004, page 22). This can be downloaded from the *People Management* archive on the CIPD's website (www.cipd.co.uk).

In this excellent opinion piece Lynda Gratton concludes that there is a very strong case for much more flexible working in the UK and in other Western economies, but that this is rather more difficult to achieve in practice than many people think. Unless we become a great deal more productive as an economy, she argues, flexible working of the kind that employees like will not be available for most.

Questions:

1 What are the major arguments in favour of flexible working?

2 Why are so many managers reluctant to move in this direction?

3 What are the implications of globalisation for the UK's prospects of expanding flexible working?

4 To what extent do you agree with Lynda Gratton's conclusion about the way forward for UK industry?

skilling. The aim is that people should increase the range of tasks which they are willing and able to perform. This may involve learning to carry out colleagues' jobs, it may involve picking up duties currently carried out either by their bosses or subordinates, or it may involve developing new skills which are anticipated to become more significant in the future.

Greater functional flexibility is associated with the following processes:

- reducing the number of different job descriptions in an organisation (ie less demarcation between jobs)
- more team-working – so that instead of employees A, B and C undertaking tasks 1, 2 and 3 respectively, all work together on all three types of task
- flatter hierarchies – fewer levels of grades defined by the type of work that is performed, more people employed on the same grades carrying out the full range of activities
- job rotation to ensure that as many people as possible are familiar with as many roles as is practicable.

It is probably best understood by illustrating how an organisation suffers when it is not functionally flexible. The following example from the past is provided by Reilly (2001:50):

A maintenance electrician would not adjust a bolt on a pipe; a mechanical craftsman would not isolate a piece of equipment. Neither of them was trained to assist production, and the operators, for their part, would not take on any craft duties.

The advantages of creating a functionally flexible workforce are evident. First, it means that people can be deployed where they are most needed at any particular time. If one area of activity is busy and another slack, multi-skilled employees based in the slack area can be moved to the busy area. This is an efficient use of staff and should mean that overall headcount can be minimised. It also makes it easier to cover for absence and lateness. Not only are costs saved, it also means that customers are served more quickly and to a higher standard. Secondly it allows faster response to change. If one area of the business grows, there is a ready supply of people familiar with its operations able to transfer over without needing extensive training.

There are, however, potential drawbacks as well. First of all, improving functional flexibility is costly. Training programmes have to be organised for larger numbers of people than in an organisation with clear lines of demarcation between jobs. In addition there are administrative costs associated with recording skills learned and organising job rotation systems. Secondly, there may be resistance to overcome – particularly where staff have been employed with the expectation that they will be specialising in one line of work. Forcing them to multi-skill against their will can then easily lead to dissatisfaction and the loss of good performers to competitors. Thirdly, it is possible that some skills are too complex or specialised to be shared by several people. Forcing the pace then leads to dilution, a group of people each being unable to carry out the job as effectively as one highly-trained individual with long experience can.

Introducing functional flexibility is thus an activity that has to be carried out with care. Employees need to be involved as much as possible, and their legitimate concerns about its effect on them addressed sensitively. It is also important to accept that there are limits to functional flexibility and that it must be introduced within reasonably defined parameters. In many organisations it is neither practicable nor desirable for everyone to be able to carry out everyone else's job.

Functional flexibility is also increasingly associated with ideas about empowerment, decentralisation and engaging employees. Multi-skilling can be introduced in such a way as to reduce the number of managers in hierarchies, creating teams who undertake management tasks as well as operational duties. Johnson (2009) writes about the development of 'post-bureaucratic organisations' which are 'flatter', 'more networked' and, importantly, 'more flexible' too. Functional flexibility can thus be seen as being central to some of the cutting-edge, more radical visions of how work will be organised in the future.

NUMERICAL FLEXIBILITY

While functional flexibility is principally intended to be promoted among the 'core' workforce, the peripheral workforce in the Atkinson model is defined in terms of numerical flexibility. The central contention is that employers seeking flexibility should employ people on different forms of 'atypical contract' so that they can deploy people where they are most needed at the times when they are needed. The extent to which different types of contractual arrangement are appropriate in different industries varies greatly. For example, part-time working is necessarily restricted in the manufacturing industry because of the need to maintain a common shift system. Sub-contracting, however, is very common. By contrast, the use of fixed-term contracts has grown most in the public services, where funding to undertake specific projects is limited in terms of time. Such contracts are also used extensively by employers whose workload increases and decreases on a seasonal basis (eg in tourism and agriculture), and have necessarily become highly significant in sectors where most employees are female, as a result of the greater take-up of the right to maternity leave in recent years.

For the HR manager, therefore, the most important questions to ask are the following:

- In respect of the particular industry and labour markets in which my organisation operates, what opportunities exist to increase the proportion of employees on non-standard contracts?

- What are the potential short- and long-term advantages and disadvantages of doing so?

Clearly the answer to these questions will vary from situation to situation.

What follows, therefore, is a brief survey of some of the factors that might need to be taken into account for each of the major categories of atypical work.

PART-TIME CONTRACTS

Part-time working is by far the most common form of atypical working. In the UK 26.6 per cent are part-timers, over 75 per cent of these being women (National Statistics 2010). Within certain sectors the figures are far higher. Over 40 per cent of all hotel and catering employees are women who work part-time; the figures for the health and education sectors are 51 per cent and 47 per cent respectively. By contrast, the numbers employed outside the service sector are considerably smaller, with a heavy concentration in clerical and secretarial roles. The biggest period of growth in part-time work was during the 1960s, when the proportion of the total workforce that worked part-time increased from 9 per cent to 16 per cent. After that it has continued to rise steadily, along with the overall female participation rate.

In past decades there were clear incentives for organisations to employ two part-timers instead of one full-timer. This resulted from an inequality of treatment in legal terms, whereby part-timers could be denied pension scheme membership and other fringe benefits and had to wait five years before they were entitled to bring cases of unfair dismissal. In the 1990s the courts ruled such practices to be indirectly discriminatory towards women, leading to several legislative amendments. Then in 2001 the UK government implemented the EU's Part Time Workers Directive which makes any discrimination on grounds that someone works part-time potentially unlawful. Treating part-timers less favourably than full-timers is thus now a risky approach to take. However, it remains the case that at the lowest pay levels, part-timers often earn less than the lower National Insurance threshold, meaning that employers do not have to pay contributions when these workers are appointed.

There are two main reasons for the creation of a part-time post. The first, and most common, is to enable an organisation to respond more efficiently to peaks and troughs in demands for its services. Hence shopworkers are hired to work part-time on busy days or to cover the busiest hours of the day. The second reason is in response to a demand from employees or potential employees for part-time jobs to be created. The most common situation in which this occurs is when a woman who has previously worked on a full-time basis wishes to return as a part-timer following her maternity leave. In many cases, organisations find ways of accommodating such requests, either by re-organising job duties or by advertising for another part-timer to share the job. However, generally speaking, the inflexibility of such arrangements makes them less easy to organise for managerial employees who need to be present throughout the week in order to supervise their departments effectively. Often a difficult choice has thus to be made between accommodating employee wishes in this regard or losing a valued member of staff. The presence of reputable childcare services can reduce the likelihood of this issue arising. Indeed there is evidence from the continent that suggests part-time working on the part of women with children is less common in countries where there is good and widely available childcare provision (Brewster *et al* 1993:17).

Creating part-time jobs can thus bring considerable advantages to an organisation. It can reduce costs dramatically by making sure that people are present only when required and can also attract well-qualified people who, because of childcare or other commitments, are looking for less than 40 hours' work each week. Other parts of the labour market to which employers can look include retired people and students in full-time education. Another possible advantage in some situations is the apparent lack of interest among part-timers for trade union activity.

There are of course potential disadvantages too. First, there is the possibility that part-timers, because of other obligations and the fact that theirs is often not the main family income, will show less commitment to their work than their full-time colleagues. The problem is potentially compounded by the lack of promotion opportunities open to them. Part-timers can also be inflexible in terms of the hours they work because of the need to honour their other commitments. They are often attracted to the job in the first place because they need to be guaranteed fixed weekly hours (eg: 12.00–2.00, or Wednesdays and Thursdays) and will thus be either unwilling or unable to change these too much. There is also the more general issue of training investment. Where two or three part-timers are employed in place of one full-timer to undertake the same role, the training time and cost will be two or three times higher. A well-rooted myth about part-time workers is the notion that they are harder to retain than full-timers, a belief that presumably arises from more general perceptions of a lack of commitment. In fact, there is little evidence to support this perception, 40 per cent staying with their employers for five years or more (IDS 1995a:4).

TEMPORARY CONTRACTS

The term 'temporary worker' covers a variety of situations. On the one hand there are staff who are employed for a fixed term or on a seasonal basis to carry out a specific job or task. This category includes well-paid or senior people such as football players or public officials, as well as individuals brought in to undertake more ordinary work on a fixed-term basis. A second group are people who are employed temporarily but for an indefinite period. Their contracts thus state that they will be employed until such time as a particular project or body of work is completed. Again, this category can encompass well-paid individuals such as TV presenters and actors, in addition to those occupying less glamorous positions. A third category includes temporary agency staff who are employed via a third party to cover short-term needs.

Currently in the UK 5.8 per cent of all employees are contracted to work on a temporary or fixed-term basis, but the figure rises somewhat during the summer months as a result of seasonal work in the tourism and agricultural sectors (National Statistics 2010). The number of such workers tends to fluctuate with economic conditions, so we saw a rise in the early 1980s, followed by a slight reduction, before the figure rose steeply again in the early 1990s. It then fell back again from the peak of 1.8 million who were employed on temporary contracts in 1998 before rising again during the most recent recession to 1.4 million. The biggest growth has been in agency working. As with part-time working, there is very great variation between the different industrial sectors, the service and agricultural sectors accounting for a high proportion of the total. As many as 10 per cent of public sector staff are now employed on a fixed-term basis, with some positions, such as those of researchers in higher education, now usually paid for through one-off grants or single allocations of funds.

While somewhat dated, the Department of Employment's Employer's Labour Use Survey (ELUS), carried out in 1987, provides a good summary of the great variety of reasons employers have for employing temporary staff:

- to give short-term cover for absent staff (55 per cent)
- to match staffing levels to peaks in demand (35 per cent)
- to deal with one-off tasks (29 per cent)
- to help adjust staffing levels (26 per cent)
- to provide specialist skills (22 per cent)
- to provide cover while staffing levels are changed (19 per cent)
- because applicants request temporary work (8 per cent)
- to screen for permanent jobs (4 per cent)
- because temporary workers are easier to recruit (4 per cent)
- to reduce wage costs (1 per cent)

- to reduce non-wage costs (1 per cent).

(Source: McGregor and Sproull 1992:227).

From the employer's perspective there are thus a number of compelling reasons to consider offering fixed-term contracts to certain groups of staff. They are particularly useful when the future is uncertain, because they avoid raising employee expectations. It is far easier, when departments close or businesses begin to fold, not to renew a fixed-term contract than it is to make permanent employees redundant. During the run-up to redundancies it is also useful to be able to draw on the services of temporary staff to cover basic tasks, freeing permanent employees who are under threat of redundancy to spend time seeking new jobs.

A note of caution is needed for those with responsibilities for the employment of staff in other EU countries, because a number have considerably greater restrictions on the employment of temps than is the case in the UK and the Irish Republic. In the UK the level of regulation is restricted to the requirements of the EU's Fixed Term Worker's Directive which was introduced into our law via the Employment Act 2002. This aims to protect people from adverse treatment at work simply by virtue of the fact that they work on a temporary contract. It also requires employers to notify their temps of any permanent vacancies and limits the number of times that a fixed term contract can be renewed without good reason. Since July 2006 if someone has been employed on a fixed-term basis for four years or more their contracts can become permanent unless the employer is able to provide objective justification for a continuation of the existing contractual arrangements.

SUBCONTRACTORS

Aside from the use of temporary agency workers, subcontracting comes in two basic forms. First, there is the use by employers of consultants and other self-employed people to undertake specific, specialised work. Such arrangements can be long-term in nature, but more frequently involve hiring someone on a one-off basis to work on a single project. The second form occurs when a substantial body of work, such as the provision of catering, cleaning or security services, is subcontracted to a separate company. The latter form is examined in the later section on outsourcing (see below). Both varieties have become more common in recent years, leading to a rise in the number of agency employees and self-employed people. Depending on which groups are included, it is estimated that around 1.3 million people are now working on an agency basis at any one time (BIS 2010:7–8), and a further 3.8 million people (13 per cent of the workforce) are self-employed (National Statistics 2010). Self-employment is focused in the fields of technical and professional services, the majority of self-employed workers being relatively well-paid men. Most of the traditional professions provide opportunities for self-employment, but the highest concentrations are in the fields of engineering, computing and business services. According to the ELUS survey described above, the main reasons given for using self-employed subcontractors were as follows:

- to provide specialist skills (60 per cent)
- to match staffing levels to peaks in demand (29 per cent)
- because workers prefer to be self-employed (28 per cent)
- to reduce wage costs (9 per cent)
- because the self-employed are more productive (8 per cent)
- to reduce non-wage costs (6 per cent)
- to reduce overheads (4 per cent)
- other reasons (11 per cent).

(Source: McGregor and Sproull 1992:227).

Again, the figures in parentheses represent the percentages of employers stating that the reason was one of significance in their use of subcontractors who are self-employed. As with temporary workers, it is interesting how cost-cutting opportunities appear to be so much less significant than the need to bring in specialists. This may be because, hour for hour, the employment of a self-employed contractor is often a good deal more expensive than hiring a temporary employee. Even when the lack of National Insurance and pension contributions are taken into account, along with other on-costs associated with standard employment contracts, it is usually more costly to bring someone in on a consultancy basis.

Aside from cost considerations, there are also other potential disadvantages from the employer's perspective. First, it is often suggested that self-employed people, like agency workers, inevitably have less reason to show a high level of commitment. They have no long-term interest in the organisation and are thus less likely than conventional employees to go beyond the letter of their contracts. In turn this leads to suspicions about the quality and reliability of the services they provide. Only where there is a clear possibility of an ongoing relationship in the form of further work does the contractor have a serious economic incentive to over-service the client. Such a perception is of course a generalisation and is probably unfair to the majority of self-employed people, but organisations have to take such thoughts into consideration when considering whether to subcontract work and to whom. In some situations there is no choice, because all the specialists in a field have chosen to work for themselves. One such example is the computer industry, where people with expertise in particular programs or operations know that they are in a sellers' market and that they can earn more, while keeping control of their own working lives, if they take up self-employed status.

Another possibility to consider, which is relatively common now, is the rehiring of retired employees on a self-employed basis. Both parties stand to gain from such arrangements where the retired person has a reasonable income from his or her pension. The company draws on organisation-specific expertise, but pays for it only when there is a particular demand. The retired person draws a pension and supplements it by undertaking a modest amount of work when he or she wishes to.

HOMEWORKING

The employment of people to work either wholly or partly from home is another trend which has aroused the interest of researchers. We are not looking here at self-employed people or casual workers, but at people whose contracts of employment are standard in other respects. The extent to which this kind of arrangement currently occurs is not easy to state with certainty because many people work from home only for a proportion of their time, but according to the most recent government statistics there are around three million people who work from home all or most of the time. This represents 8 per cent of the total UK workforce (National Statistics 2006:24), but includes within it self-employed people – a very considerable number of whom work from home. Interestingly the number of employees who are based at home appears to be very small indeed – around 200,000, a further 350,000 being mobile and working some of the time from home (IDS 2005a:2). This is surprising given the potential for growth with the expansion of computerised communication technology and improvements in telecommunications.

For the employer, the main advantage is a reduction in the size of premises required. Savings are thus made in terms of office rents, business rates, heating and lighting. The main disadvantages relate to the low morale that homeworkers often suffer as a result of their isolation from co-workers. A different kind of supervision is thus required, along with control systems that assess performance on the basis of the quantity and quality of each batch of work undertaken. Because it is clearly not possible to oversee each individual's work, there is no opportunity either to encourage or correct when mistakes are made or when the pace of work slackens. As yet there is little specific employment law concerned with protecting the rights of homeworkers. However, campaigns are launched from time to time by trade unions and other bodies concerned about low pay and lack of employment protection, so it is reasonable to expect that legislation may soon be introduced along continental lines. This will ensure that homeworkers enjoy the same terms and conditions as other employees and the same access to training, and that they are offered the full range of fringe benefits. There is also a strong case for bringing homework stations within the ambit of organisations' health and safety responsibilities.

The biggest problem in managing a home-based workforce is the maintenance of effective communication – a particularly important issue where members of the 'core' workforce are employed on a teleworking basis. If such arrangements are to work, more is needed than simple electronic communication. There is also a need to hold regular team meetings, as well as face-to-face sessions between supervisors and staff. In practice, as has been pointed out, most homeworking of this kind is carried out part-time, the employee performing some work at the office and some at home. When managed well, this can be the best of both worlds, in that effective communication is retained while savings in terms of office space and energy use are also achieved. Of course, this can occur only if employees forgo the privilege of having their own office or desk at work and accept 'hot-desking' arrangements, whereby they occupy whichever workstation or computer terminal is free when they are not working at home.

EXERCISE 3.2

EXERCISE BOX: THE AA

Read the following two articles featured in *People Management*. They can be downloaded from the *People Management* archive on the CIPD's website (www.cipd.co.uk):

- 'Home Start' by Andrew Bibby (10 January 2002, pages 36–37)

- 'Remote Control' by Catherine Edwards (16 June 2005, pages 30–32)

The first article describes the ups and downs of the Automobile Association's (AA) experiences of employing call-centre workers on a homeworking basis. Aside from initial technical problems, the company found that the main issue was the need to adapt its approaches to people management.

The second article reflects more generally on the advantages and disadvantages of introducing homeworking, suggesting ways of helping to ensure it works effectively.

Questions:

1 Why did the AA decide to employ call-centre workers on a homeworking basis?

2 What were the major problems they encountered?

3 How have they had to adjust management practices in order to make the new approach work effectively?

4 What other steps could be taken to improve the situation?

TEMPORAL FLEXIBILITY

A form of working arrangement that, evidence suggests, is becoming more common involves a move away from setting specific hours of work. While such contracts come in several different forms, all help in some way to match the presence of employees with peaks and troughs in demand. They thus help ensure that people are not being paid for being at work when there is little to do, while at the same time avoiding paying premium overtime rates to help cover the busiest periods. Three types of arrangement are common: flexitime, annual hours and zero hours schemes. Others include compressed hours and term-time working.

FLEXITIME

The most common, and least radical, departure from standard employment practices is the flexitime scheme. Precise rules vary from organisation to organisation but they typically involve employees' clocking in and out of work or recording the hours they work each day. Typically, such schemes work on a monthly basis, requiring employees to be present for 160 hours over the month, but permitting them and their managers to vary the precise times in which they are at work in order to meet business needs and, where possible, their own wishes. Often such schemes identify core hours when everyone must be at work (eg: 10–12.00 and 2–4.00 each day), but allow flexibility outside these times. It is then possible for individuals who build up a bank of hours to take a 'flexi-day' or half-day off at a quiet time.

The number of situations in which flexitime can operate and in which it is appropriate to do so are quite limited. Clearly, it is not a good idea where the presence of a whole team throughout the working day is important. It would thus not be used for roles where there is direct contact with customers or where a manufacturing process requires a large number of employees to be present at the same time. It is also inappropriate where organisational objectives and culture focus heavily on the maximisation of effort and the completion of specific tasks. In such workplaces the hours worked are often long, and there is a need to encourage employees to concentrate more on the achievement of goals and less on the actual time they are spending at work. Hence flexitime would be inappropriate for newspaper journalists, because the hours worked are inevitably determined by the requirement to chase and write stories. In any case, the whole idea of clocking in or recording hours worked on a time sheet is seen by many organisations as undesirable in itself and representative of an approach to management from which they wish to move. According to IRS (1997:7) this was the major reason for the abandoning of flexitime by Cable and Wireless following privatisation in 1981. Their objection was the way in which the system 'symbolised a relationship between management and employees far removed from the one to which it aspired – namely one based on trust and shared responsibility'.

However, flexitime remains in many organisations – particularly where large numbers of clerical and secretarial workers are employed to look after a range of different bodies of work. Where deadlines are relatively unimportant, where individuals have responsibility for carrying out a prescribed range of tasks and where there is no requirement to be available to members of the public all day long, there is a good case for using flexitime to maximise organisational efficiency. This is because it cuts out the need to pay overtime and keeps the overall headcount to a minimum. It is thus unsurprising that it is mostly used in government departments, local authorities and other public sector organisations. In the private sector it is used mainly in larger financial services companies for clerical staff working in back-office roles. Wolff (2009a) reports an IRS survey which found that flexitime was offered to some staff by 51 per cent of respondents.

ANNUAL HOURS

A more radical form of flexitime is the annual hours contract. The principle is the same, only here the amount of time worked can vary from month to month or season to season as much as from day to day. It varies from typical flexitime systems not least because variations in hours are decided by the employer without much choice being given to the employee. Each year all employees are required to work a set number of hours (usually 1,880), but to come in for much longer periods at some times than others. Pay levels, however, remain constant throughout the year. Again, from the employer's point of view, the aim is to match the demand for labour to its supply and thus avoid employing people at slack times and paying overtime in busier periods. Variations can occur seasonally, monthly or can follow no predictable pattern at all. In tourism or agriculture, where the summer is busy and the winter quiet, this can then be reflected in the time put in by employees. In an accountancy firm, where month and year-end reports need to be produced to tight deadlines, employees can then work long weeks followed by compensation in the form of shorter ones.

In the early 1990s, according to Brewster *et al* (1993), the incidence of annual hours schemes increased to a level at which they covered some 6 per cent of the UK's working population. However, more recent figures (see Bell and Hart 2003) show a rather lower level of coverage at 4.5 per cent, strongly suggesting that the incidence of such schemes has not taken off as many predicted would be the case. The 2009 IRS survey found annual hours systems to be one of the least widely-used types of flexible working and recorded little growth in their number over the previous five years (Wolff 2009a). Their relative scarcity is interesting when their potential advantages from the perspective of both employers and employees is considered. In part, this is explained by the presence of similar objections as those described above in the case of flexitime, but there are also practical difficulties. A major problem concerns what to do when an employee leaves, having worked only during a slack period, but having also drawn the full monthly salary. It can also be difficult to predict the supply of work, so that an organisation ends up either paying overtime anyway or employing more people than it actually needs to cover the work. However, where such issues can be overcome, annual hours can be attractive to employees, leading to lower levels of staff turnover and absence.

EXERCISE BOX: THE CASE FOR ANNUAL HOURS

EXERCISE 3.3

Read the article by Kevin White entitled 'Year we go, year we go' featured in *People Management* (17 June 2004, page 23). This can be downloaded from the *People Management* archive on the CIPD's website (www.cipd.co.uk).

In this article Kevin White puts a strong case for the adoption of annual hours systems, but he also considers the main reasons that they are not adopted in practice despite the potential advantages. He concludes by suggesting some possible solutions.

Questions:

1 What are the main strands of the case for the adoption of annual hours systems?

2 Why are managers and staff often resistant to changing established rostering systems?

3 What approaches is it suggested are used in order to gain support for annual hours systems among staff?

ZERO HOURS

At the other end of the scale is the zero hours contract, which organisations use in the case of casual employees who work on a regular basis. They are most suitable for situations in which there are frequent and substantial surges in demand for employees on particular days or weeks of the year, but where their instance is unpredictable. An example is the employment of couriers in the travel industry. A company needs to have a body of trained courier staff it can call on to look after clients, but is unable to predict exactly how many it will need and on what dates. It therefore hires people on a casual basis, gives them training and then calls on their services as required during the holiday season. Another common example is the employment of waiting staff for banquets and Christmas parties in hotels and restaurants. Because the staff involved have no great expectation of substantial amounts of work, they usually combine casual employment with other activities. Many have other jobs too, or are in full-time education. Employers can thus not always rely on their availability at short notice and have to ensure that enough trained people are kept on their books to cover their needs at any time.

A variation on the zero hours approach is a system that guarantees casual employees a minimum number of hours a week or days a year. IRS (1997:8) reports that Tesco uses such an approach in some of its stores. Tesco guarantees employees between 10 and 16 hours' work a week, but then adds to this if the workload increases or in order to cover absences among non-casual employees. The core guaranteed hours are fixed week by week, but additional hours are flexible and can be arranged as little as a day in advance.

Zero hours contracts are associated with the casualisation of work and are particularly criticised by those who see increased flexibility as cover for employers seeking to shift risk onto employees by making their livelihoods less secure. As such they are often seen as comprising poor practice. This is particularly true of situations in which employers move from fixed hours to zero hours as some have in recent years.

TERM-TIME WORKING

Term-time working has a great deal to offer both employers and employees, but is relatively rare in the UK. It involves employees being contracted only to work during the school term times. During school holidays they do not work, but return to their jobs again once term re-starts. It is particularly attractive to parents of younger children in two-income households, giving employers an opportunity to tap into a labour market full of talented and well-qualified potential staff who are unwilling to take a full-time year-round job. From an employer's point of view, especially for lower-skilled/semi-skilled roles, disruption needn't be a consequence because there is another group of well-motivated would-be staff who are looking to take over the jobs that have been vacated as school holidays start – namely university students looking for vacation work.

COMPRESSED HOURS

Wolff's (2009a) article on the IRS research into flexible working states that compressed hours contracts are a lot more common than they used to be. The idea is simple. Job holders work a full-time week (40 hours or whatever) but do so over fewer days, having more free days each week. The most common patterns are four-day weeks (10 hours per day) and nine day fortnights (8.88 hours per day). Such schemes avoid overtime payments, like flexitime systems rewarding people with additional time off instead of cash when they work longer hours.

OUTSOURCING

A form of flexibility that appears on the outermost peripheral circle of Atkinson's flexible firm model is 'outsourcing', a topic which has attracted a considerable amount of interest over the past 10 years. In the literature the term is usually defined in one of two subtly different ways. Some see it as involving the purchase from external providers of services which *could be* carried out internally, while others are more specific in referring to the provision of activities that *were previously* carried out internally. In fact outsourcing covers both types of situation and more besides. At one end of the spectrum it is more or less synonymous with subcontracting: an organisation purchasing a service from another which is better placed to provide it. At the other, as is shown by Kakabadse and Kakabadse (2002:31) it takes the form of a franchising arrangement or joint venture, a supplier taking over the running of core business functions. They give the example of the Virgin Group which has regularly entered into agreements 'whereby they provide the brand name and marketing flair and the other parties, the production facilities and capital'. For our purposes we will take the term to describe the situation in which an organisational function which is customarily carried out on an in-house basis by its own employees is instead purchased from a specialist provider.

In itself, like most features of the flexible firm model, outsourcing is not remotely new. Indeed, historically it was a good deal more common than is now the case. Smaller firms, in particular, have long found it necessary, even desirable, to buy in certain services rather than hire employees to carry them out on their behalf. This is because they are not large enough to be able to justify the employment of specialists such as lawyers, accountants, maintenance engineers or IT people. Some important new features are, however, clearly discernible:

- the widespread use of outsourcing by larger private sector companies
- substantial increases in the extent to which public sector organisations buy in externally provided services
- the development of a view which sees the decision to outsource a function as a central plank in an organisation's business strategy
- the extent to which organisations are prepared to replace established in-house functions, often involving large scale redundancies, with externally provided alternatives.

As far as the UK is concerned, there is extensive and compelling evidence to show that outsourcing is a form of flexibility which has become much more common in the past two decades. Colling (2005:93–95), drawing on statistics from the Workplace Employment Relations Surveys, government figures and other studies, shows that there were very substantial extensions of outsourcing during the 1990s. Kersley *et al* (2006:105–6) show that the trend has continued in the first years of the twenty-first century, but they also balance this by recording many instances of previously outsourced functions being brought back in-house. Their figures show that 16 per cent of workplaces contracted out a service in the previous five years, but that 11 per cent had also in-sourced a service that had previously been sub-contracted.

The main areas in which outsourcing occurs are as follows:

- cleaning premises
- security services
- building maintenance
- transport of documents/goods
- catering
- computing advice and maintenance
- legal services
- market research.

A great deal of the recent growth in outsourcing originated in the public sector and was the direct result of government requirements to introduce forms of competitive tendering (Reilly 2001:33), but much was also accounted for by decisions taken in private corporations. There are several different reasons that have been put forward to explain the trend. First, we have seen an increased desire on the part of organisations to focus efforts on 'core activities', by which is meant those activities which are the source of competitive advantage. It follows that where a 'marginal activity' such as security, maintenance or cleaning can be effectively provided externally it makes good business sense to employ a specialist company to provide such services. This frees the organisation to throw all its energy into seeking and maintaining competitive advantage over its rivals.

Another way in which competitive advantage can be promoted through outsourcing is in the achievement of substantial cost savings. This arises because of the economies of scale that are achieved by the providers of the outsourced services and is, according to Kakabadse and Kakabadse (2002:18) the most common reason that organisations give for considering outsourcing existing activities. A large, well-established, specialist provider of catering or security services is often able to provide as good a service (or a better one) than can be achieved by a far smaller internally run department. They have access to the newest and best equipment, are able to offer superior professional training and can readily replace staff who leave or go absent. Moreover, because they are obliged to compete for the contract to provide the service, they have an incentive to keep costs as low as possible by maximising the efficiency of their operations.

Expertise in the provision of ancillary services also leads to reduced costs. Colling (2000:71) makes the point that organisations often have 'little idea of the market rate for such activities', typically relating the pay of staff employed to carry them out to established payment systems for core employees. In doing this they commonly end up paying higher rates than is necessary given labour market conditions. This is particularly true of the public sector, where ancillary staff are frequently paid a great deal more than people carrying out equivalent roles on behalf of specialist private sector service providers. Where outsourcing has occurred, according to the Audit Commission, savings of 20 per cent or more have readily been achieved (see Stredwick and Ellis 1998:152).

It is unsurprising, therefore, that successive governments have used outsourcing as means of reducing public expenditure. Under the Conservatives in the 1980s and 1990s the terms used were 'compulsory competitive tendering' and 'market testing', under Labour we then moved to 'best value' and 'private finance initiatives'. All in their different ways involve the state (or local government institutions) seeking ways of reducing their costs by hiring private sector companies to undertake certain activities. Of course, the contracts are sometimes won by the existing public sector providing units – but only after a process in which they are obliged to compete with outsiders for the right to continue their activities. In recent years, outsourcing of public sector activities has extended well beyond the provision of ancillary services. Private sector companies are now contracted to build and provide management services in NHS hospitals, social care facilities, prisons and even military airfields.

A third major reason for outsourcing is the opportunity it gives organisations to make use of services which are provided at the desired level of quality without having to achieve this themselves. When an outsourced service is considered to be operating unsatisfactorily providers can be warned that they will lose the contract if they do not make immediate improvements. It is a great deal easier to issue such a threat than it is to manage an in-house performance improvement programme. All responsibility for achieving quality standards (along with the hassle) is passed to the supplier. The extent to which this theory operates in practice is a moot point. There have been many criticisms made of the quality standards achieved by private sector contractors operating in some public sector organisations, while private sector employees often suspect that efficiency (ie cost savings) is in fact more important than quality criteria in determining which firms win contracts to supply ancillary services.

A fourth reason for increased outsourcing activity in recent years simply derives from the fact that there is more opportunity for organisations to contract out their non-core activities. The growth during the past two decades of companies specialising in the provision of such services is itself a factor in the trend. Twenty years ago it was not so easy as it is now to find a good external supplier of security or catering services and there was less competition between the providers who were in business. Now we have large (even international) operations which are very efficiently managed, and which have access to equipment, expertise and personnel that make them a great deal more attractive as potential service suppliers. In a sense, therefore, the process has developed its own momentum. The bigger the outsourcing industries get, the more able they are to supply services at the price and of the quality that organisations require.

Table 3.1 Atkinson's model

Reasons for contracting-out	
To achieve cost savings	47%
To improve services	43%
To focus on core business activities	30%
To achieve greater flexibility	10%
Due to government regulation or policy	2%
Reasons for contracting-in	
To achieve cost savings	57%
To improve services	51%
Sufficient in-house capacity	8%
Staff/union pressure	1%

Source: Kersley *et al* (2006:105–107)

PROBLEMS WITH OUTSOURCING

The theoretical case for outsourcing is readily understood and compelling from a management point of view. However, the survey evidence suggests that the reality often disappoints in practice. Outsourcing a function, particularly where it is well established internally, is a problematic experience for many. According to Reilly (2001:135), the following difficulties are common:

- legal disputes over the meaning of contractual terms
- inability on the part of organisations to manage the relationship with contractors properly
- poor levels of service
- communication difficulties between client and contractor
- problems in evaluating/monitoring performance levels achieved.

At base there is the fundamental issue of a difference of interest between the two parties. The client (ie the outsourcer) wants a decent level of service provided, on an ongoing basis at a reasonable cost. By contrast, the contractor has a desire to maximise profits and reduce its costs wherever possible. In Reilly's view this often 'imperils the whole venture'. Where contracts are agreed on a fixed-price basis, contractors tend to 'skimp on the service as much as possible' by interpreting service level agreements quite narrowly. By contrast, where the price is variable, the client being billed according to the amount of work done in a particular week or the type of services provided (a cost-plus contract), contractors try to 'gild the lily' by over-staffing and providing too good a standard of service. Promises are often made (or half-made) during the negotiation process which do not subsequently materialise in practice, and it is frequently difficult in practice to develop a really fruitful, high-trust relationship between the two parties.

Were there perfect competition in the outsourcing industry such problems would be rare, but when contracts are signed for periods of five years or more following tendering exercises the two parties are obliged to work together. It is not easy, in practice, to ditch one contractor and immediately employ another. Aside from practical problems, legal action can easily ensue, the courts having to decide on the correct interpretation of particular contractual terms. In addition, of course, there is a range of employee relations and regulatory issues that prevent the swift dispatch either of an internally provided service or one staffed and managed by an external contractor. Such processes often result in redundancies and are, of course, governed by the requirements of the Transfer of Undertakings Regulations.

There is also some question over the extent to which outsourcing exercises save money in practice. The 1998 Workplace Employment Relations Survey (cited by Reilly 2001:136) found that costs had fallen as a result of outsourcing in only a third of the cases reported by respondents. This is because there are costs associated with outsourcing which are not immediately apparent. An example is the complexity of the contracts that need to be drawn up between the client and the contractor. Stredwick and Ellis (1998:154) state that 'contracts can, almost literally, weigh a ton', running to hundreds of pages even for the provision of quite straightforward services. These are often major deals worth millions over several years. Hence there is a need to involve firms of commercial lawyers in drafting, and subsequently interpreting, agreements. Further problems occur when contractors are not as viable commercially as they appear during the tendering process. The highly competitive nature of the businesses in which they operate means that margins are necessarily tight. Even if there are no problems at all with the performance of the contract in your organisation, your provider may have to pull out or re-negotiate terms because of difficulties in other organisations which they supply. It is not uncommon for service providers to fold altogether, leaving the client with no service at all.

Finally there are problems that result from the organisation forfeiting control over the outsourced functions. From an HRM perspective, this means losing control over who is hired to undertake roles, the approach used to performance management and the management of discipline and dismissal for unsatisfactory staff. Where problems arise (eg absence, lateness, poor service provision etc), solving them is outside the hands of the purchasing organisation. They can complain and put pressure on the contractor to address the issue, but cannot deal with it themselves. Where outsourced services have a direct impact on the effective performance of core functions this loss of control can be a major drawback with severe negative implications for the business. Colling (2005) stresses the significance of employee relations and the way that they are often damaged as a result of outsourcing. Low trust follows and, often, a reduced willingness to be flexible and work beyond contract.

OUTSOURCING P&D FUNCTIONS

Despite the presence of a great deal of hype in the HR press about the outsourcing of P&D departments, survey evidence shows that the vast majority of employers in the UK have not chosen to take this path. IDS (1999:14) was right to complain about a dangerous tendency for commentators to mistake a few high-profile examples for an 'inexorable trend'. In fact, as is demonstrated by a major CIPD survey into developments in HR provision (CIPD 2007a) the big majority of UK organisations continue to provide all the core HR activities in-house. Moreover, in recent years there have been several examples of large corporations contracting HR services back in-house (Pickard 2007). There has been some growth in the extent to which the payroll function has been contracted out in recent years, while organisations seem more willing to draw on external expertise when recruiting and training people, but there is nothing new about this at all. The truth is that organisations have long drawn on external providers in a range of HRM support roles and that they continue to do so. A number of these are directly relevant to the material covered in this book. The most commonly outsourced areas in the UK are the following:

- training
- recruitment
- payroll management
- safety and security monitoring/advice
- occupational health services
- legal advisory services
- childcare facilities
- employee welfare & counselling services
- pre-employment testing
- HR information services
- salary surveys
- benefits
- relocation
- organisational development.

Despite the patchy rate of expansion, it is true that there has been greater interest recently in the idea of outsourcing HR. It is also the case that organisations have given greater consideration to the possibility. We are seeing, for example, moves in some larger organisations towards the establishment of a 'shared services model' for their HR functions. This means that the function is set up as a separate business within the organisation and is required to sell its services to other business units. HRM departments in this position are not being outsourced, but the arrangement is a step in that direction and does require them to compete with external agencies for business. The other development which is clearly recognised in the literature is the trend for businesses which are too small to retain the services of HR employees to buy in specialist advice from outside providers. Whereas previously such organisations would have used an external pension provider and payroll administration service, they are now increasingly likely to purchase a wider range of advisory services externally. The growth in the volume of employment legislation partly explains this trend, but it also derives from the greater presence of consultancies specialising in HR issues.

Other factors may also explain the growth in interest in HR outsourcing. Reed (2001:120) sees globalisation as a significant factor. The need to expand operations internationally leads to the employment of overseas workers by employers who are not familiar with prevailing employment rights and customs in foreign countries. They are therefore obliged to hire external advisors. Another factor, according to IDS (2000a:2) is the development of new technologies:

> The increasing sophistication of HR software is enabling more routine elements of HR work to be automated. The parallel advance in corporate intranet technology is also transforming the ways in which line managers and employees can access HR information. But the investment that these developments entail in building and maintaining IT systems has led some employers to seek specialist suppliers capable of delivering this new model of HR administration on their behalf, while freeing up core HR staff to concentrate on more strategic issues.

There are therefore good reasons for believing that larger organisations may outsource more HR activity in the future than they have in the past. However, it is likely that in most cases this will be restricted to basic administrative matters that have no role in adding value. Far from allowing flexibility, such arrangements are often rather inflexible as the purchasing company is obliged to accept whatever standard package of services the contractor is set up to provide.

EXERCISE BOX: ACCENTURE AND BT

EXERCISE 3.4

Read the article by Jane Pickard entitled 'Should I Stay or Should I Go?' featured in *People Management* (25 March 2004, pages 31-36). This can be downloaded from the *People Management* archive on the CIPD's website (www.cipd.co.uk).

This article describes the experiences of BT following its decision in 2000 to outsource much of its HR administration to Accenture. The deal was initially set up as a joint venture, but BT sold its stake in 2001, so Accenture now provide the service to BT entirely on a sub-contracted basis. This was a five-year deal, so BT's managers had to decide in 2005 whether to continue the existing arrangement, whether to outsource to another company or whether to take

back some of the functions to provide on an in-house basis. In the event, they decided to sign a further agreement with Accenture. The article describes many of the problems that were encountered during the first years of the outsourcing arrangement.

Questions:

1 What features of this particular outsourcing deal gave it a good chance of succeeding?

2 What were the major problems encountered? What was their cause?

3 What changes were made some years into the arrangement to make it work better?

CRITICISMS OF FLEXIBILITY

The above discussion shows that there are many disadvantages as well as advantages associated with flexible working practices, and these probably account for the rather modest moves towards the flexible firm model undertaken by employers in practice. However, there remains a school of thought which supports the ideas associated with flexibility and argues that we *should* be moving in that direction a great deal faster than we are. Advocates of greater flexibility believe that there will be no other way to compete in a post-industrial world, and that organisations which do not maximise their flexible capabilities are likely to founder when faced competitively with others that do. This is by no means a view which is universally shared. Many take issue with the central thesis of those arguing in favour of flexibility and put forward compelling arguments in support of their position. The major strands of the critical case are set out below. All are characterised by a tendency to equate the concept of 'flexibility' with that of 'employment insecurity'. Readers seeking more detailed treatments of these debates are referred to two excellent books of articles edited by Heery & Salmon (2000) and Burchell *et al* (2002).

The major management objection to the principles of the flexible firm model relate to its supposed incompatibility with high-commitment HRM practices. It is argued that organisations cannot have it both ways in this regard. They cannot, on the one hand, create a situation in which human resources are deployed as and when required so as to maximise short-term efficiency, while also requiring staff to exhibit a high degree of commitment. It is argued that flexibility, because it creates insecurity, is associated with low commitment on the part of employees. In consequence, staff turnover rates will be higher in flexible firms, while employees are less likely to perform above and beyond the basic requirements of their contracts. There is more likely to be cynicism on the part of staff and less identification with the aims of the organisation. The result, over the long term, is a low level of performance resulting from the presence of unenthusiastic staff and recruitment and retention difficulties. In short, the suggestion is that people who perceive themselves to be peripheral to the operation (a large proportion in the flexible firm model) will act accordingly.

A development of these points forms the second major strand of the argument against flexibility. This relates to the health of the national economy as a whole, with important implications for individual organisations. It is argued that a situation in which all organisations evolve into flexible firms will have negative long-term consequences for the country. First and foremost, there is concern that in flexible organisations employers tend to seek to hire staff who are already trained, and refrain from developing people themselves. Why invest in training people who are classed as peripheral and with whom the organisation expects to have a relatively short-term relationship? Ultimately the result will be (and some would argue already is) a situation in which there are chronic skills shortages. The result is reduced output as employers find themselves unable to take up business opportunities and, over time, economic decline. Instead, the critics argue, employers should be actively encouraged (or even forced) to invest in people with whom they expect to have a long-term relationship. It follows that the best interests of economy over the longer term are met by expanding rather than contracting the size of the 'core' in the Atkinson model.

A third strand of argument brings in ethical considerations. The concern here is that managers will inevitably be tempted to use the development of a peripheral workforce to exercise too great a degree of power. People who perceive their position at work to be precarious are understandably keen to seek greater security. Peripheral workers will thus try, wherever they can, to gain admittance to the core. This, it is argued, gives employers considerable leverage over them – power which can easily be abused. The result is a situation in which managers intensify work to an unacceptable degree, require that people work longer hours than is good for them and generally exploit their vulnerability. From a management perspective, such a situation is only viable in the short term. Over time the organisation's reputation in the labour market slips, making it harder to recruit and retain people. It can potentially also lead to legal action where levels of employer-induced stress lead to ill health.

A fourth set of arguments is more political in nature, but also carries important implications for organisations. The suggestion here is that widespread adoption of the flexible firm model will lead to a more unequal society (ie even more unequal than it currently is). We will see a clearer evolution of two distinct classes of employed persons, one of which consists of people in secure, well-paid employment, the other composed of insecure, peripheral people. The result will be (and many would argue already is) a substantial rise in crime, in the incidence of family breakdown and in political alienation – all outcomes that arise when a people become less socially cohesive. This in turn requires government intervention, which necessitates higher taxation and less demand for privately produced goods and services.

Some employers also report difficulties associated with operationalising some kinds of flexible working. Wolff (2009a) reports the following findings from the most recent IRS survey of employers on the question of 'problems with flexible working':

- 50 per cent report having difficulty arranging meetings
- 48 per cent find that there is greater complexity scheduling hours
- 42 per cent report having to handle resentment from employees who do not work flexibly
- 41 per cent find difficulties in arranging training for flexible workers
- 39 per cent report internal communication difficulties
- 34 per cent find that flexible working created 'customer service' issues.

EMPLOYABILITY AND MUTUAL FLEXIBILITY

On the surface it appears that two irreconcilable positions have been summarised in this chapter. On the one hand there is a strong commercial case for moving towards greater flexibility on the grounds that it brings with it greater efficiency and the ability to cope well with change. On the other, there are serious arguments against such a trend, based on the long-term harm that results from the creation of insecurity. How, if at all, can these points of view be reconciled and a sound conclusion be reached?

First of all it is necessary to accept that the term 'flexibility' as developed in Atkinson's model of the flexible firm covers several very distinct types of employment practice. Not all of these are necessarily equated with insecurity. Indeed, functional flexibility is fully associated with the employment of 'core' workers with whom a long-term association is desirable. Secondly, many other practices are potentially as attractive to employees as to employers. The main examples are flexitime, part-time working, term-time working, compressed hours and homeworking, but it is clear from the experience of people working in the IT industry that subcontracting is also a form of relationship that some find both comfortable and profitable. It is important, therefore, not to tar all forms of flexible working with the brush of 'insecurity'.

Secondly, there is merit in the argument that in a changing world, staff have more to gain in the long term from improving their 'employability' than they do from remaining in employment with one organisation. The argument is based on the presumption that no job can be particularly secure in the contemporary business environment because technological developments are evolving at such a great speed. It follows that none of us should expect to remain employed in the same occupation through to retirement and that our best hope of remaining in work is to build up a portfolio of varied experience on which to draw as and when it is required. New opportunities should thus be welcomed and not feared, because they are the source of our future employability.

Looking at the issues from this perspective it is possible, at least in theory, to argue that organisations can become more flexible while at the same time avoiding the generation of additional insecurity. Such a conclusion is reached by Reilly (2001) in his work on the concept of 'mutual flexibility', by which he means forms which bring mutual benefits to both employees and employers. Central to Reilly's argument is the role of partnership and negotiated changes. Involving staff in decision-making about greater flexibility, and taking their concerns on board, is a good way of ensuring that the interests of both employer and employee are properly addressed.

In addition it is argued that employers should focus their attention on the types of flexible working practice which employees appreciate. Those that breed perceptions of insecurity, such as zero hours contracts and the widespread use of fixed-term contracts, should thus be avoided except where it is strictly necessary. Moreover, functional flexibility should be promoted as an alternative to the numerical and temporal forms where it is in the interests of employees that it should be. Finally, there should be a genuine commitment on the part of employers seeking more flexibility actively to enhance their people's future prospects (ie their employability) by actively developing them through the provision of relevant training and experience. In these ways insecurity can be minimised and sustainable flexibility maximised.

EXERCISE BOX

EXERCISE 3.5

Read the article by Rebecca Clake entitled 'How to make flexible working work' featured in *People Management* (11 January 2007, pages 48-49). This can be downloaded from the *People Management* archive on the CIPD's website (www.cipd. co.uk).

In this short article the author makes a series of practical and very sensible suggestions as to how an organisation should go about introducing greater flexibility if it wants to maximise the chances of its objectives being met.

People management

Questions:

1 What are the major benefits that can be gained as a result of introducing flexible working?

2 What situations can arise which hinder the success of flexible working initiatives?

3 How can these be avoided?

EXAMPLE

KEY ARTICLE BOX

'Improving working lives: flexible working and the role of employee control' by Laura Hall and Carol Atkinson. *Employee Relations*, Vol. 28 No. 4. 374–386 (2006)

In this article the authors draw on extensive semi-structured interviews and sessions with a focus group made up of staff employed in an NHS trust. Their aim is to explore employees' perceptions of flexible working practices, having been asked by the Trust's HR department to investigate why so few staff were taking advantage of the extensive range of flexible working options available to them. They found that most staff were unaware of formal flexible working policies and did not see them as being relevant to them. However, by contrast the interviewees expressed considerable interest in and satisfaction with informally arranged flexible working practices.

Questions:

1 Why were the staff in this Trust unaware of the range of flexible working opportunities available as part of formal P&D policies?

2 Why did they see these policies as being irrelevant to them?

3 Why were the informal practices of so much greater interest?

4 What practical lessons can be learned from this research about ways of introducing more flexible working opportunities in organisations?

EXPLORE FURTHER

- The topic areas looked at in this chapter are covered in several recent books. Among the most useful are *Flexible working* by John Stredwick and Steve Ellis (2005) and *Flexibility at work* by Peter Reilly (2001).

- Several textbooks contain articles looking at forms of flexible working, their advantages and disadvantages. These include work by Bryson (1999), Campos E Chuna (2002) and Colling (2005).

- Critical perspectives are well covered in recent books edited by Heery & Salmon (2000) and Burchell *et al* (2002), and in the articles by Allen (2000) and Ward *et al* (2001).

- IDS have published a series of studies focusing in detail on the experience of organisations introducing different types of flexible working. Recent studies have covered flexitime, annual hours, teleworking and the outsourcing of the HR function.

CHAPTER 4

Fairness and diversity

LEARNING OUTCOMES

By the end of this chapter, readers should be able to:

- develop policies and practices which promote equal opportunities and diversity at work
- put the case in favour of actively promoting diversity
- advise managers about legal rights and responsibilities in the field of discrimination law
- advise about how best to develop and manage culturally diverse teams of staff.

In addition, readers should be able to understand and explain:

- why unfair discrimination in the workplace continues in the twenty-first century
- the debate about the 'equal opportunities' and 'diversity management' approaches to the promotion of equality at work
- the major principles that underpin discrimination law in the UK and across the EU
- research about cultural differences between countries and their impact on expatriate workers.

DISCRIMINATION AT WORK

In Chapter 1 it was argued that when judging or evaluating resourcing policies, interventions and decisions, fairness should be one of the three major criteria used. The arguments in favour of the idea that fairness should infuse HR practice derive from 'equity theory' of the kind developed by Adams (1963) which links job satisfaction, employee commitment and superior performance to perceptions on the part of staff about fairness. When employees believe that they are being treated unfairly, they tend to redress the balance somewhat by working less hard or contributing somewhat less than they might. There is a considerable amount of research evidence to back up this theory (see Mowday 1996), allowing us to state with confidence that creating resourcing and talent systems which are perceived as being fair is necessary if an organisation is to thrive.

On one level this can be achieved simply by ensuring that 'fair dealing' is a principle that is followed across all areas of HR activity, but it is also necessary to go further. Whether we like to recognise it or not, unfair discrimination against particular groups in our society continues at one level or another, often unconsciously, and this is as true in the workplace as it is in other walks of life. Institutional sexism, racism, homophobia and ageism is present and has a habit of becoming more significant unless a conscious effort is made to recognise it and to fight against it. Organisations that wish to maximise the performance of their staff and gain a reputation for being good employers thus have to take additional steps, and be seen to be doing so, if they are to succeed. As a minimum, this means adhering to the expectations of discrimination law, but will often also involve going further than is required legally in a bid to establish a workforce and a management team that is suitably diverse in its make-up.

Despite considerable progress being made in some areas, discrimination on a number of different unfair grounds remains a significant feature of workplaces in the UK, a characteristic shared with workplaces across the world (Pocock 2008). Members of some groups enjoy greater opportunities than those from others and as a result enjoy higher rates of employment, a higher proportion of the more senior jobs and higher levels of pay. In 2008 the Equality and Human Rights Commission published two reports looking at the extent of such discrimination (Walby *et al* 2008 and Longhi & Platt 2008). Some of their findings were as follows:

- 20 per cent of white people live in low income households; the figure for black people is 41 per cent.

- Men's average gross hourly pay is £12.90; the figure for women is £10.10. Women's average pay is 78 per cent of men's.

- 81 per cent of able bodied people have jobs; the figure for disabled people is only 60 per cent.

- On average men aged 60–64 earn 24 per cent less than men aged 40–44.

- 24 per cent of able-bodied people are educated to degree level or above; the figure for disabled people is only 13 per cent.

- 19 per cent of men are employed in senior, managerial jobs; the figure for women is only 11 per cent.

- 13.5 per cent of black people perceive that they have personally suffered from discrimination at work; the figure for white people is 0.5 per cent.

There are many different explanations for the persistence of pay gaps and employment gaps between different groups despite 40 years of equality legislation, major government drives to improve matters and the now widespread acceptance across society that unfair discrimination is wholly unacceptable. Debates rage among specialists working in this field about which factors play which roles and to what degrees in explaining continued discrimination, but in truth there are no simple, single explanations. Unfair discrimination continues for a variety of reasons. The key points are summarised very effectively by Graves and Powell (2008:439–450):

i) Stereotyping

We have a tendency to associate certain characteristics with types of people. Hence women tend to be stereotyped as gentle and motherly while men are typically seen as being dominant and decisive. This plays a part in maintaining gender segregation at work and leads to men dominating the more senior jobs.

ii) Prejudice

Blatant, overt sexism, racism and homophobia are less common than they used to be, but still operate subtly. Some men tend to be hostile towards ambitious career-minded women, instead seeing women as needing their protection. Subtle sexism may be benevolent in intent, but it still sees women as inferior to men. The same is true of the subtle racism which has lower expectations of some ethnic minorities than others. Prejudice of this kind can be unconscious, but detrimental nonetheless to affected groups.

iii) Status characteristics

Western societies generally tend to accord higher social esteem to white people, able-bodied people, well-educated upper class people and to men. High status groups are expected to take up leadership roles and positions of authority, it being something that is remarked upon as unusual when someone from outside a high esteem group achieves such a position.

iv) Social roles

Social expectations vary for men and women and are established very early on in life. Men are expected to be breadwinners and women to be homemakers. As we grow up most of us develop skills that accord with these expectations, taking these with us into the workplace. As a result we have male dominated and female dominated occupations. When someone crosses over (eg a man works in a female role or vice versa) they tend to be rated unfavourably.

v) Prototype matching

Managers have a tendency to have an 'ideal prototype' in mind when looking for someone to fill a role. Prototypes tend to incorporate sex, race and especially age alongside other characteristics. This makes it easier for someone who matches the prototype to get appointed than someone who has other characteristics.

vi) Similarity attraction/social identity

People have a preference for working with others who are similar to them in terms of their social identity, background, attitudes and values. Sometimes such preferences include (perhaps unconsciously) attributes associated with gender, race, age, religion and sexual orientation. Decision-makers thus look more favourably on those who share characteristics with them than those who don't. The groups with power thus hand on that power to successive generations.

vii) Group composition

Most workplaces or parts of workplaces (departments, divisions, offices etc) tend to be dominated by majority groups. Some are male-dominated, some female-dominated, most are white-dominated. The values and preferences of the largest group tend then to become the norm, making it harder for minorities to fit in and perform as well as those who are part of the majority. The latter thus tend to advance further and faster.

TACKLING INEQUALITY AND PROMOTING DIVERSITY

There are a number of good reasons for organisations to address the issue of inequality as between different minority or underrepresented groups. They can be grouped into three distinct, if overlapping, categories.

First there is a case based on legal compliance. As will be demonstrated later in this chapter the amount of anti-discrimination law has grown substantially in recent years, providing strong incentives for employers to take the issue seriously and to avoid making decisions or pursuing policies which are detrimental to the lives or livelihoods of minority groups. Substantial compensation can be won in employment tribunals when claimants win discrimination cases, but costs accrue to employers even when they win because so much management time and effort is taken up in mounting a defence. Lawyers' fees can be high too when an organisation chooses not to provide its own representative. An alternative is to settle cases before they get to a hearing, but this too costs money and can, when a claimant's case is relatively weak, send out a signal to other would-be litigants that it is worth their while to pursue a weak claim because their employer is likely to reach a financial settlement with them. Avoiding claims, be they genuine or speculative, is thus the best alternative available and that means both acting within the law and being seen to do so.

There are also good reputational reasons for avoiding discrimination claims in the employment tribunal. Reporters from the press are frequently present and happy to report all the details of the evidence that is presented with embellishments if it helps to sell their newspapers. The results can be damaging in terms of an organisation's reputation as an employer, as a provider of goods and services and more generally in its community. The reputation of individual managers can suffer too. Under the terms of the Equality Act 2010 all public authorities are required actively to promote equality at work and to produce annual reports setting out what they have done. There is thus a particular incentive placed in the law for managements in public service organisations to take equality issues seriously and to be seen to act accordingly.

The wish to preserve and enhance corporate reputation also forms a major part of the business case for addressing equal opportunities issues. The various strands that make this up are set out with some vigour by the CIPD in its position paper on the management of diversity published in 2007. Based principally on the experience of a group of case study companies, this paper argues that initiatives taken in this field both help to support the achievement of business goals and also 'enhance overall performance' (CIPD 2007b:37). The key points are as follows:

- Staff are impressed when their employer commits to an agenda which is seen as being fair to everyone and this is reflected in lower employee turnover.
- An organisation which gains a reputation in its labour markets for treating people fairly is more likely to attract good performers to work for it.
- A wider range of employees apply for positions with organisations that are perceived to be fair employers. This means that the potential selection pool is larger when jobs are advertised allowing the organisation a better choice of candidates.
- An organisation which reflects in its make-up the diversity of its customer base is more likely to serve its clients well and to attract and retain their business.
- Local authorities as well as some other public bodies and larger private sector organisations often take account of the extent and nature of equality initiatives pursued by employing organisations when awarding contracts in competitive tendering situations.

Table 4.1 CIPD survey on motivation for diversity management

Drivers	Most important	Some importance
Legal pressures	32%	68%
To recruit and retain the best talent	13%	64%
Corporate social responsibility	13%	63%
To be an employer of choice	15%	61%
Because it makes business sense	17%	60%
Because it's morally right	13%	60%
To improve business performance	6%	48%
To address recruitment problems	8%	46%
Belief in social justice	9%	46%
Desire to improve customer relations	5%	43%
To improve products and services	10%	44%
To improve creativity and innovation	6%	43%
To reach diverse markets	6%	39%
To improve corporate branding	5%	37%
To enhance decision-making	3%	35%
Trade union activities	3%	32%
To respond to competition in the market	6%	32%
To respond to the global market	6%	30%

- Decision-making tends to be better when the senior levels of organisations are populated with people who reflect the full diversity of the communities in which they wish to do business.

- Equality initiatives can form part of a broader range of activities aimed at achieving a strong ethical or socially responsible image as an organisation. This too can help to attract customers, as well as would-be staff and investors.

This last point overlaps with the third type of case for taking an active interest in equality issues, namely the straightforward ethical or moral case. The rise of ethical consumerism in recent years as well as the growth of ethical investment funds means that there is a business case for ethical action on the part of employers, but the essence of the ethical case stands irrespective of this. Unfair discrimination is just plain wrong. It is socially unjust that some groups should succeed more than others for no good reason. The reluctance of organisations and their managers to take this on board is why there needs to be so much regulation in this area, but there is plenty of evidence to demonstrate that a purely ethical case can sometimes impress even the most hard-nosed and commercially-oriented managers. Indeed many give credit to HR managers in US and European organisations for pushing forward this whole agenda in recent decades and show that in large part the underlying motivation for doing so has been ethical rather than commercial (see Dobbin 2009). This is particularly so in respect of initiatives to promote the interests of disabled people, where the business case is sometimes a good deal less strong than it is for other categories of discrimination (Woodhams and Danieli 2000).

In practice it would seem that managers are motivated by a mixture of factors when promoting this agenda in their organisations, some legal, some commercial and some ethical. CIPD (2007b) carried out an extensive survey of its members and established that there was rarely one overriding driver that played a part, although legal compliance topped the list (see Table 4.1). This survey was notable because it demonstrated how very varied the types of motivation are that have prodded organisations into pursuing an equality agenda.

EXERCISE BOX: DEBATES ABOUT DIVERSITY

EXERCISE 4.1

Read the following two articles featured in *People Management*. They can be downloaded from the *People Management* archive on the CIPD's website (www.cipd.co.uk):

- 'Variety Performance' by Rima Evans (23 November 2006)

- 'Under the Skin' by Binna Kandola (30 July 2009)

The first of these articles surveys the UK equal opportunities/diversity scene 30 years after the passing of the Race Relations Act 1976. It concludes that considerable progress has been made, but that the record of UK workplaces in this area is still too poor. Interviewees express their belief that further progress will come if the business case for diversity is propagated more effectively. In the second article Binna Kandola challenges this view. The business case in his view is illogical. A fresh approach is necessary which starts with a recognition of how deep-seated our prejudices still are.

Questions:

1 What are the main arguments for and against the existence of a genuinely compelling business case in favour of diverse workforces and management teams?

2 Why after years of equality legislation and initiatives are UK workplaces still so unequal?

3 To what extent do you agree with Kandola's view that some form of 'prejudice awareness training' needs to form the basis of fresh approaches to building greater equality at work?

EQUAL OPPORTUNITIES V MANAGING DIVERSITY

Unquestionably one of the major developments in this field over recent years has been a switch in language from an approach labelled 'providing equal opportunities' to one labelled 'managing diversity'. Equal opportunities approaches are the longest established (see Torrington *et al* 2009:236–240). In essence they are concerned with preventing discriminatory acts which cause a detriment to members of defined socially disadvantaged groups such as women, members of ethnic minorities and disabled people. The aim is to create a level playing field so that all can compete on equal terms. Under an equal opportunities approach everyone must be treated the same by organisations, action being taken by managers to encourage the creation of a workforce which at all levels is broadly representative of the working population. The rationale for an equal opportunities approach is social justice backed by legislation which seeks to enforce compliance.

Over time, however, in many people's eyes the equal opportunities approach has fallen from favour. The chief problem is its apparent failure in practice to lead to real equality in the workplace. Equality of opportunity does not necessarily lead to equality of outcome. Organisations put in place policies, procedures and targets, but underlying attitudes don't change very much, nor do organisational cultures. There is also, according to some, a further fundamental problem. Equal opportunities approaches focus on specific groups labelled 'disadvantaged' or 'minorities' while ignoring the interests of everyone else. They have little to offer the majority, despite many of them feeling that they were not treated fairly or equally by their employers because of some other under-valued or stereotyped characteristic.

During the 1990s a different approach began to gain support and has since become dominant in many organisations. According to Greene (2010) 'managing diversity' differs from 'equal opportunities' in two key respects:

i It is less focused on minorities, seeking instead to recognise and value the differences that all people exhibit.

ii It is more dependent for its legitimacy than the equal opportunities approach on a business case rather than a moral or legal one.

Managing diversity involves the use of more positive language that embraces everyone. We are all different, is the argument, and all have diverse abilities and characteristics which the organisation can harness to its advantages. Rather than seeking to treat everyone in the same way on a level playing field as happens when an equal opportunities philosophy is developed, the immense variety of attributes that human beings have is celebrated. All can contribute in different ways. CIPD (2007a:11) sums up the attractions of the approach and the way that it differs from equal opportunities as follows:

> Managing diversity is about ensuring that all employees have the opportunity to maximise their potential and enhance their self development and their contribution to the organisation. It's not about positive or affirmative action for select groups to create a level playing field for all. By doing this we're automatically (unconsciously) not indulging in stereotyping, inaccurate perceptions and practising discrimination, but accepting that *all* employees can have a positive input into the processes and objectives of the organisation.

This shift in philosophy has itself, however, been the subject of considerable criticism. This is explored effectively by Greene (2010). First there is concern that the emphasis placed on a business case means that 'managing diversity' can only go so far in combating the effects in the workplace of deeply-rooted prejudices towards and disadvantages suffered by minority groups. All may benefit to some extent from a management philosophy that celebrates difference, but without further imposed constraints and incentives true equality of outcome will not be achieved. Secondly it is claimed that 'managing diversity' is an attractive idea that is very difficult in practice to deliver. As a concept it is quite woolly and confusing, and hence hard to operationalise. Torrington *et al* (2008:239) develop this point by looking at differences between the ways that men and women tend to behave at work. Women, it is argued, have a preference for group-working, avoiding the spotlight and forming one or two close relationships. They also dislike hierarchy and tend towards a collectivist view of employment relations. Men, by contrast, are more competitive, like to develop a high profile in an organisation, are individualistic and tend to have many more relationships that are shallower in nature. It follows, under an approach which values difference, that men and women should be managed differently by organisations in order to get the best out of them. But how can this be done in practice? And is it really desirable that it should be, given that doing so stereotypes men and women in a rough and ready way. There are plenty of men who share some of the female characteristics and vice versa.

In short, as Foster and Harris (2005) conclude, managing diversity is 'easy to say' but 'difficult to do'. This truth leads to the other major criticisms of 'managing diversity' in practice. One is that it amounts to little more than 'rhetoric' which is not matched by reality. The other is that there is little convincing evidence available linking the adoption of 'managing diversity' with positive business outcomes.

PRACTICAL EMPLOYER INITIATIVES

In practice employers vary to a considerable extent in terms of what, if anything, they do to advance either an equal opportunities or a managing diversity agenda. Torrington *et al* (2008) identify four distinct categories of employers:

i   Avoidance. These employers pay as little attention as they can to the equality/ diversity agenda, running the risk of legal action but hoping that they will be lucky and avoid it.

ii Compliance. Employers in this category do what they have to in order to comply with legislation, but little more. They have written policies and procedures, and undertake some training, but there is no high profile adoption of diversity principles.

iii Valuing diversity. These organisations appreciate the business case for managing diversity and take active steps to operationalise the underlying principles. They do more than is required by law, tackling cultural barriers and infusing their activities with diversity initiatives.

iv Sharing the value of diversity. This final group make the management of diversity a priority and actively seek to lead in this area of HR activity. Their efforts are well publicised and they tend to act as best practice exemplars for other organisations to follow.

Wolff (2009c) reports the results of an IRS survey which suggests that employers are steadily moving 'up' these categories and that more are thinking beyond legal compliance than they used to. This reflects increased diversity within organisations and the appointment of staff (often within HR departments) who have specific responsibility for driving the agenda forward. Two thirds of the employers in this survey stated that their aim was 'to put diversity and equality at the heart of what they do'. Care must be taken in reading too much into these results. The sample covered all kinds of organisations, but was quite small (140 employers). Nonetheless it does suggest that diversity issues are moving up rather than down the management agenda and that supportive rhetoric is now widespread.

What does this mean in practice? What kinds of activity or initiative do employers introduce in order to advance the equal opportunities/diversity agenda in the workplace? CIPD (2007b) found evidence of the following:

- diversity awareness training
- employee attitude surveys
- diversity training for mangers
- inclusion of diversity in mission statements
- setting diversity objectives
- building diversity into business goals
- applying diversity standards
- including diversity-related goals in performance assessments
- rewarding and recognising diversity.

Kossek and Pichler (2007:220 and 262–268) develop these points and also suggest ways in which resourcing and talent management activities can be tailored so that they accord with diversity principles. As far as recruitment is concerned their major advice is to use multiple sources so as to enhance the chances that people from a wide range of diverse social groups are made aware of job opportunities. The aim should be to gain access to as wide a 'talent pool' as possible. This will maximise the chances of highly able people being encouraged to apply, while also making sure that the existence of the opening is communicated to members of under-represented groups as well as those from which the organisation customarily recruits people. The same principle applies when the selection stage is reached. The idea here is that no single selection method should be used, but a variety. This not only has the effect of helping an organisation better predict on-the-job performance, it also makes sure that people are not 'weeded out' because of poor performance using one method. Kossek and Pichler also recommend that members of minority groups should be on interview panels, that structured interviews should be used so as to ensure consistency and that messages stressing the organisation's commitment to diversity should be included in recruitment advertisements and other literature sent to candidates. They also argue for a policy of transparency in terms of decision-making criteria so that all candidates know clearly where they stand.

Beyond the recruitment field the major recommended action is diversity training for managers and for other employees, both of a general awareness-raising kind and in preparation for interviewing or performance appraisals. Another common approach involves setting up mentoring programmes for members of disadvantaged groups so that knowledge and experience can be shared between people of a similar background. Finally, it is proposed that organisations need to monitor their progress formally by collecting statistics about the impact of interventions and about the numbers of people from under-represented groups. These can then be used as the basis of benchmarking and targeting exercises. It is necessary to collect information about perceptions as well as hard figures, and this is easily achieved by adding appropriate items to a staff attitude survey/ questionnaire.

Successive Workplace Employment Relations Surveys (WERS) sponsored by the government have tracked some of the actions being taken by UK employers over recent decades in the equal opportunities/diversity fields. Dex and Forth (2009), reviewing this data conclude that progress over the past 25 years has been slow and patchy, but that progress has nonetheless been made. For example, WERS data reveals that a good majority of employers now have formal equal opportunities policies and that these have been updated in recent years to include reference to disability, religion, sexual orientation and age in addition to sex and race. A growing minority of UK workplaces undertake formal equal opportunities monitoring, while in the public sector at least, equal opportunities statements are increasingly included in recruitment literature as a means of encouraging applications from a wider range of people. On the negative side from an equality point of view, these authors express disappointment at the continued prevalence of informal recruitment practices (see Chapter 7) and an apparent reluctance to carry out equal pay audits to establish whether or not men and women are being remunerated fairly. More generally they point out that the public sector has shown itself to be considerably more keen to adopt practices in this field than either the private or the voluntary sectors have been – a discrepancy also picked up in the CIPD survey (CIPD 2007c:5). However, according to the WERS data the biggest success story as far as diversity in UK workplaces is concerned has been the rapid adoption over the past 15 years or so of family-friendly practices and work-life balance initiatives which make it possible for people to take up jobs that would otherwise not be available to them, and subsequently to remain in those jobs for longer.

DISCRIMINATION LAW

However compelling the case for embracing diversity and equal opportunities may be in theory, there remains plenty of resistance to it. Moreover, as we saw above, the need to comply with the law is the most significant single reason that employers give when asked why they have taken action in the fields of equal opportunities/diversity. This is not surprising when it is considered how easily employers can find themselves on the wrong side of discrimination law, even when they have no intention whatever to act either unfairly or unlawfully. Moreover, compensation levels can be high. It is thus important that all HR practitioners, and particularly those with responsibility for decision-making in the fields of resourcing and talent management, are familiar with the key principles that underpin the growing regulation in this area and are able to provide their organisations with sound advice.

PROTECTED CHARACTERISTICS

The European Union's Equal Treatment Framework Directive, originally agreed in 2000, has now been introduced across all member states. This extends similar types of protection to workers in respect of six major protected characteristics, namely:

- sex
- race, ethnicity and national origin
- disability
- sexual orientation
- religion or belief
- age.

In addition, further EU law offers a measure of protection from discrimination on three other grounds, although the law in these areas is less comprehensive and operates very differently:

- fixed-term employment
- part-time work

- agency work (from October 2011).

There are then some UK statutes which provide some kind of remedy for workers who are discriminated against on one or two other grounds. These are not areas of EU competence and, here too, the principles of the law vary considerably depending on the protected characteristic:

- trade union membership/non-membership
- marital status
- ex-offenders whose convictions are spent
- whistle-blowers
- people undergoing gender re-assignment.

It is not possible in a few thousand words to cover all these areas. So we will focus on the six that are covered by the EU Equal Treatment Framework Directive and which are the major concern of the Equality Act 2010.

 EXERCISE BOX: THE SCOPE OF DISCRIMINATION LAW

 People management

EXERCISE 4.2

Read the article by Richard M. Fox entitled 'Indian air hostesses were sacked for being overweight – could it happen in the UK?' featured in *People Management* (30 January 2009). This can be downloaded from the *People Management* archive on the CIPD's website (www.cipd.co.uk).

This article uses the news that an Indian airliner had sacked stewardesses who were over a set weight as a hook for a more general debate about the extent of protected characteristics covered by discrimination law and whether or not this should be extended.

Questions:

1   Would it be lawful for a UK-based airline to dismiss cabin crew who were overweight? Would it be lawful to set slimness as an essential criterion for recruitment into such a role?

2   What are the arguments in favour of the proposal to introduce a single statute banning 'all potentially discriminatory behaviour' rather than specifying that it should be on specific grounds such as sex and race?

3   What are the main arguments against the introduction of such a statute?

TYPES OF CLAIM

There are four distinct types of claim that a worker, former worker or failed job applicant can bring against an employer when a detriment of some kind is suffered. This can be financial loss, but also a loss of dignity or status, undue stress or some other form of injury, be it physical or mental in nature. The four are as follows:

- direct discrimination
- indirect discrimination

- victimisation

- harassment.

They are best explained by making reference to sex discrimination law, but in each case the same principles apply to the other five protected characteristics covered by the European directive.

Direct sex discrimination is straightforward. It is simply defined as a situation in which a man or a woman is 'treated less favourably' on account of his/her sex. It is thus a detrimental act which is aimed at, and causes direct suffering to, an individual wholly or mainly *because of* their sex. An example would be a refusal to appoint a well-qualified man to a role because there were already too many men employed in the relevant team. Another would be a pregnancy dismissal in which a woman's contract is terminated because of the pregnancy.

The key question that tribunals ask when faced with a claim for direct sex discrimination involves applying the 'but for test'. This was established by the House of Lords in the leading case of *James v Eastleigh Borough Council* in 1990:

Would the applicant have received the same treatment *but for* his or her sex?

If the answer is 'no' then an act of direct sex discrimination has occurred. It is all very straightforward. Importantly, thanks to this case, there is no longer any need for a comparator to be cited. The question asked is a hypothetical one. The tribunal has to decide, given the evidence before it, what would have happened in the same situation had the claimant been of the opposite gender.

Employers cannot generally defend themselves if they are found to have directly discriminated on grounds of sex. There is no defence of reasonableness available or one of objective justification. As a rule it is simply considered unlawful to directly discriminate on grounds of sex in any circumstances. If the tribunal decides this has happened, the case is won by the claimant and compensation has to be paid. The only exception occurs in recruitment decisions where there is a genuine occupational requirement (GOR) meaning that only men or women are suited to a particular role.

The number of situations in which this applies is few and far between. One example is where a job must be reserved for a man or a woman for reasons of authenticity (eg acting and modelling roles); another is where considerations of decency need to be taken into account (eg toilet attendants and bra fitters).

Indirect discrimination is a very different concept from direct discrimination, not least because it often occurs entirely unintentionally. It occurs when a 'provision, criterion or practice' which is apparently gender-neutral adversely affects considerably more men than women or vice versa. In practice this means the following:

i   An employer operates a policy or practice of some kind which favours the members of one sex over those of the other.

ii The practice is generally applied (eg on all workers or all job applicants).

iii A considerable proportion of either men or women are adversely affected by the practice (ie a detriment is suffered).

The classic example is a height requirement. If a job required all its holders to be over six feet tall (as used to be the case in the police), that would be a rule which indirectly discriminated against women. On the other hand, were a job advertisement to require applicants to be under six foot tall (as is the case for cabin crew working on some airlines), it could be said to be discriminating indirectly against men.

In cases of indirect discrimination the employer is able to deploy a defence of objective justification. In other words it is possible to win a case by showing that the 'provision, criterion or practice' is (or was) genuinely necessary. It is not sufficient for the employer to show that the practice was convenient or administratively desirable – that does not amount to objective justification. To form the basis of an acceptable defence it must be shown to be genuinely necessary for the achievement of a legitimate business objective. The defence of objective justification is now specifically phrased as follows:

a proportionate means of achieving a legitimate aim.

So in order for an employer to win a case of indirect discrimination the 'provision, criterion or practice' must be shown both to exist for a good purpose and to amount to a defensible method of achieving that purpose.

The term 'victimisation' has a much more specific meaning in employment law than it does in day-to-day conversation. Victimisation provisions appear in most employment statutes, the Sex Discrimination Act being no exception. It occurs when workers suffer a detriment wholly or partly because they have taken action under an employment statute such as one relating to sex discrimination, or have assisted others in doing so. There is no need for a comparator of the opposite sex here either. The tribunal is simply concerned with establishing if someone has suffered a detriment and, if so, whether or not they would have done had they not exercised their rights under the terms of a relevant statute.

Sexual harassment is defined in terms of how far the 'victim' was offended. It thus allows for the fact that what some people take as harmless banter (or even a complement) others may find hugely offensive. The statutory definition is broad, allowing all manner of potential situations to come within the remit of the law:

a it consists of conduct of a sexual nature or based on sex affecting the dignity of men or women at work

b it can be physical, verbal or 'non-verbal'

c it must be unwanted conduct

d the conduct or the person's response to it must *either* lead to material detriment *or* create an intimidating, hostile or humiliating work environment.

Fundamental to the law of sexual harassment is the principle of 'vicarious liability.' This means that an employer is considered legally responsible for any actions taken by its employees during the course of their duties. The major practical consequence is that any legal case can be brought against the employer in the employment tribunal and not only the perpetrator. Indeed it is common for no case to be brought against the perpetrator at all, the respondent simply being named as the employer.

Once a tribunal is satisfied that an act of unlawful harassment has occurred, or indeed a campaign of sexual harassment extending over some weeks or months, there are two potential defences that an employer can deploy. One involves demonstrating that the acts being complained of did not occur 'at work' and that the test for vicarious liability is thus not satisfied. There is considerable potential here for employers to deny liability because a great deal of sexual harassment in practice occurs at social events rather than in the workplace. However, the courts have now established the principle that social events organised from the workplace (eg leaving parties, Christmas parties etc) are considered to fall within the definition of vicarious liability. So the potential for this defence to be successfully deployed is less than it once was.

The second defence thus offers much more potential from an employer's point of view. This involves satisfying the tribunal that all reasonable steps were taken to prevent unlawful harassment from occurring in the first place, and that the employer responded promptly and appropriately when the complaint was received. It is thus very helpful to have written policies on harassment, to communicate them effectively and to provide training for managers on preventing situations from developing in the first place. As soon as a complaint is received it is important to act immediately. This will usually involve separating the two people concerned so that they are not together alone. In some cases it will mean suspension on full pay while a formal investigation is undertaken. These matters are inevitably very difficult to deal with, but the last thing that an employer should do is sweep them under the carpet or delay unnecessarily.

POSITIVE ACTION

Positive discrimination occurs when an employer takes action which actively favours members of minority or under-represented groups – in the field of sex discrimination it involves positively discriminating in favour of women and against men. Despite the practice being lawful in a number of other countries and acceptable under EU law in defined circumstances, positive discrimination remains unlawful in the UK. Taking 'positive action', however, to assist members of under-represented groups has always been lawful and is considered good practice. This involves taking steps to assist members of disadvantaged or under-represented groups, but stopping short of actually discriminating in their favour. The major examples are placing recruitment advertisements in publications which target these groups alongside more mainstream media, including in advertisements equal opportunities statements which aim to encourage applications from all, and developing training or mentoring programmes that are aimed at meeting the needs of under-represented groups. Women who have recently returned to work after having taken time out to bring up young children are a group for whom tailored training is often provided.

OTHER FORMS OF UNLAWFUL DISCRIMINATION

In the case of discrimination on grounds of race discrimination and discrimination on grounds of sexual orientation and religion or belief the underlying principles are almost identical to those that apply in the case of sex discrimination. Moreover, precedents established in relation to one field of discrimination also apply to the others. So while the kinds of issues that employers have to tackle are different, understanding what the response should be is not difficult once a thorough grasp of these principles has been gained.

In the case of race discrimination it is important to remember that protection extends to workers and job applicants who suffer discrimination on grounds of ethnicity and national origin as well as their race. The term 'national origin' has been found by the courts to encompass the 'home nations', making it just as unlawful to discriminate against someone because they are from Northern Ireland or because they are Scottish, Welsh or English as it is to discriminate against someone because they are French, American or Polish. Paradoxically, given the prevalence of prejudice about regional accents and the discrimination that people suffer for this reason, it remains entirely lawful to discriminate on grounds of the region of the country that people come from.

The major issue in respect of discrimination on grounds of sexual orientation is harassment. The key point to remember here is that protection is extended to people who are harassed due to 'associative and perceptive discrimination' and not just to people who exhibit the protected characteristic itself. Hence it is unlawful to harass someone because they have gay or lesbian friends or because members of their family are gay. It is also unlawful to harass a person who appears to be gay but isn't.

The definitions are clear. Protection is extended to those who are discriminated against on grounds of 'a sexual orientation towards persons of the same sex, persons of the opposite sex, or persons of the same sex and the opposite sex'.

Some of the most interesting and difficult cases have concerned discrimination on grounds of religion or belief. Here the thorniest issue is establishing what the term 'belief' means. Initially, when the law was first introduced in 2003, in order to be protected your belief had to be philosophical in nature and similar in some way to a religious belief. This narrow interpretation was established in order to prevent members of extreme political groups from gaining protection under the law. Later, in 2006, the definition was relaxed somewhat so that people who had no religious beliefs were included, but it continues to raise difficulties. In 2009, in a controversial judgement, the boundaries were pushed into the realms of political opinion thanks to the Employment Appeal Tribunal's judgment in *Grainger PLC & others v Nicholson*. This established that someone who was discriminated against because he had a profound belief in climate change was covered by the statute. So it remains unclear exactly where the boundary lies and which 'beliefs' are and are not potentially included.

In practical terms the right of workers to take time off in order to celebrate religious festivals has proved to be problematic for some employers. Here though the law is now pretty clear and well-established. These matters are dealt with by the tribunals under the heading of 'indirect discrimination on grounds of religion or belief'. An employer has a policy in place which is generally applied, namely that permission must be asked and granted before holidays can be taken. If a detriment is suffered as a result, and a request to take holiday on a religious festival is refused, a case can be brought to the tribunal. However, the employer can defend itself if it can show that its policy and decision amounted to 'a proportionate means of achieving a legitimate aim'. In other words it remains lawful to turn down such requests if the employer concerned has a genuine and good business reason for doing so.

The law on age discrimination came into effect in October 2006 and is thus still a relatively recent development. At the time of writing (2010) many principles are still being established by the courts and so as yet there remains a degree of uncertainty about exactly what employers can and can't do while remaining within the law. The principles are broadly similar to the existing law on sex discrimination, but there are significant differences too:

i   It is possible for employers to justify *direct* as well as *indirect* discrimination on grounds of age if they can show a proportionate means of achieving a legitimate aim.

ii The regulations contain examples of situations in which age discrimination can continue to occur lawfully. These include redundancy schemes which mirror the statutory scheme but are more generous financially (see Chapter 18).

iii Age discrimination continues to be present in many employment statutes (eg national minimum wage, and compensation for unfair dismissal).

iv Complex and significant regulations have been issued concerning mandatory retirement which can be at the age of 65 or above (see Chapter 16).

Disability discrimination law is the most complex of all the six major areas. The current law dates from 1996 and has been amended on a number of occasions since then. It was substantially reformed by the Equality Act 2010, not least in establishing for the first time situations in which cases of indirect discrimination on grounds of disability can be pursued. There remain, however, significant differences between disability discrimination law and that covering discrimination on grounds of sex and race:

i   In disability discrimination law the employer can deploy a general defence of objective justification (a proportionate means of achieving a legitimate aim) in cases of direct as well as indirect discrimination.

ii Disability discrimination law only extends protection to disabled people. There is no protection provided for able-bodied people. So positive discrimination in favour of disabled people is entirely lawful.

iii The Disability Discrimination Act requires employers to make 'reasonable adjustments' to their policies, premises and/or working practices in order to accommodate the needs of a disabled person.

This concept of 'reasonable adjustment', enforceable by an Employment Tribunal, is unique to disability discrimination law. There is no equivalent measure included in any other field of discrimination law. In practice it means that employers can lawfully refuse to hire or promote a worker, or dismiss them on ill health grounds, if the adjustments that would be required to accommodate their needs would be unreasonable. There are no general rules because the size and resources of the employer concerned are taken into account in deciding reasonableness, but the employer is under a duty to take requests for adjustment seriously, and to undertake some form of formal investigation to establish whether it is practicable or not. Actions which cause a detriment (like dismissing someone) can thus only be taken after serious consideration has first been given to the possibility of making adjustments to accommodate their needs.

REMEDIES

Two types of compensation are awarded by Employment Tribunals when discrimination claims are successful:

i   compensation for financial losses caused as a result of the discrimination

ii   an award for injury to feelings.

In many cases it is this second category that accounts for the lion's share of the award. At the time of writing (2010) the minimum sum that is awarded to victorious claimants to compensate for injury to feelings is £500. For the most serious single incidents of unlawful discrimination an award of £6,000 is made, but compensation can be as high as £30,000 when someone has been subjected to a campaign of unlawful discrimination extending over some months.

EQUAL PAY

Sex discrimination law differs in one fundamental way from the other areas. This is the presence on the statute book of additional regulations that relate specifically to pay and to other forms of discrimination on grounds of sex that occur within the contract of employment (eg holiday entitlement, benefits, redundancy payments etc). In such cases there is a need for the claimant to name a comparator of the opposite sex and to show that they are being paid less than this colleague is for doing like work, work that has been rated as equivalent (ie graded at the same level) or for performing work of equal value. In most cases the colleague has to be employed by the same employer and he or she must always be of the opposite gender to the claimant. The main defence available for employers to deploy in equal pay cases involves demonstrating that there is a material factor which genuinely explains the discrepancy in pay and which is not itself gender-based in any way. Hence an employer can defend a difference in pay between a man and a woman on the grounds that his performance is better than hers or that she has longer service than he has.

CULTURAL DIVERSITY

As was established in Chapters 1 and 2, organisations and the labour markets in which they recruit are becoming increasingly international. As a result, over time, workforces are becoming more and more diverse culturally. This is most obviously true of multinational organisations which operate in a number of different locations across the world, but it is also increasingly true of UK-based organisations who have recruited people from overseas to their staff. Through mergers and acquisitions it is also now more common than it was for UK-based employees to work for an organisation which is wholly or partially owned by an overseas-based parent company. HR managers with responsibility for UK operations may thus report to American, Japanese, Chinese, Indian or Russian bosses who have different assumptions about workplace relations and different approaches to HRM. Moreover, as time passes we are seeing more people who were born and who have worked overseas being appointed to senior positions in organisations and taking responsibility for decisions in the HR field.

A culturally diverse team can be highly successful, effectively harnessing the disparate range of thinking and experience at its disposal in order to be both creative and productive. Achieving this, however, requires cultural sensitivity on the part of all concerned – managers, senior managers and the employees themselves. Where this is not achieved a culturally diverse team can easily become dysfunctional and unproductive.

TYPOLOGIES OF WORKPLACE CULTURES

While some claim that culturally the world is becoming more homogeneous, and that workplace cultures are converging over time, for the foreseeable future very substantial differences between different national cultures will continue. Getting to grips with these and developing an effective understanding of different norms, values and assumptions are therefore prerequisites for successfully doing business in the contemporary global economy. For transnational organisations, where people based in one country are managed by people based elsewhere, there is an even greater need to appreciate cultural differences and to understand how they affect resourcing practice.

In recent years a number of studies have been carried out among employees and managers in different countries in an effort to 'map' or categorise in some way the cultural variations between them. The best known and most influential are the studies by Hofstede (1980 and 2005), Lewis (1996), Trompenaars (1993) and House *et al* (2004). These are all fascinating but inevitably tend to oversimplify the picture by categorising whole nations into particular cultural groups. Hence, according to Hofstede, the UK is characterised as a 'village market', in which organisations tend to have less formal hierarchical structures than elsewhere, with much decentralisation of authority, a relatively relaxed view of change and a preference for keeping emotions hidden. Clearly there is some truth in this, especially when these characteristics are compared with those that appear prevalent elsewhere. However, there are also plenty of organisations, communities and individuals who do not share these cultural norms – so care has to be taken in simply 'reading off' a set of national characteristics from such typologies.

Lewis's studies classified national cultures into three broad categories, each of which consists of a long list of characteristics covering human relationships, work style, perception of time and preferred approaches to the collection and communication of data. The three were labelled respectively as 'linear-active', 'multi-active' and 'reactive'. Linear-active cultures, according to Lewis, include the English-speaking nations and much of Northern Europe. People originating from these areas are respectful of authority, unemotional, relatively patient and keen to keep their private lives to themselves. They also tend to be analytical, making decisions based on firm data rather than hunches or personal recommendations. In terms of work organisation, the preference is for order and planning, each task carried out separately and in accordance with agreed schedules. As a result time is seen as scarce, and great emphasis is placed on punctuality.

By contrast, multi-active cultures are shared by people originating from Southern Europe, Africa, the Middle East and Latin America. Here the social norms include a greater willingness to display emotion and to appeal to a sense of emotion rather than logic when seeking to persuade. Family relationships are closer and less likely to be kept separate from work than in linear-active cultures. Body language is far more expressive, and punctuality regarded as less important. At work there is relatively little delegation of authority, the most senior figure taking decisions according to personal perceptions. Agreed plans or procedures are thus readily altered without the need to consult others.

The third culture is labelled 'reactive', and incorporates the Eastern countries, along with Russia, Finland and Turkey. Here there is great emphasis on listening and the avoidance of confrontation in relationships with others. People are often inscrutable and will go to more extreme lengths than elsewhere to avoid losing face. Decision-making tends to take a long time but, by the same token, will be made to last for the long term. Great emphasis is placed on integrity and reliability, but it takes time to build up the trust required. Discussion and negotiation tend thus to take time, each party avoiding direct answers or even eye contact but preferring instead to listen and react after careful consideration.

Hofstede (1980) focused more directly on work organisation, and has identified four dimensions that allow different national characteristics to be classified or mapped. These are:

- power distance (the extent to which members of a society accept that power in institutions is distributed unequally)

- uncertainty avoidance (the extent to which people feel threatened by ambiguous situations and have created beliefs and institutions that try to avoid these)

- individualism (the extent to which people believe that they have responsibility for looking after themselves and their own families, as opposed to institutions)

- masculinity (the extent to which the dominant values in society are success, money and material acquisitions).

More recently, Hofstede (2005) has refined his uncertainty avoidance dimension somewhat to take account of the long-term orientation of Eastern cultures compared with those prevalent in the West. In this, like Lewis, he is recognising the important differences that exist in the field of time perception, with its implications for reactive decision-making, perseverance and face-saving. Hofstede has also produced a typology of cultures based on his first two dimensions (uncertainty avoidance and power distance), which has led him to identify four basic organisational categories associated with particular countries. These are the 'pyramid of people', the 'well-oiled machine', the 'village market' and the 'family', and are best illustrated graphically (see Figure 4.1).

Necessarily, it has been possible here only to outline some of the main contours of research findings in the field of cultural variations. Readers are referred to more specialist texts, such as those referenced above, for more detailed material on specific countries. However, it is clear even from the briefest of surveys that assumptions about work relationships and organisations vary considerably around the globe. In employee resourcing terms this means that the approaches prevalent in the UK, or even defined here as constituting 'best practice', will often be seen as foreign and ill-judged if imposed elsewhere. In managing international organisations there is thus a need to study, and gain an understanding of, the key differences in work cultures, and then to develop policies that take the variations into account.

Figure 4.1 Typology of cultures

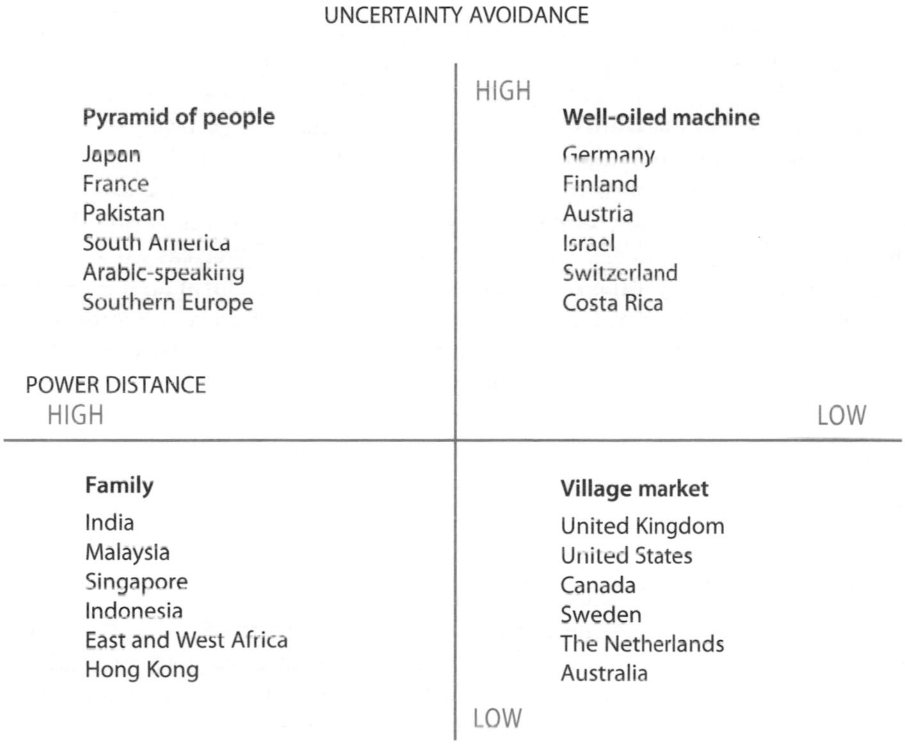

UNCERTAINTY AVOIDANCE

	HIGH	
Pyramid of people		**Well-oiled machine**
Japan		Germany
France		Finland
Pakistan		Austria
South America		Israel
Arabic-speaking		Switzerland
Southern Europe		Costa Rica

POWER DISTANCE
HIGH   LOW

Family		**Village market**
India		United Kingdom
Malaysia		United States
Singapore		Canada
Indonesia		Sweden
East and West Africa		The Netherlands
Hong Kong		Australia

LOW

Source: Hofstede (1980).

EXERCISE BOX: THE COMPASS GROUP

EXERCISE 4.3

Read the article by Rima Manocha entitled 'Bonding Agents' featured in *People Management* (11 November 2004, pages 38-39). This can be downloaded from the *People Management* archive on the CIPD's website (www.cipd.co.uk).

The article describes how the Compass Group (the ninth largest employer in the world) set about developing an international corporate identity for itself. This giant catering conglomerate has grown over the years by buying up smaller organisations based in 90 countries. As a result its staff tend to identify with their local division or brand-group rather than seeing themselves as working for a major and highly successful international company.

Questions:

1 Why did senior managers at Compass identify a need to develop an international identity among their 415,000 staff?

2 What cultural variations did they encounter during this process and how did they overcome them?

3 From a P&D perspective, what advantages do you think the company will gain over the long term as a result of the initiative described in this article?

MANAGING EXPATRIATES AT HOME AND ABROAD

The need to develop sensitivity towards and understanding of cultural differences of the kind discussed above is particularly important for expatriate workers, their colleagues and their managers. This is particularly the case when the expatriate is employed in a relatively senior position and has influence over the way things are done across a wider team of people. To survive and succeed professionally in such a situation is difficult. It is not something that will naturally occur when someone is posted overseas. There is thus a necessity to select people carefully and to make sure that they have the support they need during the period that they are abroad. In an ideal world the nature and extent of overseas working in a job will be identified at the HR planning stage. It will then form an integral part of written job descriptions and person specifications, feature in recruitment advertisements, form a major criterion at the selection stage, and then be explicitly incorporated into individual contracts of employment. This will ensure that only people with relevant language skills and whose personal circumstances are conducive to overseas working are considered for employment in such roles. Remuneration packages designed to attract and retain such staff can then be developed along with appropriate performance management systems. However, in a volatile business environment situations often arise that do not permit such a well-planned resourcing exercise to take place.

There is often a need to act speedily and opportunistically to secure business and a requirement for existing nationally-based staff to be involved. As a result, the time available for preparation is brief, and any training given has to be intensive. Where such opportunities involve staff who have not specifically been selected for overseas work there will thus often be a need to provide more structured and extensive support once the individual concerned has taken up his or her post.

That said, it is clearly not usually in the interests of an organisation to encourage people to spend time travelling or to take up a position abroad against their wishes. Wherever possible, therefore, those who are likely to be asked to do so need to be recruited, at the very least, with that possibility in mind. The following factors thus need to be included in the recruitment and selection process:

- existing language skills
- capacity to learn new languages
- awareness of relevant overseas cultures
- ability to adapt to specific overseas values and norms
- preparedness for living conditions in particular foreign counties (ie: rented accommodation or hotels)
- domestic circumstances.

This last point has to be handled very carefully to avoid breaching sex discrimination legislation. However, in most cases of overseas working it will inevitably arise and have to be dealt with at the selection stage. Of course, employers can do a great deal to help individuals to juggle international employment and family life by providing regular flights home or by making funds available for spouses and families to join employees while they are abroad. Help can also be given by granting such employees additional holidays or the opportunity to take sabbatical leave.

During the course of the past decade we have seen an increase of 70 per cent in the number of people working in the UK who originate from elsewhere. While the pace of growth may well now be declining, it is likely that overall numbers will further increase in the years to come. It follows that gaining an understanding of cultural differences in terms of workplace expectations will need to widen beyond the ranks of expatriate workers to encompass a far wider group of managers and employees. In seeking to achieve effectiveness in this area, UK-based employers stand to gain a great deal if they learn the lessons established over decades by research into the experience of UK-based staff being sent overseas on expatriate assignments.

Organisations which are able to integrate culturally-diverse teams effectively stand to benefit greatly from the development of a good reputation in overseas labour markets and among communities of people who have migrated to the UK from the same countries and regions. Moreover, they stand to gain from enhanced performance on the part of their overseas recruits.

It is partly a question of being culturally sensitive in a general sense. Not only do organisations which are serious about diversity need to eliminate unfairness or discrimination, they need to be seen to be doing so and hence perceived by their employees all the time as acting entirely equitably. The other requirement is the development on the part of managers and colleagues who originate in the UK of a full understanding of the way in which workplaces are culturally different in many overseas countries and hence that recruits coming to the UK from abroad have different expectations and different behavioural norms that need to be respected and taken into account. Laroche and Rutherford (2007) give many good examples in their book. Examples are as follows:

i   In the UK when we select people for jobs we focus primarily on the skills and experience that are necessary to do the particular job well. The better-matched the skills and the more relevant the experience, the better the chances that a candidate will be offered the job. For candidates from elsewhere in the world, particularly for people from Southern Asia and the Middle East, such an approach is alien. They are used to a business culture in which educational qualifications are far more significant, the most successful job applicants being those with the highest degrees from the most prestigious institutions. Moreover, a broad range of experience is seen as being more important than experience that is focused narrowly in one area. As a result CVs sent by people from these countries are typically very different from those that UK-based applicants would draw up. They will also tend to stress different kinds of qualities when interviewed.

ii   Inter-personal behaviour in UK workplaces appears cold and unfriendly to people from other parts of the world. We tend to like to maintain a substantial 'personal space' around us, which when it is 'invaded' by someone else makes us feel uncomfortable. Touching extends just to formal handshaking and, occasionally, perhaps a brief congratulatory pat on the back or upper arm. We rarely display emotion at work, and tend to regard such displays with suspicion, regarding the person concerned as lacking in their capacity to make cool, detached judgements. The situation in many overseas countries is very different. Personal space is much smaller, handshakes last for longer touching is common, even senior managers display plenty of emotion and people regularly kiss and hug one another at work.

iii Business cultures in UK workplaces are a great deal less hierarchical than is the case in most other countries. Managers are not, on the whole, autocratic in their approach. They consult widely before making decisions, tend to have reasonably open and genuine relationships with those they manage and will often actively encourage critical scrutiny of their thinking. Delegation of authority for decision-making is the norm, senior managers often not expecting to be informed about everything that is going on in their divisions. The situation in many other countries, including European countries, is wholly different. Hierarchy is more important, questioning the boss unacceptable and consultation far rarer. Managers expect to be informed about what is happening and delegate decision-making to a far lesser extent.

EXERCISE 4.4

EXERCISE BOX: CULTURAL DIFFERENCE AND HRM

Read the following two articles featured in *People Management*. They can be downloaded from the *People Management* archive on the CIPD's website (www.cipd.co.uk):

- 'A World of Difference' by Philip Stiles (15 November 2007)

- 'East is East' by Wes Harry (29 November 2007)

These two articles both concern the extent to which HR practices in multinational companies reflect differences in national culture. Stiles explains how his research suggests that cultural differences are becoming less important as multinational organisations increasingly adopt standardised international approaches and downplay local differences. Wes Harry, by contrast argues that cultural differences remain pronounced and that the experience of working in a Western-owned organisation is very different from working in one which has Eastern roots.

Questions:

1 In what ways does Stiles criticise Hofstede's research in the first article? How do his conclusions differ?

2 What are the major points made by Harry?

3 Can you reconcile these two points of view? If so, how?

EXAMPLE

KEY ARTICLE BOX

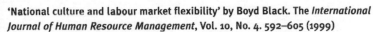

'National culture and labour market flexibility' by Boyd Black. The *International Journal of Human Resource Management*, Vol. 10, No. 4. 592–605 (1999)

In this often-cited article Boyd Black focuses both on the institutional differences between countries that affect the way that the employment relationship is managed and also on cultural differences of the kind identified by Hofstede in his research (see above). He concludes that the two should not be seen as separate dimensions of international diversity, but as two sides of the same coin. Imbedded cultural differences explain not only diversity of practices in the workplace, but many of the institutional differences too. In particular he finds that the labour market rigidities associated with many European countries (centralised bargaining, restrictive employment legislation, the level of unemployment benefit etc) are associated with the national cultures of those countries. By contrast individualistic cultures, such as the UK's, have tended to create a preference for more flexible labour markets.

Questions:

1 Make a list of the key findings that underpin Boyd Black's conclusions.

2 What criticisms could you make of his methods and conclusions?

3 What are the practical implications of the conclusions for the future development of pan-EU employment policies and institutions?

EXPLORE FURTHER

There are several good introductions to employment law which cover discrimination law effectively. The books by Lewis & Sargeant (2009), Taylor & Emir (2009) and Willey (2009) are all recommended as good introductions written primarily for an HR management audience.

The best general introduction to equality and diversity issues generally is *The dynamics of managing diversity: A critical approach* by Gill Kirton and Anne-Marie Greene (2010).

There are several good books on cultural diversity. Laroche and Rutherford (2007) are good on the integration of overseas worker into teams. Steers *et al* (2010) provide an up-to-date and very readable general introduction to the research on cultural diversity and its practical implications.

CHAPTER 5

Human resource planning

WHAT IS HR PLANNING?

The techniques of human resource planning (HRP) are some of the most involved and complex activities carried out by resourcing and talent management professionals. By contrast, the basic principles on which they are founded are straightforward, with a potential significance that is readily understood. HR planning is also an area of P&D work that has often been denigrated in recent decades, with the result that it has received relatively little attention in the literature and has become less widely used in organisations. Over the last two or three years, however, a resurgence of interest can be detected as managers have started to think about how they will secure the skills they need in the future when the large baby boom generation we discussed in Chapter 2 start to retire in larger numbers (Caruth *et al* 2009:116).

As in so many areas of HRM, there is some confusion about the precise meanings of the terms used to describe the human resource planning function. Here, as elsewhere, developments in terminology have moved on at different speeds and in different directions to developments in the activities themselves, leading to something of a mismatch between the concepts and the labels used to describe them. As with the term 'human resource management', there are in the field of human resource planning different uses of key terms by different authors. The main distinction is between those who see the term 'human resource planning' as having broadly the same meaning as the longer established terms 'workforce planning' and 'manpower planning', and those who believe 'human resource planning' to represent something rather different.

Notable among the second group are John Bramham (1988 and 1994), Sonia Liff (2000) and Hazel Williams (2002) who make a significant distinction between 'manpower planning', which they see as being primarily quantitative in nature and concerned with forecasting the demand and supply of labour, and 'human resource planning', to which they give a wider meaning, encompassing plans made across the whole range of P&D activity (including soft issues such as motivation, employee attitudes and organisational culture). For others (eg Reilly 1996, McBeath 1992 and Caruth *et al* 2009), the term 'human resource planning' is simply a more modern and gender-neutral term with essentially the same meaning as 'manpower planning'. Both are concerned with looking ahead and using systematic techniques to assess the extent to which an organisation will be able to meet its requirements for labour in the future. They are thus undertaken in order to assess whether an organisation is likely to have 'the right people, with the right skills, in the right places at the right time'. According to this definition, human resource planning is a relatively specialised sub-discipline within the

 EXERCISE BOX: THE LONDON OLYMPICS

EXERCISE 5.1

Read the article by Lucy Phillips entitled 'Games of Skill' featured in *People Management* (31 May 2007, pages 24–29). This can be downloaded from the *People Management* archive on the CIPD's website (www.cipd.co.uk).

This article discusses the major HR challenges associated with mounting a successful Olympic Games in London in 2012. The sheer size of the need for people is set out along with an explanation as to where they will be found and why.

Questions:

1   What factors make the workforce planning activities associated with the Olympic Games more complex than would be the case with a more typical commercial project involving the recruitment of thousands of people?

2   In what ways are workforce planning activities focused on a wider agenda than the Olympic Games themselves, and why?

3   What skills required for the running of the Games do managers believe are in short supply? What steps are being taken ahead of time to ameliorate this situation?

general activity undertaken by human resource managers. More recently the term 'workforce planning' appears to be being used more frequently again, while other terms which have essentially the same meaning, such as 'workforce analytics' (Schuyler 2006), 'workforce alignment' (Dyer and Ericksen 2007) and 'staffing strategy' (Bechet 2008), are finding their way into the American P&D literature.

For the purposes of this chapter we will accept this latter definition. While the term 'human resource planning' will be used throughout, it can thus be taken by readers to refer to the same disciplines and activities traditionally encompassed by the terms 'manpower' and 'workforce' planning. The focus is on forecasting the supply and demand of labour and developing plans to reconcile any future gap that is identified between the human resources an organisation needs and those to which it is likely to have access.

STAGES IN TRADITIONAL HUMAN RESOURCE PLANNING

Human resource planning is principally concerned with assessing an organisation's position in relation to its labour markets and forecasting its likely situation in years to come. It is thus mostly used to formulate the data on which plans of action can be based rather than in the actual drawing up those plans. If, for example, a supermarket chain is planning to open a large new store for which it believes there is a market, the human resource planning function would be responsible for identifying how easily – given previous experience of opening superstores of a similar size – the organisation will be able to recruit the staff it needs from internal and external sources to launch its new venture. It is thus concerned with identifying potential or likely problems with staffing the store and not with the development of specific plans to recruit and develop the employees needed. John Bramham, in defining manpower planning, has developed the metaphor of a ship at sea to illustrate the distinction between planning in general terms and the devising of specific plans of action (Bramham 1988:5–6). Seen in this way, human resource planning has more in common with navigation than piloting. It is about assessing the environment and bringing together the data required to plan the direction the organisation needs to take if it is to achieve its goals.

STAGES IN AN HR PLANNING CYCLE

1 Forecasting future demand for human resources

2 Forecasting future internal supply of human resources

3 Forecasting future external supply of human resources

4 Formulating responses to the forecasts

The forecasting function has three general stages, which will be dealt with one by one in this chapter. The fourth stage involves the formulation of a response to the forecasts. This will involve activities covered elsewhere in the book. First, there is the need to assess what demand the organisation will have for people and for what skills as its business plans unfold. This stage is therefore about distilling the human resource implications from overall organisational strategies. If the business aim is expansion to new product markets or regions, then calculations need to be made about how many people, with what training, will be required at what stage. If the business strategy emphasises consolidation and innovation rather than growth, there is still a need to assess what new skills or competencies will be required if the plan is to be met. Having determined the likely demand for labour, the next two stages involve assessing the potential supply of human resources. First, there is a need to look at internal supply – at the likelihood that those already employed by the organisation will be able, or indeed willing, to remain in their employment and develop sufficient skills and gain enough experience to be capable of meeting the demand identified in the first stage. The final stage considers any gap between likely demand and likely supply identified in stages one and two. Here the planner is concerned with forecasting how far skills and experience not available internally will be obtainable externally through the recruitment of new employees.

CASE SUMMARY

HRP AT A HIGH-STREET CHEMIST

A good illustration of the application of human resource planning principles and techniques described in this chapter was the plan drawn up by a chain of high-street chemists to cope with an expected recent shortfall in the number of pharmacists.

Here, the starting point was a change in the external environment: the expansion of the UK pharmacy degree course from three to four years after 1997. The company has always hired substantial numbers of qualified pharmacists to work in their stores straight from university, so they were faced with a significant problem in 2001, when no new pharmacists graduated.

In order to address the problem, in 1997 the company undertook a human resource planning exercise to forecast the likely demand for and internal supply of staff in the years following 2001. The demand analysis included consideration of the following factors:

- the number of new stores that were planned to open
- the staffing implications of Sunday trading and extended weekday opening hours
- the changing job roles undertaken by pharmacists.

Having worked out how many pharmacists would be required, the planners then undertook an analysis of how many they would be likely to have in post, were they to continue operating established recruitment practices. This exercise involved consideration of likely staff turnover figures for pharmacists between 1997 and 2001, but also took account of expected maternity leave and secondments out of high-street stores.

The final stage involved determining how great the shortfall was likely to be and formulating plans to match the gap with additional recruitment in the years prior to 2001. In addition, P&D policies were developed which aimed to reduce turnover among pharmacists so as to keep to a minimum the magnitude of the skill shortage.

A similar exercise has had to be carried out in the social services departments of local authorities in more recent years. Here too the main degree programme that graduate recruits complete has moved from being of three to four years' duration, creating a fallow year.

FORECASTING FUTURE DEMAND FOR HUMAN RESOURCES

The ability of human resource managers to predict accurately how many people will be required and with what skills depends on a number of factors. First, there is the timescale that the forecast is intended to cover. Except in the most turbulent of environments, it is possible to look forward one or two years and make reasonable assumptions about what staffing requirements will be. It gets far harder when timescales of three, five or ten years are contemplated. This is because relevant technological or economic developments that will have a profound effect on the level and kind of activity carried out by the organisation may not yet even have been contemplated.

The other major variable is the nature of the activities carried out by the organisation. Those in relatively stable environments are able to forecast their needs with far greater confidence than those operating in inherently unstable conditions. An example of the former might be a government department such as the Foreign Office, a prison or a local authority social services department. Here, relatively little is likely to change, except at the margins, over the foreseeable future. Such change as there is likely to be will be gradual and brought in steadily over a manageable period. It is therefore quite possible to make reasonable estimations of how many diplomats, prison officers, administrators or social workers will be needed in five or ten years' time. While there may be increases in productivity brought about through reorganisation and new working methods, such matters are predictable to a considerable degree. Numbers of staff required will only change radically as a result of well-trailed, planned changes in government policy, giving plenty of time to adjust forecasts. By contrast, a company with a relatively small market share of an international market can make such forecasts with far less confidence. Even looking forward one year, it is difficult to say for certain how many will be employed, or what roles they will be undertaking.

The timescale and the nature of the business will influence which of the various available techniques are used to forecast the demand for human resources. There are three basic categories: systematic techniques, managerial judgement and working back from costs.

SYSTEMATIC TECHNIQUES

At root, most mathematical and statistical techniques used in demand forecasting are concerned with estimating future requirements from an analysis of past and current experience. A number of distinct approaches are identified in the literature, including time series analysis, work study and productivity trend analysis. Time series or ratio-trend analyses look at past business patterns and the numbers of people employed in different roles to make judgements about how many will be required to meet business targets in the future. Such an approach is straightforward and appropriate only in relatively stable business environments. Common examples are found in the public services, where the number of school children or elderly patients that require education or treatment is predicted some years in advance on the basis of population trends. In such circumstances it is possible to project how many teachers, nurses, doctors and support staff will be needed, given the staff–student or staff–patient ratios of the past.

The method is also helpful in businesses subject to cyclical fluctuations over time. Where it is known, on the basis of past experience, that the number of customers is likely to increase and decrease seasonally or in tandem with economic cycles, it is possible to plan future staffing requirements accordingly. The principle is best illustrated graphically. In Figure 5.1 past occupancy and staffing rates in a large seaside hotel employing 250 full-timers are shown. The thin line represents occupancy rates and the thick line the number of whole-time equivalent staff employed. Future projections are shown as broken lines. Here there is a clear pattern of full or near-full occupancy in the summer and very low occupancy in the spring with an intermediate position at Christmas. The projections of future occupancy are based on the average figures for past years. The number of seasonal, temporary staff needed in the future at particular times of the year can be estimated using the scale marked on the y axis. Thus, for December 2012 the hotel will need to hire and train around 40 temporary staff to assist its 250 full-timers.

This is, of course, a very simple example used to illustrate a planning technique that is potentially far more complex. In practice, most organisations would have to analyse separate time series for different departments or grades of staff to obtain useful information. It is also likely that, for many, the fluctuations are less predictable, requiring predicted levels of business to be adjusted as the date in question approaches. The more complex the organisation and the variations in staffing levels, the more useful computer programmes designed to assist in this kind of analysis are.

The work study approach has a different basis. Here, instead of assuming that the ratio of business to staff will remain broadly constant, special studies are undertaken of individual tasks or processes carried out by the organisation in order to establish the numbers required to complete them most effectively and efficiently. The method is thus suitable in situations where there are no clear past trends to examine, or where wholly new production or service methods are being planned. Work study is most commonly associated with manufacturing industries where the work is readily divisible into discrete production-line tasks (for example, when a new plant is being brought into service using hitherto untried production methods). The work study specialist then observes employees undertaking each task involved in the manufacturing process during the development stage. Once the most productive systems have been observed, it is possible to compute the number of staff required and the type of skills they will require.

Silver (1983:49–60) argues for incorporating productivity trends into the time series calculation. This method removes from the time-series analysis described above the assumption that the ratio of staff to work (labour to capital) will remain constant over time. Instead, improvements in productivity over past years are calculated and extrapolated forward when calculating future human resource requirements. The approach is best suited to long-term forecasting, perhaps

Figure 5.1 Time series analysis: occupancy and staffing rates in a large seaside hotel

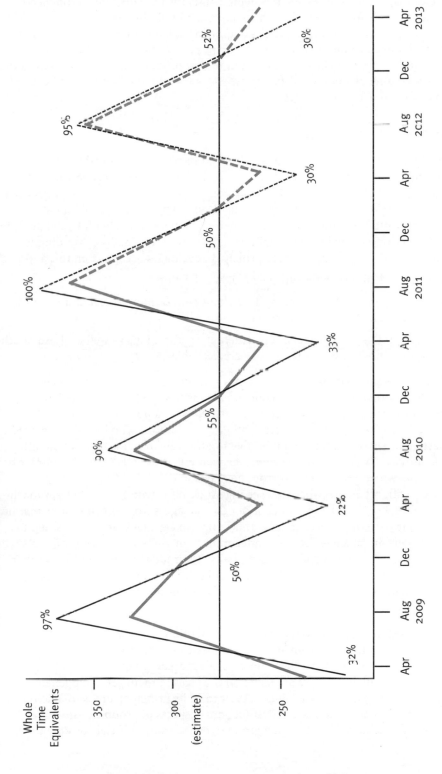

when major capital investment is being contemplated which has a long lead time. An industry for which such an approach might be feasible today would be banking, where large organisations employing skilled employees have seen very considerable productivity improvements in recent years. Given this experience, it would be appropriate to take account of that productivity trend, as well as the likely volume of work in the future, when forecasting the numbers to be hired and trained over future years.

MANAGERIAL JUDGEMENT

A different approach to forecasting demand dispenses to some degree with systematic approaches. Instead, it bases forecasts on the subjective views of managers about likely future human resource needs. Clearly, in situations where the business environment is highly volatile and where future staffing patterns may well bear little resemblance to past experience, there is no alternative, if planning is to occur, to using informed opinion as a basis for estimates. According to Stainer (1971:98) there are three principal advantages arising from this approach:

- It is quick and requires little or no data collection.

- Basically intangible factors, such as changes in fashion, social opinion and taste, can be brought into account.

- The opinions of managers from different organisations as well as those of other experts can be used, as far as they are available.

This last point is probably less relevant in the current environment, where competition between employing organisations has replaced central planning, even in much of the public sector. Nevertheless, it is possible to envisage situations in which managers from other organisations who have experienced a particular set of changes might be able to offer valuable assistance in planning for similar developments elsewhere. An example is the NHS Unit Labour Costs scheme, which puts managers from hospitals in one part of the country in touch with others elsewhere to exchange such information. Another approach commonly used is the recruitment of new managers from organisations that have a similar pattern of development. Thus a British car manufacturer wishing to adopt certain Japanese production techniques might well hire senior figures with direct experience of managing such plants. Their judgement as to the number and type of staff required in the future will clearly be invaluable. Management consultants with similar experience can also be brought in to assist in demand forecasting.

A method that has received considerable attention in the literature on human resource planning is known as the 'delphi technique'. It is a systematic approach to decision-making that aims to introduce a measure of objectivity into the process by which forecasts are made on the basis of managerial judgement. According to Jackson and Schuler (1990:163), its principal aim is to 'maximise the benefits and minimise the dysfunctional aspects of group decision-making' – achieved by removing group dynamics and political considerations from the process. In human resource planning the delphi technique requires several managers and experts to submit their own forecast in writing (often anonymously) to a central contact, who then circulates the estimates among the other members of the group. Each then revises his or her own forecasts, taking account of the factors suggested in colleagues' submissions. Sometimes several rounds of adjustments are undertaken before a consensus forecast emerges.

In Stainer's view, there are great disadvantages to relying on managerial judgement alone when conducting demand forecasting exercises (Stainer 1971:98–99). He believes that the complexity of the process and the number of factors at work are often too great for a single brain or group of brains to cope with. Furthermore, he expresses the view that organisational politics and 'emotional attachments' almost inevitably get in the way of objective decision-making when making forecasts of this kind. Kispal-Vitai and Wood (2009:176) argue that this kind of approach can amount to little more than 'a sum of the best guesses'. Where the managers involved incorrectly 'forecast the future impact of technology and of the marketplace' or lack the understanding to translate their predictions 'to HR needs in terms of numbers and skills' wildly inaccurate demand forecasts can be the result. There is therefore a good case for incorporating both statistical analysis and managerial judgement into the demand forecasting process. Computer modelling enhances the possibility of merging the two approaches successfully, because it permits many more variables to be included in the statistical formulae used than is practicable when calculations are done manually (Caruth *et al* 2009:126). Such approaches involve statistical analysis, but the assumptions made in the calculations are based on managerial or expert judgement.

WORKING BACK FROM COSTS

Bramham (1988) outlines an alternative approach to demand forecasting which removes past experience from the equation altogether. Here the process begins with the future budget – the amount of money the finance department expect to be available for staff costs in coming years. The human resource planner then works out, given that constraint, how many people at what salary level will be affordable. Current methods, ratios and productivity levels are thus ignored, the focus being on designing organisational structures and methods of working that will permit the budget to be met.

In recent years such approaches have been adopted far more frequently in the public services than in the past. With governments continually pressing for greater productivity, the emphasis in planning terms has been less on how many people are required to deliver a particular service given past experience and more on what the taxpayer is prepared to spend or the government happy to allocate, given its public-spending targets. In the jargon of politicians, resource-based provision has replaced that based on need. The future budget has thus been the starting-point in HR planning rather than the cost of providing the service in question in the past.

REFLECTIVE QUESTION

How far does your organisation go in forecasting future demand? To what extent is it possible to do so, given your business environment?

EXERCISE BOX: NOTTINGHAM CITY COUNCIL

EXERCISE 5.2

Read the news item written by Julie Griffiths entitled 'Council taps new talent pools to ease shortages' featured in *People Management* (16 September 2004, page 13). This can be downloaded from the *People Management* archive on the CIPD's website (www.cipd.co.uk).

The article describes how a chronic shortage of support staff in social services was alleviated by targeting unemployed people and providing them with training.

Questions:

1 What evidence is there in this article to suggest that the council does not carry out effective human resource planning?

2 To what extent would HRP have allowed the council to avoid the chronic staff shortages it faced?

3 What other initiatives would you advise the council to consider in order to fill its vacancies?

FORECASTING INTERNAL SUPPLY

There is a variety of techniques used to assess the extent to which the demand for human resources can be met by the existing staff employed by an organisation. However, all share the same basic characteristic: they involve analysing the current workforce department by department or grade by grade before estimating the numbers likely to remain employed and the skills they are likely to possess. As in the case of demand forecasting described above, most of the tools used rely on a mixture of statistical analysis and managerial judgement in assisting planners to make informed forecasts. The key here is detailed analysis. In forecasting internal supply, overall figures about staff turnover rates are of little help. What is important is the likely turnover rate among specific groups of staff, such as those of a particular age, those with a defined length of service or those employed at different levels to do different jobs.

Predicting likely staff turnover (better described from the perspective of P&D managers as 'wastage') with any degree of accuracy is a complex activity, because people leave their current jobs for a variety of reasons. The following list covers many of these, but is by no means exhaustive:

- internal promotion
- internal transfer

- internal demotion
- to take up a different job offer elsewhere
- to retire
- to enter full-time education
- through illness
- redundancy or end of temporary contract
- dismissal for misconduct or incapability
- to take a career break
- to set up a new business
- as a result of a spouse or partner's relocating.

While the instance of some of these can either be increased or reduced by actions taken in the employing organisation, many are linked to factors in the wider environment – social, political, economic and technological. Others are linked to the age of the employee concerned. All these factors need therefore to be considered when developing meaningful forecasts of turnover rates in the future. Edwards (1983:62) makes the following general observations, which continue to hold true:

- wastage rates decrease with increasing age
- wastage rates decrease with increasing length of service
- wastage rates decrease with increasing skill and responsibility
- wastage rates are higher for female than for male staff
- wastage rates decrease when the general level of unemployment rises.

However, the experience of particular organisations or individual departments may well not correlate with these general observations, or may do so only to a limited extent. Meaningful forecasts of turnover must thus incorporate consideration of the organisation's experience while building in assumptions about the probable future effects of environmental and demographic factors. Past figures are primarily analysed using the wastage and stability indices, together with analysis of specific employee cohorts and internal promotion patterns.

In Chapter 14 you will read about the major statistical techniques used to analyse staff turnover patterns. These are also used in HRP. The major types of analysis used are as follows:

- annual crude wastage or turnover rates (the percentage of a workforce which leaves in a year)
- stability analysis (the percentage of a workforce which stays in their current jobs across a year)
- cohort analysis (the percentage of a cohort recruited in a particular year who remain employed after each passing year)
- internal promotion analysis (the number of people in each group of staff who are promoted internally over a year).

FORECASTING EXTERNAL SUPPLY

Having established the future demand for different kinds of employee, and how far these needs will or will not be met internally, it is necessary to give attention to filling the gap and reconciling supply and demand using the external labour market. While internal data can help planners make judgements about trends in different labour markets (eg response rates to advertisements, the proportion of turnover explained by individuals leaving to join competitors, the performance of new starters), for the most part relevant information is found outside the organisation.

Most labour markets are local. That is to say, applications for vacancies will come from people already living within commuting distance of the principal place of work. The trends that are important in such circumstances, from an employer's point of view, are thus those occurring within the relevant 'travel to work area'. For other jobs, usually those requiring greater levels of skill or commanding higher salary rates, the relevant labour markets will be national or even international. In either situation there is a need for human resource planners to gain an understanding of the dynamics of these labour markets and to update their plans as trends change and develop. As far as the immediate travel to work area is concerned, the following statistics are the most helpful:

- general population density
- population movements in and out of the area
- age distribution
- unemployment rates
- school leavers
- the proportion with higher education
- skill levels.

Statistics of this nature for each local authority area are collected by the government's National Office of Statistics and published online. In addition there are commercial organisations, often specialising in particular groups of employees or industries, that collate information from other sources and undertake research themselves. An example is a consultancy set up to provide information to NHS units in England, which produces a quarterly journal as well as providing specific advice to individual trusts. In addition to the basic statistics, there is a need to apply judgement and experience to assess the potential impact of other local factors. Those that might be relevant include any developments in the local transport network that might effectively expand or contract the travel to work area, the opening or closure of other units and the construction of new housing developments.

Where employers operate in national labour markets there is far less meaningful information available, because only the more significant trends are likely to have a substantial impact on future recruitment and retention exercises. The fact that unemployment increases or decreases nationally may well have little or no impact on specific labour markets – as was shown in the recessions of the 1980s, 1990s and 2008–10, when skill shortages remained in some areas despite the large number of people seeking work. That said, there are national statistics that may be of relevance in specific circumstances, particularly for larger employers. These would include statistics on the number of individuals leaving higher education with specific qualifications and the number of employers competing for their services.

As is the case with local labour markets, there is also a need to keep an eye on any other major developments that might have an impact on the organisation's ability to recruit sufficient numbers in the future. Examples would include new government initiatives in the field of education and training, and the manner in which particular jobs or professions are portrayed by the media.

For some employers developments in international labour markets are important too.

Where there are significant skills shortages in a particular country, employers will look abroad to find the people they need. In the UK in recent years shortages of front-line medical staff has led to very substantial overseas recruitment, with particular attention being given to Spain where there is a surplus of trained medical professionals. By contrast we have seen a net outflow of executives and IT staff from the UK to the USA during the same period.

LONG-TERM FORECASTS OF LABOUR DEMAND

An important variable in estimating external labour supply is the extent to which other employers will be competing for the available talent. It is useful here to look at long-term forecasts of which professional groups are going to be most sought after and which will be easier to recruit than is currently the case.

Estimates carried out by advisors to the Leitch Review have produced estimates for the years 2004 to 2020. They calculate that UK employers will have to fill 18.4 million vacancies in total during this period, taking account of retirements, likely voluntary turnover and increases or decreases in overall demand.

The biggest growth in demand is expected in management jobs, where two million more posts will exist in 2020 than did in 2004, professional roles (one million new jobs) and lower-skilled service-sector jobs (several hundred thousand new posts). By contrast there will be rather fewer jobs overall in the administrative and secretarial fields and a fall of over 850,000 in the total number of unskilled jobs.

Source: Beaven et al 2005

EXERCISE 5.3

EXERCISE BOX: HRP CASE STUDIES

Read the following two articles featured in *People Management*. They can be downloaded from the *People Management* archive on the CIPD's website (www.cipd.co.uk).

- 'Drill Inspection' by Bruce Tulgan, 22 February 2007, pages 44–45
- 'A Bridge too far?' by Lucie Carrington, 11 August 2005, pages 24–28

These articles concern leadership development in two very different organisational scenarios – the US military and professional services firms. However, the situations described are also useful to consider from an HR planning perspective.

Questions:

1   What techniques would be best to use for forecasting the future demand for leaders in these organisations?

2   What factors described in the article might mean that internal supply forecasts might have to be adjusted from their current levels?

3   What approaches should be considered as a means of reconciling gaps between supply and demand?

IT APPLICATIONS

There are many different ways in which information technology can be used to support and undertake human resource planning. However, these can be divided into three broad categories: information provision, modelling and presentation. An important role played by computer databases is storing the information required to undertake meaningful forecasts of demand for staff and internal supply. Not only do Human Resources Information Systems (HRISs) allow more data to be stored about jobs, employees and past applicants, they also permit far swifter generation of reports summarising the data than is ever possible using manual information storage systems.

The second major application of information technology in human resource planning is in the field of modelling. The ability of a computer to handle vast quantities of data permits highly complex formulae containing numerous variables to be built up and results to be calculated in seconds. While specialist modelling programs are available on the market, most human resource forecasting can be undertaken using basic spreadsheet programmes – best illustrated with an example. Table 1 shows a fictional spreadsheet application for a computer software company. The columns each represent a different variable.

Table 5.1: Spreadsheet application

Job title	A	B	C	D	E	F	G
Manager	20	15%	20%	60%	3.6	1.44	7,200
Administrator	28	15%	20%	3%	5.04	4.9	7,350
Accountant	12	10%	20%	10%	1.44	1.3	3,250
Sales executive	40	60%	30%	5%	31.2	29.64	59,280
Software developer	35	12%	30%	20%	5.46	4.37	6,555
Software support	30	23%	30%	7'%	8.97	8.34	12,510
TOTAL:					55.71	49.99	£96,145

Key
A: Total number of whole-time equivalents in post at 1 January
B: Turnover rate based on past trends
C: Increased demand expected during the coming year
D: Number of vacancies typically filled by internal promotion
E: Number of vacancies expected in the coming year
F: Number of posts to be filled externally in the coming year
G: Recruitment costs per job group for the coming year (£s)

Columns A, B, C and D are calculated using analysis of past data, adjusted as is seen fit, given environmental changes. Columns E and F are calculated using statistical formulae that include the variables A, B, C and D. In this case E is calculated using the formula $[(A \times C) + A] \times B$. The number of vacancies is therefore calculated with reference to current numbers, likely growth and expected turnover rates. By contrast, F is calculated using the formula $E - (E \times D)$. It thus takes into account both the number of vacancies and the number of internal promotions.

Even with a small scale exercise of this kind looking at forecasts for one year in a relatively small company, the assistance of a computer makes the planning process far quicker than would be the case if the calculations were undertaken using a calculator. The advantage becomes even greater when more rows and columns are added, looking at incorporating additional variables, forecasts for a number of years ahead and the building-in of further cost assumptions. In the above example it would be very straightforward to add columns representing forecasts for future years, and others calculating the costs of training new staff members in the various categories. Spreadsheets also permit the development of far more complicated formulae involving averages, fractions, logarithms, standard deviations, variances and many other statistical tools. It is also possible to build IF...THEN...ELSE commands into the formulae used (eg IF $(A \times C) > B$ THEN E ELSE $A \times B$).

Perhaps the greatest advantage of IT in human resource planning is the ability it gives the planner to undertake 'What if?' or scenario analyses, altering figures or formulae to calculate what the implications would be were key trends to change. In the example given here, the effect of increased or reduced turnover on the future supply of and demand for labour could be calculated with great ease; it would simply be necessary to alter the figures in column B and to watch while the computer recalculated the figures in columns E and F.

The third major contribution of computer technology in the human resource planning field is in the capacity of proprietary systems to generate attractive and user-friendly reports and summaries. The advantage of innovations in this area is the relative ease with which data is interpreted. It is possible to present senior managers with well laid-out graphics that summarise forecasts without the need to spend time drawing up such documents separately.

EXERCISE 5.4

EXERCISE BOX: HR PLANNING IN THE CONTEMPORARY BUSINESS ENVIRONMENT

Read the article by Duncan Brown entitled 'Success in all shapes and sizes' featured in *People Management* (24 October 2002, page 25). This can be downloaded from the *People Management* archive on the CIPD's website (www.cipd.co.uk).

In this opinion piece Duncan Brown describes the breadth of skills shortages that employers face. He also reflects on the paradox that organisations now often need both to hire new people to work in some parts of their operation while making redundancies in others.

Questions:

1   What evidence is provided in this article of HR planning activity in organisations?

2   Why are employers apparently moving away from planning (or talent management) systems which focus uniquely on elite performers?

THE USE OF HR PLANNING IN PRACTICE

The research evidence on the issue of how many employers currently carry out systematic HR planning is unclear but tends to indicate that the majority of employers do not give the function a high profile. In recent years few surveys have looked directly at the use or lack of use of specific HR planning techniques, preferring instead to look at wider issues. It is thus necessary to make inferences about the extent to which they are in fact used from surveys on computer usage, the introduction of 'strategic HRM' and the activities of human resource managers.

The Workplace Employee Relations Surveys (WERS) ask HR managers to indicate for which of a list of management activities they are responsible. In 2004, the most recent survey, 90 per cent stated that they carried responsibility for 'staffing or manpower planning' (Kersley *et al* 2006:48). However, this term is too broad and subject to different interpretations to allow us to reach firm conclusions about the type of HR planning activity that is carried out. There is some evidence of renewed interest in traditional approaches to HR planning in the public sector, notably in the NHS where it forms an explicit part of the 'agenda for change' programme, and in local government (IRS 2003c). But no equivalent revival appears to be taking place in the private sector.

The overall picture painted by these and other research projects (see Rothwell 1995:175–178, Liff 2000:96–98 and Johnson & Brown 2004) strongly suggests that systematic HR planning carried out in the manner advocated by writers in the 1960s and 1970s is now rarely found in UK industry or elsewhere in the world. Its use is mainly restricted to large public-sector organisations and firms operating in reasonably stable, capital-intensive industries. Others, if they use it at all, do so in a more casual and irregular way – perhaps relying more on managerial judgement and intuition than on established statistical approaches.

A variety of reasons have been put forward to explain the apparent abandonment of HR planning techniques – as far as they were ever well established – by employers in the UK (see Rothwell 1995:178–180, Marchington & Wilkinson 2002:278–9, Johnson & Brown 2004:386–7). These include the following:

- a hostility to the use of statistical techniques in place of managerial judgement
- the belief that HR planning, while desirable, is not essential to organisational effectiveness; funding therefore tends to be funnelled elsewhere
- the prevalence of a short-termist outlook in UK industry, the result being a belief that individual managerial careers are unlikely to be enhanced by long-term activities such as HR planning
- practical problems associated with inadequate historical data on which to base forecasts
- ignorance of the existence of HR planning techniques and their potential advantages for organisations
- a more general ignorance or fear of mathematical methods.

It can be further argued that HR planning, as traditionally practised, simply no longer 'fits' the approach to HRM which many employers now prefer. An example can be found in the way that contemporary organisations, both in the public and private sectors have moved towards decentralised forms of structure. Responsibility for employment resourcing issues is thus no longer held centrally, but by managers operating independent business units. Their small size makes detailed HR planning impractical. Organisation structures themselves are also increasingly impermanent and are staffed by people who expect to move on after a relatively short period. Time horizons, both individual and collective are thus limited, ensuring that long-term planning is a low priority. Moreover, flexibility among staff is increasingly expected. The traditional model in which an organisation was made up of clearly defined jobs occupied by people employed on standard contracts has begun to break down. Instead organisational life is becoming more and more fluid. We are expected and expect to be members of teams rather than occupants of defined jobs and we are employed under a greater variety of contractual arrangements. None of these trends are compatible with the systematic application of the techniques outlined above. This means that gaining the co-operation of line managers is sometimes problematic, even when senior managers and the HR function decide to embark on an HRP exercise:

> Managers tend to see the process as being of limited value and complain loudly about the amount of work involved. In addition, managers are being measured and rewarded for achieving short-term objectives, and this is inconsistent with the longer-term view that strategic staffing requires.... Some managers question the validity and value of processes that ask them to provide estimates of staffing needs for points in time that are well past their ability (or need) to forecast (Bechet 2008:23).

A further probable reason for decline in the extent to which HR planning is carried out relates to complexity and turbulence in the business environment. The result is a preference on the part of managers to wait until their view of the future environment clears sufficiently for them to see the whole picture before committing resources to preparing for its arrival. This forms the background to the major academic criticisms that have been made about HR planning, a subject to which we now need to turn.

THE CASE AGAINST HR PLANNING

The essence of the argument against HR planning is based on the simple proposition that it is unfeasible to forecast the demand for and supply of labour with any accuracy – a classic case of a brilliant theory being undermined by insurmountable problems when put into practice. In recent years, the most celebrated critic of business planning processes in general (ie not just those in the HR field) has been Henry Mintzberg. In a series of books and articles he has advanced the view that, in practice, most forecasts turn out to be wrong and that, as a result, the planning process tends to impede the achievement of competitive advantage (eg Mintzberg 1976, 1994). His points were further developed and applied specifically to the P&D field by Flood *et al* (1996).

The main problem with forecasting, so the argument goes, is its reliance on past experience to predict future developments. The main techniques involve the extrapolation of past trends and predictions based on assumptions about the way organisations interact with their environments. In practice, according to Mintzberg, this means that one-off events that fundamentally alter the environment cannot be included in the forecasts:

> When it comes to one-time events – changes that never occurred before, so-called discontinuities, such as technological innovations, price increases, shifts in consumer attitudes, government legislation – Makridakis argued that forecasting becomes 'practically impossible'. In his opinion, 'very little, or nothing can be done, other than to be prepared in a general way to react quickly once a discontinuity has occurred (Mintzberg 1994:231).

The point about discontinuities is that not only is the event or trend difficult to predict itself, but there is also a whole set of problems associated with assessing its likely impact on the organisation over time. As a result, except in situations where the organisation itself is able to exert control over future developments, all forecasts are inevitably based on questionable assumptions. It therefore follows that preparations undertaken to meet inaccurate predictions may well cause the long-term interests of the organisation greater harm than would have been the case had a less definite view been taken of unfolding developments.

Competitive advantage today, according to critics of strategic planning, comes from generating responses to fast-changing circumstances that are swifter, more creative, more innovative and more flexible than those of key competitors – qualities that are stifled by the bureaucratic characteristics of planning processes (Smith 1996:31). In other words, it is claimed that because the world is increasingly complex and unpredictable it is not worth trying to predict what will happen more than a year ahead. Any plans that are made will, in all likelihood, have to be revised several times in the light of changing environmental developments. Using Mintzberg's terminology, the number of obstacles to effective planning, in the form of discontinuities, are now so legion as to render the long-term planning process effectively redundant.

Many examples of discontinuities can be cited, some of which have had negative consequences for organisations and whole industries. A prominent example is the fate of the tourist industry over the past few years. In 1998 and beyond the analysts confidently predicted steady and strong growth in the number of tourists, in air ticket sales and receipts from tourism. The Millennium Dome was widely anticipated to be capable of attracting 12 million visitors, and the UK tourist industry looked set to increase its size and wealth considerably. A number of factors then came along, one after another, which have led to a substantial contraction on a scale that no analyst, however well-informed, could have predicted. First there was the rise in the value of the pound sterling vis-à-vis other currencies in the late 1990s and early 2000s, making the UK a more expensive destination than had been the case for many years. Then in 2001 the industry was hit first by the outbreak of foot and mouth disease and then by the fall in air passenger numbers following terrorist attacks in the USA and elsewhere. Thousands of jobs were lost, while the industry contracted in size by 20 per cent.

 REFLECTIVE QUESTION

Consider what discontinuities have occurred in your organisation's business environment over the past two or three years. How far were these predicted? Would it have been possible to predict them?

THE RBS GROUP

A good example of an industry that has recently been hit by a major discontinuity is the UK's banking industry. Take the example of the Royal Bank of Scotland (RBS). In 2005 it was the second largest banking group in Europe and one of the largest companies in the world. Until 2009 it was the second largest shareholder in the Bank of China, owning several other subsidiary companies across the banking and insurance sectors. It won many awards for its activities and was generally regarded both in Scotland and across the world as a major success story. There was a corporate jet worth £17.5 million, a new HQ campus opened by the Queen in 2005 and huge bonus payments for its senior managers.

All these achievements were thrown into reverse when the financial crisis of 2008–09 occurred. RBS was left particularly exposed as it had just paid £10 billion for a major share of a Dutch Bank (ABN AMRO) – an

institution which soon proved to have been massively overvalued. The bank had also been heavily involved in trading sub-prime securities which caused it to lose a huge amount of money when their value collapsed.

In October 2008 RBS announced a loss of £28 billion, the largest ever recorded in UK corporate history, leading to a drop in its shares of 97 per cent (66 per cent in a single day).

Since then RBS has lost its chairman, its chief executive and over 20,000 staff. Several subsidiary companies have been sold, as was its share of the bank of China.

It only survives because a great deal of public money (£7 billion at least) has been used to prop it up. At the time of writing (2010) the UK government owns 84 per cent of RBS.

EXERCISE BOX: WEMBLEY STADIUM

Read the article entitled 'Underneath the Arches' by Tim Smedley, featured in *People Management* (26 July, 2007, pages 28–31) This can be downloaded from the *People Management* archive on the CIPD's website (www.cipd.co.uk).

This article describes some of the problems that faced the HR team at Wembley Stadium during the period when it was supposed to open, but didn't, and some of the key threats to smooth operations that have appeared since the opening occurred.

Questions:

1 To what extent does this episode support Henry Mintzberg's view that discontinuities will always occur, rendering HR planning useless?

2 How far could the problems have been alleviated with more effective human resource planning?

3 What future developments in the stadium's HR business environment need to be taken into account when undertaking workforce planning for the coming few years?

THE CASE FOR HR PLANNING

A number of writers working in the P&D field have taken issue with the arguments put forward by critics of business planning. In addition to generally restating the potential advantages of HR plans they also reject the assertion that because accurate forecasting is complex, difficult and subject to error it follows that organisations should abandon long-term planning altogether. Two main arguments are put forward: the need to view plans as adaptable, and the greater attention to planning required by a more turbulent environment. A third set of arguments focuses on the practical outcomes of human resource planning, suggesting that they are both useful for organisations and can make a positive contribution to the achievement of business objectives.

THE NEED TO VIEW PLANS AS ADAPTABLE

The point is made that HR planning has never been intended to produce blueprints that determine the direction that recruitment and development policy should take years in advance. Instead, it is viewed as a less deterministic activity, in which plans are continually updated in the light of environmental developments. In practice, it is said, changes in the environment rarely occur as suddenly as Mintzberg suggests. As a result, when unforeseen developments do occur, there is time for plans to be adapted and updated to enable the implications to be met. When making long-term plans for major capital investment projects (building new plants, research and development into new technologies etc), discontinuities potentially interfere far more dramatically. The time-horizons for HR practitioners are not so long, except in the case of the development of highly-skilled employees. A great deal more can be adapted and changed in six months in the HR field than is the case for capital investment in new plant and machinery. It thus follows that Mintzberg's arguments, while valid from a general management perspective, may have less relevance to P&D.

TURBULENCE REQUIRES MORE ATTENTION TO PLANNING

Linked to the first argument is the idea that because the business environment is becoming increasingly turbulent and unpredictable on account of the threat from potential discontinuities there is an even greater need for organisations to develop the capacity to plan accurately. Bramham (1988:7) puts the case as follows:

> It is of course a paradox that as it becomes more difficult to predict and select, so it becomes more necessary to do so. The 19th-century businessman would have found his 20th-century counterpart's obsession with planning strange. But, of course, the environment is now changing more rapidly and the conflicting pressures are greater. The modern manager must develop the systems and controls which increase the likelihood of the environment being controlled to a reasonable extent. Without an accurate awareness of his position, a manager will quickly lose his way in this rapidly changing environment.

In effect, what is being argued for is that it is both possible and desirable to plan for uncertainty. When faced with an unpredictable environment, employers have two basic choices: they can abandon formal planning activity and rely on intuition – reacting swiftly and decisively at the point at which a clear picture of the future comes into view – or they can plan their HR policies so as to enable them to meet the future with a variety of different responses. If the second course is taken, the emphasis in HR planning will be on maximum future flexibility. In theory, the organisation will then have the capability to respond even more quickly than rivals who pursue the first approach.

Dyer and Ericksen (2007) propose that organisations operating in turbulent environments should aim for 'workforce scalability', a concept that combines a form of HR planning labelled 'workforce alignment' with a very different idea labelled 'workforce fluidity'. Workforce alignment is concerned with ensuring that an organisation 'has the right number of the right types of people in the right places at the right times doing the right things right' (Dyer and Erickson 2007:268), but both managers and employees accept that no one configuration will last for long if competitive advantage is to be maintained. Regular re-alignments are necessary, but these should be planned strategically and are best achieved if the impetus for them comes 'from the bottom up' rather than being solely determined by senior managers and then imposed 'from the top down'. HR planning is thus effectively carried out by the employees themselves 'initiating salient moves on their own'. This will happen, it is argued, if the leaders in organisations ensure 'workforce fluidity', which essentially means a flexible mindset on the part of employees, and combine this with clear and inspirational direction from the top about the organisation's vision and its business model. The authors illustrate how the approach can work by describing its successful use by Yahoo in establishing itself as a leading internet search portal. Yahoo's success is contrasted with the failure of a rival organisation called 'Excite' which no longer exists.

REFLECTIVE QUESTION

What are the main uncertainties faced by your organisation at present? To what extent could plans be put in place to enable these to be met more effectively by you than by your competitors?

OUTCOMES OF HRP

The clearest summary of the reasoning behind HR planning in a less obviously volatile business environment was given in a discussion paper published by the government as long ago as 1968 when encouraging HRP was government policy (Department of Employment, 1971:5–7). Bramham (1987:56–57) also discusses the key objectives. Between them, six basic objectives of HR planning are identified – all of which can play a useful role in the management of organisations:

i) Recruitment

HR planning provides the information on which recruiters base their activities. It reveals what gaps there are between the demand for and supply of people with particular skills and can thus underpin decisions about whom to recruit and what methods to use in doing so. HR planning aims to ensure that there are neither too many nor too few recruits to meet the organisation's future needs.

ii) Training and development

In forecasting the type of jobs that will need to be filled in the future, as well as the number, HR planning aims to reveal what skills training and development activity need to be undertaken to ensure that existing staff and new recruits possess the required skills at the right time. The longer and more specialised the training, the more significant accurate HR planning is to the organisation's effective operation.

iii) Staff costing

The accurate forecasting of future staff costs is an important activity in its own right. HR planning assists in cost reduction by aiming to work out in advance how organisational operations can be staffed most efficiently. It is also significant when new ventures or projects are being considered, because it provides information on which to base vital decisions. Too high a labour cost, and the project will not go ahead; too low an estimate, and profit levels will be lower than expected.

iv) Redundancy

HR planning is an important tool in the anticipation of future redundancies. It therefore allows remedial action to be taken (recruitment freezes, retraining, early retirements etc) so as to reduce the numbers involved. As a result, considerable savings in the form of avoided redundancy payments can be made. While redundancies may not be avoided altogether, adequate warning will be given, thus reducing the adverse impact on employee relations associated with sudden announcements of dismissals and restructuring.

v) Collective bargaining

In organisations with a strong trade union presence, HR planning provides important information for use in the bargaining process. It is particularly significant when long-term deals are being negotiated to improve productivity and efficiency. In such situations, the information provided by HR forecasts enables calculations to be made concerning how great an increase in pay or how great a reduction in hours might be conceded in exchange for more productive working methods and processes.

vi) Accommodation

A final practical advantage associated with HR planning is the information it provides concerning the future need for office space, car parking and other workplace facilities. Such considerations are of most importance when organisations expect fast expansion or contraction of key operations. As with the other objectives described above, the basic rationale is that planning enhances cost control over the long term because it helps avoid the need to respond suddenly to unforeseen circumstances.

ADAPTING TRADITIONAL HR PLANNING

It can be argued that in this debate, as in so many featured in the management literature, there is no clear right or wrong answer. It is not a question of whether or not HR planning per se is a good or a bad thing, but of the extent to which it is appropriate in different circumstances. This is not a field in which general theories or sweeping judgements can be applied at all usefully. There remain employers for whom traditional approaches to HR planning (ie the use of systematic techniques to forecast supply and demand three to five years ahead) are very appropriate – at least for certain staff groups. These share the following characteristics:

- organisations that are large enough to be able to dedicate resources to the establishment and maintenance of an HR planning function

- organisations operating in reasonably stable product and labour markets

- organisations for which key staff groups require lengthy or expensive training

- organisations competing in industries in which decisions concerning future investment in plant and equipment are made a number of years ahead and are essential to effective product market competition (ie capital-intensive industries).

In the UK, large numbers of organisations share most or all of these distinguishing features. In addition to the major public services (health, education, social services, defence, local and central government), many larger companies would also be included (utilities, oil producers, major banks and building societies, large retailers etc). In all of these cases, while change may be occurring quickly, it is relatively predictable over the short term. The closure of departments or plants, expansion into new markets and changes in organisation do not take place overnight. Typically there will be at least six months' warning of likely changes, allowing time for established HR forecasts to be adapted and revised plans established. For such organisations, the criticisms of the HR planning process described above are applicable in relatively few situations and for relatively few staff groups. It can thus be plausibly argued that the absence of an HR planning function in such employing organisations will mean that they are not maximising their long-term efficiency and effectiveness.

The traditional approach to HR planning has a great deal less relevance for other employers (ie those that are small players in their industries, operating in a fast-changing technological field, or unable to know from one quarter to the next what turnover is likely to achieved). For such organisations the case against HR planning presented above will have greater resonance. The establishment of a formal, systematic planning function making forecasts on the basis of past trends and managerial judgement is not a cost-effective proposition. The market, as well as organisational structures, are simply too unpredictable to enable meaningful forecasts to be made and plans to be established concerning staffing needs a year or more ahead. However, that is not to say that such employers should not plan – merely that the traditional approach to planning described above has little to offer. A case for these organisations to undertake some form of HR planning can still be made, but it involves methods that have somewhat different features.

What is needed is an adaptation of the principles underlying HR planning, together with the development of newer techniques and approaches. Many of these – now well covered in the literature – are also relevant for the larger, more stable organisations, where they can be used in addition to the longer-established HR planning techniques.

MICRO-PLANNING

The first alternative is to move away from a planning function which focuses on the organisation as a whole, and instead concentrates on forecasting demand and supply of defined staff groups or on specific organisational developments (see Bechet 2008 27–40). Planning activity is thus discrete and centres on potential problem areas. The major examples are as follows:

- Tight labour markets in which the organisation is obliged to commit substantial resources to compete effectively (see the example of pharmacists above).
- Major new business developments such as an expansion/contraction, a merger or acquisition, the development of a new line of business activity or a reorganisation.
- The need to respond to a significant environmental development (eg regulation, activity of a competitor, negative publicity or a new business opportunity).
- Where it is practicable and cost effective (eg where the required information is readily available and the outcome of an HRP exercise clearly of use to the organisation).

Micro-planning is also often time-limited. It can be carried out as a one-off project, rather than on an ongoing basis. This is usually because the organisational issues themselves are transient and cease to be problem areas once the planning process has been carried out and effective responses formulated.

CONTINGENCY PLANNING

Contingency planning is rarely given more than passing reference by authors assessing the worth of HR planning, yet it can be seen as an approach that is almost universally applicable. Instead of seeing the HR planning process as one in which a single plan is developed and then adapted as the environment changes, contingency planning involves planning possible responses to a variety of potential environmental developments. The result is that HR planning effectively switches from being a reactive process undertaken in order to assist the organisation achieve its aims, and becomes a proactive process undertaken prior to the formulation of wider organisational objectives and strategies. The purpose of contingency planning in the HR field is thus the provision of information on which decisions about the future direction the organisation takes are made.

The development of IT applications that permit 'what if' analyses greatly assists the contingency planning process. They are particularly useful in their capability to calculate very rapidly the cost implications of certain courses of action or shifts in environmental conditions, a basic spreadsheet program being all that is necessary to undertake these activities. Once developed, it is a very straightforward process to alter one or more sets of figures or assumptions to forecast what would happen in HR terms were certain scenarios to unfold or be pursued.

A straightforward example would be a retailer who decides whether to open a new store and what size it should be. A spreadsheet could be constructed in which assumptions were made about the number and type of staff that would be required, the likely turnover rate in the first year and the cost of recruiting and training the new employees required to fill the posts. Different figures could then be plugged into the program representing different scenarios in terms of costs, training times, difficulty in recruiting staff, turnover, wage rates, business levels etc. Particularly useful is the capacity such approaches have for calculating, in cost terms, potential best and worst scenarios. In the case of the retail company, such analysis would produce estimates of the highest and lowest possible costs associated with opening the new store. In addition a range of other estimates could be generated, given a variety of different potential outcomes. Senior managers, charged with making the decision about whether or not to invest in a new store, would then base this partly on information provided by the HR planner.

CONTINGENCY PLANNING IN A MANUFACTURING COMPANY

An example known to the author of the effective use of contingency planning occurred recently in a major manufacturing organisation. The company produces two distinct household products under a well-known brand name, and until 1995 did so in three plants located respectively in Italy, Germany and the UK. At that time it was decided to rationalise the company's operations and concentrate the manufacturing of each item on one site, a decision that necessitated the closure of one of the three plants. The question was, which should close?

While many considerations were taken into account in making the decision, HR issues played their part. Plans were thus drawn up looking at the outcomes in cost terms of different contingencies: closing the UK plant and focusing production of one product in Italy and one in Germany, closing the Italian plant and producing the products in Germany and the UK, and so on. In the event the decision was taken to close the German factory and to produce one of the two principal products in the UK and the other in Italy. The cost in HR terms of each scenario was a significant factor in the final decision and was informed by the HR planning programme.

In the following year, managers at the UK plant had to retrain large numbers of employees in new production processes, made some redundant and hired others with particular skills. However, as a result of the contingency planning process, they had a very good idea of when each stage in the restructuring programme had to take place (ie what staff the plant needed in what jobs at what time) and a good estimate of the programme's cost in terms of recruitment, redundancy and retraining.

 LONG-TERM SCENARIO PLANNING

EXERCISE 5.6

Read the article entitled 'The Generation Game' by Anat Arkin, featured in *People Management* (29 November, 2007, pages 24–27). This can be downloaded from the *People Management* archive on the CIPD's website (www.cipd.co.uk).

This article describes some examples of organisations thinking about different future scenarios. The organisations include PricewaterhouseCoopers, BUPA and Shell.

Questions:

1 How plausible do you consider some of the long-term business scenarios described here? Why?

2 What unexpected advantages accrued to the organisations carrying out these exercises?

3 What does the article say about the decline of traditional HR planning since 1990?

SKILLS PLANNING

A further adaptation of traditional HR planning principles to meet new circumstances is a shift away from a focus on planning for people towards one that looks first and foremost at skills. Instead of forecasting the future supply of and demand for employees (expressed as the numbers of whole-time equivalents required or available), skills planning involves predicting what competences will be needed one to five years hence, leaving open the question of the form in which these will be obtained.

The approach is novel in so far as it acknowledges that as product markets have become increasingly turbulent, new forms of employment (such as those described in Chapter 3) have developed to meet the need for labour flexibility on the part of employers. It therefore abandons the assumption inherent in the traditional model of HR planning that organisations in the future will employ staff in the same manner as they have in the past. Skills-based plans thus incorporate the possibility that skill needs will be met either wholly or partially through the employment of short-term employees, outside contractors and consultants, as well as by permanent members of staff. Examples of the adoption of this approach are reported by Speechly (1994:45–47).

Skills planning is particularly appropriate in situations where there is a variety of different methods by which employee resourcing needs can be met. An example might be a computer company launching a new software package for use in industry. Managers may have a rough idea of how many licences they will sell, but are unable to predict how much training customers will require or what type of servicing operation will be necessary. They need to put in place plans that focus on their ability to provide different levels of training and service but, because these services will be provided by temporary employees and subcontractors as much as by permanent members of staff, there is no point in making plans that focus on the number of new staff posts needed. Instead, the plans focus on the possible skill requirements and form the basis of strategies designed to make sure that those skills are obtainable in one form or another.

SOFT HUMAN RESOURCE PLANNING

There is a degree of disagreement in the literature about the use of the term 'soft human resource planning' and its precise meaning. Marchington and Wilkinson (1996: 89) define it broadly as being 'synonymous with the whole subject of human resource management' while others, such as Torrington *et al* (2008:53), accept a narrower definition involving planning to meet 'soft' HR goals – particularly cultural and behavioural objectives. Torrington *et al* use the label to give meaning to a distinct range of HR activities which are similar to hard HR planning in approach, but which focus on forecasting the likely supply of and demand for particular attitudes and behaviours rather than people and skills. Soft HR planning can thus be seen as a broadening of the objectives associated with the traditional approaches described above.

Like skills planning, soft HR planning accepts that for organisations to succeed in the current environment they need more than the right people in the right place at the right time: they also need to ensure that those people have an appropriate outlook and set of attitudes to contribute to the creation of a successful organisational culture. More importantly, undertaking systematic soft HR planning can alert organisations to long-term shifts in attitudes to work among the labour force in general, allowing them to build these considerations into their general planning processes. An example might be a need on the part of an employer for sales staff who are not just appropriately trained, but who also exhibit the behaviours required to interact successfully with customers. There is thus a requirement for staff with a particular set of attitudes, so that an effective customer-focused culture develops. Traditional, hard HR planning takes no account of such issues, a deficiency corrected with the addition of a soft dimension.

Techniques for assessing the internal supply or availability of people with desired attitudes and behaviours are described by Torrington *et al* (2008:61–62). They include the use of staff surveys, questionnaires and focus groups to establish the nature of employee motivation, the general level of job satisfaction and commitment and the extent to which certain behaviours are exhibited. Methods for analysing external supply are discussed by Jackson and Schuler (1990:157). The emphasis here is on making an assessment of the likely impact of general societal attitudinal change on the future needs of the organisation. Published surveys are the main source of external data. Among the changes in attitudes they report in the USA are the following:

- Employees are becoming increasingly resistant to relocation.

- There is a general reduction in loyalty towards individual employers.

- Younger workers have considerably less trust in and respect for authority than their older counterparts.

- Younger workers tend to look for work that is fun and enjoyable, whereas older workers see it as 'a duty and a vehicle for financial support'.

- Younger workers have a different conception of 'fairness' in the work context than older colleagues. They see it as involving being tolerant towards minorities and allowing people to be different, while older workers define it as 'treating people equally'.

Advocates of soft HR planning argue that such matters can and should be considered when forecasting future needs in addition to data concerning the numbers of staff and skills that are likely to be available.

REFLECTIVE QUESTION

Which of these adaptations of traditional HRP is most relevant for your organisation? Which is least relevant?

HR PLANNING IN AN INTERNATIONAL CONTEXT

The globalisation of organisations has a number of distinct implications for the HR planning function, raising fundamental questions about the extent to which it is useful to carry it out and about the level at which such activity should be undertaken. In practical terms, there are two major implications for international organisations: the requirement for language skills and the need to move skilled employees and managers from country to country. Both complicate the planning process and make forecasting supply and demand for key groups of employees a considerably harder task. Added to this is the inherent instability associated with much international business activity. Companies are bought, reorganised and resold regularly, production is shifted from country to country as economic conditions change, and strategic alliances are formed that can easily alter a company's HR planning needs overnight.

In forecasting the demand for and supply of language skills, the HR planning function has a potentially crucial role to play, so fundamental is the need for effective communication between employees in different countries. Forecasting demand a year or so ahead is not a major problem; nor is forecasting likely internal supply. The problem arises in estimating the external supply by accessing data on the number of people in different countries proficient in different languages at different levels. As a result, accurate forecasting of the amount of language training that needs to be provided is necessarily problematic. However, the importance of the issue and the length of time needed for most people to acquire reasonable proficiency in a new language mean that factoring such considerations in to the HR planning process is an important potential source of increased organisational effectiveness.

It is hard enough, as was illustrated above, to generate accurate forecasts for the supply of and demand for employees in one country; doing so across several countries renders the process a great deal more complicated. Not only do basic labour market conditions vary considerably between countries over time, there are also, as Hofstede (1980) and others have shown, substantial differences between the attitudes and expectations of different national workforces towards their jobs, their careers and their employers. When the problems associated with obtaining access to robust external labour market data in different countries are added to the equation, it becomes clear that the operation of a single HQ-based HR planning function is unlikely to be a practical option for international companies. Instead, what is required, if HR planning is to be carried out in any meaningful way, is separate regional or national HR planning functions, each focusing on developments in their own labour markets and reporting to a central co-ordinating department. This will ensure that HR planning is carried out for each key labour market and that information is provided from each in a similar format. Planning data can then be used to inform decision-making about future investment and downsizing programmes.

EXPLORE FURTHER

- The best general introduction to the practice of human resource planning is John Bramham's well established text *Practical manpower planning* (1988). Other books which cover the topics include *The handbook of human resource planning* by Gordon McBeath (1992), *Human resource planning: A pragmatic approach to manpower staffing and development* by Elmer Burack & Nick Mathys (1996), *Human resource planning, an introduction* by Peter Reilly (1996) and *Strategic staffing* by Thomas Bechet (2008).

- The specific issue of the case for and against HR planning in the current environment has rarely been addressed in a balanced way in the literature. It is thus necessary to look in different places for the arguments on either side. The case against is best articulated by Henry Mintzberg (1994) in *The rise and fall of strategic planning*, but is also covered more briefly by Flood *et al* (1996) in *Managing without traditional methods* and by Micklethwait & Wooldridge (1996) in *The witch doctors*. The counter-arguments in favour of HR planning are best articulated in Bramham (1988), Torrington *et al* (2008) and Marchington & Wilkinson (2008). The chapter by Dyer and Ericksen (2007) in John Storey's *HRM: A critical text* is an excellent contribution to the debate as is the chapter on HRP by Zsuzsa Kispal-Vitai and Geoffrey Wood (2009) in *Human resource management: A critical approach* edited by Collings and Wood.

- Up-to-date case studies focusing on the aims and outcomes of HR planning are also relatively rare. However, Terry Hercus (1992) describes the approaches taken in eight organisations based in the UK, and Jackson & Schuler (1990) include good examples from the USA in their article entitled 'Human resource planning: Challenges for industrial/organisational psychologists', as does Thomas Bechet (2008). Current public sector developments are summarised by IRS (2003c).

EXAMPLE

KEY ARTICLE BOX

'Human resource planning and organization performance: An exploratory analysis' by Stella M. Nkomo. *Strategic Management Journal,* **Vol. 8. 387–392 (1987)**

In recent years there have been very few articles published in academic journals about human resource planning. It is not a fashionable area of research, despite the claims that are frequently made for the benefits it can bring. This article does explore the subject and, in the process, provides one possible explanation as to why human resource planning has apparently fallen off the agenda of academic researchers. The principal finding is that there is no clear link between the presence of HR planning in organisations and measures of their relative business performance.

Questions:

1 How robust do you consider the research design described in the article? How might it be improved?

2 Which of the possible explanations for the findings put forward in the concluding paragraphs do you find the most persuasive?

3 Having read the article to what extent would you agree with the view that organisations are better off not bothering to undertake human resource planning at all? Why?

Job analysis and job design

MANAGING VACANCY SCENARIOS

Effective job analysis has long been considered to be the essential foundation of any 'good practice' approach to the recruitment and selection of staff. Systematic analysis of the duties that make up any vacant or newly created job, it is argued, allows recruitment and selection to proceed drawing on objectively gathered information about the attributes required of the job holder. It thus minimises the extent to which recruiters allow subjective judgements to creep into their decision-making and helps ensure that people are selected fairly. Not only does this mean that unlawful discrimination does not occur (and is seen not to occur), it also makes sure that the best candidate is chosen for the job. In the good practice model job descriptions and person specifications are derived from job analysis and form the principal tools used by recruiters in devising their advertisements or briefing agencies, and by selectors in developing interview questions or interpreting the results of selection tests.

For many years HRM professionals have accepted an established view of what constitutes 'good practice' when an organisation decides to recruit new employees. This traditional approach is best understood as a process comprising a series of defined stages linking job analysis (the starting point) with employee induction (the final stage). It is illustrated on the left hand side of Figure 6.1.

Figure 6.1 Stages in good practice recruitment and selection

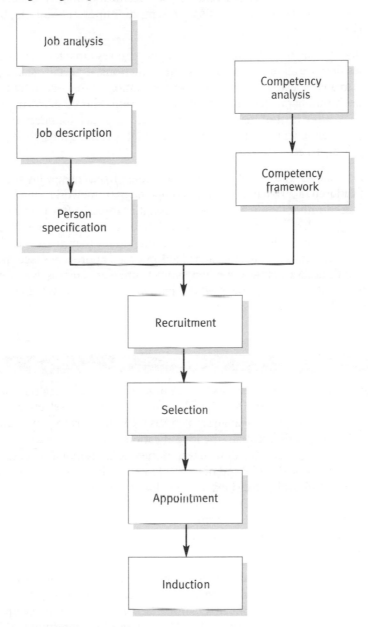

The latter stages of the traditional approach are generally accepted to be necessary, although there is a good deal of debate about how exactly they should be carried out. Most critical attention in recent years has been focused on the earlier stages, namely job analysis and the subsequent development of job descriptions and personnel specifications, which many academics and consultants now see as being outdated. Yet this traditional approach remains the most common. IRS (2003a) surveyed 250 organisations, large and small, from across the public and private sectors and found that 82 per cent of employers continue to use job descriptions and 72 per cent person specifications. This reflects a long-established view that job analysis represents an important building block for effective HRM:

> Job analysis is the most fundamental of all human resource management activities because all other human resource functions, especially staffing, depend to a large extent on the successful execution of this one activity.... There are a number of reasons why all organisations should perform job analysis. Not the least of these reasons is the creation of a foundation, through development of job descriptions and job specifications, for effective staffing (Caruth *et al* 2009:96-99).

The best articulated critiques of this view have come from those who advocate the use of different approaches based on competency frameworks which are person-focused rather than job-focused. These, it is argued, afford greater flexibility, require less administration and facilitate quicker and more effective recruitment decisions. Moreover, advocates contend that they are just as fair to potential candidates as the more established job-based approaches (see the right hand side of figure 6.1). However, competency frameworks themselves are not without their critics either, some of whom have argued persuasively that they tend to produce workforces which lack diversity.

JOB ANALYSIS

Formal analysis of the jobs that make up an organisation can form the basis of much HRM activity. Apart from its role in recruitment and selection, which is our concern here, job analysis also has a central part to play in the determination of pay differentials, the identification of training needs, the setting of performance targets and the drawing-up of new organisational structures. Furthermore, without effective and objective job analysis as their foundation, it can be difficult to justify decisions in the fields of promotion, redundancy, disciplinary action for poor performance and changes in rates of pay. As such, while essentially being a technical administrative task, job analysis (also known as occupational analysis) can be convincingly characterised as a process that adds value to an organisation's activities.

In the fields of recruitment and selection, job analysis is important because it provides the information on which to base two documents: the job description and the person specification. The first summarises the tasks that make up a job, together with statements of reporting lines, areas of responsibility and performance criteria. The second identifies those human attributes or personality traits that are considered necessary for someone holding the job in question. Of course, it is quite possible to draw up written job descriptions and person specifications without first undertaking rigorous job analysis. Indeed, it is often the case that job advertisements are compiled and interviewing processes undertaken without the assistance of these documents at all. However, in such cases, when no alternative is used, the likelihood that selection decisions will be properly objective and capable of identifying the most appropriate candidates for appointment is reduced.

Pearn and Kandola (1993:1) see job analysis as a form of considered research, and define it simply as 'a systematic procedure for obtaining detailed and objective information about a job, task or role that will be performed or is currently being performed'. It is therefore a process, or a means to an end, rather than an end in itself. This definition is a general statement of what job analysis involves. In practice, a wide variety of distinct approaches has been developed which analyse jobs in different ways and at different levels.

The first question to ask when approaching a job analysis exercise is the type of information that is sought. Only then can appropriate decisions be taken on the method that will be used. If the analysis is to form the basis of personnel selection decisions, there is a need to focus not just on the tasks carried out but also on the skills deployed in the job, the equipment used and the environment within which the various activities are carried out. Caruth *et al* (2009:101-2) list the following classes of information to collect as part of a good, comprehensive job analysis exercise:

i   job duties

ii   job responsibilities

iii machines, equipment, tools and materials used

iv   controls over work (ie nature and methods of supervision)

v   performance standards or output expectations

vi   interactions with others

vii organisational relationship (ie how the job fits into the wider structure)

viii physical factors and the job environment

ix   education, training, experience and personal requirements.

The Position Analysis Questionnaire, one of a range commercially produced for use as job analysis tools, gathers six distinct classes of information:

i   the source of information used to perform the job

ii   the kind of mental processes used to perform the job

iii the output expected and methods used

iv   the types and levels of relationships with others

v   the physical and social context in which the job is performed

vi   other job characteristics and activities not covered by the above (eg hours, payment arrangements, level of responsibility).

Job analysis is thus not merely concerned with data on the content of a job or the tasks that make it up. It also looks at how each job fits into the organisation, what its purpose is, and at the skills and personality traits required to carry it out.

A number of distinct methods of gathering job analysis data are employed – some more straightforward than others. The most basic of all simply involves observing a job holder at work over a period of time and then recording what has been observed. In most cases the observation is supplemented with an interview carried out at the same time or later to clarify points and gather information about mental activities that are less readily observable. The main drawback concerns the length of time it takes to get a full picture of the tasks carried out by any one job holder. Where the job varies from one day or week to the next, certain aspects only taking place occasionally, observation cannot be the main tool of analysis used. It is most appropriate in the case of straightforward jobs, which are primarily physical and which involve carrying out the same tasks in the same setting each day. One would thus expect to see observation used in the case of low-skilled manual work or in situations where the work, though more complex, is carried out cyclically, each day's routine broadly resembling that of the next (eg shop assistants, nursery school assistants, clerical workers).

The great weakness of the observation method is the strong possibility that the individuals being observed are unlikely to behave as they usually do, given the presence of a job analyst. Some will feel threatened, others will be out to impress; few will find themselves able to ignore the observer and continue as if no job analyst were there. Some have suggested that this kind of distorting effect can be reduced if observers are carefully trained and then introduced to the workplace tactfully. The need is to build trust with those being observed and to tell them the purpose of the exercise. Another method used to reduce the distorting effects of observation is the use of video cameras placed at a discreet distance from the place in which the observer is working. Again, this may have an effect if the individuals concerned are well prepared, but is unlikely to render an altogether accurate picture of day-to-day work, because people inevitably alter their behaviour when they know they are being watched.

The second approach is the job analysis interview. Here trained analysts ask job holders (as well as their supervisors and colleagues) to describe the job concerned, how it fits into the organisation and what it involves. Wherever possible interviewees are invited to open up and discuss particular events or occurrences to illustrate the points they are making. Interviews also provide the opportunity to probe points made by job holders and to clarify any areas of uncertainty. Information given can then be checked against answers given by colleagues and managers.

Here too there is always a danger that interviewees will 'talk up' their work in a bid to impress. They will downplay the more routine aspects of their work and seek to focus on the more interesting and significant parts. There is also a tendency for people to believe that they have greater authority and influence than they do actually enjoy – especially in situations where a degree of decision-making authority has been delegated but is still exercised under reasonably close supervision. Interviewees with a number of years' experience in the job being analysed are thus often less suitable than colleagues who have only spent one or two years in that role. As with work observation, it is possible to train job analysts to recognise such problems and to focus the attention of interviewees on the nuts and bolts aspects of what they do. Above all, it is important to make it clear that it is the job that is being analysed and not the individual's performance in the job. Where these approaches fail, another method used to ensure that individuals do not puff themselves up too much is to conduct a group interview with several job holders at the same time.

Aside from the group approach, a number of specific job analysis interviewing techniques have been developed in a bid to overcome the problems described above and to ensure that only the most important information is gathered. One of these is known as the 'critical incident technique' and involves focusing the attention of interviewees on only those aspects of their jobs that make the difference between success and failure. The starting-point here is a study of the key job objectives, so a critical incident interview always begins by establishing with the interviewee the central performance indicators or outcomes that are expected of any job holder. The interview then proceeds with the interviewee being asked to describe actual events or incidents that resulted in key objectives being either met or not met. In addition to describing the critical incident, interviewees are also asked to describe the background and to state specifically what their own contribution to the outcome was. The advantage of this approach is that it forces people to think about specific occurrences when being interviewed and not to dwell on general points. As a result, far more detailed and specific information is gathered to help the job analyst build up a picture of what the most significant job tasks are, the environment in which they are performed and what type of behaviours determine the extent to which success is achieved.

Another method that focuses on key aspects of jobs, but which requires a greater level of training, is the repertory grid approach. It involves first compiling a list of the tasks that form part of a job and then comparing and contrasting each with the others in terms of the skills or abilities needed to carry it out effectively. Random pairs or trios of tasks are usually selected and analysed by job holders, their supervisors and other colleagues until no new information on the skills required to perform the job is forthcoming. The lists of tasks and skills are then placed at right-angles to each other on a repertory grid so that each skill can be rated in terms of its significance to the achievement of each task (a very simple illustrative example is shown in Table 6.1). A seven- or five-point rating scale is usually used, a score of 1 indicating that the skill is not relevant to the accomplishment of a task and 5 or 7 signifying that the skill is crucial or essential to its successful completion.

IT programmes can then be used to analyse the scores and to establish which skills or personality attributes are most important overall. This part of the process goes beyond job analysis to the development of person specifications, but that does not negate the potential usefulness of the earlier stages as analytic tools. As with the critical incident approach, in breaking the job down into its constituent

Table 6.1 An example of a repertory grid for an office receptionist

Duties	Skills/competenciees							
	Sensitivity to customer need	Ability to plan own work	Good spoken communication skills	Reliability	Ability to analyse straightforward data	Typing skills	High level of personal presentation	Initiative
Open and close premises	1	1	1	5	1	1	1	4
Maintain filing system	1	4	1	5	4	2	1	4
Order office supplies	1	5	2	5	3	1	1	4
Deal with telephone enquiries	5	1	5	3	4	1	1	4
Welcome visitors	5	1	5	3	4	1	5	4
Type documents	1	3	1	4	5	5	1	2
Postal distribution	1	4	1	5	5	1	1	4
Arrange appointments	4	4	5	4	3	1	2	2

parts and reflecting on the detail of each the process is made more structured, thorough and objective than is the case with a straightforward interview.

The third commonly used approach is the administration of a prepared job analysis questionnaire. While it is possible for employers to develop their own, many either adapt or directly administer a proprietary scheme which they obtain a licence to use. The more reputable providers also give training in the use of the questionnaire and in its analysis. Where the jobs involved are not too unusual, this approach is probably the most efficient and straightforward to use. Because all interviewees are asked identical questions there is less opportunity for interviewer-bias to creep in, leading to a higher level of objectivity than is the case with observation or conventional job analysis interviews.

There are a number of questionnaires on the market, two of which are very well-established – the Work Profiling System and the Position Analysis Questionnaire. All the better products contain hundreds of questions and have been developed using data gathered from a very broad cross-section of job types from a number of industries. Most are now computerised, which greatly speeds up the analysis of data collected, and permits the generation of reports summarising key tasks and the competences that are most important to perform the job successfully. They also have the advantage in that where yes and no answers are inappropriate a series of descriptive statements is provided from which the most appropriate response can be chosen. The following examples come from the Medequate Job Analysis Questionnaire developed by KPMG for use in the NHS.

Why do people seek advice from the job holder?

i   First point of contact (the job holder is readily available).

ii Recognised authority (the job holder is the first source of advice within a particular function and can handle standard/routine requests for advice within their particular field. The job holder would pass on detailed/difficult/out of the ordinary requests to a senior authority).

iii Senior authority (the job holder would handle more involved/out of the ordinary requests for advice leaving the more routine requests to subordinates).

iv Acknowledged expert/specialist (the job holder is a respected source within an area of expertise/specialism; only in exceptional circumstances would the job holder need to refer to a higher source or a second opinion).

v   Ultimate authority/expert (as a result of experience and authority, the job holder is seen as the organisation's ultimate source of information in a certain field and would be expected to provide expert advice within their own speciality; the job holder would be consulted in all the most difficult/complex cases).

Describe the nature of the majority of the decisions taken by the job holder.

i   Straightforward choices (little scope for decision-making, eg yes and no answers).

ii   Few and well-established (the decisions made will be few in number and will follow well-established procedures or precedents).

iii Many and well-established (decision-making will be frequent and over a wide range of topics, but each decision will follow well-established procedures or precedents).

iv   Unprecedented (decision-making will be over a wide range of topics but will often be outside existing procedures and no precedents may exist).

Organisations also employ other methods of job analysis which do not fit into any of the three broad categories identified above. These include asking individuals to complete work diaries detailing the tasks they complete each day; the use of documentary evidence such as performance appraisal results and training manuals; and consultation with experts in particular fields. In most cases these methods will be insufficient in themselves, but may well assist in so far as they back up or contradict the results of job analysis exercises using the more conventional approaches. The use of panels of experts is particularly useful when a job that does not yet exist is to be analysed. In these circumstances, where there is no job holder to question or observe, there is no real alternative but to ask well-informed people what the key job tasks and competences are most likely to be.

REFLECTIVE QUESTION

Which of the above approaches would you consider to be most appropriate to employ when analysing complex, senior job roles?

EXERCISE BOX: HOLLYWOOD FILM MAKERS

EXERCISE 6.1

Read the article by Angus Strachan entitled 'Lights, camera, interaction' featured in *People Management* (16 September 2004, pages 44-46). This can be downloaded from the *People Management* archive on the CIPD's website (www.cipd.co.uk).

This article relates one person's experienced but subjective view about the attributes required in film directors, production co-ordinators and assistant directors working in film production in Hollywood.

Questions:

1   If a formal job analysis was to be carried out for the roles of production co-ordinator and assistant director, for what purposes could the results be used?

2   Which method (or combination of methods) of job analysis would you recommend was/were used in order to gain sufficient data to develop a useable job analysis profile?

3   What practical problems would you anticipate and how might these be overcome?

JOB DESCRIPTIONS

A written job description or job summary is the main output from the job analysis process. As has been stated, it can form the basis of a variety of decisions and processes across the range of P&D activity, including the drawing-up of training plans and the determination of pay rates. However, it is no less important in the staffing field where, once compiled and filed, it is used in five specific ways:

- *As a tool in recruitment.* Job descriptions are used to assist in the writing of job advertisements and will be given to agents hired to undertake all or part of the recruitment process. Copies are also typically sent to people who enquire about specific jobs, along with application forms and person specifications. IRS (2003a:43) found that over 75 per cent of employers include copies of job descriptions in application packs and that 82 per cent use them when drawing up job advertisements.

- *As a tool in selection.* Decisions about who to employ from among a range of possible candidates can be taken with reference to job descriptions. This helps ensure that there is a clear match between the abilities and experience of the new employee and the requirements of the job.

- *As the basis of employment contracts.* Frequently organisations make specific reference to job descriptions in their contracts of employment. They can thus have an important legal significance if someone is dismissed for failing to reach expected performance standards or resigns and claims constructive dismissal when he or she has been unreasonably told to undertake duties that lie outside the terms and conditions of his or her employment. IRS (2003a:44) found that nearly 40 per cent of employers (53 per cent in the public sector) make direct reference to job descriptions in their contracts.

- *As part of an employer's defence in cases of unfair discrimination.* Where an individual has been refused employment or promotion and believes that this is on account of direct or indirect discrimination, he or she may threaten the employer with legal action. The presentation in court of a job description can then be used as part of a case to establish that the selection decision in question was carried out objectively and that other candidates were judged to be more suitable than the complainant. As is so often the case with employment law, the existence of evidence of this kind is most important in so far as it deters people from bringing actions in the first place.

- *As a means by which the employer's expectations, priorities and values are communicated to new members of staff.* Statements can be included in job descriptions that make clear what the employee is expected to achieve and how he or she will be rewarded for so doing.

Job descriptions are one of the best-established institutions in the HRM field. As a result, a consensus has grown up about what they should include and the level of detail that should be used. They thus vary surprisingly little from one organisation to another in terms of style and coverage. Typically the following headings are included:

- job title

- grade/rate of pay
- main location
- supervisor's name/post
- details of any subordinates
- summary of the main purpose of the job
- list of principal job duties together with very brief descriptions
- reference to other documents (such as collective agreements) that may clarify or expand on other items.

Most will also include a date at the end indicating the point at which the document was last updated. In most cases they will also include some kind of general statement indicating that other duties may be carried out by the job holder from time to time. Where the job description is explicitly incorporated into the contract of employment, it is also wise to state that the content and reporting lines may be reviewed, and that they cannot be assumed to remain the same indefinitely.

ACCOUNTABILITY PROFILES

A problem with the format of job descriptions is the stress that is placed on the tasks that are performed by the job holder. This, it can be argued, encourages people to think of their jobs as being made up of defined activities or duties, rather than to think in terms of what they are responsible for achieving for their employers. In response many organisations have moved towards the adoption of 'accountability profiles' or 'role profiles' which focus on achievement rather than a straightforward description of the job.

Armstrong (2003:198-199) and Caruth *et al* (2009:107-8) advocate the use of such approaches, offering useful advice about the language that should be used in compiling the documentation and the methods that can be used to edit it down to a manageable length. They both suggest that each item in the job description/accountability profile should relate to the 'outputs' or 'key result areas' that the job holder will be expected to achieve or produce, and that each should therefore state what the job holder can be held responsible for. Where a job task is performed under supervision, such should be clearly stated. Likewise, where there are deadlines to work to, those too should be included, or at least their existence recognised. Fine and Getkate (1995:2-3) go further in proposing that the language used should always refer to 'what gets done' rather than 'what workers do', on the grounds that this allows far more effective description and less room for ambiguity. So, rather than state that the job involves 'consulting' (ie what is done), the job description should use terms such as 'communicates with', 'explains', 'clarifies', 'discusses' or 'informs', which give a more precise meaning to the activity being described.

REFLECTIVE QUESTION

Do you have a job description or accountability profile? If so, which of the above items are included? How could it be improved?

EXTRACT FROM A JOB DESCRIPTION AND AN ACCOUNTABILITY PROFILE FOR A DOCTOR'S RECEPTIONIST

Job description

Main duties:

Opening and closing the premises

Checking heating

Reconnecting the regular telephone service

Opening and distributing mail

Answering general enquiries

Registering patients

Making appointments

Filing and extracting patient records

Receiving and logging samples

Accountability profile

Key result areas:

Ensures that the premises are opened on time and secured at the end of surgery hours

Checks that heating equipment is in working order and that correct temperatures are maintained

Reconnects the regular telephone service at the start of surgery hours

Opens all mail on receipt and takes responsibility for its prompt distribution to each doctor

Ensures that all enquiries are dealt with promptly and courteously

Completes all procedures associated with the registration of new patients

Accurately maintains appointment records

Ensures the accurate extraction and filing of patient records

Receives and logs all samples received promptly and accurately

PERSON SPECIFICATIONS

The second piece of documentation that is derived from the job analysis process is the person or personnel specification. Here the emphasis is not on what the job involves but on the attributes that are required of someone aspiring to fill the role. Effectively it lists the criteria the organisation proposes to use in shortlisting and selecting an individual to fill the job concerned. Typically, person specifications include information under a number of headings such as skills, knowledge, personality attributes, education, qualifications and experience. Where the hours of work deviate from standard patterns or where the work is carried out on a number of sites, the ability and willingness to meet these requirements will also be included. It is also common for items in the person specification to be divided into 'desirable' and 'essential' characteristics.

The repertory grid method described above (see Table 6.1), is a useful tool to use in developing a person specification. An advantage is the way in which each attribute that is required by a job holder is scored in terms of its significance to the achievement of each job task. These scores can then be added up to produce a list of attributes in rank order, providing a straightforward and objective means of establishing which are 'essential' and which are 'desirable'. However, in order to ensure an accurate outcome it is necessary to weight the tasks or duties according to their relative significance in the job. Otherwise attributes of relatively minor importance can easily be given undue prominence.

Care must be taken to include in a written person specification only items that really are 'essential' or 'desirable' in someone appointed to a particular job. The presence of a professionally compiled document will be of no help in front of an employment tribunal when a case of unfair discrimination is brought by an aggrieved candidate who failed to be appointed or promoted to a new job. It is the responsibility of the P&D specialist to make sure that problems of this kind do not arise and that the items included can clearly be objectively justified.

IRS (2003a:47) found that the following areas were covered in the person specifications used by the majority of their respondents:

- skills
- experience
- qualifications
- education
- personal attributes.

Interests and motivation are not included by the majority, but according to this survey are included by 40 per cent of employers.

DISCRIMINATION LAW AND PERSON SPECIFICATIONS

Care needs to be taken when developing person specifications that items included do not indirectly discriminate on grounds of sex, race or any of the other protected grounds (see Chapter 4). If they do, aggrieved job applicants who fail to be selected on these grounds can bring their case to an employment tribunal.

The P&D professional thus needs to ensure that any criteria included in a person specification, whether 'essential' or 'desirable' in job holders, does not leave the organisation open to legal actions. In practice this means insisting that any criterion which is potentially discriminatory against a protected group is objectively justifiable. It must therefore be genuinely necessary for the performance of the job in question and not a device to benefit members of one group in the population.

Two reported cases are worth looking at in this regard. In *Hussein v Saints Complete House Furnishers* (1979) a firm limited recruitment to people living within certain postal districts of Liverpool. A tribunal ruled that this indirectly discriminated against certain ethnic minorities because applications from the postal districts in which they were concentrated were rejected. More recently, in *Northern Joint Police Board v Power* (1997), a senior police officer won his case having argued that he had been indirectly discriminated against on grounds of his national origin. Mr Power was an Englishman who had failed in his bid to be appointed as a Chief Constable because the appointment board thought it desirable that the post was occupied by a Scottish person.

EXERCISE BOX: MEMBERS OF EMPLOYMENT TRIBUNALS

EXERCISE 6.2

Read the article by Rima Manocha entitled 'Cut out for the role' featured in *People Management* (5 May 2002, pages 26-30). This can be downloaded from the *People Management* archive on the CIPD's website (www.cipd.co.uk).

This article focuses on the appointment of wing members to sit on employment tribunals. In the past these appointments were made through recommendation from employers' associations and trade unions, but more recently an open application system has been used. One of the main reasons for the change was to increase the diversity of people sitting on tribunals,

but some argue that this has led to people being appointed who lack the necessary skills and experience.

Questions:

1 Put the cases for and against using formal job analysis, job descriptions and personnel specifications in the recruitment and selection of tribunal wing members, and indeed any member of a public body. Which case do you find most persuasive and why?

2 Draw up a brief job description and a personnel specification for members of employment tribunals.

PROBLEMS WITH THE JOB ANALYSIS APPROACH

Having put the case for detailed job analysis and the production of written job descriptions and person specifications, it is now necessary to point out some of the drawbacks. One, which has already been alluded to, concerns the problems inherent in carrying out the analysis. Some argue that any exercise of this kind, even when its sole purpose is to support fair decision-making in recruitment and selection, is so difficult to achieve objectively that it is not an appropriate way to use organisational resources. According to this point of view, all the main methods used are deficient in some shape or form: observation, because of people's suspicion and their tendency to behave differently when being watched; interviewing, because of people's tendency to puff up their own importance; and questionnaires, because they are unable to include all aspects of a job role. The result, therefore, is inaccurate job descriptions and misleading person specifications – a bureaucratic procedure which takes up time and effort that could be more usefully employed elsewhere (see Searle, 2003:44-48 for a detailed discussion of accuracy in job analysis).

The problem of inaccuracy is compounded in situations where jobs change in terms of their content, character or complexity. Where this occurs, the written job descriptions can very easily become outdated, with the result that it is of little or no use as the basis of a recruitment and selection programme (let alone the other HR functions that draw on job descriptions). For organisations operating in fast-changing environments where job-roles evolve and re-evolve rapidly the problem of obsolescence of job descriptions and person specifications means that their use is of questionable value. Aside from dispensing with detailed job analysis altogether, there are two methods that can be used to minimise this effect: regular updating and looser approaches.

REGULAR UPDATING

Once job descriptions for all positions have been established, each line manager can be asked formally to review their content on an annual basis. The best time to do this is when the individual job holder is receiving his or her formal yearly appraisal. The process can then be tied in with a general review of the role, and the job description can anticipate future changes, rather than simply reflect those that have already occurred. However, this only seems to be done by a minority of organisations (IRS 2003a:46). It is more common for updates only to occur at the time that a job becomes vacant.

FUZZY DESCRIPTIONS

Where jobs are genuinely subject to substantial, ongoing change, job analysis can be undertaken on a looser basis, with the result that job descriptions are couched in less precise language than is usually the case. Parker and Wall (1998:102) describe this as making job descriptions 'fuzzy to allow for greater flexibility'. Instead of specifying the exact job duties and responsibilities, the focus is on the general level of the work and the degree of skill employed. So, instead of stating explicitly that the job involves supervising three administrators performing specific tasks, a more general statement is included simply making it clear that the job holder is expected to undertake supervisory duties across a more broadly defined field.

A third commonly cited drawback associated with job analysis and the development of written job descriptions relates to the fact that they may be used by employees as part of a case for refusing to undertake reasonable management instructions. In other words, it is argued that people cannot say 'I'm not doing that – it's not in my job description' if they have no documentation to refer to. Linked to this is the suggestion that, where job duties are written down, managers are liable to be required to negotiate changes with employees or their representatives and that this tends to decrease organisational effectiveness. Again, this problem can be minimised to a great extent if care is taken in drawing up job descriptions and person specifications. Not only should clear and explicit reference always be made to the possibility that other duties may be undertaken from time to time, but the job description can also contain some reference to the possibility that duties will change over time and that the job holder will be expected to co-operate where such changes are reasonable.

The fourth criticism is similar to one that is made about traditional approaches to human resource planning, namely that the perspective is job-based (see Chapter 5). There is an underlying assumption that organisations can usefully be seen as comprising a collection of identifiable 'jobs' into which people are slotted and remain until promoted or shifted sideways into another pre-designed and discrete 'job'. A further associated assumption is that the 'jobs' are all to be offered on a standard contractual basis, identical in terms of hours, payment arrangements, holidays and other conditions of employment. Such thinking can be convincingly characterised as being inflexible as well as inefficient on the grounds that it encourages people to see themselves as employed 'in a job' and not 'for an organisation' or 'in a team'. At best this results in a narrow focus on particular job duties, at worst in an 'I know my place' attitude which prevents people from contributing all the skills and ideas that they could if encouraged to do so.

COMPETENCY FRAMEWORKS

The major alternative approach to the job analysis/job description/person specification process involves the development of a competency framework which avoids many of the drawbacks set out above. 'Competencies' were famously defined by Boyzatis (1982:21) as 'an underlying characteristic of a person which results in effective and superior performance in a job'. Competency frameworks are therefore not very different from person specifications in terms of their broad appearance and function. What makes them different is the way that they are developed and the fact that they can be generic to an organisation (or a part of an organisation) rather than specific to defined jobs. While job descriptions and job analysis remain widely used, there is evidence to suggest that the use of competency frameworks alongside them, if not as an alternative, is growing in the UK (Rankin 2008a).

A competency approach is person-based rather than job-based. The starting point is thus not an analysis of jobs (in the manner described above) but an analysis of people and what attributes account for their 'effective and superior performance'. This involves first identifying people in the organisation whose performance is consistently impressive vis-à-vis that of average performers. Personality questionnaires, interviews or a combination of both are then used to establish what attributes the high achievers share which differentiate them from other employees. The resulting profile is then used to inform recruitment and selection processes in the same way as a person specification derived from an analysis of job tasks. Repertory grid approaches can be used here too, along with interviews that focus on individual responses to 'critical incidents' that have occurred in the past.

The precise range of competencies which explain superior performance will clearly vary from job role to job role (particularly those which are skills-based), but it is often possible to identify competencies which are more broadly present among top performers which can then be sought in all applicants for roles in the organisation. Some examples are given by Karen Moloney (2000:44):

> For companies launching on the internet, experiencing rapid market growth and change, for example, competencies such as breadth of vision, opportunism and drive will be important. For firms rethinking their strategy in the face of stiff competition – Marks and Spencer, for instance – competencies such as mental toughness, attention to detail and prudence will be crucial.

Some organisations, notably those with Japanese parent companies, go a step further and base all their recruitment and selection on generic competencies of this kind, all but dispensing with skills-based criteria altogether. Personality attributes, and particularly attitudes towards work are the major yardsticks used to judge the suitability of candidates. Recruiters want to be sure that the workforce shares the key characteristics associated with high levels of performance in current and previous employees. Having recruited people with these desired 'competencies' the employer then takes responsibility for equipping them with the skills they need to do the job. This turns established practice on its head because most organisations select primarily on the basis of skills, then subsequently use a variety of methods (performance management systems, reward systems etc) to influence attitudes.

THE MOST COMMONLY SOUGHT COMPETENCIES

According to an analysis carried out by Wood and Payne (1998:27), the most commonly adopted competencies in UK organisations were the following:

- communication
- achievement/results orientation
- customer focus

- teamwork
- leadership
- planning and organising
- commercial/business awareness
- flexibility/adaptability
- developing others
- problem solving
- analytical thinking
- building relationships.

EXERCISE BOX: LOCAL GOVERNMENT MANAGERS

EXERCISE 6.3

Read the article by Beverly Alimo-Metcalfe and John Alban-Metcalfe entitled 'Under the influence' featured in *People Management* (6 March 2003, pages 32–35). This can be downloaded from the *People Management* archive on the CIPD's website (www.cipd.co.uk).

This article describes a major research project that sought to identify the competencies associated with effective managers in the local government sector. It provides an excellent case study of the competency-based approach in action

Questions:

1 Why do you think so many senior managers in local government appear to lack the competencies their role requires?

2 To what extent would this change if recruitment and promotion processes were based around a competency framework rather than a job description/person specification approach.

3 How would you go about introducing a competency-based approach for this group of managers? What practical problems might you expect to meet when doing so?

Milsom (2009) reviews recent developments in the field of competencies. The most important in his view is the tendency for organisations to include within their frameworks statements which reflect their values as well as the know-how required to do a good job:

> By defining values in behavioural terms, a values-driven leadership framework offers an effective way for organisations to explain how they expect decisions to be made. Organisations are then able to assess the thinking style and motivations of employees to ensure that they are both rationally and emotionally engaged with their organisations' objectives and culture (Milsom (2009:3).

We are thus increasingly seeing competency frameworks which make specific reference to integrity, to commercial or customer awareness and to the development of staff. The aim is to actively recruit and select people who are not only competent to do a good job, but also share the beliefs that underpin the organisation's culture.

Milsom also discusses ways in which organisations now regularly review their competency frameworks in order to ensure that they remain up to date and reflective of current and future corporate priorities. Another interesting development he outlines is the way organisations increasingly seek to develop culturally sensitive competency frameworks, using a language that makes them equally appropriate to use in global operations in which workplace cultures vary from those prevalent in the UK (see Chapter 4).

CRITICISMS OF THE COMPETENCY APPROACH

Despite the many advantages associated with the use of competency frameworks as the basis for recruitment and selection, several significant criticisms have been made of this approach. Debates about these can be found in Wood and Payne (1998:29-33), Moloney (2000), and Whiddett and Kandola (2000).

The most persuasive critiques are those which suggest that competency-based recruitment and selection leads to a form of cloning, all new recruits tending to be similar types of people to those already in post. Over time there is a risk that everyone behaves and approaches problems in the same way. The advantages springing from the employment of a diverse group of people are thus lost. The result is less creative tension, fewer voices arguing for different ways of looking at things, and less innovative thinking. Whiddett and Kandola (2000:33) show how in many organisations competency frameworks are reflected very strongly in job advertisements, leading to a situation in which people who could play an effective role, but do not share the defined competencies, are put off from applying. They are thus not even the given the chance to impress at the selection stage.

Another criticism is the tendency for competency frameworks to reflect what attributes were needed to be effective *in the past* and not those that the organisation needs to move forward *in the future*. This occurs because the methods used to identify the competencies (especially interviews with effective performers) inevitably focus on their past activities. Not only, therefore, is there a danger of recruiting 'clones', but clones whose attributes have been superseded by developments in the business context! Other criticisms reflect bad practice in the development of competencies rather than the method itself. They serve as a reminder that establishing a meaningful competency framework is a specialised and difficult task, but do not undermine the fundamental principles of the approach.

People management

EXERCISE 6.4

EXERCISE BOX: GENDER-BIAS IN COMPETENCY FRAMEWORKS

Read the article by Julie Griffiths entitled 'Masculine Wiles' featured in *People Management* (27 October 2006, pages 20–21) This can be downloaded from the *People Management* archive on the CIPD's website (www.cipd.co.uk).

This article criticises the competency frameworks that are most frequently used by leading UK corporations in the selection of leaders and the identification of future leadership potential. They are one of the main reasons, according to the researchers quoted, that there are so few women on the boards of top companies.

Questions:

1 In what ways do competency frameworks tend to echo 'masculine' leadership attributes?

2 What alternative attributes could be included?

3 What business case can be advanced for taking action in this field?

4 What, according to commentators quoted in the article, is the case for retaining existing competency frameworks?

REFLECTIVE QUESTION

Which competencies do you consider are shared by the better performers in your organisation? To what extent do these form the basis of recruitment and selection at present?

JOB DESIGN

Job design, or job redesign as it is usually more accurately described, is concerned less with what *is* in a job or what its purpose is, and more with what duties *should* make it up. When a vacancy occurs an opportunity is often created to reorganise duties among a team, thus redesigning the vacant job. When an organisation expands it may be necessary to decide on the design of several new jobs, but the same process occurs whenever any major reorganisation occurs following redundancies or a merger between two organisations. The more volatile and unpredictable the business environment, the more frequently jobs need to be redesigned. Cordery and Parker (2007:190-192) identify six core features of work content which have to be determined for each job and which can be altered from time to time:

- scope (the breadth and level of the tasks carried out)

- discretion (the amount of control the employee exercises over the operational aspects of their work)

- variability (the extent to which a job remains the same day by day or is subject to flexibility)

- demands (workload as well as the physical and emotional demands placed on the job holder)
- feedback (the speed and effectiveness with which a job holder gains information on their level of performance)
- interdependence (how reliant on other team members the job holder is to perform tasks).

This is an interesting area of HRM to study because the central debate about the best principles for managers to use when designing (or redesigning) jobs is one of the oldest in the field, dating back to the foundations of P&D as a management discipline and field of academic enquiry in the early twentieth century. Two distinct traditions, based on totally opposing principles can be identified. The first is known as the scientific management or taylorist approach, after Frederick W. Taylor who pioneered these principles when designing jobs in the first factories to make use of large-scale production lines. The second is often referred to as the humanist approach, pioneered by managers who saw that a fundamental flaw in taylorist principles was their tendency to dehumanise work.

TAYLORIST PRINCIPLES

The taylorist approach to job design is systematic and very logical. It involves examining in great detail all the individual tasks that need to be carried out by a team of workers in order to achieve an objective. The time it takes to accomplish each task is calculated and jobs are then designed so as to maximise the efficiency of the operation. In short an analyst works out on paper how many people need to be employed, carrying out which tasks and using which machinery. Waiting time and duplication of effort is minimised to reduce costs. Moreover, work is so designed as to minimise the number of more skilled people the organisation requires. This is done by packaging all the specialised tasks to form one kind of job, which is then graded more highly than others made up of less specialised, lower skilled tasks. The workforce is thus deployed with machine-like efficiency. Each plays a very defined role in a bigger process that is overseen, supervised, controlled and maintained by managers.

While originally developed for use in engineering and car assembly plants, the principles of taylorism live on and are still widely deployed. For example, call centres are very much organised along taylorist principles, each employee having a tightly defined role and being responsible for hitting targets of number of calls made or answered in each hour of work. As a result it is planned that costs are kept as low as possible given the expected throughput of work. The public sector too makes heavy use of taylorist principles in designing and redesigning jobs so as to maximise efficiency. In recent years many skill mix reviews have been carried out in hospitals, for example, the aim being to re-allocate duties between staff and achieve cost savings in the process. This is done by seeking to ensure that highly qualified (and highly paid) staff spend 100 per cent of their time carrying out duties that only they can perform. Lower skilled activities are then packaged together into jobs carried out by support workers. Similar approaches have been used in the police and in schools with the creation of more support roles, 'freeing' qualified teachers and police officers to focus on the more demanding tasks.

REFLECTIVE QUESTION

Skill mix reviews in the public sector have often proved to be highly controversial and have been firmly resisted by trade unions and professional bodies. Why do you think this is?

HUMANIST PRINCIPLES

In the post-war era, a number of management thinkers began to challenge what had by then become the 'taylorist' orthodoxy. The major criticism made of scientific management was that it was dehumanising and therefore, ultimately, bad for business. The argument was that the adoption of taylorist principles led to the creation of jobs which were tedious, repetitive and unpleasant to perform. The result was a disengaged workforce and hence absence, high staff turnover and the development of adversarial industrial relations. It also generally created resentment among people forced into workplace straightjackets and this led to low motivation, commitment and hence performance. Some also wrote about sabotage of operations by disgruntled employees denied a 'humanistic' work environment (Fried *et al* 1998:533). Moreover, because of this, more supervisors were needed than would be the case if people were positively motivated by the content of their jobs. Ultimately, therefore, taylorism was not the most efficient approach over the long term, and an alternative set of principles were developed.

Instead of scientific management an approach evolved that draws on notions of intrinsic motivation and involves designing jobs that engage and even excite people. The alternative principles start with the idea that employees achieve higher levels of motivation, satisfaction and performance if the jobs they do are made more interesting and challenging. The key is to maximise the enjoyment that job holders derive from their work. While it must be accepted that many jobs are never going to be highly enjoyable, it can be argued that managers should nonetheless try to design them in such a way as to maximise the satisfaction that the job holder derives from his or her work.

Traditionally, the main vehicles for achieving this have been job rotation, job enlargement and job enrichment. In each case, jobs are redesigned so as to make them less monotonous. Job rotation, for example, involves training employees to undertake a variety of jobs in an organisation so that different groups of tasks are performed on different days, weeks or months. In a manufacturing plant the rotation is likely to be daily or weekly, so that each employee works on different pieces of machinery and takes responsibility for different parts of the production process at different times. In other environments, perhaps where jobs take somewhat longer to learn, the rotation may be organised on a six-monthly or yearly basis. In each case the aim is to reduce the likelihood that people undertaking routine tasks become bored and uninterested in their work.

The use of job enlargement and job enrichment to improve workforce motivation are chiefly associated with the work of Frederick Herzberg (1966, 1968). Both approaches were defined as ones by which employees were given a wider variety of tasks to undertake, but in the case of job enrichment these required the acquisition of a higher level of skill. Hence, in addition to making jobs more interesting, enrichment also opens up wider developmental and career opportunities. Further, work carried out by Eric Trist and others (eg Trist *et al* 1963) led to the evolution of the socio-technical systems perspective on job enrichment, which sought to identify the key features needed in a job if it is to be motivating. In addition to a requirement for interesting work with opportunities for development and advancement, they stressed the importance of decision-making autonomy and discretion over the way the work is organised. The implication is that the less overt control is exercised over employees at work, the more motivated they will be and the higher their standard of performance will be.

According to Buchanan (1982), job enrichment had something of an 'unhappy history' in the 1960s and 1970s, with far more interest shown in its possibilities by academic researchers than by managers in organisations. However, in recent years interest has grown substantially, so that it is now very common to hear managers talking about empowering employees, developing new work roles, multi-skilling their workforces and refashioning reporting structures. Total Quality Management (TQM), a fashionable management philosophy of the 1980s and 1990s, also draws on many of these assumptions with its emphasis on self-supervision and the 'flattening' of management hierarchies. It is probably still the case that the rhetoric is more common than the reality, but the ideas that underpin job enrichment theories are now accepted with a great deal less scepticism than was the case 15 or 20 years ago.

One method of altering work arrangements to improve efficiency and quality that has of late received a great deal of attention is teamworking. The approach is derived from Japanese management practices and involves giving autonomous or semi-autonomous groups of employees responsibility for carrying out a particular task or group of tasks. How different elements of work are divided among them is a matter for the groups themselves to determine, so it is for them to decide how best to maintain high levels of motivation and performance. Job enrichment thus goes beyond the development of challenging roles and the reduction of direct management control to include systems of social support and interdependence among members of each team. Not only is the job itself made intrinsically more pleasurable to undertake, it also provides a basis for the development of valued social relationships. However, it is not always necessary to alter working arrangements quite so radically to generate performance improvements. Rather, it is quite possible to move down this kind of route a short step at a time by adjusting the content of jobs, the level of autonomy or the amount of teamworking as opportunities to do so arrive.

REFLECTIVE QUESTION

In what ways could your job be enlarged or enriched? How far would this increase your level of motivation, and why?

These ideas were taken forward in the influential work of Hackman and Oldham (1980) with the development of their 'job characteristics model' and applied to a wider variety of job types. They propose that job satisfaction, motivation and high work effectiveness occur when five 'core job characteristics' are present. These are as follows:

- skill variety (the degree to which a job draws on a job holder's different skills and talents)

- task identity (the degree to which a job involves completing an identifiable piece of work from start to finish with a visible outcome)

- task significance (the degree to which a job has an impact on the lives of others)

- autonomy (the degree to which the job holder has freedom, independence and discretion in carrying out the work)

- job feedback (the degree to which the job provides the job holder with direct information about his or her effectiveness).

However, Hackman and Oldham (1980) also found that these job characteristics are not guaranteed to produce high work performance. Other factors also need to be present. First, the job holder must possess the knowledge and skills necessary to carry the job out effectively. If they do not, however much autonomy is given and however meaningful the job may be, they are likely to struggle. Secondly, the job holder must be psychologically in a position to appreciate the opportunities provided by the job and willing to grow through their work. In other words they must want to develop in a role and not simply be interested in working because they have to in order to earn a living. Finally, the work context must be satisfactory. Poor pay, difficult co-workers or poor managers can easily undermine the potential of the five job characteristics to deliver improved performance.

More recently Parker and Ohly (2010) have sought to take forward the Hackman and Oldham approach and make it more relevant for twenty-first century workplaces. In their view the Job Characteristics Model offers an incomplete account of the link between job design and work satisfaction because it 'rests on the assumption that individuals have needs which are fulfilled by characteristics of their jobs' (p 271). They go on to advocate the adoption by organisations of a 'social information/processing perspective' which goes beyond job characteristics to focus much more on the context in which the work is performed. Central to their argument is the view that, unless individual workers feel 'psychologically empowered' job satisfaction, and hence performance levels, cannot be maximised. They also go on to point to recent developments in work and argue that the Hackman and Oldham framework needs to be extended in order to take account of the rise of 'emotional labour', IT systems which monitor work, technologies which blur the boundaries between home and work, and increased uncertainty about the future development of jobs and organisations. These along with other developments raise the likelihood that employees will suffer stress, burnout and depression. As a result, when designing jobs, organisations need to do more than look at the tasks the job holder performs, they need to look also at the environment in which they are performed.

 EXERCISE BOX: BMW

EXERCISE 6.5

Read the article by Jon Watkins entitled 'A Mini Adventure' featured in *People Management* (6 November 2003, pages 29–32). This can be downloaded from the *People Management* archive on the CIPD's website (www.cipd.co.uk).

This article focuses on major changes made to working practices at the BMW (formerly Rover) plant at Cowley in Oxford. A major job redesign exercise placed workers into self-steering teams of 8 to 15 people, carrying out a far wider range of tasks than was the case previously.

Questions:

1   What evidence is presented in the article of job rotation, job enlargement and job enrichment?

2   What cost savings do you think are likely to have been gained as a result of the job redesign process and the other changes described?

3   From an HR perspective, what other advantages have accrued as a result of the changes?

JOB SCULPTING

Finally in this chapter we need to introduce an idea that has yet to gain much following, but may be applied more commonly in the future. Job sculpting turns almost all of the management approaches and processes discussed so far in this chapter on their heads, creating a wholly different way of managing this area of P&D work. Essentially it involves designing jobs around the needs, ambitions and capabilities of people rather than expecting people to fit themselves into a job designed for them by the organisation. Instead of recruiting someone new to fill a defined role, an effective performer is recruited and asked to develop their own role or, effectively, to write their own job description. Such an approach has always been used in the case of very talented individuals whose services an organisation wishes to secure and whose skills can be deployed in varied ways without the need to fit into any established role. It has also long been the case that long-serving staff are able, incrementally, to grow their own roles in directions that best suit them and make best use of their abilities. But job sculpting goes much further than this, beginning with the principle that contemporary organisations need to gain a capacity for flexibility and creativity above all things in order to attain competitive advantage. To achieve this they need to attract and retain effective people and develop strong, cohesive teams of individuals who can deliver changing organisational objectives. In a tight labour market, where skills are in short supply, it is argued that there is no alternative at least to move some way down the road towards job sculpting. Hirsch and Glanz (2006) see the adoption of such an approach as entirely logical. Like employer branding (see Chapter 9), job sculpting draws on the experience of consumer marketing techniques whereby customers are increasingly engaged in the design of customised products and services.

Butler and Waldroop (1999) have created a framework around which job sculpting exercises can take place. Their research, involving in depth interviews with 650 employees, has led them to conclude that there are eight major 'life interests' which motivate people as far as the content of their jobs is concerned. Most people, they claim, are primarily motivated by one or two of these. The eight can be summarised as follows:

- The application of technology. People who are interested in how things work and want to find ways of making them work more effectively.

- Quantitative analysis. People who are interested in numbers and mathematics and who like using quantitative approaches to analyse issues.

- Theory development and conceptual thinking. People who tackle problems using theory and abstract thinking.

- Creative production. Imaginative people who think original thoughts and enjoy innovating. They are particularly drawn to setting up new systems or projects.

- Counselling and mentoring. People who like to teach, coach and to guide others.

- Managing people and relationships. People who derive satisfaction from getting objectives achieved through others.

- Enterprise control. People who like leading, making decisions and taking responsibility for the completion of projects.

- Influence through language and ideas. People who gain satisfaction through writing and speaking. Excellent communicators.

A method of job sculpting involves establishing which of these eight 'life interests', or indeed others, motivate individual staff or job applicants and then seeking, as far as is practicably possible, to develop jobs which meet their particular preferences or aspirations.

REFLECTIVE QUESTION

Which of Butler and Waldroop's eight life interests carries most resonance for you? To what extent would it be possible for your current job to be re-sculpted to meet these preferences? Would this increase or decrease your effectiveness?

EXPLORE FURTHER

- Michael Pearn and Rajvinder Kandola's *Job analysis: A manager's guide* (1993) provides a thorough overview of different approaches to the topic and contains a number of short case studies outlining the methods used by four organisations. The wider issues are well covered by Caruth *et al* (2009) and by Heneman and Judge (2005).The debate about competencies is covered effectively by Robert Wood and Tim Payne in *competency based recruitment and selection* (1998) and by Gareth Roberts (2000) in r*ecruitment and selection: A competency approach*. The case for a competency approach, together with a guide to the major models used, is provided by Dalziel (2004).

- Searle (2003) contains a chapter which offers a critical perspective on job analysis, the views of its detractors and its contemporary uses.

- Job design is covered in detail by Parker and Wall (1998). The rival claims of the taylorist and humanist approaches are summarised very effectively by Fried *et al* (1998).

- A thoughtful assessment of the practice of writing job descriptions that are appropriate to the contemporary business environment is provided by Marie Gan and Brian Kleiner (2005).

EXAMPLE

KEY ARTICLE BOX

'Job analysis: a strategic human resource management practice' by C.M. Siddique. *International Journal of Human Resource Management*, Vol. 15, No. 1. 219–244 (2004).

This is a rare example of an article reporting research which seeks to test the business case for carrying out job analysis. The author is based in Dubai and the research is based on a survey of companies in the United Arab Emirates. The underlying hypothesis is straightforward. Job analysis produces information that is subsequently used to underpin a variety of other P&D practices and decisions, and hopefully improves their quality in the process. If this is so we would expect to see a correlation between the use of job analysis and the performance of organisations.

The author goes further than this, however, in distinguishing between companies that use the conventional approach to job analysis and those who have adopted the competency approach. A variety of other factors are included too as moderating, control and dependent variables. The key finding was a strong positive association between 'proactive job analysis' and firm performance. However, the extent to which a competency-based approach is associated with superior performance was less clear from the results.

Questions:

1 What measures of firm performance were found to be positively correlated with the presence in an organisation of job analysis?

2 How convincing do you find the research findings described here? How might the methodology be criticised?

3 What practical lessons can be learned from this research from the perspective of a UK-based P&D function?

CHAPTER 7

Recruitment advertising

LEARNING OUTCOMES

By the end of this chapter, readers should be able to:

- distinguish between recruitment strategies based on internal and external sources
- draft advertisements for filling vacancies and select appropriate media for specific cases
- evaluate advertising media and other methods of recruitment
- advise organisations on the options for e-recruitment.

In addition, readers should be able to understand and explain:

- the cases for and against internal and external recruitment
- different recruitment advertising strategies
- the growth, advantages and disadvantages of internet recruitment.

DEFINING RECRUITMENT

The terms 'recruitment' and 'selection' are often considered together, but they are in fact distinct human resource management activities. While recruitment involves actively soliciting applications from potential employees, selection techniques are used to decide which of the applicants is best suited to fill the vacancy in question. We can thus characterise recruitment as a positive activity requiring employers to sell themselves in the relevant labour markets so as to maximise the pool of well qualified candidates from which future employees can be chosen. By contrast, selection can be seen as a negative activity in so far as it involves picking out the best of the bunch and turning down the rest.

That said, it is equally important to understand that there is a recruitment side to selection and a selection side to recruitment. For example, there is considerable published evidence which demonstrates how heavily influenced job applicants are by the way they are treated during the selection process (Lievens and Chapman 2010:137-140). Many make direct inferences about what life would be like working for an organisation on the basis of how its recruiters treat them and the perceived fairness of selection methods used. If they are unimpressed they tend to turn down job offers and also pass on these negative impressions to colleagues.

It follows that organisations need to recognise that the process of positively attracting candidates continues beyond the stage at which applications have been received. Similarly it is increasingly recognised that good, well-designed recruitment processes include within them opportunities for people to self-select themselves out of the running for a job. No one's interests are served when unsuitable candidates pursue job applications which they stand no chance of securing, and for organisations there are major potential cost implications. It thus makes sense to ensure that recruitment literature and websites make clear to would-be candidates exactly what attributes and experience the organisation is looking for so that the number of applications from unsuitable people is kept to a minimum.

The relative significance of each stage in terms of costs, management time and organisational success varies with the state of the labour market. When labour markets are tight, as they have been in the UK in most recent years, recruitment activities assume a greater importance. This occurs because it becomes harder to find staff of the calibre and skills required, so more time and expense is necessary on the part of organisations. Conversely when labour markets are loose and jobs are in relatively short supply, as they were during the recessionary years after 2008, there is no shortage of qualified applicants for vacant positions. Less attention is thus given to recruitment and more to the selection stage as organisations look for ways of effectively differentiating between candidates. The more considered and sophisticated approaches to recruitment assume significance when unemployment among target groups is low; sophisticated selection rises up the corporate agenda when it is high.

An important question to ask whenever recruitment is being considered is whether or not there really is a need to recruit from outside the organisation at all. Giving thought to alternative approaches might lead to the development of effective solutions at considerably lower cost. Caruth *et al* (2009:137-141) give the following as the major examples:

- offer overtime to existing staff
- employ contractors
- employ temporary staff
- recruit internally.

The recruitment of new employees is an area of work in which all human resource professionals are involved in some way. According to CIPD (2009) the cost of replacing someone when they leave an organisation averages over £6,000, the large majority of which is spent on recruitment processes. The costs, of course, vary greatly from job to job. Filling a vacancy can be inexpensive if internal candidates are promoted, job centre candidates chosen or informal word-of-mouth recruitment used. But these methods, by their nature, heavily restrict the applicant pool and often mean that the 'best' available candidates are not even considered for vacant roles. To secure applications from a reasonable field of candidates more usually needs to be spent either on advertising, agency fees or attending careers events of one kind or another. It is thus not unusual for a sum equal to 2–3 per cent of an employer's total wage bill to be spent on recruitment advertising and agency fees. For a company employing 100 people at national average earnings this would mean that around £50,000 a year was committed to recruitment before taking account of administration costs. For larger organisations employing in excess of 3,000 people, the annual cost will amount to millions of pounds. Recruitment can also take up a great deal of time. One survey suggested that on average this area of work accounts for 16 per cent of a typical HR department's workload (*Personnel Today* 1996:3). It is thus important to appreciate how recruitment arrangements can be managed as efficiently as possible while making sure, at the same time, that the approaches chosen remain effective and do not breach the law.

Table 7.1: Recruitment methods

Internal methods	internal promotion lateral transfers job rotation schemes rehiring former staff
Printed media	national newspapers local newspapers trade and professional journals magazines
External agencies	job centres outplacement consultants headhunters employment agencies forces resettlement agency recruitment consultants
Education liaison	careers service careers fairs college tutors careers advisors student societies
Other media	direct mail local radio billboards internet TV and cinema
Professional contacts	conferences trade union referrals suppliers industry contacts

Other methods	'factory gate' posters
	past applicant records
	open days
	word of mouth
	poaching

INTERNAL RECRUITMENT

Most private sector employers, as a matter of course, attempt to fill vacancies internally before they consider looking for people outside the organisation (Newell 2005:122). In the public sector by contrast it is more common to advertise internally and externally at the same time. Fuller and Huber (1998:621) identify four distinct internal recruitment activities:

- promotions from within
- lateral transfers
- job rotation
- rehiring former employees.

In each case current or former staff are made aware of opportunities to develop a new role in the organisation before external candidates are considered. There are a number of advantages for organisations. First, of course, internal recruitment is very cost effective. Vacancies can be advertised at no cost at all using staff notice boards, newsletters or intranet systems. It also helps in the establishment of a strong internal labour market, giving people a reason to stay in the organisation rather than moving on to develop their careers elsewhere. This means that the organisation is maximising its return on investment in staff training, while also enhancing motivation and commitment among existing staff. Other advantages include better knowledge on the part of new recruits about the way the organisation operates and what to expect in the job. Learning times for new job holders are thus shorter, while early leaving as a result of dashed expectations is less likely. The time taken to fill a vacancy is usually less in the case of internal recruits, leading to further cost savings and greater organisational effectiveness. Finally, selection is based on greater knowledge of the individuals' merits and prospects, being less of a 'shot in the dark' than it is with external recruits.

There are also strong arguments to put against internal recruitment. Foremost is the way that it tends to perpetuate existing ways of thinking and carrying out tasks. Fresh blood is often needed to challenge the status quo, particularly at more senior levels, and this can only come through external recruitment. If all recruitment to such positions is internal the result is sterility, lack of originality and a decline in the breadth of an organisation's collective knowledge base. Secondly, it is very likely that the 'best' person for the job is not currently working for the organisation. An employer which is genuinely seeking to excel by attracting and retaining the most talented people is obliged not only to recruit externally, but to take some time and effort doing so. Finally there are arguments based on equality, the suggestion being that a reliance on internal recruitment tends to perpetuate existing imbalances in the make-up of the workforce. Hence if ethnic minorities are not currently well-represented, promoting from within will do nothing to create greater diversity, particularly among the management team.

Heneman *et al* (2000:327–331) make a useful distinction between 'traditional mobility paths' and 'innovative mobility paths' in their discussion of internal recruitment. Traditional approaches start with the assumption that individuals can expect to be promoted upwards through some form of organisational hierarchy. Internal recruitment is thus focused on people on the rung beneath that on which a new vacancy becomes available. Jobs are thus advertised narrowly, this group expecting to compete with one another for the promotion opportunity. Innovative paths are more appropriate in organisations operating in less predictable waters and in those which have sought to flatten their hierarchies by stripping out many middle management posts. Here the focus is on lateral and cross-functional moves, individuals being given the opportunity to build a broader portfolio of experience as a means of enhancing their long-term employability. In practical terms it necessitates advertising posts much more widely within an organisation and avoiding making assumptions about who could and who could not undertake the role.

IRS (2002a) correctly point to an important and problematic feature of internal recruitment, namely the need to manage situations in which candidates are unsuccessful. Turning external candidates down is a great deal more straightforward, because there are no long-term consequences for the day-to-day management of the organisation. By contrast, turning down internal candidates creates a sometimes difficult situation that needs immediate and careful management. The alternative is likely to be deeply dissatisfied staff who feel let down, unappreciated and relationships in which the level of trust has been reduced. IRS (2002a) quote the findings of an IES study into these issues (Hirsh *et al*, 2000) which recommends training managers in how to 'rehabilitate' failed internal candidates so as to avoid impaired performance, unwanted resignations and a breakdown in workplace relationships. But they also stress that these outcomes are easiest to avoid by running an open contest based on selection criteria which are both fair and seen to be fair.

REFLECTIVE QUESTION

Think about people you know who have been recruited to senior posts internally and externally. What different qualities do you think each brings to their role?

EXERCISE BOX: THE UNIVERSITY OF CUMBRIA

In December 2009 it was reported in the *Times Higher Education Supplement* (see Morgan 2009) that the University of Cumbria had an established policy of not promoting its existing academic staff into senior roles. Appointments to readerships and professorships are reserved for external applicants 'except in exceptional circumstances'. The policy led the local trade union official to describe the university as 'probably the only university in the world where a Nobel prize winner would find it difficult to progress beyond the senior lecturer level'. According to the *THES* the policy, first established in October 2007, reads as follows:

The normal process by which persons are appointed to chairs or readerships will be by external competitive advertisement..... Exceptionally, there may be an internal competitive process where such a process may assist the university in pursuit of its mission and strategic objectives.

Questions:

1 What do you think might be the reasoning behind the establishment of this policy?

2 What is the likely impact on existing staff?

3 What might well be the impact on external recruitment arising from publicising the policy in the *Times Higher Education Supplement*?

External recruitment

There are numerous different approaches used to attract applications from prospective external employees – some more conventional than others. In practice, for most jobs the formal methods can be listed under the following five headings: printed media, external agencies, education liaison, other media and professional contacts (see Table 7.1). In addition, there are informal methods that can be used whereby employees' families, suppliers or personal acquaintances get to hear about a vacancy via word of mouth or the 'grapevine'. All these methods are used to a greater or lesser degree. Some, like job centres or word of mouth, cost next to nothing. Others, including national newspaper advertising and the employment of headhunters, require considerable expenditure. A few methods, such as the use of cinema and TV, are only realistic propositions for the largest employing organisations seeking to recruit substantial numbers. An example would be the use of such media by army and navy recruiters.

When deciding which method to use, a variety of other considerations must also be taken into account. For example, it is necessary to consider how precisely the approach adopted will hit its target audience. For this reason we can safely conclude that it would be as inappropriate to advertise for a new chief executive in a job centre as it would be to place an advertisement for an engineer in a medical journal. Recruiters also need to be mindful of the image of their organisation they are portraying in the labour market. While a small local newspaper advertisement might attract large numbers of applicants, there is a case for spending rather more on a substantial advertisement set by professionals as a means of suggesting to job seekers that the organisation compares favourably with others as a place to work.

Some methods are ruled out because of time constraints. Most HR managers will at some time have experienced pressure from line managers to fill vacancies within days rather than weeks, with the result that the range of possible recruitment methods is severely restricted. In such cases the only realistic options are employment agencies, job centres, personal contacts and those local papers that advertise positions on a daily basis.

Another important consideration is the volume of applications that each method is likely to yield and the ability of the HR department to administer them effectively. While it would be grossly inefficient to choose a method that brought in hundreds of applications for a single unskilled job vacancy, there are situations in which it is necessary to attract very large numbers. One example would be advertisements seeking applications for very senior jobs where the widest possible pool of appropriately qualified individuals is needed to enable the organisation to screen out all but the very best candidates. Another common instance is the opening of a new plant or store leading to the creation of hundreds of new jobs.

 EXERCISE BOX: LONDON BOROUGHS

EXERCISE 7.2

Read the article by Rebecca Johnson entitled 'Sharing the Load' featured in *People Management* (9 August 2007, pages 40-42). This can be downloaded from the *People Management* archive on the CIPD's website (www.cipd.co.uk).

This article describes a complex project whereby 16 separate London boroughs have partially merged together their recruitment services and outsourced different parts to three separate private sector providers. The aim is to save money while also substantially improving the quality of recruitment activities.

Questions:

1 Why do you think that so many people working in the private sector have such a negative image of public sector work?

2 In what ways might the project described in this article help improve the reputation of London local authorities as employers?

3 What other advantages is it anticipated will accrue?

4 Why are some London boroughs unwilling to take part?

ADVERTISING IN THE PRINTED MEDIA

Over £1 billion is now spent each year on recruitment advertising in the UK, including £350 million on online ads. Advertising space in newspapers is generally sold in units of 3cm by 1cm. An advert measuring 10cm by 6cm will thus involve purchasing 20 of these blocks of space. The cost of each unit is known as 'the single-column centimetre rate', which varies very considerably between different publications and over time. The marketplace is highly competitive, particular newspapers offering a range of preferable rates to employers and agents who place large volumes of business with them. Over the last 20 years the *Guardian* newspaper has managed to gain a substantial share of the national market (35 to 40 per cent in most years) with very competitive pricing. As a result it now tends to dominate public sector and middle-range management job advertising. The market for senior management positions, by contrast, is divided between other quality papers like the *Sunday Times* and the *Daily Telegraph* – which charge rather more per single-column centimetre than the *Guardian*. These papers, along with the *Financial Times* carry the vast bulk of national newspaper advertising.

The choice of publication will depend very much on the target audience. Opinion poll research has indicated that around 70 per cent of people buy a different newspaper when they are looking for a new job (*Recruitment Today* 1995), so information about readership levels and profiles is only of limited use in deciding where to place a job advertisement. The first question to ask is whether or not there is a need to advertise nationally. For most jobs local newspapers are preferable, because they reach potential applicants only within the relevant travel to work area. It is only necessary to advertise on a national basis for relatively specialised vacancies for which there is a national labour market. An example of this distinction would be the labour markets for kitchen employees in expensive hotels and restaurants. In order to recruit a kitchen porter or junior chef it will probably only be necessary to advertise locally. A national advertisement might well not yield many responses, because these are not generally jobs that people would happily move house to take up. On the other hand, the market for top head chefs is national or even international – so a local paper would clearly be inappropriate in these cases. The higher the salary and the more specialised the job, the more geographically widespread the labour market will be.

Another consideration is the possibility of placing recruitment advertisements in trade and professional journals. These tend to cost rather less than either local or national papers but have a far lower readership than either. Again the decision will depend on the nature of the labour market concerned. Some industries, by nature or tradition, offer clearer career prospects to individual entrants than others. Some also tend to favour internal candidates over outsiders because of the need to recruit individuals with industry-specific skills or competencies. Where this is the case and a national or international labour market exists, there is a strong case for advertising in the relevant trade journal. An example might be the *Nursing Times*, which serves the largest single professional group of staff in the UK.

 REFLECTIVE QUESTION

Where does your organisation advertise? What considerations are taken into account in deciding which papers or journals are most appropriate?

STYLE AND WORDING

Any cursory flick through the appointments pages of newspapers and journals reveals how different one recruitment advertisement is from another. There is clearly no one best approach, because in this field 'best' can often mean 'distinctive'. Some of the key decisions that recruiters face in drawing up effective advertising copy are examined in the following paragraphs.

WIDE TRAWLS V WIDE NETS

A fundamental decision is the number of applications it is intended should be received. Wide trawls bring in lots of different fish, while wide nets only catch the biggest. According to the Newspaper Society (2005:7), 11 per cent of the of the population of working age are always actively looking for a new job, while a further 11 per cent are looking for a new job at any one time. In addition, 32 per cent of the working population say that they would consider a new job 'if they came across it'. So in principle it is not difficult to attract large numbers of applicants. The question is how useful or desirable such an approach might be.

Where a wide trawl is required the advert has to be striking in appearance. It will probably be large and make use of pictures or unusual graphics. It will then be placed prominently, on several occasions, in the places where possibly interested people are most likely to see it. By contrast the wide net approach requires less razzmatazz. The key aim here is to reach a relatively narrow audience and then to encourage self-selection on the part of job seekers. This often means including a substantial quantity of detailed information about the job and the kind of candidate being sought. It is more likely to be placed in a trade journal or on a specialist website where only the few 'big fish' the employer wants to attract will see it.

Which approach is used varies greatly from situation to situation. Wide trawls are much more costly not only in terms of advertising spend, but also in administrative time because so many applications are generated. However, they do have the advantage of giving an organisation the maximum possible choice of candidates and hence, at least in theory, increase the chances that the best possible people are recruited. The approach is most frequently used where a good number of recruits are sought at the same time and where the skills sought are relatively rare. Large PLCs, for example, use wide trawl approaches when recruiting graduates for management training programmes as do retailers when they are opening stores in new areas. Another motivation is where a more diverse workforce is sought. Hence we can observe the use of wide trawl strategies in police and civil service recruitment campaigns. By contrast wide net approaches are less expensive but result in relatively few applications being received. This is fine if those few are of high quality, but represents a waste of money if the outcome is a failure to appoint and a need to re-advertise. Wide net recruitment strategies are thus only appropriate when an employer is confident that sufficient numbers of well-qualified candidates will both see the advertisement and be sufficiently attracted to the opportunity to make an application.

REALISTIC V POSITIVE

Another important decision in designing advertisements concerns how accurate the information contained should be. One option is to use an unashamedly positive approach. The aim is to create an image of the job as an exciting and challenging opportunity for a well-motivated person. Any drawbacks in the contract or less attractive aspects of the job are thus either downplayed or left out of the advertising copy altogether. The alternative is to design a realistic advertisement which mentions all aspects of the job (potentially attractive and unattractive). It might state that the work is complex and technically demanding or that a high degree of job security is unlikely to be given.

As is the case with informal methods (see Chapter 8), the realistic approach has the advantage of encouraging people to self-select and moves some way towards the 'realistic job preview' that is said to have such a marked effect on reducing staff turnover in the first months of employment (Breaugh 2008:105-108). On the other hand, it can be argued that self-selection is often not in the interests of the employer because too heavy a dose of realism can discourage excellent potential applicants from responding. There is thus a good case for adopting a positive approach at the advertising stage and keeping back some of the potential drawbacks of a job for discussion at the selection interview once the candidates' appetites have been whetted. This is particularly true where the job is genuinely attractive in some respects, but also pretty unattractive in others. An example might be a well-paid and interesting leadership role of temporary duration. Emphasising the positive aspects is necessary to attract applicants who might otherwise be put off by the lack of guaranteed tenure. The more complex business of selling the temporary nature of the position by stressing the opportunities for enhanced long-term employability can be left until a pool of suitable applicants has been attracted.

Rankin (2008c) reports research by IRS which demonstrates considerable support for the use of realistic job previews among UK employers. Their survey showed that 61 per cent of employers believe they lead to better performance by new recruits, 58 per cent think that job satisfaction is higher, while 39 per cent assert that turnover rates are lower when realistic approaches are used.

CORPORATE IMAGE V EMPHASIS ON THE JOB

Recruitment advertisements also vary greatly in the emphasis they give on the one hand to the organisation as a potential employer and, on the other, to the nature and duties of the job. Some advertisements thus make great play out of their well-known brand names, while others put the emphasis on the job. In some cases the name of the employer is omitted altogether, with potential applicants asked to contact an agency.

In part this decision is determined by the extent to which the employer is well known in its target labour markets. People are lured towards 'big names' because they perceive that a spell of employment in such organisations will enhance their future career prospects, self-esteem or social status. However, it is also important to be mindful of the potential general publicity a recruitment advertisement incorporating well-known brand names can generate. They can thus have two purposes: to attract applicants and to increase sales of well-known products.

Research by Collins and Han (2004) demonstrates that organisations with a relatively low corporate profile benefit in terms of the quality of applications received when they use 'low involvement recruitment practices' such as traditional job advertisements. Using such approaches, however, has a much lower impact for well-known organisations with a strong reputation (positive or negative). In their case 'high involvement' approaches are required because people already tend to have a settled view about them and about whether or not they would be interested in working for them. They thus need to put the case more actively if they are 'to affect recruitment outcomes by positively affecting job seekers' beliefs about job and company attributes' (Collins and Han 2004:691).

PRECISE V VAGUE INFORMATION

Research carried out by De Witte (1989) showed above all else that job seekers like to have as much basic information as possible in job advertisements and that vague forms of words resulted in considerably lower response rates. He found that advertisements which failed to include clear information about job titles, workplace location and salary levels were significantly less attractive to potential candidates than those which were precise in this regard. Similar conclusions were reached from a huge study of 9,000 job advertisements carried out in 2000 (Focus Central London Training, reported in IRS 2004a). Here also a clear statement of all the skills required by the job holder was found to have a very positive effect on the number of suitable applications received by recruiters. So what possible justification can there be for the many advertisements that contain only imprecise information? The answer mainly lies in the frequent need to preserve confidentiality.

The absence of precise salary information is relatively common because of potential problems that can arise if other employees see the advertisement and compare their own packages unfavourably with that on offer to job applicants. There may also be a case in some circumstances for making no mention of the employer's name and using an agency to advertise the position. This would be the case if it was thought desirable for existing employees to remain ignorant of the recruitment process. An example might be a situation where an individual's contract is to be terminated with immediate effect and where a replacement is needed to take over very swiftly. In such circumstances there may be insufficient time to advertise the job and fill the vacancy after the previous job-holder has left. In extreme cases it may be deemed desirable further to disguise the organisation's identity by making only very vague references to its markets and location.

However, there is a further possible explanation for the vagueness that is characteristic of many advertisements placed by agencies on behalf of clients – namely, their wish to have on their books as many potential job applicants as possible. The aim of the vague advertisement is thus not primarily to attract candidates seeking the particular job in question, but to generate a large response from people whom the agent may be able to place in other positions at some time in the future.

There is also an argument in favour of vague approaches on the grounds that they contribute towards flexible working. According to this point of view, successful candidates are less likely to come to the job with strong preconceptions about their duties and position in the organisational hierarchy than colleagues recruited via very precise advertisements. In an age when flexible working is becoming increasingly important in many quarters, such arguments can be judged to have some validity. You could certainly use them as part of a case for omitting from advertisements details of hours of work or reporting lines. Moreover, a case can also be made for vaguer approaches on grounds of cost because imprecise wording can often take up less space than detailed information. In recruitment advertising the less wordy the advertisement, the cheaper it is to publish.

PLAIN-SPEAKING V ELABORATE

There is an ongoing debate among recruitment specialists as to the desirability or utility of incorporating expensive artwork or colour into recruitment advertisements (see IRS 2004a). Views differ greatly on this issue. At one extreme is the kind of view identified by John Courtis (1989:34) that 'too much arty input' can reduce the effectiveness of an advertisement and that the inclusion of straightforward relevant information is all that is really necessary. The alternative view, expressed by John Ainley, the former head of group personnel at WH Smith, is that refreshing and distinctive visual approaches are more eye-catching and thus yield more applicants. Blackman (2006) carried out research which involved presenting a selection of subtly different ads for the same job to a group of Australian students seeking graduate jobs. She found that the inclusion of a picture helped considerably in terms of making the ads attractive, but that this factor was less significant than the inclusion of an eye-catching heading which included the word 'graduate' and information about the career path successful applicants could look forward to following. Much probably depends on the target audience and the approaches adopted by key labour market competitors.

However elaborate in terms of artwork and presentation, it seems clear that certain types of wording are more effective whatever approach is used. Studies by Lunn (1989) and Hill & Maycock (1990), cited by IRS (2001a) suggest that the use of questions in recruitment advertisements helps to generate applications from appropriately qualified people. Instead of simply describing the role, they argue in favour of the approach in which a series of rhetorical questions are asked focusing on the attributes required for the job role (Are you ready for a new challenge? Do others judge you to be a good leader? Do you have an excellent record of achievement at the cutting edge in HRM? If so we want to hear from you' etc). Hill and Maycock's study found that response rates to advertisements were far more influenced by the presence or absence of questions than they were by the size or presentation style of the advertisement.

REFLECTIVE QUESTION

How elaborate are the advertisements for jobs used by your organisation? Could they be improved either by reducing or by increasing their visual distinctiveness?

EXERCISE BOX: ANALYSING ADVERTISEMENTS

EXERCISE 7.3

Spend some time looking in detail at the recruitment advertisements published in national newspapers or in trade journals such as *People Management*.

Analyse them in terms of the major categories set out above. See if you can find clear examples of advertisements that fit into each category (ie a wide trawl ad, a wide net ad, a realistic ad, a positive ad etc).

Then look for examples of poor advertisements which you think are unlikely to attract many applicants. You should look

for advertisements which miss out key pieces of information or those which appear dull or confusing. What is missing? What could be done to improve them?

You may find it useful when carrying out this exercise to read the article by Brian Chandler and Tony Scott entitled 'How to write a job ad'. This was featured in *People Management* on 24 November 2005 (pages 42–43). This can be downloaded from the *People Management* archive on the CIPD's website (www.cipd.co.uk).

ONLINE RECRUITMENT

The use of the internet as a recruitment medium has increased substantially in recent years. In the late 1990s the jobs advertised on the web were mainly in IT, academia or were specifically for new university graduates. At this time only a minority of people had internet access at home, so other media easily maintained their dominance of the recruitment advertising market. The position began to change in the first years of the twenty-first century, with an expansion of online recruitment activity to include vacancies across all areas of work. Yet in 2005, despite the majority of households now having access to the internet, only 12 per cent of adults first looked to the web when seeking a new job compared to 51 per cent who look first in their local newspaper (Newspaper Society 2005:50-51). Since then, and particularly since 2007, online recruitment has established itself on a much stronger footing. At the end of 2009 over 70 per cent of UK households had internet access, 63 per cent benefiting from a broadband connection. Only 21 per cent of the adult population (mainly retired people) had never used the internet, while 76 per cent had used it at some point in the three months prior to the survey (National Statistics 2009). Nearly 80 per cent of employers were advertising jobs via their own corporate websites in 2009, 29 per cent making use of commercial job boards (CIPD, 2009:9), while the providers of job-search websites were spending vast amounts of money on TV, cinema and radio advertising, sports sponsorship and public relations activities as a means of raising their public profile.

However, it must be stated also that the many confident predictions made about the growth of internet recruitment a decade ago have not proved accurate. Many believed that online recruitment would eclipse other forms entirely once most jobseekers had internet access and, in particular, that print-based media such as newspapers and trade journals would no longer be able to carry large volumes of recruitment advertising. This has not happened in practice. In 2009, despite the deepest recession for a generation, 70 per cent of employers were still advertising in the local press, 55 per cent in trade journals and 31 per cent in national newspapers. In the public sector the proportions were 82 per cent, 75 per cent and 62 per cent respectively. Job seekers are increasingly making use of the internet but, like recruiting employers, they rarely do so exclusively. A survey of 50,000 online job-seekers carried out by NORAS in 2009 found that only one in seven was *only* using the internet to look for a new job (OnRec 2009). As matters stand therefore we can conclude that while use of the internet to advertise jobs is growing year on year, other media retain an important role and are likely to do so for some time to come. Internet-based recruitment has not replaced the print media or other methods of recruitment; instead it is being used as an addition to the more traditional approaches.

Most employers now routinely advertise all jobs that are available to outside applicants on their own corporate websites. This is inexpensive and provides an opportunity to provide job-seekers with a great deal of information about both the job and the organisation. It also opens up the opportunity to invite online applications and to administer some form of selection or self-selection test as a means of establishing how suitable a candidate might be in the role. For well-known and particularly for larger well-known employers with a strong reputation in their labour markets it is possible only to advertise roles using a corporate website and to expect a good number of highly qualified applications. The most successful sites are those run by the large public sector organisations such as local authorities, the NHS and universities. These bodies, like major PLCs, can rely on their own recruitment pages to an extent because job seekers actively seek out roles in such organisations, visiting their sites in order to ascertain whether vacancies are available for which they may be suited. Such an approach, however, does not tend to yield the maximum number of strong applications because the job opportunities are only seen by people who are actively seeking a new job. If the rest of the labour market is also to be reached and informed of the existence of vacancies other approaches must also be used. Indeed, for employers who do not enjoy big-name status there is little alternative. Most small and medium sized employers will not attract sufficient numbers of hits to their corporate websites to be able to rely on this as a means of finding new recruits.

This is where the other major type of internet recruitment plays its role. In recent years online job boards (sometimes called cyber-agencies) of one kind or another have competed furiously for recognition as first choice stops for job seekers. Some are general sites advertising all kinds of different types of job (eg Monster, totaljobs and Reed), while others have managed to establish a reputation as the place to look for roles in particular industries (eg CWJobs, NHS Jobs, jobs.ac.uk and Careers in Construction). A further group of sites are run in parallel with newspaper-based operations. Examples include the *Guardian*'s JobsUnlimited site and BigBlueDog operated by the *London Evening Standard*. These sites republish on the internet advertisements that have also been carried in the job sections of newspapers and journals. It is now usual for employers to pay a fee which leads to the carrying of advertisements in both media.

ADVANTAGES AND DISADVANTAGES

There are clear potential advantages associated with internet recruitment when compared with more traditional approaches. First, as has already been stated, for bigger name employers with the potential to attract 'passing traffic' to a corporate site there are substantial cost savings to be made. These arise in part because there is no longer a need to pay for recruitment advertising in printed media, and partly because their organisations can greatly reduce the number of recruitment brochures they need to print. In addition further savings are achieved by less use of written correspondence and the need to field fewer phone calls. United Biscuits expected to cut its total resourcing costs by half with the establishment of a comprehensive new recruitment site called UBCareers.com, having already saved 85 per cent of its graduate recruitment costs by moving this online from 1999 (Roberts 2001:7).

In addition to cost savings, web-based recruitment is attractive because it gives the employer access to a potential audience of millions. This will include people who are not actively looking for a new job but who may become interested having stumbled across a particularly original or well-designed advertisement by accident when surfing the internet. The other great advantage is the speed and ease with which job seekers can respond when they see an opportunity publicised on the web. It can take seconds, and a few clicks of a mouse to send a CV by e-mail to the employer concerned. In tight labour markets, where vacancies can take months to fill, any time saved is valuable to employers. Developments in the fields of online-selection and CV-matching software are also significant as they provide a means for shortlisting of candidates to be carried out, in part, electronically. Murphy (2008a) reports the results of an IRS survey which showed that employers who use job boards are generally happy with their performance. They are seen as being cheaper and more efficient than other methods of recruitment, making it possible to fill vacancies more quickly than is possible using other methods.

However, it must also be pointed out that there are considerable disadvantages associated with internet recruitment. Some will become less significant over time as technology develops, but there will always be some important drawbacks. Parry and Tyson (2008:265-266) describe the problems their interviewees and survey respondents have experienced. Top of the list is the tendency for employers to get bombarded with applications from unsuitable candidates simply because it is so easy to respond speculatively to an advertisement. The result is a need to devote more rather than fewer resources to the shortlisting process. This problem, known as 'spamming', can only be overcome by using some form of electronic online shortlisting technology. However, in key respects these are not satisfactory. Most rely on software with the ability to reject CVs which do not include certain key words. This is a very hit and miss kind of approach which inevitably leads to applications from well-qualified candidates being electronically discarded simply because certain words do not appear. Alternative approaches require candidates to complete online application forms which ask more specific questions. Many of these now take the form of psychometric tests. They are much fairer from a candidate's perspective but are expensive to develop properly. They are thus only of great use in fields such as police, army or graduate recruitment where large numbers of people are applying for many vacancies on a year by year basis.

Another major drawback for internet recruitment relates to confidentiality and the fear many people have about allowing their CV to circulate in cyberspace outside of their own control. This may be more a problem of perception than reality, but it can act as a barrier to e-recruitment in the same way that a reluctance to submit credit card numbers acts as a barrier to the development of e-commerce more generally. The safeguards with CVs are less satisfactory than is the case with credit cards, meaning that people have good reason to worry about on whose screen their personal details will end up. A particular fear is that the CV will get sent, unsolicited, to one's own boss, who may be wholly unaware that a job search is in progress. Confidentiality issues are a particular problem for senior people who prefer to deal with traditional agencies over whom they can exercise more personal control.

A third drawback arises from the extent to which the internet is used by different groups in the population. While its use is expanding steadily, it remains the case that jobs advertised on the internet are more likely to be seen by wealthier, younger and better educated people. Older people in particular are less likely to be comfortable using the internet to look for a job, while those who do not have access to it at home (ie people on lower incomes and those living on state benefits) are necessarily at a disadvantage when compared with those who do when jobs are only advertised online. This means that internet-based recruitment scores very badly when compared to other methods of recruitment in terms of the diversity of candidates it produces.

Finally there are the whole range of technical problems associated with internet usage generally. These are summed up by IRS (2001b:5) as follows:

> Bugs in the system, computer crashes and problems caused by recruiters with poor IT skills can lose applications, delay rather than accelerate recruitment, and damage the public image of the organisation. Poorly designed or over-engineered web-sites represent a further pitfall: slow loading speeds, irritating 'movies' and faulty links are all guaranteed to

try the limited patience of online users whose expectations of fast, reliable access are very high.

It is because of the drawbacks that internet recruitment, while less expensive than other formal methods of recruitment, is not perceived as being any more effective in its capacity to produce a shortlist of appointable candidates (Parry and Tyson 2008:264).

Over time, however, it seems that the advantages of internet recruitment are steadily becoming more widely recognised, while the disadvantages are being overcome through the use of technologies and more thoughtful targeting of advertisements at appointable groups. It is clear, for example, that the recession of 2008–10 gave online recruitment a major boost as recruitment budgets were squeezed and employers were unable to afford to advertise in the printed media (Suff 2009a, Williams 2009). There is also evidence that employers are making increased use of software packages which help to improve the usefulness of online recruitment. Parry and Tyson (2008:269-70) describe some cutting edge approaches including software which improves 'back office functionality' (acknowledges applications, undertakes initial screening of applications and distributes them directly to line managers) and that which automatically creates a 'talent pool' of would-be candidates to whom future advertisements can be sent directly.

The other major contemporary developments in online recruiting are associated with the concept of 'employer branding' which we will be examining in more detail in Chapter 9. What we are seeing is employers becoming increasingly sophisticated in the approaches they are adopting to their own recruitment websites. Whereas 10 years ago these would simply be used as a place to post ads that were written for publication in newspapers and journals, recruitment pages are now far more carefully designed to attract target groups. There is extensive use of audio and video, alongside interactive features and, throughout, the repetition of core messages designed to differentiate the organisation as an employer from its competitors. The aim is to provide a great deal of information to potential candidates about the job and the experience of working for the organisation, so that they are able to evaluate for themselves whether or not they want to apply and, if so, whether or not their application would stand a good chance of success.

Another interesting development is the diversification of approaches being used by employers to 'drive online traffic' to the recruitment pages of their own corporate websites. There is nothing new about seeking to do this. For several years now organisations have been placing short, concise ads in the press or on online job boards which contain limited information plus a link to their own recruitment pages where much more information about vacancies is provided. What is still in its infancy, but growing fast, is the use of other approaches to make people aware that such pages exist and to encourage them to visit. Examples are the use of social and business networking sites such as Facebook and Linked-In as well as the establishment of a corporate presence in online games such as Second Life.

THE NAKED TRUTH INCLUSIVE

Internet recruitment is a fast-evolving field. In the early days employers tended to do no more than put their existing paper-based recruitment literature online. More recently there has been a growth in the use of interactive features such as questionnaires and games, and much more use of moving pictures and striking graphics. Humour is also being used more, as predictably are features with sexual content.

Asda pioneered these latter approaches with its 'naked truth' campaign aimed at enticing prospective graduate recruits to make applications. The website featured pictures of recent graduate recruits wearing no clothes, strategically placed pieces of fruit and cereal packets ensuring that some level of decency was retained. It also included a personality-oriented questionnaire for candidates to complete, to which instant feedback was given. Those who did not give the answers Asda was looking for were then redirected to the site of one of its supermarket rivals. Such approaches are interesting, but must be used with great care. Good candidates are just as likely to be put off as attracted by the use of this kind of imagery.

EXERCISE BOX: DEBATES ABOUT ONLINE RECRUITMENT

Read the article by Steve Smethurst entitled 'The Allure of Online' featured in *People Management* (29 July 2004, pages 38-40). This can be downloaded from the *People Management* archive on the CIPD's website (www.cipd.co.uk).

This article discusses various viewpoints on the advantages and disadvantages of online recruitment. The major point it makes is that cost savings are by no means the only reason for increased use of the internet by recruiters. It also provides a more general opportunity to review the effectiveness of recruitment strategies. Critical voices focus on diversity issues and worries that the internet is not used by many under-represented groups.

Questions:

1   Aside from reductions in cost, what other specific advantages associated with e-recruitment are cited by the people interviewed for this article?

2   Which of these points do you find most and least convincing?

3   How far do you agree with the view that internet recruitment tends to benefit groups who are already well-represented in the workforce at the expense of those who are not?

EXAMPLE

'An exploration of corporate recruitment descriptions on monster.com' by Kristin B Backhaus. *Journal of Business Communication*, Vol. 41, No. 2. 115-136 (2004)

In this article the author, who is US-based, analyses the wording of the recruitment materials posted by corporations on the leading American cyber-agency's website. Her interest is particularly in the words the companies use to describe what they offer as employers and the impression that this gives. In this respect the article is a useful contribution to the literature on employer branding (see Chapter 9), but the article is principally concerned with analysing the different recruitment tactics that are being used by different corporations.

Questions:

1 Why do you think corporations put so much more emphasis on describing themselves and their achievements rather than in explaining what they are like to work for as employers?

2 Why do such a small number make reference to pay and benefits?

3 Why is there so little attention given to ethics or diversity?

4 Why is there so little evidence of clear employer branding strategies being in use?

- Various articles in academic textbooks provide an introduction to key debates. Among the most useful are those by Thom Watson (1994), Sue Newell (2005), Julie Beardwell and T. Claydon (2007) and Lievens & Chapman (2010).

- The substantial body of American research on recruitment has been usefully summarised by Barber (1998), Orlitzky (2007) and particularly by Breaugh (2008).

- Internet recruitment has been described, discussed and debated in countless articles published in *People Management* and other journals over recent years. IRS Employment Review has given extensive coverage to online recruitment issues in recent editions, while IDS has also published major surveys on internet recruitment together with case studies. Useful books on the subject are the *Employer's guide to recruiting on the internet* by Ray Schreyer and John McCarter (1998), *E-recruitment: Is it delivering?* by Polly Kettley and Maire Kerrin (2003) and *Online recruiting and selection* by Douglas Reynolds and John Weiner (2009).

CHAPTER 8

Alternative recruitment methods

INFORMAL APPROACHES

A major government survey carried out in 2002 involved asking over a million people how they had found their current jobs (Labour Market Trends 2002). This revealed that informal channels accounted for a majority of new hires, word of mouth recruitment topping the poll by a considerable margin (see Table 8.1). By contrast, the numbers finding their positions through job centres and employment agencies is relatively small. Rather less than a third of all employees in 2002 were recruited through recruitment advertising, the large majority of whom (75 per cent) read advertisements in local newspapers. The rest of the market was split between trade journals, national newspapers and papers specialising in job advertising.

Table 8.1: Recruitment methods in practice

Recruitment method	Men	Women
Hearing from someone who worked there	30%	25%
Reply to an advertisement	25%	31%
Direct application (ie walk in/on spec)	14%	17%

Private employment agency	10%	10%
Job centre	9%	8%
Other	12%	9%

Source: Labour Market Trends (2002)

Unfortunately no similar survey has been commissioned since 2002, so similar, more up to date data is unavailable. There is, however, no evidence to suggest that matters have changed hugely since then in respect of informal recruitment. Research on smaller employers continues to show a preference on their part for informal approaches, while some surveys of larger employers suggest that informal recruitment remains widely used by them too (CIPD 2009b:9). Indeed, Suff (2009a) reports that around a third of employers have either chosen to 'rely more on word of mouth recruitment', made 'greater use of staff referrals' or both in recent years in response to recessionary conditions.

While it is clear that the use of informal methods is very widespread, opinion is divided as to how much they really have to offer employers when compared with formal approaches. Some research findings, such as those of Kirnan *et al* (1989), Blau (1990), Iles & Robertson (1989) and Castilla (2005) strongly suggest that informal recruitment methods yield a better selection of well qualified applicants than formal methods. The same studies also found a correlation between informal recruitment, low staff turnover, and high levels of subsequent employee performance (see Barber 1998:22–32 and Breaugh 2008:109–110 for a summary of US research in this area). However, the reasons for these effects are unclear. One possibility is that candidates recruited by word of mouth or by approaching organisations themselves self-select to a greater degree than those finding out about the job from other sources. They come to the job knowing more about the employer and the job duties and are better placed to decide for themselves whether or not it is suitable for them. The relatively low turnover rates are probably best explained by the likelihood that informal recruits have more realistic perceptions of what the job will be like than those recruited through formal channels.

Aside from the fact that it seems in practice to lead to better performance, other arguments in favour of informal approaches can be made. In terms of cost, they are clearly inexpensive from an organisation's point of view. Some employers offer 'bounty payments' to existing staff who introduce new recruits, but in the main these are relatively modest. Direct approaches from prospective employees cost nothing at all except for some management time. Moreover, it is also possible to argue that informally recruited people are attractive for other reasons:

....on several grounds, co-worker referrals can be desirable hires *per se*. A social tie to an existing employee provides a ready-made avenue of socialisation, training, and social support for the new hire. The co-worker responsible for the referral will also have a reputational stake in the success of the person whom he or she referred, providing an additional reason to provide assistance and support to the new hire (Baron and Kreps 1999:342).

Alec Reed (2001:23–26) also offers a robust defence of informal recruitment, going as far as to suggest that 'the oft-maligned practice of nepotism' may have a serious role to play in HR strategy. Here too the case is made, in part, with reference to the effect word of mouth recruitment has on existing employees. They like it, according to Reed, partly because they enjoy working alongside friends and partly because the practice shows 'the value the company places on them and their opinions....offering implicit praise by displaying a willingness to recruit others of the same ilk'.

Nonetheless, both word of mouth and direct approach methods are criticised on the grounds that, by definition, they only reach a very limited target audience. The employer may have a good group of candidates from which to choose but it will not be a very extensive selection – nor is it likely to be representative of the wider community. It could thus be argued that a formal method, such as a recruitment advertisement, might yield an even better pool of candidates if it was designed effectively and printed in an appropriate publication. It may not be the formal methods themselves that are ineffectual, but the manner in which they are deployed. The use of some informal methods may also cause employers to breach discrimination legislation, although the risk of facing litigation in such circumstances remains very small.

RECRUITMENT IN THE PUBLIC SECTOR

Research shows a substantial difference between preferred methods of recruitment in the public and private sectors. Although both make extensive use of advertising in the local and national press, private sector employers are more likely than their counterparts in the public sector to use other types of approach.

In particular, there is a strong aversion in public sector organisations to recruitment using informal methods (such as word of mouth, formal employee referral schemes or unsolicited applications) and headhunters. In many public sector organisations these methods are not used as a matter of policy, despite their being relatively highly rated by the employers in the private sector who use them routinely.

The main reason is the way that informal methods and headhunting tend to favour groups who are already well-represented in the workforce. While it is considered good practice for all employers to seek to reach out to all groups in the community, it is politically important that public sector organisations do so – and are seen to be doing so. This is because it is right for the demographic make-up of public servants to reflect that of the communities they serve, particularly where the individuals concerned exercise some form of statutory authority.

Source: CIPD (2009b:9)

EXERCISE BOX: WEB 2.0

Read the following two articles featured in *People Management*. They can be downloaded from the *People Management* archive on the CIPD's website (www.cipd. co.uk).

- 'Bravo Two Zero' by Andy Allen (PM Guide to Recruitment Marketing, June 2007, pages 26–28)

- 'Face to Face with Social Networking' by James Brockett, (9 August 2007, pages 15–17)

While both these articles discuss a broader range of issues, they raise some very interesting questions about the current and future use of social networking sites, blogs, viral campaigns and 'second life' as informal recruitment tools. Increasingly employers are making use of these tools,

or encouraging employees to do so, as a means of building up an employer brand or just sourcing potential recruits. They are also sometimes researching candidates' backgrounds using social networking sites such as Facebook and MySpace.

Questions:

1. What evidence is presented of employers making use of Web 2.0 applications in a formal sense as a means of recruiting informally?

2. How successful do you think these approaches could be? Why?

3. What are the major drawbacks that are identified?

4. What ethical issues does this kind of practice raise?

USING AGENTS IN THE RECRUITMENT PROCESS

A variety of different external agencies can be employed to undertake some part of the recruitment process on behalf of employers. In addition to government and voluntary agencies involved in finding jobs for people, there is now a well-established recruitment industry that exists to serve the needs of employers and job seekers in ever more complex and competitive labour markets. It is estimated to employ around 80,000 people and to have an annual turnover in excess of £27 billion (Suff 2009b). From a human resource management perspective this provides interesting opportunities for increasing the effectiveness and efficiency of recruitment activity but the use of agents also carries risks. In particular, there is a need to establish at the outset exactly what the agent can offer and precisely how much the service is going to cost. The advantages and disadvantages of agents vary considerably with the type of agency service on offer. These can broadly be categorised under four headings, each discussed below.

GOVERNMENT AGENTS

In addition to the government's employment service and its network of job centres, there also exists a number of other state-sponsored organisations which offer employers a free recruitment service. One is the Forces Resettlement Agency, which assists ex-army personnel to find jobs in civilian life. As well as providing its regular job advertising function, the Employment Service also runs a range of training programmes for people who have been out of work for a prolonged period. Its initiatives often involve placing unemployed people in workplaces free of charge in exchange for training.

Some employers are reluctant to advertise posts in job centres despite the fact that they offer free advertising. This is partly because the clientele is mainly comprised of unemployed people, the majority of whom are perceived to be unskilled or low skilled, and thus inappropriate for many jobs. The other reasons relate to poor past experiences of using job centres. Carroll *et al* (1999) found that many small employers in their qualitative study were both very willing and able to describe difficulties they had had with job centre recruitment, a 'downside' also reported in an IRS survey (2001). The main difficulties arise from candidates who come to interviews and accept posts because they are pressed into doing so by job centre staff and not because they really want to fill the vacancy. They do this because the job centres are required to ensure that people claiming state benefits are genuinely looking for work. The result is a situation in which managers spend hours interviewing people who have no real interest in the work. Often candidates do not turn up for interview or, if they are successful, subsequently fail to turn up for work.

ADVERTISING AND RECRUITMENT CONSULTANTS

These are private companies which, in return for a fee, will undertake a part of the recruitment process on behalf of employers. They act like any other management consultants, except that they specialise in the recruitment and selection functions. Perhaps the most useful are recruitment advertising agents who assist employers in the drawing up and placing of job advertisements. They are often mistakenly believed only to offer a 'Rolls Royce service' involving the production of showy artwork for publication in newspapers and careers brochures. While much of their work is at this glossy end of the market, they also have a potentially useful range of services to offer ordinary job advertisers. This is made possible by the muscle power they have in the recruitment advertising market. Because they represent large numbers of clients and consequently do a great deal of business with newspapers and trade journals, they are able to negotiate substantial bulk discounts, a portion of which can be passed on to employers. The net result is that a large agency is able to give advice on the wording and placing of advertisements while also improving the appearance of the advertising copy and charging a lower fee than would be paid were the employer dealing with the newspaper independently.

Recruitment consultants, by contrast, take over a larger part of the recruitment process. In addition to handling the advertising they will also undertake much of the administration by sifting initial applications and providing employers with a shortlist of candidates. Such arrangements are expensive, the client being charged either an hourly fee or an overall sum calculated as 10–20 per cent of the first year's annual base salary for the job in question. Sometimes both approaches are used, a retainer or advance fee being paid, followed by further payments on production of a shortlist and the appointment of a candidate. The potential advantage to the employer is access to the agent's expertise and the saving in terms of time associated with outsourcing administrative activity. Such arrangements are particularly appropriate when employers are operating in unfamiliar labour markets (eg overseas) or when a major recruitment drive is being undertaken over a limited period of time. An example might be the launch of a major new tourist attraction by a company with a relatively small HR function. In such a situation it makes more sense to buy in a one-off recruitment service than to set up a major new in-house facility.

TEMPORARY EMPLOYMENT AGENCIES

As competition has become tougher and more international, the use of temporary staff to cover peaks in business has grown. There are now large numbers of agencies that retain casual employees on their books to serve the needs of employers with short-term vacancies. Traditionally these have operated in the secretarial and clerical field, but there are increasing numbers of agencies specialising in the provision of staff to fill a variety of other functions. Examples are companies that have taken over the running of nurse banks from the hospitals, and the growing number of agencies specialising in the provision of catering and computer staff. It is also possible to find work as a personnel and development specialist on a locum basis through some agencies. In fact over 250,000 agency temps are estimated to be working in the UK at any one time (National Statistics 2006:23).

For the employer, temping agencies potentially provide a reliable source of well-qualified staff at very short notice. They will also replace an unsatisfactory temporary worker with someone more suitable if asked. While the primary purpose of such arrangements is to undertake a short-term assignment, caused perhaps by absence or a sudden increase in workload, there are also advantages for employers with longer-term vacancies to fill. First, the agency can provide someone to undertake work during the time that the search is on for a permanent replacement. This can be indispensable if an employee undertaking important work leaves at short notice. Secondly, these agencies can provide staff on a temporary basis who can later be offered full-time positions. The great advantage of such arrangements from the employer's perspective is the opportunity they give to observe an individual's work prior to making him or her an offer of employment. The employee also gets a realistic job preview and thus accepts a job less blindly than the candidate whose only knowledge of the employer derives from perceptions gained at a selection interview.

The drawback is the cost. Hourly rates for agency workers are invariably double those paid to regular employees. In addition the agencies have traditionally incorporated charges into the contract that place a financial penalty on employers who make permanent offers of employment to their temps. However, this practice is now severely limited thanks to the Conduct of Employment Agencies and Employment Businesses Regulations 2003. The regulations are too complex to describe here in detail, but they do make it possible for an offer of permanent employment to be made to a temporary worker supplied by an agency without a fee being incurred after a short period of time has passed.

CABLE AND WIRELESS

An interesting innovation introduced by Cable and Wireless PLC was the establishment a few years ago of an in-house employment agency. It has been set up as a subsidiary company with its own managing director, but unlike most agencies it is expected only to break even and not to make a profit. It exists to provide staff for other parts of the Cable and Wireless operation to undertake project work on short-term contracts.

There are two advantages for the company. First, the agency provides specialist support staff, many of whom are ex-employees of the company. Most staff on the agency's books have undertaken a number of different assignments for the company and are thus far more familiar with its business and corporate culture than ordinary agency employees would be. Perhaps more importantly, the in-house agency is far cheaper. Its requirement only to cover its own costs means that it hires staff out at approximately half the charge-out rates offered by external agencies.

Source: Walker (1996).

HEADHUNTERS AND PERMANENT EMPLOYMENT AGENTS

The fourth group of agencies offering recruitment services to employers has a number of titles. They often call themselves 'recruitment consultants' but are also known by such terms as 'headhunters' and 'executive search consultants'. They differ from the varieties of agent described above in so far as their purpose is the identification of candidates for permanent employment – often in tight labour markets. They operate on a 'no sale, no fee' basis but charge high sums (typically 30 per cent of the first year's salary) when an offer of employment is made. Essentially they act like dating agencies, selling the job to the potential candidate and then trying to sell the candidate to the employer. Their great advantage from an employer's perspective is the opportunity they give to open up confidential channels of communication with high-flying employees working for competitor organisations. As such, they allow recruitment managers to tap into a reservoir of interesting potential applicants who are not actively seeking new jobs.

While it is possible for HR professionals to build up effective relationships with trusted agents operating in this way, there is a fundamental conflict of interest which has to be managed if any association is to prove fruitful over the long term. The problem arises from the fact that the recruitment industry is highly competitive and makes money only by successfully filling vacancies. There are no prizes for coming second in this cut-throat business, commission making up a high proportion of an agent's remuneration. The competitive pressure derives from the low start-up costs or barriers to entry into the business. It is technically very easy to start up an agency – all that is needed are effective selling skills and sufficient contacts in a particular trade or labour market – so there are hundreds of agents competing for relatively scarce rewards. As a result, the agent's overwhelming aim has to be finding candidates for vacancies quickly and at the lowest possible cost. Ideally they want to place individuals already on their books so as to avoid undertaking time-consuming additional research.

By contrast, while employers may want to employ a new person quickly, they have to pay far more attention to the quality of the individual and the possibility that they will perform effectively over a prolonged period, hence the possibility of a conflict of interest and, on occasions, the presence of hard-selling and sharp practice on the part of the agent. The potential problems are outlined in some detail by Suff (2009b) who describes a recent IRS survey which found a majority of respondents to have encountered problems in their relationship with agencies during the previous year. Many of these will be familiar to any HR manager who has experience of recruiting in tight labour markets. A common example is an agent finding a new employee for you, charging a hefty fee, and then returning to poach them 12 months later on behalf of a rival employer. Others include the beefing up of CVs to make candidates appear more experienced than they really are, and agents replying to advertisements placed in professional journals that serious job-seekers would in all likelihood have seen in any event. The most common problem is simply the agents' tendency to send CVs of too many unsuitable candidates (ie recommending people who do not meet the basic specifications for the job) and their tendency to oversell the virtues of their candidates more generally.

Alec Reed (2001:26) goes as far as to refer to them as 'heat seeking missiles', urging employers to build sophisticated defences in order to match the growing sophistication of the headhunters. He describes the activities of a consultancy that has been set up with the title 'Anti-headhunting UK' which specialises in advising and training employers to improve their security systems and hence to deter headhunters from approaching their staff. These include training reception staff and telephone operators to spot calls from headhunters and to ensure that no useful information is given. It is important, for example to try to ensure that internal e-mail directories do not get into the hands of headhunters, as e-mail provides the easiest of ways to reach employees who are quite happy in their jobs but who might be interested in moving were a juicy opportunity brought to their attention.

Having pointed out the potential pitfalls, it is also necessary to stress that it is possible to develop healthy and workable long-term relationships with particular headhunters. Indeed, in some labour markets, where headhunters have gained an unassailable position, employers have few practical alternatives if they wish to recruit the best people. But here too conflicts of interest have a tendency to get in the way. This is because it does not generally make good business sense for headhunters to concentrate their time and effort on building up close relationships with one or two clients. This is a risky strategy because too much is lost if the client decides to switch to another firm. It is thus much safer to build up weaker relationships with large numbers of client employers and also necessary in this business to devote a great deal of time to developing new contacts and drumming up new business (Finlay and Coverdill 2002:76–82).

The key from the employer's perspective is to agree the ground rules from the start and to make sure that the charging structures are fully explained and understood. Courtis (1989:41–42), Jenn (2005:41–44) and Suff (2009b) make a number of helpful suggestions, including the following:

- Select a headhunter who possesses genuine expertise about your industry and who understands the needs of your organisation.
- Operate a preferred supplier list of agencies with admission criteria.
- Provide the headhunter with as much information as possible about the organisation, the job and the type of person being sought.
- Offer the agency a degree of exclusivity – never use more than one agency for any one assignment.
- Ask for temps who are prepared to become permanent when you and they fit well.
- Pay promptly.
- Explain what selection or rejection criteria you are likely to use.
- Always ask why a particular candidate is being put forward.

Over time such an arrangement should allow the negotiation of better terms than are offered by rival agencies with whom no long-term relationship has been established. The key is to gain an understanding of the labour market and the way headhunters operate. That way it is possible to avoid employing them where to do so is unnecessary, and it is also possible to save on costs.

 REFLECTIVE QUESTION

What is your experience of headhunters and recruitment consultants? To what extent have you observed situations in which a conflict of interest is apparent between the needs of employers and the aims of the agent?

 EXERCISE BOX: DITCHING THE HEADHUNTERS

EXERCISE 8.2

Read the following two articles featured in *People Management*. They can be downloaded from the *People Management* archive on the CIPD's website (www.cipd.co.uk).

- 'Research and Employ' by Jenny Hirschkorn (15 January 2004, pages 33–35)
- 'Zoom at the Top' by Jane Simms (People Management Guide to Recruitment Consultancies, April 2006, pages 27–28)

The first article explains why larger corporations are increasingly dispensing with the services of headhunters and

instead employing their own researchers to carry out the headhunting under their direction. Sometimes these researchers are directly employed by the recruiting companies, sometimes they are hired on a consultancy basis at a fixed fee.

The second article explores sharp practice among headhunters and debates the advantages and disadvantages of their use by employers.

Questions:

1 What are the major reasons cited in the first article for the move away from headhunters?

2 Why do you think representatives of companies which employ their own headhunting researchers are so reluctant to talk about it on the record?

3 What examples of poor practice on the part of headhunters are cited in these articles?

4 What are the major advantages that using headhunters can have for an employer?

CASE SUMMARY

ORIGINAL APPROACHES AT CISCO SYSTEMS

The California-based internet services firm Cisco Systems is widely quoted as being the company which has done most to develop effective new approaches to recruitment practice. Cisco grew very quickly in the late 1990s – a commercial success story that was only possible because of its ability to recruit and subsequently retain highly qualified people in extremely competitive labour markets. Today it employs 30,000 people in 60 countries, having doubled in size each year through the 1990s. Not surprisingly much of its recruitment activity has been carried out online, but other approaches have been used to raise its profile as an employer as a means of getting people to visit its recruitment websites. Some of Cisco's more interesting activities are the following:

- Cisco employs a specialised recruitment team which operates separately from the rest of its HR department. In many ways it resembles an in-house headhunting operation.

- The recruitment website includes a fake screen which prospective applicants can access instantly should their boss catch them visiting the Cisco site during working hours.

- Cisco has taken over many rival firms. One of the major motivations has been the opportunity this gives it to employ large numbers of talented new employees. Extra care is taken in the process to ensure that as many technical staff as possible are retained post take-over.

- Business cards have been distributed at brewery festivals and antique fairs after Cisco discovered that these were leisure interests of many prospective employees.

- Recruitment is considered to be an 'ongoing activity that never stops'. CVs received by jobseekers are not just filed away. Instead the senders are periodically contacted and asked to provide updates.

- Use is made of smart software which informs Cisco's system from where visitors to its website have logged on. If this is a rival firm the system directs them to the recruitment pages.

Source: Taylor and Collins (2000)

EDUCATION LIAISON

Another form of recruitment that is available to employers and is widely used involves recruiting people directly from educational institutions. Most attention is given to graduate recruitment, which has developed its own procedures and professional organisation (the Association of Graduate Recruiters), but equally important at the local level is the recruitment of young people leaving schools and colleges of further education.

Over 400,000 students now graduate from universities in the UK each year, of whom nearly 300,000 are being awarded their first degree. This figure has doubled since the 1980s and is planned over time to increase still further as the government strives for a situation in which half of all school leavers enter some form of higher education institution. Purely in terms of size, this is thus a very significant labour market in its own right, but it is made more important for employers because among the thousands of new graduates each year are most of the individuals who have the ability to make a real difference to an organisation's future fortunes. According to IDS, employers perceive about one in 60 graduates to be truly of 'high calibre', and view the process of recruiting them as resembling searching for a needle in an ever-growing haystack (IDS 1994:13). Attracting these individuals is a competitive business for the larger organisations, and is one in which they are prepared to invest substantial sums of money. This has led not only to the design of more attractive financial and development packages for new graduate recruits, but also to a refinement of the methods used to recruit and select graduates. Year on year demand for graduates continues to grow, but employers also report increasing difficulties filling their vacancies with suitable candidates. The result is simply greater competition for those who have genuine long-term potential.

Part of the problem is that all the graduate recruiters are fishing for the same types of people and are using the same range of recruitment and selection tools to identify them. IRS (2003b) shows that most graduate recruiters seek evidence of the same clusters of generic competencies, irrespective of the graduate's degree subject, communication skills, a results orientation, teamworking skills, analytical skills and business acumen being standard requirements.

The cost of recruiting graduates varies considerably depending on the size of the campaign launched and the types of methods used. Costs have reduced to an extent recently with the development of net-based graduate recruitment, but it still averages in excess of £5,000. However, this figure disguises huge variations, some organisations spending 15 or 20 times more than others (Jenner and Taylor 2000:19).

Graduate recruitment is also very time-consuming, much of the time and money being taken up with sending company representatives to the various universities to talk to groups of students, to man stands at careers fairs, and to brief careers advisors about the organisation and what it can offer to the right individuals. The more effectively these activities are carried out, the greater the organisation's prospects are of reaching that elusive creature – the well-qualified, well-motivated, intelligent, energetic and mobile graduate with management potential. In addition, there is a need to produce eye-catching literature and websites setting out what is on offer and what kinds of individual the organisation is looking for. The same fundamental decisions have to be taken in designing graduate literature as with the more conventional forms of recruitment advertising discussed above.

The major recruitment methods used are as follows:

- advertising in specialist graduate recruitment directories such as the Prospects Directories (published by the Higher Education Careers Services Unit) and GET (published by the Hobsons Group)
- attending careers fairs organised by university careers services, student industrial societies and private companies (the daily cost of a basic stand is around £2,000)
- organising employer presentations or events at universities, with 'free' food and drink to generate interest and raise the profile of the organisation
- offering work placement opportunities to students during their vacations
- sponsoring students (usually during their final years) by supplementing their allowances on condition that they subsequently join the sponsoring organisation.

Rankin (2008a) reports that recruiting former work placement students is rated as being the most effective graduate recruitment method, after internet-based advertising. Also seen as effective were recruitment fairs and campus presentation events.

GOLDEN HELLOS

One approach used to recruit people in tight labour markets is to pay them a sum of money in the form of a 'signing on bonus' or 'golden hello'. Such approaches have long been used on an ad hoc basis as a means of attracting senior staff who might otherwise hesitate about leaving their existing employment or choose some other employer instead.

In recent years some companies have formalised their procedures and extended them to graduate recruitment. The change has partly come about because of intensified competition for the very best graduate recruits, and partly because graduates are increasingly leaving university with substantial debts (an average of £15,000 according to some surveys). They are therefore considered to be more susceptible to the attractions of golden hellos and more likely to allow the prospect of a windfall payment to influence their decision to join a particular company.

Some public sector organisations have also moved down this road as a means of recruiting people to professions such as teaching and social work where there is a shortage of able graduates.

In 2009–10 leading employers were offering sums of between £2,000 and £6,000 in the form of signing-on bonuses or interest-free loans. The Training and Development Agency for Schools was offering £5,000 to trainee teachers in subjects suffering shortages, while the Department of Health was offering sums as high as £20,000 to good graduates looking to start careers in social care.

It has been argued that the cost of graduate recruitment can be reduced in a number of ways. First, employers can target their recruitment activity on a few specific universities including those in the localities where they have the greatest presence. They cannot reach such a wide pool of potential recruits this way, but they might be more successful in stimulating interest and thus making themselves attractive to students approaching graduation. Secondly, employers can question the need to take on so many graduates by analysing critically their existing training programmes and by considering other sources of graduate-calibre employees. However, while there is always the option of improving career progression and training for employees who have not completed university courses, the costs associated with such strategies may well be high.

Another approach is for graduate recruiters to develop links with universities using the methods long favoured in schools liaison. Rankin (2008a) demonstrates that the following approaches are commonly used:

- establishing relationships with staff in university departments
- sending staff to deliver/take part in lectures and seminars
- playing a role in the design of curricula
- assisting in research activities
- making financial donations
- donating equipment.

According to IDS (1998) schools recruitment drives typically involve providing work experience for students, providing industry placements for teachers, buying or donating equipment, sponsoring school events, arranging workplace visits for school parties, providing teachers with places on in-house training courses, helping out students with project work, running business understanding courses, carrying out mock interviews, mentoring students and encouraging employees to become school governors. All these activities raise the profile of the organisation in the community and, crucially, among school pupils who will be seeking jobs in the near future. It can thus be an important means by which employers improve their position in local labour markets and hope, as a result, to attract a greater number of high-quality applications than their competitors.

School leavers can also be recruited using the network of government-funded careers advisers. Several agencies, including the Learning and Skills Councils, the Training Standards Council and local/national training providers, collaborate on the development of 'work-based routes' for young people seeking to gain vocational qualifications. Through the use of government grants they encourage employers to recruit young people who are signed up to a structured training programme such as a National Traineeship or a Modern Apprenticeship. From an employer perspective these schemes provide a source of younger workers who are working towards a specific qualification in a particular field. In addition to the workplace training offered to all employees, these recruits attend further training sessions on a day or half day release basis at local colleges or the premises of private training providers. The government-funded agents help employers to identify suitable candidates and then monitor their progress in the workplace.

REFLECTIVE QUESTION

How could your organisation's educational liaison activities be improved? What arguments would you employ to persuade managers to pay greater attention to relationships with schools and colleges?

EXERCISE 8.3

EXERCISE BOX: THE END FOR TRADITIONAL GRADUATE RECRUITMENT SCHEMES?

Read the following two articles featured in *People Management*. They can be downloaded from the *People Management* archive on the CIPD's website (www.cipd.co.uk).

- 'The Fast Track Broadens' by Anna Czerny (2 September 2004, pages 14–15).

- 'Gown and Town' by Hashi Syedain (23 March 2006, pages 38–39).

The first is a news article reporting the views of delegates attending the Association of Graduate Recruiters' annual conference. It makes it clear that many employers who have recruited large numbers of fresh graduates in the past on to fast-track development schemes are fundamentally reviewing their established practices. Some are even asking whether there remains a business case for

continuing to compete for new graduates at all.

The second article paints a very different picture. It describes the National Graduate Development Programme recently established by local government organisations, its ambitions and successful record to date.

Questions:

1. What are the different factors that are combining to make some employers question the value of their graduate recruitment schemes?

2. In what ways are employers altering their approaches in practice?

3. Why is the experience of local government employers apparently so different?

EXAMPLE

KEY ARTICLE BOX

'Recruitment in small firms' by Marilyn Carroll, Mick Marchington, Jill Earnshaw and Stephen Taylor. *Employee Relations*, Vol. 21, No. 3. 236–250 (1999)

There are few articles reporting academic research about recruitment in the UK HR journals. It is not a subject which has generated a great deal of debate or sparked much interest in the academic community. This article is an exception to the rule. It describes interview-based research focused on small firms in five separate industries. The findings confirm a preference for informal methods of recruitment on the part of small business owners and managers. The reasons for this are discussed.

Questions:

1 What are the major strands of the case for the use of formal methods of recruitment on the part of small firms?

2 Why are these not used by small firms in the five sectors studied here?

3 How far do you think that the firms studied here would see their staff turnover rates decline if they were to adopt more formal recruitment methods? Why?

EXPLORE FURTHER

- Every year *People Management* produces a supplement to accompany one of its April issues that focuses on the recruitment industry. These supplements include several articles, many of which focus on developments in recruitment consultancy. They are particularly good sources of information about recruitment advertising agencies.

- Graduate recruitment is examined in depth by Jenner and Taylor in *Recruiting, developing and retaining graduate talent* (2000) and in the annual benchmarking surveys carried out by IRS and published each autumn in Employment Review. A good source of information on schools-based recruitment is the IDS Study entitled 'Business partnerships with schools' (1998).

- There is relatively little material published on headhunters. Two recent books fill the gap somewhat. Although both are written predominantly from the perspective of the headhunters and primarily give advice to them, they are useful sources of knowledge for P&D managers too. These are the books by Finlay & Coverdill (2002) and Jenn (2005).

CHAPTER 9

Employer branding

LEARNING OUTCOMES

By the end of this chapter, readers should be able to:

- distinguish between the terms 'employer branding' and 'employee branding'
- set out the major stages in an employer branding exercise
- contribute to the creation of an employer brand
- advise about approaches to the decontamination of employer brands.

In addition, readers should be able to understand and explain:

- the significance of branding in the world of consumer marketing and the possibilities it offers HR specialists in shaping resourcing strategies
- the advantages that employer branding exercises can bring to organisations in terms of improved performance against key HR indicators
- some of the major criticisms made about employer branding and arguments that can be made in its favour.

INTRODUCTION

Employer branding is a concept that was developed in the last years of the twentieth century as labour markets tightened and it became harder to recruit and retain staff. Since then interest in the idea has grown rapidly among both HRM and marketing professionals. Recent years have seen the publication of dozens of books and articles on the subject, while a number of specialist consultancies have been set up to conceive tools and techniques to help organisations develop and manage their employer brands. As a result, many if not most of the UK's larger private sector organisations are now either actively considering how they can benefit from employer branding exercises or are carrying them out. To date there has been rather less interest in the public sector and among smaller private sector and voluntary sector organisations, although there are some excellent examples of employer branding principles being put into practice by some government agencies and charities.

Despite this substantial growth in interest, employer branding remains a contested and controversial subject about which many remain sceptical. It is common, for example, for commentators to dismiss the whole idea as something of a passing fad of the kind that enthuses HR people from time to time before being forgotten. Some question its ethicality while others see it merely as a rather inconsequential development which may have minor implications for recruitment advertising but no wider significance for HRM or employment relations beyond that. Partly as a result of this hostility and indifference we have precious few reliable research findings available to demonstrate that the practical application of employer branding principles has any significant impact on organisational performance. A compelling case can be put in favour of this proposition, but it cannot as yet be supported with equally compelling evidence.

In this chapter it is argued that employer branding is neither a passing fad, an insignificant development nor one which brings with it any major ethical dilemmas.

On the contrary there are good grounds for anticipating substantial further interest developing in coming years and many more examples of implementation in practice. Indeed, at least for some organisations, it is feasible to suggest that employer branding will increasingly top the evolving HR agenda and provide the dominant focus in the making of resourcing strategies. For them employer branding can be credibly described as an idea whose time has come.

BRANDS AND BRAND MANAGEMENT

Effective branding is universally recognised to be of central importance in consumer marketing strategies. A strong brand is one which consumers recognise and trust. They are thus more likely to buy a strongly branded product than one which is just as good in terms of quality and price, but less effectively branded. Quite ordinary products such as soft drinks, soap powder or indigestion pills can only be differentiated from one another by their branding. Because brands are so fundamental to purchasing decisions, once established they have enormous value, particularly when they have global reach and are recognised instantly by the majority of consumers. This is true, for example, of BMW, Starbucks and Sony. In each case the name of the company is instantly recognisable and is associated in everyone's mind with a particular product range. In addition the brand has a clear identity signifying quality, reliability and certain expectations as regards price.

All this makes it much more likely that the average consumer will choose to purchase these heavily branded goods than an equivalent or even better product that does not have the same brand identity. There are a number of consequences:

i   The monetary value of a brand to the company that owns it is often well in excess of the value of the plant, equipment and people required to bring the relevant goods or services to the market. Martin (2009) suggests that in many cases the brand is worth at least twice as much as 'the book value of their tangible assets'. This means that brands such as Coca Cola and Microsoft are worth tens of billions of pounds.

ii It is possible to develop brand images which differentiate a product from that of its rivals and hence to target particular groups of consumers and gain competitive advantage. A good example is Häagen-Dazs ice cream, a product which in terms of its taste and quality is not very different from that produced by hundreds of other ice cream manufacturers. What makes it highly successful is its brand image which is sexy and sophisticated. This enables a premium price to be charged and helps maintain a huge international market. The brand image has also been designed to appeal to a particular segment of the market (people who are young, urban and well off) because this is where the product's marketers believe there to be most scope for sales.

iii Very substantial amounts have to be spent developing brands, but once established their power to generate sales is so great that less money has to be spent on advertising or on marketing the products concerned. It then becomes possible to extend the product range, perhaps by bringing innovative products and services to market, using the same brand at a far lower cost and with much greater success than would be the case if there was no brand to use. An example is the way that major retail chains such as Marks and Spencer and Tesco have been able to expand successfully into the provision of financial services in recent years. Another is the wide range of separate products that are branded with the 'Virgin' logo. There are also several recent examples of designer labels being used to brand products that have nothing to do with the clothing on which they originally came to prominence. Hence the Ralph Lauren brand, originally used to sell ties, has since been used to sell a wide variety of products from furniture and lighting to fragrances, watches and even restaurants.

iv Consumers have a strong tendency to become loyal to brands once they have tried them, reducing the likelihood that they will switch to products or services offered by competitors. We tend, particularly as we get older, to buy the same branded goods week by week when we visit supermarkets, use the same banks and often replace our cars with new models from the same manufacturer. We do this because we become familiar with the product and do not want to take the risk that we might be less satisfied or disappointed if we were to try something different for a change. This tendency means that branded goods can be priced rather higher than less well-branded substitutes.

v There are major risks associated with the contamination of a brand image. The more valuable a brand is, the more well-known it is and the more integral it becomes to consumer choice, the swifter its fall from grace will be if for some reason it attracts bad publicity. A classic example was the fate of the Ratner chain of jewellery stores, which were the market leaders in the 1980s. They disappeared from our high streets rapidly after their chairman (Gerald Ratner) made a speech in 1991 in which he joked that some of the products sold in the shops were 'total crap' and 'cheaper than a prawn sandwich but unlikely to last as long'. After that the value of the company's shares fell by around £500 billion and the previously strong Ratner brand was destroyed.

As product markets become increasingly global and consumers are faced with more and more potential choice of products and services, the more significant brands have become. As a result organisations are becoming increasingly sophisticated in the way that they manage their brands by taking care to protect and enhance the image created, keeping it up to date and doing everything possible to make sure that contamination is avoided (see Heding *et al* 2009). Moreover the past two decades have seen a growing recognition on the part of organisations that brand management is too important to be delegated to marketing specialists. Instead it is central to everything that is done across all organisational functions:

> If branding is treated as a cosmetic exercise only, and regarded merely as a new name/logo, stationery and possibly a new advertising campaign, it will have only a superficial effect at best.... Branding needs to start with a clear point of view on what an organisation should be about and how it will deliver sustainable competitive advantage: then it is about organising all product, service and corporate operations to deliver that. The visual (and verbal) elements of branding should, of course, then symbolise the difference, lodge it memorably in people's minds and protect it in law through the trade mark (Clifton 2009:9).

In other words, brand management is integral to organisational strategy and hence to management generally. If branding is to succeed any claims made about a product or service that are reflected in its brand image must be a genuine reflection of the organisation's objectives, culture and capabilities. As soon as the consumer perceives a mismatch between brand image and the reality of the experience they have of using the products or services, the power of the brand to drive business is much reduced. Brand management thus involves ensuring that there is no mismatch. The brand must reflect what the organisation can deliver to the consumer, while the organisation must always ensure that it lives up to the promises associated with the brand. This is why one of the most widely quoted mantras in consumer marketing is 'to thine own brand be true' – a phrase which it is equally important to bear in mind when thinking about ways in which branding concepts can help us to shape HR strategies and practices.

 ## REFLECTIVE QUESTION

Think about your own regular shopping activities. Which shops do you visit most often? When you are in a supermarket which products do you tend to buy regularly? What is it about the identity of these brands that attracts you and keeps you loyal as a customer?

DEFINING EMPLOYER BRANDING

The term 'employer brand' appears to have been invented in the early 1990s by Simon Barrow, a London-based consultant whose career has combined brand management of consumer goods with senior management roles in the advertising industry. At base what is involved is simply the application of branding techniques long used when competing in product markets (see above) to an organisation's labour markets. The idea is that what works well for organisations when marketing goods and services to consumers should also be effective when seeking to attract, retain and engage employees. Some useful definitions of the terms 'employer brand' and 'employer branding' are as follows:

> The package of functional, economic and psychological benefits provided by employment and identified with the employing company (Ambler and Barrow 1996:187).

> A targeted, long-term strategy to manage the awareness and perceptions of employees, potential employees, and related stakeholders with regards to a particular firm (Sullivan 2004, quoted in Backhaus and Tikoo 2004:501).

> Building and sustaining employment propositions that are compelling and different (Berthon *et al* 2005:153).

> A set of attributes and qualities – often intangible – that makes an organisation distinctive, promises a particular kind of employment experience, and appeals to those people who will thrive and perform to their best in its culture (Walker 2008:3).

These definitions make it clear that the concept of employer branding involves more than sharpening up recruitment advertising campaigns. It goes far wider, embracing the whole range of different ways in which an employer interacts with the labour markets from which it sources its staff. In this respect it can be argued that 'employer branding' is simply a new label being given to fundamental employment processes that organisations have always had to involve themselves with. It has long been apparent that organisations have reputations as employers and that these determine the quality and quantity of job applicants who come forward when jobs are advertised. What makes employer branding innovative is the contention that an organisation can and should take steps actively to manage its reputation as an employer in a planned and coherent manner.

As is often the case when new management ideas evolve, there tends to be a degree of disagreement among commentators and writers about how a term should precisely be used. This is true of the term 'Human Resource Management' itself and is also true of the term 'employer branding'. In the latter case some of the earlier writing on the subject is less concerned (or indeed wholly unconcerned) with labour markets and the recruitment and retention of staff. Instead the focus is on ways in which employees can be encouraged to align their behaviour at work with the requirements of consumer brands. Reference is thus made to ways in which employees can be cast as 'brand ambassadors' and persuaded in various ways 'to live the brand' (see Martin and Beaumont 2003). The emphasis is on using employees to develop and strengthen consumer brands rather than on applying understanding of consumer branding to competition in the labour market. Martin R. Edwards (2005) usefully distinguishes between these two very different types of HR activity by referring to the former as 'employee branding' and the latter as 'employer or employment branding'.

Organisations use employee branding practices as a means of building strong corporate cultures, the aim being to ensure that customers experience a consistent service which always matches the image the organisation seeks to project in its markets. Edwards quotes the following definition from Miles and Mangold (2004:68):

> The process by which employees internalise the desired brand image and are motivated to project the image to customers and other organisational constituents.

The term 'branding' in this context is being used in the way that it is used in animal husbandry, employees being psychologically 'branded' with the mark of their employers just as farmers use hot irons to brand their livestock with their mark of ownership.

'Employee branding' is an interesting and controversial issue, and is one which researchers are increasingly exploring, but it is not the same thing as 'employer branding'. This, by contrast, is externally focused and is concerned primarily with the process whereby organisations market themselves as employers in the labour market – ie as part of their people resourcing activities. Here we will thus use the term 'employer branding' in this sense.

 REFLECTIVE QUESTION

'Employer branding' and 'employee branding' are often seen as being linked processes – two sides of the same coin – and not as wholly separate from one another. Why do you think this is?

THE BENEFITS OF EMPLOYER BRANDING

RECRUITMENT

Employer branding can help to make an employer more attractive to potential recruits in general terms because it leads to a sharpening of the message conveyed in recruitment advertisements and other literature as well as helping to ensure that a consistent message is relayed about the advantages associated with working for the organisation. Ultimately the aim is to use branding in order to help achieve 'employer of choice' status in the labour market, creating a situation in which able candidates actively seek job opportunities and hold a favourable view of the organisation vis-à-vis its competitors. Importantly, of course, employer branding is also about differentiation. The purpose is not simply to attract more applicants in general terms, but to attract those who will fit in best and thus, it is hoped, perform to a higher standard. Just as consumer marketing campaigns are designed to appeal to particular groups, so employer branding exercises seek to attract interest from the candidates with the skills and attitudes each employer is keenest to employ. This occurs because candidates use the messages conveyed via branding exercises to select themselves either in or out of the running for employment with the organisation.

There is another potential advantage too, namely, the ability of a successful employer branding exercise to reduce overall recruitment costs. This occurs because the raising of an organisation's profile as an employer and the achievement of a positive reputation in the labour market means that fewer advertisements have to be placed in order to attract the applicants that are required whenever job opportunities arise. Moreover, less has to be spent on the advertisements themselves (in terms of artwork, size or positioning in a publication). When a branding exercise works particularly well managers find that they attract so much interest in the jobs they have available that they do not need to re-advertise at all for some time. Instead they simply contact the appointable candidates who were unsuccessful in previous recruitment rounds with a view to re-interviewing them. Cost savings can also be achieved, alongside an improved candidate pool, when an organisation manages to foster such a good reputation that it can staff key posts by interviewing people who have approached it looking for job opportunities.

Cost savings can be very substantial. Murphy (2008b) describes the experience of the financial services company AXA, which took the decision to alter its recruitment practices in 2004. Previously a great deal had been spent on diverse recruitment agencies dealing independently with line managers in different branches. The new approach involved centralising the process and making much greater use of the company's corporate website. A prominent feature of the AXA site is the presence of video clips in which employees talk about the experience of working for the company. A single message was then included in all recruitment literature which stressed the size of the company, the possibilities this gave people to gain promotion and development opportunities and the idea that the company's role was to act as 'an expert friend'. All recruitment literature directs would-be applicants to the website through which applications can be made directly. The aim is positively to attract those who want to work for a big international corporation and to embrace the opportunities this gives them. Conversely, it is anticipated that those seeking work in smaller more informally-run organisations will not apply and will select themselves out. By 2006 over 250,000 people were visiting the recruitment pages of the website each month. AXA estimate that the total saving achieved in the first two years in which their branding exercise operated was £1.4 million. The time taken to fill jobs also fell on average from 40 to 30 days.

RETENTION

While most employer branding activity tends to be aimed at attracting new recruits, there are important additional benefits that have been noted. One of these is the tendency of effective branding exercises to improve the perception that existing staff have of their organisation as an employer. The result is reduced rates of staff turnover as people start seeing their employer in a more positive light and compare it more favourably with possible alternative employers.

Employer branding exercises work particularly effectively when they have the effect of engendering feelings of pride in existing employees. Not only do they recognise that their jobs are of high quality and that their benefits are above average for the industry (ie higher levels of job satisfaction), but they also develop a more positive emotional relationship which results in feelings of increased self-esteem and of confidence in their employer. Branding plays a role in increasing feelings of pride through two mechanisms. First, there is the direct impact of the messages the company sends out with a view to enhancing its reputation as an employer. The primary audience may be potential recruits, but existing staff hear and see the same messages. If they are well-designed, consistently articulated, rooted in reality and genuinely serve to differentiate the lived employment experience in a positive way, the organisation's reputation in the eyes of its own existing staff should be enhanced. Secondly, there is a knock-on effect that arises from improving an organisation's reputation externally. The perception of outsiders improves and this in turn serves to make insiders proud to work for the organisation and less likely to seek alternative employment. Lievens *et al* (2007:s45) characterise this as a 'cocktail party effect':

> In social situations such as cocktail parties, dinners or alumni reunions, there is a high probability that we have to answer the question for which organisation we work. If we subsequently tell who our employer is and the conversation sways almost immediately in another direction, this might indicate that the organisation is held in low regard. However, if people express their appreciation and keep talking about the organization, this might suggest that the organisation is highly valued…. When an employer is viewed favourably by ourselves and others, membership enhances our self-esteem and our organisational identity is likely to be strong.

Bakhaus and Tikoo (2004) see the potential impact of branding exercises on existing employees as being just as significant as that on potential external recruits. Just as consumer branding is aimed both at gaining and retaining customers, so employer branding should be as concerned with employee retention as it is with recruitment. Central here is the concept of 'brand loyalty', defined as the attachment that consumers develop to favoured brands. This is of immense significance in the commercial world because it defines the value of a consumer brand. One which is not effective at engendering strong loyalty from customers is not working and hence has limited value. Of particular significance, according to Bakhaus and Tikoo (2004:508–9) is the way that 'brand loyal customers continue to purchase a product, even under less than ideal circumstances'. The same is true in the field of employment, 'brand loyal employees' remaining with their employers 'even when conditions might warrant them to consider other employers'.

PERFORMANCE

In addition to recruitment and retention there are a number of other significant benefits which managers often cite when evaluating their employer branding exercises. These include reduced absenteeism and improved levels of performance. A number of examples are provided in the case studies published by IDS in their two most recent surveys of employer branding practice in the UK (see IDS 2005b and 2008):

- Severn Trent Water recorded its highest ever response rates and scores on job satisfaction in employee surveys undertaken after its branding exercise had been launched. Higher levels of employee engagement were thought to be the result.

- QintiQ explicitly set out to rebrand itself as an employer and in so doing has found that the exercise served to help it develop a new psychological contract with its employees. This is less rule-bound and bureaucratic and is characterised by an 'enabling culture' which gives employees much more discretion over how they carry out their roles.

- The Compass Group has found its branding exercise to be a useful tool in bringing together the many diverse units across the world that make up its very global business. It has helped to develop 'shared ways of thinking and behaving'.

- Managers at Nandos believe that a significant impact of their employer branding activities has been improved levels of customer service. This has occurred because the branding exercise has contributed towards the creation of a culture which enables people to excel.

- GCHQ observed an increased willingness on the part of staff to develop 'new skills and specialisms' following its rebranding exercise.

Berthon *et al* (2005:169) suggest that a subsidiary advantage of employer branding exercises that are aimed at new recruits is the tendency for it to take longer before 'post-employment dissonance' sets in. This term refers to the tendency for people to start new jobs with enthusiasm and high expectations, but for these feelings to degenerate over time as boredom and cynicism start to develop. The negative impact on individual and team performance arising from post-employment dissonance can be significant. Employer branding helps to postpone its onset in the same way that consumer branding seeks to reassure people that they have made the right purchasing decisions after the event.

OTHER BENEFITS

One or two other distinct benefits are noted by writers who have undertaken case study or survey-based research into the outcome of employer branding exercises. Berthon *et al* (2005) give examples of what they call 'double-hit' advertising whereby job advertisements are designed in such a way as not only to sell the job to potential recruits, but also to appeal to potential customers too. They give the example of an advertisement placed by Daimler in *The Economist* which is ostensibly a recruitment ad, but which also reminds would-be corporate clients of the potential benefits associated with providing models of Daimler cars to senior staff.

Martin *et al* (2004:79) stress the role that employer branding can play more generally in building corporate reputation for different groups of stakeholders. They make reference in particular to the business press. Wilden *et al* (2004:2) stress the growing significance of a corporation's reputation as an employer to financial markets who value companies in part according to their perception of the state of their human capital. Financial journalists, opinion-formers and fund managers are thus all potential audiences for employer branding messages as well as employees and potential employees.

Finally Martin *et al* (2004:77) make an interesting point about the potential role employer branding can play in enhancing the reputation of the HR function within the organisation. By its nature, it is argued, employer branding is both a strategic activity and one which involves co-operation between HR and marketing specialists. One outcome thus tends to be greater involvement of HR managers in strategic decision-making and greater influence at board level in organisations.

 EXERCISE BOX: THE SLOW, STEADY GROWTH OF EMPLOYER BRANDING

EXERCISE 9.1

Read the article entitled 'Designs on the Dotted Line' by Lucie Carrington featured in *People Management* on 18 October 2007. This article takes a long-term look at the concept of employer branding, also raising key issues for the future. Definitional issues are discussed as well as situations in which positive branding of organisations as employers can become difficult. The experience of Orange, the tele-communications company, in developing its employer brand is also discussed.

The article can be downloaded from the *People Management* archive on the CIPD's website (www.cipd.co.uk).

Questions:

1 What advantages, according to this article, can employer branding bring to the HR function in organisations?

2 Why is the relationship between an organisation's product market brands and its employer brand sometimes incompatible?

3 Why is the impact of employer branding rarely measured?

ESTABLISHING AN EMPLOYER BRAND

There is widespread agreement among managers who have carried out successful employer branding exercises and the consultants who are employed to advise them about the steps that need to be taken. This approach is concisely and effectively articulated by the Hewitt Associates consultancy (quoted in Berthon *et al* 2005:154):

STAGE 1:   Understand your organisation

STAGE 2:   Create a compelling brand promise

STAGE 3:   Develop standards to measure the fulfilment of the brand promise

STAGE 4:   'Ruthlessly align' all HR practices to reinforce the brand promise

STAGE 5:   Execute and measure.

ANALYSIS

A common myth about strong brands is that they can be built simply through the use of effective advertising. This is not the case. Advertising has a role to play in shaping perceptions and reinforcing existing beliefs about a good or service, but it is not sufficient on its own to achieve a positive and strong brand image. The product itself must live up to expectations and deliver consistent value for the customer. Marketing text books are full of examples of companies who have tried to rebuild tarnished reputations through slick advertising campaigns, but who have failed because their advertisements simply did not reflect the reality. The starting point must therefore be the product itself, and in the case of employer branding, this means the actual, lived experience of working for a particular organisation. This point is in fact more important for employer branding than consumer branding. Unjustified hype in advertising campaigns for products will simply lead to lost business as people's experience fails to live up to expectations. However, in the employment field the costs are potentially rather greater. This is because a disgruntled employee who performs poorly or is looking for another job all the time is a direct cost to the business, not just a lost opportunity. So it is very important not to use recruitment advertising as a means of exaggerating the attractiveness of a workplace or to make any kind of misleading claim about the experience of working there. Moreover, as is pointed out by Moroko and Uncles (2008:1691), it is much harder to disguise reality from employees than is sometimes the case with consumers. In consumer branding, because customers do not see what goes on 'backstage', something of a mystique about a brand can be created and sustained by activities carried out 'front stage'. This is not an option in the case of employees. Existing staff will simply become cynical, while prospective staff to whom false messages are conveyed will build up false expectations and see them dashed soon after starting work.

All who manage, advise, study or write about employer branding seem wholly agreed about this core principle. We can thus label it as the golden rule of employer branding. Failure to follow it, which is always tempting for organisations whose employment offering is weak vis-à-vis competitors, are likely over time to worsen their market position, defeating the whole object of the exercise, and wasting a great deal of money in the process.

This is why the first stage of any effective employer branding exercise involves understanding the organisation as a workplace. It is on this foundation that the brand-building process is built. Invariably it requires formal research, involving staff attitude surveys, focus groups and in-depth interviews with employees who have remained employed in your organisation for a long period of time. The aim is to establish and then to articulate what it is about the employment experience that you offer which is particularly valued by your people and, equally importantly from a branding point of view, is distinct from the experience offered by your chief labour market competitors. Walker (2008) suggests that the following methods are the most useful and effective for gaining the required information in a systematic fashion. He also advocates carrying them out in the following order:

- senior management workshops
- an audit of existing employment-related communications material
- internal focus groups with a cross section of employees
- external focus groups with people in target groups eg graduates, members of a profession etc)
- in-depth telephone interviews with 'carefully identified individuals who have a detailed, intelligent view of the organisation'
- online surveys.

Hieronimus *et al* (2005) set out the approach that is taken by the McKinsey organisation when advising their clients. They advocate treating the start of the process of employer branding in just as rigorous a manner as corporations have long approached the development of consumer marketing strategies. Key is an analysis of your competitors, what they offer employees and how this affects their attractiveness as an employer in comparison with your organisation. Information of this kind can be gathered by looking at websites, at what has been written about key competitors and by speaking to consultants who have data on competitor organisations. A great deal can also be gleaned from interviewing members of your own staff who have, in the past, worked for competitors.

Another message that comes through clearly reading the work of experienced employer branders is the importance of going well beyond gaining an understanding of how employees view the transactional relationship they have at work, by which is meant hard features of the exchange such as money, other benefits, formal career progression opportunities and management policies and practices. These can be significant differentiators, but for a branding exercise to be truly successful it is necessary to tap into people's feelings about the organisation they work for. Once these are teased out it becomes possible to try to come up with a few sentences that truly articulate what makes the experience of working for your organisation exciting, satisfying and, above all, distinct.

Hieronimus *et al* (2005) see this process as one in which an organisation seeks to establish and then put into words the key 'emotional and intangible associations' for employees. Lievens (2007:53) agrees about the importance of 'symbolic meanings' when trying to establish a meaningful brand identity:

> Applied to a recruitment context, symbolic attributes describe the job or organisation in terms of subjective, abstract and intangible attributes. Specifically, they convey symbolic company information in the form of imagery and general trait influences that applicants assign to organisations.

These are approaches long used by market researchers seeking to develop branding strategies for consumer products. Participants are asked to ascribe personality attributes usually associated with people to products and services so that marketers can get a sense of how they feel about a product and, particularly, the ways in which consumers identify with it. The skill is then in working out how to summarise the results of the market research in a form of words or set of slogans which genuinely reflect these feelings and ways people have of identifying with a product.

The same approach can be used in employer branding. A variety of models have been advanced to provide a basis for helping to establish the nature of an employer brand identity, image or corporate personality. Lievens (2007) makes reference to the following five key sets of traits which he has used in his research:

- sincerity (honest, sincere, friendly)
- excitement (trendy, spirited, innovative)
- competence (reliable, secure, successful)
- sophistication (upper class, prestigious)
- ruggedness (masculine, tough).

Davies (2007) describes a very similar five-trait model – 'the Corporate Character Scale' – which differs from Lievens' only in some of the terms that are used. Examples are as follows:

- agreeableness (warmth, empathy, integrity)
- enterprise (cool, trendy, innovative, daring, imaginative)
- competence (leading, achievement-oriented, technical)
- chic (charming, stylish, exclusive)
- ruthlessness (arrogant, aggressive, controlling).

However, branding is not all about intangible associations of this kind. Important though they are, it is also necessary to establish what employees appreciate about the more tangible aspects of their jobs. This too is a possible avenue to explore when deciding how to differentiate your organisation's offering from that of its major labour market competitors. Fields (2001:101–102) cites ideas developed by the McKinsey consulting organisation suggesting that there are four core types of employer brand, meaning four types of proposition which employers can use in developing their brand image:

i   Prestige (ie we have a great reputation in our business, working for us will enhance your long-term career opportunities).

ii Cause (ie we undertake work which is meaningful and socially important, working for us will provide you with the opportunity to help humankind).

iii High risk/big potential (ie we are a small but growing organisation, working for us will enable you to grow alongside us to reap big long term rewards).

iv Work-life balance (ie we will provide you with a good job, but also allow you plenty of time to spend doing other things).

It is also possible to think of other types of tangible brand identity as well. One example would be an organisation that is able to offer job security, another would be opportunities to work overseas, another the opportunity to work in a close-knit friendly team.

DEFINITION

Once the research and analysis stage is complete the next task involves coming up with an agreed form of words which concisely articulates the key points that will underpin the branding exercise. This activity is variously labelled as 'defining the brand identity' (Whitenack 2001:2) and 'formulating the employee value proposition' (Michaels *et al* 2001:67). It is the creative part of the process. Walker (2008:42) uses the metaphor of stem cells to describe it:

> The task you now face is to identify and name the distinctive features that characterise your organisation as a place to work – the basic attributes of your employer brand… what you are, your individuality, the key to your uniqueness, the colour of your corporate eyes, your corporate soul…. Every other aspect of the brand – every piece of talent attraction material, every induction programme, every employee referral scheme, every campus presentation – will grow from and depend on these attributes or stem cells.

The best way of explaining what these writers mean exactly is to illustrate the approach using examples. One which most readers will be able to relate to is the BBC, which carried out an employer branding exercise in 2008. After a great deal of research managers came up with the following three attributes which they consider accurately define the essence of BBC jobs and differentiate the corporation as an employer from its major competitors. The results of their exercise were reported at the CIPD's annual conference:

- kudos
- public service
- opportunity.

From these the following form of words has been agreed by the BBC to represent a summary of the essence of its employer brand:

> Create something of value for yourself and others.

Another interesting example is provided by the Nandos restaurant chain which has managed to carve out a distinctive image for itself both in terms of its consumers and as an employer brand (IDS 2008a). Here the following five 'core values' were identified:

- pride
- passion
- integrity
- courage
- family.

The company sees itself as being informal in its approach in comparison with other restaurant companies, stronger on teamworking and better at looking after its staff. The expression that it uses to sum all this up is:

> It's the people who make the chicken.

An often quoted example is Severn Trent Water which has developed its employer brand along very different lines from the BBC and Nandos. Here the 'employer promise' is much more related to tangible benefits than to symbolic values. The message thus accepts that working for a water company may not be an especially glamorous or exciting prospect, but that the experience can nonetheless be satisfying and will provide good opportunities. IDS (2005b) sets out the eight chief themes that the company stresses in its recruitment and HR communications:

- safety, health and well-being
- work-life balance
- personal development
- competitive rewards
- teamwork
- leadership
- equality and diversity
- communication.

The statement used to sum all this up is:

> Working together to create a great place to work.

Walker (2008) explains how his consultancy developed an employer brand for the Prison Service. Like Severn Trent, the appeal in terms of kudos and glamour is not immediately obvious, but here intangible and symbolic values were identified nonetheless and a realistic and attractive brand statement developed. Extensive research resulted in the identification of the following six 'key attributes':

- human insight
- thoughtfulness
- realism
- courage
- competence
- humour.

A rather longer statement was then developed to sum up the 'brand promise':

> If you are fascinated by people and can relate to them effectively, you'll find long-term interest and satisfaction in a career with the Prison Service.

CASE SUMMARY

EMPLOYER BRANDING AT ERICSSON

The telecommunications company, Ericsson, claims to have gained substantial benefits from carrying out an extensive employer branding exercise. Its major target market was new MBA graduates from the world's top business schools. Its aims were to improve the quality of the people it recruited from this source and to retain more of its new recruits for longer.

The company started by using polling and focus group activities to establish what were the key features of the Ericksson brand from an employee perspective. Four phrases were then selected which summed these up:

- world citizenship
- forefront of technology
- connected to the best minds
- inspiring possibilities.

The 'world citizenship' idea was given particular prominence for MBA graduates, because it was found to stress the aspects of employment that they found especially appealing. The international career opportunities offered by Ericsson were thus placed at the forefront of its recruitment campaign, along with other messages about exposure to newest technology and the practice of board level directors acting as mentors.

The result was a greatly improved retention rate among new graduate recruits (perhaps because more appropriate people were self-selecting into the applicant pool), a substantial reduction in recruitment costs (because advertising and other approaches were more effective) and lower employment costs (because people wanted to work for Ericsson sufficiently to accept a lower initial salary).

Source: Presentation by Sven-Ake Damgaard at the 2001 CIPD Conference, Harrogate.

COMMUNICATION

The key here is to ensure that consistency is achieved and that all forms of communication with potential recruits, job applicants (successful and unsuccessful), new starters and existing employees are aligned appropriately to help communicate the core brand message that has been settled on. Only by doing this determinedly and doggedly over time will the effectiveness of the branding exercise be fully realised. Central to achieving effective communication is the corporate website, and particularly those parts of it which are aimed at employees and potential employees. Pictures, logos and sound can be used alongside written content to reinforce the 'core attributes' of the brand that have been identified. Writers on employer branding also stress the significance of organising effective interactive launch events and of ensuring that the most senior figures in an organisation are conspicuously involved so as to communicate seriousness of intent.

Sometimes the means of communication and the precise use of words need to be adapted for different potential audiences. This is necessary and need not deflect from the effectiveness of the communication effort, but it must be handled carefully to ensure that consistency is achieved as far as the communication of those core values or attributes is concerned. For example, where an organisation employs large numbers of highly educated professional workers and lower-skilled people too, there will be a case for tailoring rather different messages in rather different forms to each. IDS (2008a:6) gives the example of QinetiQ who tailored its message to make it appropriate for the many specialised scientists and engineers that it employs. For this group it adopted a '30/70 approach' in communications: 'here 30 per cent of any message consists of content and 70 per cent describes the rationale behind the change'. A similar need to vary the message somewhat, while remaining true to the ideas behind it, faces international companies with audiences from a variety of different cultural backgrounds. IDS (2005b) give examples showing how this was achieved at Motorola and Unilever following their employer branding exercises.

Further ideas about effective communication, like the branding concept itself, can be borrowed from the experience of consumer marketing. Both Barrow & Mosley (2005) and Martin (2009) stress the significance of story-telling in communicating a brand's values to key audiences. Barrow and Mosely (2005:137–8) illustrate their point with the example of a communication exercise undertaken by the London Borough of Ealing which involved the production of a five-minute video called 'Making a World of Difference' which drew on the story of the movie 'It's a Wonderful Life':

> What Ealing did was to film different groups of employees telling the story to each other while going about their daily activities. What the film dramatised, in a gently humorous but also very moving way, was how the thousands of daily activities carried out by the Council's employees contribute towards the community's collective quality of life. The film was both highly imaginative and down to earth. It highlighted Ealing's service proposition while, at the same time, celebrating the vital role of employees in contributing something of real value to people's lives.

MEASUREMENT

IDS (2008a) suggest that the following HR metrics are used in order to measure the impact of an employer branding exercise and to justify the expense of carrying it out:

- number of job applications (overall)
- number of speculative applications
- number of applications in response to specific campaigns
- time it takes to fill vacancies
- ratio of job offers to acceptances
- number of employee referrals
- staff retention levels
- number of internal promotions.

In addition, especially where a great deal of time and money has been invested in developing and communicating an employer brand, there is a strong case for designing and carrying out bespoke surveys to establish what impact the branding exercise has had on employees. Tools such as these can also be used to measure how far the brand values have penetrated into people's perceptions of the organisation as an employer and to establish whether or not they have served to improve levels of employee engagement or pride in working for the organisation.

EXERCISE BOX: EMPLOYER BRANDING CASE STUDIES

EXERCISE 9.2

Read the following three articles featured in *People Management*. Each represents a good case study of an organisation seeking to establish a clear, well-differentiated, positive brand image in its labour markets. The organisations are Axa, the Environment Agency and McDonalds. The articles can be downloaded from the *People Management* archive on the CIPD's website (www.cipd. co.uk).

- 'Image Conscious' by Karen Higginbottom (6 February 2003, pages 44–45)

- 'Blue Skies Thinking' by Jane Simms (8 December 2005, pages 24–26)

- 'Fast Forward' by Stephen Overrell (9 February 2006, pages 26–31)

Questions:

1 How would you define in a few sentences the different types of employer brand that each of these organisations is seeking to develop?

2 How far do you find their values to be attractive brand propositions from an employment perspective?

3 What evidence is provided of actual or potential problems being encountered in the process of establishing a positive employer brand image?

REFLECTIVE QUESTION

Think about your own organisation. What is its reputation as an employer in its key labour markets? What distinguishes the experience of working at your organisation from working at others in the same industry? How could that difference be encapsulated in a statement of your 'brand promise'.

EMPLOYER REBRANDING EXERCISES

An interesting and important part of the published literature on employer branding is less concerned with establishing a brand in the first place, and more with altering perceptions when an organisation gains a poor reputation as an employer. The problem here is not that there is no brand that can be easily articulated, but that one does already exist and it is damagingly negative. The aim is thus to de-contaminate the employer brand so that potential recruits are attracted rather than put off of working for the organisation because of its poor image in the labour market.

In order to achieve de-contamination and successfully rebrand, the starting point must always be improving the actual experience of working for the organisation. Whatever it is that has led to the establishing of the negative brand image must be corrected. As is wisely pointed out by Clifton (2009:9) 'reputation is, after all, reality with a lag effect' and no amount of slick image-making will be effective if the actual lived reality of the work is not first improved. That having been put in train, it becomes necessary to carry out an extensive employer branding exercise in order that the improvement is communicated to potential workers.

There have been a number of high profile examples of effective employer rebranding exercises in recent years. The most widely-cited is the experience of the UK division of the McDonalds fast food restaurant chain, which has invested large sums of money in turning round its reputation as an employer. Despite being the market leader in the industry and a very profitable, growing company, McDonalds had long-suffered from high levels of staff turnover and an image as a provider of low-paid jobs with few prospects that people avoid unless they have no alternative. There were particular problems attracting senior staff from other organisations and graduate recruits, despite these jobs being competitively rewarded and offering good career development prospects. Indeed so poor had the company's reputation as an employer fallen that the term 'McJob' had found its way into the Oxford English Dictionary accompanied by the following definition:

> An unstimulating, low-paid job with few prospects, especially one created by the expansion of the service sector.

Turning round this poor labour market reputation is a long-term task, but is one that is well in train and has begun to bring significant gains to the company. In 2006 substantial improvements were reported in staff turnover levels (down 50 per cent), numbers of unsolicited applications and in the proportion of employees who stated that they were proud to work for the company (86 per cent). In part, according to Suff (2006), the process partly involved articulating the positive aspects of working for the company that were always there, but often not appreciated. McDonalds has always been able to provide plenty of flexible working opportunities, for example, and has always promoted people internally up its career ladder at a fast rate. It also not only holds the Investors in People award, but has achieved the highest scores for people management.

The 'employee value proposition' that was decided on as the basis for the branding exercise comprised the following simple points:

- improvement opportunities
- flexibility
- energising environment
- continuous learning.

These points were communicated using a series of posters and job advertisements which made explicit use of the 'McJob' label and sought to turn round perceptions very directly. The campaign was not at all subtle. Each poster set out an advantage of working for the company and included the slogan 'not bad for a McJob.'

Other examples of rebranding exercises that have met with measurable success are the following:

- British American Tobacco is a large and very successful company which employs people all over the world and provides good quality jobs for workers in several developing countries. However, because it is a cigarette manufacturer it has always suffered from a negative image in the labour market. The company is addressing this issue by improving its performance management and talent management processes and actively taking steps to develop a distinct employer brand. This stresses two attractive features of the company, its professionalism and the diversity of its workforce using the slogans 'winning with integrity' and 'bring your difference' (see Suff 2009c).

- Lloyds of London is the world's premier insurance market, providing insurance services to the world's leading insurance companies. It employs 800 people in London and Kent, as well as in smaller international offices all over the world. Lloyds is a highly successful, very modern business, yet because it traces its origins back several centuries and because of the presence in its syndicates of so-called 'names' (ie wealthy people looking for high returns on their investments) it has retained an image as an elitist and socially exclusive organisation. Its rebranding exercise was thus aimed at ridding itself of this stuffy reputation. The core values that it identified were 'commercial, accountable, clarity, collaboration, flexible and excellence'. These translated into expressions used in recruitment communications such as 'constant originality' and 'do something that matters' (see IDS 2008a).

- The British Library is the UK's national library and one of a handful of 'copyright libraries' which hold in their collections copies of all printed materials published in the UK. It employs 2,000 people and serves 16,000 users every day. It has never had any difficulty recruiting good people to its more specialist, academic roles, but it has had problems attracting staff into the more customer-service roles and in staffing its commercial operations. The reason according to Walker (2008:32–3) was 'negative perceptions of a bureaucratic, boring and static organisation which only employed librarians'. Managers thus set about re-tuning their image as an employer by embarking on a branding exercise. This stresses the library's 'world-class well-being offer' and the excellent opportunities staff have to develop themselves while working for the library. The overall message is summed up in the simple expression 'a great place to work'.

 REFLECTIVE QUESTION

Think about your own industry. Which employers have the best reputations and which have the poorest? What explains the difference? What would you advise those with poor or weak employer brands to do to improve their reputations as employers?

DEBATES ABOUT EMPLOYER BRANDING

Employer branding, as a relatively recent development in HRM, has yet to become the subject of a clearly defined debate among either HR professionals or academic researchers. However, it is not at all difficult to anticipate the lines of debate that are likely to open up in the future as more employers undertake exercises of the kind we have described in this chapter. We are now beginning to see the development of two criticisms, both of which can be contested, and hence can be predicted to lead to significant debates in the field:

1 A strong case to be made on principle against the whole concept of employer branding and the role it can be seen as playing in the employment relationship.

2 It can be argued that employer branding is no more than a 'management fad', a passing fashion in HRM which will soon run out of steam and cease to have major relevance.

The principled case against employer branding rests on the view that this kind of marketing activity is inherently manipulative, serving the interests of employers while harming those of employees. Indeed, it could be argued to be something of a new frontier in the extent and nature of the control which employers seek to gain over employees because it goes so far beyond the use of incentives and disincentives to gain compliance by appealing to people's emotions, sense of self-worth and self-identity in order to affect their behaviour in the labour market. Put crudely a critical view would be that employers use branding techniques in order to recruit and retain without increasing wages. Costs of production are thus reduced to the benefit of shareholders and taxpayers at the expense of workers. Aside from an economic argument of this kind, more generally there is a great deal of suspicion about branding activity simply because it is widely seen as being unpleasantly manipulative in nature. House (2007:10) writes about the reaction he sometimes gets from audiences of senior HR professionals when he speaks about branding in the context of employment:

> I was surprised to find myself being challenged on the perception that the word brand is a 'dirty' word. Some felt that it was all about spin and was some sort of black art and not something that HR professionals should be thinking about or associated with.

Negative views of 'branding' partly stem from the apparently trivial nature of some of the slogans and images that companies have developed in order to advertise and sell their products. People who see themselves as intelligent and discerning believe that they themselves are not influenced by such trivia in their purchasing decisions and are thus suspicious of the claims made for the power of branding more generally. For the more politically committed, and particularly those who oppose globalisation and the spread of international capitalism, the major global consumer brands are the principal target of their anger. This is very much the view expressed forward by the journalist Naomi Klein (2000) in her best selling book *No logo: taking aim at the brand bullies*. In this highly influential book, Klein argues that brands are not only anti-competitive in their impact, damaging to society and hugely negative in their impact on developing economies, but also doomed to fail over the long term. Sooner or later, she argues, people will wake up to the way they are being manipulated by corporations through branding and will rebel by purchasing unbranded products.

A number of points can be made in response which are in favour of employer branding. First it should be accepted that employer branding, like much HR activity, is in part aimed at achieving greater return for the employer per pound spent on employing people. One aim is to improve recruitment and retention while limiting the costs associated with competing for staff with other employees in tight labour markets. It is also true that employer branding can be manipulative in nature, and perhaps have the effect of hoodwinking unwary recruits into accepting jobs on a false premise. However, as is repeatedly stated in all the publications on employer branding, branding exercises which are dishonest in nature invariably fail. As Martin (2009:224) points out, where branding is used to increase the 'gap between rhetoric and reality' in employee relations rather than to narrow it the result will be 'employee cynicism and opposition to change'. It is reasonable to argue that it is these poor employer branding exercises which seek to mask the truth about working in an organisation rather than to build on that truth, which are manipulative in nature. It is thus an unfair criticism to make of exercises which do no more than to identify what employees themselves consider to be the distinct and positive advantages associated with their employment and then to develop resourcing strategies around these perceptions.

Part of the problem may well be the term 'employer branding' which can be misleading, suggesting triviality and manipulative recruitment advertising, when the process is actually far more serious, complex and ethical. What we are really focusing on when we talk about 'employer branding exercises' is an attempt by the HR function to take a long-term, strategic approach to the management of an organisation's reputation in key labour markets. If we were to use the term 'reputation management' instead of 'employer branding', it is likely that there would be a great deal less principled suspicion on ethical grounds and fewer accusations made about the triviality of employer branding activity. There is little or no criticism levied at organisations who seek to be seen as 'employers of choice' in order to recruit and retain more effectively, yet employer branding, when carried out honestly, is really no more than a process whereby managers seek to achieve that status.

The view that employer branding is no more than a temporary, passing fashion in HR circles is also commonly expressed (see CIPD 2007d & 2009a). Here the argument runs that the idea came to prominence recently in response to the emergence of unusually tight labour market conditions. In the decade before 2008, unemployment fell to historically low levels, severe skills shortages emerged and employers were forced to compete very much harder with one another to recruit and retain the people they required. According to this view the far looser labour market conditions and higher levels of unemployment that developed after the onset of recession in 2008 have brought fundamental changes that are likely to last for several years. In other words, it is argued that the boom years of the late 1990s and early 2000s were the exception in historical terms and we are now back to a 'normal' state of affairs in which as far as most labour markets are concerned it is the employer and not the employee who enjoys the whip hand. Skills shortages are far fewer, employees have less choice of alternative jobs and employers can recruit and retain the people they need without the need for costly branding exercises.

A number of arguments can be made in response to this point of view. First, it can reasonably be asked why if employer branding is a fad whose time has passed so many organisations claim to have or to be actively working on employer branding activities. According to the CIPD's 2009 Survey on Recruitment and Retention, 45 per cent of respondents were using employer brands in order to address recruitment difficulties, while 38 per cent saw 'regaining control of the employer brand' as a major reason for bringing previously outsourced resourcing activities back in-house (CIPD 2009a:7 and 17). Secondly, as was pointed out in Chapter 2, there are good grounds over the longer term for anticipating tighter labour markets as far as skilled staff are concerned and hence a need for organisations to address recruitment and retention issues more strategically. Organisations are going to have to think more carefully about how they position themselves in their labour markets vis–à–vis competitors, and employer branding will play an important role in helping them to do this. Finally it is worth considering the points made by some leading sociologists about apparent changes in the way that employees and would-be employees view the labour market and the whole business of choosing where to work and how long to stay with their employers (see Chapter 2). If it is true, as du Gay (1996), Bauman (2005) and Svendsen (2008) argue that we are increasingly viewing decisions about where to work in the manner of consumers choosing what to purchase, it follows that the techniques used by organisations to market goods and services are likely to be increasingly adopted by recruiters seeking skills in tight labour market conditions.

REFLECTIVE QUESTION

The advantages of employer branding are most obvious in organisations facing tight and competitive labour market conditions. Does the concept have anything to offer employers who have few problems recruiting and retaining? If so what are they?

EXAMPLE

'Conceptualizing and researching employer branding' by Kristin Backhaus and Surinder Tikoo. *Career Development International*, Vol. 9, No. 4/5, 501–516 (2004)

This is one of relatively few academic journal articles focusing specifically and exclusively on the subject of employer branding. It is interesting and useful because it discusses the idea of employer brands in the context of established theories in the fields of marketing and HRM. Towards the end a future research agenda is set out.

Questions:

1 Explain how our understanding of 'employer branding' can be enhanced with reference to theories about:

   i   the resource-based view of the firm

   ii the psychological contract

   iii brand equity

   iv social identity theory

   v   brand loyalty.

2 How, in theory, does employer branding serve to enhance an organisation's performance?

3 What type of research study would be required to test whether or not there is a link between employer branding and organisational performance?

- CIPD has published several papers on employer branding as well as a practical guide about steps to take when developing an employer brand. These can be downloaded from the institute's website (www.cipd.co.uk). The publications entitled 'Employer branding: Maintaining momentum in a recession' and 'Employer branding: The latest fad or the future for HR?' are particularly good introductions to debates about employer branding and its future prospects.

- Martin Edwards's chapter in *Managing human resources: Personnel management in transition* edited by Stephen Bach (2005) is a particularly thoughtful examination of developments in this field from an academic perspective.

- IDS has devoted two editions in its 'HR Studies' series to employer branding. Both contain several case studies describing the approaches taken and the benefits gained by organisations from different sectors who have carried out employer branding exercises. The relevant studies are number 809 (2005b) and 872 (2008a).

CHAPTER 10

Selection: the classic trio

LEARNING OUTCOMES

By the end of this chapter, readers should be able to:

- devise application forms
- draw up a shortlist of candidates
- conduct a selection interview
- make effective use of employment references
- advise on the effectiveness of traditional selection tools.

In addition, readers should be able to understand and explain:

- the theoretical advantages and disadvantages of different selection methods
- employer objectives in the use of interviews, references and application forms.

RESEARCH IN EMPLOYEE SELECTION

The choice of appropriate employee selection techniques is a field in which there is great divergence between the recommendations of academic writers and day-to-day practice in organisations. When applying for a job, most people expect to have to fill in an application form, attend one or more interviews and then receive an offer of employment subject to satisfactory references being provided by the referees they have named. These three methods are labelled 'the classic trio' by Mark Cook (2004). It is the expectation because in most cases this is the approach taken by organisations. What is interesting is that this traditional approach continues to dominate in the face of apparently conclusive evidence that other tools of selection have far greater predictive power and are fairer to most candidates.

There is a long tradition, going back to the beginning of the last century, of academic research into the relative merits of different selection tools. For the most part, the field has been dominated by occupational psychologists who have worked with a shared set of assumptions concerning personality traits and their relationship to job performance. Foremost among the approaches undertaken have been validity studies, in which a selection process that results in the appointment of several individuals is observed. The scores given to candidates at the selection stage are recorded and compared with their actual performance on the job some months or years later. Different selection methods can then be compared according to how accurately they predict job performance (ie the extent to which candidates who score particularly well at selection achieve higher levels of performance than colleagues who impressed less at the selection stage).

The unit of measurement used in these studies is the correlation co-efficient – a measure of how closely scores at the selection stage correlate with those awarded for later performance. Were a selection process to be found to have resulted in a correlation co-efficient of 1, it would have predicted the relative performance of employees with perfect accuracy. Conversely, a correlation co-efficient score equal to 0 indicates the absence of any predictive accuracy at all – the employer might as well have picked candidates at random. A modest validity study looking at a small group of employees chosen using one selection tool, while interesting, is not especially helpful in allowing generalised judgements to be made about the predictive qualities of any particular selection method. However, over the years many hundreds of such studies have been carried out in many countries which can be combined and assessed together using computer programs. It is the results of such exercises, known as meta-analyses, that have apparently confirmed what many have long believed, namely that traditional methods of selection such as interviews are markedly poorer at accurately predicting job performance than more sophisticated techniques such as personality tests and assessment centres. The results of meta-analyses are illustrated in Table 10.1. More recent meta-analytic studies have given a rather better press to structured interviews, but provide continuing evidence of the poor predictive powers of the traditional formats that are the more commonly used (see Buckley & Russell 1999, Rynes *et al* 2000, Salgado 2001, Dipboye *et al* 2001, Cooper *et al* 2003 and Morgeson *et al* 2007).

Despite the presence of this research and the accompanying bad publicity for traditional selection methods, there is plenty of evidence to show that they remain very widely used in the appointment of new employees. Successive CIPD surveys looking at recruitment and selection practices show that interviews of one kind or another are almost universally used, that application forms are completed by candidates seeking work in over 80 per cent of organisations, and that references are taken up either before or after interviews by at least three quarters of employers (CIPD 2007 and 2009). The current picture would thus appear to confirm the observation made by Robertson and Makin (1986) that in the UK 'the frequency of a method's use is inversely related to its known validity'.

However, what is particularly interesting in these surveys is the response of employers when asked to reflect on which selection techniques they find to be most useful. For all grades of staff, a very clear majority stated that the interview was the most important tool for them in making selection decisions. There is thus clearly a great gulf between the considered views of academics and practitioners about the relative usefulness and value of different selection methods. Possible reasons for this disagreement will be explored in relation to each of the selection

Table 10.1 Meta-analyses, various selection methods

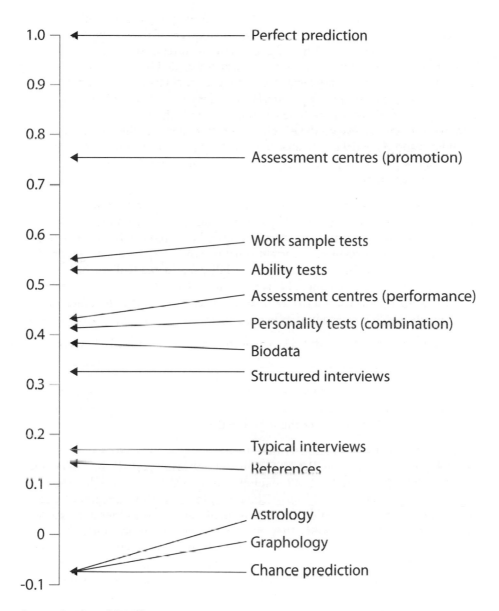

Source: Smith et al (1989).

methods described in this and the subsequent chapter. It is, however, useful to make one or two general observations at this stage.

First, it should be pointed out that the 'classic trio' are the most straightforward and least expensive of the range of selection methods available to employers. The use of reputable personality and ability tests requires costly training or the employment of trained consultants, to which is added the cost of the tests themselves. The potential expense of an assessment centre is clearly far higher and is not in any case a practical option for small organisations or for the selection of relatively low-skilled personnel. Secondly, it is important for employers to have an eye on the effect the selection methods they use have on candidates and potential candidates. Such matters have not historically concerned psychologists, who have preferred to concentrate purely on the predictive qualities of each tool.

Furthermore, because application forms, interviews and references are so commonly used, they are expected by job applicants. Too much innovation in the selection procedure might be disorienting and thus reduce the effectiveness of a candidate's performance. In certain situations the prospect of being judged by the selection methods with the highest validity may actually dissuade good candidates from applying. This is particularly true of assessment centres which require attendance at a two or three day event and which often include assignments which are perceived as being tough.

The reluctance from the candidates' perspective springs from the lack of control they can exercise over the process when the more scientific approaches are adopted. Not only, therefore, are we more comfortable with the classic trio because we expect them and have experienced them before, we also prefer them because we think we understand how they work, and feel that they give us a greater degree of influence over the selection decision.

Mention should also be made of criticisms that have been made of the psychological research itself. Iles and Salaman (1995:219–224), Searle (2003) and Iles (2007:99–100) suggest that the assumptions on which much validity research is based are open to question. In particular, they take issue with the notion that personality is on the one hand readily measurable, and on the other necessarily stable over time. In other words, they question the very basis on which psychometric studies of selection are based. They also draw attention to the fact that job content varies to a great extent over a period of years, or even months, and that the individual attributes candidates display when selected may be less and less relevant as time passes and the nature of the job develops and changes. It follows from this argument that what is important at selection is finding an individual who generally 'fits in' with the culture and values of the organisation and is sufficiently well qualified to undertake a range of possible tasks. The aim is thus less to 'match' a personality with a job than to screen out people perceived as likely to be dishonest, lazy, difficult to work with or unsatisfactory for a variety of other reasons.

THE USE OF GRAPHOLOGY

An interesting example of the use of selection methods that are neither scientific nor systematic is the use of graphology or handwriting analysis. Despite firm evidence of its poor predictability (Smith *et al* 1989:86–88 and Ben-Shakhar 1989), it appears to be used surprisingly widely. In the UK it is rare for employers to admit to its use in selection, although some have confirmed that they use it as one of a range of techniques (Cooper *et al* 2003: 149–152). However, on the continent it is much more common, with over three quarters of smaller French companies believed to use it in employee selection, whilst a good proportion of employers in Belgium and Germany also apparently believe it to have an effective role to play.

A possible reason for the use of graphology is its apparent 'reliability' as a selection tool. People's handwriting tends not to change to any great extent during their adult life, although it can be made neater with effort. It is also a 'reliable' method in so far as different graphologists have been found to reach similar conclusions about a candidate's personality when given the same handwriting sample to analyse – not a situation that typically occurs when several people interview the same candidate at different times.

However, reliability should not be confused with validity. There is also evidence to show that graphology is a poor diviner of important personality traits and is thus probably a poor predictor of job performance. According to Smith *et al* (1989), when tested, graphologists were unable to distinguish between real and faked suicide notes, and failed to identify which of a range of handwriting samples had been submitted by people diagnosed as neurotic. Further research reported by Watson (1994:208) and Edenborough (2005:29–30) supports this view, leading them to conclude that, as yet, there is insufficient evidence to support the use of graphology as part of a fair and objective selection procedure.

EXERCISE 10.1

EXERCISE BOX: PERFORMANCE-BASED SELECTION

Read the article by Lou Adler entitled 'Outside Chance' featured in *People Management* (10 March 2005, pages 38–39). This can be downloaded from the *People Management* archive on the CIPD's website (www.cipd.co.uk).

In this opinion piece, Lou Adler draws on many years of recruiting experience to suggest ways in which decision-making about who to hire can be improved in organisations.

Questions:

1 What, according to Adler, are the major common errors made by recruiters when selecting staff?

2 To what extent do you agree with Adler's five easy-to-learn principles for improving employee selection decisions?

3 What other action could be taken by organisations seeking to improve their capabilities in this area of practice?

APPLICATION FORMS

Surveys report that application forms are used in some shape or form by 80 per cent of employers in the UK (CIPD 2003a). In many larger organisations and in the public sector they appear to be used for all jobs except those at senior management level, and there are examples of universal usage for all jobs including the most senior. The alternative is to allow or encourage applicants to compose their own curriculum vitae or CV. This practice is widespread in the private sector, but only permitted in 50 per cent of public and voluntary sector organisations. Many employers make use of both approaches, accepting CVs as well as application forms, the CV being the preferred approach in smaller organisations. It might have been expected that the use of CVs in job applications would become rarer with the widespread introduction of online applications in recent years. However, this does not appear to be the case. CVs remain commonly used in several sectors (Murphy 2008c).

From an employer's perspective there are advantages and disadvantages both to application forms and CVs. In principle, the CV is preferable because it gives applicants the freedom to sell themselves in their own way. They are thus able to tailor their applications to their own strengths and are not restricted to fitting relevant information into boxes of predetermined size. Some application forms, because they are so restrictive in their design, may lead to excellent candidates being overlooked. An example might be a form that contains a set of questions and several blank spaces under the heading 'Present employment'. In putting so much emphasis in the form on this aspect, the likelihood is that otherwise good candidates who are not currently in full-time employment will be disadvantaged. A similar problem confronts an applicant who, while in work, is unhappy and is perhaps seeking a new position after just a few weeks or months in this employment. Indeed, a poorly designed application form has been shown to put many applicants off applying in the first place (Jenkins 1983).

However, CVs can be criticised for giving job applicants the opportunity to sell themselves to a potential employer by including material in their applications that is wholly irrelevant to the position being advertised. Similar 'contamination' effects can occur when a CV is particularly attractively presented or structured, leading unwary selectors, perhaps unconsciously, to favour applications from otherwise unimpressive candidates over those of their better-qualified rivals. In extreme cases, candidates engage in sophisticated 'impression management', going to great lengths to dazzle with well-bound, professionally produced CVs with career and other achievements highlighted and a judicious mix of leisure interests. It is for this reason that many public sector organisations refuse to accept CVs at all.

Perhaps the best solution is to design separate application forms for each vacancy advertised. This gets round the problem of inappropriate design and allows specific questions to be posed relevant to the job in question. With the development of more sophisticated word-processing and printing equipment, such an approach should be used more frequently, but as yet there is little evidence to suggest that employers have moved away from the standard organisation-wide form that has long been used across the whole range of jobs on offer. Individualisation would also permit the inclusion, where appropriate, of spaces for candidates to write longer descriptive answers to more involved questions.

Whether the application form used is standard or original to the job advertised, it will fill a number of distinct functions. According to Smith and Robertson (1993:81–82) these are the following:

- to enable a shortlist of candidates for interview to be drawn up
- to provide information that can be drawn on during the interview
- as a means by which information about good but unsuccessful candidates can be filed away for future reference
- as a means of analysing the effectiveness of the various alternative recruitment media used (see Chapters 7 and 8)
- as a public relations tool enhancing the employer's image as 'an efficient, fair and well-run organisation'.

Employers also use forms 'to capture sensitive information in a non-intimidating way' as a means of undertaking equal opportunities monitoring and gathering sensitive medical information (IRS 1999:8).

It follows that the best application forms are designed so as to fulfil each of the above functions as effectively as possible. The first three factors require the presence of clear, concise language and a layout that allows candidates sufficient space to include all relevant information. The public relations function is best served by the use of good quality paper and typesetting.

A typical application form would include questions asking for basic biographical information, previous work experience, educational background, vocational training undertaken and future career aspirations. Forms often ask about previous convictions and the applicant's state of health. Asking candidates to include a passport-size photograph used to be common, although in practice candidates often failed to do so, and is now much less common. Another development in recent years is the request for information concerning gender and ethnic background to enable organisations to undertake equal opportunities monitoring. More often than not, this is included on a separate form that is detached or removed from the original prior to shortlisting. The question of nationality, by contrast, is usually included in the main body of the form to allow the employer to discuss matters relating to work permits with candidates at their interviews.

There are a number of questions commonly included in application forms that are controversial and that are often the subject of heated discussion among recruiters. Examples are those asking applicants to state their age or date of birth, and those asking them to list their hobbies and interests. The latter is a peculiar type of question because it usually has no relevance at all to the ability

THE STANDARD APPLICATION FORM (SAF)

Many employers recruiting graduates prefer applicants to complete the standard application form provided by the university careers service. The SAF has been used extensively for many years now, proving to be an effective and fair shortlisting tool. Being designed specifically for new graduates, it is updated each year and is competence-based.

Copies are available at all university careers services establishments and can also be downloaded from the CSU website at www.prospects.csu.ac.uk. The following appears on the current version:

- personal details (name, contact address/numbers, date of birth, driving licence, work permit etc)
- higher education (dates, courses, expected and achieved results)
- prior education (A levels, number and dates of GCSE passes at C and above, grades in English and maths, number of GCSE A grades)
- work experience (dates, jobs, responsibilities and achievements)
- geographical location (preferred work locations)
- personal interests/achievements (spare-time activities, specifically those which included organising and leading or those requiring initiative and creativity)
- evidence of 'planning, implementation and achieving results' (specific examples required together with an estimation of 'how you measured your success')
- evidence of 'influencing, communication and team work' (specific examples required with a statement of why the outcomes were satisfactory)
- evidence of 'analysis, problem solving and creative thinking' (specific example of a problem required, together with information about alternative approaches that could have been used in solving it)
- additional information (space for the candidate to write what they wish plus a question about where they heard about the vacancy)
- specific skills (languages, IT packages etc)
- career choice (a requirement for candidates to state their reasons for applying and evidence of their suitability)
- health declaration
- referees (x2)
- availability for interview
- equal opportunities monitoring form.

of candidates to fulfil the requirements of the job. It is also very likely indeed to be answered untruthfully, candidates taking care to include only mainstream or 'politically correct' interests. If candidates' main hobbies are eating fast-food, watching adult movies and smoking illegal substances, they are unlikely to include them in the response.

The question of age is more interesting, not least because since 2006 it has become possible to bring an age discrimination claim before an employment tribunal. The new law serves to restrict the extent to which age can be used as a selection criterion, but it does not outlaw such practices altogether. Employers remain free to continue discriminating on grounds of age when they can objectively justify so doing, the test being that the practice in a particular case constitutes 'a proportionate means of achieving a legitimate aim'. Ahead of the passing of the relevant regulations, the government's consultation documents suggested that age discrimination would be lawful on the following grounds:

- for health, safety and welfare reasons

- in order to facilitate employment planning

- to encourage or reward loyalty

- to take account of the need for a reasonable period of employment prior to retirement.

At the time of writing (late 2009) we are still waiting for more test cases on these issues to reach the appeal courts, so it is not yet possible to know exactly how far the judges will ultimately permit continued discrimination on grounds of age, and hence whether or not some long-standing selection practices will have to be abandoned. For example as matters stood it was lawful for age to be taken into account when a vacancy for a position as a supervisor of a group of middle-aged employees is advertised. While the presence of a young supervisor might not necessarily cause problems, many employers might think it very reasonable to include age as one of the criteria used in deciding who to invite for interview. It would then be possible to ensure that there were at least some older people shortlisted. Alternatively, to what extent will it be considered lawful for an organisation whose customers are either predominantly from younger or older age groups to reflect these demographic bases when selecting staff for marketing and customer-facing roles?

Perhaps these are further situations in which there is a case for designing different applications for different jobs. The question about age or date of birth would then be included only when judged strictly necessary.

 REFLECTIVE QUESTION

Where do you stand in this debate? Can you think of other circumstances in which it might be appropriate to request information about dates of birth?

In the next chapter we examine the use of weighted application forms and biodata. These are methods that enhance the role of application forms in the selection process and that have been found to have relatively high validities when compared with other selection methods.

EXERCISE BOX: FRAUDULENT APPLICATIONS

Read the article by Steve Smethurst entitled 'Faking It' featured in *People Management* (16 June 2005, pages 35–36). This can be downloaded from the *People Management* archive on the CIPD's website (www.cipd.co.uk).

This short article reports the views of various commentators on the subject of untruths being included by job applicants in their CVs and on application forms. It concludes that the problem is widespread, but that employers can take steps to reduce the extent to which it affects them.

Questions:

1 What proportion of CVs are thought to contain inaccurate information which makes candidates appear more impressive than they actually are?

2 Why do you think so few employers carry out checks to ascertain the truth of the information candidates submit to them?

3 What measures does the article suggest could be taken? How far do you think these would reduce the extent of fraud and why?

SHORTLISTING

The next stage in the traditional approach to selection is to boil down the applications received to a shortlist of candidates to invite for interview. Here again, as so often in employee selection, there is a potential tension between the relative merits of methodical and more informal approaches. All descriptions of best practice, advocate a systematic approach to shortlisting whereby a list of criteria are drawn up from the person specification. Each application form is then judged and scored against these standards. Torrington *et al* (2008) suggest that the drawing up of criteria is best done by a panel, but that the shortlisting itself should be undertaken on an individual basis, each panel member looking at all application forms separately and drawing up his or her own list. Any candidate chosen by all the screeners is then invited to interview, while any discarded by all is rejected. Panel members then debate the merits of the remaining applicants with regard to the requirements of the person specification until a consensus is reached about who should and who should not be interviewed.

The argument in favour of such an approach is its inherent fairness. It discourages selectors, either consciously or unconsciously, from discriminating unfairly on the basis of factors unrelated to the content of the job. It thus reduces the chances of well-qualified candidates being screened out on account of peculiar handwriting, marital status or place of birth. Research quoted by Cook (2004:4) found evidence of unfair discrimination on grounds of sex occurring at the shortlisting stage through the stereotyping of men and women as suitable or unsuitable for particular jobs. It goes without saying that it is easier for individual managers who are racially prejudiced to screen out members of ethnic minorities if there is no panel to whom they must justify their actions.

Having put the case for a systematic approach, it also reasonable to point out the drawbacks. The main problem arises if the criteria drawn up are too exacting, leading to the screening out of good candidates who fail to respond to questions on the application form with precisely the answers required. An example might be a situation in which the agreed criteria include a requirement for shortlisted candidates to have had some years' experience in a particular role or at a specified level in an organisation. A typical case might be one in which applicants for a personnel management job are required to have worked for a minimum of three years in a senior HR role in manufacturing. While relevant and justifiable, such a parameter might lead to the rejection of the best candidate on the grounds that he or she has only two years' experience as a general manager in a service industry.

There is thus a strong case for allowing a degree of flexibility in the screening of application forms and for avoiding too narrow or bureaucratic an approach. If a candidate looks interesting, for whatever reason, it does no great harm to invite him or her to interview. To reject purely on the basis of an arbitrary set of criteria may be theoretically justifiable, but might well not be in the long-term interests of the organisation.

Wood and Payne (1998:77–81) advocate a simple scoring approach which, they argue, allows recruiters to sift hundreds of application forms at a rate of less than two minutes per form, while maintaining a high degree of fairness. Their starting point is the presence of an agreed list of competencies being sought for the job. Each candidate's application form is then rated on a three point scale (A, B or C) against each competence, an A indicating strong evidence of the competence being sought, B indicating moderate evidence and C indicating little or no evidence. Once two C scores have been awarded the form is rejected. Those with most As are then shortlisted for interview.

REFLECTIVE QUESTION

How systematic are the approaches to shortlisting used in your experience? What examples of stereotyping have you come across?

ONLINE SIFTING

As was explained in Chapter 7, among the disadvantages associated with online recruitment is the sheer number of unsuitable applications that employers can receive when jobs are advertised to a potential audience of several million internet users. According to Parry and Tyson (2008) this is by some margin the most significant problem for employers who use online recruitment – many of their respondents had experienced difficulties dealing with large volumes of applications from unsuitable candidates. The problem is particularly acute in areas such as graduate recruitment where employers actively seek to encourage applications from people who have yet to gain much work experience and thus employ broad criteria (a wide-trawl rather than a wide-net approach). In such circumstances some form of electronic screening technologies need to be used so that the cost of printing off completed forms and/or CVs, and subsequently reading them, does not become prohibitive. Several approaches can be used, although the evidence suggests that to date they have only been adopted by a minority of organisations (see CIPD 2009b).

ONLINE APPLICATION/BIODATA FORMS

These require job applicants to complete an application form which is questionnaire-based. Its first purpose is to collect straightforward factual information about achievements and personal career history (eg class of degree, years of relevant work experience, current salary etc). Secondly, forms usually ask direct questions designed to establish how far the candidate possesses the attributes or competencies the employer wants for the job in question. Once completed, the candidate submits the form and it is scored electronically. Those which do not reach a threshold score are rejected electronically (but hopefully with courtesy), while the others are sent on into the employer's database. IRS (2003d) describes online application procedures which include 'killer questions' designed to sift out unsuitable candidates before they have even completed the form. If one or two of these are answered 'wrongly' the procedure terminates and the candidate is directed to another site.

ONLINE PERSONALITY QUESTIONNAIRES

These are generally established psychometric tests developed by reputable providers which have been adapted for use online from their original paper and pencil formats. Their advantages and disadvantages as tools of selection are debated in Chapter 11. Our purpose here is to explain how they can be used as a means of screening out (or screening in) candidates who make applications via a website. As with online application forms, personality questionnaires can be scored electronically, those candidates who do not meet the employer's criteria being sifted out within a few minutes of completing the test.

There are drawbacks to the use of personality tests in this way. First, they are not completed within a set time limit. This allows the candidate greater opportunity to think carefully about what answer is sought and to give that rather than an answer which is truthful. Secondly, the employer cannot know that it is the candidate himself or herself who is completing the inventory. Finally, as has been pointed out by McHenry (see Lamb 2000:12) online testing gives no opportunity for face to face feedback which has always been considered good practice in the administration of personality tests.

ONLINE ABILITY TESTS

The fact that online tests can be completed by anyone, and not necessarily the candidates themselves, is a particularly acute problem in the case of online ability testing. However, this has not stopped some test providers from developing tools of this kind. As with the other forms of test identified above, these allow poorer candidates to be screened out, meaning that only those achieving the highest scores proceed to the next stage. Two methods seem to be used as a means of reducing the likelihood of 'cheating' (see IRS 2001d:9). First, the tests are designed to be 'game-like in appearance and functionality', so that applicants are not necessarily aware that they are in fact screening tests. Secondly they are deliberately designed to be enjoyable exercises so that individuals will want to complete them and will be less inclined to get someone else to do so on their behalf.

Whatever drawbacks such tests have at the shortlisting stage, they remain potentially useful later in the selection procedure when candidates can be asked to complete them while sitting in front of a terminal on the employer's own premises.

CV-MATCHING TECHNOLOGIES

The fourth approach differs from the first three in that it makes use of IT to screen out CVs submitted by candidates rather than a form designed by the employer. Here use is made of software which searches for key-words in each CV that is submitted (examples would be 'teamwork', 'initiative', 'self-confidence' or 'leadership'). Those which mention enough of the key words identified as being desirable by the employer are then sent on to the recruiter for further analysis. Those which mention none or insufficient of the key words are rejected electronically with a polite but definitive e-mail.

This whole concept is highly questionable professionally as it introduces a strong element of chance into the shortlisting procedure. Good candidates are rejected simply because they have used one word rather than another, while poor ones slip through the net by chance having chosen a lucky turn of phrase. It is only really justifiable when an employer receives far more CVs electronically than it can begin to cope with. In such circumstances, there is no practicable alternative if applications are to be considered and then answered at all. It is the HR equivalent of a highly popular sporting event for which demand is so great that organisers are forced to allocate tickets via a ballot.

SELF-TEST QUESTIONNAIRES

The final approach differs somewhat from the first four in that the employer does not itself use the results of online testing for shortlisting purposes. Instead a questionnaire is provided which prospective candidates complete, but which is designed to encourage those who score 'poorly' to select themselves out by refraining from making an application. Questionnaires of this kind are 'marked' electronically, allowing e-mail based feedback to be given. A candidate who does not answer the questions in the desired way is then advised that their application, were they to make one, would be unlikely to succeed.

EXERCISE BOX: SHORTLISTING GRADUATES ONLINE

Read the article by Victor Dulewicz entitled 'Give full details' featured in *People Management* (26 February 2004, page 23). This can be downloaded from the *People Management* archive on the CIPD's website (www.cipd.co.uk).

In this opinion piece Victor Dulewicz of Henley Management College makes a number of very serious criticisms about some employers' practices when using online shortlisting for candidates applying to join their graduate schemes.

Questions:

1 In what ways do the practices described in the article fall short of those you would expect to see adopted by professional graduate recruiters?

2 Aside from the ethical issues, what business case could be made to persuade these employers to reconsider their approaches?

3 In his penultimate paragraph Dulewicz bemoans the failure of recruiters to implement a joint approach to graduate recruitment in which candidates would all take the same tests and complete the same application forms. What would be the advantages and disadvantages of such a scheme from the perspective of graduate employers?

PROBLEMS WITH INTERVIEWS

As was stated above, there is plenty of apparently authoritative research in support of the claim that traditional selection interviews are poor predictors of future job performance. The term 'traditional' refers to typical, unstructured interviews in which different candidates may be asked quite different questions. The traditional interviewer thus gathers information in a relatively unsystematic manner, and may reach judgements about candidates on a number of different grounds. Anderson and Shackleton (1993), drawing on a wide variety of academic studies from several countries, very effectively summarise the reasons put forward to explain why such interviews have been criticised for their poor predictive validity. The following list is based on their summary:

- The expectancy effect: undue influence being given to positive or negative expectations of a candidate formed from his or her CV or application form.

- The self-fulfilling prophecy effect: interviewers asking questions designed to confirm initial impressions of candidates gained either before the interview or in its early stages.

- The primacy effect: interviewers putting too much emphasis on impressions gained and information assimilated early in the interview.

- The stereotyping effect: interviewers assuming that particular characteristics are typical of members of a particular group. In the case of sex, race, disability, marital status or ex-offenders, decisions made on this basis are often illegal. However, the effect occurs in the case of all kinds of social groups.

- The prototyping effect: interviewers looking for or favouring a particular type of personality regardless of job-related factors.
- The halo and horns effect: interviewers rating candidates as 'good' or 'bad' across the board and thus reaching very unbalanced decisions.
- The contrast effect: interviewers allowing the experience of interviewing one candidate to affect the way they interview others seen later in the selection process.
- Negative information bias effects: interviewers giving more weight to perceived negative points about candidates than to those that are more positive.
- The similar-to-me effect: interviewers giving preference to candidates they perceive as having a similar background, career history, personality or attitudes to themselves.
- The personal liking effect: interviewers making decisions on the basis of whether or not they personally like or dislike the candidate.
- The information overload effect: interviewers forming judgements based on only a fraction of the data available to them about each individual candidate.
- The fundamental attribution error effect: interviewers incorrectly assuming that some action on the part of the candidate is or was caused by an aspect of his or her personality rather than by a simple response to events.
- The temporal extension effect: interviewers assuming that a candidate's behaviour at interview (eg nervousness) is typical of his or her general disposition.

What are we to conclude from this litany of criticisms? The most tempting and apparently rational conclusion would be to consign the traditional interview to the personnel management dustbin on the grounds that selection decisions reached in this manner are inevitably infused with subjectivity, prejudice and displays of cognitive dissonance. However, such action would be hasty. A different conclusion is an acceptance that the validity of some traditional interviews is probably higher than others. In other words, we might acknowledge that interviews in which the above traps are avoided are likely to have greater predictive power than those in which they feature strongly. It follows that it may not be the interview as a selection tool that is faulty so much as the interviewer. With thought, care, experience and training it should then be possible consciously to avoid making many of the basic errors that have been described.

 REFLECTIVE QUESTION

Where do you stand in this debate? Is it the traditional interview that is faulty or is it the typical interviewer who is responsible for giving the method such a bad press?

THE SURVIVAL OF THE TRADITIONAL INTERVIEW

Another reason for hesitating before abandoning traditional approaches to interviewing is their continued popularity as tools of selection among both managers and candidates. Despite the presence for a number of years of evidence that suggests they are extremely poor predictors of performance, they continue to be the most favoured and frequently used of the available selection techniques. It is wise, therefore, at least to consider whether managers may in fact be right to continue swearing by the interview.

A number of alternative explanations can be put forward to explain the survival of traditional interviewing, some of which have already been touched on. One possibility is that managers have simply remained unaware of the research evidence amassed over the years. Another is that they are aware of the defects of traditional interviews but feel it to be counter-intuitive and therefore discount its relevance. Others accept some of the research evidence but regard themselves as exceptions (ie good, intuitive interviewers who avoid making the classic errors).

Another explanation is the relatively low cost of carrying out simple one-to-one interviews and the consequent perception that their efficiency outweighs their ineffectiveness as predictive techniques. In some cases it is also true that unstructured interviews are used as one of a range of selection tools, and that their principal role is to confirm impressions or clear up points left unresolved from the other selection methods used. However, the most straightforward and significant explanation is that interviews are not only arranged for the purpose of enabling managers to make predictions about future performance on the job. According to Herriot (1989a), there are in fact three key objectives for selection interviews, of which only one is their function as tools of assessment. The others are labelled 'mutual preview' and 'negotiation'.

The mutual preview function refers to the opportunity the interview gives both employer and applicant to meet face to face and exchange information unrelated to the prediction of performance, but nevertheless essential to any recruitment and selection process. In particular, it gives candidates the opportunity to ask questions about the job and the organisation as part of the process whereby they decide whether or not they wish to take the job. Interviewers also have the opportunity to inform candidates about the duties they can expect to undertake and the role they would be expected to fill, were they successful. It must be appreciated that in order to make effective choices about whether or not to accept the position on the terms offered, any candidate needs sufficient information about how the type of work and the organisational environment compare with those of existing or other employers.

The negotiation function is another part of the selection process that can only realistically occur by means of an interview. Here we are concerned with the processes that have to be gone through prior to the issuing and subsequent acceptance of a contract of employment. According to Anderson and Shackleton (1993:42), matters up for negotiation include start dates, relocation procedures and allowances, training provisions and all other terms and conditions of employment.

A further role played by an interview is that of a labour market public relations exercise. There is every advantage to be gained from sending candidates away (a) believing that they would like the job if subsequently offered it, (b) determined to seek other positions within the organisation if other opportunities present themselves, and (c) willing to speak well of the organisation because of the efficiency, effectiveness, fairness and courtesy displayed towards them. The interview provides the only real opportunity for organisations to carry out this PR function with any degree of success.

Poor selection, on the other hand, leads to damaging, negative PR. If individuals depart perceiving that they have been treated unfairly, incompetently or harshly, they are likely to share their experiences with others. As the word spreads, it almost inevitably becomes embellished and distorted with repetition, which is exactly what we find in the field of consumer affairs. In 1986, the Ford Motor Company discovered that people who are pleased about their cars tell an average of eight others, whereas dissatisfied customers boast about their experiences to at least 22 others (who in turn tell 22 others, and so on). The result is that, in the realm of products and services, organisations lose customers; in the field of selection, organisations lose potential talent. It is not even absurd to believe that individuals treated badly as candidates might withdraw their business from the offending organisation, and that they might encourage others to do so as well. It can thus be contended that giving no interview, as much as giving a bad one, is likely to lead to such occurrences. People expect to be interviewed, and will not feel that they have had a fair hearing or respectful treatment if one is denied.

It can therefore be concluded that the interview has a number of distinct objectives, and that these can be summarised as follows:

- to predict future job performance and behaviour
- to focus on aspects of behaviour and performance that cannot easily be addressed by other methods
- to supply information to the candidate
- to persuade suitable candidates to accept the job offered and join the organisation
- to create good will for the organisation.

For these reasons, whatever the potential dangers of relying too heavily on traditional interviews, there is no practical substitute for some form of informal face-to-face meeting between employer and candidate. The interview is the only way in which the range of fragmented information about candidates gathered from the use of other selection techniques can be integrated into a meaningful pattern.

IMPRESSION MANAGEMENT

In 1998 Liz Whalley and Mike Smith published a fascinating book called *Deception in Selection* which examined the different ways in which both employers and potential employees seek to manipulate selection processes and mislead one another. One of their chapters concerns interviews. Here they set out how candidates for jobs use impression management techniques to impress interviewers – activities that are far easier to undertake in traditional than in structured types of interview.

One technique involves taking an assertive or pro-active approach. Here the candidate confidently exaggerates their past achievements or elaborates them somewhat so as to appear more impressive. There is also a tendency for candidates to talk assuredly, but not truthfully, about exciting future plans. When carried out convincingly interviewers are impressed not only by the achievements themselves, but also by the implication that they provide evidence of attributes such as assertiveness and natural leadership ability. Common examples are a willingness to claim personal credit for some kind of positive outcome or to make out that an outcome was more positive than was the case in truth.

The other major impression management technique used is defensive or reactive in nature. Here the candidate seeks to minimise the significance of their perceived weaknesses in a form of 'damage limitation exercise'. In interviews these often focus on reasons for leaving past jobs. Candidates will, for example, frequently be reluctant to admit they were fired or, if they admit that, will want to make out it was not their fault. They will say either that they were made redundant, or that all the fault was on the part of the manager.

Whalley and Smith argue that impression management of this kind is not necessarily a bad thing. It may reduce the predictive validity of the interview (if interviewers are sufficiently taken in), but it can also provide strong evidence of the ability to create a good impression – a necessary attribute in many management and customer-facing roles.

VARIETIES OF INTERVIEW FORMAT

Interviews and interview questions come in diverse forms. For this reason, when one is about to be interviewed, it is very difficult to predict exactly what will be involved or the general approach to questioning that will be taken. An obvious variable is the number of interviewers – will the interview be conducted by one person, by two, or by a panel?

The one-to-one interview has the advantage of informality and thus helps reduce the artificiality of the process. The intimacy makes it relatively straightforward to gain an interviewee's trust and thus to encourage them to relax. In the view of Munro Fraser (1979:140), this is the most important objective of any interview:

> The first requirement of a selection interview is that the interviewee should feel at ease and that he should talk freely and frankly. In practically every case, this will depend on the skill of the interviewer. If he behaves in a formal manner, asking questions and appearing to evaluate the answers, he will cease to be an interviewer and become an interrogator. There will thus be little chance that the interviewee will behave in his normal manner, and the amount of information he supplies will be minimal.

However, against this are the considerable drawbacks of cosy one-to-one interviews. First, there is the danger alluded to above of information overload. It is very difficult for one interviewer simultaneously to encourage openness by relaxing the candidate while concentrating on what he or she is saying and considering what question is best to ask next. What is gained in informality is lost in effectiveness. Secondly, having just one interviewer greatly increases the possibility of unfair bias in the final decision. Many of the problems with traditional interviews discussed above – particularly the halo and horns effect, the similar-to-me effect and the personal liking effect – are far less likely to play a part in the evaluation of candidates if multiple interviewers have to justify their thinking to one another.

While drawbacks can be ameliorated to an extent by the presence of two interviewers, it is only in the panel format that information overload and unfair bias are excluded to a satisfactory degree. However, the panel interview (when up to a dozen interviewers are present together) suffers from the very artificiality and formality that are such positive features of the one-to-one and two-to-one formats.

Panel interviews are also difficult to arrange, as so many people have to make sure they are available at the same time over a day or two while a series of candidates are seen. According to Anderson and Shackleton (1993:75), they are also frequently controlled poorly, leading to the presence of unprofessional practices. Perhaps the best solution of all is the sequential interview, in which the candidate is interviewed by several people over a period of time, but only sees one or two at a time. In principle, such an approach is the best of both worlds. The danger here, however, is that each interviewer or duo simply ask the same questions as each other. The result is a bored candidate and less information on which to make selection decisions. Sequential interviewing thus only lives up to expectations when different interviewers agree in advance which areas of questioning each will cover.

PUBLIC SECTOR V PRIVATE SECTOR APPROACHES

In 2007 IRS Employment Review carried out an extensive survey of selection practices used in UK organisations. One of the most interesting findings was the difference in approaches used in most public sector and private sector organisations. In pretty well all areas public sector employers take greater care to adhere to approaches which are commonly defined as constituting 'best practice', but which also tend to be more bureaucratic and more costly than the less formal approaches used in some, but by no means all, private sector organisations.

Nowhere is the contrast greater than in selection interviewing. For example, it is very rare indeed for anyone applying for a public sector job to be interviewed by a single person on a one-to-one basis. IRS found that only 3 per cent of public sector organisations ever use such an approach, while 100 per cent make use of panel-based interviews. In the private sector there is a much greater variety of practice. In the service sector 35 per cent of employers use one-to-one interviews, the figure being 47 per cent in the manufacturing sector.

There are also big differences in other areas. In the public sector interviewing duties are much more likely to be carried out by line managers without the presence of an HR manager. Moreover in 81 per cent of cases it is the line manager who is expected to 'take the lead in the interview process'. Here too practice is far more diverse in the private sector. Managers in the public sector are also twice as likely as their private sector counterparts to be trained in interviewing practice via specialised, in-house training courses.

Source: Murphy (2007a)

VARIETIES OF INTERVIEW QUESTION

Another way that interviews vary is in the type of questions asked. While there are many approaches, three types are given particular attention in the literature: hypothetical, behavioural and stress questions.

HYPOTHETICAL QUESTIONS

Also referred to as problem-solving or situational questioning, this method involves asking candidates how they would react or behave in specific situations. The problems posed will usually be examples of those that might be encountered in the job in question, but there may be situations in which examples from outside work could be used in an attempt to obtain evidence of the candidate's customary reactions to pressured or unusual circumstances. The obvious problem, of course, is the opportunity that such questions give the quick-witted candidate to think of the best answer, or that which is expected. When asked how you would react if a customer complained loudly about sloppy service, it is very easy to say that you would deal with the situation calmly and cool-headedly by taking the complainant to a private area and listening carefully to their points, before judiciously offering discounts or complimentary products. The extent to which people would really manage the situation so professionally and effectively remains open to question: it is far easier said than done.

There is also the problem of asking candidates about situations that they cannot have encountered and would not be expected to deal with anyway without relevant training. In such cases honest candidates will say, 'I don't honestly know', or 'I would ask head office what to do' – answers that are likely to gain them little credit. Others will make up a plausible response without having any idea about whether they have answered correctly. To that extent, hypothetical questioning can be said to introduce an unsatisfactory element of chance into the interview. Perhaps it is best to use hypothetical questioning only in order to test basic knowledge about the tasks that make up the job in question, and not to ask about social situations or those that are particularly complex.

Examples of hypothetical questions that might be used for an HR post are as follows:

- A customer reports the loss of a wallet or purse. A manager subsequently finds a wallet which matches the description in a locker allocated to a member of staff. what would you do if confronted with this situation?

- Absence rates in Department A are three times higher than in Department B. What steps would you take to analyse the reasons and reduce absence in Department A?

- A female member of staff comes to talk to you confidentially. She claims to have suffered harassment from two work colleagues who have used intimidating language with a sexual content. What do you do?

BEHAVIOURAL/COMPETENCY-BASED QUESTIONS

Increasingly commonly used, and often more effective, are questions that focus on past events in a candidate's life, the aim being to establish whether or not they have the attributes or competencies required for the job. These are also referred to as Patterned Behaviour Description Interview (PBDI) questions, which seek to focus the candidate's attention on critical incidents from his or her past. In so doing, the interviewer hopes to hear of occasions when the interviewee has demonstrated those abilities or behaviours that are most relevant to the job for which he or she is applying. An example might be a job in which decisiveness was seen as a crucial attribute. A behavioural question would then involve asking candidates to describe an occasion when they took a particularly difficult decision or were forced to make an important decision without having as much information as they would have liked.

In putting this question, the interviewer is looking for hard evidence that candidates have acted with sufficient decisiveness in the past. The assumption is then made that, put in a similar situation, they would display the same behaviour in the future.

When asking behavioural questions, it is often necessary to home in on the detail of a critical incident by seeking supplementary information. Once the candidate has given a broad description of a relevant occasion, the interviewer probes more deeply by asking, 'What exactly happened?', 'What was your personal contribution?' or 'Tell me more about how you reacted'. Only when hard evidence of the behaviour in question has been gained can the candidate be deemed acceptable on that count. It is harder to make up answers to behavioural than hypothetical questions because of the need to give believable answers to the probing supplementaries. They also have the advantage, from the interviewer's point of view, of providing a good basis on which to justify an appointment or promotion. When asked why someone was unsuccessful, it can simply be pointed out that there was no hard evidence given of sensitivity, persuasiveness, creativity or whatever other attributes were deemed important for a job holder to possess. A very positive review of behavioural interviewing is provided in Jean Barclay's (2001) account of her research into the subject, while Murphy (2007b & 2008d) reports increased usage of these types of approach among UK employers.

There are few disadvantages of this approach to interviewing recorded in the research literature although, as was shown in Chapter 6, there are criticisms of the competency frameworks which underpin many of the questions that are asked. However, problems can arise when the behaviours asked about in the interview are not strictly those required to undertake the job effectively. It is actually very difficult to pick three or four key attributes or personality dimensions for any one job and, as a result, different interviewers often end up asking very different questions. There is thus clearly a need to base such questioning on the contents of agreed person specifications, or ideally on discussions with a current holder of the job in question.

REFLECTIVE QUESTION

Would you like to be interviewed using behavioural questions? What are the advantages and disadvantages from the perspective of the candidate?

STRESS QUESTIONS

A third type of question apparently used quite regularly is one that is disparaging or aggressive. These 'stress' questions can also involve deliberately contradicting something the interviewee has said. Sometimes, one suspects, this practice has no real purpose and is carried out only because it is hugely enjoyable for a particular type of sadistic selector. However, some argue that stress interviews are necessary in some circumstances in order to observe, at first hand, reactions to stressful or uncomfortable situations. There is also no clear agreement as to what exactly is encompassed by the term 'stress' in these circumstances. Some people might find being asked to 'sell themselves' highly stressful, while others will not blink an eyelid when given a thorough interrogation.

In general this author would argue that there are precious few circumstances in which there is any case for deliberately putting a candidate under undue stress. Reactions are likely to be as artificial as the behavioural patterns of individuals in any kind of selection interview; moreover, candidates are being asked to produce spontaneous responses in unfamiliar circumstances when, in practice, they would have the opportunity to think about options in advance. There is also a grave danger that the interviewee will react badly, assume that the interviewer has acted unprofessionally and share their negative experiences with others. In this respect the stress interview can be said to generate bad labour-market PR of the kind described earlier.

Of course, not all interview questions fit neatly into one of these three categories. There is a case for asking easy-going and chatty questions to which there are obvious answers in order to put candidates at their ease and hence glean more meaningful information. Such approaches are particularly useful at the start of interviews when candidates may be less than forthcoming, because they are apprehensive.

However, at all times, there are certain basic rules to follow in posing interview questions. According to Goodworth (1979:51–61), these include the following:

- Ask open-ended questions, ie those starting with the words 'what', 'when', 'why', 'where', 'which' and 'how'.

- Avoid direct (or 'closed') questions to which the candidate can answer simply yes, no, or 'That's right'.

- Avoid asking questions that reveal the answer you want. An example given by Goodworth is, 'We place great faith in our house magazine as a medium of communication – are you in favour of house journals?'

- Avoid engaging in arguments with interviewees. Restrict yourself to restrained and courteous discussion about issues of importance in the job.

- Ask one question at a time. Avoid the temptation to string one or two together, as this will confuse the candidate.

STRUCTURING INTERVIEWS

The one constructive and consistent message that emerges from the large body of research into selection interviewing is the finding that structured interviews have considerably higher predictive validity than their unstructured equivalents, and recent years seem to have seen a substantial growth in the number of employers taking up this approach (CIPD 2007e:13). However, academic commentators differ in their interpretations of how substantial an improvement is made by structuring. Smith *et al* (1989:9) suggest that structured interviews have validity co-efficients of approximately 0.3, although they also refer to studies that have found them to have greater predictive qualities. Anderson & Shackleton (1993:49–51), Eder & Harris (1999:16–18) and Rynes *et al* (2000), on the other hand, give structured approaches a far better press. They quote meta-analyses that suggest validity co-efficients in excess of 0.6 – as effective as any selection technique can ever reasonably be expected to be.

The term 'structured' in the context of selection interviewing has a number of distinguishing features:

- questions are planned carefully before the interview
- all candidates are asked the same questions
- answers are scored according to agreed rating systems
- questions focus on the attributes and behaviours needed to succeed in the job.

While structuring interviews in this way may be a highly effective method of improving their predictive quality, it is not necessarily conducive to the creation of a relaxed atmosphere in which the candidate can easily open up. There is evidence to suggest that unless handled carefully by trained interviewers, structured interviews can be unsatisfactory:

> The main disadvantage of using a structured interview is that its rigidity can limit the information-gathering process. Instead of exploring an applicant's responses by further questioning during the interview, the process is often

rushed in order to get through all the questions on the schedule, and the assessment of the individual can be inaccurate as a result. Also, since the interviewer takes the lead, he or she may dominate the process, denying the applicant sufficient time to provide a considered and accurate response (Du Plessis 2003:179).

The artificiality of these approaches may also dissuade candidates from entering into a two-way exchange by asking their own questions. In short, the mutual exchange and negotiation functions are less well served than the assessment function. There are two compromise solutions that help ameliorate these problems: semi-structuring and mixed approaches.

SEMI-STRUCTURING

The interviewer can opt for the approach referred to by Anderson and Shackleton (1993:72) as 'focused', in which there is a degree of structuring, but also a greater degree of flexibility than a fully structured approach would allow. The interviewer thus plans a series of topics to cover in the interview but follows up what individual interviewees say with supplementary questions. A degree of spontaneity is therefore made possible which permits the candidate some control over the direction of the interview. Meaningful two-way exchange is thus retained.

MIXED APPROACHES

The interviewer can use different questioning techniques at different stages in the interview. Hence, at the start, in order to facilitate mutual exchange and to help the candidate relax, unstructured spontaneous questions are asked. Later, in order to maximise the effectiveness of the assessment function, a greater degree of structuring is introduced, with all candidates asked the same questions. Unstructured approaches are then returned to in the final stages when the negotiation function becomes significant.

APPLICANT REACTIONS

In recent years as labour markets have tightened and employers have had to work harder at attracting staff, researchers have focused more extensively on the recruitment aspects of selection interviewing. Several projects have thus been carried out looking at the perceptions of applicants and at which forms and types of interview experience give them the most favourable impression of the organisation.

Among the qualities that applicants rate highly is warmth. They like an interviewer who appears friendly and supportive rather than distant and cold. Secondly, the research shows that candidates greatly appreciate being interviewed by someone who is informative, who answers their questions frankly and gives them a full picture of the job and the organisation. Candidates are suspicious of interviewers who seem to be overselling the job, because they assume that they are covering something up. They also tend to be put off by interviews which are very heavily structured and give them little opportunity to put their own case in the way that they want to. Aside from being personable and informative, applicants also want to be assured that their interviewer is competent and is clearly listening to what they are saying.

Body language thus matters a great deal as does effective preparation on the part of interviewers. These studies provide further evidence of the gains that can be made for organisations who invest time and money in training their interviewers. Perhaps the most dangerous beast of all is the arrogant manager who believes he or she is a 'natural' interviewer whose style cannot be improved with training or thorough preparation.

Sources: Whalley & Smith (1998:96) and Rynes *et al* (2000:260–266)

EXERCISE BOX: SELECTING PEOPLE TO WORK WITH CHILDREN

EXERCISE 10.4

Read the article by Catherine Waldon of the NSPCC entitled 'Questions of Trust' featured in *People Management* (7 March 2002, page 27. This can be downloaded from the *People Management* archive on the CIPD's website (www.cipd.co.uk).

This article raises a number of interesting and important issues about the selection of staff to work in schools, children's homes and other children's organisations – situations in which choosing the wrong person can have extremely serious consequences.

Questions:

1 Why do some people have concerns about the equal opportunities implications of in-depth preliminary interviewing of the kind advocated in this article?

2 What kind of interview and interview questions do you think would be most appropriate to ask candidates applying to work with children and why?

3 Aside from interviewing, what other methods of selection should be used when recruiting for these kinds of jobs?

TELEPHONE INTERVIEWING

Telephone interviews are becoming increasingly common, being used mainly by employers as a quick and relatively cheap method of deciding which candidates to invite to a formal face to face interview. CIPD (2007e:13) reports that over 60 per cent of employers now use this approach for some of their jobs, a very substantial growth being recorded in the use of telephone interviewing in recent years.

Aside from cost, the main advantage that supporters of telephone interviewing point to is a supposed reduction in the opportunity for unfair bias on grounds of race, age, disability and other factors that might be unlawful to take into account or simply mean that good candidates are rejected for insignificant reasons. The extent to which this is true is debatable, and there appears to be little academic research which backs it up. When speaking to someone on the telephone who we have not met, we have a strong tendency to picture someone in our minds based on the characteristics of his or her voice. These impressions are often wildly inaccurate as we later find out to our surprise when we meet someone who we have only got to know on the telephone (the same is true when a radio presenter we are very familiar with appears on television). The suggestion that telephone interviewing reduces the extent to which interviewers leap to conclusions about people must be questionable. In fact they are often more likely to gain an inaccurate impression.

A rather more sound, evidence-based argument is that telephone interviews tend to be more business-like, interviewers and interviewees focusing on the key questions from the start. There is less general chit chat and hence a greater focus on the job role itself. It is also argued that the quality of someone's argument comes through more clearly by telephone than it does in a face to face interview, because interpersonal factors such as the way someone looks, is dressed or carries themselves physically cannot get in the way of judgements about what they are actually saying.

Research carried out by Joanne Silvester (reported by IRS 2002b) found that candidates were consistently rated more poorly in telephone interviews than when interviewed face to face. Interviewers, it would seem, are happier to be critical of someone they have not met personally. This strongly suggests that there is a likelihood of unfair bias occurring where some candidates are interviewed by telephone for a job, while others are seen face to face. The latter invariably achieve greater success rates.

EMPLOYMENT REFERENCES

The reference letter of recommendation or testimonial is the third of the three selection techniques that make up the 'classic trio'. Like interviews and application forms, it is very widely used but has been found to be of limited value by researchers. As a predictor of job performance it has low validity and has often been found to contain more information about its author than about its subject.

A number of reasons have been put forward to explain the limitations of references. According to Cooper *et al* (2003:154), they are 'highly subjective' and 'open to error and abuse' because 'the flow of information is between two people who are unlikely to meet and about an applicant who will never know what is written'. The implication is that employers, when asked, are generally disinclined to regard the giving of a fair, considered assessment of a former employee to be a high priority. The result is carelessness and a reluctance to put a great deal of time or thought into the writing of the reference. Interestingly, only around half of all reference requests sent out by post ever receive a response (IRS 2001e:11). Furthermore, a number of specific problems have been identified:

- A tendency to give individuals a similar rating when asked about different aspects of their work and personality. If asked to comment separately about someone's social skills, conscientiousness, initiative and attendance records, referees tend to rate candidates as good, moderate or poor on all counts.

- A tendency to give good ratings. It is comparatively rare for employers to receive poor references. While this could be simply because candidates name only people who, they believe, will write a positive assessment, there is also evidence to suggest that employers are generally reluctant to mark someone down in a reference report. A range of average or non-committal ratings or statements thus often indicates a weak performer.

- A tendency, when given a five-point scale, to rank individuals in the centre. Employers seem reluctant to give excellent ratings.

Suff (2008) reports the results of research which suggests that employers are 'lukewarm' about the effectiveness of references and rarely find them to be useful when making selection decisions. A great deal of time and effort is put in by some employers to chasing them up, only to find that they have little practical value. Negative or even semi-negative comments are very rarely made, while many employers now have a policy of only providing factual information and making no comment about someone's suitability at all. This state of affairs has undoubtedly arisen because of the Data Protection Act 2000, and rulings made by the Information Commissioner in favour of unsuccessful candidates who have asked for copies of their references. In short the law now makes it very difficult for a reference-writer to know for certain that what they write will remain confidential. Fear of further litigation under defamation or discrimination laws means that a very cautious approach tends to be taken.

As was the case with interviews, given these damning research findings it is reasonable to ask why references retain their near universal appeal for employers. Here, too, the answer probably lies in the function that references fulfil. According to CIPD (2009b:10), only 19 per cent of employers take up references before the selection decision has been made. The aim is therefore less to assist in the prediction of job performance and more to do with double-checking factual information and seeking confirmation of general impressions gained during the selection process. The reference provides one more piece of information, but is rarely crucial in determining who will get a job.

There are three exceptions to this. The first is the case of internal candidates. In large organisations where people compete for in-house promotions, references are likely to play a more fundamental part of the selection process. In such situations both the selector and the referee will take the process of writing references more seriously. The same kind of influences also come into play in the case of applicants for jobs in professions occupied by relatively few people. Here, although job transfers are occurring between organisations, the chances are that referees know those responsible for the selection of candidates. As a result, references are generally more reliable than they are when the writers and recipients are anonymous to each other. Examples include academic and senior medical appointments. The other exception is the case when a reference reveals that candidates have been less than honest in statements they have made in interviews or on their application forms. Common examples include misleading information about dates of employment, salary, seniority and reasons for leaving previous jobs. Where references bring dishonesty of this kind to light, they can be crucial in determining that offers of employment are not made. Perhaps the most useful question of all is 'would you re-employ this person?' If former employers answer negatively, there is a need to probe further and find out why.

There are four improvements to the process of reference-gathering that researchers have found increase the quality of the information gathered. The first is to contact former employers and named referees by telephone. Doing so is less anonymous and thus increases the chances of a candid and balanced assessment. Confidentiality vis-à-vis the candidates themselves is also ensured making disclosure and litigation impossible (unless verbatim notes are made and retained). Provided that the questions asked over the phone are precise and job-related, this approach can work well. It also has the advantage of making it harder for ex-employers to avoid giving references. According to Suff (2008) 48 per cent of employers take up references by telephone, but it appears generally to be much used as a fallback rather than as a formal part of regular procedures.

The second widely mooted improvement is to design structured assessment forms that relate specifically to the skills and experience necessary to perform well in the job under consideration (Dobson 1989). As with structured interviewing, this requires much more preparation than the placing of a pre-printed form in an envelope. It requires separate forms to be constructed for different jobs, with questions related to the criteria agreed in the job specification.

The third means by which references can be made more useful is to request more than just one or two. Asking a candidate for permission to approach half a dozen referees increases the chances of receiving meaningful information. It also makes it harder for the candidate to name only people who are likely to give unblemished reports. It is for this reason that applicants for positions in the security services are asked to name several referees, including employers whom they left many years previously. Cook (2004:70–72) gives a positive review to the practice of including peers as well as former supervisors in the list of people to whom references are sent.

Finally it is possible to improve the quality of references simply by providing the referee with plenty of information about the role in the form of a job description and/or person specification, together with guidance notes about how to fill in the forms or what areas to cover.

Perhaps the best approach to the use of references, like so many tools and techniques in human resource management, is not to have too great expectations about them. They are not a panacea; nor are they a substitute for managerial judgement. They have very great limitations, but can nevertheless be useful and informative provided they are treated warily. If they are approached in the full knowledge that they are less than perfect and likely to be overgenerous towards candidates, they have a positive role to play in selection. The danger is relying too heavily on them.

People management

EXERCISE BOX

EXERCISE 10.5

Read the article by Anat Arkin entitled 'Burden of Proof' featured in *People Management* (24 February 2005, pages 30–32). This can be downloaded from the *People Management* archive on the CIPD's website (www.cipd.co.uk).

In this article contributions made to an online discussion forum set up by CIPD are set out and discussed. Contributors debated the future of the job reference in the context of 'today's litigious society'.

Questions:

1 What are 'tombstone references' and why have they become more common in recent years?

2 What, according to the article, are effective ways of eliciting full and accurate information from referees?

3 Why is it argued that we tend to be more cautious about giving full and accurate references than we need be?

CRIMINAL RECORD CHECKS

One of the more significant, time consuming and sometimes controversial recent developments in selection practices is the need, for some roles, to undertake formal checks on a job applicant's background in terms of criminal records before a job offer can be made. In England and Wales applications are made to the Criminal Records Bureau (CRB), Scotland and Northern Ireland operating similar regimes using different disclosure institutions. Whenever a job involves its holder in working either with children or vulnerable adults a request for 'standard' disclosure needs to be made. This will list all previous convictions, including those which are spent, as well as any warnings, cautions or reprimands held on the Police National Computer. A request for 'enhanced disclosure' has to be made where job holders are involved in caring for, training or supervising children or vulnerable adults, or where a job puts people in sole charge of these groups. Enhanced disclosure includes further information held by local police forces as well as that held on the national computer database.

The number of checks carried out each year is currently running at around three million, leading to frequent delays on the part of the records bureaus which cause inconvenience to employers and would-be employees alike. According to Suff (2008) over half of the employers responding to a recent IRS survey complained that delays in getting access to an individual's record were causing difficulties for them, including cases of new recruits withdrawing because they are not prepared to wait any longer to hear if their applications have or have not been successful. Of greater concern are situations in which the agencies make mistakes and send the wrong person's record, often someone with a similar name or who has lived at the same address.

EXAMPLE

'Selecting hotel staff: why best practice does not always work' by Cliff Lockyer and Dora Scholarios. *International Journal of Contemporary Hospitality Management* Vol. 16, No. 2. 125–135 (2004).

This article persuasively questions the universal utility of the conventional 'best practice' approach to recruitment and selection. It combines a questionnaire survey of practice in 81 Scottish hotels with a case study approach focusing in some detail on the selection practices used in nine hotels. The findings are somewhat contrary to those that are usually reported in the selection and 'best practice' literatures. Hotels which are part of larger chains with centralised P&D functions tend to use the more formal, sophisticated approaches to selection recommended in the best practice literature. Independent hotels, as well as those which are part of chains but which are characterised by very high standards of customer service, tend, on the contrary, to recruit and select using informal methods of the kind damned in the literature for lacking predictive validity. Yet staff turnover is lower in the case of the hotels using informal processes, while they also have far fewer recruitment difficulties. In other words, in this industry it appears that failing to adopt 'best practice' leads to the best staffing outcomes.

Questions:

1 Why do independently managed hotels persist with the use of informal recruitment and selection methods?

2 What explanations do Lockyer and Scholarios give for concluding that informal methods can amount to 'best practice' in the hotel industry?

3 How persuasive do you find the conclusion? Why?

4 To what extent might the findings be generalised beyond the Scottish hotel industry and why?

KEY ARTICLE BOX

EXPLORE FURTHER

- There is good coverage given to the general topic of research into employee selection in all the current personnel management text books. The most accessible books on the topic are *Selection and assessment: a new appraisal* by Mike Smith, Mike Gregg and Dick Andrews (1989), *Recruitment and selection: a framework for success* by Dominic Cooper, Ivan Robinson and Gordon Tinline (2003), *Personnel selection: adding value through people* by Mark Cook (2004) and *Assessment methods in recruitment, selection and performance* by Robert Edenborough (2005). Lievens and Chapman (2010) are good on current developments in academic research on employee selection.

- There has been a great deal published on the topic of selection interviewing. All the above texts discuss the topic in detail as do two specialist academic books of edited articles: *Assessment and selection in organisations* edited by Peter Herriot (1989b), and *The employment interview handbook* edited by Robert Eder and Michael Harris (1999). More recent research is reviewed by Schmitt and Chan (1998), Rynes *et al* (2000), Salgado (2001) and Cook & Cripps (2005).

- The best general guide to interviewing practice is *Successful selection interviewing* by Neil Anderson and Vivian Shackleton (1993). While being somewhat dated now, this is rooted in academic research but is aimed at students and practitioners, and is very accessible.

- Comparatively little has been written on the subjects of application forms and references. However, Paul Dobson's article on references in the book of articles edited by Herriot (1989a) is useful, as are the relevant sections of Mark Cook's general text on selection referred to above. A useful critical perspective on all these approaches is provided by Rosalind Searle (2003). Online application processes are discussed effectively by Reynolds & Weiner (2009).

- The subjects covered in this chapter, particularly selection interviewing, have long been the focus of extensive academic research and debate among occupational psychologists. Online searches of the psychological journals always yield dozens of examples of academic papers on these subjects, including original validity studies.

CHAPTER 11

Advanced methods of employee selection

LEARNING OUTCOMES

By the end of this chapter, readers should be able to:

- advise on the sources and standards for biodata, assessment centres, aptitude and personality tests
- recommend and assist in devising a variety of exercises for use in an assessment centre
- seek and evaluate sources of professional advice about psychometric testing and other 'high-validity' selection methods.

In addition readers should be able to understand and explain the:

- benefits and shortcomings of biodata, aptitude tests, personality tests and assessment centres
- different situations in which each would or would not be appropriate.

In recent years, despite the continued prevalence of traditional methods in employee selection, there has been increased interest shown by employers in a range of other techniques. While few have dispensed altogether with interviews, references and application forms, substantial numbers now supplement information gathered from their use with a range of more sophisticated assessment techniques (CIPD 2009b:10). Such methods cost a great deal more to operate fairly and effectively, but have all performed comparatively well when subjected to analysis by occupational psychologists. As a result, they can probably be said to be the most accurate techniques available in terms of their ability to predict job performance. In this chapter we complete our discussion of employee selection by examining four specific 'high-validity' selection methods: biodata analysis, ability tests, personality tests and assessment centres.

BIODATA

The use of biodata (biographical data) to predict job performance has a long history. According to Furnham (2005:196–7), its use can be traced to the early twentieth century, and it has attracted the attention of researchers ever since. However, in the UK the method has only ever been used by a small minority of employers. The most recent CIPD surveys have not registered any use at all, although it is clear that employers are moving in this broad direction through the design of lengthier and more sophisticated application forms, often completed online (Reynolds and Weiner 2009:82–83). The lack of usage is probably because, in spite of its apparent high validity, biodata remains both controversial and costly to develop. In practice it thus tends to be used only in the limited number of situations to which it is most suited.

Selection using biodata takes a number of forms, but at base all involve using detailed information concerning an applicant's past to make deductions about his or her likely performance in a future job. Typically, the employer using the approach requires applicants to fill in a detailed questionnaire that contains a large number of items about their work and personal lives. These often take a multiple choice form, allowing for ease of analysis. The questionnaire is usually sent to applicants in the post with a request that it should be returned within a few days. The data collected is then fed into a computer and a score generated. Some companies now take a more direct approach and read out the questions over the telephone, while others use online tests which contain questions of the biodata type. The candidate's answers are then fed directly into the computer for immediate analysis.

The scoring system operates in a similar manner to those operated by insurers and actuaries, the employer screening applicants according to how closely their history or characteristics match those of the better existing employees. Just as an insurance company determines its prices and willingness to insure property according to the age of applicant, location of house, type of property, type of employment and number of previous claims, the employer using biodata seeks to predict from a range of factual data how effective an employee each applicant is likely to be if appointed. In both cases, experience of the characteristics of previous clients or employees is being used to make predictions about whom to insure or employ in the future.

A biodata questionnaire is effective only if designed separately for each job type. Typically, it involves an employer choosing a sample of existing employees that includes the best and poorest performers. These individuals then complete very extensive questionnaires covering a whole range of issues related to their work history, hobbies and personal circumstances. The results are then analysed and conclusions drawn about which questions most effectively delineate between the good and poor performers. The process can throw up some extraordinary results, as is illustrated by the following quotation:

> Mosel (1952) found the ideal saleswoman was: between 35 and 54 years old, had 13–16 years' formal education, had over five years' selling experience, weighed over 160 pounds, had worked in her next to last job for under 5 years, lived in a boarding house, had worked in her next to last job for over 5 years, had her principal previous experience as a minor executive, was between 4 feet 11 inches and 5 feet 2 inches high, had between 1 and 3 dependants, was widowed and had lost no time from work during the past two years (Cook 2004:75).

Having established which attributes are shared by the best existing employees, a biodata questionnaire is drawn up containing the questions found to have elicited information about the relevant characteristics. If, for example, it is found that the best employees tend to have achieved GCSE level in maths and English and that poor employees have not, questions would be included about educational attainment in these subjects. By contrast, if it was found that the age at which employees left school had no statistically significant bearing on whether they were good or poor performers, then no such question would be included.

The use of biodata can be criticised from a number of perspectives. First, it can be perceived as unfair by rejected candidates and may thus have adverse effects on an organisation's image in the labour market. An example known to the author concerns a major UK company which uses biodata to screen out large numbers of applicants for its graduate trainee programme. One of the questions applicants are asked is to identify which university awarded their first degree. The company then rejects all applicants who did not attend one of 10 specific universities. This is very rough on otherwise excellent candidates who may spend a great deal of time completing application forms and researching the company before being rejected on grounds over which they have no control at all. In one case, an applicant who had gained a post-graduate degree at one of the approved institutions was rejected because her first degree had been awarded elsewhere. Another example is quoted by Cooper and Robertson (1995:124). Here an employer found that there was a significant correlation between an individual's work performance and their preferred holiday location. The result was a negative score for future applicants who stated that they enjoyed holidays in Spain.

It is the apparently arbitrary nature of making selection decisions on the basis of such questions that is disturbing, however effective the approach may be at predicting effective job performance. The result can very easily be strong feelings of unfairness and injustice. For these reasons, employers using biodata approaches have to take very great care to avoid using questions that might be construed as unfairly discriminating against one sex, any racial group or people with disabilities. Whatever the validity of the method in terms of its ability to predict job performance, it may easily also fall foul of discrimination law.

Biodata has also been criticised on practical grounds. In particular, detractors have pointed to its lack of portability between job types. A questionnaire that is good at predicting the performance of airline stewards will be very different from one that aims to forecast how effective pilots are likely to be. Researchers have also found that biodata questionnaires age fairly rapidly, and thus need to be revised every few years if they are to retain their predictive power. These factors, combined with the need for large numbers of existing employees to take part at the development stage, greatly limits the number of situations in which it is practicable to employ the approach. Smith *et al* (1989:56) suggest that, in order for a questionnaire to be effective, the sample of existing employees should not generally be less than 300, 'and in any event should be at least four times the number of items in the questionnaire'. It can therefore be concluded that biodata is best used in the following circumstances:

- where large numbers of applications are received for a particular job
- where there are large numbers of existing staff employed in the same position
- where the nature of the work performed is not likely to change to any great degree over time
- where job applications are screened centrally (ie where the process has not been dissolved to separate divisions or business units).

Its use is thus effectively restricted to large organisations aiming to employ the most systematic and valid technique to screen candidates prior to inviting them to an interview or assessment centre.

REFLECTIVE QUESTION

For which particular jobs or professions would you consider biodata to be an effective and efficient selection method?

ABILITY TESTING

According to CIPD (2009b), around half of larger employers now use some form of ability testing when selecting at least some of their employees, some use tests of general ability (such as IQ tests), others focus only on literacy or numeracy, while a third group test skills in areas that are more specific to the particular job. Results from such tests seem most often to be used as a back-up to other selection techniques rather than as the main determinant of hiring decisions. Tests of basic literacy and numeracy tend to be used to weed out the poorest candidates rather than as a means of distinguishing between those considered appointable. It should not be surprising that ability testing is becoming increasingly widely used, as it is the least controversial of the high-validity selection methods, with great potential advantages over other approaches. According to Smith *et al* (1989:9), Cook (2004: 99) and Furnham (2005:204), validity co-efficients of over 0.5 are achievable using such approaches. Moreover it is a relatively inexpensive technique, making it the selection technique which 'delivers the biggest bang for the buck' in the words of Wood and Payne (1998:131).

A broad distinction can be made between tests of specific job-related abilities and the more general tests of mental or cognitive ability. The former category includes the use of typing and shorthand tests in the case of applicants for secretarial appointments, tests of hand-eye co-ordination for manual workers and driving tests for potential drivers of heavy goods vehicles. In practice, employers who use such methods are making selection decisions on the basis of a sample of the quality of the work candidates will be able to offer if successful in their applications. However, in many cases people apply for jobs made up of tasks they have not undertaken previously. In manufacturing this is very common because of the specialised machinery that is often used. In such situations it would clearly be impractical and unfair to expect candidates to be able to demonstrate ability in the principal job duties.

One means of getting round this problem is the trainability test. Here the aim is to make deductions about future performance by observing how effectively candidates learn a job-related task when given a standard set of instructions or training from an instructor. It is particularly suited to jobs in which new recruits are required to master new and complex machinery. An example given by Downs (1989:394) is a test designed by British Airways to assess how quickly aspiring electricians might become sufficiently well-qualified to maintain aircraft engines. Her advice is to develop tests that stretch candidates to the full and, when scoring their performance, to focus on the number and type of errors made.

CASE SUMMARY

PRE-EMPLOYMENT TRAINING AT COURTAULDS

An interesting experiment in employee selection was reported in 1997 when Courtaulds set out to select around a hundred new process technicians to work at a new textiles plant in the north-east of England. Prior to opening the plant, the company operated an intensive evening training programme for prospective employees running over 12 weeks. The courses were held in sessions of four hours on two nights a week and took place at a local college. Participants were not paid for attending, but completed a level 3 NVQ qualification, whether or not they were taken on to work in the new plant. The course was run by managers and cost just £1,000 per candidate to provide. The topics covered included process control, safety, basic science, computing and team-building.

Participants were assessed according to their performance in a written examination but were also scored for team working ability and leadership potential. Inferences were also made, from participants' approach to the course, about motivation levels and likely attendance records. The managers responsible were happy with the experiment (though they have stated that in future they will be cutting the length of the programme). Not only did the course successfully identify the most effective employees, it also ensured that a good part of their initial training was already completed when they took up their new posts.

Source: Burke (1997:29–30)

A substantial amount of research has been carried out in the field of mental ability testing, with apparently encouraging results. Meta-analyses of many small-scale validity studies carried out in the 1980s seem now to have established, to the satisfaction of most researchers, that tests of intelligence or intellectual ability are among the most effective predictors of job performance available. The main controversy seems to be between those who believe it is possible to devise fairly short pencil-and-paper tests that can deliver meaningful measurements of general intelligence in less than an hour (see Toplis *et al* 2005:20–21) and those who argue that a more sophisticated battery of different tests is required to achieve reliable results (Cook 2004:117–119).

In theory, tests of mental ability are superior to other selection methods on a variety of counts. The biggest advantage is their transportability – they do not have to be designed afresh for each job, each organisation or even each country. Once a test is accepted as being a valid measurement tool, it can be used across a wide variety of job types in all manner of organisations. There is thus no need for extensive job analysis, as in the case of personality testing, or for development among a specific group of staff, as in the case of biodata. Tests can be bought from a supplier, and training in their use undertaken before they are administered to job applicants at all levels in an organisation.

Test questions come in a variety of forms and are forever being updated and improved by suppliers who operate in a very competitive market. However, most share the same basic format. First, they all contain questions to which there is a right answer – in most cases requiring candidates to pick from a set of multiple choice options. Secondly, all tests are designed to be taken under examination conditions with a set time limit and standard instructions. Typically, before applicants undertake each type of question, there are practice examples given which can be checked by the instructor to ensure that everyone fully understands what exactly they are expected to do. Another feature shared by all reputable tests is the process by which they are developed. This is a lengthy and costly operation involving hundreds of volunteers to enable the scoring system to reflect the performance of certain 'norm' groups. Norming allows the employer marking the test to know how well a particular candidate has done in comparison with a specified population such as graduates, school-leavers or senior managers.

Some of the most common types of question are illustrated below (Byron and Modha 1991, 1993).

1 Verbal Reasoning

  i Ocean is to Pond as Deep is to

    a) Shallow b) Well c) Sea d) Lake

  ii Early is the Opposite of

    a) Evening b) Late c) Postpone d) Breakfast

  iii What means the same as Portion?

    a) Whole b) Part c) Chip d) None

  iv Which would be the third in alphabetical order?

    a) Sevene b) Severn c) Seveen d) Seven

  v Which is the odd one out?

    a) Lock b) Quay c) Bollard d) Anchor

  vi Which is the penultimate letter in the word REST?

    a) R b) E c) S d) T

2 Numerical Reasoning

  Which number comes next in the following series:

  i 12 10 8 6 4

    a) 3 b) 2 c) 1 d) 0

ii 1   1   2   3   5

    a)   7   b) 10   c) 8   d) 9

iii 10 25 12 30 14

    a)   16   b) 50   c) 24   d) 35

iv 81 27 9 3 1

    a)   0.5   b) 1   c) 0.33   d) 0.166

v If a set of five screwdrivers costs £4, how much does each one cost?

    a)   50p   b) 60p   c) 70p   d) 80p   e) 90p

vi If a 90-litre tank needs to be filled up using a hose pipe that allows water to flow at 2 litres per second, how many seconds would be needed to fill up the tank?

    a)   180   b) 90   c) 45   d) 22.5   e) 11.25

3 Analytical Ability

Janet, Marcus, Eric and Angela sit in this order in a row left to right. Janet changes places with Eric and then Eric changes places with Marcus.

i Who is at the right end of the row?

ii Who is to the left of Eric?

James is eight years old and half as old as his brother Humphrey. Jenny is two years younger than James and the same number of years older than Mark.

iii Who is the oldest?

iv Who is the youngest?

v How old is Mark?

Furnham (2005:207–208) distinguishes between questions that measure 'crystallised intelligence' and those which measure 'fluid intelligence'. The former consists of specific bits and pieces of knowledge that are picked up over a lifetime. Older people, because they have had more life experience, tend to do well in such tests. Fluid intelligence, on the other hand, is defined as 'the ability to perceive relationships, deal with unfamiliar problems and gain new types of knowledge'. Questions of this type are answered better by younger people, because 'it peaks at the age of twenty'.

Furnham gives examples of the two types of question:

a Which of these numbers does not belong with the others?

    625   361   256   193   144

This requires fluid intelligence to answer and will often be answered more quickly by a schoolchild than a retired person.

b Which of the following towns is the odd one out?

    Oslo   London   New York   Cairo   Bombay   Caracas   Madrid

By contrast, this requires crystallised intelligence. You know the answer if you are able to draw on knowledge picked up or learned over time. It is fluid intelligence that seems to be the best predictor of success in a job, particularly among senior managers, and hence contemporary ability tests increasingly feature that type of question. But in practice, the two types of intelligence are correlated. Someone who scores well on one type of test tends also to score well on the other.

Often the questions in tests of mental ability are not in themselves particularly difficult, but become far harder when part of a long questionnaire which has to be completed in a limited period of time. There is also a tendency for the questions to get very much trickier as the test proceeds. This makes it possible for people with a wide range of mental ability to be scored after sitting the same test. A recent innovation in abilities testing is the use of IT. In such situations the candidate answers using a keyboard, and the score is automatically recorded. The great advantage of these packages is the capability they have to tailor the standard of questions to the appropriate level for each individual applicant. If a candidate performs well in the early questions the computer starts generating more difficult problems. As a result, less time is taken to establish the level of mental ability demonstrated in each individual case.

An issue of significance with this kind of test is the extent to which candidates can raise their performance with practice. Opinion is divided on this issue, writers of books aimed at helping candidates to prepare claiming that practice improves performance (eg Byron and Modha 1991:9), while psychologists and test-providers downplay the extent to which this can in fact occur. Toplis et al (2005:73) suggest that retesting candidates with the same test a few days after their first attempt usually leads only to a marginal improvement in performance, a conclusion underlined by research quoted by Wood & Payne (1998:136) and Whalley & Smith (1998:120). Moreover it appears that candidates are quite likely to encounter the same test on a number of occasions, particularly if they are applying for many jobs at the same time. Silvester and Brown (1993) found that 40 per cent of the graduate job-seekers in their sample had completed the same test twice or more for different prospective employers. As a result, the rise of online testing has led, according to Dulewicz (see Allen 2007:7), to the existence of a 'Harry Potter' problem. The title derives from the tendency of would-be recruits signing up under the name 'Harry Potter' repeatedly to practice the same test again and again. Clearly the extent to which candidates can prepare will vary from test to test, with some forms of ability test more susceptible than others to this kind of effect. Another variable is the effectiveness of any feedback that a candidate may be given on their performance when first attempting a particular type of test.

Whalley and Smith (1998) show that candidates often end up under-performing in ability tests – which is just as problematic for an employer seeking the most able candidate as is over-performance by candidates who are practised test takers. The reasons for poor performance can relate to anxiety or can derive from the adoption of failed 'test-taking strategies' involving 'a trade-off between speed and accuracy'. Here candidates opt to complete the test on time by rushing or even guessing answers rather than risk failing because they have not managed to complete all the questions. Some tests also appear to disfavour members of lower socio-economic groups and some ethnic minorities, while others are biased against people whose first language is not English because of the requirement to complete them speedily (Wood and Payne 1998:138). That said, research carried out in the USA shows that it is quite possible to design tests which favour members of some ethnic minorities (Cooper *et al* 2003:128) and that with care and extensive research unbiased tests can be developed.

Kandola *et al* (2000) raise doubts about the way that ability tests are used in practice. Their principal concern relates to the common use of mental ability tests in the selection of senior managers, which they suggest may be inappropriate because factors other than mental ability tend to determine success or failure in such job roles. The studies showing that ability tests have high predictive validity relate to whole populations and not specifically to senior managers, yet employers continue to use them in the selection of their senior people. Their conclusion is that other types of selection method such as assessment centres are probably better than ability tests at predicting managerial competence. Others argue that ability tests, and particularly those designed to measure cognitive ability, are unsuitable when all applicants for a particular job are likely to share a similar level of general intelligence (Cooper *et al* 2003:127–8).

Ultimately, it is probably wise to accept that no method can be perfect, and that some candidates may perform better than others for a variety of reasons. No predictive selection method is a panacea, and management decisions in this field are bound to contain a measure of error. It can nevertheless be said that, according to current research and against a range of criteria, ability testing is more effective than other methods. Furthermore, it would appear to be a least-worst option across a wide range of selection situations. That said, there are of course plenty of jobs for which too high a level of intelligence would be a drawback. Where duties are purely manual or highly simplistic and repetitive, and where there is no clear upward career path to more interesting work, it can plausibly be argued that they are not best undertaken by people who score highly in tests of mental ability. The result would be boredom, low levels of commitment and high staff turnover. Wood and Payne (1998:139–40) thus give good advice when they argue that ability tests are best used conservatively as a means of excluding unsuitable people rather than for identifying top performers.

 REFLECTIVE QUESTION

For what jobs in your organisation would mental ability tests be appropriate? For which would they be inappropriate?

EXERCISE BOX: ONLINE TESTING

Read the article by Vivienne Riddoch entitled 'Safety Net' featured in the *People Management Guide to Assessment* (October 2007, pages 21–24). This can be downloaded from the *People Management* archive on the CIPD's website (www.cipd.co.uk).

This article considers the vigorous debate that exists over the use of online ability tests completed by candidates at home rather than under exam conditions on an employer's premises. Is it possible, the article asks, to devise mechanisms and approaches that either substantially reduce or rule out cheating?

Questions:

1 What mechanisms are being developed which seek to prevent cheating from taking place?

2 What other potential problems with online testing are identified?

3 To what extent do you agree with the view that online ability testing has no future and that employers will soon choose to revert back to pencil and paper tests?

PERSONALITY TESTING

The use of tests that purport to measure personality in the selection process is a field of activity that has generated a vast literature and that remains highly controversial. It is not within the scope of this book to deal with the very many issues that this long-lasting and wide-ranging debate has encompassed. The aim here is to introduce the topic in general terms and to give a general assessment of the effectiveness of using personality tests in different situations. While a number of distinct approaches to personality testing have been developed by psychologists, in most selection situations inferences are made about candidates' suitability for a particular position from responses given in answer to personality questionnaires or inventories (mostly pencil-and-paper or on-screen tests produced by commercial organisations). The validity of personality testing ultimately rests on a number of basic assumptions about which psychologists and other researchers have very different ideas, namely that:

● human personality is measurable or 'mappable'

● our underlying human personality remains stable over time and across different situations

● individual jobs can be usefully analysed in terms of the personality traits that would be most desirable for the job holder to possess

● a personality questionnaire, completed in 30 to 60 minutes, provides sufficient information about an individual's personality to make meaningful inferences about their suitability for a job.

A large body of research into these questions and the validity of the various psychological instruments developed to map personality has been undertaken. Nevertheless, opinions among specialists in the field – let alone lay people – differ considerably, making it difficult to come to firm conclusions about the validity of the personality test per se. To a great extent the jury is still out, test providers and their supporters claiming them to be effective predictors of various aspects of job performance, and others questioning their claims. For reasonably accessible introductions to these debates the following are recommended: Cook & Cripps (2005), Furnham (2005:170–196), Cook (2004:133–172) and Searle (2003:191–225).

For the purposes of this text, and while acknowledging its controversial nature, the broad thrust of the case for personality testing is accepted. When used carefully and professionally, personality tests at least have a potentially useful role to play in the selection procedure. This position appears broadly to be shared by most occupational psychologists working in the field of employee selection. The general consensus is that well-designed tests can, if used properly, predict aspects of job performance reasonably accurately. The problem is the large number of poorly designed tests on the market and misuse by untrained assessors (Smith *et al* 1989:77–78, Allen 2007:10).

THE BARNUM EFFECT

A classic piece of research carried out in 1958 should act as a warning to those who place great faith in the power of personality testing. In Dr R. Stagner's study – written up under the heading The Gullibility of Personnel Managers – 68 managers completed a personality questionnaire. At the end, each was presented with a written profile summarising the main characteristics of their personalities. They then completed a further questionnaire asking how accurate they believed the profile to be. 50 per cent ranked the profile overall as being 'amazingly accurate' and a further 40 per cent as 'rather good'. However, the researchers had tricked the managers by giving them all the same faked personality profile to assess, instead of genuine summaries of their own personalities.

The experiment shows how very easy it is for the devisers of personality tests to profit from their high face-validity by taking advantage of the fact that the results can appear a great deal more accurate and meaningful than they actually are. Personality tests of this type are said to sell as a result of the 'Barnum effect' – the belief that 'you can fool most of the people most of the time'. Prospective purchasers of tests should, therefore, be highly suspicious of tests that produce profiles similar to those written by astrologers in the tabloid newspapers!

Source: Jackson (1996:37–38)

IRS (1997:13) reported that the use of personality testing remained stable during the 1990s, approximately three fifths of organisations stating that the method formed part of selection procedures for some positions. They were used for all appointments by fewer than 10 per cent of employers. Interestingly, this finding contrasts with the great growth in the use of ability tests over the same period, and may well reflect unease about their accuracy in terms of predicting job performance.

CIPD (2007e), drawing on a larger sample of employers, reported that 56 per cent use personality questionnaires for some selection of candidates, the figure being broadly similar for all industrial sectors. CIPD's equivalent survey in 2009 showed usage in only 35 per cent of organisations, while Murphy (2008) reported an IRS survey which demonstrated increased usage in recent years. Whatever the overall pattern, evidence strongly suggests that their use within organisations is mainly restricted to applicants for management and trainee management roles, jobs for which a majority of applicants can now expect to complete personality tests. An exception appears to be the finance sector where their use is particularly heavy, over 85 per cent of employers stating that they employ them in the selection of some staff. However, managers appear not to allow the results to have too much influence in actual selection decision-making, preferring to use them to back up or inform decisions made primarily using other methods.

All the major personality questionnaires available on the market employ the same basic methodology, the aim being to help assessors in making inferences about an individual's psychological make-up from answers given to a standard set of questions. Underlying this is an acceptance of the idea that people differ one from the other in terms of their personality traits. According to Cooper *et al* (2003:22–24) and Furnham (2005:180–186), it is now possible to state with some confidence that there are five basic psychological constructs or 'traits' which form the building-blocks of our personalities and explain the differences between us:

- extroversion introversion (the extent to which we enjoy socialising with others, excitement and change)
- emotional stability (the extent to which we exhibit tension and anxiety)
- agreeableness (the extent to which we avoid conflict and exhibit good-nature, warmth and compassion)
- conscientiousness (the extent to which we are well-organised, concerned with meeting deadlines and the making and implementation of plans)
- openness to experience (the extent to which we are imaginative, flexible and view new experiences positively).

Of these emotional stability and conscientiousness appear to be the two which are consistently important determinants of effective performance across the vast majority of job roles. This has led some to argue that the other three are less significant and that personality tests need not be concerned with their measurement. Such views are firmly criticised by Robertson (2001) on the grounds that they are often more important in some jobs than conscientiousness and emotional stability. Lievens and Chapman (2010) agree, citing a series of studies which show that high levels of conscientiousness are associated with low levels of job performance when individuals simultaneously demonstrate low levels of extraversion or agreeableness, or inadequate social skills.

Another theory states that the most significant single personality trait as far as predicting effective work performance is concerned is self-esteem (see Furnham 2005:211–213) and that a relatively simple test that measures it is thus all that is required. This too is a controversial idea although there is evidence to support it. The problem here is that psychologists have yet to agree among themselves as to why people with high levels of self-esteem perform better than those with low levels. Is it because they really perform better, or is it because they tend to believe they do and persuade others of this?

Personality questionnaires are designed to assist selectors in finding out where individuals lie on scales like the big five. In so doing, it is claimed, it is possible to predict the manner in which people are predisposed to react in given situations. Using this knowledge, selectors can make inferences about a number of important matters:

- how well the individual's personality matches that believed to be ideal for the job
- how well the individual will fit in with the general organisational culture
- how well an individual's personality or predisposition to behave in a particular way might complement those of existing team members
- whether an individual, otherwise well-qualified, might in fact be unsuitable for a post because he or she scores too high or too low in terms of a particular personality trait.

Even if the results of the personality questionnaire are not themselves crucial determinants of the selection decision, they can flag areas to raise and discuss at the interview stage.

Like mental ability tests, the better personality questionnaires are developed using large numbers of volunteers. Aside from testing the validity of the instrument, this also enables each individual's scores to be compared with those typical of humanity in general or a particular sector of the population. However, personality tests differ in that individuals completing them are not usually given strict time limits. Indeed, it is essential that applicants complete all questions in order to enable a full and well-balanced assessment to be made of their psychological make-up.

There are a number of different forms of question asked in personality inventories, most of which require applicants to agree or disagree with a statement. In some cases this simply involves choosing one of two options: true or false, yes or no. In others, a three-point scale is used, allowing candidates to state that they are uncertain about the statement or that their answer is 'in between' yes and no. These fictitious examples are from Jackson (1996:154):

1 I lose my temper over minor incidents.

   a) True   b) In Between   c) False

2 I like giving practical demonstrations in front of others.

   a) True   b) Uncertain   c) False

3 I double-check for errors when I perform calculations.

   a) True   b) Sometimes   c) False

A further development of this approach is to give the applicant five options in response to each question. Such questionnaires often make use of a Likert scale, as in the following examples:

1 I like working to strict time deadlines

  a strongly agree

  b agree

  c unsure

  d disagree

  e strongly disagree

2 On TV, drama series are more interesting than factual series

  a strongly agree

  b agree

  c unsure

  d disagree

  e strongly disagree

A problem with these approaches is the apparent ease with which candidates can fake their responses in an attempt to make themselves appear more appropriate for the job. If applying for a position as a senior manager, no serious candidate will want to give the impression that they lack decisiveness or assertiveness. On a Likert scale it is not difficult to spot which questions are concerned with these traits and to tailor answers accordingly. In an attempt to reduce faking of this kind, some questionnaires use ipsative or forced-choice questions, in which applicants are required to choose between a number of statements or descriptive words that appear equally desirable or undesirable. The following examples are typical:

1 Would you rather work with people who are:

  a) generous   b) hard-working

2 Do you feel that it is best:

  a) to be too assertive   b) not to be sufficiently assertive

3 Which word appeals to you most in each of the following pairs?

  a) effective   b) pleasant

  a) loyal   b) ambitious

4 Rank the following characteristics in order of preference:

Characteristics	Rank Order
Arrogant	
Controlling	
Irritable	
Reticent	
Smooth	

In tests such as these candidates have to choose one or other option, so they cannot say that they are 'unsure' or that their preference is 'in between'. Another ipsative format asks candidates to choose which of four descriptive words is most, and which is least, appropriate as a description of their personality:

1 a) kind   b) influential   c) respectful   d) inventive

2 a) refined   b) adventurous   c) tactful   d) content

However, ipsative questions have also been criticised because they set one psychological construct against another. In such a questionnaire, a question does not, for example, simply assess how conscientious someone is: it forces the candidate to choose between a statement concerning conscientiousness and another concerning extroversion. As a result, the fact that someone is both relatively extroverted and relatively conscientious is not recorded. For this reason the scoring and meaningful interpretation of ipsative tests is particularly difficult to carry out, and raw results can be highly misleading. The extent to which, in practice, they deter faking is also questionable. While it is harder to spot which traits the forced-choice questions are focusing on, to do so is not an impossible task for anyone familiar with the way personality questionnaires work.

An alternative approach to the problem of faking personality questionnaires is to include a 'lie-index' – also known as a 'social desirability index'. While these do not deter candidates from faking responses, they can help indicate to the assessor that the truth has been embellished in some way by sending warning signals concerning honesty. The approach used is to include in the questionnaire a number of questions to which there is, for the vast majority of individuals, only one honest answer. An example from one of the most widely used tests is a question that invites people to agree or disagree with the following statement:

> I sometimes talk about people behind their backs.

Anyone claiming to disagree – or even strongly disagree – with this statement is considered by the test devisers to be giving a socially desirable response, as opposed to a true one. If several questions of a similar kind are answered in the same manner a high social desirability score will show up when the test is analysed. There are two implications for the employer:

- There is an indication that the test in general may not have been completed accurately.

- It may be possible to infer that the candidate is not a particularly honest individual.

Unfortunately for test designers, research has sometimes shown that people who occupy jobs which require very high standards of integrity tend to score badly on lie scales, suggesting that they are not particularly trustworthy. Examples given by Whalley and Smith (1998:114) include civil servants, bank managers and church ministers. This implies either that these people are major-league liars or that they are genuinely decent characters who really do 'never talk about people behind their backs', who 'never lose their tempers' or who are 'never late for meetings'. If the latter is the case, as it may well be, lie indexes of this kind actually serve to screen out as 'untrustworthy' people those who are actually the most conscientious and upright. It is important that test users are aware of this possibility when they come across candidates who have achieved low marks on one of these indices. It is also possible, of course, to make more general inferences about someone's integrity from their answers to other questions in personality tests. Cooper *et al* (2003:141–2) describe a study in which a group of ordinary white-collar employees were tested using different methods against a group of convicted white-collar criminals. The criminals were found to score poorly on measures of social conscientiousness, responsibility/irresponsibility and reliability/unreliability. They also had a disregard for rules and social norms.

A significant and more recent development in personality testing is the use of computer-based and online administration of tests. As in the case of ability testing, software is available that permits candidates to answer questions generated on the screen using the keyboard. The result is far greater speed and accuracy in the scoring of tests. These have now largely replaced paper-and-pencil tests read by computer scanners. Perhaps the greatest advance made possible by computer technology is the extensive print-outs that are now generated summarising the main features of the candidate's personality. To some extent this obviates the need for a trained psychologist to be present to interpret the results of the questionnaire. The print-out permits individuals with far less extensive training to make meaningful inferences from the results of personality tests. By way of illustration the following extract is taken from a print-out generated following the completion of one such test:

> Temperamentally, Mr **** has quite a trusting nature and is inclined to believe that people are basically genuine and honest. An easy-going, affable group member, he may occasionally be accused of being overindulgent, and consequently may be taken advantage of. He will generally give people the benefit of the doubt (without being unduly credulous). Social demands do not play a significant part in determining his behaviour. Not being particularly concerned about how others view him, he will prefer to relate casually to others rather than be constantly alert for the need to observe social etiquette. Although his affinity with group activities is above average, he may have difficulty conforming to its rules. He is unlikely to make a popular group member in situations where individualism is strictly discouraged. Somewhat unpretentious, genuine and rather outspoken, when asked for an opinion, Mr **** may on occasions, unintentionally (or otherwise), express himself in a direct and uncalculated manner.

EXERCISE 11.2

EXERCISE BOX: PERSONALITY TESTS IN AN INTERNATIONAL CONTEXT

Read the article by Fons Trompenaars and Peter Woolliams entitled 'Model Behaviour' featured in *People Management* (5 December 2002, pages 31–35). This can be downloaded from the *People Management* archive on the CIPD's website (www.cipd.co.uk).

In this important article the authors draw on the results of their research to question the value of established approaches to personality testing, particularly with reference to the employment of people to work in overseas countries. In calling for the development of tests which focus on the identification of 'trans-cultural competence', they argue that different types of questions are needed from those that feature on the best established, market-leading personality tests.

Questions:

1 What is Trompenaars and Wolliams's major criticism of existing psychometric tests?

2 How do they suggest these can be improved so that they effectively test for 'trans cultural competence'?

3 To what extent do the arguments presented hold true for selection within a UK context?

PROFESSIONAL ISSUES IN THE USE OF SELECTION TESTS

In the absence of any detailed statutory regulation, professional bodies such as the CIPD and the British Psychological Society (BPS) have drawn up guides to professional usage. A 'Quick Facts' download is also provided at the CIPD website which includes advice on ethical issues as well as achieving value for money when choosing selection tests. The following six points summarise the most significant points set out in the CIPD guide:

● Selection decisions should not be made using psychological tests alone. If used, they should always form a part of a wider selection process. Inferences made from test results should always be backed up with data from other sources.

● Anyone in the organisation who has responsibility for supervising applicants taking tests, evaluating results, or giving feedback should have gained the relevant certificate of competence from the British Psychological Society. In the case of ability tests, these people should be trained and certificated to level A, and in the case of personality tests, to level B.

● Feedback from tests should be given to all candidates – successful as well as unsuccessful – concerning their performance in tests. However, such feedback should be given only by individuals who have been professionally trained in interpreting test results and who are skilled at giving appropriate feedback.

● The only tests that should be used are those 'which have been through a rigorous development process with proper regard to psychological knowledge and processes'. It is also important to ensure that any test used does not discriminate unfairly on grounds of gender, ethnicity or disability.

- Test users should maintain the highest possible standards of confidentiality, with results made available only to those with 'a genuine need to know'.

- Test results should be used only to make decisions between candidates when they are shown to have a clear potential impact on likely performance in the job in question. Test results should not therefore be used as the basis for making decisions based on personal preference for a particular character type.

Perhaps the biggest problem for HRM practitioners is making sure that what they are being sold by the test providers does in fact conform to the above standards. It is very tempting, when being offered an apparently plausible product at a competitive price, to overlook the lack of evidence of BPS approval or the lack of professional training needed to operate the test. The best advice in such circumstances is to seek professional assistance from a chartered psychologist. The British Psychological Society can recommend appropriate professionals for this purpose. When considering introducing tests or replacing existing products, it is also a good idea to research the issues explored above thoroughly and to familiarise yourself with the alternative products on the market. The bigger and more reputable providers of tests have now formed a professional body (the Business Test Publishers Association) to which the publishers of less sophisticated testing instruments are not admitted. The British Psychological Society has also set up an extensive website which provides a good source of information on professional issues in selection testing (www.psychtesting.org.uk). Sources of further reading on this and other relevant topics chapter are given at the end of the chapter.

SIMULATIONS

The most significant contemporary development in the practice areas covered in this chapter is the increasing use of simulation exercises. Sometimes these are used as part of an assessment centre, candidates being asked to react to unexpected occurrences such as might occur if they were to be selected to do the job. More often, however, simulations take the form of sophisticated computer-based exercises which are used to shortlist candidates for interview. Some are bespoke (ie designed for a particular corporation), but it is possible to purchase packages 'off the shelf' which are designed to help weed out the less suitable candidates. In either case the simulation aims to test how far a candidate is comfortable taking decisions and operating in an environment that is similar to the one that they have applied to work in. Producers and users of simulations argue that aside from being useful and effective selection tools, a good simulation also acts as a realistic job preview and thus helps candidates to decide for themselves whether or not they are really suited to a job and if they will enjoy it.

Sources: Smethurst (2006) and Allen (2007b)

ASSESSMENT CENTRES

The assessment centre has been referred to as 'the Rolls Royce' of selection methods, and is the approach that has received the best all-round press of any surveyed in this and the previous chapter. Validity studies have consistently found assessment centre techniques to have good predictive ability, and they appear to be liked by candidates too. Perhaps the only drawback, albeit an important one, is the cost associated with their preparation and administration.

Assessment centres involve assembling in one place several candidates who are applying for the same position and putting them through a variety of different tests. Centres can be operated over one day, but usually involve an overnight stay. They will typically include a conventional interview, together with paper-and-pencil tests both of mental ability and personality. In addition, a range of other exercises are included to test a variety of specific competencies. It is the presence of so many different selection tools acting together that is thought to account for the high validity that the approach has been found to possess. This permits assessors to observe candidates' behaviour in a number of distinct situations, removing the need to make inferences based on only one technique (interview, psychometric test, application form etc).

However, most centres are not exclusively concerned with the identification of underlying personality traits or constructs, as is the case with personality testing. Instead, the aim is to observe actual behaviour in a work-related situation. The concern is not therefore with identifying an underlying predisposition to be assertive, conscientious, sociable or whatever, but to assess each candidate's actual actions and reactions when they are placed in job-related situations. A particular feature of the method is its ability to focus on potential rather than on achievement. Unlike the other commonly used selection methods, assessment centres are not concerned with making inferences about the candidates' likely future performance from evidence of their past activities. Instead, the focus is on anticipating how potential employees are likely to behave, if appointed, from direct observation of their behaviour in circumstances similar to those they are likely to encounter on the job.

A number of researchers have pointed out that, in practice, assessors tend to resist scoring candidates according to specific psychological dimensions, but instead prefer to judge their general performance in each exercise (Woodruffe 1993:199–203). In other words, managers who are supposed to be looking out for evidence of specific behaviours when observing an assessment centre activity end up giving high scores to those candidates of whom they have formed a generally good impression, whatever specific behaviours are demonstrated. The result is an apparent preference on the part of managers to see the assessment centre as an extended interview or work sample rather than as a psychometric selection technique.

According to CIPD (2009b), assessment centres are used for the selection of some staff by over a third of organisations. However, the extent of their usage increases very steeply with the size of employer (they are used by 75 per cent of organisations employing over 5,000 people, but only by 20 per cent of those employing fewer than 200 staff). There seems to be little variation between industrial sectors, most larger private- and public-sector organisations employing the assessment centre approach in the selection of managers, professional grades and new graduates.

The fact that assessment centres are mainly used by larger organisations is not surprising when the costs associated with the development and running of an effective centre are considered. At the very least, the following activities have to be undertaken and either paid for directly or accounted for in terms of management time:

- analysis of the key competences required to perform the job in question
- the development of appropriate exercises to measure or permit observation of the competencies
- the purchase of psychometric tests or other proprietary products to use at the assessment centre
- shortlisting of applicants to be invited to the centre
- training of assessors and other employees actively involved in conducting the exercises
- food and accommodation at the centre for candidates and assessors
- the presence of senior managers to act as observers and interviewers
- the giving of meaningful feedback to successful and unsuccessful candidates
- evaluation and validation.

When it is considered that, to run an effective assessment centre it is necessary to have a candidate–assessor ratio of around 2:1, it is easy to see how the costs can mount up – especially when a number of centres are set up for the selection of different staff groups. For this reason, the approach is only really appropriate for the selection of individuals who fall into one or more of the following categories:

- people who will be employed in the most senior positions with large staffs to supervise or sizeable budgets to manage
- people who will be employed to undertake work which is absolutely crucial to the success of the organisation (perhaps jobs in which the making of errors has unusually important consequences)
- people (like graduates) who are expected to remain employed by the organisation for a long period and in whom significant investment will be made.

IN-TRAY EXERCISES

A common exercise used in assessment centres is the in-tray or in-basket test. Here each candidate sits at a desk and is given a pile of documents to read through. The pile consists of a mixture of memos, letters, notes, telephone messages, e-mails and other documents related to the job for which candidates attending the centre are applying. Participants are then given a limited amount of time to read the documents and state what action they would take in each situation. In some tests they are explicitly required to prioritise their actions by listing what they would do, and in what order, on an answer sheet. Tests of this kind are increasingly administered electronically.

The more sophisticated in-tray tests take place over a two- or three-hour period and require candidates to digest fairly complex written material before recommending courses of action. It is also possible for assessors to add extra pieces of paper to the in-tray and to take away completed work (the out-tray) at set time-intervals. A further variation involves instructing candidates to demonstrate writing skills by composing a letter or report in reaction to an item in the in-tray. In some centres, candidates are interviewed after completing the test to allow assessors to explore their thinking and the reasons for the decisions they have made.

In-tray exercises have a number of very useful functions. They are relatively straightforward to develop and can be undertaken by all candidates at the same time. However, their greatest advantage is the number of different competencies they require candidates to demonstrate. According to Jansen and de Jongh (1997:36), these include intelligence, interpersonal sensitivity, planning and organising ability, delegation skills, problem analysis, problem-solving ability and decisiveness. While the test requires candidates to give an indication of their interpersonal style and approach to dealing with colleagues and customers, it clearly does not directly test social skills such as assertiveness or a candidate's ability to negotiate effectively. On the other hand, as Edenborough (2005:146) points out, there is huge and very valuable scope to tailoring the content quite closely to the organisation's actual day-to-day activities.

GROUP EXERCISES

Interpersonal competence is usually tested by means of a variety of group exercises which a group of four or five candidates carry out together. A common approach is the 'leaderless' project, in which the group is given instructions to carry out a particular task and a time limit, but are left to decide for themselves how the project is to be tackled and who is to do what. The aim here is to allow assessors to observe how each candidate behaves in relation to the others. The kind of questions they will be looking for answers to are: Does someone take the lead? Does someone hold back but contribute effectively later? Does someone negotiate between opposing views? Is one candidate more persuasive than the others?

Some assessment centres give groups fairly involved tasks to complete, some of which resemble management games more commonly used for developmental purposes. In some cases the group is presented with a problem to which there is a definite right answer. The assessors then observe which of the candidates played the greatest part in reaching it, and how this was achieved. Other group exercises are open-ended, the instruction being simply to design or build something, to draw up a strategy or action plan, or to agree among themselves a common position on some issue. Often the group is then required to present their solution to the panel of assessors. Such exercises test creativity and the ability to present ideas confidently, as well as a wide range of interpersonal skills. An interesting feature of some group exercises is the use of the outdoors to allow for greater flexibility in the type of tasks the group is required to undertake.

Other group exercises differ in that candidates are, in turn, assigned leadership roles. The content of the tests is similar but the type of behaviours being observed are different, the emphasis being on how well and using which methods the leader motivates others, exercises effective control or delegates tasks. The difficulty with such approaches arises from the unavoidable presence of competition between candidates who are, after all, applying for the same job. To discourage other group members from undermining the 'leader' it is necessary to point out that other behaviours are also being observed (eg the ability to work as an effective team member).

PRESENTATIONS

Most assessment centres also contain exercises that require candidates to make some kind of presentation or put a case to other participants and assessors. Again, these come in many different forms. At one extreme is the highly unpleasant exercise in which candidates are required to speak off-the-cuff for a few minutes on a subject, without notice. In turn they are simply given a subject and asked to respond immediately. Understandably, many find this very difficult and find themselves either waffling or drying up completely. At the other end of the scale are exercises that test the candidates' ability to make a longer and more considered presentation. Typically this approach involves giving each candidate some information to read – perhaps concerning a specific organisational problem – before explaining that they have a limited period of time to prepare a presentation.

ROLE-PLAYING

A variety of assessment centre exercises employ the services of staff members to play roles of one kind or another. The classic exercise involves observing how a candidate deals with an irate customer, but there is no reason why other job-related scenarios should not be included. Role-playing is a good way of observing how effectively someone deals with subordinates in need of emotional support or effective counselling. It could also be used as a means of scoring candidates in terms of their ability to handle the disciplining of subordinates or negotiations with hard-bargaining suppliers. Another test that makes use of role-playing is the fact-finding exercise, in which candidates are given incomplete written information about an organisational problem. They then each have a limited time to question a role-player with a view to discovering the missing information. In some versions, the person playing the role is under instructions to be evasive or to challenge the line of questioning. According to Jansen and de Jongh (1997:39), when properly designed, fact-finding exercises allow assessors to evaluate candidates in terms of their intelligence, thoroughness and decisiveness, as well as their interpersonal skills.

Other tests used include exercises requiring candidates to compile an extensive piece of written work in the form of a report, and all manner of problem-solving exercises carried out alone rather than in groups. Other organisation-specific exercises include some of the work-sample and trainability selection techniques identified above. Ideally, more than one exercise will be devised to test each of the key behaviours the assessment centre is concerned with identifying. The aim here is to reduce the extent to which situational factors may obscure a candidate's abilities. It is possible, for example, that one participant might appear to have poor skills of persuasion when observed carrying out a group activity, but will subsequently show considerable persuasive skills in giving a presentation. The more tests that are included to test each key attribute, the more chance there is of seeing the whole picture.

A common method used to demonstrate which exercises are testing which competences is the assessment centre matrix. An example is shown in Table 11.1.

Table 11.1: Barclays personnel procedures manual – sample assessment centre matrix

Competencies	Exercises						Total
	GE	IT	PRES	IV	OPQ	WR	
Analysis		X	X			X	3
Business awareness		X		X			2
Competitive	X			X	X		3
Decision-making	X	X					2
Drive/enthusiasm			X	X			2
Leadership	X				X		2
Oral communication	X		X				2
Written communication		X			X		2
Planning/organising		X			X		2
Interpersonal sensitivity	X			X	X		3
Achievement/motivation			X		X		2
Total	5	5	4	4	5	2	25

Key	
GE = Group Exercise	IV = Interview
IT = In-Tray	OPQ = Occupational Personality Questionnaire
PRES = Presentation	WR = Written Report

Source: IDS (1995b)

Assessment centres throw up particular issues concerning fairness. Aside from the need to ensure that equal opportunities law is complied with and that tests do not unfairly discriminate on grounds of sex, race or disability, there is also a potential problem of unfair bias towards candidates with relevant work experience. A special difficulty arises when internal as well as external candidates are present at the same assessment centre. There are two alternative approaches to coping with this:

- Take care to design exercises that are job-related but do not give a particular advantage to those with extensive knowledge of the job or the organisation.
- Retain the organisation-specific exercises while taking account of the advantages to internal and experienced candidates at the scoring stage.

CASE SUMMARY

THE CIVIL SERVICE SELECTION BOARD

The selection procedures for entry into the UK Civil Service 'fast-stream' are notoriously tough and rigorous. Around 80 per cent of applicants are turned down after the first stage on the basis of biodata analysis and performance in a series of mental ability tests sat at regional testing centres. Those who successfully negotiate these first hurdles are invited to a two-day assessment centre known as the Civil Service Selection Board (CSSB).

Before they arrive at the assessment centre, candidates are informed of the key qualities the service is looking for in new recruits. These include:

- the ability to communicate effectively at all levels
- a strong intellect coupled with common sense
- the ability to think quantitatively

- drive and determination
- readiness to accept responsibility
- awareness of the outside world.

In order to test for these qualities, the CSSB includes two group exercises: an in-tray exercise and a series of written tests which resemble Civil Service work. Candidates are required to assimilate information from several documents, make recommendations, summarise information, draft letters and participate in the running of a committee. At the end, each candidate is given three interviews: two with senior civil servants and one with a psychologist. Eight hundred candidates are invited to CSSBs each year. Of these, 22 per cent go on to the final stage in the selection procedure – a panel interview lasting approximately one hour.

Source: IDS (1995b)

EXERCISE 11.3

EXERCISE BOX: SELECTING SPIES

Read the article by Charles Woodruffe entitled 'Intelligence Test' featured in *People Management* (16 May 2002, pages 36–37). This can be downloaded from the *People Management* archive on the CIPD's website (www.cipd.co.uk).

This article discusses the recent experiences of MI5 in developing an assessment centre for use in the selection of graduate recruits. The author says very little about what the assessment centre actually contains, but the way it was put together and continues to be managed are explained very effectively.

Questions:

1 What aspects of the MI5 assessment centre have led the author to conclude that it is a good example of best practice?

2 How would you define poor practice in the development and management of assessment centres?

3 What characteristics do you think the MI5 centres are designed to identify in applicants? What types of exercise would test for these most effectively?

CONTEMPORARY DEVELOPMENTS IN SELECTION

Lievens and Chapman (2010:141–148) discuss some significant contemporary trends in research on employee selection, the aims being to improve the quality of the tools that are available for organisations to use and to gain greater acceptance among managers for psychometric-based testing. Among the more significant developments they cite are the following:

- The development of online ability tests which do not require the presence of a test administrator and can be completed at home by a job applicant. The main problem with 'unproctored testing' of this kind is the impossibility of verifying that it is the candidate who is completing the test, but there are also potential problems associated with unsuitable individuals repeatedly doing the same test until they stumble across the right answers and hence pass the screening process at a fifth or sixth attempt. While these problems will always remain, the next generation of online tests tackles them firstly by creating new combinations of questions of equivalent difficulty each time a candidate carries out a test. Another innovation involves candidates carrying out separate tests, the first unproctored, then another for those who pass which is proctored. The software then uses 'sophisticated verification procedures' to establish that the same person took both tests.

- The development of personality tests which are valid across cultures. A major problem for selectors in international companies has long been the lack of transportability of tests that work effectively in one cultural setting to others. For example, it is the case that some assessment centre exercises predict performance better than others in different countries. Role-plays are poor predictors in countries with 'high power distance cultures' (see Chapter 4), while in Japan presentations work badly as a means of predicting job performance. Recent studies suggest that tools which map personality are valid across cultures, although different types of score will be sought in successful managers in different countries. An international company may want to employ people with different types of personality in different countries, but it is useful to be able to use the same tests to establish the attributes that candidates possess. Valid tests of this kind, developed using panels of experts from many different cultures, are now beginning to be produced for use by multinational organisations.

- Tests that measure emotional intelligence effectively are being developed and used more widely, as are 'situational judgement tests'. The latter are scenario-based and can be administered online. They present candidates with a series of problematic situations of a kind that they may encounter in the job if successful. Some of these tests are simply scored in a straightforward way, there being a 'correct answer' to each problem which candidates with the best judgement will tend to choose. Others do not have correct or incorrect choices, but instead operate like personality tests, the answers chosen by candidates being used to make assumptions about their personalities.

- Research is increasingly being carried out that goes beyond simply demonstrating that selection tests predict performance accurately. Metrics are now being used to estimate what the actual value is to an organisation, over time, if it uses well-validated tests in selecting staff rather than traditional interviews. These involve looking at the concept of 'validity' in a more nuanced and complex way, going beyond an analysis of individual performance to look at a broader range of organisational outcomes. The aim is to demonstrate that investing in a sophisticated and expensive set of tests will yield financial benefits over time, will bring genuine 'strategic value' to the firm and will also reduce the likelihood of successful legal action being taken by unsuccessful candidates making use of discrimination law.

EXAMPLE

KEY ARTICLE BOX

'Explaining greater test use for selection: the role of HR professionals in a world of expanding regulation' by Alison Wolf and Andrew Jenkins. *Human Resource Management Journal*, Vol. 16, No. 2. 193–213 (2006)

In this article the authors describe their research into the reasons why UK employers are using ability and personality tests more frequently than they used to. Drawing on their own case study research and on data from the Workplace Employment Relations Survey, they conclude that contrary to the commonly held view, the reasons have little to do with the increased sophistication and validity of the most widely used proprietary tests, and indeed nothing much to do with their psychometric properties at all.

Questions:

1 What three major reasons are identified in this research to explain increased usage of psychometric testing in the UK?

2 What implications do these findings have for the commercial producers of the tests?

- A number of texts cover all four of the selection methods discussed in this chapter as well as the legal and ethical issues. The most comprehensive are *Assessment methods in recruitment, selection and performance* by Robert Edenborough, *Personnel selection: adding value through people* by Mark Cook (2004), *Competency-based recruitment and selection* by Robert Wood and Tim Payne (1998) and the book of articles edited by Peter Herriot entitled *A handbook of assessment in organizations* (1989a).

- Aside from coverage in these texts, the application of biodata in selection has received relatively little attention. An exception is two articles in the first issue of *Recruitment and development bulletin* (IRS 1990), and the research reported by Neal Schmitt and David Chan in their book on selection (1998). IRS also published a useful article on biodata in 2004 (IRS 2004b). Searle (2003) and Furnham (2005) both include substantial sections on the subject in their books.

- There are numerous specialist texts and a great deal of academic literature covering psychological testing. In addition to coverage in the texts mentioned above, two useful and accessible books are *Psychological testing: A manager's guide* (3rd edn) by Toplis, Dulewicz and Fletcher (2005) and *Understanding psychological testing* by Charles Jackson (1996).

- There are two good books that deal specifically with the subject of assessment centres. These are *Assessment centres: identifying and developing competence* by Charles Woodruffe (1993) and *Assessment centres: a practical handbook* by Paul Jansen and Ferry de Jongh (1997). IDS published a study of assessment centres in 2002 including summaries of the approaches used by a number of companies and public bodies (IDS 2002).

- Readers seeking information about particular psychological tests are referred to the guides produced by the British Psychological Society and to their website. These are expensive but contain detailed and authoritative reviews of all personality and ability tests recommended by the society. Another useful and unbiased review of the major tests is contained in the article by Richard Bell in *Professional issues in selection and assessment* edited by Mike Smith and Valerie Sutherland (1993).

CHAPTER 12

The new employee

LEARNING OUTCOMES

By the end of this chapter, readers should be able to:

- draw up basic contracts of employment
- write offer letters and written statements of terms and conditions of employment
- advise on legal questions relating to the establishment of employment contracts
- influence the evolution of psychological contracts in their organisations
- give advice about how to convey organisational expectations to new employees most effectively
- design and deliver induction and orientation programmes
- evaluate and review established approaches to induction.

In addition, readers should be able to understand and explain:

- the principles of the law as it relates to contracts of employment and employment status
- the concept of the psychological contract and its development over time
- debates about good practice in induction
- the reasons for the continuation of inadequate induction programmes in organisations.

EXERCISE 12.1

EXERCISE BOX: THE BRITISH ANTARCTIC SURVEY

Read the article by Becky Allen entitled 'Anoraks Welcome' featured in *People Management* (13 July 2006, pages 28–30). This can be downloaded from the *People Management* archive on the CIPD's website (www.cipd.co.uk).

This article describes the particular problems faced by an organisation based in Cambridge which employs teams of scientists to work in Antarctica. A number of issues relevant to those covered in this chapter are discussed.

Questions:

1 What particular issues arise in this organisation in relation to the drawing up of legal contracts?

2 How would you describe the major features of the psychological contract established with workers employed at staff bases in the Antarctic over the winter period?

3 What are the major aims of the induction programme? What particular problems can you identify which would make induction processes difficult to handle in this organisation?

CONTRACTS OF EMPLOYMENT

One of the most common fallacies that people continue to believe is that a contract of employment can exist only as a written document. This leads even those who have worked somewhere for months or years to state quite falsely that they 'do not have a contract', when a contractual relationship was in fact formed on the day they first accepted the offer of employment. As a P&D manager it is therefore often necessary continually to remind people that the contract of employment is no more or less than an agreement between two parties to create an employment relationship. It can thus quite easily exist only in an oral form or with an offer letter and acceptance forming the only written evidence of its existence.

There are in fact four simple legal tests as to whether or not a contract exists:

- Has an offer of employment been made?

- Has the offer been accepted?

- Does consideration exist (see below)?

- Is there an intention to create legal relations?

The question of consideration relates to the law of England and Wales. In the modern context it means that the employee agrees to perform the job and that the employer agrees to make payments in the form of wages. In other words, the employment relationship can be likened to a bargain in which both parties give something up (time and effort in the case of the employee, and money in the case of the employer). According to Aikin (2001:10), under Scottish law it is insufficient simply to show that 'consideration' exists. The employment relationship is seen as something more than an economic bargain. Instead, there has to be 'causa', which also includes an acceptance of moral obligations on behalf of the two parties.

Legally this is significant, because once a contract of employment exists, both parties are said to owe certain duties to one another that are enforceable at law. These are known as 'implied terms' because they are held by the courts to exist even though neither party has agreed to them in writing. In addition, all employees are entitled to the protection of some statutory employment legislation (ie laws passed by Parliament). While much dismissal law currently applies only to employees with over a year's continuous service, other legislation applies from day one and is relevant wherever a contract of employment has been agreed. Examples include the right to Statutory Sick Pay, to maternity leave and to a minimum period of notice.

The question of implied terms is more complex because they can vary from situation to situation – for example, where over a period of time employer and employee have both acted as if there was an agreed term or where certain obligations can be said to have emerged through custom and practice. That said, there are common-law implied terms that exist simply because a contract of employment has been agreed. For example, the employer is obliged to pay wages, to treat employees courteously, to provide support to help employees undertake their work, to reimburse expenses incurred in the performance of the job and to provide a safe working environment. In return, employees are expected to be willing to work, to be honest, to co-operate with an employer's reasonable instructions, to be loyal and to take care in performing their duties (ie not to be careless with the employer's property).

While it is important to appreciate that contracts of employment – and therefore duties and obligations – exist whether or not they are agreed in writing, it is far more satisfactory for all parties if there is evidence in writing of both the existence of the contract and its main terms. This will not make the contract any more valid, but will make it far easier to prove if challenged, and puts the relationship on an open, clear footing from the start. There are three types of written document which are most commonly used to provide evidence of the contract and its contents: an offer letter and acceptance, written particulars of the terms and conditions, and other documents expressly incorporated into the contract (eg collective agreements).

MUTUAL TRUST AND CONFIDENCE

One of the most significant contemporary developments in UK employment law is the steady evolution of the implied term labelled 'mutual trust and confidence'. It is a recent development and one which assumes greater and greater significance each year as new cases raising new types of situation are brought before tribunals and appeal courts.

Like other implied terms, the requirement to maintain a relationship of mutual trust and confidence is an invention of the courts and is not mentioned at all in any Act of Parliament. It was originally invented in the 1980s, being expressly approved by the House of Lords (now the Supreme Court) in 1997 in its landmark ruling in the case of *Mahmud v Bank of Credit and Commerce International*.

For the following 10 years the precise formulation was that neither party to an employment relationship would 'without reasonable or proper cause, conduct itself in a manner calculated *and* likely to destroy or seriously damage the relationship of confidence and trust between employer and employee'. The use of the word 'calculated' in this formulation limited the number of situations in which breaches of the term could be said to have occurred to those in which either the employer or employee had intended to damage the relationship. However, since 2007 the courts have decided that the word '*or*' instead of '*and*' should be read in, meaning that calculation was no longer needed. This has fundamentally altered the situation and means that whenever either party does something which has the effect of 'seriously damaging' confidence and trust, it amounts to a breach of contract.

The implications in practical terms are huge. Alleged breaches of the term are now routinely used as the basis of cases in which an employee resigns and claims constructive dismissal, for example when 'bullied', not informed about a decision or required to change work duties/work location without enough notice. Conversely employers are increasingly using the term as the basis for summarily dismissing employees without notice in circumstances where it is difficult to show that an act of gross misconduct has clearly and *knowingly* been committed.

OFFER LETTERS

The style and length of offer letters clearly vary greatly from position to position. Where the terms and conditions of employment are standard across the organisation, the offer letter itself can be short and to the point. A copy of the standard terms and conditions can then be enclosed or sent a short time later. Where the contract is unusual or particularly different from the standard, there is a need to write longer and more detailed offer letters. In any case, the following should always be included:

- job title
- start date
- starting salary
- pay date (ie weekly or monthly)
- hours of work
- any probationary or fixed-term arrangements.

Some employers go further at this stage and make specific mention of bonus schemes, sick pay arrangements, holiday entitlements, pension schemes, periods of notice and other matters. By and large, unless the employee concerned is to be treated differently from others, or unless he or she has specifically asked about these matters at interview, there is no need to include them in the offer letter. What is important is that the letter is dated and that a reply is requested within so many weeks of receipt. Where this is not done, potential employees are liable to wait several weeks before replying, by which time the job has been offered to another candidate.

WRITTEN PARTICULARS OF EMPLOYMENT

According to the terms of the Employment Rights Act 1996 as amended by the Employment Act 2002 new employees have to be informed in writing of their main terms and conditions within eight weeks of the start of their employment. The written particulars must cover the following in a single document:

- the names of the employer and employee between whom a contractual relationship has been formed
- the date the employment commenced
- the job title or a brief description of the work concerned
- the amount of pay
- the dates on which pay will be received
- details of bonuses or commission to be paid
- the hours of work
- holiday and holiday pay entitlements
- the place of work.

Where an employee moves to a new job with a new employer but remains in the same parent organisation, continuity of employment is retained. In other words, the employee is not required to work for a further year before being entitled to full employment rights. Where internal moves of this kind have occurred, the written statement is also required to state that such is the case.

Employees have also to receive other documentation which can be incorporated into the principal statement described above or can be sent separately. These are the following:

- sick pay arrangements and other terms and conditions relating to sickness
- notice periods for both employer and employee
- details of any occupational pension arrangements
- the anticipated duration of the contract, if it is temporary
- details of any collective agreements which govern the terms and conditions of employment.

In the case of employees working abroad, there is also a requirement to indicate the duration of the period to be spent overseas and the currency in which payments will be made. Additional allowances and benefits for overseas workers have also to be included.

Finally, the written particulars must include details of relevant disciplinary and grievance arrangements. The full procedures do not need to be sent to everyone, but everyone needs to be informed of where they can have access to these documents. As a rule, disciplinary and grievance procedures do not themselves form part of the contract of employment, which is stated clearly in the written particulars. Employees thus have a contractual right to be informed that they exist but cannot use the law either as a means of forcing an employer to apply them or to sue for breach of contract where this has not occurred.

It must again be stressed that the written particulars do not amount to a contract of employment. Even when signed by an employee and returned for filing, they are seen legally only as written evidence of the contract and as such representative only of the employer's view of what the contract itself contains. However, in practice, they are generally accepted by the courts as good evidence of a contract's details, and it is very difficult for employees to suggest otherwise when they have not complained of any inaccuracy previously.

Until 2004 there was little by way of a legal incentive to persuade employers to comply with the requirement to issue written particulars. Where the employer failed to do so, all the employee could do was to ask an Employment Tribunal to require that a statement was issued. This remains the case, but an additional incentive has now been introduced under regulations that form part of the Employment Act 2002. These include a right for Employment Tribunals to award compensation of between two and four weeks' pay to anyone who wins a case of another kind and is found not to have been issued with the written particulars or has not been informed of important changes that mean that any original statement is now out of date. Importantly, however, these regulations also free employers of the obligation to issue a separate statement of terms and conditions when they have already communicated all the relevant information to a new employee in an offer letter or have included it in a single, written contract of employment.

INCORPORATED DOCUMENTS

Notwithstanding the minimum requirements described above, employers often expressly incorporate other documents into contracts of employment. The most common examples are job descriptions, collective agreements and staff handbooks, but there is no reason why other material such as a disciplinary procedure or a set of health and safety rules should not also be incorporated. Whether or not this is done is a matter for the employer, and there are arguments for and against doing so.

Once procedures are incorporated, an employee gains the right to sue the employer if those procedures are not followed. For example, if the staff handbook is incorporated and it states that all employees are entitled to a month's notice, then any employee, even if he or she has not yet completed a month's service, could sue for damages if summarily dismissed. In incorporating these documents, the employer is in effect conveying on employees more generous terms and more extensive rights than they are entitled to at law. The argument against doing so is therefore that this amounts to an unnecessary risk.

However, where an employer wishes to be seen as being fair and applying best practice, there is a good case for incorporating such documents as a means of indicating that all employees will be treated equally well from the start of their employment. Incorporation ensures that this is the case and that exceptions are not made in the case of recent starters. The rationale, as with all commitment to best practice, is that as a result the organisation will be better able to attract, retain and motivate the best available people. Incorporation, if done conspicuously, can make a sizeable contribution to the achievement of this objective.

The second argument in favour of incorporation is the clarity that it can bring to the employment relationship. Provided the documents concerned are written unambiguously, they should act to set out exactly what is expected of each party and thus avoid disputes breaking out about interpretation. For example, where a grievance procedure exists but is not incorporated, and an employee with less than two years' service wishes to complain about his or her manager's actions, there will always be a temptation among some managers either to threaten dismissal if the allegation is not withdrawn, or actually to dismiss the employee. Such action could very easily lead to anger or less co-operation on the part of others, or to calls for collective action. Where the policy is incorporated into contracts of employment everyone should know where they stand from the start, thus avoiding such situations.

SPECIFIC CONTRACTUAL TERMS

Employers are free in principle to seek to include whatever terms they wish into a contract, and will be able to enforce these at law provided they are not superseded by statutory employment rights. Similarly, in principle, employees are free to accept or reject any offer that is made to them. However, in practice, for the vast majority of people contracts take a pretty standard form and it is only in relatively exceptional cases that there is a need to require lengthy notice periods, unusual patterns of hours or peculiar payment arrangements. However, where such is the case, there will be a need to draw up a more substantial, individual written contract rather than relying simply on an offer letter and written particulars.

That said, there are a number of potential express terms that most P&D practitioners are likely to come across at some stage and about which it is wise to have some knowledge. In some cases they can simply be inserted into an offer letter; in others it may be felt more appropriate to include them in a separate written contract. They include the clauses discussed below.

FIXED-TERM CLAUSES

Employing people on a fixed-term basis is common where funding is limited or where the job is clearly of fixed duration. In such cases a termination date clearly needs to be stated in the contract. It is, however, important to remember that the Employment Act 2002 limits the length of time that employers can employ people on a succession of fixed-term contracts to four years unless they can justify their actions.

PROBATIONARY CLAUSES

Many employers initially hire people for a probationary period of six months or a year, at which point their performance is reviewed and a decision taken on whether or not to confirm the appointment. Where this is the case it is important to gain the employee's agreement and to ensure that he or she understands the probationary arrangements together with the consequences of failure.

RESTRAINT OF TRADE CLAUSES

Another common express term that is incorporated into contracts seeks to deter employees from working for rival employers in their spare time or using information gained in their employment to help business competitors (eg by leaking trade secrets).

RESTRICTIVE COVENANTS

These are like restraint of trade clauses, but refer to the period after the employment has ended. They usually seek to prevent employees from taking up employment with competitors for a certain period of time after they leave. They are covered in greater detail in Chapter 17.

FLEXIBILITY CLAUSES

It is wise when drawing up a written contract, or indeed when writing an offer letter which sets out the principal terms and conditions under which someone is to be employed, to include a flexibility clause or a number of distinct flexibility clauses. The aim is to ensure that should the need arise, necessary changes can be made by the employer to the contract without a legal breach occurring. Where an employer unilaterally changes a contract without the employee's express consent, causing a detriment in the process, the employee can sue for breach of contract or resign and claim constructive dismissal (see Chapter 18). Flexibility clauses both reduce the risks of this happening and provide a means whereby changes can be made to contracts from time to time without undue hassle and expense.

Flexibility clauses can be quite specifically framed, as for example is the case with a mobility clause which permits an employer to alter the location of an employee's work without breaching their contract. More often they are general in nature referring to 'pay, hours of work, work location and other terms and conditions of employment'. It is important to remember that a flexibility clause, however broadly expressed, will never give an employer the right in law to make whatever changes it wants to in whatever fashion. As is clearly demonstrated by IDS (2009:319–329), the courts have shown an increasing willingness in recent years to restrict the use of flexibility clauses in situations where unilateral changes are made which cause a considerable detriment to an employee (such as loss of income or a requirement to move house). While we have not quite reached the point at which employers' actions are subject to a general test of reasonableness in this area, case law has established that implied terms should not be 'exercised for an improper purpose, capriciously or arbitrarily, or in a way in which no reasonable employer, acting reasonably, would exercise it' (*Birmingham City Council v Wetherill and others* 2007). Moreover, we are increasingly seeing situations in which a change made to terms and conditions is seen as amounting to a breach of the duty to maintain a relationship of mutual trust and confidence, despite the presence of a flexibility clause (see the boxed text above).

CONTRACTS FOR SERVICES

As was seen in Chapter 3, it is increasingly common for people to take on 'atypical' work which does not resemble the traditional 40-hour, Monday–Friday, 9–5.00 form that has dominated for generations.

In these cases it is not always easy to state with certainty that a contract of employment actually exists. It may be that even though the employees believe themselves to have contracts of employment, albeit on an atypical basis, they are in fact employed as an independent contractor through a 'contract for services', which is a very different legal beast. In this case, because the individual concerned is technically self-employed, there are fewer obligations, but far fewer rights too.

In determining whether the relationship is governed by a 'contract of service' (employees) or a 'contract for services' (all workers), employment tribunals are required to look at the facts of each case. It is therefore difficult to identify any overriding general principles that are applied. However, according to Macdonald (1995:2) the following questions are some of those usually asked when a case falls into the grey area between the two types of status:

Is the person in business on his or her own account?

- Is the work performed an integral part of the company's business?

- Is the work performed under the direction and control of the company?

- Is the person obliged to do any work given or can he or she choose whether to do so?

- Is the company obliged to give the individual work to do?

- Is the individual required to do the work personally or can he or she see that it is done by someone else?

- To whom do the tools and equipment belong?

- Is a fixed wage or salary paid?

- Is work also taken from other employers?

- Is tax and national insurance deducted by the company?

- Are company benefits such as pensions or holiday pay received?

In recent years the concept of 'mutuality of obligation' has become increasingly significant when the courts are deciding these issues (see *O'Kelly and Others v Trusthouse Forte* 1983 and *Carmichael v National Power* 1999). The focus here is on whether or not the employee is able, in practice, to turn down offers of work without ending the employment relationship. Where the answer to this question is 'yes' the likelihood is that a court will judge the applicant to be a 'worker' and not an 'employee'. Some employment rights apply to 'all workers, such as the right not to suffer unfair discrimination, but many others do not. Foremost among these is the right not to be unfairly dismissed which is a prerogative of employees working under contracts 'of service'.

EXERCISE BOX: INTERNSHIPS

EXERCISE 12.2

Read the article by Helen Beckett entitled 'All Good Practice' featured in *People Management* (9 March 2006, pages 38–40). This can be downloaded from the *People Management* archive on the CIPD's website (www.cipd.co.uk).

This article discusses the growing recruitment practice whereby large employers take on a number of 'interns' – mainly university students during their summer vacations – to undertake a period of work experience. The practice raises a number of questions about contractual issues.

Questions:

1 Why do employers hire interns?

2 What factors would determine the employment status of an intern as far as legal rights are concerned? Why is this a significant issue?

3 What would be the major elements you would include if drawing up a contract for an intern? Why?

THE PSYCHOLOGICAL CONTRACT

Formulating and agreeing legally enforceable terms and conditions of employment is not the only form of contract that is established with new employees. Equally important, but rather harder to pin down, are the 'terms' that make up the psychological contract. This concept was first discussed in the 1960s and has since been refined and debated extensively by writers such as Edgar Schein (1980). They see the psychological contract as being concerned with the expectations that employers and employees have of their relationship – what each expects the other to deliver, what each expects to get from the working experience, how each expects to be treated by the other party. By their nature such expectations are perceived and exist only in people's heads. Unlike contracts of employment, they are unwritten. But this does not mean that the terms of the psychological contract can be breached without important consequences. Where employees' expectations are not met, or worse, where changes made by managers mean that long established sets of expectations are dashed, the result is dissatisfaction, demotivation and higher levels of staff turnover. Loyalty and commitment are lost because employees perceive that their employer has been disloyal in breaching their psychological contract. Rousseau (1995) goes further than Schein and the earlier researchers in stating that the psychological contract contains more than just expectations. She sees it as containing more significant 'promissory and reciprocal obligations', which lead to anger and alienation among employees if breached by the employer. Guest (2007) and Boxall & Purcell (2008) have taken the idea further still by arguing that the psychological contract contains shared (ie between employer and employee) understandings which explicitly go *beyond* those set out in a written contract. This is an important contribution because it suggests that a positive psychological contract is a necessary condition if employees are to demonstrate discretionary effort and willingly 'work beyond contract' on behalf of their employers.

In recent years there has been a great deal of debate about 'the state of the psychological contract' in the UK and elsewhere in the world. Many influential voices claim that we are seeing a steady and identifiable shift across industry towards the replacement of an 'old' psychological contract with a 'new' one that is different in important respects. In other words, it is claimed that the expectations and perceived obligations that employees have of and to employers (and vice versa) are changing fundamentally. The old psychological contract is usually characterised as being 'relational' in nature. The expectation is of a long-term relationship on the part of employers and employees, in which job security and career progression are offered by employers in return for loyalty, commitment and discretionary effort on the part of employees. By contrast, the new psychological contract is typically characterised as being 'transactional' in nature. The employer offers employment for a limited period, together with pay and some developmental opportunities, while in return employees undertake a defined set of duties to an agreed standard until such time as their career aspirations are better met by an alternative employer. The relationship is thus less emotional in nature and much more a case of a simple economic exchange. The shift from old to new is said to be being driven by greater volatility in product markets of the kind discussed in Chapter 2. Because the business environment is becoming increasingly unpredictable and subject to sudden and profound change, this is also reflected in the employment relationship. The result is greater flexibility for employers, but less job security for employees. Commitment is lost in the process as employees increasingly see their employment as being a short-term opportunity to earn money and develop skills and experience, rather than as the start of a longer-term relationship with their current employer.

The extent to which we are seeing the replacement of relational psychological contracts with those which are transactional is an issue about which researchers are divided. Different studies undertaken in different industries come up with findings that are at variance with one another. Atkinson (2003) shows that most evidence for change comes from smaller-scale studies in which managers, employees and trade union officials are interviewed in depth about their experiences. These tend to produce more evidence of change and of 'breaches' in psychological contracts than the larger-scale questionnaire-based studies such as those conducted by David Guest on behalf of the CIPD. The latter, by contrast have tended to find evidence of the persistence of the 'old' relational contracts as far as most organisations and most jobs are concerned.

REFLECTIVE QUESTION

Think about workplaces in which you have been employed and others with which you are familiar. Can you think of occasions in which someone's psychological contract was breached by their employer? Why did the breach occur? What were the consequences?

Where employers are seeking to change the content (or terms) of psychological contracts, as is the case with contracts of employment, this can in part be achieved by altering the expectations of new employees. The recruitment, selection and induction processes provide an opportunity for the organisation to shape expectations and state what obligations it expects to shoulder in return for the effort, commitment and initiative of employees. It is in the weeks leading up to the start date of employment and particularly in the first few weeks of employment that organisations have an opportunity to establish the psychological contract that they would like to see operating, or at least to influence it profoundly. A failure to take this opportunity, as is the case when no written terms and conditions of employment are issued, does not mean that no psychological contract exists. But the expectations will be shaped by fellow employees, past employment experiences and general impressions rather than by managers taking a lead and focusing on the needs of the organisation.

In practical terms this means setting out clearly and consistently, using a range of communication methods what are the employer's expectations of the new employee and what he/she can expect to receive in return. This is not something that can be left entirely to line managers because of the need for consistency. Mixed messages can easily be given out if different people convey different nuances in their communication with employees. It is best if a clear organisation-wide set of expectations is established and communicated effectively to everyone in the same way. Above all this gives managers an opportunity to convey their priorities to new starters and thus can over time help to deliver cultural change. Examples of the kind of expectations that managers might want to shape on the part of employees could include the following:

- reliability (in terms of lateness and absence)
- honesty and integrity
- professionalism in terms of manners, appearance etc
- customer focus
- quality of work v quantity of work
- flexibility
- organisational focus v departmental focus.

In order to help ensure that the organisational expectations of this kind are met, it is necessary to communicate the other side of the bargain too. Without two sides there is no contract. So it is important to give equal stress to what the organisation offers people who meet its expectations. Examples would be rewards of various kinds, career development opportunities, flexibility in terms of hours, time off and holidays, a decent work-life balance, a pleasant/supportive/exciting/relaxed/dynamic working environment, genuine employee involvement, a fair-minded, open and straight management style and as much job security as can be offered.

Establishing a positive psychological contract and delivering on it should, at least in theory, be easier to establish with an employee hired on a permanent contract than with someone taken on on a fixed-term or agency basis. The lack of job security and short nature of assignments means that less effort and money is likely to be invested in members of the latter group than the former. The psychological contract is likely to be heavily transactional in nature with little opportunity to establish relational terms. It follows that temporary staff are likely to be less committed and that the likelihood of them happily working beyond contract is lower. This conventional, long-held view has been challenged recently by researchers focusing on the psychological contracts of temporary staff (see Gallagher 2008, De Cuyper & De Witte 2008). Two key points are made. First it is argued that temporary staff are not a homogenous group. They comprise people with quite distinct sets of expectations about what they want from jobs. Some are working on an agency or fixed-term basis because they cannot find permanent employment, others are taking up temporary posts in the hope that they may impress and subsequently secure a permanent contract, while a third group have chosen temporary work because of the control it gives them over the way they organise their time. Secondly, it is argued that temporary staff, because they are temporary, enter employment in a workplace with a completely different set of expectations from those typically held by permanent staff. They tend to have lower expectations and to invest less emotional capital in the relationship. As a result, their psychological contracts are different and, crucially, less likely to be breached by an employer. They may have an expectation of increased employability, but will not anticipate job security and will not expect the employer to invest in them personally for the longer term by, for example, spending money on career development activities. It follows that while it may be harder to establish a positive psychological contract with temporary staff, once established such contracts are less likely to be breached causing disengagement or even active disengagement of the kinds which tend to result from breaches of permanent psychological contracts.

EXERCISE BOX: CAN WE MANAGE PSYCHOLOGICAL CONTRACTS?

EXERCISE 12.3

Read the article by Rob Briner and Neil Conway entitled 'Promises, Promises' featured in *People Management* (25 November 2004, pages 42–43). This can be downloaded from the *People Management* archive on the CIPD's website (www.cipd. co.uk).

In this article the authors briefly summarise the history of research into psychological contracts before questioning the wisdom of organisations trying to manage psychological contracts in their own organisations or to use the concept as a management tool.

Questions:

1 Why is it often problematic in practice to set out explicitly what the organisation perceives its own psychological contracts to contain?

2 What are the major features of your psychological contract?

3 To what extent could these be written down and communicated explicitly by your employer? What purpose would it serve?

INDUCTION

Once the offer letter has been sent and the basic terms of contract agreed, the final stage in the recruitment and selection process can begin – namely, the induction of new employees. There is some confusion between different writers in the terminology used to describe events and procedures surrounding the arrival of new staff, so it is important to distinguish between different aspects of the subject. For the purposes of this chapter, 'induction' is used as a general term describing the whole process whereby new employees adjust or acclimatise to their jobs and working environments; 'orientation' refers to a specific course or training event which new starters attend; and the term 'socialisation' is used to describe the way in which new employees build up working relationships and find roles for themselves within their new teams.

There is nothing easier than giving new starters a poor induction, achieved simply by neglecting them and failing to consider their basic needs. On the other hand, making it work well is both difficult to achieve consistently and time-consuming. There is also a need to persuade others of the value a well-designed induction has for the organisation. The following quotation puts the nub of the case most effectively:

> Few things affect employees more than the way they are first introduced to their job, to their workplace, and to their co-workers. If new employees are treated with indifference, considered a necessary nuisance, left to wait interminably 'till people get around to you', loaded down with incomprehensible policy and procedure manuals, given sketchy introductions to the people and things they encounter, left with their questions unanswered and their curiosity unslaked, they are likely to be far less than fully productive new employees. However, if a new person's and the organisation's human resources department staff carefully plan and implement an effective programme for proper induction and orientation, they are making a wise investment in that person's growth, development and output, and in the organisation's efficiency, productivity and future success (Shea 1985:591).

It is not just a question of creating the conditions for employees to reach their full potential as soon as is possible. Important though that is, there is also a need to minimise the other effects of 'induction crises', such as low morale and resignation. In some industries, as will be seen in Chapter 14, staff turnover is particularly high in the first months of appointment. The result for the organisation is the presence of avoidable costs, as jobs have to be re-advertised and selection procedures used more often than is necessary. Of course, not all early leaving is avoidable, but there is evidence to suggest that effective initial induction has an important contribution to make in encouraging employees to stay who might otherwise have been tempted to leave (see Fowler 1996:1–6).

At base, it is a question of recognising, as Wanous (1992) argues, that starting a new job is often a pretty stressful experience for the average employee. Adjusting to a new environment, and taking in and committing to memory new procedures and terminology while building up relationships with new colleagues, is an onerous, confusing and tiring process. It is made all the more difficult when the employees concerned have moved to new locations or are starting work in an industry with which they are unfamiliar. That said, it is also the case that employees have very different requirements when they join a new organisation, and there are thus dangers in making blanket assumptions about what they need to know and how much assistance they will need in adjusting. Putting everyone, regardless of rank or experience, through an extensive, identical, centrally controlled induction programme can well be counter-productive, whatever its intentions, as it will inevitably be inappropriate for some participants.

On the other hand, there are some aspects of induction which, if they are to be managed efficiently, have to be organised on a collective basis and must be provided for all new starters. Examples are fire regulations, security arrangements, canteen facilities, the distribution of organisation handbooks, the setting up of payment arrangements and the completion of forms detailing next of kin in case of emergency. There is thus a good case in larger organisations for running a general induction session covering these matters on a weekly basis and making sure that all new members of staff definitely attend.

Other matters that are traditionally dealt with at orientation sessions held in the first few weeks include a formal welcome from senior management, the setting-up of occupational pension arrangements and general tours of the premises. There is also a need to appraise new employees of current organisation-wide trends and key strategies and to let them know about centralised administrative arrangements such as expense claims, welfare services and rules covering absence, discipline, holidays and the making of telephone calls. Because these activities do not have to be covered on an employee's first day, and because they are likely to lead to discussion and questioning, they are probably best organised for small groups of new employees to attend some days after their start date. This also allows flexibility in terms of who is invited to each session, so that school-leavers, graduate recruits, senior staff and junior employees are invited to separate sessions. Differentiation of this kind will, of course, not be an option for smaller employers who have relatively few new employees starting each month.

Other matters to be covered during an employee's induction are specific to each department or job. They are therefore the responsibility of line managers to organise. Aside from the basic issues of performance standards, training arrangements and introductions to colleagues, some also argue that there is a need for employers consciously to use the induction period to ensure that the organisation's values and culture is assimilated by the new employee. Achieving this is easier said than done, and there are dangers that too regular a repetition of such points can demotivate and actually increase the time it takes an employee to adjust and reach a good standard of performance.

For organisations seeking, and then trying to hold on to, the Investors in People (IiP) Award, induction is particularly important, as they need to be able to show that there are effective systems in place for introducing new employees to their jobs and organisations. The need to provide evidence inevitably leads HR managers to develop control systems designed to ensure that the departmental orientation and socialisation processes are carried out to a sufficiently high standard. The most common mechanism for achieving this is a check-list of points that supervisors are required to cover which new employees tick off or sign when completed. Another means of making sure that induction procedures are being followed is for HR specialists to see new staff formally a month or two after they have started work in order to ascertain how they are getting on and whether or not they have any outstanding questions about what is expected of them.

The other aspect of induction that needs to be worked at is the need for new starters to be made to feel comfortable socially. For strong extroverts this aspect of starting a new job is not a problem: they will relish the opportunity to meet new people and will quickly ensure that they fit in with the prevailing social norms. For others, being new in a department filled with old hands is daunting and can very easily hold back the speed with which they adjust and reach their full potential. More fundamentally, a lack of social ease is likely to discourage new starters from asking questions or being honest about their training needs. Again, there is no great strategy needed to deal with this issue. It is simply a question of reminding people of its existence, asking them to recall how they felt when they started jobs, and suggesting that attention is given to making new starters feel welcome. According to Skeats (1991:56), an approach that can be successful is the identification of an established staff member to act as mentor or 'buddy' to each new employee. This person should be approximately the same age and have similar status to the new starter, and should have a good working knowledge of the job the newcomer will be doing. The buddy then makes contact before the start date to introduce him or herself and is responsible for showing the newcomer where facilities are located. Ideally they will also take meals together in the first days and discuss some of the prevailing norms and unwritten rules that govern the way the department operates. Buddy schemes appear to be common in the UK, Wolff (2009d) reporting research that suggests around 60 per cent of employers operate an arrangement of this type. She sets out the following features of successful schemes:

- choose the buddy with care
- offer training and clear guidelines
- keep it flexible (ie over timescales and the scope of the role)
- provide support to buddies
- reward people who take on the buddy role (eg by making it a first step on the route to becoming a team leader or manager).

Wolff (2009e) reports on a large IRS survey looking at current induction arrangements in UK organisations. One way in which practice varies considerably from organisation to organisation is in the extent of standardisation. Around a third of respondents to this survey put every new recruit through the same standard induction programme. The other two thirds vary the induction to an extent depending on the employee, but there are standard elements in most cases. Some tailor to fit the needs of types of job, others vary content from department to department. Some take different approaches depending on the seniority of the employee, while others offer completely customised programmes for each individual without any standard organisation-wide content. Only a small minority offer tailored inductions for employees with special needs. Only 24 per cent or so of all organisations adopt full customisation, the majority putting most, if not all, new employees through an induction programme which is to some degree standardised across their organisations. Rankin (2006) found that while most UK employers evaluate the effectiveness of their orientation programmes by asking new employees to comment on them at the time, few undertake sophisticated evaluation, for example by surveying managers or employees once they are established in their roles. His survey also, perhaps surprisingly, found little evidence of a move towards electronic forms of induction training.

A common problem raised in relation to induction is concern among P&D managers that line managers do not give sufficient attention to induction processes and often fail to carry out the procedure fully or properly. Induction is too often seen as being a personnel affair with the result that new employees are given little personal attention by their direct supervisors, given a full workload immediately and are forced to turn to colleagues for assistance. It is also sometimes difficult to persuade line managers of the need to release new starters so that they can attend orientation events such as visits to parts of the organisation that they do not work in. Getting line managers to appreciate the significance of an effective induction and to carry it through with enthusiasm, let alone take responsibility for improving it, appears to be a distant ambition for many working in HR.

This tension between the perspectives of P&D and line managers is interesting to observe and not easy to explain. It may be because many line managers necessarily have a shorter-term focus than P&D people. Their overwhelming need is to ensure that work gets done now, and they are placed under continual pressure to reduce costs. So releasing valuable new people for orientation training is something they can only do with enthusiasm when they have sufficient other staff to cover. It is thus something of an unaffordable luxury. Another explanation for the lack of enthusiasm on the part of line managers for carrying through induction procedures is that they are often quite tedious, and by their nature need to be repeated regularly. There is thus a tendency to see them as routine aspects of the management role and to delegate them whenever possible. Indeed the same point can be made about the approach taken by many larger corporate HR functions. Running orientation programmes is rarely seen as being glamorous, cutting edge or important work. Instead it is routine, regular and standardised. As a result the task tends to be given to junior training managers, while management attention and resources are focused on other training and development interventions. This is understandable, but does not make good business sense. Few P&D activities are more important than ensuring that new employees receive a timely and effective induction. Failing to provide one is the best way of ensuring that people are ineffective in their roles for longer than they need to be when they first start, unable to maximise their contribution, lacking in confidence when dealing with customers and generally demotivated. Moreover, the likelihood of early leaving is vastly increased by a failure to induct new staff properly.

Good practice in induction was established in an IRS survey conducted in 2003. This identified a number of features which employers have found serve to improve the experiences of their new starters. These include the following:

- regular updating of induction procedures
- direct consultation with new recruits about how to improve induction
- keeping improvement of induction on the organisational agenda
- making use of several communications methods (eg intranets)
- including job-related training as part of orientation programmes
- producing an accompanying 'welcome' resource pack
- involving senior managers in orientation sessions
- covering informal rules and norms as well as the formal ones.

REFLECTIVE QUESTION

Reflect on the induction you have received when starting new jobs. Which aspects were helpful? How could the process have been improved?

CASE SUMMARY

THE TEXAS INSTRUMENTS STUDIES

A classic research exercise designed to investigate the benefits of induction was carried out in the USA in the 1960s by two occupational psychologists called Gomersall and Myers. Working among employees at an electrical assembly plant, they started by ascertaining from existing employees what aspects of the work they had found to be most stressful when they first took up their jobs. Acting on this information, they designed a six-hour orientation programme designed to reduce stress among new starters. The course covered four areas:

- New recruits were assured that failure rates were very low and that the vast majority of starters quickly learned to perform to a satisfactory level.

- They were told to expect some baiting from established employees, but to ignore it because the same treatment tended to be given to all new starters.

- It was suggested that they took the initiative in terms of communication with others, including their new supervisors.

- They were each given some specific advice about how to build up a good working relationship with their particular supervisors.

A hundred new starters, selected at random, were then put through the new orientation programme, and a further hundred given the standard two-hour course offered by the company. The result was a substantial divergence between the performance of the two groups, those who had attended the six-hour session achieving higher productivity rates. They also had better attendance records and required less training time than those who had been given the standard two-hour introduction.

Source: Wanous (1992:178–179)

EXERCISE 12.4

EXERCISE BOX: INDUCTION TIPS

Read the article by Guy Browning entitled 'New Kid on the Block' featured in *People Management* (15 July 2004, page 98). This can be downloaded from the *People Management* archive on the CIPD's website (www.cipd.co.uk).

In this short and amusing article Guy Browning makes a number of serious points about the experience of new employees in an entertaining fashion.

Questions:

1 What examples of good and bad practice in handling new employees are described in the article?

2 How many of the poorer types of new employee experience are provided by your organisation?

3 What changes would you recommend were made to your organisation's induction practices? What business case could you advance to justify your recommendations?

EXAMPLE

'Employee orientation – the Japanese approach' by Michel Mestre, Alan Stainer & Lorice Stainer. *Employee Relations* Vol. 19, No. 5. 443–458 (1997)

Induction, socialisation and orientation of new employees is an under-researched area. This is a rare example of an interesting recent article published in an academic journal on the subject. The writers are based in UK and Canadian universities, but their subject is the approach to the management of new employees that is typically taken in Japanese companies. They contrast these approaches with those that are common in Western organisations and discuss the implications.

Questions:

1 Why do you think Japanese approaches to the induction of new employees are so very different to those we tend to use in the UK?

2 To what extent do you think it is sensible to 'select for attitude and train for skill'? Why?

3 How far in practice would it be possible for a UK firm to adopt the Japanese approach to induction? Why?

- *Contracts* by Olga Aikin (2001) is a good starting point for further reading on the topic of contracts of employment. Useful information can also be found in most general texts covering employment law. While somewhat dated, *Hired, fired or sick and tired?* by Lynda Macdonald (1995) provides the most readable and easily understood guide to basic contract law as it applies practically to employment relationships. More detailed guides to legal obligations are found in IDS (2009).

- The psychological contract is introduced very effectively in many HR textbooks. Sparrow (1998), Osborn-Jones (2004) and Taylor & Tekleab (2004) all provide helpful guides drawing on the work of the leading researchers. Conway & Briner (2005) have written the best introductory book on the subject.

- Two general management guides to employee induction are *Successful induction* by Judy Skeats (1991) and *Employee induction: a good start* by Alan Fowler (1996). Established academic research on the topic is summarised by John Parcher Wanous in *Organizational entry* (1992).

Succession planning

INTRODUCTION

In Chapter 5 we introduced Human Resource Planning (HRP), a process which involves forecasting an organisation's future demand for and supply of people in general terms. Succession planning is a similar kind of activity, but is much more focused. It involves planning thoughtfully and systematically for the time when people holding the most senior and pivotal positions in an organisation leave, the aim being to ensure as seamless a transition as possible. According to Jackson and Schuler (1990:171), succession planning differs from traditional HR planning in that 'the prediction task changes from one of estimating the percentage of a pool of employees who are likely to be with the company x years into the future, to one of estimating the probability that a few particular individuals will be with the company x years into the future'. In other words, the planning process covers a narrower group of employees but does so with a higher degree of intensity. Moreover, because plans concern relatively few, they can be considerably more sophisticated. The time-horizons involved are also longer than is the case with traditional HR planning.

There is evidence to show that interest in succession planning is growing again. New terms are entering the HR vocabulary – succession management, talent management, talent planning – which bring along with them some new thinking about ways of renewing and modernising traditional approaches with a view to making them more appropriate for the contemporary business environment. This is therefore an area of resourcing practice which is the subject of much debate. It is also one in which the debates are particularly interesting because they have an ethical angle, there being quite serious ethical question marks over some of the longer-established approaches to succession planning used in some organisations. Wendy Hirsh (2000:8) in her excellent short book about these matters makes the following observation:

It is a curiosity of succession planning that it is simultaneously seen as a crucial process and as a most dubious one.

WHAT IS SUCCESSION PLANNING?

Succession planning encompasses a group of activities which aim to ensure that at any time an organisation has sufficient numbers of people with the ability, knowledge, personal attributes and experience necessary to step into senior roles when they become vacant. When successfully carried out, succession planning ensures a smooth transfer when one senior person leaves and is replaced by another. Gaps during which people 'act up' on a temporary basis are avoided as are situations in which someone who is ill-prepared has to take up the reins in a senior post at short notice. As a result there is less uncertainty and much less disruption. Projects, priorities and strategies continue as before, while the level of confidence that investors and other stakeholders have in the organisation is maintained.

However, there is much more to succession planning than this, because in part it is about developing a new generation of potential leaders who will have the capacity to succeed into senior roles in several years' time. Like HRP it thus requires a future focus, pushing managers into looking forward long-term and investing in the development of people who they think will be best placed to take the organisation forward over rather longer time horizons than they are accustomed to considering. This longer-term aspect of succession planning activity has major implications for an organisation's culture, on its capacity to recruit and retain staff, and on the level of performance that individuals lower down the management hierarchy achieve.

On one level, therefore, succession planning can be seen as being relatively short-term, technical and focused on who will succeed Mr X or Mrs Y when they retire or move on to another role. At this level it is highly political, but affects only the senior team and those who report to them directly. However, on another level it is a process which has direct, strategic relevance across much of the organisation and for most people employed in it, informing practice in the areas of recruitment, employee development and performance management.

The process is best understood as a series of distinct stages. Bechet (2008:247–8) outlines the following:

1) Identify the critical positions that are to be included in the process.

In theory it would be quite possible to plan in this way for the succession to all posts in an organisation, but it would be an overly elaborate and costly process in most cases. The tendency is thus to focus on the most senior jobs and on those which are critical to the organisation and which require considerable organisation-specific expertise and experience to be carried out effectively. Murphy (2009a), reporting the results of an IRS survey into succession planning in UK organisations, found that in 93 per cent of cases management posts were the focus of succession plans. 60 per cent of organisations who carried out succession planning also covered professional jobs of some kind, the figures for other types of role being far smaller. In small businesses succession plans are often exclusively focused on the owner-manager or managing director, typically being restricted to family members and a handful of others with the potential to take on the senior role. In the largest companies several hundred posts will be identified on a succession plan and a small team employed within the HR department whose job is to maintain the plan and keep it up to date. For many the focus of attention is on 'once-in-a-generation' appointments such as the chief executive, board-level directors, hospital consultants, professors, newspaper editors, ambassadors and top civil servants. These jobs typically represent the pinnacle of an individual's career, and tend to be occupied by a single employee for between five and 20 years.

Public sector organisations tend not to undertake formal succession planning, preferring to advertise all jobs that become available even at the most senior levels, and to appoint following an open competition among internal and external candidates. This has the advantage of being fair and transparent, but it does mean that lengthy periods of uncertainty and stagnation occur while the selection procedure is carried out. Uncertainty then typically continues for a longer period still while any successful external candidate works his or her notice in his or her previous job. During this time someone 'acts up' into the senior role and tends to be reluctant to make major strategic decisions, believing that it is right for these to be left until the new permanent incumbent takes up the post. Were private sector organisations to take such an approach the likelihood is that they would suffer commercially during inter-regnums and lose the confidence of investors and opinion-formers such as financial journalists. This risk is too great, so proper succession plans are formulated and acted upon.

2) Define the capabilities that each of these positions will require in the future.

Pretty well everyone who has written about succession planning in recent years has stressed the importance of thinking about the attributes that will be required to do a good job in a senior role in the future, and hence of avoiding looking for a like-for-like replacement. Organisational priorities will change over time, as will aspects of the business environment. Fashions in leadership vary and develop over time for good reason and what is needed now may very well not be what is needed in the future. Succession planners need to bear this in mind and operate from a starting point which sets out what the attributes needed will be in the future. Only this way, as Bowick (1996:180) points out, will the organisation be in a position to 'choose a successor who is right for the time at which they are going to succeed'. Bechet (2008:248) goes further in advocating a contingency-based approach to succession planning. Because the future is uncertain, he argues, organisations need to plan for a number of different possible scenarios and ensure that people with a range of distinct talents appropriate to each are developed. Only that way will the organisation give itself the best possible chance of picking the best successor for the priorities and conditions that pertain at the time of succession. Blass (2009:290) sets out the argument for careful consideration of future needs very clearly and concisely, showing how a failure to do so makes matters worse than it would have been had no succession planning been carried out at all:

> It is not impossible to see a situation where an organisation puts in place its talent management system with a clear, objective process for identifying talent, but that process measures the wrong things and the 'wrong' sort of talent is recognised and developed within the organisation. Not only will the organisation end up with a management team that is incongruent with its future aims, but it will also have extinguished the 'right' talent from the organisation.

3) Identify and assess possible candidates for these positions.

Some organisations, particularly those who see succession planning as being an integral part of wider talent management processes, choose not to identify any particular group of staff to include in their succession plans. Instead they take the very principled and democratic decision to label all employees 'talented' and to develop everyone at the same pace, investing no more in the development of an outstanding performer with huge potential than in that of someone who is unlikely ever to move up the management ranks any further. According to Blass (2009:24) this is approach taken at Accenture, the professional services provider. Elsewhere it is much more common to restrict the numbers only to people who have demonstrated serious long-term or short-term senior management competence. Because Accenture's business is very people-based, all its staff are thus considered to be 'talent'. Using the water metaphors that are very common in this area of HR work, it could be argued that Accenture operates a reservoir approach, whereas most organisations restrict their planning to a mere pool.

Identifying the pool and hence who will become a participant in the succession plan is most commonly achieved by scoring staff against two key criteria – performance and potential. Blass (2009:26 and 286) argues for the use of a nine-box grid allowing each employee to be rated as having good, satisfactory or poor performance in their present roles and as having high, moderate or limited future management potential. Others argue in favour of the same approach, but suggest that a simpler four-box grid is all that is necessary on the grounds that the only people who will ever be included in the succession plan are those who are judged both to be good performers and to have a high level of potential. Odiorne (1984) (see Figure 13.1) gave the four boxes names which are memorable and helpful if not flattering. Here it is those in the 'star' category who would be included in the plan.

Figure 13.1 Odiorne's typology

	High Performance	
STARS High Potential	WORKHORSES	
		Low Potential
PROBLEM EMPLOYEES Low Performance	DEADWOOD	

It must be recognised that the identity of people who are included in the succession plan must be flexible and hence is subject to relatively frequent review. It makes sense to review someone's status at least once a year. This is because people can and do move from box to box on a grid such as Odiorne's. Performance or potential ratings can readily change as jobs change and, particularly, as people get promoted up an organisational hierarchy. A person rated as a 'star' in one job, may become a 'problem employee' or more of a 'workhorse' when given more managerial responsibility. The same can happen when a 'star' is shifted sideways in order to broaden his or her experience. By contrast of course employees placed in one of the non-star categories can make themselves into 'stars' given new opportunities or even just a new manager to work for. Moreover, of course, as organisations develop and change over time, new circumstances and contexts suit some more than others. The identity of people included in a succession plan must thus be viewed as dynamic. People should not expect to stay there forever irrespective of their performance as time proceeds. Blass (2009:10) also cautions about confusing 'potential' with 'promotability'. It is only once an employee has fully developed sufficient potential that it becomes safe to promote them.

4) Provide these individuals with focused development that will prepare them so that, if desired, they could assume these positions in the future.

The type of development that individuals require in order to prepare them for succession into senior roles will clearly vary hugely. There is the world of difference between the needs of a recently recruited graduate trainee with huge potential but limited experience who will succeed into a senior job in 15 years' time and those of an experienced executive who is being groomed to succeed the chief executive on his retirement in six months' time. Both feature on a succession plan, but their immediate training and development requirements are as different as chalk from cheese. The key is therefore to individualise the drawing up and review of development plans.

It is generally accepted that a well designed competency framework (see Chapter 6) should form the basis of development plans, but that it too must be kept under review and reflect future requirements and not just the kind of attributes, experience and knowledge-base needed by today's occupants of senior roles. There is less agreement on whether the development of individuals should be designed around their strengths or their weaknesses (see Blass 2009:11–12). An argument can be made in favour of either approach, but in practice it is of course necessary to focus on both. The aim when developing future leaders must be to capitalise on and harness someone's strengths in the interests of the organisation, while also seeking over time to improve in the weaker areas. When dealing with people of this calibre getting them motivated is not a problem: they would not be participants in the succession plan if they were not committed, professional employees. It is thus largely a question of giving them the opportunity to develop by including them on project teams, asking them to lead working groups and moving them up and across the organisational hierarchy as and when they are ready for new assignments. Senior managers need to spend time working in a number of organisational functions and, in the case of larger organisations, a number of subsidiary businesses. International assignments will form an important part of the development of high potentials as will periods spent undertaking short-term assignments of one kind or another. These career steps serve to broaden experience, increase understanding of different areas of the business and to build character more generally. These are then combined with coaching and mentoring sessions, alongside formal training programmes designed to increase relevant knowledge. Many organisations, for example, will sponsor people with senior management potential through an MBA or professional doctorate programme.

5) *Regularly review the progress of identified successors.*

This final stage in the process is as important as all the others, but needs much less explanation. The key point is simply that it is necessary to undertake regular reviews with the individual and among the wider management team about progress. Formal performance appraisal plays an important role here, as does 360 degree appraisal if it is used by the organisation. Formal evaluation against a competency matrix needs to take place along with more general qualitative evaluation with a view to addressing any problem areas in the future. In order to achieve this fifth stage files have to be kept containing information about training programmes, results of performance appraisals, career histories and qualifications, as well as details of any potential constraints that might hold an individual's development back (such as a disinclination to move to a new region or country). Customised and proprietary computer systems are now available to help match people to jobs, although some of these appear to be too sophisticated and prescriptive to be of any great practical use (O'Reilly 1997:4).

EXERCISE 13.1

EXERCISE BOX: NURTURING SENIOR MANAGERS

Read the article by Jane Simms entitled 'The Generation Game' featured *in People Management* (6 February 2003, pages 26–31). This can be downloaded from the *People Management* archive on the CIPD's website (www.cipd.co.uk).

In the article it is argued that traditional approaches to succession planning that fell out of fashion in the 1980s and 1990s are making a comeback under the new title of 'talent management'. It also considers whether it is better to recruit senior

managers externally or to promote people from within.

Questions:

1 Why did succession planning become unfashionable over the past 20 years?

2 Why is it now undergoing a renaissance in many organisations?

3 Summarise the arguments for and against promoting senior managers from inside the organisation rather than recruiting them from outside.

TRADITIONAL APPROACHES

Hirsh (2000), Murphy (2009a) and Blass (2009) all distinguish between 'traditional approaches' to succession planning and modern, 'new style' approaches which better fit the needs of the contemporary business context. Traditional approaches are those which are associated with practice in larger corporations during the 1960s and 1970s when the business environment was much more stable and predictable. At that time it was also much more common than is now the case for people to pursue their careers largely within a single organisation, joining in their 20s and then advancing steadily up a hierarchy. This type of situation does still exist in some parts of the public sector, but it is now much less common than it was in the private sector. Downsizing, outsourcing, off shoring as well as mergers and acquisitions of one kind or another have become the norm, making it hard for anyone to pursue a single-company career even if they wanted to. However, it has also become less common for people to choose to build their careers in this way. The norm now in most professions is to advance by moving from organisation to organisation every five years or so, broadening one's experience and enhancing one's employability with each move. The faster pace of change also means that people commonly now change careers as well as jobs from time to time during their working lives. They are also much more likely than they were to take early retirement or at least not to retire at a predictable age.

Traditional approaches to succession planning are not only distinct from more contemporary approaches in the type of organisations they are designed to suit. They also differ in respect of the style of management of which they form a part. To start with they involved 'grooming a selected few'. Managers identify people they believe to have senior management potential and then take steps to foster their careers. This involves fast-tracking future leaders through career steps so that by their late 30s they have a wide enough understanding of the organisation's operations to be given a job with substantial responsibility. Thereafter they are promoted every three to five years. The fast-tracking process involves sideways moves as well as vertical moves. Identified successors work for periods in several functional areas and, in international companies, will usually spend time overseas.

The result is continuity of leadership. Successful corporations aim to continue to be successful by ensuring that their leaders are nurtured in the way that princes are trained to succeed to the throne after the death of a king or queen. Alongside that advantage, however, aspects of the traditional approach increasingly jar against ethical standards that now prevail in many organisations and modern approaches to management:

- selection is subjective
- it tends to produce clones of existing leaders
- it disfavours women and members of ethnic minorities
- it is unashamedly elitist
- it does not conform with principles of 'best practice' HRM.

For these reasons traditional approaches have fallen out of fashion in the wider HR world and are less commonly carried out in a formal way. However, because succession planning is still a necessary activity, traditional approaches do continue informally. Senior managers still identify their likely successors typically as people who share their values, beliefs and who agree with their vision for the organisation's future and do then groom them to succeed via fast-tracking career advancement. It would be surprising to find that this kind of activity did not continue, not least because senior people like, if they can, to protect their own legacies and do not want to be succeeded by people whose aim is to take things in a radically different direction. Informality can, though, lead to secrecy and a lack of transparency which is damaging and can have the effect of lowering morale generally among ambitious staff who resent not being able to compete openly and on a level playing field with those who have been 'chosen'. Bowick (1996:181) is particularly critical of secrecy in succession planning, especially of approaches which are so secret that the individuals being earmarked as successors are not aware that they are in that position, or at least are not actively involved themselves in the process.

Murphy (2009a) reports IRS research that suggests just over half of UK organisations do now carry out succession planning of some kind. Their sample size was small, but the results are useful as a general guide to existing practice. The figures were as follows:

A formal process is in place:	28%
An informal process is used:	28%
Never operated a succession planning process:	41%
No longer has a process, but did so in the past:	3%

She goes on to set out the four main reasons organisations that do not carry out succession planning at all, formal or informal, give as their reasons. The first is a concern about the compatibility of succession planning with a commitment to diversity. Size is the second reason given. Many organisations say they are just too small to be able to offer clear internal career paths, there being far too few opportunities for people, however talented they may be, to progress their careers internally. The third reason is a lack of resources. As is the case with HRP more generally, managers can see the benefits and would like to do it if they could, but other more pressing, shorter-term priorities account for all the time and money available. Finally, some companies told IRS that they planned one day to develop formal succession planning systems, but they were not a current priority because they are 'young companies with big plans'. Once they have grown and consolidated their positions they intend to introduce HR policies and practices such as succession planning.

Other writers in this field have identified further more human reasons. Cohn *et al* (2008:49) state that in many organisations it is something of a taboo, a subject that no one wants to raise because it involves looking beyond the time when the currently powerful individuals will have gone:

> Planning your exit is like scheduling your own funeral; it evokes fears and emotions long hidden under layers of defence mechanisms and imperceptible habits. Perversely, the desire to avoid the issue is strongest in the most successful CEOs. Their standard operating procedure is to always look for the next mountain to climb, not to step down from the mountain and look for a replacement.

CONTEMPORARY APPROACHES

Having explained some of the unsatisfactory points about traditional approaches to succession planning it is necessary to stress that there are considerable advantages in carrying out this type of activity and that this explains why a sizeable proportion of UK businesses still do operate some form of formal system. Despite the problems discussed above, there remains a need to develop effective managers and to ensure a transfer of authority from one leader to the next that is smooth and stable. A corporation's reputation on the stock market can be made or un-made by such episodes. Moreover there is research evidence that demonstrates a link between the presence of formal succession planning with superior business performance (Kispal-Vitai & Wood 2009:183). This is unsurprising when you consider what potential advantages flow from having a formal succession plan:

- improved retention of strong performers
- enhanced reputation as an employer
- well-targeted, individualised employee development initiatives
- stronger organisational development.

The renewed interest in succession planning in recent years can partly be accounted for by an understanding of these advantages. However, there are also some developments in the contemporary business environment which are responsible for moving it up the list of HR priorities in some organisations:

i   Population ageing. The baby boom generation are now starting to retire, and there are fewer people in the younger generations to replace them (see Chapters 2 and 16).

ii Tighter labour markets generally mean that talented people know they are rarer and are happy to move from organisation to organisation if the 'personal terms' are sufficiently attractive.

iii More generally, the experience of downsizing has made people less inclined to be loyal to one organisation and to have a preference for careers developing across employments.

iv The complexity of organisations and of their environments, the unpredictability and the pace of technological change, and the intensity of market and media scrutiny have reduced the size of the pool of people who are both willing and able to take on senior positions in pressured modern organisations.

As a result of these trends recruiting and retaining people with senior management potential has simultaneously become harder and more important. CIPD research shows that replacing senior people in a timely and effective manner has become much harder in recent years. There has been a huge growth in the market for 'interim managers' and many more examples of people 'acting up' temporarily before a permanent replacement for a senior person is found.

We are thus seeing the evolution of new approaches to succession planning (see Hirsh, 2000). The objectives remain the same as is the case with the traditional approaches, but the methods are different. They are more in tune with contemporary ethics, do not conflict with the diversity agenda and also meet the needs of a more flexible labour market. The key features are as follows:

i   Less secrecy

    Organisations are now a good deal more open about their succession plans. There is open competition for places on fast-track career development schemes and plenty of communication about their purpose. The aim is to ensure greater fairness in selection and a more diverse senior management team.

ii Devolution

    New-style approaches are less centralised. Instead of a single succession planner or team of succession planners carrying out the work centrally of behalf of a whole corporation, line managers generally are encouraged to identify and develop talent locally. This should result in less cloning and the development of people who have different ideas and who challenge the status quo.

iii Less precision

Because it is now generally accepted that there should be open competition for senior posts modern succession plans do not identify specific successors, although emergency actors-up are still specifically identified. Instead the aim is to create a sufficiently strong 'pool of talent' internally who are in a position to apply for the senior jobs.

iv Formal selection

Instead of selecting people who look as if they may have potential, modern succession planning involves the use of sophisticated selection techniques. Assessment centres are used, activities being carefully designed to help spot competencies associated with effective leaders.

v Range of developmental techniques

More management development techniques are used including mentoring, coaching, appraisal, secondments etc, and are used in a more formal way.

vi Encompasses all

Increasingly organisations are including all in their succession plans by merging them with career development activities generally. Future leaders are identified in the process, but everyone's career ambitions are established formally and appropriate developmental plans drawn up accordingly.

In practical terms most organisations who carry out succession planning formally end up with a written document which is then regularly reviewed and updated. Its key feature is a list of all the jobs in the organisation that are deemed sufficiently critical to require named successors. For each the plan sets out the following:

- At least one named individual who is ready now to succeed if necessary.

- This is the person who would step into the shoes of the current job holder if that person was to depart suddenly or 'go under a bus' as the euphemism has it.

- Two or three named individuals who will be in a position to succeed in three to five years' time. These are generally going to be people from the generation below that of the job holder, one of whom will be promoted into the senior role when the current job holder retires or moves on to another position in a planned manner. Ideally an appointment can then be made a few months before the departure, allowing a smooth transfer when the time comes.

- A larger group of named individuals who are considered to have the capacity to succeed into top jobs in perhaps seven or 10 years' time. These will generally be younger people who are performing well in junior management posts and have serious senior management potential. The current priority is to provide them with the development opportunities needed to move up into the second category in a few years' time.

TALENT MANAGEMENT AT COCA COLA

CASE SUMMARY

In 2005 managers in the marketing function at Coca Cola's European operation established that they had a talent management problem. While it had on its staff many highly competent and well motivated junior marketing managers, relatively few were in a position to take on the senior roles when they became vacant. Instead the company was recruiting from outside. The effect was to reduce morale among its own staff and led to many people with strong potential leaving the company to take up positions elsewhere.

The issue was addressed by organising a two-day development centre for eight junior managers who were thought to have senior management potential. Although being chosen to attend the centre was an acknowledgement that a participant was considered to have 'high potential', some were quite suspicious initially, thinking that

they were 'on trial' in some way. It thus took some convincing that the purpose was developmental and that an outcome would be the drawing up of personal development plans designed to help people advance more quickly and effectively within the company.

Coca Cola considered this initiative to be a considerable success and has since run similar centres for marketing managers in other parts of the world. Of the 31 participants in the first round of centres, 17 had been promoted by 2008, while all 31 remained employed by the company. Feedback from the participants has been good, attending the centre and drawing up development plans serving to raise their confidence as well as their skills levels.

Source: Martindale (2008)

EXERCISE BOX: ACCELERATION POOLS

EXERCISE 13.2

Read the article by William Byham entitled 'Pools Winners' featured in *People Management* (24 August 2000, pages 38–40). This can be downloaded from the *People Management* archive on the CIPD's website (www.cipd.co.uk).

In this article the author, an HR consultant, puts the case for replacing traditional succession planning approaches with 'acceleration pools'. He concludes that this approach has more to offer both employers and employees.

Questions:

1. Why do companies prefer to fill senior jobs with internal candidates rather than to bring new recruits in from outside?

2. Why is this becoming increasingly difficult to achieve?

3. What does an 'accelerated pool system' have to offer over succession planning? What are the potential disadvantages?

KEY ARTICLE BOX

EXAMPLE

'Exploring succession planning in small, growing firms' by Sally Sambrook. *Journal of Small Business and Enterprise Development*. Vol. 12, No. 4. 579–594 (2005)

In this article the author discusses her interviews with four senior managers (two of whom are owner-managers) of small but fast-growing firms based in Wales. The issues associated with identifying and developing successors to top roles in small organisations are explored in detail. Particular problems are identified along with steps that need to be taken to ensure an effective transition over time from one leader to another.

Questions:

1 Why is succession planning a particularly necessary activity in small, growing firms like those featured in this article?

2 Why is it a more problematic process than in larger organisations?

3 What key steps are identified as being necessary if succession planning is to be effective in small firms?

4 What might larger organisations learn from the discussion about effective succession planning in this article?

EXPLORE FURTHER

- The best single source of information on succession planning is Wendy Hirsh's short book on the subject published by IES in 2000. This explains the key stages and sets out the major contemporary trends towards 'new style' approaches. The more recent book on talent management edited by Eddie Blass (2009) also debates these issues. It sets out good practice in succession planning and provides a series of case studies about this and talent management more generally.

- There are three useful American books which cover the practicalities of drawing up succession plans written by consultants with extensive experience in this field of work. All cover wider topics as well. These are *Strategic staffing* by Thomas Bechet (2008), *Effective succession planning* by William J Rothwell (2005) and *The talent management handbook* edited by Lance and Dorothy Berger (2004).

CHAPTER 14

Measuring and analysing employee turnover

LEARNING OUTCOMES

By the end of this chapter readers should be able to:

- distinguish between different types of employee turnover
- implement different approaches to measuring and monitoring staff turnover
- advise on sources of turnover data for benchmarking purposes
- estimate the costs associated with staff turnover in an organisation.

In addition, readers should be able to understand and explain:

- debates about the significance of employee turnover in organisations
- key trends of employee turnover across different industries in the UK
- the distinction between rudimentary and sophisticated approaches to turnover costing.

DEFINING VOLUNTARY TURNOVER

Distinguishing between departures from employment initiated by employees and those initiated by the employer is not straightforward. It is important, however, as it is necessary to understand the drivers behind voluntary turnover in order to improve staff retention rates. While some cases are clear-cut (eg dismissal for gross misconduct or resignation to take up a job with a competitor), many others result from a mixture of factors. A common example is the resignation of an employee on grounds of serious ill-health when dismissal would have resulted in any event. Another situation arises with retirement, when it is not always easy to tell how keen individual employees are to quit at a predetermined retirement age. It is also difficult to say with any degree of certainty whether someone 'was pushed' or 'jumped' if they resign when redundancies are threatened. Perhaps the simplest approach is to use the very broad definition that includes all resignations not formally initiated by the employer. Data of this kind is straightforward to collect and is thus unlikely to take up a great deal of management time. Results can then be adjusted or re-interpreted at the analysis stage to take account of any grey areas such as those identified above.

A further distinction to be made in deciding how to manage turnover levels is that between resignations that might have been avoided and those that would have occurred anyway, irrespective of employer actions. These are often referred to as, respectively, 'controllable' and 'uncontrollable' reasons. The former category includes employees who quit primarily because of dissatisfaction with some aspect of their job or the organisation in comparison with perceived alternative employment opportunities, while the latter encompasses resignations that result from factors such as ill-health, the relocation of spouses and other domestic responsibilities. Naturally, it is the controllable resignations to which most attention is given when organisations seek to reduce turnover levels. However, there are grey areas here too. Often employers will label a particular resignation as 'unavoidable' when in truth a mixture of avoidable and unavoidable factors caused it to occur. The most common examples involve employees resigning to relocate so as to live with a partner or spouse based elsewhere. On the surface this appears like unavoidable turnover, but couples often weigh up the advantages and disadvantages of either one of them relocating. The one who stays put is usually the one with the best career prospects, highest pay or greatest level of job satisfaction. Good employers lose fewer people for these kinds of 'personal reasons' than poorer ones.

 REFLECTIVE QUESTION

What factors explained your decision to resign from positions you have held? To what extent are these readily categorised as voluntary/involuntary or controllable/uncontrollable?

 EXERCISE BOX

EXERCISE 14.1

Read the opinion column by Penny de Valk entitled 'High staff turnover means employers must give staff "a new deal" on working arrangements and development' featured in *People Management* (6 November 2003, page 24). This can be downloaded from the *People Management* archive on the CIPD's website (www.cipd.co.uk).

In this article Penny de Valk raises some very interesting issues about long-term trends in employee turnover patterns. She also assesses changes in employer priorities and concludes by calling for the development of a new model to underpin talent management in the future.

Questions:

1 What developments are leading employees to be less loyal to their employers and to move from job to job more regularly?

2 Why is employee turnover tending to become more problematic from an employer perspective?

3 Is it possible for employers today to achieve both high levels of flexibility and high levels of employee retention? If so, how?

DOES TURNOVER MATTER?

A fundamental debate that managers have about employee turnover and retention concerns the extent to which the issue should be a matter of concern. While most would agree that too high a level of turnover has negative implications for an organisation, there is disagreement about how significant these implications are.

A recent CIPD survey found that 9 per cent of respondents thought that labour turnover had a 'serious negative effect' on organisational performance, 51 per cent thought that it had 'a minor negative effect', 29 per cent thought it had no effect at all, while 10 per cent believed it to have a positive effect (CIPD 2009b:28). For many HR specialists, therefore, rising staff turnover is seen as being an important organisational problem. It follows that improving retention rates should be high on the management agenda and that it is proper for resources to be devoted to achieving this aim. Others disagree. For them staff turnover is at most an irritation, well down their lists of priorities for action. Moreover, a certain amount of turnover is actively welcomed by some managers. There are no right or wrong answers in this debate. In the end the extent to which staff retention difficulties constitute an important organisational problem depends entirely on the type of organisation and its particular business circumstances.

The view that staff turnover has essentially negative implications derives first from an appreciation of the costs that are associated with it. We examine this issue in some detail below, but it is useful to point out at this stage just how costly to an organisation excessive turnover can be. Nine times out of 10 when someone leaves, a vacancy is created which is subsequently filled externally. A range of different costs are necessarily associated with this process. In many cases the most significant element will be the cost of recruiting a new person. It may be necessary to place an advertisement in the press, to pay agency fees or both. At the very least there will be a cost in terms of management time associated with administering the recruitment process, shortlisting candidates and selecting a replacement. For some types of job several interviews may be arranged or some kind of assessment centre. Interview expenses will often be paid and recruitment literature printed and posted to candidates. Then there is the cost of inducting and training the new employee, the cost of administering the entry of a new starter (payroll, personnel records, offer letters, issuing contracts etc). In addition, while all this is going on there is a vacancy. This may mean that the organisation is less productive or effective for a few weeks, or it may result in further expenditure on overtime or temporary staff employed at a premium hourly rate. The total cost is difficult to calculate accurately and varies substantially from job to job, but has to be absorbed by the organisation in virtually every case of voluntary turnover. In most cases the cost will not be especially high for one individual leaver. However, when assessed cumulatively across an organisation, the total cost associated with staff turnover can mount to hundreds of thousands or even millions each year.

In addition to direct costs such as these, a voluntary resignation also represents a waste of organisational resources in other ways. This is particularly so when someone is given intensive or extensive training at the organisation's expense and then leaves before a proper return on the investment is attained. The situation is made worse when one of your employees resigns in order to take up a post with a rival organisation. The training and experience gained at your expense is then not just lost, but can actively be deployed in competition with you. The more extensive and commercially useful the knowledge that resignees take with them when they leave, the more significant is the potential damage done.

The other major negative consequences of voluntary turnover result from its impact on the staff who remain employed. The resignation of a colleague often means more work for those left behind. New duties have to be taken and project work taken forward. Some see this as an opportunity, but others find it difficult to cope and become resentful. They are also typically required to help train the new employee in addition to their existing duties. Taking on this kind of extra burden is not a problem when it occurs occasionally. The consequences in terms of lost morale and commitment can be a great deal more damaging where there is high turnover and where a near-continual shortage of staff results. High turnover is also bad from the point of view of labour market competition. A reputation for being unable to keep people rapidly translates into a poor reputation as an employer generally. The result is a disinclination on the part of good people looking for jobs even to consider applying. This effect is strongest where an employer relies heavily on recruitment from a defined geographical area and the local job centre or newspaper always seems to be advertising its vacancies.

Finally we can point to the negative perceptions that staff turnover can have from the perspective of customers. The impact here is in jobs where familiarity with the individual needs or preferences of a customer on the part of employees is central to an organisation's reputation. This is the case wherever professional services are being provided on an ongoing basis; it is as true of hairdressing and restaurants as it is of schools and firms of solicitors. Too much chopping and changing of personnel in such workplaces, at the very least, tends to diminish customer loyalty. At worst it leads to a genuine reduction in perceived standards of customer service which translates, in turn, to the development of a poor reputation in key markets.

The case against staff turnover and for retention initiatives is thus strong and has considerable resonance in most types of workplace. However, we can also construct an alternative argument which serves to downplay the negative impact of turnover from a management point of view. First, it is important to acknowledge that a good employee retention record is not necessarily needed in order to achieve substantial commercial success. McDonald's, for example, is by anyone's standards a highly successful international corporation. Yet it reportedly managed to grow spectacularly over recent decades despite, for many years, having a staff turnover rate of over 300 per cent (see Ritzer 1996:130 and Cappelli 2000:106). Average length of service of just four months was not so great a handicap as to stop McDonald's becoming the dominant player in its industry during the last 20 years of the twentieth century. The reverse is also true. Some public sector corporations in the UK which by common consent provide a pretty dire level of customer service have some of the highest rates of staff retention in the country.

A second argument concerns the need for organisations to have regular infusions of fresh blood from time to time. Too high a retention rate can lead to organisational decay as it stops new ideas from entering and circulating. New people bring with them alternative perspectives and varied types of experience on which organisations can profitably draw. They also frequently bring to their jobs a burst of enthusiasm and idealism. The fresh blood argument in favour of employee turnover is especially true of senior people in an organisation. As a general rule there is little more damaging to the interests of an organisation than leaders who have run out of new ideas or have outstayed their welcome in other ways. Unless senior teams get periodically rejuvenated with suitable people from outside, they can very easily stagnate or become essentially self-serving. Moreover, of course, it is only because of turnover at senior levels that more junior staff get an opportunity for promotion. Where turnover rates are too low, not only can fresh blood not get in, but existing blood can not circulate healthily either.

The third strand of the argument in favour of a measure of staff turnover simply reflects the fact that some resignations are welcomed by managers because they result in the replacement of a relatively weak performer with a better one. This is the most common example of a resignation which is 'functional' rather than 'dysfunctional'. Others include the departure of people who did not fit in particularly well, whose attendance was poor, who had ceased to enjoy their work or who had developed destructive relationships with colleagues. Griffeth and Hom (2001:6–7) quote research evidence gathered in a US bank which showed that over 40 per cent of voluntary turnover was appropriately classed as 'functional'. The precise proportion varies from workplace to workplace, but it is reasonable to presume that 40 per cent is a good estimate for most workplaces. This is because a fair number of all resignees quit because they are dissatisfied with some aspect of their work, which in turn is likely to be reflected in their relative work performance prior to the resignation.

Finally it must be acknowledged that in some situations relatively high staff turnover allows managers to exercise greater control than would otherwise be the case over their wage bills. This is particularly true of organisations whose business levels are subject to regular fluctuation. It means that when the level of income drops for a few weeks or months, wage costs can be made simultaneously and painlessly to fall simply by holding back from recruiting replacements. Profitability is thus maintained without the need to lay people off at a cost to the organisation.

With strong arguments on either side of the debate it is reasonable to conclude that the significance of turnover varies from organisation to organisation. There are some situations in which it matters a great deal and can have a real impact on the employer's competitive position, but also others in which the impact is neutral or even positive. A third type of situation is one in which staff turnover is acknowledged to have a damaging effect but where the costs associated with its reduction outweigh those being created by the turnover itself.

Empirical research focusing primarily on the nature of the link between turnover rates and organisational performance is relatively rare. There is a general assumption among HR researchers that too much staff turnover is damaging, so the research effort has instead been put into establishing why people leave jobs and what can be done to reduce turnover. Some years ago now Abelson and Baysinger (1984) proposed a model in which the relationship between turnover and firm performance was broadly shaped like an inverted U. In other words their suggestion was that turnover could be too high and also too low and that the best performing organisations were those whose staff turnover rates were close to a theoretical 'ideal level' somewhere in between the two extremes. In more recent years a number of papers have been published reporting attempts to test the validity of the Abelson and Baysinger model. Meier and Hicklin (2007) looked at the relationship between staff turnover and performance in over 1000 Texas schools, while Michele Kacmar and her colleagues (2006) undertook a similar analysis in 262 Burger King restaurants. A third study, by Glebbeek and Bax (2004) focused on branches of a Dutch employment agency, a fourth by Ton and Huckman (2008) looked at a retail chain. The results varied somewhat but all found a very clear, statistically significant correlation between high turnover and relatively weak performance. There is now thus reasonably strong support in the published literature for the view that where staff turnover is relatively high, the higher it gets the more of an adverse impact it has on organisations. These studies are, however, less clear on the question of how much low staff turnover has a similarly damaging effect. They are much less confident in making that assertion. Instead the studies suggest that there is relatively little negative impact on performance generally when turnover levels are low or moderate, the problems only begin once turnover increases beyond levels which are easily manageable. Meier and Hicklin (2007) concluded that turnover was more damaging in its impact on performance among higher skilled staff than it was when lower level employees left, while Ton and Hickman (2008) noted that the impact of high turnover in retail stores could be mitigated through the imposition by managers of standardised operating procedures. In other words, the less discretion employees have about how to do things, the less significant it is when any individual leaves. Their conclusion, essentially, is thus the same. The more knowledgeable and experienced employees have to be in order to do their jobs well, the more problematic turnover tends to be. This is because such people are harder to replace and because it takes longer for their successors to reach the same levels of performance as they had reached by the time they left.

So what can we conclude about the impact of turnover on performance? By and large if the following applies, it is fair to argue that organisations should be concerned about turnover levels which are higher than those of their competitors or which are rising significantly:

- where labour markets are tight, making it hard to recruit the people with the skills your organisation needs

- where recruitment costs are substantial (eg where agencies or press advertisements are used or sophisticated approaches to selection)

- where training has to be provided to new starters at some cost to the organisation
- where a new starter takes several weeks or months to reach full effectiveness in the job
- where patterns of business are reasonably stable on a week to week and month to month basis
- where leavers take with them (in their heads) knowledge which would be very useful to a competitor
- where an organisation is growing and does not anticipate a need to make compulsory redundancies in the foreseeable future.

In these kinds of situation staff turnover over 10 per cent or so is seen as being a management issue which needs to be tackled. It is likely that substantial resources are currently being wasted as a direct result of excessive voluntary resignations. There is thus a strong business case for investment in retention initiatives. Conversely, in the following situations relatively high rates of turnover are more likely to be sustainable:

- where labour markets are loose, making it easy to find replacement staff of the required quality when someone resigns
- where new staff can be hired at relatively low cost (eg via a job centre or through word of mouth recruitment)
- where selection can be carried out easily and cheaply (eg a simple interview with one or two managers)
- where training costs for new starters are low
- where new starters are able to become fully effective in their jobs within a few days or weeks
- where patterns of business are reasonably unstable or unpredictable on a week by week or month by month basis
- where it is likely that compulsory redundancies will have to be made in the coming months
- where leavers do not generally walk out of the door in possession of knowledge that would be of use to a competitor.

MEASURING TURNOVER

Measuring staff turnover, calculating (or at least estimating) its cost and benchmarking these figures against those of other comparable organisations are activities which form the starting point for developing a programme aimed at improving staff retention rates. By gaining a clear understanding of the size of the problem and the potential benefits associated with addressing it, HR managers are well placed to persuade their colleagues that there will be a return on investment if money is spent on a turnover reduction programme.

Published evidence demonstrates that despite the generally acknowledged significance of employee turnover and retention as an issue, many employers in the UK take no formal steps to manage it systematically. Rankin (2008d) quotes research which suggests over a third of employers in the UK are unable to state their annual turnover level, while 70 per cent do not know how their rate compares with others in their industry. For most employee retention initiatives are short-term, ad hoc activities introduced in response to rising staff turnover rates. There are few examples of employers taking a pro-active approach to prevent increasing turnover before it happens, and relatively few examples of organisations undertaking any kind of cost-benefit analysis of the initiatives they bring forward. Part of the problem is that in order to embark on a meaningful, strategically-driven programme to improve employee retention, calculating the likely costs and benefits, a fair amount of data has to be collected first. Where organisations have not in the past collected information about turnover, they need to start doing so before they can start thinking about the best methods of tackling it.

Generating meaningful turnover statistics that form a robust basis for the development of remedial plans is an inexact science. It is easy to misinterpret figures, which can lead to problems in multi-divisional organisations where one unit's turnover rates are compared with others. A classic example arises from the tendency for turnover to be at its highest in the first months of an individual's employment. For this reason, units that are performing well (and are thus expanding) are very likely to have higher figures than those in relative decline. So great care has to be taken in analysing raw turnover statistics and in using them as a means of formally assessing the performance of particular personnel functions or line managers. Nonetheless, finding a satisfactory way of measuring staff turnover in your organisation is important as this allows you to do the following:

- compare turnover rates between different departments, business units or occupational groups

- benchmark turnover rates against those of your competitors or norms for your industry

- track over time the success or failure of interventions aimed at reducing turnover

- draw on past data in order to predict likely future turnover rates

- estimate the cost of turnover to the organisation over a specific period of time.

The most straightforward method of measuring staff turnover involves calculating 'crude turnover rates' (also known as wastage rates). The basic formula is simple:

$$\frac{\text{Total number of leavers in the year to date x}}{\text{Total number of employees at date x}} \times 100$$

A crude turnover rate of 30 per cent thus indicates that 30 out of every 100 people employed left during the course of the past year. It provides a good rough 'rule of thumb' guide but can be criticised for being too blunt an instrument to facilitate effective management action. This is because it fails to reveal the detail of the comings and goings in an organisation (or part of an organisation), characterising all turnover as being of equal significance. For example, it acknowledges no distinction between the loss of someone after two days' service and someone who has left after five years. It also fails to distinguish between the functional and dysfunctional, avoidable and unavoidable, or voluntary and involuntary varieties of turnover. It is particularly misleading for organisations who employ people on a seasonal basis or whose headcount tends to fluctuate markedly at different times in response to commercial opportunities. For such organisations the crude rate is heavily influenced by the time of year that the measurement is taken. An organisation which employs large numbers in the summer months but then reduces its headcount in the winter will be shown to have a far higher turnover rate if the year end date is 31 December than if the date chosen is 1 July when the number of employees is high. For this reason it makes sense to use a modified formula which includes an average annual figure for total headcount:

$$\frac{\text{Total number of leavers in the past year}}{\text{Average total number employed in the past year}} \times 100$$

Adjusting the formula in this way cannot capture the distinction between early turnover and turnover of relatively long serving employees. This can be important when thinking about what prescriptions are most appropriate to help reduce turnover. It also makes meaningful comparisons between different units difficult. For example, two regional divisions of a bank might both report crude turnover rates of 20 per cent, yet be experiencing very different kinds of turnover. In one the vast majority of the turnover could be accounted for by people leaving after a few weeks of employment, the majority of employees having much longer service. By contrast, in the other, the 20 per cent could represent the loss of a fifth of the most experienced staff. While is possible to argue about whether or not the second situation is more damaging than the first, it must be conceded that the two regions are experiencing different patterns of turnover with different effects and requiring different types of management action.

The most common approach used to deal with this defect in the crude turnover rate is to calculate a stability rate. Some organisations use this instead of the crude turnover rate, but most see it as an additional tool of analysis. The commonly used formula is as follows:

$$\frac{\text{Number of staff with service of a year or more}}{\text{Total number of staff employed a year ago}} \times 100$$

Effectively this gives you the proportion of staff in the unit concerned who have more than a year's service. The result is an index which removes early leavers from the equation. It is thus possible to have a high crude turnover rate (eg: 60 per cent) while also having a high stability rate (eg 90 per cent). Nine out of every 10 employees in such a situation have been employed for over a year, but there is also a very substantial turnover of staff in the first months of their employment. The same situation would be true of an organisation which employed a substantial number of employees on fixed-term contracts of less than a year. The stability index does not allow their departures to 'contaminate' the overall picture of a stable workforce.

It is possible, of course, to carry out analyses of the stability index using any number of years as the basis (ie proportion of staff with two years' service, five years, 10 years etc). This type of calculation can then form the basis of cohort analysis – a third commonly used approach. This is a more complex method of measuring turnover, but one which gives a richer picture and which you can use as a predictive tool. It can be applied to the whole workforce or to a particular grouping. Either way the aim is to assess what happened in turnover terms to a defined group of employees who started working at around the same time. It could be all new recruits in a particular year, a group of graduate trainees commencing at the same time or the employees who were recruited when a new unit first opened. The cohort analysis tells you what proportion were still employed after one year, two years, three years, four years and so on. The analysis is readily illustrated graphically with the production of a 'survival curve'.

Another feature of cohort analyses is the calculation of a 'half life' figure. This is the number of months it takes for half the members of a defined cohort (ie people who started at the same time) to leave. Because it is a single figure (eg 10 months, 30 months, 60 months etc) it allows you to make ready comparisons between different groups and over time. Hence, an organisation which takes action to reduce turnover among graduate recruits can usefully judge its effectiveness by calculating the half life for successive cohorts. A rising figure shows that turnover rates are declining.

A more complex approach to stability analysis, but one which has a good deal to offer, is defined by IDS (1995c:3). This could be labelled a 'grading approach' because it effectively awards a mark out of 100 to an organisation or part of an organisation on its performance as far as employee turnover is concerned. Central is the notion that turnover among long-standing staff is more damaging than that among new entrants, presumably on the grounds that experience is being lost. The method skews the calculation accordingly. The formula is as follows:

$$\frac{\text{Total length of service of all employees at date X}}{\text{Total length of service had no turnover occurred in the year to date X}} \times 100$$

Its effect is best understood by means of a simple example. Assume that there is a company which employed nine people one year ago. At that time the newest member of staff had one year's service, the longest serving had nine years', while each of the others started working for the company in successive years. The total number of years' service a year ago was thus 45. If nobody was to have left during the subsequent year the total number of years' service at the date under consideration (date X) would be 54 years. This is illustrated in Figure 14.1. However, what really happened was that three people left at the start of the year (those with five, six and seven years' service respectively), each being replaced by a new employee. This means that the total length of service at date X was *in fact* 36 years. This is illustrated in Figure 14.2. This gives us a figure for the index of 67 per cent (ie 36 divided by 54 and multiplied by 100). Had no one left at all the score would have been a perfect 100 per cent. Had the three most junior employees left instead of those who did the total number of years' service at date X would have been 48, giving an index score of 89 per cent.

Table 14.1 Stability analysis: 1

Employees	Length of service a year ago	Length of service at date x if there was no turnover
Annie	1 year	2 years
Ben	2 years	3 years
Cecilia	3 years	4 years
Deborah	4 years	5 years
Emma	5 years	6 years
Fiona	6 years	7 years
Gill	7 years	8 years
Hamish	8 years	9 years
Irene	9 years	10 years
TOTAL:	45 years	54 years

Table 14.2 Stability analysis: 2

Employees	Length of service a year ago	Actual length of service at date x
Annie	1 year	2 years
Ben	2 years	3 years
Cecilia	3 years	4 years
Deborah	4 years	5 years
Emma	5 years	–
Fiona	6 years	–
Gill	7 years	–
Hamish	8 years	9 years
Irene	9 years	10 years
John	–	1 year
Kieron	–	1 year
Linda	–	1 year
TOTAL:	45 years	36 years

There are clearly disadvantages as well as advantages to this approach. First there is its complexity, although getting access to the required information is not difficult where a good personnel information system is in operation. Secondly, it can be criticised for over-egging the significance of turnover among long-standing staff vis-à-vis those who are less experienced. The differential between them in practice is often a good deal less than is supposed in the method of calculation. For this reason it is particularly important to remove retirees from the analysis. A couple of retirements of long-standing staff, even though wholly unavoidable, can badly affect a department's figure if this is not done.

Despite the possibility of using all these other approaches in addition, it remains the case that the crude wastage rate (or one of its closest relatives) must remain the central index of turnover in organisations. This is partly because it is so readily understood and partly because it facilitates necessary costing exercises such as those described below. It is also the standard unit of measurement used in most of the published turnover surveys, so it has to be calculated to allow meaningful benchmarking with other organisations to occur.

Griffeth and Hom (2001) suggest that there is merit in removing from the analysis all turnover which is functional as well as that which is clearly unavoidable. The upshot is a final figure a good deal lower than the crude wastage percentage, which measures only that turnover which is both damaging from a corporate perspective *and* which it is in the organisation's power to avert. Ultimately, it can be argued, this is the only figure that really matters – the true measure of how effectively an employer is managing to compete in its key labour markets.

LEVELS OF TURNOVER MEASUREMENT

In their article entitled 'Unweaving leaving' Morrell *et al* (2001:223) distinguish between three distinct 'levels' of turnover measurement. Level 1 involves developing a basic awareness of the problem. A general turnover rate for the organisation is calculated and benchmarked in a broad brush way against national figures or industry norms. At this level managers can be said to be doing little more than monitoring turnover in their organisations.

Level 2 involves planning, predicting and controlling turnover. Rates are calculated for different departments or units within the organisation and targets set for reducing them. There is a move away from a reliance on crude wastage rates as measures are developed to take account of voluntary and involuntary leaving in working out the figures. Figures are compared with those of direct competitors, especially those competing in the same local labour markets.

At Level 3 turnover can be said to be truly managed. Measurement is much more sophisticated. Account is taken of functional and dysfunctional turnover as well as that which is avoidable and unavoidable. Moreover, an 'ongoing dialogue' is established with staff and with leavers to develop the most effective retention measures.

REFLECTIVE QUESTION

Does your organisation measure its turnover rates? How varied are the figures for different occupational groups?

COSTING TURNOVER

People have different ideas about the cost that an organisation bears each time an employee leaves. Even when asked to estimate the costs associated with the loss of the same types of staff, managerial estimates can vary hugely. An example was a survey of retention issues in the NHS which asked respondents at different hospital trusts to estimate the costs associated with filling 'a typical vacancy'. Respondents suggested figures ranging from £150 up to £9,500 (Health Service Report 2001:6). The average figure was £2,300. In 2009, when IRS asked respondents to their annual survey to estimate the costs only 11 per cent replied to that question. The fact that the average estimate was £739 and the median only £371 indicates just how very wide apart estimates generally are (Rankin 2009). Moreover, all these figures fall way below estimates of the total turnover cost calculated by academic researchers and consultants who have looked at the issue in greater detail. Most put the lowest figure at around 50 per cent of the annual salary for the job in question, with upper figures climbing as high as 200 per cent or even 250 per cent (see Cascio and Boudreau 2008, *The Economist* 2000). Surveys of employers indicate that while costs are not generally perceived to be this high, they are nevertheless very significant. Employers participating in the 2007 CIPD survey on labour turnover estimated the average cost of turnover to be £4,333 (see Table 14.3), but the figures for senior staff were a good deal higher than for those paid at lower rates.

Table 14.3 Turnover costs

Median turnover costs for different occupational groups (2007)	
Managers and professionals	£11,000
Technical and administrative	£5,000
Services	£5,000
Manual and craft	£1,174
Average for all employees	£7,750

Much depends on the type of job that someone is leaving. Where it is easy to find a replacement quickly and inexpensively, and where it takes a matter of days to train them up fully, costs are going to be low. At the other end of the scale, there is the loss of highly skilled employees who go to work for competitors, taking their expertise and organisational knowledge with them. When such people's skills are in short supply or where they have been developed over some years at the organisation's expense, the costs can easily run into hundreds of thousands of pounds. The other key variable is the method used to calculate the cost associated with the resignation. Several different approaches can be used here. You can simply tot up the most obvious direct costs (eg recruiting and training a replacement) or you can try to estimate the total real cost in terms of staff time spent administering the resignation and covering while there is a vacancy. The most sophisticated approaches seek to quantify matters such as lost productivity and unrealised opportunities resulting from resignations.

The truth is that it is very difficult to estimate the overall total cost of turnover within an organisation. Many of the elements are not easily quantified, while organisations may not record data which enable ready quantification of the more basic, direct types of cost. Further complexity is added when you start trying to distinguish between functional and dysfunctional turnover or try to add in cost savings associated with staff turnover as well as financial losses. Examples are redundancy payments that no longer have to be made, salaries saved during a 'quiet period' and fewer contributions needed for the company's final salary pension scheme. In short, no absolutely accurate figure will ever be reached. But this does not mean that there is no point in making reasoned estimates. Staff turnover in most organisations does have an expensive price tag attached, meaning that there are substantial savings to be achieved from its reduction. Measuring these allows progress to be tracked in financial terms, but also greatly enhances the chances that funds will be made available by finance directors to help tackle the issue. HR managers' chances of success are a good deal higher if they can say 'we calculate that avoidable resignations cost the company £3.8 million last year' than if they make some vague claim about the benefits that could accrue if turnover levels were lowered.

Several approaches can be taken to the costing of turnover. The most straightforward involves focusing solely on the basic, direct costs that result when an individual leaves the organisation either voluntarily or involuntarily. This approach has the virtue of accuracy as far as it goes, but is likely to underestimate the actual total cost by a considerable margin. The results are believable and easily justified to a sceptical audience, but will not usually reflect the reality. The proportion of the total cost reflected in basic, direct costs is a matter of opinion, but several American studies have estimated 'hidden' or 'indirect' costs to account for as much as 85 per cent of the total (see Douglas Phillips 1990). There is thus a good case for trying to make a reasonable estimate of indirect costs, accepting that here accuracy is a good deal harder to achieve. Beyond this, it is possible to opt for 'an all-singing-all-dancing' approach which takes into account all matters which impact on the cost of turnover including cost savings. The aim is to achieve accuracy in estimating *both* the hard direct and the soft indirect costs. Calculations of this kind are complex and involve detailed research. By their nature they require in-depth analysis of factors that relate to particular jobs, making them impractical to carry out for all types of role in larger organisations. However, there is a case for carrying out focused analysis of this kind in the case of groups of employees who are highly valued, costly to replace and prone to leave a good deal more often than is good for the organisation. Where you want to target retention drives at such people and need funds to bring about a marked reduction in turnover, it makes sense to make use of the most sophisticated form of cost analysis as a means of convincing doubters that substantial investment is worth making.

EXERCISE 14.2

EXERCISE BOX: HR AND STAFF TURNOVER

Read the opinion column by Lara Ashworth entitled 'How can we hang on to top performers, while maintaining a healthy employee churn?' featured in *People Management* (19 April 2007, page 54). This can be downloaded from the *People Management* archive on the CIPD's website (www.cipd.co.uk).

In this short piece Lara Ashworth considers the extent to which measures of employee turnover rates are a good proxy for measuring the relative success of an HR function in organisations. She concludes, with some minor reservations, that they are.

Questions:

1   What are the main points made in favour of using turnover statistics as a measure for HR success more generally?

2   What points can be made against this point of view?

3   Thinking about your own organisation and its turnover trends, to what extent do you think it would be fair or valid to use these to judge the performance of your HR function?

IDENTIFYING THE COSTS

Over the years analysts have developed a range of different checklists setting out the different types of cost that organisations sustain when staff leave. Some are more comprehensive than others, and different terminology is used, but all focus broadly on the same areas. Reading this work serves to concentrate the mind by revealing the magnitude of potential savings when turnover levels are reduced in larger organisations – even by a just few percentage points. The following has been compiled with reference to the work of Douglas Phillips (1990), Fair (1992), Hom and Griffeth (1995) and Cascio and Boudreau (2008).

POTENTIAL DIRECT COSTS

- redundancy pay
- pay in lieu of holidays not taken
- advertising the vacancy
- recruitment agency fees
- recruitment literature (paper-based or web-based)
- overtime payments while there is a vacancy

- temporary cover while there is a vacancy
- interview expenses for candidates
- cost of psychometric tests
- assessment centre costs
- relocation allowances
- induction programme
- initial training programme
- literature provided to new starters
- sign-on bonuses/employee referral bonuses
- uniforms for new starters
- litigation costs when tribunal applications are made
- security badges/car parking permits/keys issued etc.

POTENTIAL ADMINISTRATIVE COSTS AND MANAGEMENT TIME

- administration of the resignation (filing, personnel information system etc)
- payroll activity associated with the resignation/dismissal
- pension fund transfers
- conducting exit interviews (manager and departing employee)
- writing references
- meetings to discuss vacancy/job description and person specification
- liaising with external agencies (eg job centres, headhunters, advertisers)
- direct recruitment costs (eg employer presentation at a job fair)
- sending out documentation to potential candidates
- shortlisting
- arranging interviews
- chasing up references
- management preparation for selection interviews/assessment centres
- time spent interviewing and assessing potential replacements
- pre-employment medical examinations
- issuing contracts
- personnel administration associated with new starters
- payroll administration
- pension fund administration
- orientation of new starter
- company car arrangements

- informal training of new starter by experienced staff.

POTENTIAL EFFICIENCY-RELATED COSTS

- inefficiency prior to termination (ie absence, slackness, failure to meet deadlines etc)
- inefficiency while there is a vacancy (ie temporary cover less effective)
- inefficiency of new starter vis-à-vis experienced employees
- inefficiency of colleagues affected by the resignation/with responsibility for the new starter.

POTENTIAL LOST OPPORTUNITIES

- business lost due to lower standards of service from new starters
- impaired standards due to low morale of staff left to cover
- knowledge, skills and experience developed now made available to a competitor
- investment in ex-employee (training, experience etc) wasted
- restrictions on/delays to growth due to shortages of skills, knowledge and experience.

RUDIMENTARY APPROACHES TO TURNOVER COSTING

There is a real danger, thinking about how to put a figure on some of the items listed above, that the analysis of turnover costs itself could be seen as an inefficient activity. Better use, it could be said, can be made of management time than developing very sophisticated models to estimate the true cost of turnover. There is truth in this observation. Some of the attempts made which are described in the academic literature are hugely involved and would be difficult to justify in many organisations. This is especially true of those which are undergoing sustained periods of change which mean that organisational activity and job content is continually being altered. In such circumstances calculating the cost of turnover among a particular group of staff can be meaningless 12 months later when skills shortages are faced elsewhere in the organisation. So there are many circumstances in which the only need is to get a broad handle on turnover costs by making rough but credible estimates.

The most straightforward approach is to focus uniquely on the costs which are readily measured. For the most part this will be those items listed above under the first two headings which are applicable to your own organisational context. It is not necessary to measure staff and management time down to the last minute. Instead rough estimates can be made about the number of hours spent in total on recruitment, selection and induction activity, as well as on administration which is linked to a resignation. The direct costs are by their nature straightforward to compute. For an experienced HR manager with responsibility for the key activities, estimations of this kind need only take a few minutes to carry out.

It is wise to focus on the major staff groups that are employed, and particularly on those which suffer the highest level of turnover. However, some companies try to work out an estimate for the whole organisation (ie all types of staff) by calculating an estimate of turnover costs for 'the typical post'. This is then multiplied by the annual overall turnover for the organisation to reach a final 'total turnover cost' figure. The following example illustrates how the costs mount up, even in the case of quite junior, low paid jobs. The organisation here is a chain of clothing stores employing 200 retail assistants at several UK locations. The aim of the exercise is to estimate the total cost of turnover among that particular staff group in a typical year. There is an annual turnover rate of 30 per cent.

ESTIMATION OF BASIC TURNOVER COST FOR A RETAIL ASSISTANT

Staff time administering the resignation	2 hours	£20.00
Management time on exit interview	1 hour	£20.00
Other resignation-related management activities	2 hours	£40.00
Holiday not taken by the resignee	7 days	£400.00
Management time writing and placing ad	1 hour	£20.00
Recruitment ad in local paper		£900.00
Postage and application forms sent to candidates		£30.00
Management time shortlisting	1 hour	£20.00
Staff time administering interviews	3 hours	£30.00
Management time interviewing (x 2 managers)	10 hours	£200.00
Interview expenses		£50.00
Staff time administering new starter	2 hours	£20.00
Management time on new starter	1 hour	£20.00
Induction day for new starter	6 hours	£60.00
Management time on induction/orientation activities	4 hours	£80.00
Staff time for on the job training	12 hours	£120.00
TOTAL COST PER INDIVIDUAL TURNOVER EPISODE		£2,030
TOTAL NUMBER OF TURNOVER EPISODES IN A YEAR		60
TOTAL TURNOVER COST FOR THE YEAR		£121,800

An alternative approach simply involves estimating the total costs incurred by the organisation (or part of it) on resignation, recruitment, selection and induction activities over the course of a year. This is readily done by working out, broadly, the percentage of each player's time which is spent on these activities in a typical week before adding in recruitment costs (ie advertising, agencies etc). The next step is to estimate the percentage of recruitment activity that results from expansion and not from turnover. The final figure is reached by deducting from the total that element. It is then very straightforward to work out the cost incurred each time a 'typical' employee leaves. This process is illustrated in the following simple example. Here we have a hotel employing 150 people. There is one HRl manager employed (total annual employment cost £28,000) and a part-time personnel assistant who deals with payroll matters (cost £12,000). Line management salaries (plus on-costs) average £25,000, while the average staff salary cost is £17,000. The hotel has an annual turnover rate of 35 per cent. It has not expanded or contracted at all in the past year, so every recruitment episode resulted from a resignation or dismissal. No redundancy payments were made, no overtime payments made and no temporary cover hired while there were vacancies.

Percentage of time spent on resignation, recruitment, selection and induction activities		Cost
Personnel manager	30%	£8,400
Personnel assistant	40%	£4,800
Line managers (x7)	5%	£8,750
Staff (x 150)	2%	£51,000
Annual recruitment advertising bill		£25,000
TOTAL ANNUAL TURNOVER COST		£97,950

These approaches have the virtue of being simple to carry out, but the results can only amount to rough estimates. Moreover, of course, they underestimate the total true cost of turnover considerably because they do not take account of the 'soft' costs incurred such as loss of productivity or lost customers due to poorer service levels than could have been achieved with a more stable staff. There are two alternative approaches to take in acknowledgement of these deficiencies. First, it is possible to present the figures to managers on a 'not less than' basis. This is what the Audit Commission does when it carries out assessments of turnover costs in public sector organisations. In other words, it is stated that the figure represents a minimum estimate of the likely total cost incurred in the year. Alternatively it is possible to make an attempt at quantifying the percentage of total turnover costs which are 'soft' costs. As stated above, estimates vary, but most suggest that for average non-managerial jobs soft costs account for half to two thirds of total costs. The figure is rather higher for management and professional occupations where efficiency losses deriving from resignations are higher.

In recent years a number of consulting firms have set up free web-based turnover costing tools which anyone with internet access can use. Some are sophisticated, building in assumptions about soft costs to give a more accurate estimate of total costs for you. There are numerous tools of this kind on the web now, most originating in the USA. Several dozen can be discovered simply by typing 'employee turnover cost' into a search engine.

SOPHISTICATED APPROACHES TO TURNOVER COSTING

The sophisticated approaches to turnover costing include the types of analysis in the rudimentary approaches, but examine each item in greater detail. Broad assumptions are avoided, so that at each stage a figure is reached which is as accurate as possible. In addition, an attempt is made to put a figure on the 'hidden' or 'soft' costs. Some of the methods that have been evolved are quite involved, but are necessary if any kind of accurate estimate is to be made.

An important component of hidden turnover costs is reduced efficiency or productivity. The most significant chunk relates to the performance of new starters as they learn their new jobs, but it is also important not to forget impaired productivity on the part of co-workers and supervisors who have to devote time to initial development of the new employee. Then there is lower productivity on the part of the leaver in the weeks leading up to their departure. When someone is working their notice out, productivity can dip very substantially as people slow down, complete existing projects and are not involved in new ones. In the few jobs where individual performance is measured easily and objectively costs of this kind can be easily calculated. For most, however, efficiency measurements have to be a matter of human judgement.

In his influential article, Douglas Phillips (1990) sets out, with worked examples, methods that can be used to quantify reduced productivity in such jobs. His suggested method draws on two detailed research projects. It is not by any means perfect, but it does provide a means of making a convincing calculation of these types of costs. He suggests that 'incoming employee inefficiency' is best estimated by asking employees in particular job groups (or their supervisors) to estimate the number of weeks or months it took when they started in the role before they were able to work at full efficiency. The method recommended involves estimating productivity during the learning-curve period.

The approach is best understood by means of two simple examples. First, let us assume that a new junior manager arrives to start a job with relevant technical experience but no prior knowledge of how the organisation operates politically, culturally or structurally. A year and a half later she is asked to estimate how many months were required before she was working at 25 per cent efficiency, 50 per cent efficiency, 75 per cent efficiency and 100 per cent efficiency respectively. Thinking back she says that it took a year to reach 100 per cent efficiency in the job. She estimates that she was 25 per cent proficient after two months, 50 per cent proficient after six months and 75 per cent proficient after nine months. These figures allow the following analysis to be undertaken:

Efficiency level	Average efficiency		Months required		Months of full productivity
0–25%	.125	×	2	=	0.25
25%–50%	.375	×	4	=	1.5
50%–75%	.625	×	3	=	1.875
75%–100%	.875	×	3	=	2.625
TOTALS:			12		6.25

For the first two months our manager was working, on average, at 12.5 per cent efficiency. This translates into .25 months of full productivity. She then works four months at an average efficiency of 37.5 per cent (equivalent to 1.5 months) and so on until she reaches full efficiency at 12 months. It is thus estimated that during the first year she was fully productive for a period equivalent to 6.25 months. The remainder of the time (5.75 months) represents 'lost' productivity or the difference between the efficiency level of an experienced long term employee and that of a new starter moving up the learning curve. It is then straightforward to convert this figure into a percentage and to work out a total 'cost of lost efficiency' that can be accounted for because the post is held by a new starter. In this case, with an annual employment cost of £20,000, the cost recorded would be £9,600 (48 per cent of 20,000). For jobs with a faster learning curve, you are best setting the unit of calculation at weeks or days rather than months.

You can use the same approach to calculate a cost associated with declining productivity of a departing employee. Here though the estimates have to be made by supervisors and work colleagues. The following example focuses on the declining productivity of a clerical worker who costs his employers £1,000 to employ each month.

Efficiency level	Average efficiency		Weeks at level		Weeks of full productivity
100%–75%	.875	×	3	=	2.65
75%–50%	.625	×	2	=	1.25
50%–25%	.375	×	2	=	0.75
25%–0%	.125	×	1	=	0.125
TOTALS:			8		4.775

In this case our worker's efficiency took eight weeks to decline from 100 per cent to zero. During this time we estimate that he was averaging 87.5 per cent efficiency for three weeks, 62.5 per cent efficiency for two weeks, 37.5 per cent efficiency for one week and 12.5 per cent efficiency for one week. Over the eight weeks we thus calculate that he was fully efficient for a period equivalent to 4.775 weeks or around 60 per cent of the time. The lost efficiency due to his impending departure is thus 40 per cent of £4,000 (the cost of employing him during the eight weeks). That is £1,600 worth of work that is 'lost' because of an impending resignation.

Clearly these figures can only be broad estimates, but the method represents a credible and reasonably straightforward way of assessing losses sustained due to reduced operational effectiveness when people leave and are replaced with relatively inexperienced successors.

When carrying out this kind of project the most effective method involves focusing in detail on actual 'turnover episodes' experienced in your organisation. Analysts typically carry out at least three or four separate analyses for each major job group. Resulting costs are then averaged to give a credible 'typical' figure for lost efficiency each time someone leaves that type of job.

It is a great deal harder to estimate costs associated with lost business opportunities when people leave – the fourth category in the list set out above. There are no standard approaches available here, because these factors affect each organisation very differently. For many jobs the effect in these terms is negligible when one person leaves. No customers are lost and no business opportunities passed up. However, the impact can be significant when a particularly effective performer leaves. Examples would include a solicitor whose personal reputation attracts clients to a law firm, a well-known and respected head teacher or a particularly successful sales executive. In each case the departure of the individual can be seen, in practice, to have a measurable negative impact on the organisation. Where this is the case it would be negligent not to include some kind of damage estimation in any calculation of turnover costs. The only way it can be done is to examine, in detail, what happened when such an individual left. Reasoned costings are then applied and totalled up.

The final feature of sophisticated approaches is the inclusion of the pluses as well as the minuses. There is thus a recognition that some turnover in some circumstances can lead to cost savings. Examples are as follows:

- where new starters enter employment at the bottom of an incremental scale, replacing leavers who had reached the top (this is a very common situation in the public sector)

- where the opportunity is taken, when there is a vacancy, not to recruit for a few weeks (ie by freezing the post)

- where employer pension fund contributions are lower for a new recruit than for the leaver (eg where entry to a final salary scheme is barred for new starters)

- where a particularly unproductive employee is replaced by a highly productive new starter.

BENCHMARKING TURNOVER

Measuring and costing turnover are useful activities for the reasons given above. Those activities allow an organisation to track its progress over time and hence to calculate savings achieved as a result of staff turnover reduction exercises. They also allow inter-departmental comparisons to be made. The figures can, however, be put to another use too, namely comparing an organisation's performance on turnover and retention with those of other organisations, and particularly with those of competitors in the same industry. This is particularly useful where involuntary turnover is seriously damaging to an organisation because the figures can be used as a useful proxy for the performance of the HR function more generally.

Job tenure figures for the UK as a whole are occasionally published by the government using data from the Labour Force Survey. The most recent figures, according to the DTI, later DBERR and now DBIS (2006), are as follows:

Length of service	% of the workforce
1 month–2 years	27%
2–5 years	24%
5–8 years	13%
8–12 years	9%
Over 12 years	24%

Interestingly, despite what we read about the 'end of jobs for life' and decreasing employer – employee loyalty, these figures have remained remarkably stable over time. There have been no dramatic reductions in job tenure trends in recent years.

A number of surveys are undertaken each year in the UK to establish overall turnover rates. The largest are those carried out by the CIPD and by the Confederation of British Industry (CBI), but there are also many others that are organised by consultancies and employers' organisations which focus on specific industries. An excellent summary of the data from these and other one-off surveys is published each year in *IRS Employment Review*.

All the surveys reveal considerable fluctuations in turnover rates over time, in different regions and between different industries. However, the different methodologies and definitions of turnover used mean that the figures can vary quite considerably from survey to survey. Between the late 1990s and 2008 the overall national figure reported by the CIPD and CBI surveys has been between 17 per cent and 20 per cent, which is quite high by historical standards, reflecting strong economic conditions and the presence of tight labour markets. The more opportunity people have to move employers, the more likely they are to do so. By contrast, in the early 1990s recessionary conditions led to a national turnover rate of only 10 per cent (IFF Research 1993) and we have seen a similar, if somewhat smaller, dip in 2009 and 2010 as the impact of the latest recession reduced opportunities for people to find new jobs.

Of particular interest to employers seeking to benchmark their turnover rates against appropriate comparators are the figures for turnover in specific industrial sectors, regions and occupational groups. Retention is always hard in the most prosperous areas of the country where unemployment is lowest. The highest levels are invariably found in London, the South East and East Anglia where rates in excess of 25 per cent are regularly reported (see Rankin 2009). By contrast, in Northern Ireland, Merseyside and the North East figures are some 40 per cent lower.

For data on variations between specific industrial sectors it is necessary to rely on smaller-scale surveys such as that carried out each year by the CIPD. One should not read too much into these results, because of the very small sample sizes used. They do, however, give a general indication of substantial variations between industries, particularly when it is considered that the same industries (call centres, retailing and catering) top the table in most years (see Table 14.4).

They are thus very helpful when carrying out benchmarking exercises, provided not too much weight is placed on any one year's figures.

Table 14.4 Turnover rates, various industries

Industry	Average total turnover 2009 (%)	Average voluntary turnover 2009 (%)
Hotels and catering	34%	16%
Call centres	34%	19%
Media and publishing	23%	12%
Communications	23%	13%
IT industry	22%	14%
Construction	18%	10%
Retail and wholesale	17%	10%
Financial services	17%	10%
Community and voluntary	16%	11%
Manufacturing	15%	5%
Education	15%	9%
Professional services	14%	11%
Local government	14%	10%
Utilities	13%	7%
Transport/storage	11%	5%
Health	11%	6%
Central government	4%	4%

Data from these and other surveys suggest that turnover figures also vary quite considerably between people in different occupations. Perhaps unsurprisingly, it appears to be highest among sales staff and those employed to do routine, unskilled work (30–50 per cent), and lowest among management and craft workers (10–20 per cent). In other words, turnover rates are highest among those who possess fewest industry-specific skills. By contrast, there is less movement where individuals are more restricted in their choice of alternative jobs because their skills and experience are less readily transferable. Despite recent rises the lowest turnover levels of all are found in the public sector, where jobs tend to be reasonably well paid and terms and conditions of employment are good.

EXERCISE BOX: LABOUR TURNOVER IN LAW FIRMS AND BARRISTERS' CHAMBERS

Read the article by Karen Moloney entitled 'Lines of Defence' featured in *People Management* (11 July, 2002, pages 48–49). This can be downloaded from the *People Management* archive on the CIPD's website (www.cipd.co.uk).

This article reports the views of managers in law firms and barristers' chambers about labour turnover trends and some other associated issues.

Questions:

1 Why is labour turnover so much higher among solicitors than it was 10 years ago? Why might it be considered more damaging in this industry than in many others?

2 Aside from reducing staff turnover rates, what other advantages accrue to the firms who invest in training and developing their junior staff?

3 Once barristers have secured a place in a chambers, it is rare for them to leave. Turnover rates are very low indeed. Why do you think this is? Can other employers learn anything from the pupilage system operated by barristers' chambers?

EXAMPLE

KEY ARTICLE BOX

'The real costs of turnover: Lessons from a call center' by Steve Hillmer, Barbara Hillmer and Gale McRoberts (2004). *Human Resource Planning.* **Vol. 27, No. 3. 34–41**

There are few articles which examine in detail the costs associated with voluntary staff turnover in particular workplaces. Here the authors have done so, using data they have gathered from a call centre in the USA. They conclude, having made conservative estimates for intangible as well as tangible costs, that the true cost of turnover in this workplace is equivalent to a sum not less than a year's salary.

Questions:

1 Why is staff turnover both so high in call centres and so problematic for their managers?

2 To what extent do you think that the researchers have included all the possible sources of cost in their calculations?

3 How far could this methodology be employed in other types of organisational setting?

EXPLORE FURTHER

- *Employee turnover* by Peter Hom and Rodger Griffeth (1995) is by far the most comprehensive publication on the topic. All aspects are explored and all the established research reviewed. Their more recent book entitled *Retaining valued employees* (2001) is more user-friendly, but also draws on robust academic research.

- The best source of data on turnover levels in different regions, industries and occupational groups is the online journal *IRS Employment Review*, which regularly publishes statistics and useful articles on the subject. Their annual benchmarking survey is published early every year. Incomes Data Services has also produced a number of useful publications on the management of turnover. The annual CIPD survey covering recruitment and retention is also a good source of benchmarking data.

CHAPTER 15

Improving employee retention

LEARNING OUTCOMES

By the end of this chapter readers should be able to:

- distinguish between different types of resignation and explain their significance
- advise managers about the major causes of staff turnover in their organisations and departments
- conduct effective exit interviews and staff attitude surveys
- develop and secure commitment for plans aimed at reducing turnover levels
- recommend effective methods of improving employee retention.

In addition, readers should be able to understand and explain:

- the main theories and models explaining staff turnover
- debates about how best to reduce staff turnover
- the strengths and weaknesses of the major diagnostic tools used to underpin employee retention initiatives
- major theories and research findings concerning effective approaches to employee retention.

 EXERCISE BOX: PEEBLES HYDRO HOTEL

EXERCISE 15.1

Read the article by Jim Dow entitled 'Spa Attraction' featured in *People Management* (29 May 2003, pages 34–35). This can be downloaded from the *People Management* archive on the CIPD's website (www.cipd.co.uk).

This article describes the experiences of a large, privately owned country house hotel in the Scottish borders. It has very low staff turnover in comparison with its competitors, many of its staff having over 10 years' service.

Questions:

1. Why do you think staff turnover is generally so high in the hotel industry?

2. What factors cited in the article help explain why this particular hotel enjoys low staff turnover? What other factors are likely to have played a part?

3. What problems has the hotel encountered because of its low turnover? What has it done to tackle these?

4. What lessons could be learned from the experience of the Peebles Hydro Hotel by organisations in other industries?

REASONS FOR LEAVING

The major causes of employee turnover fall into four categories. Each is fundamentally different from the other and demands a different type of organisational response when it is identified as the major explanation for turnover among members of particular occupational groups:

PULL FACTORS

Pull-type resignations occur when the major cause is the positive attraction of alternative employment. The employee concerned may be wholly satisfied with their existing organisation and happy in their job, but nonetheless decides to move on in search of something even better. It may be a higher rate of pay, a more valued benefits package, more job security, better long-term career opportunities, a less pressured existence, the opportunity to work overseas, a shorter commute or more convenient hours of work. Alternatively it may be the desire to work with particular colleagues or for a particular management team. People also move in order to spend some time working in a high-profile or well-respected employer so as to build, over time, a portfolio of such experience.

Where pull factors are at work, the organisation seeking to reduce quit-rates will gain little by seeking to enhance job satisfaction. This may delay the inevitable for a few months, but will not in itself serve to deter resignations. Instead it is necessary to find out what employees really value, what they are looking for in their careers, and to enhance the organisation's ability to provide it.

PUSH FACTORS

By contrast, in the case of push factors, the major underlying cause of resignations is the perception that something is wrong with the existing employer. The person concerned may move in order to secure a 'better job', but they are as likely to join another organisation without knowing a great deal about it just because they no longer enjoy their current one. In doing so they hope working life will improve but they cannot be sure that it will. A range of different push factors can be identified ranging from a dislike of the prevailing organisational culture, to disapproval of changed structures and straightforward personality clashes with colleagues. Perceptions of unfairness often underlie these types of departure, but they can also occur simply because the employee is bored or generally fed up with their day-to-day work. They thus start looking for something (or anything) different and leave when they find a suitable alternative. In the more extreme cases of dissatisfaction people leave before securing another position.

Where push factors are pre-eminent the required organisational response is to address the root causes of dissatisfaction. This may mean selecting supervisors with greater care, providing them with better training and appraising them more effectively in terms of their supervisory skills. It may mean examining organisational policy with a view to improving the fairness of its operation or it may mean simply paying greater attention to enhancing the quality of working life. Above all it requires the creation of what Freeman and Medoff (1984) famously characterised as an employment relationship of 'voice' as opposed to one of 'exit'. This means providing structures (both collective and individual), as well as a culture, which encourages the resolution of disaffection internally before it generates unwelcome resignations.

UNAVOIDABLE TURNOVER

This category comprises reasons for leaving which are wholly or mainly outside the control of the organisation. The resignation does not occur because of dissatisfaction with the job, or the perceived opportunities provided elsewhere, but for reasons which are unconnected to work in any direct sense. The most common is retirement which affects almost everyone at some stage, but there are many others too. Illness is often a cause, either because it incapacitates the employee or a relative for whom they have caring responsibilities. Maternity is another, women preferring not to return to the same job after their leave either to take a break from work altogether or in order to secure a job which makes it easier for them to combine work with childcare arrangements. A fourth common reason is relocation – usually in order to follow or join up with a spouse or partner. Finally there is the desire to take a career break for a period in order to travel, re-enter full-time education or pursue some other interest.

Organisations often conclude that nothing can be done to reduce turnover of this kind. This is only partially true, because in many situations the employee who leaves for an 'unavoidable reason' could choose to continue working in the same job if they really wanted to. People choose to take a career break, choose not to return to work after maternity leave and often choose to retire. This suggests that if the job was more valued and attractive they might choose not to exercise the option of leaving.

INVOLUNTARY TURNOVER

The final category includes departures which are involuntary and initiated by the organisation. The employee would have remained employed had they not been asked or required to leave. Redundancies clearly fall into this category along with short-term layoffs, the ending of fixed-term contracts and other dismissals of one kind or another. Many resignations are also in fact largely involuntary because people often prefer to 'jump before they are pushed'. Hence someone who knows he or she is to be made redundant in a few months seeks alternative employment ahead of time, while a colleague who believes his employment will soon be terminated on grounds of poor performance secures another job before being formally dismissed.

While such turnover can sometimes be characterised as being 'functional' rather than 'dysfunctional' it still carries a cost and is thus best avoided where possible. The main aim should be to stop the situations which cause it to happen from arising in the first place. Except in the case of some dismissals on grounds of illness, measures can be taken to reduce the incidence of involuntary turnover. These largely focus on recruitment and selection practices, the aim being to ensure as far as is possible that a large pool of potential candidates comes forward and that poor decisions are avoided when deciding who to offer jobs to. However, good supervision plays a role too. Well-managed employees tend to 'give of their best', resulting in fewer examples of poor performance and hence fewer dismissals.

Exit routes

For some employees the decision to leave is taken on the spur of the moment, some incident occurring or a management decision being confirmed that leaves little room for second thoughts. In other cases the process is drawn out over a longer period of time. There may well be months or even years separating the actual resignation from the first thoughts about the possibility of leaving. In between there are a series of stages, some more complex in nature than others, at which the decision to quit comes a step closer. At each of these stages an organisational intervention of some kind may have the effect of halting progress towards the resignation either temporarily or permanently.

Researchers specialising in the study of employee turnover have long debated the nature of the multi-staged decision-making process which precedes the final decision to quit. Some have put forward universal models which claim to cover all turnover scenarios, while others have specified different types of exit route. One of the most influential approaches has been that of William Mobley (1977) who found evidence to support the validity of the following 10 stage model:

a Evaluate existing job.

b Experience job dissatisfaction.

c Think of quitting.

d Evaluate expected utility of search for a new job and the cost of quitting.

e Decide to search for alternatives.

f Search for alternatives.

g Evaluate alternatives.

h Compare best alternative with present job.

i Decide whether to stay or quit.

j Quit.

Mobley's was the first academic work undertaken in the modern business environment to draw proper attention to the complexity of most resignation decisions. His model includes both push and pull factors, suggesting that in practice the former come before the latter. In other words, his view is that in most cases dissatisfaction occurs first and that this precipitates the search for a new job. While few would argue with the items Mobley includes in his model, there is doubt about the extent to which the ten stages tend, in practice, to follow one another in linear sequence. It is plausible to argue, for example, that employees who perceive themselves to enjoy plenty of alternative job opportunities enter a workplace with a wholly different mindset to those who believe their career options to be severely limited. The first group will judge their employers harshly, will be quicker to criticise and more likely to feel discontented. They are also less likely to seek to develop feelings of commitment. From the start they know that as soon as they cease to enjoy their jobs, they can and will move on. By contrast, the second group will instinctively seek (literally) to make the best out of a bad job. They will be prepared for knocks, will expect to go through periods of dissatisfaction and will put up with poor treatment from supervisors.

Other models, such as those put forward by Steers & Mowday (1981) and Price & Mueller (1986), identify the different elements that can combine to bring about a resignation, but remove the concept of linear stages. Their purpose is to identify all the different types of factor that lead to employee turnover and to suggest how each relates to each other. The Steers and Mowday model is illustrated in Figure 15.1.

Figure 15.1 Steers & Mowday's model

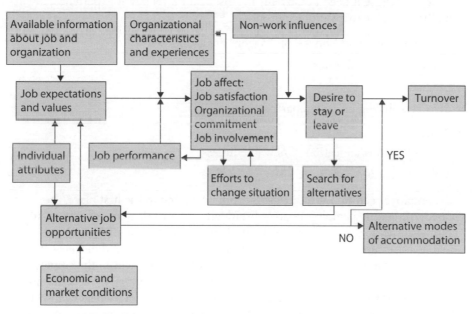

Source: Steers and Mowday, in L. Cummings and B. Straw (eds) (1981), Research in Organizational Behavior. Greenwich, CT. JAI Press. p242. Quoted in Hom and Griffeth (1995)

A useful feature of the Price and Mueller model is the clear separation of the notions of 'job satisfaction' and 'organisational commitment'. In doing this they are asserting that it is possible to be broadly satisfied in your job and yet simultaneously uncommitted to the organisation you work for. Reduced commitment leads to turnover, but this can be brought about as a result of *both* dissatisfaction with a job and other factors such as a disapproval of company policy or the growing importance of issues in one's non-work life. This is a vital distinction for managers who want to get a better grip on turnover in their organisations to take on board. A rather different model has been developed by Thomas Lee, Terence Mitchell and their colleagues (see Lee & Mitchell 1994 and Lee *et al* 1999). Their 'unfolding model' is notable for its suggestion that employee turnover rarely occurs after careful, rational consideration on the part of employees. Drawing on image theory, these researchers have found that what actually happens in many cases is that individuals experience some kind of 'shock' which jolts them very quickly into thinking about leaving when they have not seriously given it much thought in the past.

Far from weighing up alternatives and thinking carefully about advantages and disadvantages of quitting, employees tend often to make the decision very quickly. The term 'shock' can refer to any event, personal or organisational, which has the effect of bringing continued employment with the current employer into question. Because it need not, by any means, be an unpleasant experience, the term 'trigger' is perhaps more appropriate.

Common examples of 'shocks' or 'triggers' are as follows:

- a call from a headhunter
- pregnancy
- divorce/splitting up with a partner
- mergers
- reorganisations/allocation of new job duties
- appointment of a new supervisor.

If the employer can stop these 'triggers' from occurring in the first place, the chances of retaining employees are substantially enhanced. Some, of course, are genuinely outside the organisation's control, but many can be influenced. It is possible, for example, in very competitive labour markets to build defences that are hard for headhunters to penetrate (see Chapter 8). It is also within the employer's power to lessen the extent to which the trigger has 'shock-impact'. There are no one-off easy answers to these predicaments. It is a question of managers knowing what makes their staff tick, understanding the nature of the most common exit routes, and anticipating possible turnover triggers ahead of time.

DIAGNOSTIC TOOLS

There are a number of different methods available for managers to use in collecting evidence about the reasons people have for leaving different parts of their organisations. By far the most commonly used tool is the 'exit interview' or some variation that uses questionnaires rather than face to face interviews. These ask people directly, at the time of leaving, what major explanations underlie their decision to quit. Unfortunately, while helpful, there is plenty of evidence to show that exit interviews can be a highly unreliable source of information. There is thus a need to consider using other methods alongside them.

EXIT INTERVIEWS

The aim here is to establish and record the main reasons for resignations. Ideally the interviewer will also discover if the organisation could have done anything to postpone or prevent the resignation with a view to avoiding others in the future. For those employers who re-hire ex-employees from time to time, a third aim will be to leave a favourable impression of the organisation in the leaver's mind. There is nothing wrong with carrying out exit interviews, especially if they are the only diagnostic tool being used in turnover management, but managers need to be mindful of their weaknesses as well as their strengths. It is wise both to treat data collected in this manner with some caution and to search out alternative sources of information about reasons for leaving.

The most recent CIPD survey on employee retention practices reported that exit interviews were employed 'to investigate the reasons as to why people leave' by 89 per cent of respondents, a further 28 per cent using anonymous exit surveys either in addition or as an alternative (CIPD 2009b:30). IRS (2002c:34) reported that 92 per cent of their respondents used exit interviews and that 13 per cent used a mixture of exit interviews and separation questionnaires. Of these, nine out of 10 stated that they 'had acted' on the information gathered in their exit interviews, as many as 99 per cent agreeing that the main purpose was to discover why employees had chosen to tender their resignations. A later IRS survey looking at retention management reported that 65.4 per cent of employers evaluate the data they gather from exit interviews and surveys every month and that 25.6 per cent do so once a year. The information is then used for a variety of purposes including 'reward management', 'evaluating the effectiveness of training', 'workforce planning', 'evaluating recruitment' and 'evaluating the performance of line managers' (IRS 2004a:44–45). While employers accept that there are problems associated with the use of the data they collect about labour turnover in their organisations, these are typically seen as being technical in nature. Only 14.6 per cent of respondents to the IRS survey considered that the 'data is not sufficiently trusted (ie it lacks credibility)'. We can thus conclude with some confidence not only that the use of exit interviews and questionnaires is standard practice in larger UK organisations, but that managers rarely question the validity of these approaches and make extensive use of the data they collect by these means in developing their HR policies.

The most straightforward approach is to take the resignee through a questionnaire of direct questions concerning his or her satisfaction with pay, supervisor, development opportunities, relationships with colleagues and job content. The results are then recorded and analysed annually to see if there are any patterns that provide pointers to how the organisation should change things if it wants to improve its employee retention rates. However, many UK organisations either fail altogether to record the reasons people leave their organisation or do so in such an unsophisticated way as to provide little by way of a useful platform on which to build robust employee retention practices. The typical approach involves managers talking briefly and formally to their departing staff to confirm the reason for leaving and the identity of their new employer (if there is one). The commonly used name for these encounters is 'exit interviews', but they are often too short and peremptory to justify such a title.

In theory exit interviews should work well and provide accurate information on which to base employee retention initiatives. The problem is their reliability. There are two key assumptions on which claims in their favour rest:

i   Departing employees give their managers full and accurate accounts of their reasons for leaving at exit interviews.

ii   It is possible to identify, for each departing employee, a single 'most salient' reason to explain their resignation.

There now is a considerable volume of published evidence which strongly suggests that these assumptions are highly questionable, particularly the first.

As long ago as 1969 in an IPM publication, Samual stated that 'research has indicated that the validity of reasons stated by employees at the point of leaving a company is highly suspect' (Samual 1969), while Giacalone and his colleagues, in a series of articles published in the 1980s and 1990s cast doubt on the accuracy of such data, arguing that employees have a strong tendency to distort the responses they give (see Giacalone 1989, Giacalone & Knouse 1989 and Giacalone & Duhon 1991). Steen (1999), Furnham (2001) and Findlay (2003) have also all made strident criticisms of the exit interview, the latter's contempt for the practice being particularly colourful. Describing the exit interviews as 'the cockroach of the HR world', he says that 'no one knows why they exist, no one can justify or eliminate them, and they will likely survive into the third millennium'.

The results of these studies suggest consistently that many employees fail to tell the whole truth to their managers at the time of leaving about why they have resigned. First, there is a tendency for resignees to give equivocal answers in interviews when they actually have clear and definite reasons for going. Secondly, employees tend to down play push factors and play up the pull factors and 'unavoidable' reasons when explaining their departure to their managers. Thirdly, it is the case that departing employees are a great deal more likely to cite pay levels as the main reason for leaving when asked by managers than is the case when the interview is conducted by a neutral party.

Furnham (2001) argues that the central problem is that exit interviews potentially have far more to offer employers than their departing employees. There is no incentive for resignees to explain in full why they are leaving, but often very good reasons from an employee perspective to avoid telling the whole truth. He goes on to advise departing employees that it is probably in their best interests to avoid total honesty and candour when being interviewed.

Opinion is divided about in what way the information given in exit interviews is likely to be distorted. Giacalone *et al* (1999) believe that negative points are often over-emphasised, interviewees and survey respondents taking the opportunity to 'retaliate against disliked members of the organisation via responses that are stated in direct contradiction to actual sentiments'. In some circumstances, they argue, inaccurate information may be given because of a desire on the part of the resignee to be unhelpful to a disliked employer.

A more common view is that employees have every reason, and hence a strong tendency, to downplay the significance of their negative reasons for leaving and to play up positive or neutral reasons. There are several good reasons for this:

- A reluctance on the part of the employees to criticise managers who they have worked closely with and may personally like.

- Fear that the interviewing manager will take criticisms personally and will rebut them in the interview.

- A wish not to 'burn bridges' because a favourable reference may be sought in the future.

- A wish to leave wide open the possibility of returning to work with the employer at a later date.

- Embarrassment that the true reason for leaving will seem trivial or pathetic when articulated to a manager.

- A reluctance to reveal what the manager may see as weaknesses were the genuine reasons for leaving to be revealed.

- A wish to protect colleagues who are not leaving.

- Due to feelings of generosity and goodwill towards colleagues who are marking the employee's departure with leaving cards, presents or parties.

- Because the true reasons for leaving are personal and therefore considered confidential.

- Because of a perception that the real reason for leaving would make the employee appear ungrateful for opportunities given and exercised while in the job.

For all these reasons it is easier for departing staff (whose real reasons for leaving are complex or which imply criticism of their managers) to state that they are leaving to gain more pay or because they are relocating to move in with a partner, than it is to set out the genuine causes of the resignation.

 REFLECTIVE QUESTION

Have you been responsible for conducting exit interviews? If you have, to what extent have you experienced the problems identified above?

THE VALIDITY OF EXIT INTERVIEWS AND QUESTIONNAIRES

Wilkinson (2004) investigated the accuracy of responses given in exit questionnaires by carrying out in-depth telephone interviews with 50 people who had previously been employed as nurses at a large NHS Hospital Trust, all of whom had resigned voluntarily within the past four years. Questions were put to them about their reasons for leaving in the same order as they appeared on the original leavers' questionnaire and in the same format. This enabled a direct comparison to be made between the responses made by each interviewee to the Trust at the time of resignation and those made some months or years later confidentially to an independent researcher.

The results clearly showed substantial differences between the two responses. In fact only 36 per cent of the reasons given for leaving on questionnaires completed at the time of resignation were confirmed in the follow-up interviews. Moreover, of those responses that changed 88.9 per cent were altered from reasons that could be categorised as 'pull' factors to those which were essentially 'push factors'. By far the most common reason for leaving given in the interviews was dissatisfaction with management, yet this was only stated as being the reason on the questionnaires by a small minority.

This study appears to confirm that departing employees are reluctant to voice the real reasons for their resignations when these are negative. In particular there is a strong reluctance on the part of leavers to make criticisms of their line managers or to complain about matters within the control of line managers. As a result the employer is given a highly misleading impression of why its employees are resigning.

In order to maximise the likelihood that leavers will talk frankly in their exit interviews you can take a number of steps. First, the interview should not be carried out by the individual's immediate line manager, or by any manager who has exercised direct authority over them. Instead the interviewer should be someone with whom there has been no prior reporting relationship and who will not be required to give a reference in the future. Human resources staff are often ideally placed to carry out the role, but it can equally well be performed by managers based elsewhere in the organisation. The less contact the manager concerned has had with the leaver, the better. However, very senior personnel should not be used, simply because people can be overawed when talking to them (the headmaster syndrome). Some organisations go as far as to outsource the exit interviewing function entirely to a consultant, while others simply apply common sense and ask the employee concerned with whom they would prefer to conduct the interview. Both approaches significantly increase the chances that valuable information will be obtained.

Secondly, as far as is possible, confidentiality must be ensured. If the real reason for the resignation is some perceived failure on the part of management, few employees will come clean for fear of burning their bridges unless they believe that any comments they make will not subsequently be relayed to the individuals of whom actual or implied criticism is being made. Confidentiality can never be 100 per cent guaranteed, but steps can be taken to reassure leavers:

● If an organisation ensures that its exit interviews are confidential, the practice will be seen to as such by existing employees. When their turn comes, they are more likely to have confidence in the system.

- Explaining that maintaining confidentiality is as much in the interests of the employer as the ex-employee, enhances the leaver's belief that what they say will not get back to those they criticise.

Thirdly, the timing of exit interviews is important. Organisations should avoid the last day or two of employment. This is because they are abnormal days for the leaver, tending to be a more pleasant and exciting experience. The imminent prospect of a break between jobs or of new employment naturally weighs highly in our minds on our last days. To this is added the tendency for leaving events of one kind or another to be organised and anticipated, at which cards and presents are given and generous speeches made. The messages conveyed are often designed by co-workers to be both touching and memorable. They thus have the effect of engendering in the leaver feelings of generosity towards people and a job that they may actually have detested and couldn't wait to leave a week or two earlier. Conversely, where these rituals do not occur or are apparently organised under some sufferance by colleagues, the leaving employee will often be disappointed. The emotions generated in the final days are thus too strong to make this a good time to carry out the interview.

In theory exit interviews are best carried out as close as possible to the date of resignation when the reasons are clearest in the leaver's mind and best articulated. The problem here is that the resignation may occur some weeks before the physical departure because of notice provisions. This means that there are plenty of working days still to go and hence a reluctance to jeopardise working relationships by voicing criticism of managers or colleagues. So a balance has to be struck. The best time is probably a week or so prior to the last day. There are a few days work left; not enough to worry about the fallout associated with critical remarks, but a sufficiently long period before the more emotionally charged atmosphere of the last days begins to kick in.

A final point to make about exit interviews concerns their content. Here too the traditional approach involving the use of standard questionnaires should be avoided. This is because they tend to pre judge the responses that departing employees will give through the presence of prompts. In many cases a list of reasons for leaving is given and the resignee required to state which one was the most significant in their case. Such approaches make for easy analysis and collation of data, but they are unlikely to reflect the true picture. Prompting must therefore be avoided as should any attempt to simplify for data collection purposes the complex reality of the decision to leave. For most people a number of factors come together, often over a long period, to cause a resignation. Some will be pull-factors, others push-factors; some will be work-based, others rooted in personal circumstances. Each will interact with others in different ways and at different times. It is only via unstructured exit interviews that the employee will be able to articulate their reasons properly and in their own words. The interviewer needs to explain the organisation's purpose in completing exit interviews with leavers, before asking the departing employee to explain step by step and in their own words why they are resigning. Supplementary questions can then be asked as a means of clarifying points made and probing a little more deeply, or to encourage the interviewee to keep talking. At the end the interviewer should sum up what they think has been stated and check with the employee that this represents a fair summary of their words. After this has been done, a further question can be asked along the following lines:

> What, if anything, could the organisation have done differently which would have led you to remain an employee?

Here again the leaver should be left to answer in their own words without prompting. Supplementary questions should only be asked to clarify points, to ask for something to be repeated or to probe for more detail. The urge to contradict or to enter into any kind of discussion about the answer given to the question has to be avoided. What matters, after all, in terms of retention management (as in customer retention) is what ex-employees actually perceive, not what managers hope that they should perceive.

Further good general advice about how to conduct a good exit interview, including ways of encouraging honesty, is provided by Macafee (2007).

STAFF ATTITUDE SURVEYS

Questionnaire-based attitude or opinion surveys circulated among all employees are a widely employed communication mechanism in the UK. They are used to gauge morale in the workforce generally as well as to help managers pick up on specific issues that need attention. In many organisations the results are quantified to allow progress to be tracked over time and comparisons to be made between different business units.

The problem with attitude surveys, as is made clear by Levin and Rosse (2001:115–6), is that in order to be effective they must be anonymous. In other words, if you want your employees to answer the questions in the survey frankly and fully, their completed forms must not be traceable back to them. However, if the survey is anonymous it prevents the organisation from identifying individual problems and acting upon them. It also means that it is not possible to compare the answers given by people who subsequently leave with those of colleagues who stay. Yet, from a retention management perspective it is this kind of data which is most valuable. Attitude surveys often reveal general dissatisfaction with some aspects of an organisation and general satisfaction with others. This information is useful to know but does not allow you to establish which types of dissatisfaction lead to turnover and which do not. Nor does it allow you to see what forms of positive assessment of the organisation are associated with people who stay a long time and those which have no impact on the propensity to leave. For example, a survey may well reveal that 50 per cent of the staff are dissatisfied with their pay level, while 50 per cent are satisfied. But it is impossible to tell from this data alone whether or not there is a higher turnover rate among those who are dissatisfied with their pay. The survey's analysts could easily make such judgements if we were to require staff to identify themselves on the survey questionnaire, but that would compromise the accuracy of the survey. So managers cannot know whether or not an increase in pay would or would not have any actual impact on staff retention rates.

For attitude surveys to be useful as a tool for diagnosing the causes of turnover, ways have to be found around this conundrum. Four approaches are worth considering:

1 Issuing an attitude survey to all staff on a regular basis, but also asking leavers to complete the questionnaire before they depart. The leavers' forms can then be compared with those of the staff as a whole. The problem here is the same as for exit interviews, namely a tendency to inaccuracy. However much the organisation guarantees confidentiality, departing employees will perceive their answers to be traceable back to them.

2 Using an independent, external body to issue the attitude survey and to collate the results. Provided employees trust the consultancy concerned to protect their confidentiality, this can work well. Employees write their name and job title on the attitude survey form and, hopefully, go on to give full and honest answers. A list of leavers is then given to the consultants on a regular basis and comparisons made in their report between the attitudes of leavers and those of stayers. The disadvantage, of course, is the cost.

3 Asking leavers to complete a confidential attitude survey (as above) and then administering the same survey to a group of stayers from the same job groups. Ideally you want to look for pairs of people (one leaver and one stayer) with broadly the same characteristics in terms of job tenure and job duties.

4 Including in a confidential attitude survey a question about intention to leave (eg 'Are you actively seeking alternative employment at present?' or 'Do you intend to leave your job in the next 12 months?'). The American research suggests that such questions are good predictors of actual resignations, making it useful to compare attitude survey responses to questions about job satisfaction/dissatisfaction of those who express an intention to leave with those who do not (see Griffeth & Hom 2001:121–4).

SURVEYS OF FORMER EMPLOYEES

One way round some of the problems associated with exit interviews is to survey staff some weeks or months after they have left. This can be done using a standard questionnaire, but is better able to tap into the mix of factors and their interaction with each other if it is conducted as an interview. The assumption here is that ex-employees will be both more willing and more able to identify and articulate their real reasons for leaving once they have successfully settled into a new job. They are less emotionally involved in the affairs of the organisation than is the case at the time of leaving and may well be more inclined to give a clear-headed, considered response to questions about their reasons for leaving. Moreover, because they are able to compare their new organisation with their previous one, they are in a better position to give advice about how retention rates could be improved in the future.

However, a number of the problems associated with exit interviews remain in the case of surveys of ex-employees. There endures in many cases a reluctance to give the appearance of criticising a former employer or individual managers for whom one has previously worked. References may still be needed in the future, while in some cases there is a wish to keep open the possibility of a return in the future. In many industries, of course, managers move regularly too, leading to a situation in which people find themselves working with or for ex-managers in new workplaces. For all these reasons assurances of confidentiality are necessary and best guaranteed through the employment of an independent consultant to carry out the survey.

STAYERS' SURVEYS

Bramham (2001:73) suggests that organisations have much to gain from looking 'at the other side of the coin' and investigating what makes people stay rather than what makes them leave.

A number of approaches could be taken, each of which is attractive in theory, but which do not appear to be widely used in practice. Each starts with the identification of a sample of employees who are *both* long serving and above average performers. The first approach involves issuing an attitude survey to the members of this group. A few days later the same survey is issued to another group of staff, in similar jobs but with below average length of service. The responses are then compared and a report written identifying how characteristics or attitudes differ between the two groups. An alternative approach is less systematic, but could be just as useful. This simply involves establishing a focus group made up of long-stayers and asking them why they have remained employed for so long. Each member should be asked to describe a time when they thought about leaving and to articulate the reasons for their eventual decision not to quit. A third type of 'stayer survey' is interview based. This is more time consuming, but may induce some long stayers to be more frank about their 'near-leaving experiences' than they would be in a focus-group situation.

Stayers' surveys do not tell managers exactly why people leave their organisations, although the long stayers may well have an informed and accurate view about this issue. They do however provide information which can be used to shape retention initiatives. If, for example, stayers state that a major reason they chose not to leave when they had the opportunity was because of the relatively generous pension scheme or the flexible working arrangements or the crèche, managers learn that these features are key to their organisation's competitive position in its labour market. Communicating their value to the workforce should then form part of the retention strategy. Alternatively it may be discovered that long stayers share certain competencies or attitudes which are present to a lesser extent in other employees. If so, this can help inform future selection exercises. More ambitious employers seeking to develop a full blown employer branding exercise, will also find information gained by these means to be a useful contribution (see Chapter 9).

LAST-JOB-MOVE SURVEYS

Useful if less directly relevant information can be assembled by asking new employees to talk frankly about their last job moves (ie the decision to leave their former employer and to join your organisation). This is not going to inform an organisation about what it is doing right or wrong as an employer, but it does help to build a clear picture of the dynamics that operate in key labour markets. It may, for example, be found that more recent employees applied not because of any positive attraction to your organisation, but simply because they hated their previous jobs and needed to work somewhere. This information suggests that push factors are more significant than pull factors in the particular labour market concerned. Alternatively the survey may reveal that the main reason employees left their previous jobs and joined you was because you offered them 50p an hour more for their efforts. This informs you that your labour markets are highly pay-sensitive and that it is important to keep a close eye on what competitors are paying if you are to retain people. As with the other methods, surveys of this kind can either be questionnaire-based or interview-based.

QUANTITATIVE APPROACHES

An alternative method to the use of surveys is to make use of employee records to compare the data or characteristics of those who leave with those who stay. Although quantitative approaches are unlikely in themselves to give a particularly clear picture of reasons for turnover, they may reveal some interesting general trends, and can usefully supplement information gathered using the three other methods outlined above.

Any number of ratios can be investigated using quantitative analyses. Examples might include comparing leavers with stayers in terms of their age, the distance they travel to work, their shift-patterns, pay levels, performance record or length of service. It is also possible to use these techniques to identify the extent to which turnover varies with the type of job undertaken or with the supervision of different managers. As with all quantitative analyses, the data is really useful only when there are large sample sizes available. Such approaches are thus inappropriate for smaller organisations.

 EXERCISE BOX

EXERCISE 15.2

Read the article by Tracey Evans entitled 'Australian employers are losing $20 billion a year as staff turnover increases dramatically' featured in a publication of the Australian Human Resources Institute (1 March 2008). This can be downloaded from the *People Management* archive on the CIPD's website (www.cipd.co.uk).

This article is in two parts. The first half concerns employee retention management (or lack of it) in Australia generally. The

second half considers the initiatives being taken by the Australian National University in Canberra to improve its staff retention record.

Questions:

1 Why are people management problems such as reducing retention rates given low priority by senior managers in Australian organisations?

2 Why are initiatives that involve 'throwing money at the problem' seen as ineffective as means of addressing skills shortage issues?

3 In what ways should the ANU's survey into why people stay and leave help the university to improve its retention rates?

REDUCING TURNOVER

Once the reasons for resignations have been established and analysed, the next step is to formulate plans to reduce them. Clearly, it is impossible to generalise about the form such plans will take, because they will vary dramatically depending on the causes of turnover in specific organisations. Employers may often find that very different factors explain resignations in each department or business unit. However, there are several possible courses of remedial action that can usefully be considered and which have been shown by researchers to have a positive effect in some circumstances. Two books by Peter Hom and Rodger Griffeth cover this ground particularly well. Hom and Griffeth (1995) is a comprehensive review of recent US research into the management of turnover, while Griffeth and Hom (2001) is a more accessible guide for managers drawing on their earlier research. They describe nine areas for employers to consider. The first six are described as 'robust' methods of controlling turnover, for which there is strong research evidence, and the final three as 'promising' methods:

- realistic job previews
- job enrichment
- workspace characteristics
- induction practices
- leader-member exchange
- employee selection
- reward practices
- demographic diversity
- managing inter-role conflict.

Some of these areas are investigated elsewhere in this book (eg: realistic job previews, selection and induction). In the following paragraphs, we therefore focus on the other areas identified by Hom and Griffeth as worthy of consideration.

JOB ENRICHMENT

Psychological research has strongly suggested that employees are far less likely to consider looking for new jobs when they feel fulfilled in their existing roles.

According to Hom and Griffeth (1995:203), the following perceptions of jobs by job holders are particularly significant:

- There are opportunities for self- and career development.
- The job is meaningful or significant.
- A variety of skills is used.
- There is a high degree of personal responsibility.
- There is the ability to work with a degree of autonomy.
- Positive feedback on performance is given.

Increasing the extent to which these features are present in a job leads to its 'enrichment'. There is thus a good case, where retention rates need to be improved, for looking at ways in which job content can be refined in some or all of these directions. In many cases the costs associated with such actions will not be particularly high.

WORKSPACE CHARACTERISTICS

In a series of research papers G.R. Oldham and his colleagues have reported research findings on working environments and their effect on employee satisfaction (see Hom and Griffeth 1995:203–205). Their experiments have involved providing similar groups of employees working for the same organisation with radically different office designs, which has led to interesting results. Other studies have pointed to the significance of office design, temperature level, ventilation, room size, lighting and decoration. A series of articles on these themes edited by Clements-Croome (2000) suggested that quite substantial improvements could be made to productivity if proper attention was given to the design of appropriate office environments. There is a link here to employee retention as productivity tends to decline when good, experienced performers or those with potential leave due to dissatisfaction with their work environments.

While one or two specific recommendations are made, such as the suggestion that a building depth of 12 metres is optimal (Leaman and Bordass 2000:180), the main finding is that people vary in their preferences. The best results are achieved where staff have a high degree of personal control over their own immediate environment. Where this is not possible it is necessary to have survey opinion regularly and to follow up complaints about the environment to compensate for an absence of direct control on the part of individuals. The research also suggests that the maximum number of people who should occupy one office is four or five (Leaman and Bordass 2000:184–5). Once the number becomes bigger than this people perceive a loss of control over their environment and become less productive. Hom and Griffeth (1995) also stress the finding that large open-plan offices with few dividing walls or partitions tend to reduce employees' feelings of autonomy and significance, and therefore increase dissatisfaction significantly. Overcrowding and darkness make matters worse. It can thus be argued that, except where it clearly matches the established workplace culture, the idea of doing away with partitions to decrease feelings of isolation and to encourage people to identify and socialise with other group members may be mistaken. This research also suggests strongly that the tendency to develop large open-plan office arrangements, partly in a bid to raise productivity, may in fact have the opposite effect.

LEADER-MEMBER EXCHANGE

The suggestion here is that turnover is reduced, particularly in the first months of appointment, if managers have been trained to develop high 'leader-member exchanges' with their subordinates. This term is defined as paying new starters particular attention and actively trying to develop high-trust relationships with them from the start. This involves taking special care to ask employees their opinion about operational matters, giving them influence in decision-making processes and allowing them as much latitude as possible to undertake their job roles in the way they prefer. Essentially it means resisting the display of any feelings of suspicion managers may have, and relying on 'social exchange' rather than 'formal authority' to ensure that work gets done.

Such techniques might be regarded as simply attributes of effective supervisors. The point made by researchers working in the field is that they do not necessarily come naturally to managers and that it is possible to develop appropriate characteristics with formal training.

DEMOGRAPHIC DIVERSITY

Research in the USA reported by Hom and Griffeth (1995:239–252) has indicated that, on average, women and members of ethnic minorities are more likely than white males to leave jobs voluntarily. Furthermore, studies have shown that this is partly explained by perceptions on the part of these groups that they have been unfairly discriminated against while in their jobs. The point is made that it is irrelevant from a management perspective whether the discrimination is 'imagined' or 'real': it is the perception of inequality that is significant, and that needs to be tackled if turnover is to be reduced. The US research has found that perceptions of supervisor bias, inequality in pay awards, unsupportive colleagues and blocked careers all contribute towards high turnover among women and ethnic minorities. Others identified extra pressure to perform well, and a tendency for the most interesting and highly visible tasks or projects to be given to whites and males as factors in their decision to resign voluntarily.

Such problems are familiar in the UK but, as yet, little formal research appears to have been undertaken here as regards their specific effect on employee turnover. However, it is reasonable to assume that, at least in some cases, involuntary resignations could be explained by perceptions of unfair discrimination. Clearly the way to tackle this is to introduce and communicate effective equal opportunities policies that managers at all levels are obliged to accept. There is a need not just to monitor the pay and job progression among members of the relevant groups but also to communicate results and plans of action to employees. Problems with particular supervisors or departments could be effectively identified using the survey techniques described above. A good start would be for questions relating to unfair discrimination to be included in exit interview questionnaires.

MANAGING INTER-ROLE CONFLICT

Another reason for turnover identified by Hom and Griffeth (1995:252–255) relates to conflicts between the demands of work and family – a problem made worse with recent increases in the number of single-parent families. Research into turnover in the USA suggests that whereas 33 per cent of women cite such conflicts as contributing to their reasons for quitting a job, it was significant for only 1 per cent of men.

Such findings may back a business case for employers to go further than the minimum standard required by the law in the provision of maternity leave (paid or unpaid), career breaks, childcare, day-care for elderly dependants, flexible work schedules and forms of homeworking. Although some of these may be expensive for employers to introduce (particularly in small organisations), they are at least worthy of consideration where the costs do not outweigh those associated with high levels of staff turnover.

In addition to organisation-wide policy initiatives such as those outlined above, employers can also improve staff retention rates simply by giving the issue a far higher profile in the organisation than is often the case. This involves securing senior management commitment by developing a robust business case and then giving responsibility for turnover reduction to individual line managers. It is possible to go as far as to incorporate departmental turnover records into performance appraisal criteria for supervisors, so that career progression or bonus levels are determined in part by success in this area.

EXERCISE 15.3

EXERCISE BOX: PRET A MANGER

Read the article by Lucy Carrington entitled 'At the Cutting Edge' featured in *People Management* (16 May 2002, pages 30–31). This can be downloaded from the *People Management* archive on the CIPD's website (www.cipd.co.uk).

This article describes the approach to recruitment that has been adopted by the chain of cafes Pret a Manger. Its thoroughness is highly unusual in the industry, but appears to result in substantially reduced staff turnover – from 130 per cent to 98 per cent.

Questions:

1 How can organisations such as Pret a Manger sustain their operations with such high staff turnover rates?

2 Why do you think the recruitment procedure the company has adopted leads to fewer voluntary resignations?

3 What further advantages does the company enjoy as a result of its approach to recruitment?

EMPLOYEE RETENTION AND REWARD

Common sense tells us that the link between pay and staff turnover is both clear and significant. Most people, we suppose, work in order to earn money. Payment considerations must therefore play a major role in guiding their decision-making about which employer to work for. It follows that low-paying employers will suffer most from staff shortages. People will avoid working for them if they can and will quit to take up better paying positions at the earliest opportunity. These are the basic laws of supply and demand in a material world. It is therefore assumed that staff turnover is highest where pay is lowest and that a sure-fire way of retaining staff for longer is to pay above the market rate.

This is a commonly held view, but it is not an accurate one. In practice things are a great deal more complicated. There is plenty of evidence to suggest that employers can enjoy high rates of retention among their staff without paying particularly well. Conversely we know that high-paying employers can by no means guarantee the long-term commitment of their employees. Raising pay rates will not therefore *necessarily* bring about reduced levels of turnover. In some situations there will be a marked effect, but in others, especially where there are other sources of discontent, there will be no impact at all.

There is a big divide in the academic literature between writers who see remuneration as central to an organisation's ability to retain staff and those who downplay its importance vis-à-vis other areas of management practice. It is thus impossible to reach firm conclusions. As a rule, the role of pay is stressed by economists and researchers whose focus is on pay policy, its importance being under-emphasised by occupational psychologists and by those whose research concentrates on employee retention in more general terms.

Research studies carried out over decades on human motivation, job satisfaction and the factors that influence employee decision-making at work generally tend to suggest that payment is a good deal less powerful as a positive motivator than intrinsic rewards (ie the 'pleasures' people gain from doing the job itself). The conclusion reached is that raising pay rates buys only short-term job satisfaction. If there are underlying problems causing unhappiness among employees, these will not be 'bought off' in most cases. In terms of employee turnover and retention this suggests the following:

i employees who are dissatisfied and minded to look for another job will only be deterred from doing so in the short term if they are given a pay rise

ii employees who are otherwise happy in their jobs are unlikely to leave purely in order to secure a higher hourly rate.

However, this same body of research points out that while pay rarely motivates positively, its capacity to demotivate is substantial. Herzberg (1966) famously described pay, along with other extrinsic rewards, as a 'hygiene factor'. It is something that people tend only to act upon if it is absent – like the cleanliness of a house. In practical management terms this suggests that the capacity of pay to act as a 'push factor' in employee turnover terms is a great deal more powerful than its capacity to work as a 'pull factor'. It is therefore helpful to see these as two separate types of situation. In the first employees are unhappy either with the level of pay they are receiving or with the distribution of rewards in the organisation. The issue of what other employers are paying is a second order consideration. Whatever the market rate, the dissatisfaction is likely to lead to voluntary quits. The second situation is one in which employees are content with their rate of pay in terms of the living standard it buys and regard it as being broadly 'fair' vis-à-vis co-workers, but in which a higher rate could be secured by moving jobs. Voluntary turnover, according to the research evidence, is a good deal less likely to occur where such conditions apply. Dissatisfaction with payment arrangements in an organisation is a bigger cause of employee turnover than the simple desire to earn more money. The amount of pay that is given to each employee is seen by them as a powerful indicator of their individual worth to the organisation.

It can also be a significant status symbol and acts as an important form of tit-for-tat compensation when burdens are shouldered by particular employees. For the majority of people these are far more salient issues and have greater capacity to affect their behaviour than concerns about the purchasing power of their pay packets. Perceptions of unfairness or injustice in payment matters are thus the big turnover drivers when it comes to reward policy. Eliminating these, as far as it is possible to, must therefore be a priority for organisations wishing to improve their staff retention records.

This may well be one reason why staff turnover rates are lowest in those public sector organisations which are widely perceived to pay poorly vis-à-vis comparable roles in the private sector. The pay may be relatively poor, but the employers have in place payment systems which are transparent, rational and which by and large operate fairly. People know what one another earn in the public sector and are clear about the rationale that underlies decisions about who is paid what. The systems are cumbersome and bureaucratic, making the organisations concerned slow to embrace change, but they have the advantage of acting to reduce avoidable turnover. Conversely in most private sector organisations, particularly for the more highly skilled jobs in non-union firms, the opposite situation tends to prevail. Pay levels are individually negotiated and then kept secret. People are paid what their managers think they are worth and can afford to pay. A great deal thus hinges on what people ask for on joining the organisation and can persuade the organisation to pay them subsequently. External market rates have to play a greater role when such approaches are used than concerns about internal differentials. Hence in many private sector organisations a situation is created in which people working together and undertaking roles of broadly similar value are paid differently. The result is high turnover rates, despite relatively high rates of pay. This kind of approach is sustainable where pay levels are kept confidential. If nobody knows exactly what their colleagues are getting, no sense of injustice is able to develop. The problem is that pay levels rarely do stay confidential in practice. People want to know and thus find ways of finding out what their colleagues are paid. Where the differences are more (or indeed less) marked than they think they ought to be, the result can be dissatisfaction or a seething sense of injustice.

Finding out about how your pay measures up to that of your colleagues can even be sufficiently 'shocking', using the terminology used above, to set in motion the process which leads to a voluntary quit. Worse still are situations in which false information about what individuals are paid gets spread around by means of a rumour mill. Where pay is kept confidential this happens a great deal, misinformation frequently originating from the mouths of employees who think that their status will be enhanced among colleagues if they are believed to be earning more than they are.

Employees who know that they are being paid less than a colleague who engaged in a similar role are not the only people for whom payment arrangements are perceived as unfair. Severe dissatisfaction can also result from a situation in which employees consider differentials to be too small. This also results from informality and subjectivity in payment arrangements. Hence you get situations where a supervisor is paid only a tiny amount more than her subordinates or where an employee of many years' service who carries major responsibilities is paid the same as younger, more recent appointees who he is responsible for training. Here the problem is one in which a genuine individual contribution is not being sufficiently recognised in the relative remuneration being paid.

In terms of improving staff retention, it is most important that managers do not underplay the significance of these kinds of issues by dismissing them as trivial. From a management perspective things tend to look a great deal more rational, objective and fair than they do from the employee perspective. But this is an irrelevance when it comes to reducing staff turnover levels. What matters is that *they* perceive the payment arrangements to be fair.

At base the problem that all organisations inevitably face is a difference of opinion about the worth of individual contributions. Most employees genuinely believe that they:

a are above average performers

b contribute as much, if not more, than their colleagues

c deserve to be recognised accordingly.

This is particularly true of employees who are seen by their managers as good, solid, reliable, but also unexceptional performers. Dissatisfaction thus occurs whenever the employee is told or reminded of the fact that their managers consider their contribution to be only average. Pay rates and pay rises are the most powerful ways that an organisation communicates this kind of judgement. Hence their importance as a potential driver of staff turnover among the groups of staff on whom organisations rely (ie solid, reliable performers).

FOLLOWING THE MARKET

Where it becomes impossible to pay the market rate it remains possible for employers to attract and retain sufficient staff of the right calibre. This is achieved by paying below the market rate (following or lagging the market), while working a great deal harder in other areas to create a workplace which people are reluctant to leave. This is by no means an easy option, but it can be achieved with creative and effective managers who know how to motivate their staff and are given the opportunity to do so.

The approach involves taking a 'total reward perspective', which involves thinking about 'reward' in the widest sense rather than simply as money in the pocket. It recognises that people often value all kinds of things about their work in addition to the pay that they receive. It follows that many will happily 'trade' a certain amount of potential pay in order to secure the other things that they value. The employers that retain people most effectively, according to this view, are not those who pay most, but those who offer the highest level of 'total reward'. The following are some features of working life which people value and can thus aid retention where pay rises are not affordable:

- job security
- flexible working arrangements
- benefits such as free car parking or staff discounts
- short commutes to work
- work which is satisfying or meaningful
- a pleasant working environment
- career development opportunities
- the opportunity to work for a respected 'big name' employer
- a respectful and considerate boss.

Where an organisation can *genuinely* offer several of these, it will often find that it is able to retain people without the need to pay at or above the market rate.

EMPLOYEE RETENTION AND DEVELOPMENTAL OPPORTUNITIES

One of the most interesting debates in the field of employee retention relates to the impact of training on the propensity of staff to quit. Two entirely logical, but wholly contradictory points of view are often put when this issue is discussed:

i It can be argued that investment in training for employees is essential if you want to encourage them to stay. A failure to train, or at least to offer training opportunities, will lead career-minded people to look start looking for an alternative employer who will provide training.

ii It can be argued that providing employees with training makes them more likely to leave because it provides them with skills which are sought by other employers. It opens up opportunities for quits which were not available to the employees concerned before they received the training.

Greenhalgh and Mavrotas (1996) make the following points in reporting UK-based research:

- A study by Wadsworth published in 1989 using Labour Force survey data found no evidence of a link between training and job mobility.

- Dolton and Kidd's (1991) study of graduates found evidence to suggest that training reduces job mobility provided it does not result in the achievement of 'generally recognised' qualifications.

- Elias (1994) found that training reduced female job mobility somewhat, but had no significant impact on turnover among men.

- Greenhalgh and Mavrotas (1996), drawing on data from the 1980s, found that younger men had a higher propensity to quit after receiving training (more so than women). However this effect was not observed in the public sector where mobility remained low despite a high level of training. They also found a higher incidence of turnover in smaller firms than in larger ones.

Green *et al* (2000) in another large scale study found that overall the effect of training on the propensity to leave was neutral, but that the type of training made a big difference. Their research was questionnaire-based and involved asking over 1,500 employees about their perceptions. 19 per cent of their respondents stated that receiving training was 'more likely to make them actively look for another job' while 18 per cent said that it was less likely to. The rest, comprising the substantial majority, saw training provision as making no difference to their interest in leaving. The key findings were as follows:

i   training paid for by the employer appears to reduce the desire to quit

ii   training paid for by the government or the employees themselves tends to raise job mobility

iii firm-specific training is associated with relatively low levels of turnover

iv   training which results in the acquisition of transferable skills is more likely to lead to turnover.

This body of research allows us to reach a number of conclusions. First it seems clear that a distinction has to be made between training which relates to activity which is particular to the organisation and that which results in the employee gaining skills or knowledge that are sought by competing organisations. The former, as far as it has any major effect, appears to increase the likelihood that an employee will stay rather than leave. We are talking here principally about training which is designed and delivered in-house or which is developed by consultants to meet specific organisational needs. Providing employees with the opportunity to undergo such courses will not, all things being equal, enhance the chances of them leaving. Instead it acts as an effective means of communicating to staff that they are valued and that the organisation wishes to invest in their development. Because it does not result in the award of any qualification that is 'generally recognised', such training does not hugely enhance employees' ability to secure work elsewhere.

A rather different picture emerges in the case of training which leads to the achievement of a recognised external qualification. Here it does seem to be the case that one outcome is an increased propensity on the part of some employees to resign. However, quit rates are a good deal lower when the employer pays for the training and actively encourages staff to gain the qualification concerned. This could be because of the widespread use of pay-back penalty arrangements, but is more likely simply to reflect greater commitment being given to employers who are prepared to invest time and money in their people. The opposite is the case when the employer refuses to pay and thus obliges the employee either to stump up their own course fees or to rely on state funding. Where this happens there is a far greater likelihood of a subsequent quit. The employee enhances their ability to find a better job and senses no obligation to the employer to hold them back. It thus makes sense, where a valuable employee is determined to attain a recognised qualification, to sponsor them either in whole or in part.

Also potentially significant is the extent of the opportunity people are given to develop their careers in an organisation. Some staff (often the better performers who organisations are keenest to retain) are very career-minded and will not stay for long in an organisation which denies them the opportunity to advance upwards at the speed which they perceive to be their due. Some professional groups, particularly those which are managerial in nature, tend to attract people who want to build a career in this way. Failing to provide proper opportunities for them to do so will lead to a continually high rate of attrition. Care must thus be taken when designing organisation structures to make sure that promotion opportunities can be provided.

A career ladder which provides steps which people can reasonably aspire to climb will provide some incentive for them to remain. Structures also matter because they affect the way people think about their future careers from the first day of work. If insufficient promotion opportunities *appear* to be available, the relationship will be considered by the employee as likely to last a relatively short time. The probability of a move in the foreseeable future is thus high, so the relationship is established on relatively weak foundations. The opposite is the case where structures provide good grounds for anticipating that career aspirations can be satisfied internally. For these reasons organisational restructuring exercises which bring greater efficiency can often be criticised for removing career development opportunities. Damage is done not just because people subsequently have to leave to achieve their ambitions, but also because the nature of their psychological contract is changed. People who now think they may have to leave (when they previously thought in terms of a long stay) see their relationship with the organisation differently and are likely to display less commitment as a result.

We must recognise, however, that there is more to the management of career expectations than the provision of suitable organisational structures. People also need to be given reason to believe that they have a good chance of being promoted should a vacancy arise. Managers thus have to be *seen* to be running things in a promotion-oriented manner. The following are examples of the types of activity that will encourage retention among people who aspire to be promoted:

- Ensure that jobs are filled by internal promotion where it is practicable. Try to achieve a balance in recruitment between the employment of fresh blood from outside and the need to satisfy the legitimate aspirations of existing staff.

- Engage in succession planning exercises, identifying individuals with the attributes required to be promoted and giving them the necessary experience when the opportunity arises.

- Encourage first line managers and supervisors to discuss promotion possibilities with their staff during formal performance reviews or performance appraisal interviews.

- Provide the opportunity to attend formal training courses which set out to develop skills which are relevant to possible future (as well as current) roles.

- Allow/encourage staff who are candidates for future promotion to expand their current roles over time so as to enhance their chances of promotion.

EMPLOYEE RETENTION AND EFFECTIVE LINE MANAGEMENT

It is often said that employees are more likely to leave their managers than they are to leave their organisations. They may be happy with their pay, the developmental opportunities open to them and find their jobs interesting and fulfilling, but nonetheless decide to leave because they no longer wish to work for a line manager or senior manager who they dislike, disrespect or perceive to have treated them unfairly. In research carried out by the author and colleagues (Taylor 2002), dissatisfaction with management in various forms was found to be a major cause of unwanted staff turnover across a range of different professional groups. The key problems articulated by leavers are the following:

i   Supervisors who fail to respond to grievances. Resignations that are triggered because managers avoid confronting issues that are important to employees. They often prefer to sweep problems under their office carpets.

ii   Supervisors who act autocratically. These are situations in which, apparently for no good reason, managers impose their views on their subordinates without discussion, irrespective of the effect such decisions have on their working lives.

iii Supervisors who abuse their positions. There is a tendency for supervisors to treat subordinates rudely, to make jokes at their expense or to criticise them unfairly (often when they are under pressure) without subsequently issuing any kind of apology.

iv   Supervisors who show undue favouritism to some staff. Those who see their colleagues being given more responsibility, praise, interesting tasks or pay than they are getting – *when this is not justified* – develop very negative feelings and often quit.

v   Supervisors who fail to appreciate their subordinates' efforts. Another common cause of dissatisfaction, and hence of voluntary leaving, is situations in which people put in extra effort, complete a project or make a special contribution in other ways and get insufficient recognition or feedback.

vi   Supervisors who are very self-centred. Another common situation is one in which career-minded supervisors give the appearance of running their domain in their own interests rather than for the good of their teams, or in some cases their customers.

vii Supervisors who fail to deliver on their promises. This covers situations where indications are given that things will improve in the near future or that other commitments will be met. If in practice the promises are not subsequently delivered, the result is greater resentment than was felt at the start. This can push people over the edge into looking for a new job.

Good supervision is difficult and good supervisors are therefore a rarity. Like good parenting, good supervision is not something that comes naturally to everyone. It is a skill that is gained over time through experience and by learning from one's own and others' mistakes. Yet despite this evident truth, organisations rarely offer people formal training in supervisory skills either before or after they take up their first posts which carry responsibility for the management of others. It should therefore come as no surprise that so many supervisors are ineffective. The problem is compounded by our tendency to appoint people into supervisory positions for the wrong reasons. We tend to promote people who are good at doing their present jobs, assuming wrongly that this will make them good supervisors of others doing that job. Such people are often respected for their technical abilities, which helps, but many turn out to be poor managers of others. Another common situation involves the promotion of the longest serving member of a team into a supervisory role, or the most highly paid. Sometimes we simply choose the person who wants the supervisor's role most, or worse still, allow the former occupant of the post to select their 'favourite' as their successor.

The same is true in the case of many external appointments. Proficiency in the current role is used as the yardstick as much as or more than someone's supervisory potential. The result is an inexperienced and ineffective supervisory cadre in the organisation, often more concerned with establishing their own authority over disrespectful subordinates than motivating a team of individuals to achieve organisational objectives. Finally, having appointed someone for poor reasons, we have a tendency to judge their subsequent performance without reference to their achievements as supervisors. Provided organisational goals are accomplished, we see no need to question how effectively someone manages their team. Because managers who lose their staff as a result of their incompetence as supervisors pay no penalty, they do not concern themselves too much when their people quit. As always when seeking to reduce staff turnover, it is the perceptions of staff that are important and not the reality. If employees are given reason to believe that they are being treated poorly or unfairly, and this subsequently leads to resignations, the organisation must count this as a failure.

So, whilst bettering the quality of supervision is important as a basis for improving staff retention, being seen to do so is just as necessary. Because supervisory skills do not usually come naturally, they need to be learned. This means formally training people in the principles of effective supervision both before and after they take up posts which carry responsibility for the management of others. The following are six 'golden rules' long recognised as being attributes of effective supervision, but often not achieved in practice:

1) Give praise where praise is due

Supervisors often forget to praise staff when they do their jobs well. It's almost as if we expect our employees to perform at the highest level consistently and expect no less. Why praise someone just for doing their job? The same principle, of course, does not apply when people slip up or perform badly. Then the supervisor steps in and is quick to criticise. This is a tendency which all supervisors must guard against. As a general rule, except in the case of genuinely poor performers, managers should try to praise twice as often as they criticise. Giving people a 'kick up the arse' while failing to give them the requisite 'pat on the back' leads to resentment and precipitates resignations.

2) Avoid the perception of favouritism

Treating people fairly is a fundamental principle of effective supervision. Again it is a question of managers looking at what goes on, as far as possible, through the eyes of their subordinates. Managers will inevitably have views about the relative merits of their team members. Some will be liked and trusted more than others, but it is essential that this does not lead to unfairness. Once the perception of favouritism is established it is difficult to regain the trust and support of those who believe they are being denied opportunities that are their due. Some will be more likely to leave as a result. More often than not, it will be the more able who are lost first because they are best placed to secure an alternative job.

3) Talk to every team member regularly

Another common reason that supervisor-subordinate relationships deteriorate is simply a lack of contact between the parties. It is above all necessary that managers notice their staff, show an interest in what they are doing, and give them feedback.

People are more likely to quit when they think that their absence will not be noticed or where they see themselves as being undervalued as human beings. It is not necessary to be over-friendly or gushing in any way. It is just a question of ensuring that some kind of genuine relationship of mutual respect is established and continues over time.

4) Act when you suspect there are problems

It is very easy for busy supervisors who have important work of their own to do to 'act deaf' or 'turn a blind eye' when they believe their subordinates to be unhappy with some aspect of their work. Sometimes this means that small problems grow into very much bigger ones, making them far harder to deal with later on. The aim should always be to sort out difficulties at an early stage. People often leave jobs as a result of personality clashes with colleagues, an inability to cope with a workload or as a result of strain caused by problems originating outside the workplace. In many cases judicious and early intervention by a well-meaning supervisor can defuse such problems and serve to retain individuals for longer.

5) Give people as much autonomy as you possibly can

A view that it is pretty well unanimously shared by management researchers across all disciplines is the damaging effect of overly-close supervision. The good supervisor should therefore minimise the extent to which their subordinates perceive themselves to be supervised at all. Wherever possible they should find ways of allowing their staff freedom to carry out their own work in the way that they want to. They should be encouraged to use their own judgement and to develop systems of working with which they are comfortable. Where standardisation across an organisation or part of an organisation is genuinely necessary, then rules should be drawn up and agreed with the consent of the supervisees. The more highly qualified and experienced your staff are, the more advantage is to be gained from allowing them the strongest possible measure of autonomy. A sure way to demotivate and to precipitate voluntary resignations is to give the impression that you are standing over people and watching them unnecessarily. Some management control usually needs to be exercised to ensure that an organisation achieves its objectives effectively, efficiently and fairly. But control for the sake of control is unhealthy and simply serves to make an organisation less effective.

6) Involve people in decision-making

As well as allowing people, and indeed encouraging them, to take responsibility for their own areas of work, good supervisors also involve staff in the decisions that they have to take themselves. This need not be done in a formal way. All that is usually required is to ask employees their views ahead of time. Doing so shows in a very direct way that each individual's contribution is valued and that management is carried out by consensus rather than diktat. Involving people in decision-making serves to boost their self-esteem, while failing to do so serves to depress and de-motivate. It is particularly important to involve new staff as far as is possible. Asking someone who has just joined your team to contribute their views helps to build trust in the early weeks when a lot of voluntary resignations occur. That said, merely going through the motions for the sake of appearances may well actually make matters worse than if decisions are simply imposed from above. Pseudo-consultation builds mistrust and makes voluntary resignations more rather than less likely.

EXERCISE BOX: SUCCESSFUL STAFF RETENTION INITIATIVES

EXERCISE 15.4

Read the following articles featured in *People Management*. They can be downloaded from the *People Management* archive on the CIPD's website (www.cipd.co.uk):

- 'Batteries Recharged' by Steve Smethurst (5 May 2005, pages 24–27)
- 'In Their Shoes' by Jane Simms (20 April 2006, pages 36–38)
- 'Safety in Numbers' by Emma Clarke (11 January 2007, pages 44–46)

Each article describes a case study of an organisation which has managed to reduce staff turnover rates. The organisations and the type of staff they employ are diverse

(accountants, managers and retail workers), but in each case carefully thought through management interventions have had a striking impact.

Questions:

1 What are the major interventions which are credited with improving staff retention rates in each of these cases?

2 Why were different approaches called for in each of the cases?

3 What general lessons can be learned from the experience of these three organisations?

EXAMPLE

KEY ARTICLE BOX

'Recruitment and retention in front-line services: the case of childcare' by Marilyn Carroll, Mark Smith, Gwen Oliver and Sirin Sung (2008). *Human Resource Management Journal.* **Vol. 19, No. 1. 59–74**

This article reports the results of a substantial interview-based research programme involving staff and managers in 33 day nurseries. It demonstrates that all four of the push, pull, unavoidable and involuntary varieties of turnover play a role in contributing to high turnover among this group of staff. Other reasons rooted in the specific business environments of day nurseries are also identified and used to explain why managers in this industry tend to have quite a pessimistic and fatalistic view about their ability to improve employee retention rates.

Questions:

1 Why are skills shortages particularly acute in this industry? What could be done by employers to help reduce their impact in practice?

2 Why are childcare difficulties one of the major reasons that employees leave the childcare industry?

3 What are the major 'push' and 'pull' factors that explain high turnover in the industry? What major industry-wide initiatives would need to be taken to reduce their significance?

- Good books based on robust research are few and far between in the area of employee retention. *Employee turnover* by Peter Hom and Rodger Griffeth (1995) remains by far the most comprehensive publication on the topic. All aspects are explored and all the established research reviewed. Their more recent book entitled *Retaining valued employees* (2001) is shorter, but more user-friendly.

- Interesting and useful contributions by academic writers researching in this field include articles by Hiltrop (1999), Cappelli (2000), Maertz & Campion (2001) and Lawler (2008). IDS regularly publish HR studies about turnover and retention issues. These include case studies discussing employer initiatives. The most recent was published in 2008.

- Information about initiatives taken by particular employers is often featured in articles published in the CIPD's twice-monthly journal, *People Management*. The CIPD also carries out a large survey each year focusing on employee retention and turnover. This can be downloaded, free of charge if you are a member, from their website.

Retirement

INTRODUCTION

One of the most interesting contemporary social trends affecting most countries in the world is population ageing. The process is particularly well-advanced in the most industrially developed countries where life expectancy is increasing rapidly at the same time as average family size is falling. As a result we see the average age increasing each year. The trend is about to accelerate in countries such as the UK, propelling us into what commentators refer to as 'the age of the old', in which power and wealth will be increasingly in the hands of older people comprising a much more substantial portion of the population than has been the case in more recent youth-obsessed times (Pearce 2009). There are profound and as yet not fully appreciated consequences for public policy, family life, business strategies and employment practices.

The trend towards older populations raises particular issues for employers who have traditionally sought to employ younger people where they can and have tended to release people from their jobs, whether they like it or not, at a fixed retirement age. In the near future, when there will be fewer younger people seeking work and more older people potentially available to work, it is likely that these traditional approaches will have to change. Indeed we already see evidence in some companies of a preference for employing older staff, particularly where customers tend to be older too. We are thus potentially about to see quite a shift in practice whereby employers will actively seek to both attract and retain skilled people in their 50s, 60s and even 70s.

The question of how to fund pensions in a society when there are more older people and fewer people of working age is becoming an increasingly difficult problem. Government is pushing employers to play more of a role in contributing and facilitating saving into pension funds, while also increasing the age at which the state pension can be drawn. The ability of established pension funds to provide a good standard of living for the increasing number of years that people live after retiring is also coming under pressure, leaving older people less able to take early retirement and pushing many into working beyond the typical retirement age simply because they cannot afford to live on their pensions.

A linked issue is age discrimination which is most significant in its impact on people who are entering the labour market at relatively young ages and on those who are nearing the end of their working lives. Since 2006 a measure of protection has been available as far as employment is concerned thanks to age discrimination law. However, due to the way the legislation in the UK operates, it remains possible for employers quite lawfully to discriminate directly against people on grounds of their age. Nowhere is this more true than in the area of retirement where, at least at the time of writing (2010), it remains entirely lawful to dismiss someone at the age of 65 for no good reason, against their will, and as a matter of policy.

POPULATION AGEING

Organisational practices in relation to retirement and to the employment of older people, as well as pension policies, are being profoundly influenced by the ageing of the population. As is the case across the developed world, and increasingly in developing countries too, the UK has recently seen a steady increase in the proportion of its population who are older and a relative decrease in the number of younger people. To date the trend in this direction has been slow and steady, but over the next two or three decades it is going to speed up and have a far more considerable practical impact in the HR field. The reasons are as follows:

1)   *Longer life expectancy*

As each year passes the average age at which people die goes up by a few weeks. At present it is around 77 for men and 82 for women. What matters as far as retirement and pensions are concerned though is the average length of time that people live after reaching retirement age. In 2008 this figure was officially calculated as being 17.4 years for men and 20 years for women. However, for those who reached the age of 65 in 2008 the projected average life span extends to 21 years for men and 23.6 years for women. This means that people retiring at 65 now can expect, on average, to live until they are 86 or 89 depending on their sex (ONS 2009). Back in the 1950s the average man lived just 12 years after retiring at 65 and this had increased to 16 years by 1990. After this the rate of increase accelerated markedly, meaning that average life expectancy in the UK is now increasing by over two years with each passing decade. Internationally the figure is closer to four years, reflecting steep falls in death rates among the populations of developing countries. We are living longer primarily because of advances in medical science, but healthier eating and improved sanitation are also playing a part.

2)   Lower fertility rates

In order to maintain a stable level of population, each couple needs to produce on average 2.1 children. The 0.1 is necessary to account for the now mercifully small number of children who die before reaching adulthood. Internationally the fertility rate is currently around 2.6, which is why global population is rising quite steeply. However, this is much lower than was the case 30 years ago when women on average had over four children (*The Economist* 2009), and it also masks major variations across different countries. Fertility rates since the 1970s have fallen particularly steeply in the industrialised countries. United Nations figures show fertility rates in the UK to be 1.8 for 2005–10, which is a little higher than earlier in the century and considerably higher than the rates in many other countries. In Spain, Germany and Italy the figure is now less than 1.4, while in Poland and Singapore it is only 1.23. The lowest fertility rates in the world are found in Hong Kong and Macau where the figure is now below 1, meaning that a good majority of women in those countries are not having any children at all. The UK figure is higher than elsewhere in Europe mainly because of the multi-cultural make-up of our population. Fertility rates among UK-born women are similar to those recorded elsewhere, the overall average figure being lifted by the tendency of families who have moved to the UK from overseas to have considerably larger families. A quarter of all babies born in England and 55 per cent of those born in London have mothers who were themselves born overseas (Kelly 2009).

There are several reasons for the steep falls in fertility rates over recent decades. It is partly simply because people are now better able to control their own fertility than they used to be. Contraception became more widely available from the late 1960s, while the legalisation of abortion also had a big impact, around a fifth of all pregnancies in the UK now being medically terminated. Women are also increasingly waiting until later in life before having children, while a larger proportion than previously (now over 20 per cent in the UK) are choosing not to have a family at all.

While fertility rates are currently below replacement levels, this was by no means the case in the 1940s, 1950s and 1960s when the UK, like many countries, experienced a baby boom. At its peak in 1964 over a million babies were born in the UK, but the numbers were high for a good 20 years. Between 1945 and 1964 there were 17.6 million live births in the UK, an average of 880,000 a year. This compares with 16.1 million births (average 803,000 a year) between 1965 and 1984 and just 14.8 million (738,000 a year) between 1985 and 2004.

The net result of these two trends is a situation in which the proportion of our population which is made up of older people is steadily growing, while the proportion accounted for by younger people is falling. The median age in the UK in 1950 was 34.6, meaning that half the population was over that age and half below it. By 2005, according to UN figures, the median age had increased to 39, representing a steady increase over five decades. Predictions for the next 50 years show this continuing, a median age of 43 being projected for the UK in 2050.

An important consequence will be a steep increase in the dependency ratio, meaning that the proportion of the population who are over the current retirement age vis-à-vis those of working age will be much larger than at present. As the baby boomer generation retires we will see this rise from the current level of 27 per cent (ie: roughly three workers for each retired person) to 50 per cent in 2030. This inevitably poses important questions for public policy, the need being to ensure that pensions are available for this large number of retired people.

What does all this mean for the practicalities of HRM and the need to staff organisations with skilled and experienced people? A number of points can be made about the near future:

- Employers will find it harder to recruit and retain younger employees as they have traditionally preferred to and so will be forced to look to older people as a source of staff.

- Employers will seek to discourage experienced staff from taking early retirement, instead encouraging them to stay on in some capacity for longer.

- Employers will look to the population who are over the age of retirement as a potential source of people, recruiting staff in their late 60s and 70s.

- The state pension age is likely to rise as governments struggle to pay decent pensions to the increasing number of older people.

- Pension issues will rise up both organisational and public policy agendas as the ability to finance income in old age becomes harder and people become more aware of the role occupational pensions can play in providing a slice of their income in old age.

EXERCISE BOX: POSTPONING RETIREMENT

EXERCISE 16.1

Read the following two articles featured in *People Management*. They can be downloaded from the *People Management* archive on the CIPD's website (www.cipd.co.uk).

A Life's Work' by Roger Trapp (6 May 2004, pages 38–39)

'An Idea Past its Sell-By Date?' by Rebecca Johnson (1 November 2007, pages 26–39)

These articles cite several reasons for expecting many more older people to remain in the workforce in the future than has traditionally been the case. Examples are given of organisations that have offered flexible retirement options, or even abandoned fixed retirement altogether, and of the consequences.

Questions:

1 What are the main factors that are making people more willing and able to work beyond the 'normal' retirement age for their occupation?

2 Why have some employers been reluctant to accede to requests from individuals to work beyond their normal retirement date while others have actively encouraged later retirement?

3 Why are employers still so reluctant to appoint new staff over the age of 50?

4 Think about an individual you know who was forced to retire at a certain age. What would have been the advantages and disadvantages from the employer's point of view of continuing to employ that person for some years?

EMPLOYING OLDER WORKERS

At present a good majority of people retire fully once they reach state pension age. In 2009 only 10 per cent of men over the age of 65 and 11 per cent of women over the age of 60 were working in the UK. A substantial number also take early retirement. For some this is a matter of choice. They can afford to retire early and so decide to do so. Others are made offers by their employers, often as part of a redundancy package, that they find sufficiently attractive. Ill health forces a third group to retire, while a fourth simply find themselves out of work and unable to secure a new job. In total around 30 per cent of people (both men and women) over the age of 50 but below state retirement age are not currently working (ONS 2009:4–6). However, as was explained above, skills shortages among younger workers as well as less secure incomes from pensions will mean that more people in these age categories will be in work in the future. Indeed, a marked trend in this direction has already begun. Until 2002 the average age at which men retired had been falling steadily for 20 years (since official records were first maintained in 1983). Since then the age has started rising again. For women, the average retirement age has been continuously rising since 1984, there having been a particularly sharp increase since 2000 (ONS 2009:4–7).

Over time it is thus likely that employers will increasingly employ older people. Fewer will retire early or at the state pension age, while employers will also bring in new hires in their late 50s and 60s. Undoubtedly for some older people, there will be a need to continue working later than planned simply in order to build up a large enough pension. For others though, particularly those over the state retirement age, working or not working will be a matter of choice. This is likely to be particularly the case with the more highly skilled and experienced people who will be in most demand. It follows that a key question for HR managers specialising in resourcing is how best to go about attracting and retaining people who, due to the presence of a pension, have a choice about whether they want to work or not?

> Making employment attractive to older workers will become urgent. This will not just be a matter of good HR practice: in the face of tight labour markets it will be a commercial priority (Moynagh and Worsley 2005:45).

Attracting older workers back into economic activity is also a priority for governments who are seeking to reduce welfare bills and help ease skills shortages while reducing the extent of overseas immigration. As a result quite a lot of research has been carried out in recent years across the world looking into how employers should best go about recruiting and retaining older people.

Studies of this kind all tend to agree that flexibility in terms of hours worked is the most important single factor. Older people tend to have a particular wish to balance work and other aspects of their lives. They often take on responsibility for looking after grandchildren while their children are at work and increasingly, due to rising life expectancy, have caring responsibilities for their own parents. They also very naturally have an interest in enjoying the leisure time which retirement gives them. It thus follows that employers seeking to successfully employ older people must first and foremost offer them forms of flexible employment. This may be part-time work or a more casual type of contract that allows them to work as and when they want to. Others are attracted by short-term assignments which are of limited duration. A third group seek full-time work, but put a premium on the ability to combine this with longer periods of annual leave than is associated with most jobs. This is why Asda, for example, has famously introduced so-called 'Benidorm leave' for its older staff, allowing them to take unpaid sabbaticals each year between January and March. Such schemes have been common in the USA for some time where they are known as 'snowbird' programmes. In some cases larger organisations are able to provide older workers with employment opportunities both in their main place of residence and close to their winter holiday homes in Florida.

Employees who are nearing the state retirement age and have a choice about exactly when they retire will often choose to wind down slowly given the opportunity, moving on to part-time hours or shifting into roles which carry rather less responsibility and hence allow them to work shorter hours than they are accustomed to. Phased retirement is discussed in greater detail below, for now it is useful to point out that a good majority of people in the UK who are over state retirement age and still working do so on a part-time basis (ONS 2009:4–6).

It is important to recognise, however, that the provision of flexible working opportunities such as these is by no means the only type of initiative that employers need to take if they are successfully to recruit and retain people who have a choice about whether or not to retire. The work itself must also be attractive. Amanda Griffiths (2007:121) in her recent work in this area sums up this broad point most effectively:

> It is recognised that work can be a source of much satisfaction. It can provide purpose, meaning and challenge, a vehicle for learning, creativity and growth, opportunities to use skills and to demonstrate expertise, to exert control and to achieve success.

This is key. Unless the work is satisfying and meaningful – rewarding in the broadest sense of the word – someone who has no strict need to work for financial reasons will not enter or stay in employment for long. It further follows that older workers need to be treated well by their managers, accorded proper respect and included in decision-making.

Moen (2007) calls for flexible job opportunities for older workers, but also stresses the attraction of work which has a meaning and clearly contributes to the 'greater good' of a community. She also demonstrates that older employees are often much less concerned than younger counterparts with career building. She argues in favour of providing them with 'not so big jobs' which are less stressful and require less energy than those they may have done earlier in their careers. According to the Economist (2009:13) it is common in Japan for this kind of approach to be followed, managers reaching the retirement age being rehired to carry out more junior roles in divisions other than those they were previously employed in. As many as two thirds of Hitachi's employees in Tokyo apparently apply to be rehired under the terms of this kind of scheme.

Hirsch (2007) stresses the importance of providing a comfortable physical environment for older workers who are often at greater risk of developing ill health problems than their more youthful counterparts. He also shows how the need for workers to exercise control over their work is an important factor in encouraging retention as people near retirement. It is for this reason, perhaps, that older workers seem to be particularly suited to and attracted by work in smaller enterprises where there is typically much greater informality, flexibility and control exercised by workers over their own work (Bitman *et al* 2006).

Another stream of research looks at the characteristics of retired people who choose to re-enter work and compare these with those who remain retired. Studies of this kind carried out in the USA have found, somewhat surprisingly, that the overall financial position makes relatively little difference (see Lahey *et al* 2006). Those who have a good, generous pension are just as likely to go back to work after retiring as those who are struggling financially. In the USA, unlike the UK, health insurance plays a major role in influencing these decisions, with those who have not got access to health care plans provided through former employers being much more likely to return to work than those who do. The other key factors concern satisfaction with retirement. Those who are unhappy being retired are much more likely to return to work than those who are happy, while people who have been forced to retire are more likely to want to look for new jobs once they have retired than those who have chosen to retire. The experience of being pushed out of a job seems not to reduce the desire to work at all.

PENSION ISSUES

At present most skilled people retiring from jobs in which they have clocked up a fair number of years' service are retiring with good, reasonably generous pensions. This is particularly true of people who have been employed in the public sector or larger private sector companies, men being more likely than women to have been a member of an occupational pension scheme for a long period of time. As time goes by, however, the situation will begin to change.

Fewer younger people are being given the opportunity to join generous private sector schemes, while there remains a serious question mark over the capacity of the state to continue funding public sector schemes as generously as is currently the case. Change is being brought about because of the rising level of life expectancy discussed above. Employers simply cannot afford, as they used to, to guarantee the funds necessary to keep paying people generous pensions over the 20 or 30 years that they now typically live after retiring.

Current retirees, in addition to their state pension, often have private pension income or an occupational pension provided by their employer to which they have made contributions over their years of employment. Traditionally in the UK these have been provided on a final salary basis, meaning that the level of pension received is determined by the level of salary at the time of retirement and the number of years of membership an individual has behind them. In the private sector a so-called 60ths formula tends to be used. This divides the final salary by 60 and multiplies the result by the number of years pensionable service to determine an annual pension which is then uprated in line with inflation. Hence someone with 30 years service retires on a pension worth half their annual salary at the time of retirement. In the public sector the same approach is used but with a formula based on eightieths. This produces a lower level of pension, but employees are compensated by a tax-free lump sum which is received on retirement. Final salary pensions thus provide a good level of pension income to people who have contributed for a decent length of time, as is the case for many retiring now.

Younger colleagues, however, are not being so generously provided for. Over the past 10 years most companies have closed their final salary schemes to new entrants, replacing them with defined contribution schemes. These are simpler to administer, employers and employees both contributing a set sum into the fund each month, but almost always produce a lower level of pension. Moreover, and more importantly, the level of pension received bears no relationship to the salary at the time of retirement. Things are much riskier. On retirement the pensioner receives the accumulated income from their pension pot and is advised about how to use it to purchase an annuity that will provide an income for the rest of their life. The level of pension received is thus hugely influenced by how well the investment has performed and by prevailing annuity rates at the time of retirement. This is one of the reasons that may well mean that employees are less able to take early retirement in the future and may well feel the need to work on past the state pension age in order to accumulate a higher level of pension.

Increased life expectancy and the anticipated widening of the dependency ratio also mean that pensions are a major public policy issue. At present around 60 per cent of all pension income in the UK is provided by the taxpayer, mainly taking the form of a basic state pension paid to all men after they are 65 and to women once they are 60.

In 2010 this was worth £97.65 for a single person and £156.16 for a couple. The remaining 40 per cent comes from savings and investments, a good deal of which takes the form of occupational pensions. However, over time as the number of retirees grows vis-à-vis the number of people of working age, the government wishes to switch the ratios so that 40 per cent is funded from the state and 60 per cent from other sources. A number of policy initiatives are in the process of being introduced in order to achieve this, all of which will impact on HR management over the coming few years.

First it is planned that the female state pension age will rise in stages to 65 between 2010 and 2020. There are also plans to increase the male age to 66 and thereafter for a new equalised pension age to rise to 67 in 2034 and then to 68 from 2044 although in practice these changes may well come into effect a good deal sooner. Secondly, after April 2012 new regulations are being phased in which will require employers automatically to enrol their employees either in an established occupational pension scheme or, if there is none, in a new government-sponsored personal pension account scheme. As a minimum employees will then contribute 4 per cent of their salaries and employers 3 per cent into the scheme. A further 1 per cent will come through tax relief. The idea is thus that a sum that is equivalent to at least 8 per cent of everyone's salary will be invested in a pension, substantially increasing the amount of privately saved retirement income in the future. People will, however, be able to opt out if they wish to. Only time will tell how many actually choose to do so and the extent to which employers seeking to avoid their 3 per cent contribution will find ways of encouraging opt-outs.

 EXERCISE BOX: THE 2012 PENSION CHANGES

EXERCISE 16.2

Read the article by Sarah Campbell entitled 'Pensions: Now it's personal' featured in *People Management* (18 June 2009, page 24). This can be downloaded from the *People Management* archive on the CIPD's website (www.cipd.co.uk).

Questions:

1 How could you summarise in a few points the 'optimistic' and 'pessimistic' visions for the future of occupational pension provision set out in this article?

2 Which do you think will prevail and why?

3 What do you think of the suggestion that saving for a pension should become compulsory?

AGE DISCRIMINATION LAW

Above the case was made for targeting older workers in recruitment campaigns and for retaining people, as far as is possible, up to and beyond the state pension age. Such a case has to be made because for many employers there is a strong preference for youth when recruiting and a willingness to retire older staff early in order to make room for the promotion of younger colleagues. Age discrimination of this kind is widespread all over the world and has a very real, negative impact on the opportunities available to people over the age of about 50 as far as work is concerned. Ageism has some economic logic to it when employment is seen as an investment in an individual over the longer term. It is inevitably true that the return on investment from giving an older person training and experience is going to be less than for a younger person, but when it is considered that staff turnover rates are much higher among the young, the extent to which such arguments stand up in a practical rather than a theoretical sense can be questioned.

Older workers suffer, above all, from stereotyping effects. In some respects they come out quite well from comparisons with younger colleagues. Older people are, for example, typically seen as more mature, reliable, conscientious and experienced as workers, as well as more likely to remain in their jobs. However, there also very widely-held negative stereotypes too which serve to damage career prospects considerably. According to a summary of research on ageism in the UK by Marshall and Taylor (2005:576–578), substantial numbers of HR managers believe older people to be difficult to train, unable to adapt to new technologies, slower to learn, more overly-cautious and more prone to ill health. As a result 'though older workers' recruitment potential was recognised, traditional sources of labour, eg younger people, were viewed by management as the primary source when future recruitment needs were considered' (Marshall and Taylor 2005:577).

It was in response to this long-standing state of affairs that the European Union decided in 2000 to introduce regulation aimed at diminishing the extent of age discrimination in the workplace. The resulting UK legislation, The Employment Equality (Age) Regulations 2006, goes some way to deterring employers from acting in an ageist fashion, but they are by no means as far-reaching as equivalent regulations covering sex and race discrimination. Particularly important is the opportunity employers have in the regulations to defend themselves against any act of age discrimination (direct or indirect) by arguing that they have a good business reason for their approach. In both cases the requirement is on the employer to show that their actions constituted 'a proportionate means of achieving a legitimate aim'. This means, in practice, that age discrimination remains lawful if a court can be persuaded that there is a sound, justifiable reason that it should be.

In relation to retirement, however, the 2006 Regulations introduced special procedures which permit employers to dismiss their employees entirely lawfully via mandatory retirement on their 65th birthday or at a later date. Since their introduction the mandatory retirement rules have been highly controversial and have been the subject of a high profile challenge in the courts by the charity Age Concern. At the time of writing (2010) the legal issue has still not been finally resolved, although the government has succeeded in its argument that the maintenance of mandatory retirement is lawful if it can be justified on social and economic grounds. It is highly likely that these regulations will be repealed in the not-too-distant future, ministers having announced a formal review into their operations to take place soon. For the time being, however, the scheme remains and is something that HR managers need to be aware of. The key features are the following:

- It is lawful to dismiss at a set retirement age of 65 or higher, provided a statutory procedure is followed.

- Mandatory retirement ages between 60 and 65 can continue, but only if the employer can objectively justify them.

- There is a duty on employers to write to employees between six months and a year before they reach retirement age informing them that they will be retired unless they exercise their right to request to continue working.

- If the employee replies requesting to work beyond the set date, the employer must give the request serious consideration, hold a meeting to discuss the matter with the employee if the request is not granted, give a final decision in writing within 14 days and allow an appeal.

- There is no list of reasons given in the regulations for legitimately turning down requests, so in practice an employer can simply make it its policy to mandatorily retire everyone at a set age.

- When a request is accepted it is possible for the employer to set a new retirement date and to go through the procedure again six months before the employee reaches that age.

The main reason that this is so controversial and unsatisfactory arises from the fact that at the same time that the new procedure was introduced, thanks to age discrimination law, the exemption that previously prevented people who were over 65 (or the normal age for retirement in an organisation if lower than 65) from bringing cases of unfair dismissal was abolished. Previously employers were encouraged to keep people on past 65 because it was so easy to dismiss them lawfully if, perhaps as a result of age, their performance or absence became problematic. Now that unfair dismissal law applies to all of whatever age, employers face the need to take people through lengthy capability procedures and to give warnings before they can lawfully dismiss someone who is over 65 and whose performance has begun to decline. However, at the same time a procedure which permits mandatory retirement at 65 with no good reason has also been introduced. Surely, the critics quite reasonably argue, the effect in practice is to encourage employers to dismiss at 65 when previously, before the advent of age discrimination law, they would have kept people on. In other words, the practical result of age discrimination law is to make it more rather than less likely that employers will mandatorily retire people.

Under the current regime the temptation on the part of an organisation to refuse all requests from employees to work beyond 65 as a matter of policy is considerable. Dismissing people lawfully on grounds of capability is often a difficult, time-consuming and clumsy process, but it is harder still when the dismissee is a 75-year-old who has served the organisation in a senior capacity for decades and now has to be dismissed due to declining mental or physical capacity.

One feature of the mandatory retirement procedures which is often forgotten, but which is important for many employers, is the way that they only apply to 'employees' by which is meant working under a contract of service. Workers with other types of contractual status are not covered – groups which include many agency staff, casuals, partners in a firm, contractors and office holders. In their cases mandatory retirement is not possible lawfully unless the decision can be justified objectively. Case law on this subject is beginning to be established by the higher courts, so we are beginning to get a better picture of which types of reasons are justifiable and which are not. To date the courts, including the European Court of Justice, have tended to accept defences based on the need to provide promotion opportunities for younger staff, but to reject those based on any assumption that older workers are likely to suffer from declining mental or physical ability after a set age.

THE IMPACT OF AGE DISCRIMINATION LAW

In 2008, two years after age discrimination law was first introduced, IRS carried out a survey of 97 UK employers from across the industrial sectors focusing on its practical impact. Their findings were interesting and their conclusions optimistic about the ability of regulation to improve organisational practices in the field of equal opportunities and diversity.

Employers were evenly divided overall about whether the age discrimination legislation had benefited their organisation, a majority claiming that policies and practices did not have to change because they were already compliant. Of those who did make changes over half sought to use the opportunity to refresh their practices on age discrimination more generally by going beyond the requirements so as to promote age diversity.

As far as retirement is concerned the most striking finding of the survey was the way they had led to an increase in retirement ages to 65 in organisations where younger ages had been the norm previously. Others took the opportunity to do away with a fixed retirement age altogether, 24 per cent now adopting this position.

Within the first two years of the new regulations' operation a good majority of the surveyed employers had received requests from staff to work beyond 65. 44 per cent claimed to have agreed all requests, 49 per cent agreed to some but refused others, while only 7 per cent admitted to turning down all requests from employees to work on after 65.

The general impression conveyed by the findings is one of HR managers embracing the opportunity provided by the new law to move the diversity agenda forward in their organisations.

Source: Rankin (2008e)

EARLY RETIREMENT

Many larger employers offer employees the opportunity, if they so wish, to retire early. A survey undertaken by the CIPD (2003b) indicates that a clear majority welcomes the opportunity to take early retirement, and that very few choose to carry on working having made the decision to retire. Although people with private savings or personal pensions that have performed particularly well may be able to retire before their contractual dates, the term 'early retirement' is more commonly associated with membership of the employer's occupational pension scheme. Precise terms and methods of calculation vary from organisation to organisation, but most employers will in some circumstances pay a reduced pension to retirees who leave before the contractual retirement age. Where employees have accrued sufficient pension rights to provide a satisfactory income, such offers are very tempting – especially if there is a possibility of continuing to work on a part-time or consultancy basis.

However, in order to prevent a general exodus of highly valued employees, most employers also reserve the right to refuse requests for early retirement. Where the financial liability for the pension fund is increased by such arrangements, scheme trustees also have a right of veto. Where redundancies are in the offing, managers often improve the early retirement provisions somewhat in order to provide an incentive for older employees to take up the opportunity. In so doing, they reduce the number of compulsory redundancies, while much of the cost is shouldered by pension scheme funds.

XR ASSOCIATES

CASE SUMMARY

In 1991, in order to sweeten the incentive to take early retirement at a time when large numbers of redundancies were being made, Ford UK set up a consultancy company called XR Associates. It was unusual in that it was staffed entirely by ex-Ford employees over the age of 50 who had accepted offers of early retirement. In return, they were guaranteed 90 days' work a year on a consultancy basis with either Ford or one of its suppliers. After two years of operation, it was reported that XR employed 400 people, including a third of the managers who had left Ford in that period. By 1996 there were 600 consultants.

XR people work on one-off projects on behalf of the company, rather than simply working in their pre-retirement roles again. They are paid daily rates at a level commensurate with the type of work undertaken. They can take as much or as little work as they please, some opting to work three or four days a week and others reducing their commitment to one day. The advantage for the company is the ability that it gives to call on experienced people with a knowledge of the business to undertake project work. This leaves full-time managers free to carry out day-to-day duties.

Source: IDS (1996:17)

PREPARING EMPLOYEES FOR RETIREMENT

In her book on retirement, Phil Long (1981:38–50) puts a very good case for the provision by employers of effective pre-retirement training. Without it, she claims, employees often experience shock and prolonged depression when they suddenly find that they no longer have jobs to go to. The sense of loss and lack of purpose in life leads many to deteriorate mentally and physically:

> The emergence from the world of work is as much a culture shock as the entry, yet in neither situation is there much preparation. The young school leaver, entering his or her first job, usually finds a supportive environment, however informal this might be. By contrast, the newly retired have to adjust to an equally novel situation unaided and for many the transition can be a difficult one .... Three score years of being indoctrinated in the

Protestant work ethic, which stresses the virtues and values of work, is no preparation for what should be a period in which to do one's own thing. Unfortunately few have been educated to use their leisure in a creative way.

In France and in the Scandinavian countries governments are actively involved either in providing or promoting pre-retirement training courses. In the UK, although some local authorities operate events of this kind, it is mainly up to employers to do so.

The contents of pre-retirement training courses appear to be fairly standard. In practice, there is usually a need to blend group-based training with individual counselling and advisory sessions. Wherever possible, spouses should be invited to attend along with the prospective retirees. According to Long (1981:49), the following are typical issues to be covered:

- understanding pension provision
- taxation of savings
- investment of lump sums and annuities
- social security entitlements
- health and nutrition
- safety in the home
- developing leisure activities
- re-employment and part-time working
- moving house
- drawing up wills.

In addition, courses include sessions designed to help people to adjust psychologically to the idea of retiring. These involve explaining what difficulties might be encountered and suggesting approaches to managing the transition. Reynolds and Bailey (1993), in their book on pre-retirement training, give a good deal of attention to this topic and offer helpful advice for those delivering training of this kind. Drawing on their experience, they provide a depressing description of the emotional problems that people suffer when they are required to retire. However, they also show how it is possible to work through the initial feelings of shock, denial and depression in order to adjust and accept retirement as the new, normal state of affairs. Unsurprisingly, a major part of this process is the development of new interests and the revival of those left dormant during busy working lives. The taking-up of voluntary work or part-time paid work is also a possibility. By all accounts, one method of avoiding the psychological problems associated with retirement is to find ways of phasing it in over a period of a year or two. A number of larger organisations have well-established schemes of this kind which permit employees gradually to reduce their working hours as they approach the date of retirement. Ideally, in order to attract employees, such schemes should not involve too great a loss in income.

The importance of pre-retirement preparation is also stressed by Vickerstaff *et al* (2004), but their research among older people from three large organisations found that it tends to be offered rather too late to be of maximum value. They also found much support for the idea of 'downshifting' in the years immediately prior to retirement, but established that many employers and employees think that it is not a serious option due to its impact on subsequent pension entitlements.

POST-RETIREMENT CONTACT

The final area of activity that contributes to the smooth transition into retirement is the maintenance of formal contacts with the organisation. These can take a wide variety of forms. At one extreme, there is the continuation of an economic relationship, whereby the retiree is hired again, but on a casual or part-time basis, and thus continues to come in to work from time to time. For professional and managerial staff, an option is to work on a consultancy basis. In such cases the employee is freed from having to come to work at set times, but is still required to provide advice or to undertake specific projects.

At the other end of the scale is the organisation of social events. Where organisations operate social clubs or provide weekend trips, Christmas parties and evening functions for staff, it is possible to invite retired employees, too. The larger, more paternalistic organisations go further, setting up benevolent funds for retirees in order to provide, or assist in the provision of, private health care, sheltered housing and holidays.

REFLECTIVE QUESTION

What formal contact does your organisation maintain with retirees? To what extent could greater use be made of retirees' skills and expertise?

EXAMPLE

KEY ARTICLE BOX

'Organisational practices and the post-retirement employment experience of older workers' by Marjorie Armstrong-Strassen (2008) *Human Resource Management Journal*. **Vol. 18, No. 1. 36–53**

This article starts with the premise that as the population in many countries ages significantly over the coming decades and labour markets tighten, organisations will need to attract older people into jobs (including those who are past normal retirement ages) and will also be keen to retain existing employees in employment until and beyond such ages. Using a large sample of older Canadian workers, the research described sought to establish how big an impact HR practices that are tailored to meet the needs of older people can have on decisions by people in these age groups to continue working or to return to work after retiring. The significance of other factors was also tested such as 'perceived fair treatment by the organisation' and 'perceived respect from one's work group'. The main finding was that HR practices are very important indeed as factors which influence people's decision about whether to retire and whether to return to work after having retired. Moreover, and significantly, it was not just HR practices in the fields of flexible working and reward that were significant. The whole range of 'good practice' approaches have just as big an impact in practice, including access to training and development opportunities.

Questions:

1   Why do you think people who have retired and then returned to work in a different job are more committed to their employers on average than those who have remained employed in the same organisation past the normal retirement age?

2   Why does the way that people perceive their last pre-retirement job have such a big impact on their decision about whether to return to the workforce post-retirement?

3   What lessons can be learned from this research by employers who are of the view that the main way of attracting and retaining older workers is to provide them with flexible working options?

EXPLORE FURTHER

- Two publications on the preparation of employees for retirement are *How to design and deliver retirement training* by Peter Reynolds & Marcella Bailey (1993) and *Retirement: Planned liberation?* by Phil Long (1981). The CIPD's 2003 survey of attitudes to ageing, pensions and retirement is a good guide to the perceptions and preferences of the working population (CIPD 2003b). Vickerstaff *et al* (2004) contains extensive analysis of qualitative data looking at the same issues.

- The impact of age discrimination law on retirement is covered effectively in the CIPD's *Managing age: A guide to good practice* (2007f) and by the IS Employment Law Supplement on age discrimination (2006).

- Two chapters focusing on contemporary developments in occupational pensions are 'Occupational Pensions' by Stephen Taylor in *Reward management: A critical text*, edited by Geoff White and Jan Druker (2009), and 'The pensions revolution' by Sue Field and her colleagues in *Rethinking reward* (2009) edited by Sue Corby, Steve Palmer and Esmond Lindop.

CHAPTER 17

Dismissals

By the end of this chapter, readers should be able to:

- manage the process for dismissing employees on grounds of ill-health and misconduct
- compile the documentation required in the dismissal process
- advise line managers and other colleagues about the major requirements of the law as it relates to dismissal
- distinguish between gross and 'ordinary' misconduct
- distinguish between unfair and wrongful dismissal.

In addition, readers should be able to understand and explain:

- the legal concept of 'reasonableness'
- automatically fair, automatically unfair and potentially fair reasons for dismissal
- the importance of following correct procedures when dismissing employees
- the role of the ACAS code of practice and the role that can be played by ACAS itself.

INTRODUCTION

Dismissing individual employees, however strong the justification, is undoubtedly the most difficult task that HR practitioners are required to undertake. Since 1971, as the law of unfair dismissal has developed, it has become a task that can very easily lead to costly and time-consuming legal actions when carried out poorly. For both these reasons it tends to be an area of work that other managers have little inclination to take over. When carried out effectively, it enhances the reputation and authority of HR practitioners in the organisation, raising their profile and giving them greater influence. By contrast, when carried out sloppily, the result is tribunal claims, bad publicity, ill-feeling and even industrial action.

Inevitably, given its centrality to the topic, the law occupies much of this chapter – in particular, its requirements as to the handling of dismissals. In this field, recourse to legal action is very common indeed. Between a million and two million people are technically dismissed from their jobs in the UK every year (many through compulsory retirements), of whom around 10 per cent subsequently bring employment tribunal claims (Knight and Latreille 2000, National Statistics 2006:11). This means that a majority of UK employers face unfair dismissal claims in any one five-year period, while a quarter find themselves on the losing side (IDS 1995c:5).

INTRODUCTION TO THE LAW OF UNFAIR DISMISSAL

The law of unfair dismissal in the UK dates from 1971, when it was included among a host of other measures in the Industrial Relations Act of that year. Although much of this legislation was later repealed, the measures relating to dismissal and the employment tribunal system have remained on the statute book and have developed over time as new regulations have been introduced and legal precedents set. For some time, the basic principles have been well established and they now form the basis of the manner in which dismissals are carried out by most employers. To an extent, therefore, it is possible to argue that best practice in this field is synonymous with the principles of the law. The only substantial way in which best practice and legislation part company arises from current regulations that exclude certain groups of employees from protection. By far the largest of these is employees who have completed less than a year's continuous service, but many casual workers, sub-contractors and office holders are also excluded.

For these reasons, it is essential for anybody with responsibility for the dismissal process to gain a sound basic knowledge of unfair dismissal law. The best way of avoiding the time, expense and inconvenience of appearing in court to justify one's action in dismissing someone is to anticipate the consequences of that action and to make sure that there is no case to answer. This is why even though only a minority of HR managers are ever called to give evidence to a tribunal, they should all be familiar with the relevant law and legal processes, and allow this knowledge to guide their actions.

When an employment tribunal is faced with a claim of unfair dismissal, and when it is satisfied that a dismissal has actually taken place, it is required to ask two main questions:

- Is the reason for the dismissal one of the potentially fair reasons identified in law?
- Did the employer act reasonably in treating the reason as sufficient to justify the dismissal?

Only if the answer to the first question is yes will the second even be considered. In other words, if it cannot be established at the outset that the dismissal has actually occurred for a lawful reason, the employer's case will fail, and the tribunal will not get round to considering the issue of the employer's 'reasonableness'.

When reaching a judgement about the first question, the burden of proof is on the employer. The tribunal thus expects the employer's representatives to show that they dismissed the individual for one of the reasons laid down as fair or potentially fair in the relevant statutes. For the second question, the burden of proof shifts and becomes neutral, so that the tribunal considers the facts and makes its decision without requiring either side to prove its case. In employment tribunals, as in all civil courts, the standard of proof is 'on the balance of probabilities' and not, as in criminal courts, 'beyond reasonable doubt'.

FAIR AND UNFAIR REASONS

In considering the reason for dismissal, the tribunal has to decide into which of three categories a particular case can be classified. These are: automatically unfair, automatically fair and potentially fair. Only if they decide that the reason is 'potentially fair' will the second question (ie reasonableness) be considered. If they find the reason to be either automatically fair or unfair they will reach an immediate judgement.

The list of automatically unfair reasons has grown over the years. At the time of writing (2010) it comprises the following:

- dismissal for a reason relating to pregnancy or maternity
- dismissal for a health and safety reason (eg refusing to work in unsafe conditions)
- dismissal because of a spent conviction
- dismissal for refusing to work on a Sunday (retail and betting workers only)
- dismissal for a trade union reason
- dismissal for taking official industrial action (during the first 12 weeks of the action)
- dismissal in contravention of the part-time workers or fixed-term employees regulations
- dismissal for undertaking duties as an occupational pension fund trustee, employee representative, member of a European Works Council or in connection with jury service
- dismissal for asserting a statutory right (including rights exercised under the Employment Rights Act, as well as those connected with the Working Time Regulations, the National Minimum Wage Regulations, the Public Interest Disclosure Act and the Information and Consultation of Employees Regulations; the right to request flexible working, the right to time off for dependants, the right to adoptive, parental or paternity leave, the right to be accompanied at disciplinary and grievance hearings and the claiming of working tax credits).

In cases of automatically unfair dismissal there is no one year qualifying period, so the right not to be unfairly dismissed applies to all who work under contracts of employment from their first day of work.

There are now only two automatically fair reasons for dismissing employees. The first concerns situations in which employees take unofficial industrial action, by which is meant action that has not been sanctioned by a union executive. Effectively, employers have immunity from liability where a dismissal occurs directly as a result of unofficial industrial action. The other category of dismissals over which employers can dismiss automatically without breaching unfair dismissal law are those that relate to safeguarding national security. In most cases, this will apply only to certain government employees working in the intelligence services or armed forces, but may also conceivably be relevant to some private sector employers, such as those engaged in weapons production.

The vast majority of cases fall into the third category of potentially fair dismissals, and it is in these that the issue of the employer's reasonableness and the circumstances of individual cases become relevant issues. The law states that there are five potentially fair reasons: capability, conduct, redundancy, statutory restrictions, and 'some other substantial reason'. A new category comprising dismissals taking place after eight weeks of official industrial action was effectively created in 1999, the period being increased to 12 weeks in 2004, and a further one comprising dismissals that take place for a reason relating to the transfer of an undertaking where an economic, technical or organisational reason applied from 2006. Mandatory retirement as discussed in Chapter 16 effectively now forms a further form of potentially fair dismissal. The original five potentially fair reasons are defined as follows:

CAPABILITY

This term is defined broadly as encompassing skill, aptitude, health or 'any other mental or physical quality'. In other words, it is potentially fair to dismiss someone who, in the judgement of the employer, is incapable of carrying out their work because they are ill-qualified, incompetent or too sick to do so.

CONDUCT

Poor conduct or misconduct on the part of an employee is also deemed to be a potentially fair reason for dismissal. The most common instances involve absenteeism, lateness, disloyalty, refusal to carry out reasonable instructions, dishonesty, fighting, harassment, drunkenness and swearing.

REDUNDANCY

This term relates to economic dismissals that meet the definitions laid down. They are discussed at length in Chapter 18.

STATUTORY RESTRICTIONS

This category is intended to cover situations in which employers cannot continue to employ particular individuals in a job because they are legally barred from doing so. The two examples most frequently given relate to foreign nationals who do not have work permits (or whose permits have run out) and drivers who lose their licences.

'SOME OTHER SUBSTANTIAL REASON'

The final category has attracted criticism in so far as it is seen as being something of a 'catch-all', permitting employers to dismiss on a variety of grounds not covered by the other fair or potentially fair reasons. The question of how substantial the reason is in practice is a matter for the courts. Over the years the following reasons for dismissal have been included:

- business re-organisations that do not result in redundancies
- pressure from customers
- termination of temporary contracts
- staff mutinies
- misrepresentation of qualifications at interview.

 REFLECTIVE QUESTION

What other cases have you come across that could be classed as 'some other substantial reason'?

REASONABLENESS

Having established that the reason for the dismissal is indeed one of the above 'potentially fair' ones, employment tribunals go on next to judge how reasonable the employer has been, given the circumstances of the case, in deciding to dismiss the employee concerned. It is thus on the issue of 'reasonableness' that most unfair dismissal cases hang. The following quotation from the Employment Rights Act 1996 sets out the approach that is taken:

> The determination of the question of whether a dismissal was fair or unfair, having regard to the reasons shown by the employer, shall depend on whether in the circumstances (including the size and administrative resources of the employer's undertaking) the employer acted reasonably or unreasonably in treating it as a sufficient reason for dismissing the employee; and that question shall be determined in accordance with equity and the substantial merits of the case.

For a number of years tribunals interpreted these words in different ways, but since the judgment in the case of *Iceland Foods v Jones* (1983), an accepted standard test has operated. Since that time, members of tribunals have not simply asked whether, in their view, the course of action taken by the employer was what they themselves would have done in the circumstances, but whether or not it fell within a band of reasonable responses. It is thus quite possible that a decision to dismiss might not be what the members of the tribunal believe should have occurred, given the facts of the case, but will nevertheless be found fair because the employer's action was one that fell within a range of approaches that *could* be considered reasonable.

In judging reasonableness, tribunals look at a number of factors relating to the individual and the organisation concerned. They will, for example, wish to satisfy themselves that the employer treats all staff alike in deciding to dismiss. Where it is shown that, in similar circumstances, an employer has acted inconsistently in dismissing one employee while retaining the services of another, it is likely that the dismissal will not be found to have been 'reasonable'. However, tribunals also like to see account taken of an employee's past record, especially in questions of conduct. This means that staff who have been employed for a good number of years and have impeccable disciplinary records are expected to be treated rather more leniently than colleagues with less service and records of poor conduct. Where relevant, tribunals will also investigate how far employers have sought to avoid the dismissal. Such matters are particularly associated with dismissals due to ill-health, where there may be alternative jobs or duties that employees can carry out, even though they are no longer fit to undertake their existing job.

The size and relative resources of the employer concerned are also issues considered when judging 'reasonableness'. A large organisation employing hundreds of people will thus be judged against different standards from those expected of a small business employing half a dozen. In the former case, it would probably be unreasonable to dismiss someone who was sick but expected to return to work in five or six months' time. For a small business, by contrast, such an action might be necessary to permit it to continue in operation. Similarly, a large employer will have more opportunities than a small counterpart to find alternative work for an employee struck down with a serious illness such as multiple sclerosis or a severe neck injury.

The other major issue that tribunals are currently required to look at in judging 'reasonableness' is the procedure used. Since the landmark case of *Polkey v Deyton Services Ltd* (1987), the question of the procedure used to carry out the dismissal has become central to tribunal decision-making. Prior to that date, there were cases of tribunals disregarding procedural deficiencies on the grounds that it made no difference to the final outcome – namely the decision to dismiss. For a time, between 2004 and 2009, thanks to legislation known as the Dispute Resolution Regulations (2004), the position in respect of procedure became complex and not always entirely clear. However, as from April 2009 when these regulations were repealed, we have returned to the situation as set out in the *Polkey* judgement. In practice, this means that, in dealing with employees in matters of ill-health, misconduct or poor performance, as well as redundancy and the other potentially fair reasons, employers are obliged to adopt the procedures recommended by ACAS in its code of practice. Although these are not prescribed by law, they are still the yardstick by which tribunals judge reasonableness, and so have formed the approach used by most employers. Furthermore, employers will be found to have dismissed unfairly if they do not follow their own prescribed procedures in significant respects.

The most widely used ACAS code is that concerned with discipline. The current version dates from 2009 and forms the model that employers are expected to follow when dealing with poor conduct, work performance and poor attendance. Based on the principles of natural justice, it includes the following basic features, the last of which is now a statutory requirement:

- Organisations should have written disciplinary procedures, and not handle cases on an ad hoc basis.

- There is a need to state who has the authority to take what action at each stage of the procedure.

- The procedure should clearly specify what employee action or lack of action will be treated as sufficiently serious for formal procedures to be invoked.

- Action should be taken promptly following the receipt of any complaint about an employee's conduct.

- Provision must be made for employees to be informed of the complaint against them and to have every opportunity to state their case.

- In the case of poor performance a fair-warnings system must be in place to ensure that employees are given at least one warning and thus the opportunity to improve before being dismissed.

- Provision should be made for a right to appeal, and an individual or committee should be specified to whom appeal may be made.

- Employees should have the opportunity to be accompanied and represented at any serious formal hearing by a trade union representative or work colleague of their choice.

THE DISCIPLINARY CONUNDRUM

A problem for P&D practitioners managing disciplinary issues is how to resolve the tensions inherent in procedures such as those recommended by ACAS – tensions that pull in two very different directions. The problem arises from a situation in which the procedure is supposed to be at once corrective in intent and also the mechanism by which lawful dismissals take place. Often the two aims conflict.

The problem is best illustrated with an example. A common situation is that of an employee who has become seriously demotivated (for whatever reason) and whose standard of performance drops. He or she starts arriving late, phones in sick on Mondays, ceases to complete work tasks on time and becomes a disruptive influence on other members of the department. In theory, such a situation needs action to be taken that addresses the employee's lack of motivation and seeks to provide new challenges and incentives. Giving a formal oral warning and setting attendance and performance targets is thus an inappropriate course of action, because it is likely to demotivate further. It may also lead to a breakdown in trust between the employee concerned and his or her line manager.

Yet any P&D manager who has seen many such situations in the past knows that, in all likelihood, there is no practical means by which the employee's level of motivation can be lifted. He or she is unsuitable for promotion, has already alienated work colleagues and has formed an apathetic attitude towards training and development opportunities. There is thus a strong probability that this situation will lead to dismissal if the employee concerned does not voluntarily resign first. In order for the dismissal to be fair, and to protect the organisation from possible legal challenge, the P&D response is to start the disciplinary procedure.

Therein lies the problem. There are two conflicting requirements. First there is a need to meet with the employee formally, to inform him or her that he or she can be represented or accompanied by a colleague or union official, to warn that his or her performance is unsatisfactory, to give an opportunity to state his or her own case, and then to send a letter that confirms the outcome and informs the employee of the right to appeal.

Secondly, however, there is a need to find ways of looking forward positively, of offering opportunities, and of seeking to remotivate the employee concerned. In practice, this is fiendishly hard to achieve. The very act of setting up a formal hearing, particularly in the case of relatively senior staff, signals a breakdown in trust. However positive and helpful the managers present at the hearing try to be, invariably the fact that the procedure has started at all will have the opposite effect.

MISCONDUCT AND POOR PERFORMANCE

A common misconception is that an employer must always start disciplinary proceedings at the start of the ACAS-recommended procedure with an oral warning. In most cases, such as those involving poor attendance, persistent lateness, minor mistakes or instances of negligence, or failure to carry out legitimate instructions, this is indeed the appropriate approach to take. However, where more serious instances of poor performance or breaches of discipline occur, it is well within the definition of 'reasonableness' to start the procedure with a written warning, final written warning or even summary dismissal (ie dismissal without notice), when the circumstances are apt. This latter situation occurs where the breach of discipline comes within the definition of 'gross misconduct'. There is no clear statutory definition of this term, and employers are within their rights to decide for themselves what is to be treated as gross misconduct in their own workplaces. Provided their list is broadly reasonable and provided people know that breaches may lead to summary dismissal, it is acceptable in principle to dismiss without notice on these grounds – provided, of course, that all employees are treated alike. These offences typically include the following:

- theft, fraud or deliberate falsification of records
- fighting or assault on another person
- deliberate damage to company property
- serious incapability through alcohol or drug use
- serious negligence causing unacceptable loss, damage or injury
- serious acts of insubordination.

This list is meant to provide examples, and is therefore not definitive or exhaustive. It does, however, indicate the degree of seriousness that an incident must reach if it is to justify summary dismissal. Whether or not misconduct is to be construed as 'gross' inevitably depends on particular circumstances. Drinking three pints of beer at lunch-time may not even qualify as any kind of misconduct in many jobs, but where someone works as a driver, dispensing chemist, or operator of dangerous machinery, it would in all likelihood justify summary dismissal. Similarly, depending on the job and organisation, careless breaches of confidentiality can either be irrelevant or highly damaging.

Often managers do not find themselves debating whether or not an act of gross misconduct has occurred. That much is usually pretty clear. The problem is deciding whether the organisation's response should be to dismiss the individual or individuals concerned (which it would be within its rights to do) or to give written warning. Factors to take into account include whether it is a first breach of discipline, the nature of any mitigating circumstances, the extent to which the employee shows remorse, and their persuasiveness in stating that the offence will not be committed again. It is inevitable that subjective judgements come into play here, with employees who have potential, who are hard to replace or whose work is generally valued treated more leniently than less-favoured colleagues. Provided there are genuine, defensible reasons for this, some inconsistency will be justifiable should the matter be raised in a tribunal. What is important is that these judgements not be clouded by personal likes and dislikes or grudges.

Procedure also plays a significant role in tribunal decisions concerning the reasonableness of dismissals for gross misconduct. It is not acceptable to fire someone in a fit of temper on the spot (however tempting that course of action can be on occasions). If the dismissal is to meet the legal definition of 'fairness', the following eight steps need to be taken:

- Inform the employee or employees concerned that they are under suspicion of committing an act of gross misconduct.

- State that a full and fair investigation will now take place to establish exactly what has occurred.

- State that the individuals will be suspended on full pay while the investigation proceeds.

- Inform them that a formal hearing will be held when the investigation has been completed at which they have the right to be represented and will have every opportunity to state their case.

- Formally investigate the issue, taking formal statements from any witnesses and keeping a written record of all relevant evidence.

- Hold a hearing within five working days.

- Put the case to the employee or employees and allow them to respond.

- Make a decision either to dismiss or to take other action short of dismissal.

In addition to the above, organisations are expected to make provision for dismissed employees to appeal to a more senior manager, and to inform them of this right at the time of their dismissal.

In recent years we have seen the development in the courts of an alternative approach for employers to use in justifying summary dismissals. This does not require reference to lists of reasons set out in staff handbooks or written procedures, nor does it require an employer to show that the employee either knew or should have known when they committed 'the act' that it might lead to summary dismissal. Instead it encompasses all manner of possible situations, some of which go well beyond the realms of misconduct and are more properly considered as acts of professional mis-judgement. The approach involves demonstrating that the employees' actions were so intolerable as to constitute a fundamental breach of trust and confidence.

Since the late 1990s the duty to maintain a relationship of mutual trust and confidence has been considered by the courts to constitute an 'implied term of contract', by which is meant a term that is deemed to be present in everyone's contracts whether expressly agreed or not. It follows that when an employee acts in such a way as to destroy trust and confidence, the employer is entitled to consider it as a fundamental breach of contract. Provided the employer takes prompt action this can then form the basis of a lawful summary dismissal.

This development is very helpful from an employer perspective and also controversial. The problem is that it is a very nebulous concept. What one tribunal panel will consider to be an act that breaches trust and confidence will not always accord with the judgement of another panel. As yet we have very little guidance on this point in the judgements made by higher courts, and so we have a situation in which the law is unpredictable. This is generally a bad thing as it makes it hard in the workplace to decide what to do in any given case. It is also important to remember that the duty to maintain a relationship of trust and confidence is *mutual* and that legal consequences also follow when an employer acts in such a way as to cause a breach. In this situation the employee can resign and rely on the breach to bring and potentially win a claim of constructive dismissal.

Dismissals on grounds of poor performance are classed as being for a reason of incapability, but in practice they are dealt with in a very similar way to acts of ordinary misconduct (ie those which do not give rise to summary dismissal). In both cases employers are required to give at least one warning prior to dismissal, and to allow the employee concerned sufficient time to show that their conduct or capability has improved. In cases of poor performance employers are expected to provide constructive assistance to the employee in the form of training or additional support where to do so would be reasonable. Only after these efforts have been made and a formal warning given is it safe to dismiss. Here, as with cases of gross misconduct it is necessary to hold proper hearings at which representatives can be present, and to allow an appeal.

WHITBREAD PLC V HALL

The significance of procedure in determining the outcome of unfair dismissal cases was firmly reiterated in the case of *Whitbread v Hall* (2001). This concerned the dismissal on grounds of gross misconduct of an employee who admitted falsifying stock control records. The reason was found to be one which was potentially fair, but the manner of the dismissal was unreasonable because there were deficiencies in the procedure adopted. The main problem here was the way that the same area manager both investigated the issue and subsequently conducted the disciplinary hearing herself. Moreover, proper consideration was not given to all the facts of the case. So the employer was found to have dismissed the employee unfairly even though he had openly admitted carrying out the offence. The employer appealed to the Employment Appeals Tribunal and then to the Court of Appeal. At all stages the claimant won his case.

ILL-HEALTH DISMISSALS

Of all the tasks that HR professionals have to undertake, by far the most unpleasant is to dismiss employees because they are no longer fit to work. It is particularly hard when the individuals involved are supporting other family members and when there is no possibility of providing financial assistance through a pension or other insurance scheme. Where it is believed that the illness is terminal, the process becomes even more difficult. However, that said, it remains a task that has to be carried out from time to time, and one that has to be done lawfully as well as sensitively.

It is very difficult to give any kind of general definition of 'reasonableness' in such cases, because the law requires above all that each individual case is treated on its own merits. However, the basic considerations are the following:

- Long-term illness is a potentially fair reason for dismissal.

- The decision to dismiss need not be taken on medical grounds alone. It is at root a management issue, which has to be determined against the background of the available medical evidence.

- Jobs should be kept open for sick individuals for as long as is practically possible wherever there is a reasonable expectation that they will be able to return to work in the foreseeable future.

- Sick pay arrangements are wholly distinct. There is no right for an employee to have his or her job held open until sick pay ends, nor are employers permitted to dismiss at this point for no other reason than that no further payments are being made.

The decision to dismiss has thus to be taken in the light of individual circumstances and so cannot be determined by written policy. Where the employee's duties cannot practically be covered by others, the employer will be justified in dismissing the sick employee in order to hire a replacement after a relatively short period of time. By contrast, where covering through the use of temporary employees, overtime or departmental reorganisation is possible, and where the employee's illness is believed to be long-term and yet temporary, the 'reasonable' employer is expected to keep the job open, and not to dismiss.

Such judgements are impossible without medical evidence, so tribunals expect employers to take all possible steps to obtain it. In most cases this is no problem, because employees have no objection to a letter of enquiry being sent to their GP or specialist. Indeed, they themselves will often provide copies of medical reports to their employers. However, employees are not obliged to do so, and are legally entitled to refuse their employer access to a report once it has been written. There are also situations in which doctors refuse to send reports to employers because they believe that to do so would be potentially damaging to the employee's health and/or chances of speedy recovery. Often these arise when doctors do not wish their patients to see the full content of such reports. Employees who are sick can also be invited to see a company doctor or medical practitioner employed by an employer's occupational health service. Here too, though, they are under no obligation to attend.

From the HR manager's perspective, the more information that is provided the better, but the tribunals only require that efforts be made to obtain that evidence. Often this will include formally warning employees concerned that their job is at risk if they do not co-operate. Where no medical evidence is forthcoming despite taking all reasonable steps to obtain it, and the employer has good reason to believe the illness to be sufficiently serious to justify dismissal, the decision to dismiss will generally be held to be fair by a tribunal. Where it is written into contracts of employment that employees are obliged to submit to a medical examination when they are sick for a prolonged period, the issuing of formal warnings is more easily accomplished.

As in other cases of unfair dismissal, tribunals also pay attention to the procedural arrangements when judging the employer's reasonableness. In ill-health cases, they will look at how far the employer has kept in touch with employees during their illness, how far they have been consulted and informed about the possible consequences of their continued ill-health, and whether or not colleagues or trade union representatives have been present at meetings. Here too there is a need, wherever possible, to give formal consideration to taking action short of dismissal. Among the questions that ACAS suggests should be asked are these:

- Could the employee return to work if some assistance were provided?

- Could some reorganisation or redesign of the job speed up a return to work?

- Is alternative, lighter or less stressful work available, with retraining if necessary?

- Could reorganisation of the work group produce a more suitable job?

- Could early retirement be considered, perhaps with an enhanced pension or an ex gratia payment?

- Have all possibilities been discussed with the employee and his or her representative?

To these could be added the possibility that a temporary replacement could be appointed on a fixed-term basis, or the suggestion that the employee works part-time or from home during his or her recovery. It may also be possible to offer help in bringing the employee in to work and taking him or her back home at the end of the day.

All the above are the kind of questions a tribunal will ask when judging reasonableness in a case of dismissal on grounds of ill-health. These issues become a great deal more important where the dismissed employee is able to bring a claim under the Disability Discrimination Act 1995. Compensation levels are often considerably higher in these cases, particularly where the individual concerned is unlikely to find new employment for some time. In these cases employers will be found to have discriminated unlawfully if they do not make 'reasonable adjustments' to working practices or the physical working environment to accommodate the needs of a disabled employee. The burden of proof in these matters is on the employer, although its size and resources are taken into account in judging reasonableness. For larger employers there is thus an expectation that wheelchair ramps and disabled toilets will be installed, that duties will be reorganised to allow a disabled person to occupy a post, that the employee concerned will be allowed to take more absence (eg to attend medical appointments) and that in some circumstances he/she will be allowed to work from home. In other words the law expects that employers will not prevent a disabled person from continuing to work unless it would be unreasonable to expect the required adjustments to be made.

Where someone is believed to fall into the category of 'disabled' under the terms of this Act, it is essential that great care is taken in managing their case. They should certainly not be dismissed without first consulting with them about possible adjustments that could be made to enable them to continue working in some capacity. No assumptions should be made about their willingness to work and serious consideration must be given to requests for reasonable adjustments to be made. Only once these possibilities have been discarded as clearly unreasonable is it safe to dismiss. Failure to do so is likely to lead to legal action which is a good deal more costly than typical unfair dismissal cases. DDA claims also succeed much more often in practice. In addition there are risks of attracting adverse publicity in the local press.

In some respects, greater difficulties are caused in situations where employees who are sick continue to come into work despite the fact that they are incapable of adequately performing their jobs. The problem is made worse when such staff have to take time off to undergo medical examinations or to be treated in hospital. In the case of a long-term sickness that results in poor performance and intermittent periods of absence, it is not always easy to judge under which procedure (misconduct, performance or ill-health) it should be managed. It is made all the harder when employees are unwilling to admit that they are seriously ill, for fear of losing their jobs. In such situations, the principles set out above are the same. There is a need to reassure the employees concerned and to deal with the situation as sensitively as possible but, ultimately, if no recovery materialises, there is a need to take all reasonable steps to obtain medical evidence and to consider dismissing on grounds of ill-health. Again, provided the above procedural steps have been followed, the dismissal would be defensible at a tribunal, and a legal challenge would therefore be unlikely.

REFLECTIVE QUESTION

How far does your organisation follow the above principles in handling ill-health dismissals? In what ways could your procedures be improved?

DOCUMENTATION

As has already been made clear, it is necessary, in managing and carrying out individual dismissals, to bear in mind the possibility that a tribunal case might be brought. It is therefore important that affairs are dealt with in such a way as to ensure that, if the dismissed employee decides to launch a legal action, the organisation is well placed to defend it. In any event, where the dismissal has been carried out lawfully and the procedure used has been fair, the aggrieved employee will be less likely to take the organisation to tribunal. Making sure that the documentation associated with the dismissal is in order has a significant role to play in the deterrence process, because documentary evidence is crucial for a tribunal seeking to judge how reasonable the procedural aspects of the dismissal were. There is no point in undertaking all the necessary procedural steps if at the end of the day it cannot be shown that this actually occurred. Documentary evidence, as well as that given by witnesses, is the only means open to a tribunal to make such judgements, and documents tend to be rather more reliable.

Perhaps the most important document of all is the organisation's disciplinary procedure. Since 1993 all employers with more than 20 staff have been obliged to have a written disciplinary procedure, and to make it available to staff through incorporation in an employee handbook or inclusion among the various pieces of information that now have to be given to all new starters within two months of the beginning of their employment (see Chapter 12). If no such document exists, or if a dismissal has been carried out without adopting these procedures, the organisation will lose credibility in the eyes of a tribunal, and may not be seen to have acted 'reasonably'. Ex-employees could also quite honestly claim that they did not know what the procedure was and were put at a disadvantage as a result.

In practice, most organisations base their written procedures on that outlined in the ACAS code of practice on discipline at work, although they may adapt it to meet local needs. In particular, the list of offences considered to be acts of 'gross misconduct' may be extended to cover the particular circumstances of the organisation concerned.

Other documents that it is important to draw up correctly are any letters sent to the employee prior to his or her dismissal. Here again there is a need to be able to demonstrate that the employee was made fully aware of his or her rights and of the consequences of future actions, and had been issued with clear warnings. The same is true in cases of ill-health and in many of the occurrences that fall under the heading 'some other substantial reason'. It is necessary not only to keep employees informed of their rights and obligations, but to be able to prove that this occurred and thus that any dismissal was carried out with procedural fairness. To that end, employers are well advised to write to employees after any meeting or formal hearing, stating the outcome and the reasons for any decisions taken. Above all, there is a need for clarity so that there is no room for debate later about what was said. If the warning is final, it is vital that the letter confirming the outcome of the hearing states that such is the case.

When writing to employees who either are under threat of dismissal or have been dismissed it is necessary to stress the right to appeal and the right to representation at any formal hearing. In the case of formal letters to employees, it is good practice to send two copies and to ask the member of staff concerned to sign one, stating that they have received it and understood its contents, before returning it. There is then no possibility of an employee's claiming later that no correspondence was received.

A further consideration to bear in mind is the right of tribunal claimants to 'discovery and inspection' of documentary evidence. This means that, in preparing their case, they have a right not only to ask only what documents exist but also to see any that are relevant, and to take copies. Where confidential matters are included, the employment judge can be given the disputed papers and makes a judgement as to whether or not they should be made available to the claimant. For this reason, care must be taken in compiling minutes of any meetings or hearings that took place, to ensure that their content is clear and not readily misinterpreted.

 EXERCISE BOX: AVOIDING UNFAIR DISMISSAL CLAIMS

EXERCISE 17.1

Read the article by Emma Grace entitled 'How to avoid unfair dismissal claims' featured in *People Management* (7 February 2002, pages 48–49). This can be downloaded from the *People Management* archive on the CIPD's website (www.cipd.co.uk).

This article gives employers a simple checklist of actions to take and pitfalls to avoid when handling disciplinary cases. It stresses the importance of procedures and of being seen to have acted in a procedurally correct manner.

Questions:

1   Why are employers who follow all the steps set out in this article less likely to face tribunal claims than those who do not?

2   In your view should employers be able to defend themselves in situations when they have not followed the full procedure on the grounds that it would have made no difference to the final outcome?

3   Why has the organisation of the appeal stage become a more significant issue for employers than was the case until recently?

NOTICE PERIODS

One of the classes of information that has to be provided for all employees within two months of their start date is the period of notice that they have to give their employer when they resign and which they can expect to receive if dismissed. This is not simply a matter for the contract of employment, because there are also minimum notice periods required by statute (Employment Rights Act 1996) linked to an employee's length of service:

- Continuous service of between four weeks and two years entitles the employee to a minimum of one week's notice.

- Continuous service of between two and 12 years entitles the employee to one week's notice for each completed year.

- After 12 years' continuous service the minimum notice period remains 12 weeks.

These limits apply wherever no specific mention of notice periods is made in contracts of employment. However, if the contract specifies longer (eg 12 weeks for everyone), then that overrides the statutory minimum and must be given, whatever the circumstances of the case. It is interesting to note that employees voluntarily resigning are required to give only a week's notice where no separate contractual agreement has been made.

As was explained above there are effectively two situations in which an employer can summarily dismiss an employee without notice. The first is where the dismissal results from gross misconduct, defined as a breach of defined rules. The second is where the employee has acted in such a way as to have effectively 'repudiated' the contract of employment. In most cases, these two categories overlap, but there are situations in which courts have found repudiation to have occurred even though it could not be said that the employee concerned had committed an act of gross misconduct. Examples include a sportswriter who publicly criticised his employers at a press conference, and a shop steward who made unauthorised use of a password to enter a colleague's computer.

In practice of course, with the exception of redundancies, most dismissals are intended to take immediate effect. Employees are thus not required to work the notice to which they are entitled. What usually happens is that employees are offered 'pay in lieu of notice', a lump sum covering the number of weeks to which they are entitled. The law accepts such payments as marking the end of the contractual employment relationship, and judges their receipt by employees as marking the effective date of termination.

In the case of more senior jobs, perhaps where the individuals employed have access to sensitive or confidential commercial information, it is not in the employer's interest to dismiss with pay in lieu of notice. To do so would immediately free the individual concerned of all contractual obligation and permit him or her to take up a post with a competitor within a few days or weeks of the dismissal. For jobs where this situation could arise, employers insert into the original contract of employment a clause that gives them the option of requiring the dismissed employee to take 'garden leave'. In practice this means that the employee, once dismissed, remains on the payroll during the period of notice but is not required to undertake any work. Instead he or she is expected to stay at home (gardening or undertaking some other pastime – hence the above expression) until the period of notice has been completed. Often this occurs where the employees concerned have held very senior positions and have been entitled to six or 12 months' notice.

UNFAIR DISMISSAL CLAIMS

As was mentioned in the introduction to this chapter, it is not at all unusual for organisations to have unfair dismissal cases launched against them by aggrieved ex-employees. The cost to the individuals concerned is low, so they may feel that they have nothing to lose and everything to gain by bringing an action. At the very least, many hope to receive something by way of an out-of-court settlement, even where their case is comparatively weak.

Dismissed employees are required to make a claim in writing to the secretary of tribunals via their regional tribunal office. In cases of alleged unfair dismissal, the application must be received by the office within three months of the effective date of termination. A standard ET1 form must now be used to launch a claim. The tribunal officer then sends a copy of this form to the employer, who is required to issue a 'notice of appearance' within 14 days using the ET3 form. A notice of appearance states whether the claim is to be contested, and, if so, on what grounds. At this stage, all that is required is a brief statement of which statutory provisions form the basis of the defence, and not a detailed statement describing events surrounding the dismissal. That said, the notice of response is significant because, once completed, the grounds of any defence cannot easily be changed. Employers who later embellish their 'stories' to present at tribunal will invariably be asked why they did not make reference to new salient points at the time that they completed their ET3. Failure to provide a good explanation suggests unreliability and will not impress the tribunal.

The next stage involves the setting of a date for the hearing and the preparation of cases. In many circumstances this will be preceded by a case management discussion with an employment judge at which arrangements for the exchange documents, schedule of loss and witness statements are determined. The purpose is to clarify beforehand the issues about which there is a dispute, so as to reduce the length of time the hearing actually takes. Where the crux of the matter is clear and the issues in dispute straightforward, tribunals will proceed to a hearing without need for lengthy 'pleadings' of this kind.

In practice, most cases brought never get so far as a hearing, either because they are withdrawn or because they are settled out of court beforehand. Intervention from officers employed by ACAS facilitates most withdrawals and settlements, making their role crucial to the way the system operates. The conciliation arm of ACAS becomes involved as a result of its statutory duty to seek settlements between parties before cases are formally presented before a tribunal. All ET1 applications and notices of response are copied to ACAS, together with other relevant documents, to allow officers to judge the prospects of reaching such a settlement. Where they decide to proceed, they contact the parties, review the strength of the respective cases, and then either advise one party to withdraw or seek to negotiate a financial settlement. Of the cases received by ACAS for conciliation, fewer than a third actually go on to a full tribunal hearing. Where agreement between the parties is reached in this way, it is deemed binding in law only where it has been confirmed in writing. ACAS provide a COT3 form for this purpose.

QUALIFICATIONS AND REMEDIES

All those who have been employed by the organisation from which they are dismissed for a period of a year or more have the right not to be unfairly dismissed, and are therefore able to bring a tribunal case against their former employers. There are a few exceptions (eg crown employees, police officers, some domestic servants) but, in most cases, provided the individual is an employee and not a self-employed contractor, the same statutory rights apply. There is also a need to have been employed continuously for a year without contractual breaks. Only when the reason for dismissal is one of those classed as 'automatically unfair' is there no one-year qualifying period.

In cases of unfair dismissal, where a tribunal finds in favour of an employee, a number of options is open to it by way of remedy. First, it can require that the applicant is re-employed either in the same position (reinstatement) or in a comparable one (re-engagement). However, in practice, this occurs in only a handful of cases, because the vast majority seek compensation. In determining the sum the applicant is to receive, tribunals make two distinct calculations: the basic award and the compensatory award. The first is calculated in the same way as a statutory redundancy payment (see Chapter 18), taking into account the salary level and the length of service of the individual concerned. To this is added the compensatory award, which seeks to take account of losses sustained by the employee as a result of the dismissal. At present (ie 2010) there is a ceiling of £11,400 on basic awards and £65,300 on compensatory awards, but in practice average awards in cases of unfair dismissal fall well below these maximum figures. In 2008–09 the median figure was only £4,269, in part reflecting the way that tribunals reduce the value of compensation to reflect any contributory fault on the part of the applicant. The cost to the employer thus derives less from the award itself, and more from legal costs and management time expended in the preparation of a case.

The one-year qualifying period, together with the statutory maximum payments and the restricted way that compensation is calculated, have been criticised on the grounds that it tips the balance of justice heavily in favour of the employer. Prior to 1999 a two-year qualifying period was required, but back in the 1970s it was only six months. The reasons for the continued requirement to have completed a full year's service remain controversial. The major reasons given are as follows:

- the belief that less than a year is too short a period of time for employers to determine whether they wished to employ someone over the long term

- the belief that employment protection legislation increases unemployment by acting as a deterrent to employers considering the employment of new staff.

In both cases, it was concern for the needs of small and growing businesses that most appears to have influenced government thinking over the years (see Davies and Friedland 1993:561).

Despite these arguments, many disagree with the qualifying period and maximum penalties. It can thus be expected that campaigns to change the law in these areas will continue to be run.

REFLECTIVE QUESTION

What is your view about these issues? What effect would a return to the pre-1980 regulations have for your organisation?

THE ACT OF DISMISSAL

There is no definite right or wrong way to inform people that they are being dismissed, because the circumstances of each case are very different. In cases of gross misconduct, the news may well come as a shock to some employees whereas, in other cases, where a lengthy procedure has been followed, the response is more likely to be anguish. Employees may become abusive, but such cases are relatively rare.

Whatever the circumstances, this is a difficult and cheerless task. Some of the general rules to follow are these:

- Prepare for the meeting at which the dismissal is to take place very thoroughly.

- Be certain of the facts of the case and the precise reasons the decision to dismiss has been arrived at.

- Organise practical matters such as pay in lieu of notice before the meeting takes place.

- Consider in advance the likely reaction of the individual and prepare an appropriate response.

- Talk to employees concerned firmly but sympathetically. It is important that they understand that the decision is final, but they should be given as much practical assistance in planning for their future as is possible. Where the services of outplacement specialists would be helpful, consider offering these.

- Wherever possible, avoid the need for employees to leave immediately. There is nothing more humiliating and liable to cause ill-feeling than being frogmarched off the premises like a criminal when there is no intention on employees' part of causing damage or removing company property.

EXERCISE 17.2

EXERCISE BOX: LIFTING THE CAP

Read the news article by Zoe Roberts entitled 'Lords call for unfair dismissal review' featured in *People Management* (29 July 2004, page 8). This can be downloaded from the *People Management* archive on the CIPD's website (www.cipd.co.uk).

In this article it is explained that the Law Lords have expressed concern about the cap of £55,000 on compensatory awards that then applied in cases of unfair dismissal. The cap (£65,300 in 2010) means that some victorious claimants who have lost out financially by much higher sums cannot be recompensed. To gain more by way of an award they are required to take a separate claim to the county or high court alleging breach of the implied term of contract known as 'trust and confidence' (see Chapter 12).

Questions:

1 Do you think that employees who are dismissed unjustly should have the right to claim for injury to feelings as is the case in discrimination cases?

2 What arguments could be advanced for leaving the cap on compensatory awards at its present level?

3 Why is the cap on unfair dismissal described in the article as being 'a political hot potato'?

WRONGFUL DISMISSAL

In some situations employees who do not qualify for unfair dismissal rights or who believe they should receive more by way of compensation than is permitted under unfair dismissal law can choose instead to sue their ex-employers for damages under the law of wrongful dismissal. Until 1994 such cases could be heard in the civil courts only, requiring considerable expenditure on the part of the applicant. However, since then jurisdiction over claims worth up to £25,000 has passed to employment tribunals, making the wrongful dismissal route more attractive.

Cases of wrongful dismissal differ from those of unfair dismissal in that they do not rely on statute. The question of how reasonably an employer has acted is thus not at issue. What matters is whether or not the dismissal contravened the terms of the employee's contract of employment. The court is thus asked to rule whether the employer was entitled to dismiss the employee for a particular reason in the way that occurred, given the nature of the particular contractual terms agreed.

There are two situations in which someone who has been dismissed might choose to sue for wrongful rather than unfair dismissal. The first is where the employee, for whatever reason, does not have the protection of unfair dismissal law. This might apply to people with less than a year's service or where a longer period of employment has been temporarily interrupted. Secondly, it might apply in cases where the damages that could be gained might reasonably be expected to exceed those likely to be offered as an unfair dismissal award. An example would be a highly paid person who was summarily dismissed and whose contract entitles him or her to three months' notice.

However, no claim of wrongful dismissal can be successful unless the terms of the contract of employment have been breached by the employer. In practice, this can happen very easily, because many employers explicitly incorporate disciplinary procedures into all contracts. In some cases, it is the contents of an employee rule book or staff handbook that are incorporated, in others it is the terms of collective agreements with trade unions. Often these documents include lists of offences that may be considered to constitute gross misconduct, rules for selecting people for redundancy and details of ACAS-type disciplinary procedures. Where that is the case, any employee of whatever age, whether or not he or she has a year's continuous service, can expect the terms of the contract to be honoured. If he or she is then dismissed in contravention of those terms, there is a possibility that there will be a sound case under wrongful dismissal law.

BEST PRACTICE

As has been shown, in most situations good practice in the field of dismissal is effectively defined by law. It is thus only at the margins that employers seeking to implement 'best practice' approaches across all fields of employee-resourcing activity can improve on the legal requirements as far as procedure is concerned. Perhaps the only major area where improvement can be made is in applying the same principles to all employees regardless of length of service. In making it clear that everyone will be treated according to the ACAS code from the very start of their employment, an employer extends the principles of natural justice to all, and could claim to be going as far as it is possible to go in treating employees fairly when conduct or capability are in need of improvement.

That said, best practice in dismissal should not be concerned just with procedural matters – the manner in which the procedures are operated is also important. Employers could therefore look at improving the training of managers in these fields, at the clarity of documentation and at ways of improving the investigation stage of any enquiry.

Moreover, in the field of dismissals on account of ill-health there are a number of improvements that can be made on the statutory requirements. Here it is a question of handling matters sensitively and seeking to give as much practical and financial assistance as is possible. No employer who terminates contracts in these circumstances without making appropriate and adequate provision for a sick employee's future, either through a pension scheme or other funds, can reasonably claim to be operating 'best practice'.

EXAMPLE

'Unfair dismissal disputes: a comparative study of Great Britain and New Zealand' by Sue Corby (2000) *Human Resource Management Journal.* **Vol. 10, No. 1. 79–92**

In this interesting article the author describes her in-depth comparative study between different aspects of unfair dismissal law in the UK and in New Zealand, where it is known as 'unjustified dismissal'. She shows how the two systems are similar, while pointing out the main differences and their practical impact. The article concludes with a discussion about how the UK system might be improved were some aspects of the New Zealand approach to be adopted.

Questions:

1 How do the UK and New Zealand systems compare in terms of:

- accessibility?
- speed?
- informality?
- potential cost to the claimant?
- likely outcome?

2 To what extent do you agree with Sue Corby's recommendations as to how the UK system might be improved by taking on some features of the New Zealand system? Why?

- There are many books on the market that offer a straightforward guide to unfair dismissal law. Good starting points are *Employment law* by Deborah Lockton (2006), *Employment law in context* by Brian Willey (2009), *Employment law: An introduction* by Stephen Taylor & Astra Emir (2009) and *Essentials of employment law* by David Lewis and Malcolm Sargeant (2010).

- More detailed treatments by specialist lawyers and academics are found in Labour Law by Simon Deakin and Gillian Morris (2009), *Unfair dismissal: Law practice and guidance* by Michael Duggan (1999), *Dismissals: Law and practice* by Julian Yew and in the IDS *Handbook on unfair dismissal* (2005c).

- The law in this field develops at a fair pace, often rendering books more than a year or two old out of date. Readers are therefore advised to turn also to journals for details of new legislation and case law. *People Management, IDS Brief* and IRS *Industrial Relations Law Bulletin* regularly include guidance notes focusing on key legal issues geared for practitioners rather than lawyers.

CHAPTER 18

Redundancy

LEARNING OUTCOMES

By the end of this chapter readers should be able to:

- define the term 'redundancy'
- calculate redundancy payments
- organise job-search courses
- run or commission the provision of outplacement services
- draw up policies on the management of redundancy
- determine fair criteria for selecting employees to be made compulsorily redundant.

In addition, readers should be able to understand and explain:

- the main legal issues relating to the management of redundancy
- the impact of age discrimination law on redundancy
- best-practice approaches to handling redundancy over and above what is required by law.

 EXERCISE BOX: THE LEGAL SERVICES COMMISSION

EXERCISE 18.1

Read the article by Hashi Syedain entitled 'A Judicious Review' featured in *People Management* (4 October 2007, page 37). This can be downloaded from the *People Management* archive on the CIPD's website (www.cipd.co.uk).

This brief article describes how the LSC managed to cut a third of its workforce over five years, while also ensuring that it did not lose its best people.

Questions:

1 Why do strong performers tend to leave an organisation voluntarily when future redundancies are rumoured?

2 Why was the approach used by the LSC successful in preventing this from occurring?

3 What other types of initiative might have been used to achieve the same effect or to complement the approach that was taken?

DEFINING REDUNDANCY

In the UK, the term 'redundancy' is defined by law as a situation in which, for economic reasons, there is no longer a need for the job in question to be carried out in the place where it is currently carried out. Although the selection of employees to be made redundant can take into account the ability to perform the job, individual failings are not the main reason that a job is being lost. The Employment Rights Act (1996) states that redundancy occurs only when a dismissal arises either mainly or wholly for one of the following reasons:

- where the employer has ceased, or intends to cease, carrying on the business in which the employee is or was employed
- where the employer ceases, or intends to cease, carrying out this business at the place where the employee is or was employed
- where the requirements for employees to carry out work of a particular kind have ceased or diminished (or are expected to), and where the employee is employed to carry that work out
- where the requirements to carry out work of a particular kind have ceased or diminished at the place where the employee is employed.

The starting point is, therefore, a reduction in the need for employees (ie headcount) either in general or at a particular location. If such is not the case, whatever the dismissal might be called by those involved, it is not considered a 'redundancy' in legal terms. Although a reduction in the requirement for employees usually results from a reduction in the volume of work, that is not a necessary condition for a legal redundancy to occur. It is quite possible for an expanding business to make redundancies, provided certain types of work are becoming less necessary and the employees concerned are unable to transfer to other jobs. A common example would be a situation in which new technology is introduced to meet increased demand, leading to a requirement for fewer low-skilled employees.

It is important to grasp the legal definition, because it sets out the circumstances in which employees are entitled, as of right, to a redundancy payment. Where the dismissal is mainly for other reasons, such as misconduct or incapability, the employer is not obliged to pay compensation, except in cases where individual contracts of employment require it. Redundancies also require a wholly different procedural approach if they are to be judged to have been carried out reasonably by employment tribunals. Moreover, the distinction between true redundancies and other dismissals is also a matter of interest to the Inland Revenue, because redundancy payments below £30,000 are tax-free. The practice of making someone redundant and paying a redundancy payment when the above definitions do not in fact apply can thus lead to as much difficulty as situations in which payments are not made to dismissed employees who are truly redundant.

Redundancies fall into the category of 'potentially fair dismissals' as far as employment tribunals are concerned. Like the other kinds of dismissal discussed in the last chapter, employers are therefore legally able to dismiss employees on account of redundancy provided they meet the tribunal's standards of 'reasonableness'. In other words, a redundancy will be judged fair as long as the correct procedures are followed and as long as people are treated equitably. As is the case with all kinds of dismissal, employment tribunals can hear only cases brought by employees with over a year's continuous service after the age of 18.

THE IMPACT OF RECESSION

In recent years the number of redundancies recorded each year has tended to increase somewhat due to greater turbulence and unpredictability in the business environment. In the industries most affected, downsizing, streamlining, rationalising, delayering, outsourcing and offshoring have all occurred, alongside the creation of economies of scale following mergers and acquisitions. All tend to result in redundancies.

The numbers of people being made redundant, however, varies depending on economic conditions. When the economy is growing as it did throughout the late 1990s and early 2000s redundancies are far less common than they are during downturns and recessions.

The total number of redundancies in the UK in most years when the economy is growing averages at around 400,000. In 2008 it increased to 660,000 and in 2009 reached 939,000 as the recession took grip and deepened.

A better way of seeing the impact of recession is to look at the figures the Office of National Statistics publishes in each quarter about the number of employees per 1,000 who have been made redundant. This allows for more accurate comparison across time as it takes account of rises and falls in the total number of jobs. The changes here are more striking.

In the years following 2000 redundancy rates per thousand declined steadily from about eight to five. This indicates a low rate of redundancy due to a good steady level of economic growth being achieved. The rates increased very steeply once recessionary conditions hit the UK economy after 2007. By the first quarter of 2009 the rate of redundancies per thousand employees had risen to 12.2 per thousand employees.

AVOIDING REDUNDANCIES

One of the issues that tribunals look at in judging the reasonableness with which a redundancy programme has been carried out is the extent and nature of the steps taken either to minimise the number of redundancies or to avoid them altogether. A variety of management actions can be taken to avoid making people compulsorily redundant, some of a general nature that help prevent redundancy situations arising in the first place and others that come into play once it becomes apparent that redundancies are likely or necessary.

LONG-TERM APPROACHES

In publications on redundancy, authors rightly give considerable attention to the approaches that managers can take to prevent, or reduce the likelihood of, redundancies (eg: Lewis 1993, Redman and Wilkinson 2009). Each involves planning in order to avoid as far as possible scenarios in which the employer has no alternative but to dismiss employees whose jobs have become redundant. The approaches fall into three broad but distinct categories: effective human resource planning, flexible working practices, and the sponsorship of early retirement incentives.

The arguments for and against human resource planning were explored at length in Chapter 5. One strong argument in favour of carrying out formal forecasting of staffing needs is the assistance that the development of human resource plans give in avoiding redundancy. If one can foresee months or even years ahead a downturn in business levels or a change in business processes likely to reduce an organisation's need to employ people or to undertake work of a particular kind, then one can take steps to reduce the number of compulsory redundancies that will have to be made. For example, an organisation can reduce the number of new employees taken on and focus its attention on retraining and developing existing employees for new roles that they may have to undertake in the future. Such a course of action also permits natural wastage to occur, so that over time the size of the workforce diminishes as people leave voluntarily and are not replaced.

The second long-term activity is the maximisation of flexibility in an organisation, so that where work of a particular kind is expected to grow less, the employees engaged in that work are able to develop new job roles. We explored these issues in Chapter 3. Fowler (1999:24–26) usefully distinguishes between 'organisational flexibility', which involves both reducing the number of steps in organisational hierarchies and also organising employees into multifunctional teams, and 'job flexibility', which requires enlarging and enriching individual jobs so that each employee becomes multiskilled. Such courses of action make modern organisations more efficient and the employees working within them more adaptable to changing circumstances. Each of these consequences contributes to the avoidance of redundancies.

Other kinds of flexibility with a role to play are the employment of subcontractors to carry out peripheral tasks and the development of flexible contractual terms. Because subcontractors are hired on a temporary or fixed-term basis, it is clearly less expensive to dispense with their services or to renegotiate new terms than is the case with established employees. However, the introduction of such outsourcing may itself reduce job security and increase the likelihood that individual employees will be made redundant. Over time, though, it can be accomplished without harming the prospects of current employees, as long as retraining opportunities are offered to those affected. In smaller, growing organisations such forms of flexibility can be developed as the business expands. Contractual flexibility also contributes by ensuring that an organisation is able to maximise its efficiency through reducing its inherent rigidity. Wherever possible, therefore, staff can be employed on contracts that do not define job content or hours of work too narrowly.

Early retirement is often an attractive way of reducing the extent to which compulsory redundancies are necessary. The Inland Revenue permits organisations to release people after the age of 50 with enhanced pensions, so in most cases such schemes apply only to employees who have reached that age. Many employees find it an attractive option, because it permits them to draw their occupational pensions early (if at a reduced rate) but also permits them to continue working either as a full-time employee or on a part-time basis. In practice, they are made voluntarily redundant, but are better off financially than they would have been with a straightforward redundancy payment. In most cases the costs are met by using pension fund assets, and so do not have to be drawn from current organisational budgets. In theory, therefore, everyone benefits: the employer loses employees amicably and at low cost, the retiree leaves on acceptable financial terms, and fewer compulsory redundancies are needed from the ranks of other employees. Early retirement is, of course, an option only for organisations with an established occupational pension fund that has successfully attracted members from among its employees. For this reason, it is best categorised as a long-term activity that can help reduce the need to make compulsory redundancies. There is also a significant cost incurred to the pension fund, making it an option that is only realistic for employers whose funds are in surplus.

SHORT-TERM APPROACHES

The above preventative measures will not always have been introduced and will, in any case, often fail to prevent the need for compulsory redundancies. In these circumstances most employers will seek to minimise their number by using a range of other established tools and practices. The most common of these is to ask formally for volunteers – to give long-serving employees in line to receive substantial redundancy payments the opportunity to claim them. However, there are problems. First, this is often more expensive for the employer than a situation in which the employees to be made redundant are not volunteers but are identified by management. Secondly, it often allows the most employable and valuable staff to depart, leaving less effective employees in place after the programme of redundancies has been completed.

In practice, the process of seeking volunteers is fraught with difficulty and has to be managed with great care if the many pitfalls are to be avoided. A common problem arises when too many people volunteer for redundancy, leading to a situation in which weaker performers appear to have been rewarded with redundancy while more valued volunteers are left to soldier on until they reach 65 (or whatever the contractual retirement age is). Such situations are common where redundancy terms are excessively enhanced in order to attract a pool of candidates. The result is demotivation among those required to stay on. Another problem relates to people's fear that their careers may suffer or that their relationships with line managers may deteriorate if they are known to have applied unsuccessfully for voluntary redundancy. This may deter people from applying in the first place, but can also lead to further problems of morale if the employee is kept on.

These and other problems can be overcome provided the volunteering process is carefully controlled and planned. The first decision to make involves establishing the coverage of the voluntary scheme. To whom is voluntary redundancy to be offered? Should it be to everyone in the organisation or just to selected grades or departments? Some organisations, particularly those having to effect large numbers of redundancies in a short period of time, will make a blanket offer to all employees, or may exclude only a few groups – such as people in jobs that are to remain and into which others could not be redeployed. By contrast, where the redundancies are restricted to limited areas of the organisation it makes sense to target these alone so as to avoid raising expectations among those working in other areas.

It is also possible to target offers on individuals who are performing poorly and who have built up a number of years' service. This can be done by developing a package specifically designed to appeal to them, perhaps including early retirement options. Offers can then be made individually ahead of any general announcement, with a view to developing tailored settlements to suit those whom the organisation most wants to lose. Flexibility over the timing can also be discussed to increase the incentive to volunteer. The other approach is to use the stick as well as the carrot, by indicating that the people concerned are likely to find their jobs disappearing in the post-redundancy structure anyway. As with so much practice in this area employers need to keep half an eye on age discrimination law, but that should not be an insurmountable obstacle provided a clear business case can be advanced to justify a policy.

The next step is to establish the criteria for selecting candidates for redundancy from among those who volunteer. It is important that these are drawn up before the offer is made, in order to avoid raising the hopes of people whom the organisation has no intention of selecting. It can, for example, be made clear that those with good performance and attendance records, long service and valuable skills are unlikely to be selected. A general offer can then be made to all staff within affected departments, which will nevertheless deter from applying those who are still very much wanted.

Other approaches to avoid or minimise redundancies are rather more straightforward. Where there exists several months' warning, it is possible to institute a general restriction on all recruitment of new employees. A post that becomes vacant that will continue after the redundancy programme has been completed may only be advertised internally and be filled by someone at risk of redundancy. Another approach is to fill vacancies externally but to do so only on a fixed-term basis. If it is known that redundancies are likely in six months' time, new starters are hired on six-month contracts which can later be extended but which are occupied by people with no expectation of longer-term employment. Where the period is shorter than six months it is better to bring in agency staff or subcontractors.

A recruitment freeze effectively allows the organisation to minimise the number of redundancies it will have to make in that it allows the size of the permanent workforce to diminish by natural wastage. When redundancies are expected, individual employees will often take steps to look for other work in any case, and many will thus resign of their own accord rather than wait to see whether their job will survive the programme of staff reduction. This has cost advantages for employers, in so far as it reduces the number of redundancy payments, but it can be risky if more valuable employees resign leaving the poorer performers in place.

A further means of reducing redundancies is to cut staff costs in general. The commonest approach is to cut or radically reduce overtime or to cut hours more generally. The result is less pay for employees in return for greater job security. Other approaches include pay freezes, or even pay cuts and the abandonment of profit-based bonus schemes. Where negotiated with staff representatives, such methods of redundancy avoidance can be the most satisfactory. The reduction of non-pay costs can also be considered: for example, the amount of office space occupied can be reduced or less expensive premises rented.

CASE SUMMARY

AVOIDING REDUNDANCIES AT KPMG

When recessionary conditions hit the world economy in 2007 and 2008 and it became clear that staffing costs would have to be cut, HR managers at the professional services provider KPMG decided to avoid having to make compulsory redundancies if at all possible. The firm had made a lot of redundancies in 2002 only to find a year or two later that it had lost many of the skilled people it then needed. The fact that many of its employees are well-paid also means that making redundancies in a firm like KPMG is itself very expensive.

The aim in 2008 was to retain as many people with specialised skills that it could while reducing its staffing costs substantially. This was achieved through a variety of distinct initiatives:

- redeploying people across its international offices where skills were in most need

- retraining people so that they are able to work in growing areas of the business (eg corporate restructuring)

- allowing people to move onto a four-day week or nine-day fortnight contract

- encouraging people to take sabbaticals (at 30 per cent of pay) for periods of between four and 12 weeks.

Eighty-five per cent of KPMG's partners signed up either to the reduced hours or sabbatical programmes. The savings achieved in the first three months of these initiatives was £1.2 million.

Source: Wolff (2009f)

The final approach is redeployment, or finding jobs elsewhere in the organisation for those whose jobs are redundant. Frequently this will mean placing people in posts which are very different from those they currently hold or relocating them to different premises. Where there are flexibility or mobility clauses in the contract of employment, employers are able to redeploy people as they deem appropriate. If individuals refuse a reasonable offer of alternative employment in such circumstances there is no obligation on the employer to pay a redundancy payment. Where there is uncertainty about the suitability of a post, in law employees have the right to a four week trial period before deciding whether or not to accept. A different situation arises where there are jobs available elsewhere in the organisation but these are thought unsuitable to offer to redundant workers because they are lower paid, of lower status or located hundreds of miles away. Employers should not make any assumptions about people's interest or willingness to take up such jobs. All possibilities need to be explored before redundancies take effect.

SELECTING PEOPLE FOR REDUNDANCY

The body of case law on the selection of employees for redundancy is now substantial but remains based on straightforward principles: that the employer, in choosing which staff to make redundant, must use criteria that are fair and objective. If this is judged not to be the case, the test of 'reasonableness' will have failed and the dismissals will be declared unfair by an employment tribunal. Some selection criteria fall into the 'automatically unfair' category. If these are found to have been used, the tribunal will not even get as far as debating the issue of reasonableness. Automatically unfair criteria, as in all cases of unfair dismissal, include the following:

- a trade union reason (ie selection either because a member is or is not a member of a trade union, or took part in trade union activities or refused to take part)

- pregnancy

- sex, marital status, race, disability, sexual orientation or religion/belief

- as a means of victimising an employee who has asserted legitimate statutory rights.

Aside from these unfair selection methods, many others are acceptable provided they are fair and objective.

For many years in the twentieth century the standard approach used was known as LIFO – standing for 'last in first out'. This involved selecting the most recent starters for redundancy, protecting longer-serving staff and hence rewarding seniority. Trade unions have tended to favour such an approach, and it has the great virtue from a management perspective of minimising the costs while also being administratively straightforward. However, in more recent years it has been used less and less. By 2004 this once common approach was only being used exclusively by one in five employers (IRS 2004e) and its use has declined further since then. There are three main reasons for this:

i   LIFO is a very blunt selection tool. It tends to lead to the loss of good performers alongside people who have joined an organisation recently and who have potential to become good performers. Meanwhile poorer performers with more years' service are retained.

ii   Until 1994 employers were under a legal duty to select for redundancy in line with their customary practice. This effectively forced many to apply LIFO criteria simply because that was what they had traditionally done in the past. The abolition of this law allowed greater freedom for managers.

iii Since 2006 age discrimination law has left the lawfulness of LIFO selection in some doubt. Clearly it favours older employees over younger colleagues and so does tend to discriminate on grounds of age, but could it nonetheless be justifiable as a 'proportionate means of achieving a legitimate aim'? At the time of writing (2010) this matter has not yet been settled in the courts. In one test case, *Rolls Royce v Unite* (2009) the High Court ruled that LIFO was justifiable where it was one of several criteria used and where the policy had been agreed with a recognised trade union, but we have no definitive ruling yet on the lawfulness of a pure LIFO system where no union agreement has been struck.

Instead of LIFO two other methods are now commonly used. The first, sometimes called the 'matrix approach', involves scoring employees in the at risk group according to a variety of criteria. These typically include the following:

- skill or competence
- performance records
- attendance records
- record of conduct
- qualifications
- attitude.

While some of the above, such as attendance, are easy to verify objectively, others are not. How, for example, is it possible to judge an employee's attitude or commitment in an objective fashion? The answer, according to Fowler (1999:108), is to ensure that there is evidence to back the decision up and that the latter is not based on a subjective judgement and does not arise from a personality clash. He suggests that where a choice has to be made between two employees, and only one has volunteered for unpleasant tasks in the past or taken the initiative in a specific case, it will be reasonable to take that into account when deciding which person is to be made redundant. What is important is the presence of some kind of evidence (letters, reports, mentions in performance-appraisal records etc) that could be used to show a tribunal that the selection was based on objective criteria.

The same care must be taken when using other methods. Attendance, for example, is a potentially fair criterion. Where there are grounds for believing that an employee's state of health is likely to lead to poor attendance in the future, it is reasonable to take that into account. What is important is that the judgement is made on objective grounds and can be justified if necessary at a tribunal. What is not acceptable is to single out one employee for redundancy on health grounds while failing to apply the same criterion to others. Moreover, it would be unfair to base a redundancy on a poor health record in past years where there was evidence that a full recovery had been made. Where the employee concerned falls under the definition of 'disabled' in the Disability Discrimination Act 1995, very great care must be taken in using attendance or estimations of future health as criteria. It is unlawful to select a disabled person for redundancy for a reason connected to their disability.

Where matrix or points-based systems are used it is important, wherever possible, to avoid any perception of subjectivity. It must thus be decided at the beginning what points are to be awarded for what factors. So defined numbers of points must be awarded (or deducted from a base starting point) for each day of absence in a particular period, for numbers of GCSEs, for written warnings, for performance appraisal scores and so on. It is essential that everyone in the selection pool is treated the same way by being scored fairly against identical criteria. A wholly different approach to the selection of staff for redundancy is to start by developing a new organisational structure, identifying which jobs will be present in the organisation, undertaking which roles or duties, after the redundancy programme has been completed. This is the kind of approach used by organisations undergoing a planned downsizing operation, and has been used extensively in public-sector organisations, as well as those that have been privatised. In such situations, the new structure is agreed and job descriptions and person specifications, or competency frameworks, drawn up for the jobs that remain. Where a job remains essentially unchanged and is currently undertaken by a single person, that person is then 'slotted in' and told that he or she will not be made redundant. Others then apply for the jobs in the new structure and, if necessary, undergo a competitive selection process. Where two or three jobs of a particular type are disappearing, to be replaced by a single job, the application procedure is 'ring-fenced' so that only those currently employed to undertake the roles in question compete for the new position. Those that are unsuccessful are then selected for redundancy. The advantage of this arrangement is the control that it gives managers over the selection process. Its great disadvantage is its effect on morale and teamworking, as employees compete with one another for positions in their own organisations. Of course, it remains the case that the selection criteria have to be both fair and objective, and capable of being justified in court if necessary.

REFLECTIVE QUESTION

Which of these approaches to the management of redundancy have you experienced or observed? In your view, which is least distressing for the individuals involved, and why?

BREAKING THE NEWS

Telling people that they are at risk of redundancy and then subsequently that they have been selected is a very difficult task. Except where very large redundancy payments are on offer, it is probably impossible to carry out this task without causing substantial disquiet. However, the stress suffered can be reduced with careful planning and by following a few sound rules. Rothwell (2000) suggests the following:

- make the process as transparent as possible

- keep people informed throughout periods of uncertainty
- plan for any meetings with great care, anticipating questions and ensuring that you are fully aware of how selection criteria are to be applied
- hold one to one meetings as well as larger collective sessions
- choose a suitable time so that individuals are not faced with major responsibilities immediately after hearing the bad news
- arrange a follow up meeting to discuss detailed matters a day or two after the meeting at which the news is broken.

PROVIDING HELP FOR REDUNDANT EMPLOYEES

One area of redundancy management in which the law does not intervene to any great extent is the provision of counselling and assistance to employees who are under notice of redundancy. All the law requires is that such employees should be given reasonable time off work to look for a new position or to undergo job-search training once they have received notice of redundancy. However, because few cases have been brought, it remains unclear what exactly 'reasonable time off' means. At present, it depends on the facts in particular cases (eg the nature of the job, the extent of expected difficulties in finding comparable work and the need for retraining). That said, the survey evidence suggests that most large employers offer further practical assistance to employees who are going to be dismissed on account of redundancy, and many also provide counselling where necessary (IDS 2001, IRS 2004e).

According to Fowler (1999), there are two broad stages in counselling redundant employees. The first is helping them to come to terms with their fate and to understand the reasons. The second is future-oriented, and involves assisting them to see the future as an opportunity to make new plans for their careers. Although in practice both issues are dealt with together, the first is a prerequisite for the second. It is only when people have successfully 'put initial feelings of resentment, anger and fear behind them' that they are psychologically able to face the future constructively. For this reason, Fowler argues strongly that professional, trained counsellors should be employed to carry out this work. Where well-meaning but untrained people attempt to carry out counselling the result is often counter-productive. If there are no trained counsellors in-house there is, therefore, a good case for hiring external specialists. The other great advantage of bringing in outsiders is the experience they have of dealing specifically with redundancy situations. Moreover, employees are more likely to open up and talk freely to outsiders than they are to colleagues who will be remaining with the organisation. Established Employee Assistance Programmes (EAPs), should an organisation have them in operation, can obviously be used as providers of counselling services.

A number of employers also offer to provide services of a more practical kind for employees under notice of redundancy. These are usually known as outplacement or career consultants, who specialise, on the one hand, in the provision of advice to individuals and, on the other, in running job-search courses or workshops for groups of employees. In both cases, the content of outplacement programmes covers similar grounds. The following is a typical list:

- sources of further employment
- options concerning part-time and self-employed work
- analysis of skills
- application forms or CV preparation
- interviewee skills
- advice about retraining
- salary negotiation.

Some outplacement consultants also operate as headhunters and are thus in a position to give more assistance than simply advice. This raises a potential conflict of interest, which may mean that the advice given is not sufficiently unbiased. The CIPD Code of Conduct for Career and Outplacement Consultants deals with this issue, along with others concerning the appropriate system of payment and the question of proper qualifications. Managers considering employing consultants should thus take note of the Code and make sure that potential providers adhere to its contents and are CIPD members.

Aside from formal outplacement and counselling, there are many other ways in which employers can give helpful and practical assistance to employees seeking new positions. First and foremost, they can offer more than just time off to look for a job by permitting the use of company facilities as well. Secretarial assistance can be given in the preparation of CVs and in other aspects of the job-search process; company cars can be used; and employers can waive any routine restraint-of-trade clauses that might otherwise prevent employees from working for competitors. Larger companies can also offer retraining courses or pay for redundant employees to attend training events elsewhere. Managers can also get in touch with professional contacts and other employers in the area to see whether opportunities exist for those whose jobs are going.

Another option, as mentioned above, is redeployment to another location within the same organisation, if necessary with further training provided. Employees are more likely to show interest in such opportunities if allowances are paid to assist with removal expenses and if the career prospects are perceived as good. Employers also sometimes negotiate rehire agreements, whereby ex-employees are employed as subcontractors or consultants after they have been made redundant. Again, such arrangements are unlikely to be attractive or feasible for most, but may prove satisfactory for some redundant employees. Another approach is the establishment of a recall arrangement, whereby employees are given advance notice of any jobs advertised at their old place of work following their redundancy.

The final area of support that employers often choose to give reflects the possibility that ex-employees will spend a period without work following their redundancies. For some, this will mean applying for state benefits and surviving with a greatly reduced standard of living. For others, such as those leaving with substantial redundancy payments, a period out of the workforce may be more welcome. In either situation, there is a need for psychological preparation and sound financial advice. Some organisations make funds available to employees to organise their own counselling or training in these areas. They might, for example, add a sum of a few hundred pounds to the final redundancy payment to fund individual financial advice. Others take a more pro-active role, laying on courses covering benefit entitlements and investment for employees who are leaving without a job to go to.

REFLECTIVE QUESTION

If you were to be made redundant, what other forms of help and support would you like to have? Which of those described here would be of most use to you?

EXERCISE BOX: GOOD AND BAD PRACTICE IN REDUNDANCY MANAGEMENT

EXERCISE 18.2

Read the article by Jane Pickard entitled 'When Push Comes To Shove' featured in *People Management* (22 November 2001, pages 30-35). This can be downloaded from the *People Management* archive on the CIPD's website (www.cipd.co.uk).

This article debates what exactly is good practice and bad practice in the handling of redundancies. It questions some of the commonly held views about good practice and reflects on the advantages that can be gained from taking extra care over how redundancies are planned and executed.

Questions:

1 On what grounds does the article question the use of performance measures as the basis for selecting people for redundancy?

2 Is there a better alternative? If so what is it?

3 What different strands could make up a business case in favour of treating people as well as possible during a redundancy exercise?

REDUNDANCY PAYMENTS

Since 1965, the law has set out minimum levels of compensation to which redundant employees are entitled. In most cases, the rules are straightforward and have remained unchanged for 30 years. The main features as at 2010 are as follows:

● The amount due to redundant employees depends on their length of service with the employer.

- The calculation is based on the number of continuous years' service and the employee's weekly salary at the time the notice period expires.
- If the weekly salary varies, the average figure for the 12 weeks preceding termination is taken into account.
- Only completed years count.
- The maximum weekly salary that can be used as the basis for the calculation is determined by the government. At the time of writing (2010) it is £380.
- The maximum number of years' service that can be used as the basis of the calculation is 20.
- Only employees with more than two years' continuous service are entitled to redundancy payments.
- The formula for the calculation is as follows:
  - For every completed year between the ages of 41 and 65 = 1.5 weeks' pay
  - For every completed year between the ages of 22 and 41 = 1 week's pay
  - For every completed year between the ages of 18 and 22 = 0.5 week's pay

However, the statutory scheme is widely recognised as very much a minimum standard. The CIPD's guide on redundancy recommends that higher redundancy payments are made 'if at all possible, as the statutory sums are often too small to adequately compensate for the loss of a job'. The 20-year rule, combined with the £380 earnings limit, mean that the largest payment that employers are currently obliged to make is £11,400 – not a great deal for someone in his or her 60s with over 20 years' service. As a result, many have introduced more generous arrangements to ensure that those leaving are treated fairly. According to IRS (2004e:15-17), the ways in which improvements to the statutory package are made vary from organisation to organisation. Examples from their survey include the following:

- doubling the statutory minimum
- increasing the number of weeks' pay used in the calculation (often to one month per year of service)
- making additional ex gratia payments for each completed year of service (eg 5 per cent of salary per year)
- disregarding the statutory earnings limit.

There are rarely any problems in calculating and communicating the entitlements due to full-time employees with unbroken periods of service. However, difficulties often arise where work patterns take a less standard form and where periods of employment have been temporarily broken. Cases have also been brought over the question of what figure represents a week's pay. Is it just base pay, or are overtime payments and bonuses to be considered too? The law states that all contractual payments should be included but is silent on the question of what figure should be used as the basis of calculations where weekly earnings fluctuate from one month to the next. In such cases, tribunals are forced to look at the facts in each individual case with a view to establishing what is 'reasonable'.

Another common problem occurs in the case of employees who have completed a number of years' service as full-timers but have then opted for part-time work. Unjust though it may be, at present employers are permitted to calculate redundancy compensation on the basis of the current part-time salary, thus disregarding however many years have been completed as a full-time employee. In all such cases it must be stressed that employers have the discretion to award more generous terms, and they often choose to do so as a means of avoiding additional unpleasantness and bad feeling.

The continued presence of age-based criteria in the calculation of redundancy payments is surprising given the introduction of age discrimination law in 2006. The opportunity was not taken at this time to amend the statutory minimum redundancy payments scheme simply because the EU directive covering age discrimination did not require this. Interestingly, however, the government specifically included in the age discrimination regulations the right for employers to retain schemes which are more generous than the state scheme and which mirror its key features.

REFLECTIVE QUESTION

What level of redundancy payments does your organisation pay? What are the reasons for calculating them in the way that it does?

MANAGING THE SURVIVORS

An important feature of the successful management of a redundancy programme is the attention given to those who remain employed in the organisation after the dismissals have taken place. Ultimately, the long-term success or failure of the redundancy programme depends on these people's ability to come to terms with new structures and working practices. In practice, as anyone who has experienced such a situation can verify, it is not always easy to bring about a soft landing. Like soldiers who have survived a bloody battle, employees left to run organisations in the absence of colleagues can suffer from strong feelings of guilt and shell shock. Added to this, it is likely that there will be some who would have preferred to take voluntary redundancy had they been given the chance, and who experience demotivation as a result.

The CIPD Guide on Redundancy (CIPD 2003c) provides sound advice on approaches to managing these issues and reducing the likelihood that survivors will lack 'commitment, enthusiasm and initiative'. First and foremost, the guide stresses the need to manage the redundancy process in a fair and open way. Survivors are more likely to recover and look forward if they are satisfied that the dismissal of colleagues was truly unavoidable in the circumstances and was handled professionally. There is thus a need not only to select redundant employees fairly, to provide fair levels of compensation and to offer practical assistance, but also to make sure that these matters are communicated effectively to all employees, whether or not they are individually affected by the redundancy programme. Secondly, it is important that communication with staff is two-way and that managers respond to suggestions and criticisms from employees at different stages throughout the process.

The other emotion that survivors often display is fear arising from concern that further redundancies will follow and that they may be next in line. If this is not dealt with, organisations will find that they have difficulty retaining the very individuals they most need to ensure future prosperity. Extra attention has to be given to reassuring employees of their value and continued employment prospects. The CIPD guide suggests that this is best achieved by line managers putting time aside to meet employees individually both to reassure and to listen. Once more, two-way communication is vital to success.

Murphy (2009b) reports the results of a survey carried out by IRS into 'survivor syndrome'. This confirms the importance of effective, regular communication both during and after the redundancy programme. The survey also showed that the most common symptom of survivor syndrome is a tendency for employees to become alienated and less trusting of management. Morale tends to drop, stress tends to increase, absence rates to go up and the result is a drop in productivity. This all arises because survivors are less secure in their jobs and unwilling to take risks or decisions that may backfire. Avoiding situations in which they may get blamed becomes more of a priority. Such responses can be minimised if the messages that are communicated are framed carefully and if plenty of opportunity for frank two-way communication is provided. Employees who had survived rounds of redundancy were also surveyed by IRS about what they needed from management. The overwhelming response was 'honesty'.

EXERCISE BOX: RBS

EXERCISE 18.2

Read the article by Jane Pickard entitled 'Heavy Interest' featured in *People Management* (3 December 2009, page 18). This can be downloaded from the *People Management* archive on the CIPD's website (www.cipd.co.uk).

This article reports an interview with Neil Roden, HR Director at the Royal Bank of Scotland, a company that has been through a very difficult period in recent years. The focus is on measures taken by the company to keep levels of staff morale and engagement up following the near-collapse of the bank and its effective takeover by the government in 2008.

Questions:

1 Why might it be expected that 'survivor syndrome' would be more pronounced in RBS than in other organisations affected by the recent recession?

2 What measures did RBS managers take in order to address the insecurities felt by survivors?

3 What evidence is provided of success in the management of survivors?

OTHER LEGAL ISSUES

As in many areas of resourcing practice, in the field of redundancy there is a great deal of relevant employment law which it is beyond the scope of this book to explore in detail. Readers are thus recommended to turn to specialised texts, such as those identified at the end of this chapter, for more detail on these topics. Here, therefore, we simply give a short description of a number of significant legal issues that P&D managers should be aware of when approaching the management of a redundancy programme.

COLLECTIVE CONSULTATION

The law requires employers to undertake meaningful consultation exercises with trade unions in situations where they are recognised and where members are under threat of redundancy. To that end employers have to disclose in writing to relevant trade union representatives the number of employees likely to be dismissed and details of the groups of employees at risk. Moreover, the proposed selection criteria must be outlined, together with the method that will be used in selection and the proposed redundancy payments. Where trade unions are not recognised employers are obliged to arrange for the election of workforce representatives to carry out the same function. Sufficient numbers must be elected to allow representation of all key groups who are to be affected.

The timescale for consultation is a minimum of 30 days where between 20 and 99 employees are to be made redundant, and 90 days if more than 100 are affected. Where fewer than 20 redundancies are proposed there is still a requirement to consult, but not to any predetermined timescale and not on a collective basis. The consultation process has to be more than a formality. In other words, employers are required to seek agreement with trade union representatives on such issues as ways of minimising numbers and of mitigating the consequences.

INDIVIDUAL CONSULTATION

Irrespective of whether or not collective consultation is being undertaken, and additional to it, is the requirement on employers to undertake reasonable consultation with individual employees who are at risk of redundancy. Each should be seen formally, at regular intervals, during the weeks or months leading up to the redundancies. The purpose is to explore possibilities for redeployment, to allow the employees to comment on selection criteria or scoring processes, and to discuss ways of ameliorating the effects of the redundancies. Where proper consultation of this kind does not occur, it is possible for employers to lose subsequent unfair dismissal claims on the grounds that they have not met all the procedural requirements expected by the law.

NOTIFICATION

Whether or not a trade union is recognised, employers proposing to make 20 or more employees redundant are obliged to notify the relevant government department in writing. In the past few years it has changed its name twice from the Department of Trade and Industry (DTI), to the Department for Business Enterprise and Regulatory Reform (DBERR) and then to the Department for Buisness, Innovation and Skills (DBIS). Standard forms are produced for this purpose and the timescales are the same as those for trade union consultation.

THE NEED TO DISMISS

An important legal technicality is the requirement that employees have to be formally dismissed in order to qualify for the receipt of a tax-free redundancy payment. Employees who volunteer for redundancy must, therefore, not resign. Instead they have to express an interest in being made redundant and then must wait to be dismissed by the employer.

'BUMPING'

'Bumped' or transferred redundancies occur when an employee whose job is to be made redundant is given a position elsewhere in the organisation, leading to the dismissal of someone else. In other words, an occupant of a position whose own job is not being made redundant is dismissed in order to retain the services of an employee whose job is being removed.

The courts have ruled that such manoeuvres are potentially 'reasonable' where it can be shown that the business clearly benefits as a result. It is thus unacceptable to bump simply in order to find a job for a particularly liked person who would otherwise be redundant; it has to be shown that there are sound operational reasons to justify the action. Where that is the case, it is acceptable to pay a redundancy payment to the bumped individual, despite the fact that his or her job is not itself affected.

MURRAY V FOYLE MEATS (1999)

The question of whether or not bumping was a lawful practice has been the subject of much debate in legal circles, some cases suggesting that it was acceptable and others that it was not. In 1999 the House of Lords reached a judgment in a landmark case called *Murray v Foyle Meats* which appears to have settled both this, and a range of other thorny legal issues.

The Law Lords ruled that when faced with a situation in which it was not clear whether a dismissal was or was not for legitimate reasons of redundancy, tribunals should ask three straightforward questions:

i Has the employee been dismissed?

ii Has there been an actual or prospective cessation or diminution in the need for employees to carry out work of a particular kind?

iii Is the dismissal wholly or mainly attributable to this state of affairs?

If the answer to all three questions is 'yes', then it is a redundancy and the tribunal can proceed to consider the question of reasonableness (ie the manner of the dismissal, fairness of selection, procedure used etc).

This ruling suggests that bumped redundancies are acceptable in principle (ie are potentially fair reasons for dismissal). However, procedures used and selection methods adopted must operate fairly in practice.

OFFERS OF ALTERNATIVE WORK

Where employees under threat of redundancy are offered suitable alternative work by their employer before they are dismissed and refuse to take the offer up, the employer is under no obligation to pay them a redundancy payment. Where redundancy payments are substantial, the suitability of the new job offer is often a contentious issue. Tribunals have tended to avoid applying general principles in cases of this kind, preferring to look at the facts and take into consideration the employee's reasons for rejecting the offer. Where the job is in the same location, pays the same salary, is of a similar status and is within the capability of the employee concerned, it is likely that a refusal to accept would be found unreasonable by a tribunal.

The law also provides for four-week trial periods to be offered to employees where new jobs are offered on terms different from those on which the previous contract was based. At the end the employee has to decide whether or not the work is suitable. Again, where an employee who has been given every assistance to settle into the new position resigns for trivial reasons, the employer is entitled to refuse the redundancy payment. Here, too, tribunals judge reasonableness by looking at the particular facts in each case rather than setting down hard-and-fast principles.

LAY-OFFS

When a firm runs out of work for people to do, due for example to a lack of orders, but where it is anticipated that the situation will be temporary it is lawful for management to lay off staff without paying any redundancy payments. There are two conditions:

i there must be no work for the individual concerned to do

ii it must be genuinely anticipated that the lay-off will be temporary.

Once laid off, the employees are entitled to write to their employers to claim a redundancy payment, but to do so there is a need to follow quite a strict procedure which involves giving a week's notice in writing.

INDIVIDUAL CASES

So far in this chapter the topic of redundancy has been examined from a collective perspective. The topic has therefore been seen from the perspective of managers faced with decisions involving groups of employees. However, there are also occasions when individuals are dismissed for reasons of redundancy – situations that tend to be handled rather differently. Although the basic legal principles remain the same, there is no requirement to inform the Secretary of State, and the process may be managed in a less formal and standardised fashion.

The kind of situation under consideration here arises when, for example, one member of a team has to be dismissed. Examples might be losing one teacher from a school when the number of pupils declines, or needing to dismiss one of a pool of clerical workers following the introduction of new technology. In such circumstances, the use of impersonal approaches, such as putting people under formal notice that they are at risk of redundancy and making them undergo highly formalised selection procedures is too brutal. What is needed is a great deal more sensitivity and confidentiality.

First, where they are not already laid down in a redundancy policy, it is necessary to agree the selection criteria that will be used in choosing the individual to be dismissed. Instead of asking generally for volunteers, the next step involves privately approaching individuals who might be interested in taking voluntary redundancy and establishing whether or not this is the case. If no one expresses an interest in leaving, the individual to be compulsorily dismissed should then be informed and discussions carried out with him or her personally to explore alternative opportunities and the extent to which practical assistance can be given to help him or her find a new position. The principles of reasonableness are thus adhered to, just as in the case of collective redundancies, but the manner in which the process is managed is made more appropriate to the case of the individual concerned.

CASE SUMMARY

THE MAZE PRISON REDUNDANCY PROGRAMME

Between 1998 and 2000 the prison service in Northern Ireland faced a very difficult P&D situation. As the peace process proceeded nearly all prisoners who were members of paramilitary groups were released, stage by stage, from the top security Maze Prison. This meant the disappearance of 1,300 jobs out of a total workforce of 3,271 (ie a 40 per cent reduction). However the redundancy process was complicated by the fact that it could have been stopped and thrown into reverse at any stage should paramilitary ceasefires come to an end. Managers had to be prepared for this eventuality, but also needed to be mindful of their responsibility to run an effective prison service for the Province over the long term.

In the event, mainly due to very generous redundancy packages provided by the government, around 200 more people volunteered for redundancy than was necessary. Unfortunately these tended to be the more senior and experienced officers, leaving the Service with a dilemma. Should it refuse some of the requests for voluntary redundancy (ie senior people) while making compulsory redundancies among more junior staff? Or should it allow all those who volunteered to take redundancy and promote people into their roles? In the event the latter route was chosen, leading to a situation after 2000 in which many senior officers were newly recruited.

The opportunity was taken to restructure the organisation and to improve its record on managing diversity. A big investment in training was made and fresh blood brought in at all levels.

A substantial outplacement programme was used in the early stages of the process which involved families of staff as well as the officers themselves. Consultants provided this service over a two-year period, giving advice in workshops to 900 employees. The total cost of the redundancy programme, including payments, was £147 million – considerably over £100,000 per redundant employee. At that price, it could be argued, it is just as well that the programme has been judged a success.

Source: Johnson (2001)

EXAMPLE

'Deciding on promotions and redundancies' by Adrian Furnham and K.V. Petrides (2006) *Journal of Managerial Psychology* Vol. 21, No. 1. 6–18

This is a fascinating article. Its findings are not at all unexpected, but research questions are important ones that have rarely been asked, and the methodology used is unusual. The researchers put together 16 separate 'vignettes' of information about fictional employees which made reference to their intelligence, length of experience and motivation. Their gender was apparent from their names and their age indicated by their length of experience. One hundred and eighty-three volunteer managers were asked to imagine that they were running their own company and employed the people described in the vignettes. They were then asked to rate them in turn according to a seven point rating scale in terms of their suitability for promotion and the likelihood that they would be made redundant should such a situation arise.

Questions:

1 Why do you think the managers might have rated experienced men more highly than experienced women, but unintelligent men more poorly than unintelligent women?

2 Why do people rate motivation more highly than intelligence or experience when thinking about who should be selected for redundancy?

3 What are the major strengths and weaknesses of the methodology adopted by these researchers?

KEY ARTICLE BOX

EXPLORE FURTHER

- Two excellent general texts covering all aspects of redundancy management are 'Redundancy handling' (2009), an ACAS advisory booklet, *Managing redundancy* by Alan Fowler (1999) and *The successful management of redundancy* by Paul Lewis (1993). A good introduction to the issues, together with some critical analysis, is provided by Redman & Wilkinson (2009) and, with an international perspective, by Cascio (2009).

- Legal aspects are well covered in employment law handbooks and textbooks. The most up to date case-law is described in the various loose-leaf subscription services covering legal issues. Incomes Data Services publish a superb handbook which covers all the legal aspects of redundancy handling in a comprehensive but readable manner (IDS 2008c). A broad summary is provided by the CIPD's *Guide to redundancy handling* written by lawyers from Hammonds (2003).

- Surveys and case studies looking at redundancy and retirement practices are published from time to time by IRS in *Employment Review* and by the IDS Studies. IDS (2007) is a recent edition of their HR study series which contains several useful case studies on effective redundancy handling.

CHAPTER 19

Resourcing strategy

LEARNING OUTCOMES

By the end of this chapter readers should be able to:

- identify the different ways in which organisations can take a strategic approach to the management activities discussed in this book

- state how organisations can take steps to align their people resourcing activities with the business strategies being pursued by their organisations

- develop a strategy for effectively competing in the labour market.

In addition, readers should be able to understand and explain:

- the major theories concerning linkages between business strategy and HR strategy

- critiques of approaches to HR strategy making which focus on altering HR practice so as to match strategic organisational objectives

- the determinants of effective labour market competition.

TAKING A STRATEGIC APPROACH

On one level it is possible to describe an organisation's people resourcing activities as having a strategic character simply because of the manner in which they are carried out by management. The term 'strategy' in this context means taking a planned, well thought out, evidence-based approach to the various HR activities explored in this book. Instead of activities being carried out in a reactive, ad hoc or ill-considered manner, there is a clearly defined coherence and purpose. Hence an organisation might have developed and put into practice a succession management strategy, an employee retention strategy or an employer branding strategy. In each case a long-term objective or set of objectives needs to be set, and decisions made about how those objectives are going to be met in practice. These will be influenced by the context of the organisation and by the expectations of staff, managers, shareholders and customers.

Strategic thinking and practice in the resourcing and talent management area is most commonly evident when organisations embark on discrete episodes or projects such as expansions, retractions, reorganisations and structural change management exercises. Here it is usual for a project management team to be assembled and a well thought through, if adaptable, plan drawn up which is then followed.

Hence when large retailers open new stores they are more likely to act strategically than they are to act in an ad hoc manner in the way they go about the staffing process. Human resource planning exercises are undertaken to establish how many people will be required with what level of skills and experience. Care is then taken to ensure that these people are recruited at the right time so that a new team can be selected, inducted and trained in time for the date the new store or branch opens. Similar care tends to be taken when organisations are required to downsize. Layoffs are planned at some length, consultation taking place as required by law, and the most appropriate method chosen for the selection of staff to be made redundant. It is usual for a recruitment freeze to be introduced, for a redeployment register to be established and not at all uncommon for outplacement training to be provided too. Cascio (2002 and 2010) provides several examples of strategic downsizing in practice, going on to set out some rules to follow and mistakes to avoid.

Cultural change is harder to bring about and to plan strategically in any kind of systematic way. But here too there is evidence that many organisations at least attempt to take a strategic approach. Campaigns of activity are planned by teams of managers which involve communicating messages to staff and consulting with them. Reward mechanisms are established to encourage new ways of thinking and these are included explicitly as individual objectives in performance appraisal exercises. Several examples of successful programmes of this kind are provided by Millmore *et al* (2007:225–232), drawing on a range of published case studies. They argue that in many instances the most effective approaches are 'bottom up' in nature rather than 'top down'. By this they mean that initiatives are taken in parts of the organisation rather than being very publicly co-ordinated centrally. Initiatives are taken by line managers, involving their staff and resulting in the establishment of a shared vision of some kind. The HR function then becomes involved by developing interventions, policies and practices which support this, for example by providing appropriate training and development opportunities.

 EXERCISE BOX: MIDLAND HEART

EXERCISE 19.1

Read the article by Penny Cottee entitled 'Change of Heart' featured in *People Management* (10 August 2006, pages 42–44). This can be downloaded from the *People Management* archive on the CIPD's website (www.cipd.co.uk).

The article describes a carefully planned change-management project that met with an apparent high level of success at a large

city-based housing association. It involved the merger of four regional offices, the introduction of new technology, further cost-saving measures and major changes to established procedures.

Questions:

1 What were the strategic objectives identified by managers at the start of the process described in the article?

2 What evidence is provided of a 'strategic approach' being taken to the management of the project?

3 What do you think might have happened if a more 'ad hoc' approach had been taken?

Such evidence as there is therefore suggests that when people resourcing activities are carried out as part of a distinct project, an approach that can be labelled 'strategic' is typically taken. However, this is not the case when it comes to the way that organisations manage the same resourcing activities over the long term on a day-to-day basis. Here, it would seem, most organisations take an approach to core resourcing activities that is closer to the 'ad hoc' than to the 'strategic' end of the scale. We saw in Chapter 5, for example, how much less prevalent the practice of formal human resource planning is nowadays when compared with the position two or three decades ago, in Chapter 16 how rarely organisations plan the retirement of staff in a considered manner (despite the known advantages of doing so) and in Chapter 9 how many managers remain sceptical about employer branding and the idea that an organisation can benefit from positioning itself strategically in its key labour markets. Millmore (2003) reached the same conclusion in his study investigating the extent to which UK organisations take a strategic approach to recruitment and selection. His work is particularly useful because of the way he has developed tests of 'strategicness' against which to judge organisational practice. The criteria he suggests should be used as a means of judging whether organisations are or are not 'strategic' in the way they handle the recruitment and selection of staff are as follows:

- Recruitment and selection practices should reflect the organisations' strategic plans. In other words, the job descriptions and person specifications used should clearly link to current and future organisational priorities. Hence, if the adoption of new technologies is a key component of organisational strategy, a need for people with the competence and experience to work with them, or at least to learn to work with them, should be central to recruitment practices and selection decisions.

- A long-term focus should be apparent. The organisation is not simply seeking to fill its need for staff quickly with like-for-like replacements 'with the emphasis on meeting the immediate needs of a vacancy at a highly localised level', but is thinking longer-term about recruiting people with the attributes that will be required increasingly in the future.

- A 'bridging-mechanism' for translating long-term plans and organisational priorities into practical recruitment and selection policies and practices. In most cases this will take the form of some kind of formal human resource planning activity, the organisation being in a position to forecast its likely future demand for and supply (internal and external) of labour with reasonable accuracy.

Millmore terms these criteria 'three interdependent primary features', necessary minimum attributes of an approach to recruitment and selection that can be labelled 'strategic'. However, he goes on to suggest further secondary criteria which emerge from the adoption of the first three. In other words he argues that where an organisation operates practices which have the three primary features, it is very likely that two further features of the recruitment and selection policies will follow, will hence be apparent and can therefore form further criteria against which the extent to which the approach being used can be judged as having a 'strategic character':

- A sophisticated and complex approach to recruitment and selection, a reasonably wide array of methods being used as appropriate and a relatively 'diverse and exacting' set of person specifications being in use when recruiting for different categories of job.

- Recruitment and selection processes which are accorded high status as activities within the organisation. Evidence for this can be found in the relative level of expenditure on recruitment and selection activities and the involvement of many stakeholders (ie not just the immediate supervisor assisted by an HR officer).

- The use of approaches which are clearly sensitive to the impact on candidates and which, in particular, facilitate 'informed self-selection decisions'.

Millmore's research found precious little evidence of any 'strategic' recruitment and selection being carried out in the organisations he surveyed when judged against these simple criteria. Indeed he found no examples whatever of any recruitment exercises meeting all his criteria at the same time. As far as the primary criteria were concerned 'taken together it could be argued, perhaps very generously, that 8 per cent of recruitment and selection exercises are being strategically driven' (Millmore 2003:101).

ALIGNING HR PRACTICES WITH BUSINESS STRATEGY

A prominent theme in the academic literature on HRM strategy has long been the idea that organisations should explicitly align their HR activities with their long-term strategic objectives. Indeed, for many writers and consultants this has become the major test used to establish the extent to which an organisation's HR function is or is not acting 'strategically'. The clearer the alignment between HR activity and organisational strategic objectives, the clearer it is that a coherent HR strategy is being pursued (see Boxall and Purcell 2008:56). The idea of strategic alignment is closely associated with contingency or 'best fit' approaches to HRM, in which HR practices and approaches are quite deliberately selected from a range of alternative possibilities so as to ensure that they 'fit' most comfortably with the organisation's strategic objectives. When fully achieved, it can be shown that the organisations which have the 'best fit' as far as their HR practices are concerned also prosper financially and stand a better chance of gaining competitive advantage. This happens because the HR practices in use are most appropriate as a means of supporting the achievement of the organisation's competitive strategy. Hence, where an organisation's business strategy is focused on achieving steady, continuous, long-term organic growth (ie growth from within rather than by acquiring other firms), the appropriate HR strategy involves prioritising the development of people through effective career management activities. The aim is to select people with potential, to provide them with attractive internal career progression opportunities, to invest in their development and to find ways of tying them into the business for the long term through the use of share options and other longer-term profit-related rewards. On the employee relations side partnership approaches designed to engender high-trust relationships and a shared long-term interest between employer and employee are most appropriate. Achieving a fit of this kind will enhance business performance vis-à-vis competitors whose HR practices fit less well with the organisation's strategy.

Over recent years a number of academics and consultants have published contingency models which set out, albeit often in a somewhat simplistic manner, the major different types of business strategy and the most appropriate packages of HR practices which align most closely with them. Some of these models have become highly influential and have spawned a considerable literature comprising research studies that aim to evaluate their utility in practice (Marchington & Wilkinson 2008 and Boxall & Purcell 2008 both provide an extensive survey of this body of literature). The models range across the whole HR field, including many areas of practice which are beyond the scope of this book. But resourcing activities often play a central role, and it is thus appropriate that a chapter on 'resourcing and talent management strategy' should focus in some detail on the content of the major models.

MILES AND SNOW

The model advocated by Miles and Snow (1978) has been influential in the business strategy literature and has had a particularly significant impact on thinking about HR strategy over the past few decades. This is due in large part to an often-cited study by Doty *et al* (1993) which provided good evidence that organisations whose HR practices were aligned appropriately to the contingencies in the Miles and Snow model out-performed competitors whose practices were less well aligned.

Miles and Snow identify three major types of business strategy: the defender strategy, the prospector strategy and the analyser strategy. Organisations which do not pursue one of these are labelled 'reactors'. This fourth group consists of organisations that do not have a clearly identifiable organisational strategy. The assertion is that they tend to perform badly in competitive environments and so their approach is not presented alongside the other three as an 'ideal' type.

The defender strategy involves the organisation protecting its existing market share and growing slowly, steadily and incrementally. Surplus profits are reinvested in the organisation to build up its strength vis-à-vis would-be competitors, the major purpose being to maintain competitive advantage. A suitable military metaphor would be a mediaeval castle with thick walls and full of soldiers able to withstand attack from any who dared to try to seize ground that is already held. Examples of defender organisations are the large clearing banks, the major retail organisations and international organisations which are the established market leaders in their fields. The McDonald's restaurant chain is a good example. They are leading players in their industry, established, strong and capable of withstanding competitive charges from smaller rivals. The Pearl Group is a major financial services provider that meets the definition of a defender. One of its major office buildings located near to Peterborough is built like a modern-day castle, with a drawbridge, turrets and a courtyard – a very visual statement of the organisation's long-established strategy.

By contrast prospectors are highly opportunistic and flexible. Innovation and the search for new market opportunities are the chief features. They have an entrepreneurial approach, take risks and have a tendency to move in and out of industries. Manufacturing organisations frequently take this approach, particularly those operating in high-tech environments where continual innovation is essential to survival. The appropriate military metaphor here is the armoured tank. These organisations move across battlefields, taking ground for short periods of time before moving on in search of new conquests. Smaller start-up organisations have no choice but to take this approach, as do larger organisations whose competitive environments are unpredictable and volatile. Drugs companies, electronics manufacturers and private sector media organisations are all examples.

The third strategic approach categorised by Miles and Snow is the 'analyser'. These organisations combine features of the other two types. On the one hand they tend to be a sizeable, established presence in an industry, but they also diversify into new markets and indeed new industries when opportunities present themselves. They are like castles from which tanks occasionally emerge to seek new ground to conquer. Analysers are often known for being 'second-to-market' which means that they wait and watch the prospectors carve out new markets (and make all the mistakes) before coming in themselves a few years later to compete with them making full use of their well-known brand names and financial largesse. The Virgin Group is often cited as a classic example of a company which follows this strategy, the result being that it has a presence in many industries, some for the long term, others for relatively short periods.

In the case of each of these three strategies different kinds of people resourcing strategy are appropriate. In order to maximise their success they need to adopt approaches which are aligned with their business strategies. In the case of the defender, the need is for a stable organisational structure in which jobs are well-defined and quite specialised. Their market power enables them to exercise a degree of control over their business environments, so flexibility is not as important as it is in smaller organisations. Instead there is a need to maximise efficiency, so the structures are designed to achieve this. It is in organisations of this kind that traditional approaches to human resource planning and succession planning remain in use. There are well-developed internal labour markets, people often being appointed into junior positions early in their careers and then promoted up the career ladder internally over time. Graduate recruitment is thus highly significant and will have a great deal of resources allocated to it.

Selection methods tend to be sophisticated, enough time being taken to ensure that the right people are offered jobs. Subsequent investment in training and development is also extensive, the psychological contract being rooted in the notion of long-term commitment on both sides. Jobs are designed quite narrowly so as to maximise the machine-like efficiency which defender organisations require. Performance appraisal systems will be standardised and linked directly to organisational objectives, while HR bureaucratic policies and a central HR function tend to play a leading role.

The opposite approach is necessarily taken by prospectors. Here flexibility is key, so contracts of both the legal and psychological variety tend to be short-term. Multi-skilling is the norm, job descriptions (if they exist) being broad and subject to regular change. People are recruited as and when particular expertise or experience is required, opportunistic and informal recruitment and selection being used much of the time. Costs are kept to a minimum, so bureaucratic approaches to HRM do not make sense. Formal HR planning is unlikely to occur and neither are substantial annual recruitment programmes aimed at graduates or school leavers. Instead a variety of recruitment methods are used to bring people in at different levels. Use is made of recruitment agents, different types of advertising and informal approaches. Decision-making in the people resourcing field is delegated to line managers wherever possible as is responsibility for performance management. HR managers see their role as to provide advice and support rather than to determine how managers carry out their jobs. Prospectors regularly work in networks of other organisations, collaborating on projects and forming alliances. Outsourcing of activities is common as is the use of subcontractors and agency staff.

In the case of analysers a mixture of the two extreme approaches outlined above is appropriate. The model of the 'flexible firm' we looked at in Chapter 3 is appropriate for them because of its clear core-periphery distinction. In analyser companies there will always be a need for a core of long-term employees to manage the organisation's more stable, core businesses and to staff its corporate HQ. But beyond that opportunism and flexibility are needed to maximise the ability to compete in new markets when opportunities are identified. Analysers are thus divisional in terms of their structure, and while they often have a well-defined corporate image and a pronounced set of corporate values, each part will necessarily pursue rather different HR policies and practices within that broad framework.

PORTER

Michael Porter's (1985) model of generic business strategies has been as influential as Miles and Snow's, and like theirs has been taken up by researchers specialising in HRM to test the idea that organisations enjoy greater success when their P&D practices are closely aligned with their overall business strategies. In the case of Porter's model, studies of the HR implications are particularly associated with Schuler and Jackson (1987), but many others have carried out research using the same premises. Porter identifies two major types of business strategy which he suggests organisations must choose from. The first is a strategy based on 'cost leadership' which means that the key source of competitive advantage lies in providing goods or services at a highly competitive price. Consumers are attracted to the organisation because it can provide them with what they are looking for more cheaply than competitors can. Low cost retailers such as Kwik Save, Aldi and those which sell everything at discount rates are examples of organisations that compete in this way. The major alternative is a strategy based on 'differentiation'. This involves charging higher prices for goods and services that are either of higher quality than those provided by competitors or more innovative in some way. In the retail world a high quality department store or a supermarket like Waitrose or Marks and Spencer are examples of differentiators. Porter goes on to argue that each of the two strategies can be applied to a broad market (eg national or international) or to a niche or narrowly-focused market, for example one which is very localised or specialised in terms of its tastes. These ideas are not controversial. What has attracted criticism is the further claim that companies will do less well financially if they fall in between the two stools, for example by seeking to compete on price and quality at the same time. A mixed strategy, according to Porter, invariably leads to poorer financial performance than one which is clearly either cost-based or which involves clear differentiation. The extent to which this holds true is questionable in the UK retailing market where the market is now dominated by chains which specifically appeal because they stick a range of products which are both cheap and of high quality, alongside those which are either cheap or of high quality.

Despite the criticisms, the Porter/Schuler and Jackson models are important and influential as far as the determination of HR strategy is concerned. Where an organisation is clearly intent on pursuing a cost-leadership strategy it makes sense for its P&D policies and practices to be low cost too. Otherwise it will find it hard to make sufficient profit to thrive. This does not necessarily mean that wage levels need to be low because it is possible to employ fewer people more efficiently and to gain a cost advantage that way. It does, however, tend to require resourcing and talent management systems that are less comfortable from an employee's perspective and which are often associated with higher levels of turnover as a result. In order to maximise efficiency jobs tend to be quite specific and narrowly defined. This keeps training costs to a minimum and makes it possible to operate a standardised, routine approach to recruitment, selection and induction. Organisational rhetoric in such organisations can often be enlightened, forward-looking and employee-friendly, but the reality tends to be different simply because at the local level managers are given strict budget targets to meet which have very little slack. So efforts are continually focused on keeping staffing costs down. There is, as a result, a reluctance to give people overtime and a continual intensification of work so that each employee expends greater effort and is increasingly productive. Cost leaders are typically intolerant of absence, taking a firm disciplinary line, have no interest in sophisticated approaches to selection or performance management, and will be happy to risk dismissing employees in an unlawful way on the grounds that few cases actually go to tribunal and that it is possible to settle most ahead of any hearing. It is hard to maintain a high standard of ethics in the way that people are managed while also pursuing a competitive strategy that requires continual pressure to reduce costs.

By contrast where a strategy of differentiation is pursued, cost control is a less all-embracing feature of organisational life. More important is the effective recruitment, retention and motivation of the best people. Without them, the strategy cannot work. Hence budgets are made available for sophisticated recruitment campaigns, lengthy selection processes and five-star, gold-plated induction experiences. Where innovation is central a great deal of time, attention and money is given to appropriate training and development activities, while performance management practices are tailored to meet the needs of the key groups. The last thing an organisation pursuing a strategy of this type needs is the development of low trust relationships between staff and management. There is a need to encourage the sharing of knowledge, so reward and recognition of individual contribution is needed. People need to feel valued, so they are managed as individuals rather than as one of a group of staff.

EXERCISE BOX: ITV

EXERCISE 18.2

Read the article by Rima Evans entitled 'Telly Vision' featured in *People Management* (22 March 2007, pages 24–29). This can be downloaded from the *People Management* archive on the CIPD's website (www.cipd.co.uk). This article focuses on a major new HR initiative called 'Imagine' that has been introduced by HR managers at the broadcaster ITV. The objectives and origins of the initiative are explored in some detail.

Questions:

1 How would you characterise ITV's current business strategy using the Porter and Miles & Snow models?

2 To what extent do you think the 'Imagine' project can be seen as being well-aligned to the organisation's business strategy?

3 To what extent can the 'Imagine' project be seen as a strategic intervention designed to bring about cultural change in the organisation?

OTHER MODELS

Several other academics and consultants have published other models over the years all of which in rather different ways link HR policy and practice to organisations' strategic objectives or to their position in competitive product markets. Some have achieved greater influence than others, but none have generated as much interest as the two outlined above in terms of attempts being made to test their validity with reference to financial outcomes. It is beyond the scope of this chapter to look in detail at each of these models, but it is worth mentioning some of them and how they differ from those derived from the Porter and Miles & Snow models.

One approach that has attracted the interest of several commentators is to focus on the stages in the life-cycle of a typical firm (see Sisson & Storey 2000:41–3). Here it is very plausibly argued that organisations that are small and growing require rather different HR practices from those that are large, successful and in their maturity, and from those which are in decline. Affordability plays a role here because firms that are struggling to survive in their present form as well as small start-up organisations will inevitably have fewer resources to devote to HR activities than those which are successful, sizeable and resource-rich. Hence we find many more examples of sophisticated approaches to the major people resourcing functions (HRP, recruitment, selection, induction, performance management, absence management retirement etc) being used in large corporations than we do in smaller organisations and in those which are declining in terms of their market share. The same broad principles are reflected in the Boston Consulting Group model (see Purcell 1989) and in the Lengnick-Hall model (Lengnick-Hall and Lengnick-Hall 1988), both of which focus in large part on the extent to which an organisation is expanding and expects to expand further in the future. They go on to argue that the focus of HR policy ought to be different in each case in order to achieve strategic alignment.

A rather different set of assumptions underpins James Walker's contingency model (Walker 1992). Here the focus is on the rate of environmental change to which an organisation is subject and to the extent of its complexity. This has the advantage over the other modes of incorporating of public sector organisations and others that are non-commercial in nature. In terms of people resourcing practices the big difference between organisations operating in fast-changing, volatile environments and those whose environments are reasonably stable and predictable is the extent to which flexibility is central. Where the environment is stable a long-term approach can be taken to resourcing the organisation. Reasonably sophisticated policies can be established and bureaucratic systems set up to administer HR matters. Change occurs in defined, manageable episodes, and it is feasible to structure organisations in an efficient (if inflexible) hierarchical manner. The less stable the environment the greater the need for a capacity for flexibility.

ALTERNATIVE VIEWS OF THE HR-BUSINESS STRATEGY LINK

In terms of academic fashion the thinking that lies behind the models described above had its heyday in the 1980s and 1990s. That does not mean to say that they have no relevance today – that is far from the case – but it is true to say that the assumptions that underlie the models are no longer universally accepted as being the best way for the P&D function in organisations to contribute towards the achievement of competitive advantage. Two major alternative schools of thought about the link between HR policy and practice and organisational strategy have developed, both of which have proved highly influential. These can be termed the 'best practice school' and the 'resource-based view school'. In both cases there are particular implications for the development of practice in the area of resourcing policy.

BEST PRACTICE APPROACHES

Over the past 20 years a group of researchers have challenged the basic idea that organisations maximise their financial success by adopting approaches in the HR field which are explicitly 'aligned' to their business strategies. One of the leading figures in the development of 'best practice thinking' is Jeffery Pfeffer:

> Contrary to some academic writing and to popular belief, there is little evidence that effective management practices are 1) particularly faddish (although their implementation may well be), 2) difficult to understand or to comprehend why they work, or 3) necessarily contingent on an organisation's particular competitive strategy (Pfeffer 1994:27).

Pfeffer's research in this area has involved identifying the most successful organisations in terms of growth and profitability, and then seeking to establish through interviews with managers and staff in what ways their HR activities contribute to that success. In other words he has sought to discover what it is HR-wise that the most successful organisations do and which less successful organisations do not. In carrying out his research he looked at organisations that were of very different sizes and which were pursuing varied business strategies. His major finding was that these contextual factors had much less relevance than is often thought. In practice the most successful organisations all pursued a similar broad approach to HRM which, in his view, was a major determinant of their success.

Similar conclusions were reached by Mark Huselid (1995) using a different methodology. His studies have involved large-scale distribution of questionnaires across most major industries in the US which ask managers in some detail about their HRM practices. He has then taken this data and analysed it with reference to indicators of the organisations' business performance. Here too a clear link has been established between superior financial performance and particular approaches to HRM. Similar approaches have been used by UK-based researchers (see Wood and Albanese 1995, Fernie and Metcalf 1996, Guest 2000). The upshot is a situation in which there is now a considerable body of evidence which backs up the idea that there is a definable approach to HRM which can be termed 'best practice' and which appears to help all organisations, whatever their business strategy or market position, to maximise their financial performance over the long term. Guest (2000) sums the case up as follows:

> human resource practices exercise their positive impact by: (i) ensuring and enhancing the competence of employees, (ii) by tapping their motivation and commitment, and (iii) by designing work to encourage the fullest contribution from employees. Borrowing from elements of expectancy theory (Vroom 1964, Lawler 1971), the model implies that all three elements should be present to ensure the best outcome. Positive employee behaviour should in turn impact upon establishment level outcomes such as low absence, quit rates and wastage, as well as high quality and productivity (Guest 2000:2).

Important elements of the 'bundle' of best practice approaches that these researchers have identified relate to resourcing activities. First, in order to maximise motivation and commitment it is important that employees perceive themselves to be in secure jobs. Clearly it is never possible to guarantee people full security, and it is becoming steadily harder and harder to do so as the product markets that organisations operate in become increasingly global, competitive and volatile. However, this body of research clearly indicates that a response which involves ditching job security and replacing it with a highly flexible approach to staffing is likely to hinder the achievement of a strong financial performance. In other words, organisations which wish to thrive need to find ways of becoming more flexible, while also retaining high levels of commitment on the part of their staff – people for whom job security is important. It is a difficult balance to achieve, but it is by no means impossible. To start with some of the ideas put forward by Peter Reilly (2001) under the heading 'mutual flexibility' can be adopted (see Chapter 3). The focus here is on the adoption of flexible working practices that benefit both employers and employees and the avoidance of those which are unattractive to employees. Secondly, it is possible to commit to internal recruitment policies so that people whose jobs are no longer viable can be redeployed into new jobs and be given new opportunities within the same organisation. Thirdly it is possible to carry out human resource planning exercises so that the extent of redundancies or job losses caused through reorganisation are planned for well ahead of time, remedial action being taken to reduce wherever possible the extent of compulsory redundancies.

A second commonly-cited element in the 'best practice bundle' is a sophisticated approach to recruitment and selection when external candidates are being sought. The approaches that should be used are those which are known to maximise the chances of the best performers being selected. Inevitably this means that recruitment and selection need to be carried out with care and that sufficient time needs to be taken in order to get the decision right. As far as recruitment is concerned, 'best practice' requires that applications are solicited from a reasonably wide field of appointable people. This is achieved partly through the use of carefully planned and well-targeted advertising campaigns, and partly by taking steps more generally to maintain a good reputation in core labour markets. At the selection stage the techniques which are known to have the highest predictive validity should be used to support in-depth, structured interviews. Ideally this will include psychometric testing and, if affordable, some form of assessment centre or work-sample exercises. Key is the involvement of a variety of people and decision-making based primarily on the experience and attributes required to do the job rather than on any personal 'gut feelings' or subjective criteria.

RESOURCE-BASED VIEWS

The resource-based view of the firm (often abbreviated to 'RBV') has its origins in the 1950s and has always had considerable influence in thinking about business strategy. However, it is only over the last 15 years or so that its application to HRM has become prominent (Allen & Wright 2008). This is largely because it provides an alternative perspective on the link between HRM and business strategy than those advanced either by proponents of strategic alignment or by those who favour best practice thinking. Key is the notion articulated very effectively by Cappelli and Singh (1992) that organisations are often better off developing business strategies which reflect their existing human resource-base than they are seeking continually to re-align their HR practices and workforce so that they 'match' the business strategy. So what we have here is a way of thinking about business strategy, HRM strategy and the link between them that is fundamentally different from those more traditional approaches outlined above. The starting point is not the external environment, but the existing internal resources or assets that the organisation has, including in large part its people. First and foremost RBV involves identifying what attributes the organisation's existing resources have which make them distinctly beneficial when compared to those of competitors. Barney (1991) suggested that the focus should be on understanding which resources are:

- valuable

- rare

- inimitable (ie hard for competitors to replicate)

- non-substitutable.

These provide the basis of existing competitive advantage and can be improved further so as to sustain and strengthen that competitive advantage.

A good number of the assets that give organisations a degree of competitive advantage are resources of a nun-human kind, like location of activities or buildings, brand reputations and financial solvency. But increasingly it is accepted that the key differentiators are human in nature, particularly knowledge of one kind or another, experience and specialised skills. Increasingly the term 'human capital' is used to describe these attributes, the implication being that long-term competitive advantage is best attained and sustained by those organisations that are able to find ways of developing and growing their stock of human capital. Under RBV thinking, business strategies emerge, often quite opportunistically, as a result of competitive processes. The organisations which are best placed to provide a service or manufacture a product get the business, and their capacity to do so depends on their internal resources.

What contribution can resourcing and talent management activities make? The answer inevitably will vary from organisation to organisation depending on its current situation. The aim will always be to reinforce and further develop the human assets that the organisation has at its disposal which give it its competitive advantage. Hence, where a particular knowledge base is identified as providing a key source of advantage in the market, the people resourcing contribution will involve taking steps which foster it and help in its further development. There is thus a role for quite sophisticated human resource planning, and in particular for the planning of individual developmental activities, the aim always being to ensure that the key areas of knowledge are not lost, but are enhanced. Recruitment and selection is also key, the aim being to replenish the organisation with people who are both willing and able to absorb and assimilate the knowledge needed to maintain the organisation's position when existing staff resign or retire. Effective employee retention is crucial to resource-based approaches to strategy-making because a failure to keep key human assets, and particularly their loss to competitors, can profoundly weaken the resource base which creates competitive advantage.

Beyond the knowledge base, another key attribute of organisations which often gives them competitive advantage is their unique culture. Knowledge can be readily replicated by a competitor, but cultures are far harder to create. It is not in the gift of managers to do so, the best they can aim for is influence over the development of an organisational culture. So, if an organisation is lucky enough to have a culture which contributes towards its competitive edge, there is under RBV thinking a good case for identifying this, treasuring it and fostering it. For example, an organisation may have developed a culture which is characterised by a 'can-do' attitude on the part of people, where discretionary effort is regularly deployed, where people co-operate and collaborate willingly, where there are high-trust, open relationships between staff and managers and where people interact creatively. Such a culture is an enormous asset. It is difficult for a competitor which is less fortunate to create, so the need is to find ways of fostering it, encouraging its further development and celebrating it. Key here is a need for managers to consider very carefully how structural or policy changes they may be planning might disturb the culture or weaken it in such a way that it is diminished. It is also important not to bring forward interventions which have the effect of triggering voluntary resignations among people who are immersed in the positive culture and help to foster its further development.

COMPETING IN THE LABOUR MARKET

So far in this chapter the idea of 'resourcing and talent management strategy' has been seen either as deriving from or contributing to the wider HR and business strategy of an organisation. In other words we have defined 'strategicness' in the resourcing context in terms of the extent to which relevant HR activities in some way link with an organisation's wider business strategy – either deriving from a defined business strategy, or supporting an emerging business strategy. These are the assumptions that underlie most recent research on HR strategy and which are reflected in the examples of practical applications which are published in professional journals and publicised at conferences attended by HR managers. There is, however, a completely different perspective that can be taken. This involves defining people resourcing strategy less in terms of its relationship with business strategy, and more in terms of an organisation's strategy vis-à-vis its labour markets.

When labour market conditions are tight, unemployment low, and skilled, experienced recruits relatively hard to find, the freedom of manoeuvre for organisations as far as recruiting and retaining people becomes severely constrained. Such conditions have prevailed in the UK for several years now and are likely to re-establish themselves in the future as the economy emerges from recession (Leitch 2006). In such circumstances resourcing activities inevitably become more important, consuming more expenditure and rising up the HR agenda ahead of other priorities. The tighter an organisation's labour markets, the more significant it becomes to recruit and then to retain more effective and committed performers than its competitors are able to.

Higgs (2004) suggests that employers have much to gain from 'segmenting' their employment markets and positioning themselves strategically in accordance with such an analysis. He presents a model which suggests four potential basic strategic choices (see Figure 19.1). There are two variables. One is the amount of money the employer is willing or able to pay. The other is not fully explained, but is labelled 'culture', and appears to refer to the extent to which employees are treated in a professional or ethical manner. One strategic choice is therefore to be 'an employer of cash' whereby employees are treated quite harshly, perhaps autocratically or by being expected to work excessive hours, but are nonetheless rewarded well. Such a strategy involves attracting good recruits with large pay packets and then retaining them by ensuring that they will have to take a pay cut if they opt to work elsewhere. According to Neil (1996:184 and 192), such an approach is used at the News International publishing group, allowing the company to buy acceptance from its employees of a range of 'low-commitment/ high-control' HR practices. The opposite strategy involves paying poorly, perhaps rather less than the going market rate, but to compensate by treating staff conspicuously better than would-be competitors do. Higgs labels this 'the employer of values' strategy. Such approaches have traditionally been associated with work in the public services, where pay has tended to be relatively low, but the work remains attractive because it is perceived as meaningful and rewarding by employees who also enjoy a superior level of job security.

The top right quadrant in Figure 19.1 is labelled 'employer of choice', a term which is increasingly commonly used to describe an organisation which sets out to achieve an excellent labour market reputation by both paying well and treating people well too. Examples of such organisations, many of which operate in the professional and financial services sectors, are found in the annual *Sunday Times* survey of the best 100 companies to work for in the UK (see www.timesonline. co.uk/tol/life_and_style /career_and_jobs/best_100_companies/). Finally, in the bottom left hand corner is the box labelled 'employer of churn'. In such organisations pay is lousy as is the way that employees are treated. The result is high staff turnover. In a tight labour market, where people have choice about where they work, such organisations find it hard to recruit and keep good staff. In recent years they have tended to rely on workers recruited overseas as well as on people who have very low skills and are thus incapable of finding alternative jobs. As a result, a number of companies that have traditionally been 'employers of churn' have taken the decision to reposition themselves. A good example is the McDonald's fast food restaurant chain which had been forced to witness the ignominy of having the term 'McJob' included in the Oxford English Dictionary and defined as meaning a poorly paid job without prospects. In recent years the company has actively sought to improve its labour market image, aiming to become an employer of choice (Overell 2006).

Figure 19.1 Higgs' model

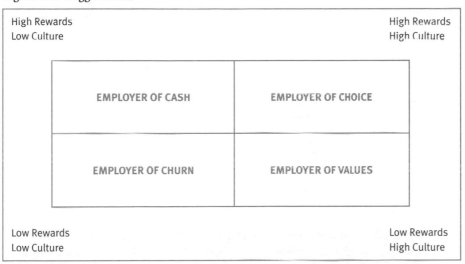

Within the 'employer of choice' category, it is possible to identify further divisions, the idea here being that there are distinctly different ways of achieving 'employer of choice' status. Which a particular organisation chooses will in large part be determined by the type of labour market conditions it faces. A potentially useful approach involves simply classifying organisations according to the relative strengths of their internal and external labour markets, the rationale being that different approaches to HR in general, and people resourcing activities in particular, are appropriate in each case. Figure 19.2 represents a simple two axis, four-way illustration. The top left quadrant represents employers whose external labour markets are tight and who thus struggle to recruit people, but who are in a position to offer long-term career development opportunities because their internal labour markets function effectively. They are labelled 'developers' because the best option available to them is to sell themselves to potential recruits as employers who will help people develop themselves and their careers. By contrast, moving to the top right quadrant we have employers whose external labour markets are tight, but who cannot for one reason or another provide many attractive career development opportunities. Such organisations often tend to be small and specialised. The only option open to them if they want to recruit and retain the best people is thus to pay at above the market rate, hence the label 'high payers'.

In the lower half of Figure 19.2 we can place organisations who have relatively little difficulty recruiting and retaining. On the left hand side are larger organisations with plenty of career paths available to people. In a loose labour market such organisations are highly attractive to job-seekers, the consequence being that they receive large numbers of applications whenever they advertise jobs and plenty of unsolicited applications when they don't. They therefore have the luxury of being able to pick carefully who they wish to employ. As a result, employee selection is the focus of their resourcing activities, plenty of money being spent on graduate recruitment exercises and on sophisticated selection techniques, so that they can maintain their position as an employer of choice.

Figure 19.2 Taylor's model

Tight market/career opportunities **DEVELOPERS**	Tight market/few career opportunities **HIGH PAYERS**
Loose market/career opportunities **SELECTORS**	Loose market/few career opportunities **INVOLVERS**

Finally on the bottom right are 'involvers'. These are employers who are able to offer most employees few development opportunities but who also, often because they are one of relatively few employers of particular types of staff in a region, find that they have relatively few problems recruiting new people. The main problem they face is thus the presence of dissatisfied staff who are trapped in their jobs, unable to move up the career ladder internally, but who also have few alternative job opportunities open to them. The danger in such circumstances is that low levels of trust will develop between staff and management, leading in some cases to the establishment of an adversarial industrial relations climate. The priority therefore, for an aspiring employer of choice, is to involve staff in decision-making, to ensure that jobs are well-designed and to try as hard as possible to maintain good levels of job satisfaction.

 EXERCISE BOX: ONLINE GAMING

EXERCISE 19.3

Read the article by Catherine Edwards entitled 'Raised Stakes' featured in *People Management* (9 March 2006, pages 25–27). This can be downloaded from the *People Management* archive on the CIPD's website (www.cipd.co.uk).

This article concerns the HR practices being developed in two organisations operating in the international online gaming industry. The industry is growing very rapidly, as are the organisations which operate the best-used web sites. However, they are also characterised by an unusual extent of uncertainty about their future.

Questions:

1 What different factors make the future uncertain for online gambling companies?

2 Using the models described in this chapter, how would you characterise their business and employment market strategies?

3 To what extent are the resourcing policies and practices being developed appropriate to these strategies?

QUEEN BEE RESOURCING STRATEGIES

Finally in this chapter it is necessary to assess an approach to talent and resourcing strategy that is controversial, but also apparently increasingly common. This involves organisations focusing their efforts in terms of labour market competition not on the generality of employees but very much on the few who are identified as being highly talented. Such approaches are advocated to different degrees by Hiltrop (1999), Woodruffe (1999), Williams (2000), Cappelli (2000), Pfeffer & Sutton (2006) and Larkan (2007).

The case for a 'queen bee' approach rests on the assumption that there are in all areas of work individuals who have particularly rare and sought-after skills which give them the capacity to 'make a real difference' to an organisation's performance. Their individual contribution is often rated by managers as being five or 10 times more useful to them and their organisations than the average performer. Not only are they exceptional performers in their current roles, but they also have considerable potential for further development in the future. Queen bees typically have a reputation that spreads well beyond the organisations they work for, making them desirable 'catches' as far as headhunters are concerned and the targets of poaching raids by rival employers. Recruiting and retaining such people clearly gives an organisation a competitive advantage in its industry, but to do so particular efforts have to be made. A queen bee resourcing strategy thus involves lavishing particular attention, opportunities, perks and often money on these relatively few, highly talented individuals. The strategy is judged to be successful when the queen bees are retained for substantial periods and the organisation is successful in attracting the services of further queen bees.

Some of the more thoughtful contributions to this debate borrow ideas from the marketing function and from the way organisations segment their customers into distinct groups, those who spend most and remain loyal being valued more than others. Ferguson and Brohaugh (2009) put the case for developing 'B2E marketing strategies' (ie business to employee) based on long established approaches used by marketers:

> B2E marketers can take a page from consumer loyalty marketing by building a performance database and mining it to build a talent segmentation matrix. Just as customer segmentation allows you to squeeze maximum efficiency out of your marketing budget, so can employee segmentation deliver maximum benefit from your bonus compensation and recognition budget.
>
> (Ferguson and Brohaugh 2009:360).

Cardy et al (2007) also argue in favour of employee segmentation, suggesting that a four-way categorisation used by marketers to segment customers could be applied to the HR world. In their model the most valuable employees are labelled 'platinum', followed by 'gold', and 'iron'. The least valuable are labelled 'lead employees' who it is suggested should be either required to improve or be managed out of the organisation. They argue that the organisation stands everything to gain and nothing to lose by establishing what it takes to retain and maximise the performance of platinum employees and to deliver it.

The problem with this approach is its capacity for demotivating average performers who may well be less enamoured of the talents of their queen bee colleagues and hence resent the 'special treatment' they enjoy. The danger arises because there are many more average performers than there are queen bees and thus considerable potential damage that can be done if they become demotivated and dissatisfied. An organisation can thus readily end up retaining its outstanding performers, but losing many more of the kind who are solid, reliable and effective, and on whom the organisation relies over time to deliver a good level of service to its customers. The problem is compounded by the way that queen bees understandably tend to have a keen sense of their own worth and thus display little natural loyalty to any one organisation. Keeping them thus tends to be expensive and time consuming.

An alternative approach which has much to recommend it is outlined by Huselid *et al* (2005). They argue that lavishing attention, incentives and benefits on 'A players' is 'putting the horse before the cart'. Instead, they suggest, the key step is to identify the 'A positions' by which is meant the jobs which have 'a disproportionate importance to a company's ability to execute some part of its strategy'. Effort should then be put into trying to ensure that these are occupied by the people who perform *them* best. In other words, there is nothing much to be gained from investing in good people per se, what matters is that people who have the capacity to perform to a superior level in key roles are identified and then placed in those roles.

Suff (2004) describes the development and execution of such a strategy by managers at Signet, the parent company of the Ernest Jones, Leslie Davies and H. Samuel jewellery retailers. The sales people working in their stores are the people who really make a difference as they deal face to face with customers who are often making purchases which are both expensive and emotionally significant. The difference in terms of value to the organisation between an excellent and an average sales person is thus very significant. Using Huselid *et al*'s (2005) language, these are the 'A positions' in the company. Signet has therefore invested a considerable amount of time and effort in establishing the precise type of person who is most suited to the role. They found that two attributes were necessary and that while common, they are not that often combined together in the same person. One is 'excellent rapport-building skills', the other is a need to 'be happy working in a rules-driven environment' (ie one that is very security conscious). The company then went about finding the 'A people' needed to fill these roles using targeted recruitment literature, sophisticated selection methods, the building of a distinct employer brand, a carefully designed induction programme, numerous training opportunities and the development of internal career paths. The vast majority of the company's managers are internally recruited and employee retention levels are good.

EXAMPLE

KEY ARTICLE BOX

'The adoption of family-friendly HRM policies: Competing for scarce resources in the labour market' by Steven Poelmans, Nuria Chinchilla and Pablo Cardona (2003) *International Journal of Manpower.* Vol. 24, No. 2. 128–147

This article reports the results of a questionnaire survey undertaken in Spain which aims to establish what factors lead organisations to commit to family-friendly employment practices. Various hypotheses are tested, several of which surprisingly are found not to be proven. The key finding is that the tightness of the labour market is a major determinant of whether or not organisations adopt family-friendly policies.

Questions:

1 Why do the authors argue that Spanish employers face rather different issues when it comes to adopting family-friendly employment practices than is the case in other countries?

2 Why do you think that this study found so little support for the proposition that organisations adopt family-friendly policies in order to improve performance and reduce absenteeism?

3 What are the major weaknesses you can identify with this study? To what extent do these undermine the validity of its conclusions?

4 Using the models presented above, explain in what circumstances the adoption of conspicuously generous family-friendly practices might contribute most to a resourcing strategy.

EXPLORE FURTHER

- To the author's knowledge there are no books, book chapters or journal articles that focus on the idea of 'people resourcing strategy' in general terms. There are, however, many excellent books which provide comprehensive introductions to the idea of strategic HRM more generally. Schuler & Jackson (2007), Millmore *et al* (2007) and Boxall & Purcell (2008) are all recent and recommended.

- Marchington & Wilkinson (2008) contains good, accessible chapters covering best fit models, best practice thinking and the resource-based view of the firm. The resource-based view is covered succinctly by Allen & Wright (2008).

CHAPTER 20

The future of work

INTRODUCTION

The writer Mark Twain famously observed that 'prediction is difficult, especially when the predictions relate to the future', while George Eliot cautioned that 'of all the forms of mistake, prophesy is the most gratuitous'. But this has never stopped people trying to predict how the world will develop by thinking through the consequences of a continuation of current trends. A great deal of future gazing has always gone on in the fields of management and business because so much rides on the ability to anticipate coming trends so as to enable your organisation to cash in more quickly and effectively than your competitors. In recent years the attention of the futurologists has increasingly turned to people management issues and to many of the areas of employment practice covered in this book. This principally stems from a belief that the contribution made by individuals and indeed by an organisation's human resources in general is becoming increasingly central to the achievement of competitive advantage. For a large proportion of organisations, human capital is now the key determinant of long-term business success, outweighing or at least equalling in significance other forms of capital (land, buildings, equipment, finance etc). The way people are managed is thus accepted as being a central determinant of business success. Moreover, governments have become increasingly interested as they seek to bolster their nations' fortunes in a global economy. Government ministers are as keen as managers of organisations to grasp the significance of current and future trends, so that they can regulate and develop interventions which help to create and sustain international competitive advantage. As a result a great deal of government research funding is now being channelled into projects which contribute to our understanding of the future of work.

In this final chapter we explore the major debates that are developing about the future of work and raise questions about the accuracy of some of the more prominent recent predictions. The case is put for and against the likelihood that we are about to witness very radical change. We then go on to look at some topic areas of general significance to resourcing and talent management activities which are likely to become more important in the future. These are the concept of emotional intelligence, the management of knowledge and work-life balance initiatives. Finally we look briefly at the practice of scenario planning.

DEBATES ABOUT THE FUTURE OF WORK

Debates about the future of work and how the HR function will look as the coming decades unfold are necessarily different from the others which have been explored in this book. Self-evidently this is because the arguments cannot be based on hard evidence and must be speculative in nature. We can extrapolate current trends forward and we can also place firm bets on likely future technological advances, but we cannot know with any certainty whether our predictions will in fact be realised. As was shown in Chapter 5, discontinuities have a habit of occurring and surprising even the most well-informed authorities, rendering formerly confident forecasts obsolete. There are also of course very different views about what *should* happen in the future and it is not at all clear which of today's competing visions about paths to take, if any, will ultimately win the day.

However, a lack of hard evidence about the future has not stopped many writers from developing quite sophisticated theses about what we can expect over the coming decades. Indeed, helping managers to understand and come to terms with the evolving business environment has developed into a highly profitable industry. Thousands of books are published each year aiming to assist managers in this task, top authors becoming multi-millionaires in the process (see Collins 2000:19). Hundreds of thousands of managers contribute towards further fat cheques for so-called 'management gurus' to hear them speak on the international conference circuit, while millions of pounds more are spent each year on consultants' fees with the same aim in mind. Much of what these people have to say is useful and interesting, but it is important to remember that they are not impartial observers. They have a vested interest in persuading us that the world is changing rapidly and that if we do not radically alter what we are doing we, and our organisations, have a bleak future to look forward to. The more successful they are at persuading us of the 'ever accelerating pace of change', the more opportunities there are for new editions of books, the emergence of new buzzwords and the further development of the gurus' own industry. This would not matter too much were the message to fall on thoughtful and sceptical ears. Unfortunately the rhetoric is deployed with such evangelical fervour and is repeated so frequently through different forms of media that managers tend to accept it as received wisdom in quite an unquestioning way. This means that faulty assumptions sometimes cloud decision-making and that the gurus' messages can become self-fulfilling prophecies.

In the last few years these messages have been authoritatively challenged in some of the publications that have been written by participants in the ESRC's (Economic and Social Research Council) future of work programme. Led by Peter Nolan of Leeds University, this is a large scale government funded research programme which has involved some 30 teams of researchers in many UK universities. Their findings have, on the whole, been a great deal more cautious than the views of the management gurus, suggesting a future for working life which is not so different from the one we currently experience. Evolution rather than revolution is their message. As yet, however, despite the appearance of hundreds of publications deriving from ESRC future of work projects, their message continues to be muffled out somewhat by sexier, but less well-founded, predictions of radical change just around the corner.

Having called for a dose of hard-headed scepticism about claims made for the future, it is important not to ignore everything that is being said by professional futurologists. HR professionals need to have a view about the way their work may evolve during their careers and can only gain in credibility by developing robust views about the debates that rage in this field. It is difficult to sum these up in a few hundred words, without over-simplifying the arguments. A whole book is really necessary to do proper justice to the various claims that are made about the future, so recommendations for further reading are given at the end of the chapter. However, it is possible to summarise some of the key strands in the arguments that are put forward, many of which build on ideas explored earlier in the book about internationalisation, technological change and flexibility.

Central to the future of work debate is the notion of 'a new economy' which is said to be in the process of replacing 'the old economy' in western, industrialised countries. The new economy is sometimes conceived as being service-based (ie principally consisting of non-manufacturing activities), but more often nowadays as being 'knowledge-based'. This means that organisations exist for the purpose of making and distributing knowledge (ie information or intellectual-services). The main thrust of the predictions is that most people will, in the future, be engaged in different types of work than has historically been the case. The claim is based on the idea that most manufacturing jobs, along with more routine administrative work, will no longer exist in the countries such as the UK. Labour-saving new technology will account for some of these jobs, while millions of others will effectively be 'exported' to developing countries. The work that we will carry out instead will be of two basic types:

- knowledge-work (developing new technologies, creating new knowledge, R&D etc)

- people-based service provision of the kind which machines cannot carry out (care work, work which leads and inspires others, creative work).

There is considerable evidence to support this point of view. As was shown in Chapter 2, the vast majority of new jobs being created are of these two types.

What is more questionable is the further claim that the way work will be organised in 'the new economy' will be fundamentally different from the way we currently do things in 'the old economy'. While different commentators use different terms to describe what they think will happen, several of the most influential (eg Susan Greenfield, Charles Handy, Jeremy Rifkin, William Bridges) argue that the concept of 'the job' as we have come to know it is on the way out. In its place will come a variety of other arrangements which have more in common with forms of self-employment. Instead of perceiving ourselves as belonging to an organisation, we will have 'portfolio careers', undertaking different assignments on a temporary basis for many different organisations. Handy likens this future state of affairs to the life of an actor playing different types of roles for a limited period of time for different sorts of organisation (TV, film, advertising, theatre etc). Flexible working through agency work, temporary contracts and self-employment will thus become the norm. This will happen, it is claimed, first because of the increasing volatility of the business environment. The less organisations are able to forecast their own futures with any degree of certainty, the less able they will be to make any kind of long-term commitment to employees. Moreover, technological developments and the rise of knowledge-work will mean that the work we do is increasingly suited to a jobless economy. Much of the work will be able to be carried out at home on a teleworking basis and will be project-based. Knowledge workers with expertise will thus be required to sell their services to organisations as and when they can, and will not be able to anticipate a lengthy employment relationship. Linked to these predictions is a further one which has been downplayed recently, but which was confidently asserted 10 years ago. This is the belief that we will all have a great deal more leisure time in the new economy than we have been accustomed to enjoying in the old one. More holidays, more time out in further education, earlier retirement and shorter hours have all been forecast by one or more authors in this context.

If these analyses are right, there are clearly major implications for HR managers. The way we attract people, select them, seek to retain them, motivate them, develop them and reward them will in the future be utterly different from the way things are today. The most significant consequence will be a change in the basic power relationship between employers and employees. With a host of potential employers to work for, the possibility of working largely from home and sought-after expert knowledge in their heads, people will be able to choose who they work for and under what types of terms and conditions. They may choose to enter into a long-term relationship with one organisation, but it will not necessarily be exclusive and could be terminated very easily at any time. Administrative requirements will be wholly different in such a world too. There would be no more standard contracts of employment or organisation-wide HR policies to implement. Payment would be individualised to a far greater degree than at present, while the concept of determining and recording holiday entitlements would seem very old-fashioned indeed.

It is interesting to speculate on the shape of a typical HR function in such a world. It is likely that most of the activities would themselves be outsourced and that all efforts would be focused on developing a strong corporate reputation for providing interesting and challenging work. But is this really going to happen? Are we really heading fast towards a world in which people no longer have or desire 'jobs' and in which staff choose their employers rather than the other way round? How accurate are the predictions that are being made about the 'new economy'? As was stated above, it is impossible to say with a strong degree of confidence. Some of these predictions are based on a very logical analysis of what can be expected to occur as new technologies and the process of globalisation develop further. However, there are grounds for doubting some of the wilder claims, or at least for concluding that their significance for the workforce as a whole is severely exaggerated.

An important source of evidence is the trend towards atypical working examined in Chapter 3, a phenomenon that is often used by proponents of paradigm shifts in workplace relations themselves to justify earlier predictions. The following quotation from one of Charles Handy's books on the future is typical:

> It had been foolhardy then, at the start of the Thatcher years in Britain [ie 1981], to prophesy that by the year 2000 less than half of the working population would be in conventional full-time jobs on what are called 'indefinite period contracts'. The rest of us would either be self employed, or part-timers, perhaps temps of one sort or another, or out of paid work altogether. We would need, I said, a portfolio of different bits and pieces of paid work, or a collection of clients and customers, if we wanted to earn a living.... As it turned out, by the year 2000 the British labour force on those indefinite period contracts in full time employment had fallen to 40 per cent and the BBC World Service was running programmes on the theme 'What Future for Men?' (Handy, 2001:3–5)

Unfortunately, such claims are highly misleading (see Coats 2009). It is true that if you add together part-time workers, temporary workers, self-employed people, people in full-time education, unemployed people and those who have taken early retirement, you have a sum that is higher than the number employed on a full-time permanent basis. But this situation was not actually that different in 1981 when Handy made his 'foolhardy' forecast. There have been modest increases in atypical forms of working since then, mainly in part-time contracts, but these were largely continuations of existing trends. To use this as the basis for a claim that we are now largely a workforce made up of portfolio workers as defined in the quotation is simply untrue. We would have to have witnessed a vastly greater increase in temporary working and self-employment for this prediction to have been substantiated. In fact, the 1990s saw a modest decline in self-employment, while the period since 1997 has seen a sharp decline in temporary employment as a proportion of total employment (McOrmond 2004:30, National Statistics 2006:24–25), remaining a great deal lower than in most other industrialised economies. The number of self-employed people has begun to increase again, but the rate of increase is gradual and is largely accounted for by the banking and finance sectors, where jobs have been shed leading people to set up their own businesses, and in the building and construction industries, which provide excellent opportunities for self-employed people (Lindsay and McCaulay 2004, National Statistics 2006:23). There is no evidence whatever of major underlying shifts away from permanent employment towards short-term contracts and self-employment.

A second source of information on current trends which can furnish evidence for the future of work debate are the figures on job tenure. If it were true that we are heading towards a world of temporary assignments instead of permanent full-time jobs, we would expect to see a substantial decline occurring over recent years in the length of time we spend in each of our jobs. However this is not at all clear from the government's statistics. Average job tenure has fluctuated up and down with economic conditions over the years, but has remained within the same broad bands throughout the past 30 years (Gregg and Wadsworth, 1999:115, DTI 2006). There is no evidence of any dramatic shift here. Moreover, a quarter of the UK workforce has already been employed in the same place for over 12 years. It is true that average male job tenure has fallen somewhat and that the biggest increases have been in the figures for women with children, but we would expect to have seen substantially greater changes to judge the 'new economy' thesis to be proven. In short, while some sectors have seen a shift towards shorter periods of employment, the overall picture for the labour force is not greatly different. We can thus conclude that as yet, despite the claims of some gurus, there is little evidence of any kind of fundamental shift in working relationships along the lines of their forecasts.

Another objection to some of the 'future of work' predictions is their apparent determinism. Proponents argue that the changes they anticipate are going to be technologically driven and that they are therefore in some way inevitable. The fact that people themselves may object and seek to stop the developments happening (or limit their effects) does not seem to be considered. Linked to this is an assumption that people will soon learn to be comfortable with portfolio working, or may even welcome it. No consideration seems to be given to the inherent insecurity of these types of employment and the probability that people will act in such a way as to gain greater security. It may well turn out to be the case that the majority of people will opt for employment rather than the promise of 'employability' wherever they can. It follows that workers with considerable market power derived from their specialist knowledge will actively seek a traditional 'job' where it is on offer and will tend to steer clear of employers offering only temporary assignments. The result will be an incentive for employers to offer contracts of the full-time, open-ended variety that are supposedly on the way out. It will take a significant shift in established attitudes towards work for people readily to accept life as a portfolio worker. It is true that there is some evidence of a more flexible mindset on the part of the 'Generation Y' people in their early 20s (see Brown *et al* 2007, Twenge & Campbell 2008), but only time will tell whether their avowed comfort with insecurity will remain when they begin to shoulder domestic responsibilities. All the current evidence suggests that people seek security and prefer to develop their careers with their existing employers. Moreover, employers continue in the large majority of cases to meet their expectations in these respects (see White *et al* 2004).

In addition there is the question of regulation – another factor that is largely ignored in the visions of the futurologists. It is quite possible to envisage a situation in which work insecurity becomes a major political issue and that politicians are required to respond with legislation that seeks to deter employers from moving towards atypical contractual arrangements. At the European level such debates are already well rehearsed. A great deal of work has already been carried out both in Brussels and through other EU governments to examine ways of bringing greater regulation to the labour market using regulatory mechanisms. The following quotation from a European Commission publication on 'the Future of Work' illustrates the kind of thinking that is dominant:

> The question is whether Europe, after the establishment of economic and monetary union, will have the resources – and whether it wishes to use them as part of its social policy – to put a halt to this creeping job insecurity which flies in the face of its values of solidarity (including solidarity between men and women). What balance should it strike between much-needed adaptation of its labour force to international competition and the social cohesion it sees as vital? (European Commission 2000:33).

It is thus reasonable to conclude that HRM specialists should be cautious in responding to the cries of 'change now or die' emanating from conference platforms and management books with dramatic titles. They may be right in their messages about the future, but there is little evidence to date of any kind of fundamental changes occurring and reasons to doubt that the 'new world of work' will ever materialise in the way its advocates suggest. A 'new economy' is emerging but it seems clear, at least for the foreseeable future, that it will co-exist alongside the 'old economy' rather than replacing it. It might be a good thing for the UK economy if the transformation occurred more rapidly, particularly in respect of skills acquisition, but it is the slowness of change that tends to concern contemporary commentators and not its rapidity.

In fact, a compelling case can be made in favour of the view that the UK employment scene has already gone through its major transformation and that the period ahead will be characterised by relative stability in comparison with the past two decades. We may actually see a deceleration rather than an acceleration of the pace of change. It is easy when looking to the future to forget just how major the changes that have occurred since the 1970s have been. These have included a substantial fall in manufacturing employment and the rise of the service sector, large-scale privatisation of state-owned enterprises, the demolition of the established system of national-level collective bargaining as a means of determining terms and conditions, increases in immigration from overseas, huge falls in trade union membership, the establishment and growth of the internet, huge increases in regulation, the feminisation of many workplaces, globalisation of many industries and a tightening of labour markets due to lower birth rates. The practices that managers have had to develop in response to these and other trends have been a major focus of this book. Could it be that the future of work 'has already happened' to a great extent and that consolidation rather than further change is the likely dominant theme for the next 20 years?

Above it was argued that there is little disagreement between commentators about one prediction. That is that the industries that will dominate economies such as the UK's over the coming decades will be of two major types: personal care and knowledge-based. There will be less unskilled work, while some existing skills will become less desirable from an employer's perspective. The effective management of people employed to work in the personal care and knowledge-based industries is thus likely to move up the HR agenda – and indeed already is doing so in many organisations. Below three topic areas of relevance to these trends are introduced: emotional intelligence, knowledge management and work-life balance initiatives.

EXERCISE 20.1

EXXERCISE BOX: SUSAN GREENFIELD'S PREDICTIONS

Read the article by Susan Greenfield entitled 'Flexible Futures' featured in *People Management* (23 October 2003, pages 52–53). This can be downloaded from the *People Management* archive on the CIPD's website (www.ipd.co.uk)

In this short article Baroness Greenfield of Oxford University sets out some of her thoughts about the future of work. Some of her views are similar to those of Charles Handy and others who believe in a radically different future working environment In other respects her predictions differ somewhat.

Questions:

1 What different factors does Greenfield identify which will bring about the changes she envisages?

2 What major weaknesses can you identify in her arguments?

3 What do you think would be the major implications for you as an HR professional if her predictions of 'imminent change' were to prove accurate?

KEY ARTICLE BOX

'Shaping the future: the political economy of work and employment' by Peter Nolan (2004) Industrial Relations Journal. Vol. 35, No. 5. 378–387.

This article is the editorial which opened a special edition of the *Industrial Relations Journal* on different aspects of the 'future of work debate'. In it, as well as introducing some of the key points from the articles which followed, Peter Nolan takes the opportunity to introduce the ESRC's Future of Work research programme and to tackle head-on some of the myths perpetuated by people he describes as 'well-paid visionaries' about contemporary labour market trends. In particular he takes aim at those who argue that a move away from employment (ie the death of the job) is at all imminent.

Questions:

1 Why, according to Nolan, is it plain wrong to argue that new technologies will replace people, leaving a world in which there are too few jobs to occupy for the population of western industrialised countries such as the UK?

> 2 Why is it wrong to assert that self-employment and temporary work will increasingly replace traditional employment in the future?
>
> 3 On what basis does Nolan argue that the research commissioned by the Future of Work programme 'reveals good and bad news for paid and unpaid work in the UK'?

EMOTIONAL INTELLIGENCE

The concept of emotional intelligence came to prominence in the 1980s and 1990s through the work of American psychologists such as Howard Gardner, Peter Salovey and John Mayer. However, credit for bringing the term to a wider audience must be given to Daniel Goleman, who wrote several very accessible books and articles on the subject in the late 1990s and continues to preach his message. Goleman has also carried out his own research which suggests that emotional intelligence is a particularly significant ingredient in effective leadership and is not something that is necessarily associated with intelligence as conventionally conceived (see Goleman 1998, Cook & Cripps 2005:51). Salovey and Mayer (1989) describe four distinct elements:

- the ability to perceive how oneself and other people are feeling

- the ability to access or generate emotions in oneself as means of assisting thought

- the ability to understand emotions and emotional reactions to events

- the ability to manage or regulate emotions in oneself and others.

Goleman (1998) defines EQ slightly differently with reference to five separate components:

- self-awareness (ie of motivations, strengths and weaknesses)

- self-regulation (ie controlling emotions and channelling them constructively)

- motivation (ie being internally driven to achieve goals)

- empathy (ie understanding emotional reactions in others)

- social skill (ie working well with others, building rapport etc).

Emotional intelligence differs from IQ in that it takes account of irrational as well as rational reactions to different types of situation. But it is also about making intelligent use of one's own emotions and responding effectively to emotional responses in others.

The claim that emotional intelligence (or something very similar) exists and is significant is not new or revolutionary, being rooted in centuries of psychological research and practice (Woodruffe 2001:27–28). What is new is the *extent* to which proponents of the theory now believe EQ to contribute to effective performance in the workplace. Goleman, in his research on effective leaders, goes as far as to claim that up to 85 per cent of success in the contemporary business world can be accounted for by emotional intelligence and only 15 per cent by cognitive ability (ie IQ). It follows that organisations should ascribe greater prominence than they have done historically to this group of competencies when recruiting, selecting, managing and developing their staff.

While many more cautious analysts have questioned the magnitude of Goleman's claims and believe him to be exaggerating its importance, few dispute the basic idea that the intelligent use of emotions is an attribute that helps raise standards of performance in a number of roles – namely those which hinge to a good degree on the effectiveness of dealings with other people. EQ is not especially useful for people whose main interaction at work is with machines, land or animals. Technical competences are clearly more important for them. However, for those whose jobs involve managing or serving others in more than a routine manner, a compelling case in favour of the significance of emotional intelligence can be made. The increase we continue to see in the number and prominence of people-oriented jobs thus also accounts for the growth in interest in the EQ concept.

While most of the writing on emotional intelligence has focused on its part in effective leadership, it is clear that the same broad principles apply to many service-sector jobs involving direct and prolonged contact with customers. It therefore stands to reason that these types of competences should be influential factors in recruitment and development practices for such roles. The use of emotional competencies in employee selection is controversial and is apparently opposed by Goleman himself (IRS 2000:8). However, case study evidence suggests that it is being increasingly used and that positive results can be identified:

- In the 1990s L'Oreal, a cosmetics company, tried selecting some of its sales agents on the basis of their emotional intelligence, while retaining existing selection practices for others. They subsequently found that the first group outsold the second to the tune of $90,000 per year. Staff turnover rates were also 63 per cent lower in the first group than in the second (IRS 2000).

- In 2002 it was reported that British Telecom was boasting of a 36 per cent rise in its customer satisfaction rates. Apparently this occurred after a reorganisation of their service management centres using assessments of emotional intelligence to select staff for different roles. Structured interviews and a competency-based questionnaire were used to identify which staff were best suited to roles which involved customer contact, and which were best allocated to administrative jobs. BT concluded that 80 per cent of its employees' success in serving customers derived from emotional intelligence, and 20 per cent from technical competences.

The major providers of personality tests are now developing instruments which specifically seek to measure emotional intelligence, and a number are already on the market. Those developed by reputable companies using proper validation mechanisms are likely to be used with increasing success in the selection of people for customer-oriented roles.

More generally, EQ would seem to comprise a set of competencies which HR specialists themselves should seek to develop. This is particularly true for those whose jobs involve frequent interaction with staff in circumstances which precipitate emotional responses. Those with responsibility for hands-on handling of disciplinary issues, cases of poor performance, dismissals and absence particularly stand to benefit. Development programmes which focus on the effective handling of emotion (in oneself and others) are thus worthy of serious consideration. It is true that these competencies can be learned with experience and proper training, raising the effectiveness of the P&D function and the respect in which it is held. The following quotation illustrates the type of understanding which can be usefully developed and applied in more tense encounters:

> There are only two ways to deal with emotion. If you have aroused the emotion because of something you did which you now accept is wrong, then an *early* apology will defuse the situation. On many occasions, however, this may not be appropriate. In these circumstances the only solution is to let the emotion run its course. This can be encouraged in two ways. Attentive, but silent listening, and the occasional use of *reflective* questions. Silence can be difficult to maintain as there is a strong temptation to jump in and correct inaccuracies. Reflective questions do what their name suggests; they use a summary of what the person has just said and reflect it back, without evaluation. For example, 'You feel you've been undervalued by the firm – is that it?' The effect is to allow the emotion to run its course. High levels of emotion are difficult to maintain without support from others, either in the form of agreement or argument. With no evaluation, the emotional level tends to steadily decrease (Makin, Cooper and Cox 1996:202).

In some books on emotional intelligence, writers go on to explore the notion of the 'emotionally intelligent organisation' (see Goleman 1998, Weisinger 1998). Although it is always stated that it will take some years for research on this topic to be fully established, the idea is attractive in principle and could assist in the achievement of competitive advantage. On one level an emotionally intelligent organisation can simply be characterised as one which is made up of emotionally intelligent people, but it also goes a great deal further. Such organisations, because of the orientation of their people, are said to have developed strong values which combine to make them more effective and understanding workplaces. These include the following:

- a commitment to the work-life balance
- openness/high-trust working relationships
- creativity and innovation formed through collaborative working
- a willingness to share ideas and resources
- a supportive as opposed to a competitive climate.

REFLECTIVE QUESTION

To what extent would you characterise your organisation (or parts of it) as 'emotionally intelligent'? What steps would need to be taken in order to encourage the development of such characteristics?

EXERCISE BOX: EQ IN CALL CENTRES

EXERCISE 20.2

Read the article by Malcolm Higgs entitled 'Good Call' featured in *People Management* (23 January 2003, pages 48–49). This can be downloaded from the *People Management* archive on the CIPD's website (www.cipd.co.uk).

In this article Malcolm Higgs describes a programme of research in which he and his colleagues sought to establish a link between emotional intelligence and effective performance on the part of call centre workers. Their results suggest that call centre managers should alter their traditional approaches to recruitment.

Questions:

1 In what ways are the personality traits shared by effective call centre workers any different from those you would expect to find shared by most good employees working in customer service roles?

2 To what extent do you agree with the argument that call centres should avoid recruiting intuitive people and why?

3 Why do you think older women make the best call centre workers?

KNOWLEDGE MANAGEMENT

Knowledge management is another notion of general relevance to the material included in this book, and this chapter in particular, which has attracted a great deal of interest in recent years. Originating in the 1980s, the term is linked to a range of other fashionable buzzwords such as 'intellectual capital' and 'the learning organisation'. Like other recent additions to the vocabulary of management thinkers, knowledge management and the ideas that flow from an understanding of its aims are compelling in theory. However, as is the often the case, there is a tendency to exaggerate both the extent to which the idea is new and its significance for managers operating in the real (as opposed to the theoretical) world.

At base we are concerned here with the consequences of the view that our business environment is changing fundamentally from being essentially 'industrial' in nature to 'post-industrial'. The new world differs from the old one in several respects, but central is its knowledge-based nature. Wealth is now principally generated, so it is argued, through the creation and application of knowledge:

In these environments, wealth creation is less dependent on the control of resources and more dependent on the exercise of specialist knowledge, or the management of organisational competences. We can no longer blame the mismanagement of tangible resources for failures in a knowledge-based society. We now need to turn our attention to the management of the intangible. Managerial systems remain important, but it is the management of intangible assets that is now argued to be at the heart of the managerial process (Swart 2007:450–1).

The trend is most clearly apparent in the nature of the work which we are now required to perform. Historically, the majority of the working population were not obliged to use their minds to any great extent in the workplace. Most people went in to work and performed a range of routine tasks that were prescribed for them by managers. They were not required or even invited to be creative, or to innovate, or to make use of their knowledge in any other way. It is argued that the position today is wholly different. Most of us can now be categorised, in some shape or form, as 'knowledge workers', fitting in somewhere to the following four-way classification provided by Laudon and Starbuck (1997:299):

i   people who process or preserve data

ii   people who interpret information and act upon it

iii people who generate new information

iv   people who apply accumulated knowledge.

We are hired less for what we can offer in physical terms and more because of what we know and our ability to apply that knowledge. Brinkley and Lee (2006) estimate that 48 per cent of the UK workforce is employed in knowledge-based industries, the number having grown significantly over the past decades, and up from only 17 per cent at the start of the twentieth century (see Storey and Quintas 2001:346). It follows that organisations depend to an increasing extent on the knowledge that is held in the heads of its employees in order to develop and retain competitive advantage. 'Intellectual capital', by which is meant the relevant content of human brains, is thus a more significant determinant of commercial success than the ownership of land, tools and machines.

What does all this mean for human resource management? An answer is provided in the following two quotations from Holbeche (1999:424) and Micklethwait and Wooldridge (1996:147) respectively:

> The challenge of managing intellectual capital is ensuring that it does not walk out of the door.

> The secret of managing knowledge workers, like the secret of making a martini, lies in the mixing.

One result is some shifting in the traditional power relationship between employers and employees. Micklethwait and Wooldridge (1996:136) rightly state that 'the modern masters of the universe are the gilded few who have had the good fortune to be born bright – lawyers, scientists, stockbrokers, skilled mechanics, indeed everyone who can make connections and generate ideas more rapidly and imaginatively than his peers'. The more useful your knowledge, and the rarer your capacity to apply it, the more desirable you are from an employer's point of view. In a knowledge economy employees are less readily dispensable than they once were. Losing an employee involves losing some portion of the organisation's intellectual capital. There are clear implications for P&D professionals in general, and resourcing specialists in particular:

- The retention of knowledge workers becomes a central organisational objective. It follows that they must be managed effectively and that substantial effort needs to be put into motivating them and enhancing their job satisfaction. A degree of turnover, however, is needed in order to bring new knowledge into the organisation from outside.

- A sophisticated approach must be taken to performance management. Knowledge workers do not have to submit to clumsy, bullying or incompetent treatment. If they do not like the way they are being managed, they can go and work elsewhere.

- Recruitment and selection are crucial processes. It is essential that organisations engaged in knowledge work attract the best possible pool of candidates and devise methods of selecting new employees which are able correctly to identify those with appropriate knowledge or the ability to develop it.

- Redundancy management processes need to focus on the need to retain significant or valuable knowledge at the disposal of the organisation.

Aside from the effective management of knowledge workers, organisations also need to ensure that they are managed in such a way as to foster the sharing of existing knowledge and the creation of new knowledge. This is important firstly because it is through sharing knowledge among groups of people that new knowledge is created. Innovation and creative thinking, both central capacities for organisations competing in a knowledge economy, are a great deal more likely to occur when people spark ideas off one another, argue out their differences and put their expertise at the disposal of one another. The result is a situation in which human capital is converted into intellectual capital (Swart 2007:453). Secondly, sharing knowledge is important because it helps to increase the stock of knowledge available to the organisation. It means that the organisation as a whole is better qualified to address problems, develop future strategies and prosper in an increasingly volatile environment. In short, the more staff know about more things, the more effective they are at performing their knowledge-based roles.

It is useful here to introduce the distinction between explicit and tacit forms of knowledge. Explicit forms of knowledge are those which can be readily identified. The material contained in this book is one example, as is any set of ideas or information that can be readily communicated through books, briefing documents, articles, TV programmes, lectures, training events or computer programmes. Explicit knowledge is relatively easily grasped and transferred from one person to another. It can also be measured to an extent (ie organisations can maintain databases on who has completed certain training courses, who has particular qualifications etc). Tacit knowledge, by contrast is much harder to get a handle on, but is thought by many to be equally important to organisations. Nonaka and Takeuchi (1995) say that it includes 'subjective insights, intuitions and hunches', while Holbeche (1999) sees it as consisting of 'intangibles such as know-how, information on stakeholder relationships, experiences and ideas'. Micklethwait and Wooldridge (1996:143) prefer the following starker definition:

> The informal, occupational lore generated by workers grappling with everyday problems and passed on in cafeterias, not the official rules written down in company manuals and transmitted in compulsory training sessions.

This kind of informal knowledge is seen by many analysts to be equally, if not more important, than explicit knowledge in cultivating organisational learning. Tacit knowledge is also often the ultimate source of new knowledge. A business idea starts as a hunch, is shared informally with colleagues who assess its possibilities and bring their experience to bear on it. It is then raised more formally and discussed at formal meetings before being developed further. At some stage in the process it becomes explicit knowledge, but it did not start out that way.

Encouraging people to have ideas and to share them is thus an important role for P&D professionals in knowledge-based organisations. This can be done in a number of different ways. First, opportunities need to be provided for people to gain a range of experiences. In so doing their minds are stimulated, new ways of approaching familiar issues are observed and more knowledge created. Job rotation schemes achieve these aims, but are not always practical or desirable. Secondments to other parts of the organisation (if possible internationally) are a good way of developing knowledge, but much can also be achieved through inter-disciplinary team-working, mentoring and attendance at training events which include participants from different branches of the business. Attendance at conferences and external training events also achieve the same outcomes. When it comes to tacit knowledge, all that can be done to facilitate its transfer around the organisation is to provide sufficient opportunity. Social events are important here as are recreational activities. We are just as likely to learn useful things from someone visiting from overseas at the dinner table as we are from formal meetings with them.

There also needs to be active encouragement for people to share knowledge, and this should be reflected in reward and recognition systems. It is not easy to achieve because knowledge is so difficult to measure and pin down. However, it is not impossible to include an estimate of knowledge sharing prominently in employees' performance objectives (either formally or informally) and subsequently to allow assessments to influence decisions about pay or promotion. Scarbrough *et al* (1999:39–40) draw attention to less tangible forms of reward such as 'status, reputation and recognition which can be conferred on knowledge-leaders in a particular field'. However, formal systems are often not necessary. What is needed is the creation of a culture in which sharing is encouraged. Praise and genuine gratitude from managers and colleagues are sometimes all that is necessary by way of reward.

A third way that HR people can encourage sharing of knowledge is by helping to promote a high-trust/high-security culture. Where levels of trust are low and where people fear unnecessarily for their future job security they are much more likely to hoard knowledge. This is because doing so enhances their status and makes them more indispensable as individuals. Why help to develop other people by sharing knowledge if this increases the likelihood that you (rather than others) will lose your job or lose some element of your role which you value? In a volatile business environment there will always be an element of job insecurity, but a great deal can be done to minimise the extent to which it becomes a factor in determining the actions of employees. Where knowledge workers are concerned, for example, it does not make sense to employ people on fixed-term contracts or to withhold information about future human resource plans. Perceptions of insecurity are also minimised through the genuine promotion of employee involvement, and generally through the use of an open style of management.

EXERCISE 20.3

EXERCISE BOX· FROM THEORY TO PRACTICE

Read the following two articles published in *People Management*. They can be downloaded from the *People Management* archive on the CIPD's website (www.cipd.co.uk):

- 'The Alchemists' by Nick Kinnie and Juani Swart (6 April 2006, pages 42–45)

- 'Sphere of Influence' by Peter Williamson (12 October 2006, pages 32–34)

Both these articles describe simple tools which can be used by P&D managers to think about what they can do practically to make knowledge management more effective in their organisations. In addition, the article by Peter Williamson contains several examples of how international organisations have been able to harness knowledge to their advantage.

Questions:

1 To what extent are the approaches set out in these articles currently used in your organisation, either formally or informally?

2 In what ways could more formal use be made of them in practice?

3 What business case could you put forward for the adoption of more formal knowledge management activities in your organisation?

A CRITIQUE OF KNOWLEDGE MANAGEMENT

It is difficult to take issue with the central ideas put forward by the proponents of knowledge management. They are right to remind us that knowledge (explicit and tacit) is the source of much competitive advantage and that this should be recognised in our approach to the management of organisations. They are also correct in identifying a breed of 'knowledge workers' who require different types of supervision or leadership from traditional approaches if their talents are to be fully harnessed. However, it is also the case that the ideas are too frequently dressed up in evangelical rhetoric which only serves to dazzle audiences and to exaggerate the significance of what is being said.

In truth, while many of us can now be loosely defined as 'knowledge workers', we are not for the most part individually indispensable to our employers. Nor, alas, are most of us members of headhunted classes who are actively sought by competing employers because of our exceptional knowledge. Talk of fundamental shifts in the power balance between employers and employees is thus untrue in most organisations. Some sectors which have these characteristics have grown in recent years, mainly those in the professional services sector (advertising, public relations, consultancy, IT, law etc). For these the knowledge management literature has a great deal to offer. The same is true of departments (such as R&D or engineering) in larger organisations operating in other sectors. However, for most employees in most organisations this is not the case. Their knowledge is not as invaluable to their organisations as is suggested in the literature. Most of the recent growth in employment has been in the provision of other types of services. While expertise and qualifications are required to undertake these jobs, it is not true to say that the capacity to innovate or leverage knowledge is any kind of pre-requisite for success. Such organisations will benefit from shared ideas and new thinking on ways of attracting business or organising things more efficiently, but the capacity to harness the knowledge of employees is less of a priority than getting on with the job of serving their customers.

We can thus conclude by saying that knowledge management theory provides the basis of a useful contribution to HRM practice. It is not, however, as universal in its application as many commentators lead us to believe. There is a 'knowledge economy' and there are 'knowledge workers' who require careful management, but as yet these represent a relatively small section of the total economy. There is nothing to be gained, and may be some danger, in applying knowledge management principles in situations where they are not appropriate.

 EXERCISE BOX: SHELL

EXERCISE 20.4

Read the article by Lucie Carrington entitled 'Oiling the Wheels' featured in *People Management* (27 June 2002, pages 31–34). This can be downloaded from the *People Management* archive on the CIPD's website (www.cipd.co.uk).

This article provides an excellent case study of a knowledge management project which has developed over time and yielded major benefits. It also explores some of the problems encountered and explains how these were managed.

Questions:

1 Why is the approach described in the article particularly appropriate for large, international organisations?

2 Aside from the savings that have been made as result of the knowledge-sharing networks, what other business benefits have accrued because of Shell's use of a web-based approach to knowledge management?

3 How has the problem of 'knowledge hoarding' been overcome?

WORK-LIFE BALANCE

Work-life balance initiatives have become prominent in recent years for several reasons. In some situations they are primarily introduced to meet operational requirements of organisations rather than the preferences of employees. Much of the growth in part-time working, for example, has come about because employers in the service sector require additional staff over and above their full-time cohort to help them meet peaks in demand that occur at certain times of the week or day. The fact that such initiatives can also serve to meet the needs of employees with caring and childcare responsibilities is essentially coincidental. A second important factor is the move we have increasingly witnessed in recent years towards far longer hours of operation for many organisations. Only a few years ago most shops opened just during office hours, closing on Wednesday afternoons. On the other hand, the pubs, bars, restaurants and other leisure services opened only once the shops and offices had closed. Working hours thus equated to hours of operation. An organisation did business for 40–45 hours a week, employing managers and staff to work those hours. The norm now is for such organisations and all the others that provide services of one kind or another to operate at full pace throughout the daytime and evenings, not to mention Sundays and bank holidays. This trend has provided opportunities for the employment of staff on unconventional shift patterns, some of which can help people achieve a better balance between the needs of their work and those of their home-based activities. For example, they allow older people to reduce their hours of work steadily over a number of years rather than transferring from full-time working to total retirement in one jump. Regulation has played a major part in pushing work-life balance issues up the HRM agenda and will continue to do so further (see Chapter 2), while major social changes are also having an important impact. Organisations can no longer assume, as they could largely a generation ago, that most of their employees lived in households in which men were the breadwinners and the women primarily looked after the home and children. Dual income earning is now the norm, many women earning more than their male partners, while single parent households are commonplace.

Despite the presence of all these factors, it remains the case that most work-life balance initiatives are introduced for labour market reasons. In other words, employers are moving in this direction because their employees and potential employees are seeking a greater work-life balance and helping them to achieve it is thus a good way of acquiring a loyal and effective workforce. CIPD (2005) shows clearly that the major reasons for the introduction of work-life balance options for employees are in order to better recruit and especially to retain staff. However, it is not just a question of providing existing employees with a more desirable package in order to dissuade them from looking elsewhere for employment. Importantly, initiatives in the field of work-life balance also help to provide organisations with an entrée into parts of the labour market from which they have hitherto been unable to gain access. Organisations suffering from skills shortages are obliged to look beyond their customary recruitment sources (typically people looking for full-time employment during conventional working hours). Once a more flexible approach is adopted interest can be engendered among groups of people who are interested in working some hours each week or year, but who are either unwilling or unable to take up a traditional full-time role.

IDS (2000b) provides an excellent survey of the various types of elements that make up a work-life balance policy. They identify four major categories of initiative:

FLEXIBLE WORKING

This comprises patterns of working hours which differ from the traditional 9–5 working week. Part-time working is the most common, but there it is also possible to offer compressed hours whereby people work a full complement of hours each week, but concentrate them into three or four days. Term-time working is attractive to parents with children of school age as are shifts which allow parents to divide childcare responsibilities between them. Job-sharing, flexitime (see Chapter 7) and homeworking are other types of arrangement which can be adopted. Finally, of course, it is possible simply to meet the needs of particular individuals either for a temporary period or permanently by altering established patterns of working.

LEAVE AND TIME OFF

Allowing staff to take extended periods of leave on an unpaid basis and to return to their jobs at a later date is another significant type of work-life balance initiative which is valued by employees. In practice the vast majority will never take up the opportunities offered to them, but many find it comforting to know that the possibility is there and are likely to opt to work for organisations that have schemes of this kind. The law now requires organisations to allow people a few days off at short notice to make arrangements for the care of dependants when they become ill, but it does not provide for any longer periods away. If it can be afforded and does not reduce productivity it can make good business sense in labour market terms to go beyond the minimum requirements of the law and offer a more generous entitlement. Permitting people to take career breaks or sabbaticals for longer periods (eg six months or a year) once they have become established employees is also a valued benefit.

CHILDCARE FACILITIES

The third type of initiative which forms part of a work-life balance policy involves providing direct assistance with childcare. It is common for larger organisations to provide nurseries for children who are below school age, but other types of approach are also in operation. After school clubs and school holiday clubs are the major examples. Some organisations also provide equivalent facilities to help meet the needs of older people for whom employees have a caring responsibility. The Peugeot 'granny crèche' in Coventry is a well-publicised example.

HEALTH AND WELL-BEING

The final category includes the provision of any other service which aims to assist employees to reach a better work-life balance for themselves. Occupational Health Services have long been run by larger employers as a means of helping to ensure that employees remain fit and well. But it is possible to extend these so that they also provide confidential counselling and advisory services which provide practical assistance to employees who are finding it difficult to juggle their domestic and working lives.

While the extent of work-life balance initiatives has grown considerably in recent years (Fleetwood 2007) many commentators agree that a great deal more benefit could be gained for employers than is currently the case. This is because there remains a strong tendency for managers and employees alike to perceive them as only being relevant for women with young children and not for the generality of people. This leads to the presence of strong cultural barriers which prevent men and women who do not have young children from taking up opportunities offered by the initiatives that might help them to achieve a better work-life balance. While many state that they would be interested in working fewer hours or taking a sabbatical, they chose in practice not to because they perceive that they would suffer career-wise over the long term. Kodz *et al* (2002) found substantial evidence of such effects in their research as well as a lack of enthusiasm on the part of first line managers. Organisations, it would seem, are happy to embrace the principles of work-life balance and develop initiatives centrally, but are less able to develop a supportive culture which enables the idea to become a reality.

EXERCISE BOX: BT

EXERCISE 20.5

Read the article by Claire Seneviratna entitled 'Dependant's Day' featured in *People Management* (6 December 2001, pages 38–40). This can be downloaded from the *People Management* archive on the CIPD's website (www.cipd.co.uk).

The article describes the development of a wide suite of family-friendly policies at BT designed to help its employees achieve a better work-life balance. The positive results of the policies are also set out.

Questions:

1 Write down a list of the various different work-life balance initiatives that are mentioned or alluded to in the article.

2 What were the main reasons for their introduction?

3 What benefits does BT point to in its evaluation of its policies?

Scenario planning

It is impossible to predict something as complex as 'the world of work' with any serious degree of confidence in one's accuracy. Yet it is as important as ever, because the pace of change in our business environment is increasing so much, that organisations think seriously about the future and plan so that when the future becomes the present they are in a position to maximise the opportunities and meet the threats more effectively than their competitors. This is as important for managers of people as it is for those whose primary concerns lie in other fields of management practice.

The most effective approach is to think in terms of 'multiple futures' rather than just a single future. This enables organisations to plan for a range of possible future scenarios rather than putting all eggs in the one basket and betting on one particular scenario being fulfilled. HR consultants at PriceWaterhouseCoopers recently worked with academics at Oxford University to develop scenario thinking about how the world of work may develop between now and 2020 (PWC 2007). They surveyed 3,000 recent graduates before eventually coming up with three distinct bundles of ideas. These were each labelled with colours:

- An orange world of work in which the dominant trend is the growth of small, specialised organisations working in a networked fashion. In this scenario larger organisations, particularly multinationals have less power and significance in the world economy than they do at present.

- A green world of work in which the large corporations grow in influence, but are increasingly regulated and restricted by an expectation on the part of customers that they will act in a socially responsible manner. The need to tackle climate change and ensure environmental sustainability dominate the corporate HR agenda.

- A blue world of work in which huge global corporations dominate markets and have greater power than many states. Skills shortages mean that the packages and careers provided for those who work for these corporations are very generous, but technology also permits closer supervision of them.

In practice, of course, no one such scenario may turn out to dominate in quite the way this body of work implies. Elements of each coloured scenario may well turn out to progress in tandem with others from a different colour to forge a more complex and varied future. Alternatively, of course, other unforeseen developments may come to dominate. However, the process of engaging in this kind of thinking and the collection of evidence to back up the ideas remains useful and interesting. Not only is it useful to think about and prepare for different possible futures on behalf of your organisation and the areas of P&D practice you are responsible for, it is also very helpful when planning your own career and in determining what choices you are going to make now in order to make sure that you are best placed to take up future opportunities when they arise.

EXAMPLE

KEY ARTICLE BOX

'Working to live or living to work? Work life balance early in the career' by Jane Sturges and David Guest. *Human Resource Management Journal*, Vol. 14, No. 4. 5–20 (2004)

This article looks in detail at the perspective of young graduate recruits on the issue of work-life balance. The results of two surveys are presented, one questionnaire-based and one interview-based. The article is interesting because of the way the authors try to reconcile two apparently contradictory findings. Why is it, they ask, that graduate recruits profess to be very interested in achieving a good work-life balance, but at the same time stay in jobs which require them to work long hours and hence prevent them from achieving one?

Questions:

1 What do the findings presented show about the employees' attitudes towards work-life balance?

2 Why are they prepared to work such long hours?

3 What are the major lessons to be learned from these findings from a practical HRM management perspective?

EXPLORE FURTHER

- There are numerous books and articles in print that deal with aspects of the 'future of work debate. A good starting point is the work of *Economist* journalists John Micklethwait and Adrian Wooldridge. Their two books published in 1996 and 2000 introduce the debates and discuss them. Another recommended book is Colin Williams' (2007) book on the future of work, particularly Chapter 11. Storey (2001) and Coats (2009) also provide good summaries of the debate. Taylor (2002 and 2004) and Moynagh & Worsley (2005 and 2008) draw effectively on the research emanating from the ESRC future of work project to summarise current trends. The case against revolutionary change is put best by Nolan (2004).

- The best introduction to emotional intelligence is found in the books and articles of Daniel Goleman. His original book was published in 1996 under the title *Emotional intelligence: Why it can matter more than IQ*. This was followed by *Working with emotional intelligence* in 1998. Both books sold millions of copies. An excellent summary of research in the field and its implications for P&D managers is provided by IRS (2000). More critical perspectives are developed by Davie *et al* (1998) and Woodruffe (2001).

- Knowledge management is the subject of hundreds of texts published in recent years. A good general introduction is provided by Hislop (2009). Armstrong (2009) includes a helpful introductory chapter, a more comprehensive treatment being provided by Storey and Quintas (2001). Summaries of more recent research and the interesting points about the HR implications are provided by Swart (2007) and Salaman (2007).

- Work-life balance issues are well covered in the literature. CIPD publish a wide-ranging guide (CIPD 2002) in which several authors write about different aspects of introducing initiatives in the field. The Institute of Employment Studies research report by Kodz and her colleagues (2002) provides much food for thought about the practical and cultural barriers which often prevent organisations from reaping the full benefit from such policies. In more recent years a lively critical perspective has been developed. The articles by Fleetwood (2007) and Eikof *et al* (2007) and the book by Gambles *et al* (2006) are useful introductions.

References

ABELSON, M. and BAYSINGER, B. (1984) Optimal and dysfunctional turnover: Toward an organizational level model. *Academy of Management Review*. Vol. 9, No. 2. 331–342.

ACAS (2009) Redundancy handling. Advisory booklet. London: ACAS.

ADAMS, J.S. (1963) Toward an understanding of inequity. *Journal of Abnormal and Social Psychology*. No. 67. 422–436.

ADLER, L. (2005) Outside Chance. *People Management*. 10 March. 38–39.

AIKIN, O. (2001) *Contracts*. Second edition. London: IPD.

ALIMO-METCALFE, B. and ALBAN-METCALFE, J. (2003) Under the influence. *People Management*. 6 March. 32–35.

ALLEN, A. (2007) Bravo two zero. *People Management Guide to Recruitment Marketing*. June. 26–28.

ALLEN, A. (2007) Niche work if you can get it. *People Management Guide to Assessment*. October. 4–11.

ALLEN, B. (2006) Anoraks welcome. *People Management*. 13 July.

ALLEN, C. (2000) The hidden organisational costs of using non-standard employment. *Personnel Review*. Vol. 29, No. 2.

ALLEN, M. and WRIGHT, P. (2007) Strategic management and HRM, in P. BOXALL, J. PURCELL and P. WRIGHT (eds.) *The Oxford handbook of human resource management*. Oxford, Oxford University Press.

AMBLER, T. and BARROW, S. (1996) The employer brand. *Journal of Brand Management*. Vol. 4, No. 3. 185–206.

ANDERSON, N. and SHACKLETON, V. (1993) *Successful selection interviewing*. Oxford: Blackwell.

ARKIN, A. (2005) Burden of proof. *People Management*. 24 February. 30–32.

ARKIN, A. (2007) The generation game. *People Management*. 29 November. 24–27.

ARMSTRONG, M. (2003) *A handbook of human resource management practice*. Ninth edition. London: Kogan Page.

ARMSTRONG, M. (2009) *A handbook of human resource management practice*. Eleventh edition. London: Kogan Page.

ASHWORTH, L. (2007) How can we hang on to top performers, while maintaining a healthy employee churn? *People Management*. 19 April. 54.

ATKINSON, C. (2003) *Exploring the state of the psychological contract: the impact of research strategies on outcomes*. Paper presented to the CIPD Professional Standards Conference, Keele University.

ATKINSON, J. (1984) Manpower strategies for the flexible organisation. *Personnel Management*. August.

BACKHAUS, K. (2004) An exploration of corporate recruitment descriptions on monster.com. *Journal of Business Communication*, Vol. 41, No. 2. 115–136.

BACKHAUS, K. and TIKOO, S. (2004) Conceptualising and researching employer branding. *Career Development International*. Vol. 9, No. 5. 501–517.

BARBER, A. (1998) *Recruiting employees*. Thousand Oaks, California: Sage.

BARCLAY, J. (2001) Improving selection interviews with structure: Organisations' use of behavioural interviews. *Personnel Review*. Vol. 30, No. 1.

BARNEY, J. (1991) Firm resources and sustained competitive advantage. *Journal of Management*. Vol. 17, No. 1. 99–120.

BARON, J. & KREPS, D. (1999) *Strategic human resources: Frameworks for general managers*. New York: Wiley.

BARROW, S. and MOSELY, R. (2005) *The employer brand*. Chichester: Wiley.

BAUMAN, Z. (2005) *Work, consumerism and the new poor*. Second edition. Maidenhead: Open University Press.

BEARDWELL, J. and CLAYDON, T. (2007) *Human resource management: A contemporary approach*. Fifth edition. London: FT/Pitman.

BEAVAN, R., BOSWORTH, D., LEWNEY, R. and WILSON, R. (2005) *Alternative skills scenarios to 2020 for the UK economy*. Cambridge: Cambridge Econometrics.

BECHET, T. (2008) *Strategic staffing: A comprehensive system for effective workforce planning*. Second edition. New York: AMACOM.

BECKETT, H. (2006) All good practice. *People Management*. 9 March. 38–40.

BELL, D. and HART, R. (2003) Annualised hours contracts: The way forward in labour market flexibility. *National Institute Economic Review*. Vol. 185, No.1. 64–77.

BEN-SHAKHAR, G. (1989) Non-conventional methods in personnel selection, in P. Herriot (ed.) *Assessment and selection in organisations*. Chichester: Wiley.

BERGER, L. and BERGER, D. (eds.) (2004) *The talent management handbook*. New York: McGraw Hill.

BERTHON, P., EWING, M. and HAH, L.L. (2005) Captivating company: Dimensions of attractiveness in employer branding. *International Journal of Advertising*. Vol. 24, No. 2. 151–172.

BIBBY, A. (2002) Home start. *People Management*. 10 January. 36–37.

BIS (2010) *European Parliament and Council directive on working conditions for temporary agency workers. Impact Assessment*. London: Department for Business, Innovation and Skills.

BITMAN, M., FLICK, M. and RICE, J. (2006) *The recruitment of older Australian Workers: a survey of employers in a high growth industry*. University of New South Wales. Social Policy Research Centre. (www.sprc.unsw.edu.au).

BLACK, B. (1999) National culture and labour market flexibility. *International Journal of Human Resource Management*. Vol. 10, No. 4. 592–605.

BLACKMAN, A. (2006) Graduating students' responses to recruitment advertisements. *Journal of Business Communication*. Vol. 43, No. 4. 367–388.

BLASS, E. (ed.) (2009) *Talent management: Cases and commentary*. Basingstoke: Palgrave Macmillan.

BLAU, D.M. (1990) An empirical analysis of employed and unemployed job search behavior. *Industrial and Labor Relations Review*. Vol. 45, No. 4. July. 738–752.

BLYTON, P. (1998) Flexibility, in M. POOLE and M. WARNER (eds.) *The handbook of human resource management*. London: Thomson Business Press

BOSELIE, P., DIETZ, G. and BOON, C. (2005) Commonalities and contradictions in research on human resource management and performance. *Human Resource Management Journal*. Vol. 15, No. 3. 67–94.

BOWICK, C. (1996) Eight ways to assess succession plans, in G. FERRIS and M.R. BUCKLEY (eds.) Human resource management: Perspectives, context, functions and outcomes. Third edition. Engelwood Cliffs, New Jersey: Prentice-Hall.

BOXALL, P. and PURCELL, J. (2008) *Strategy and human resource management*. Second edition. Basingstoke: Palgrave Macmillan.

BOYZATIS, R.E. (1982) *The competent manager*. New York: Wiley.

BRAMHAM, J. (1987) Manpower planning, in S. HARPER (ed.) *Personnel management handbook*. London: Gower.

BRAMHAM, J. (1988) *Practical manpower planning*. Fourth edition. London: IPM.

BRAMHAM, J. (1994) *Human resource planning*. Second edition. London: IPD.

BRAMHAM, L. (2001) *Keeping the people who keep you in business*. New York: Amacom.

BREAUGH, J.A. (2008) Employee recruitment: Current knowledge and important areas for future research. *Human Resource Management Review*. Vol. 18, No. 3. 103–118.

BREWSTER, C., HEDGEWISCH, A., LOCKHART, T. and MAYNE, L. (1993) *Flexible working patterns in Europe*. London: IPM.

BRINER, R. and CONWAY, N. (2004) Promises, promises. *People Management*. 25 November.

BRINKLEY, I. and LEE, N. (2006) *The knowledge economy in Europe*. London: The Work Foundation.

BROCKETT, J. (2007) Flexicurity knocks. *People Management*. 19 April. 16–17.

BROCKETT, K. (2007) Face to face with social networking, *People Management*. 9 August. 15–17.

BROWN, D. (2002) Success in all shapes and sizes. *People Management*. 24 October. 25.

BROWN, A., RODDAN, M., JORDAN, S. and NILSSON, I. (2007) The time of your life. *People Management*, 26 July. 40–43.

BROWNING, G. (2004) New kid on the block. *People Management*. 15 July.

BRYSON, C. (1999) Managing uncertainty or managing uncertainly? in J. LEOPOLD, L. HARRIS and T. WATSON (eds.) *Strategic human resourcing*. London: FT/Pitman.

BUCHANAN, D. (1982) High performance: New boundaries of acceptability in worker control, in J. HURRELL and C. COOPER (eds.) *Job control and worker health*. Chichester: John Wiley.

BUCKLEY, M.R. and RUSSELL, C.J. (1999) Validity evidence, in R.W. EDER and M.M. HARRIS (eds.) *The employment interview handbook*. Thousand Oaks, California: Sage.

BURACK, E. and MATHYS, N. (1996) *Human resource planning: A pragmatic approach to manpower staffing and development*. Third edition. Northbrook, Illinois: Brace-Park Press

BURCHELL, B., LADIPO, D. and WILKINSON, F. (eds.) (2002) *Job insecurity and work intensification*. London: Routledge.

BUTLER, T. and WALDROOP, J. (1999) Job sculpting: The art of retaining your best people. *Harvard Business Review*. September/October.

BYHAM, W. (2000) Pools winners. *People Management*. 24 August. 38–40.

BYRON, M. and MODHA, S. (1991) How to pass selection tests. London: Kogan Page.

BYRON, M. and MODHA, S. (1993) *Technical selection tests and how to pass them*. London: Kogan Page.

CAMPBELL, S. (2009) Pensions: now it's personal. *People Management*. 18 June. 24.

CAMPOS, E. and CHUNA, R. (2002) Privatization and outsourcing, in C. COOPER and R. BURKE (eds.) *The new world of work: Challenges and opportunities*. Oxford: Blackwell.

CAPPELLI, P. (2000) A market driven approach to retaining talent. *Harvard Business Review*. January–February.

CAPPELLI, P. and SINGH, H. (1992) Integrating strategic human resources and strategic management, in D. LEWIN, O. MITCHELL and P. SHERER (eds.) *Research frontiers in industrial relations and human resources*. Madison: IRRA.

CARDY, R., MILLER, J. and ELLIS, A. (2007) Employee equity: Toward a person-based approach to HRM. *Human Resource Management Review*. No. 17. 140–151.

CARRINGTON, L. (2002) At the cutting edge. *People Management*. 16 May.

CARRINGTON, L. (2002) Oiling the wheels. *People Management*. 27 June. 31–34.

CARRINGTON, L. (2005) A bridge too far? *People Management*. 11 August. 24–28.

CARRINGTON, L. (2007) The skills equation. *People Management*. 23 August. 24–28.

CARRINGTON, L (2007) Designs on the dotted line. *People Management*. 18 October.

CARROLL, M., MARCHINGTON, M., EARNSHAW, J. and TAYLOR, S. (1999) Recruitment in small firms: processes, methods and problems. *Employee Relations*. Vol. 21, No. 3.

CARROLL, M., SMITH, M., OLIVER, G. and SUNG, S. (2008) Recruitment and retention in front-line services: The case of childcare. *Human Resource Management Journal*. Vol. 19, No. 1. 59–74.

CARUTH D., CARUTH, G. and PANE, S. (2009) *Staffing the contemporary organization*. Third edition. Westport, Connecticut: Praeger.

CASCIO, W. (2002) Strategies for responsible downsizing. *Academy of Management Executive*. Vol. 16, No. 3. 80–91.

CASCIO, W. (2010) Downsizing and redundancy, in A. WILKINSON, N. BACON, T. REDMAN and S. SNELL (eds.) *The Sage handbook of human resource management. London*: Sage.

CASCIO, W.F. and BOUDREAU, J. (2008) *Investing in people: The financial impact of human resource initiatives*. Upper Saddle River, New Jersey: FT/Pearson.

CASTILLA, E.J. (2005) Social networks and employee performance in a call center. *American Journal of Sociology*, Vol. 110. 1243–1283.

CHANDLER, B. and SCOTT, T. (2005) How to write a job ad. *People Management*, 24 November. 42–43.

CIPD (2002) *The guide to work life balance*. London: Chartered Institute of Personnel and Development.

CIPD (2003a) *Labour turnover: Survey report*. London: Chartered Institute of Personnel and Development.

CIPD (2003b) *Age, pensions and retirement: Attitudes and expectations. Survey Report*. London: Chartered Institute of Personnel and Development.

CIPD (2003c) *Redundancy*. London: Chartered Institute of Personnel and Development.

CIPD (2005) *Flexible working: Impact and implementation. An employer survey*. London: Chartered Institute of Personnel and Development.

CIPD (2007a) *The changing HR function: Transforming HR?* London: Chartered Institute of Personnel and Development.

CIPD (2007b) *Managing Diversity: People make the difference at work, but everyone is different*. London: Chartered Institute of Personnel and Development.

CIPD (2007c) *Diversity in business: A focus for progress*. London: Chartered Institute of Personnel and Development.

CIPD (2007d) *Employer branding: The latest fad or the future for HR?* London: Chartered Institute of Personnel and Development.

CIPD (2007e) *Recruitment, retention and turnover*. London: Chartered Institute of Personnel and Development.

CIPD (2007f) *Managing age: A guide to good practice*. CIPD and TUC. Middlesex University and the Centre for Research into the Older Workforce (CROW).

CIPD (2009a) *Employer branding: Maintaining momentum in a recession*. London: Chartered Institute of Personnel and Development.

CIPD (2009b) *Recruitment, retention and turnover: Annual survey report*. London: Chartered Institute of Personnel and Development.

CLAKE, R. (2007) How to make flexible working work. *People Management*. 11 January. 48–9.

CLARKE, E. (2007) Safety in numbers. *People Management*. 11 January. 44–46.

CLEMENTS-CROOME, D (ed.) (2000) *Creating the productive workplace*. London: E & FN Spon.

CLIFTON, R. (2009) *Brands and branding*. Second Edition. London, *The Economist*: Profile Books.

COATS, D. (2009) Changing labour markets and the future of work, in J. STOREY, P. WRIGHT and D. ULRICH (eds.) *The Routledge companion to human resource management*. London: Routledge.

COHN, J., KHRANA, R. and REEVES, L. (2008) Growing talent as if your business depended on it, in *Harvard business review on talent management*. Cambridge, Massachusetts: HBS Press.

COLLING, T. (2000) Personnel management in the extended organization, in S. BACH and K. SISSON (eds.) *Personnel management: A comprehensive guide to theory and practice*. Third Edition. Oxford: Blackwell.

COLLING, T. (2005) Managing human resources in the networked organisation, in S. BACH (ed.) *Managing human resources: Personnel management in transition*. Fourth edition. Oxford: Blackwell.

COLLINS, D. (2000) *Management fads and buzzwords: Critical-practical perspectives*. London: Routledge.

COLLINS, C.J. and HAN, J. (2004) Exploring applicant pool quantity and quality: The effects of early recruitment practice strategies, corporate advertising and firm reputation. *Personnel Psychology*. Vol. 57. 685–717.

CONFEDERATION OF BRITISH INDUSTRY (2000) *Cutting through red tape: The impact of employment legislation*. London: CBI.

CONWAY, N. and BRINER, R. (2005) *Understanding psychological contracts at work*. Oxford: Oxford University Press.

COOK, M. (2004) *Personnel selection: Adding value through people*. Fourth edition. Chichester: John Wiley.

COOK, M. and CRIPPS, B. (2005) *Psychological assessment in the workplace: A manager's guide*. Chichester: John Wiley.

COOPER, D. and ROBERTSON, I. (1995) The psychology of personnel selection. London: Routledge.

COOPER, D., ROBERTSON, I. and TINLINE, G. (2003) *Recruitment and selection: A framework for success*. London: Thomson.

CORBY, S. (2000) Unfair dismissal disputes: A comparative study of Great Britain and New Zealand. *Human Resource Management Journal*. Vol. 10, No. 1. 79–92.

CORDERY, J. and PARKER, S.K. (2007) Work organisation, in P. BOXALL, J. PURCELL and P. WRIGHT (eds.) *The Oxford handbook of human resource management*. Oxford: Oxford University Press.

COTTEE, P. (2006) Change of heart. *People Management*. 10 August. 42–44.

COURTIS, J. (1989) *Recruiting for profit*. London: IPM.

CZERNY, A. (2004) The fast track broadens. *People Management*. 2 September.

CZERNY, A. (2005) Double trouble. *People Management*. 24 February. 14–15.

DALZIEL, M.M. (2004) Competencies: The first building block of talent management, in L. BERGER and D. BERGER (eds.) *The talent management handbook: Creating organizational excellence by identifying, developing and promoting your best people*. New York: McGraw Hill.

DAVIDSON, E. (2003) A break with tradition. *People Management*. 10 July. 38–40.

DAVIE, M., STANKOV, L. and ROBERTS, R. (1998) Emotional intelligence: In search of an elusive construct. *Journal of Personality and Social Psychology*. Vol. 75, No. 4.

DAVIES, A.C.L. (2009) *Perspectives on labour law*. Second edition. Cambridge: Cambridge University Press

DAVIES, G. (2007) Employer branding and its influence on managers. *European Journal of Marketing*. Vol. 42, No. 5/6. 667–681.

DAVIES, P. and FREEDLAND, M. (1993) *Labour legislation and public policy*. Oxford: Clarendon Press.

DEAKIN, S. and MORRIS, G. (2009) *Labour law*. Fifth edition. Oxford: Hart Publishing.

DEAKIN, S. and WILKINSON, F. (1996) *Labour standards – essential to economic and social progress*. London: Institute of Employment Rights.

DE CUYPER, N. and DE WITTE, H. (2008) Job insecurity and employability among temporary workers: A theoretical approach based on the psychological contract, in K. NASWALL, J. HELLGREN and M. SVERKE (eds.) *The individual in the changing working life*. Cambridge: Cambridge University Press.

DEPARTMENT FOR TRADE AND INDUSTRY (2006) *Collective redundancies – Employer's duty to notify the Secretary of State. Full regulatory impact assessment.* London: DTI.

DEPARTMENT OF EMPLOYMENT (1971) *Company manpower planning.* London: HMSO.

DE VALK, P. (2003) High staff turnover means employers must give staff 'a new deal' on working arrangements and development. *People Management.* 6 November. 24.

DE WITTE, K. (1989) Recruiting and advertising, in P. HERRIOT (ed.) *Assessment and selection in organisations.* Chichester: Wiley

DEX, S. and FORTH, J. (2009) Equality and diversity at work, in W. BROWN, A. BRYSON, J. FORTH and K. WHITFIELD (eds.) *The evolution of the modern workplace.* Cambridge: Cambridge University Press.

DIPBOYE, R.L., GAUGLER, B.B., HAYES, T.L. and PARKER, D. (2001) The validity of unstructured panel interviews: More than meets the eye. *Journal of Business and Psychology.* Vol. 16, No. 1. 35–49.

DOBBIN, F. (2009) *Inventing equal opportunity.* Princeton: Princeton University Press.

DOBSON, P. (1989) Reference reports, in P. HERRIOT (ed.) *Handbook of assessment in organisations.* Chichester: John Wiley.

DOLTON, P. and KIDD, M. (1991) *Job changes, occupational mobility and human capital acquisition.* Mimeo University of Newcastle.

DOTY, D.H., GLICK, W.H. and HUBER, G.P. (1993) Fit, equifinality and organizational effectiveness: A test of two configurational theories. *Academy of Management Journal.* Vol. 36. 1196–1250.

DOUGLAS PHILLIPS, J. (1990) The price tag on turnover. *Personnel Journal.* December.

DOW, J. (2003) Spa attraction. *People Management.* 29 May.

DOWNS, S. (1989) Job sample and trainability tests, in P. HERRIOT (ed.) *Handbook of assessment in organisations.* Chichester: John Wiley.

DRAKELEY, R. (1989) Biographical data, in P. HERRIOT (ed.) *Handbook of assessment in organisations.* Chichester: John Wiley.

DU GAY, P. (1996) *Consumption and identity at work.* London: Sage.

DUGGAN, M. (1999) *Unfair dismissal: Law, practice and guidance.* Welwyn Garden City: CLT Professional Publishing.

DULEWICZ, V. (2004) Give full details. *People Management.* 26 February. 23.

DU PLESSIS, D. (2003) Contemporary issues in recruitment and selection, in R. WEISNER and B. MILLETT (eds.) *Human resource management: Challenges and future directions.* Sydney: Wiley.

DYER, L. and ERICKSON, J. (2007) Dynamic organizations: achieving marketplace agility through workforce scalability, in J. STOREY (ed.) *Human resource management: A critical text.* Third edition. London: Thomson.

ECONOMIST (2000) Labours lost. *The Economist.* 13 July.

ECONOMIST (2009) A slow burning fuse: A special report on ageing populations. *The Economist.* 27 June.

EDENBOROUGH, R. (2005) *Assessment methods in recruitment, selection and performance.* London: Kogan Page.

EDER, R. and FERRIS, G. (eds.) (1989) *The employment interview: Theory, research and practice.* Newbury Park, California: Sage.

EDWARDS, C. (2005) Remote control. *People Management.* 16 June. 30–32.

EDWARDS, C. (2006) Raised stakes. *People Management.* 9 March. 24–27

EDWARDS, J. (1983) Models of manpower stocks and flows, in J. EDWARDS *et al* (eds.) *Manpower planning: Strategy and techniques in an organisational context.* Chichester: John Wiley.

EDWARDS, M.R. (2005) Employer and employee branding: HR or PR? in S. BACH (ed.) *Managing human resources: Personnel management in transition.* Fourth edition. Oxford: Blackwell Publishing.

EDWARDS, C.Y. and ROBINSON, O. (2001) Better part-time jobs? A study of part-time working in nursing and the police. *Employee Relations*. Vol. 23, No. 5.

EIKHOF, D.R., WARHYURST, C. and HAUNSCHILD, A. (2007) What work? What life? What balance?: Critical reflections on the work-life balance debate. *Employee Relations*. Vol. 29, No. 4. 325–333.

ELIAS, P. (1994) *Job-related training, trade union membership and labour mobility: A longitudinal study*. Oxford Economic Papers. No. 46.

EMPLOYMENT TRIBUNAL SERVICE (2009) *Annual report and accounts*. London: HMSO.

EUROPEAN COMMISSION (2000) *The future of work*. London: Kogan Page.

EVANS, R. (2006) Variety performance. *People Management*. 23 November. 26–30.

EVANS, R. (2007) Telly vision. *People Management*. 22 March. 24–29.

EVANS, T. (2008) *Australian employers are losing $20 billion a year as staff turnover increases dramatically*. Australian Human Resources Institute. 1 March.

FAIR, H. (1992) *Personnel and profit: The pay-off from people*. London: CIPD.

FEINBERG, R.A. and JEPPESON, N. (2000) The validity of exit interviews. *Journal of Retailing and Consumer Services*. Vol. 7, No. 3.

FERGUSON, R. and BROHAUGH, B. (2009) The talent wars. *Journal of Consumer Marketing*. Vol. 26, No. 5. 358–362.

FERNIE, S. and METCALF, D. (1996) Participation, contingent pay, representation & workplace performance: Evidence from Great Britain. Discussion Paper 232. Centre for Economic Performance, London School of Economics.

FIELD, S., OLSEN, C. and WILLIAMS, R. (2009) The pensions revolution, in S. CORBY, S. PALMER and E. LINDOP (eds.) *Rethinking reward*. Basingstoke: Palgrave.

FIELDS, M. (2001) *Indispensable employees*. Franklin Lakes, New Jersey: Career Press.

FINDLAY, J. (2003) Cockroaches of human resource practice? Exit interviews and knowledge management. *Business Information Review*. Vol. 20, No. 3.

FINE, S. and GETKATE, M. (1995) *Benchmark tasks for job analysis*. New Jersey: Lawrence Erlbaum.

FINLAY, W. and COVERDILL, J.E. (2002) *Headhunters: Matchmaking in the labor Market*. Cornell: Cornell University Press.

FLEETWOOD, S. (2007) Why work-life balance now? *International Journal of Human Resource Management*. Vol. 18, No. 3. 387–400.

FLOOD, P., GANNON, M. and PAAUWE, J. (1996) *Managing without traditional methods: International innovations in human resource management*. Wokingham: Addison Wesley.

FORDE, C. and SLATER, C. (2005) Agency working in Britain. Causes, character and consequences. *British Journal of Industrial Relations* Vol. 43, No. 2. 249–271.

FOSTER, C. and HARRIS, L. (2005) Easy to say, difficult to do: Diversity management in retail. *Human Resource Management Journal*. Vol. 15, No. 3. 4–17.

FOWLER, A. (1996) *Employee induction: A good start*. Third edition. London: CIPD.

FOWLER, A. (1999) *Managing redundancy*. London: IPD

FOX, R.M. (2009) Indian air hostesses were sacked for being overweight – could it happen in the UK? *People Management*. 30 January.

FREEMAN, R.B. and MEDOFF, J.L. (1984) *What do unions do?* New York: Basic Books.

FRIED, Y, CUMMINGS, A. and OLDHAM, G.R. (1998) Job design, in M. POOLE and M. WARNER (eds.) *The handbook of human resource management*. London: Thomson Business Press.

FULLER, S.R. and HUBER, V. (1998) Recruitment and selection, in M. POOLE and M. WARNER (eds.) *The handbook of human resource management*. London: Thomson Business Press.

FURNHAM, A. (2001) Catharsis with your cards: Exit interviews with departing employees help companies to learn about themselves. *Financial Times*. 28 August.

FURNHAM, A. (2005) *The psychology of behaviour at work*. Hove: The Psychology Press.

FURNHAM, A. and PETRIDES, K.V. (2006) Deciding on promotions and redundancies. *Journal of Managerial Psychology*. Vol. 21, No. 1. 6–18.

GALLAGER, D. (2008) Contingent work arrangements, in P. BLYTON, N. BACON, J. FIORITO and E. HEERY (eds.) *The Sage handbook of industrial relations*. London: Sage.

GAMBLES, R., LEWIS, S. and RAPOPORT, R. (2006) *The myth of the work-life balance. The challenge of our time for men, women and societies*. Chichester: John Wiley & Sons.

GAN, M. and KLEINER, B.H. (2005) How to write job descriptions effectively. *Management Research News*, Vol. 28, No. 8. 48–54.

GIACALONE, R.A. (1989) The exit interview: Changing your expectations. *Supervision Magazine*.

GIACALONE, R.A. and DUHON, D. (1991) Assessing intended employee behaviour in exit interviews. *Journal of Psychology*. Vol. 125, No. 1.

GIACALONE, R.A. and KNOUSE, S.B. (1989) Farewell to the fruitless exit interview. *Personnel*. Vol. 66, No. 9.

GIACALONE, R.A., KNOUSE, S.B. and POLLARD, H.G. (1999) Willingness to report unethical behaviour in exit surveys. *Teaching Business Ethics*. Vol. 3, No. 4.

GLEBBEEK, A. and BAX, E. (2004) Is high employee turnover really harmful? An empirical test using company records. *Academy of Management Journal*. Vol. 47, No. 2. 277–286.

GOODWORTH, C. (1979) Effective interviewing for employment selection. London: Hutchinson.

GOLEMAN, D. (1998) *Working with emotional intelligence*. London: Bloomsbury.

GRACE, E. (2002) How to avoid unfair dismissal claims. *People Management*. 7 February.

GRATTON, L. (2004) Feel the burnout. *People Management*. 15 July.

GRAVES, L. and POWELL, G. (2008) Sex and race discrimination in personnel decisions, in S. CARTWRIGHT and C. COOPER (eds.) *The Oxford handbook of personnel psychology*. Oxford: Oxford University Press.

GREEN, F., FELSTEAD, A., MAYHEW, K. and PACK, A. (2000) The impact of training on labour mobility: Individual and firm-level evidence from Britain. *British Journal of Industrial Relations*. Vol. 38, No. 2.

GREENE, A.M. (2010) HRM and equal opportunities, in A. WILKINSON, N. BACON, T., REDMAN and S. SNELL (eds.) *The Sage handbook of human resource management*. London: Sage.

GREENFIELD, S. (2003) Flexible futures. *People Management*. 23 October. 52–53.

GREENHALGH, C. and MAVOTAS, G. (1996) Job training, new technology and labour turnover. *British Journal of Industrial Relations*. Vol. 34, No. 1.

GREGG, P. and WADSWORTH, J. (1999) Job tenure 1975–98, in P. GREGG and J. WADSWORTH (eds.) *The state of working Britain*. Manchester: Manchester University Press.

GRIFFETH, R.W. and HOM, P.W. (2001) *Retaining valued employees*. Thousand Oaks, California: Sage.

GRIFFITHS, A. (2007) Healthy work for older workers: Work design and management factors, in W. LORETTO, S. VICKERSTAFF and P. WHITE (eds.) *The future of older workers: New perspectives*. Bristol: The Policy Press.

GRIFFITHS, J. (2006) Masculine wiles. *People Management*, 27 October. 20–21.

GUEST, D. (2000) Human resource management, employee well-being and organisational performance. Paper given at the CIPD Professional Standards Conference, University of Warwick.

GUEST, D. (2007) Human resource management and the worker: Towards a new psychological contract, in P. BOXALL, J. PURCELL and P. WRIGHT (eds.) *The Oxford handbook of human resource management*. Oxford: Oxford University Press.

GUEST, D. and CONWAY, N. (2002) Communicating the psychological contract: An employer perspective. *Human Resource Management Journal*. Vol. 12, No. 2. 22–38.

HACKMAN, J.R. and OLDHAM, G.R. (1980) *Work redesign*. Reading, Massachusetts: Addison-Wesley.

HALL, L. and ATKINSON, C. (2006) Improving working lives: Flexible working and the role of employee control. *Employee Relations*. Vol. 28, No. 4. 374–386.

HANDY, C. (1989) *The age of unreason*. London: Business Books.

HANDY, C. (2001) *The elephant and the flea: Looking backwards to the future*. London: Hutchinson.

HARRY, W. (2007) East is east. *People Management*. 29 November. 36–38.

HEALTH SERVICE REPORT (2001) *Recruitment, retention and return in the NHS still an uphill climb*. Health Service Report. Summer.

HEDING, T., KNUDTZEN, C.F. and BJERRE, M. (2009) *Brand management: Research, theory and practice*. Abingdon: Routledge.

HEERY, E. and SALMON, J. (eds.) (2000) *The insecure workforce*. London: Routledge

HENEMAN, H. and JUDGE, T. (2005) *Staffing organizations*. Fifth edition. Boston, Mass: Irwin McGraw-Hill.

HENEMAN, H., JUDGE, T. and HENEMAN, R. (2000) *Staffing organizations*. Boston, Mass: Irwin McGraw-Hill.

HERCUS, T. (1992) Human resource planning in eight British organisations: a Canadian perspective, in B. TOWERS (ed.) *The handbook of human resource management*. Oxford: Blackwell.

HERRIOT, P. (ed.) (1989a) *A handbook of assessment in organizations*. Chichester: John Wiley.

HERRIOT, P. (ed.) (1989b) *Assessment and selection in organizations*. Chichester: John Wiley.

HERZBERG, F. (1966) *Work and the nature of man*. Cleveland: World Publishing.

HERZBERG, F. (1968) One more time: How do you motivate employees? *Harvard Business Review*. January–February.

HIERONIMUS, F., SCHAEFER, K. and SCHRODER, J. (2005) Using branding to attract talent. *The McKinsey Quarterly*. 28 September.

HIGGS, M. (2003) Good call. *People Management*. 23 January. 48–49.

HIGGS, M. (2004) Future trends in HRM, in D. REES and R. McBAIN (eds.) *People management: Challenges and opportunities*. Basingstoke: Palgrave Macmillan.

HILL, J. and MAYCOCK, A. (1990) *The design of recruitment advertising featuring questions which have a thematic content*. Paper presented to the British Psychological Society Conference.

HILTROP, J M. (1999) The quest for the best: Human resource practices to attract and retain. *European Management Journal*. Vol. 17, No. 4.

HINRICHS, J.R. (1971) Employees coming and going. *Personnel*. Vol. 48. 30–35.

HIRSCH, D. (2007) Sustaining working lives: The challenge of retention, in W. LORETTO, S. VICKERSTAFF and P. WHITE (eds.) *The future of older workers: New perspectives*. Bristol: The Policy Press.

HIRSCH, M.S. and GLANZ, E. (2006) Tomorrow's world of recruitment. *People Management*. 18 May. 48.

HIRSCHKORN, J. (2004) Research and employ. *People Management*. 15 January.

HIRSH, W. (2000) Succession planning demystified. *IES Report*. No. 372. Brighton: Institute for Employment Studies.

HIRSH, W., POLLARD, E. and TAMKIN, P. (2000) *Free fair and efficient? Open internal job advertising*. Brighton: Institute of Employment Studies.

HISLOP, D. (2009) *Knowledge management in organisations: A critical introduction*. Second edition. Oxford: Oxford University Press.

HODGE, N. (2009) Viva la visa. *Financial Management*. November/December. 12–16.

HOFSTEDE, G. (1980) *Culture's consequences: International differences in work-related values*. Beverley Hills, California: Sage.

HOFSTEDE, G. and HOFSTEDE, G.F. (2005) *Culture and organisations: Software for the mind*. Second edition. London: McGraw-Hill

HOLBECHE, L. (1999) *Aligning human resources and business strategy*. London: Butterworth Heinemann.

HOM, P. and GRIFFETH, R. (1995) *Employee turnover*. Cincinnati: South Western College Publishing.

HOPE, K. (2005) Scots Missed. *People Management*. 13 October. 16–17.

HOUSE, G. (2007) The changing world of employment brands and HR, in CIPD (ed.) *Employer branding: The latest fad or the future for HR?* London: CIPD.

HOUSE, R., HANGES, P., JAVIDAN, M., DORFMAN, P. and GUPTA, V. (2004) *Culture, leadership and organisations: The GLOBE Study of 62 Societies*. Thousand Oaks: California, Sage

HUSELID, M. (1995) The impact of human resource practices on turnover, productivity and corporate financial performance. *Academy of Management Journal*. Vol. 38, No. 3. 635–672.

HUSELID, M., BEATTY, R. and BECKER, B. (2005) A players or A positions. *Harvard Business Review*. December. 110–117.

IDS (1994) Graduates. *IDS Focus*, 71. August. London: Incomes Data Services.

IDS (1995a) The jobs mythology. *IDS Focus*. No. 74. March. London: Incomes Data Services.

IDS (1995b) Assessment centres. *IDS Study*. No. 569. January. London: Incomes Data Services.

IDS (1995c) Managing labour turnover. *IDS Study*. No. 577. May. London: Incomes Data Services.

IDS (1996) Older workers. *IDS Study*. No. 595. February. London: Incomes Data Services.

IDS (1998) Business partnerships with schools. *IDS Study*. No. 658. November. London: Incomes Data Services.

IDS (1999) The changing shape of personnel management. *IDS Focus*. No. 90. Summer.

IDS (2000a) Outsourcing HR administration. *IDS Study*. No. 700. December. London: Incomes Data Services.

IDS (2000b) Work-life balance. *IDS Study*. No. 698 (November). London: Incomes Data Services.

IDS (2001) Managing redundancy. *IDS Study Plus*. Autumn. London: Incomes Data Services.

IDS (2002) Assessment Centres. *IDS Study*. No. 735. September. London: Incomes Data Services.

IDS (2005a) Homeworking. *IDS Study*. No. 793, March. London: Incomes Data Services.

IDS (2005b) Employer branding. *IDS Study*. No. 809. November. London: Incomes Data Services.

IDS (2005c) Unfair dismissal. *Employment law handbook*. London: Incomes Data Services.

IDS (2006) Age discrimination. *Employment Law Supplement*. London: Incomes Data Services.

IDS (2007) Managing redundancy. *IDS HR Studies Plus*. No. 860. December. London: Incomes Data Services.

IDS (2008a) Employer branding. *IDS Study*. No. 872. June. London: Incomes Data Services.

IDS (2008b) Improving staff retention. *HR Studies*. No 863. London: Incomes Data Services.

IDS (2008c) Redundancy. *Employment law handbook*. London: Incomes Data Services.

IDS (2009) *Contracts of Employment*. London: Incomes Data Services.

IFF Research (1993) Skills needs in Britain 1993. *Annual survey produced for the DFEE*. London: IFF Research.

ILES, P. (2007) Employee resourcing and talent management, in J. STOREY (ed.) *Human resource management: A critical text*. Third edition. London: Thomson.

ILES, P. and ROBERTSON, I. (1989) The impact of selection procedures on candidates in P. HERRIOT (ed.) *Assessment and selection in organisations*. Chichester: Wiley.

ILES, P. and SALAMAN, G. (1995) Recruitment, selection and assessment, in J. STOREY (ed.) *Human resource management: A critical text*. London: Routledge.

INSTITUTE OF EMPLOYMENT RIGHTS (2000) *Social justice and economic efficiency*. London: Institute of Employment Rights.

IRS (1990) Biodata. *Recruitment and Development Report*. No. 1. January. London: Industrial Relations Services.

IRS (1997) The state of selection: An IRS survey. *Employee Development Bulletin*. No. 85. January. London: Industrial Relations Services.

IRS (1999) The business of selection: An IRS survey. *Employee Development Bulletin*. No. 117. November. London: Industrial Relations Services.

IRS (2000) Emotional intelligence – mind games for the future of work. *Employee Development Bulletin*. No. 122. January. London: Industrial Relations Services.

IRS (2001a) Putting on a brave face. *Employment Review*. No. 738. October. London: Industrial Relations Services.

IRS (2001b) All aboard the online express. *Employee Development Bulletin*. No. 134. February. London: Industrial Relations Services.

IRS (2001c) Think local: Using job centres for recruitment. *Employee Development Bulletin*. No. 139. July. London: Industrial Relations Services.

IRS (2001d) Screen test. *Employee Development Bulletin*. No. 140. August. London: Industrial Relations Services.

IRS (2001e) Checking out new recruits. *Employee Development Bulletin*. No. 135. March. London: Industrial Relations Services.

IRS (2002a) Internal applicants – handle with care. *Employment Review*. No. 748. 35–38. London: Industrial Relations Services.

IRS (2002b) I've got your number: Telephone interviewing. *Employment Review*. No. 756. 34–36. London: Industrial Relations Services.

IRS (2002c) Don't leave us this way. *Employment Review*. No. 757. 5 August. London: Industrial Relations Services.

IRS (2003a) Setting the tone: Job descriptions and person specifications. *Employment Review*. No. 776. 42–48. London: Industrial Relations Services.

IRS (2003b) Competencies in graduate recruitment and selection. *Employment Review* 783. 44–48. London: Industrial Relations Services.

IRS (2003c) Fail to plan, plan to fail. *Employment Review*. No. 790. 42–48. London: Industrial Relations Services.

IRS (2003d) Spinning the recruitment web. *Employment Review*. No. 767. 34–40. London: Industrial Relations Services.

IRS (2003e) Induction to perfection: The start of a beautiful friendship. *Employment Review*. No. 772. London: Industrial Relations Services.

IRS (2004a) A graphic illustration: Getting the best from recruitment ads. *Employment Review*. No. 805. 42–48. London: Industrial Relations Services.

IRS (2004b) Biodata: This is your life. *Employment Review*. No. 795. 42–44. London: Industrial Relations Services.

IRS (2004c) Measuring and managing labour turnover: Part 1. *Employment Review*. No. 793. February. London: Industrial Relations Services.

IRS (2004d) Research – measuring and managing labour turnover: Part 2. *Employment Review*. No. 794. March. London: Industrial Relations Services.

IRS (2004e) Communicating bad news: Managing redundancy. *Employment Review*. No. 803. 11 17. London: Industrial Relations Services.

JACKSON, C. (1996) *Understanding psychological testing*. Leicester: British Psychological Society.

JACKSON, S.E. and SCHULER, R.S. (1990) Human resource planning: Challenges for industrial/ organisational psychologists. *American Psychologist*. Vol. 45. Reprinted in G R FERRIS and M.R. BUCKLEY (1996) (eds.) *Human resources management: perspectives, context, functions and outcomes*. Third edition. Englewood Cliffs. New Jersey: Prentice Hall.

JANSEN, P. and DE JONGH, F. (1997) *Assessment centres: A practical handbook*. Chichester: John Wiley.

JENKINS, J. (1983) Management trainees in retailing, in B. UNGERSON (ed.) *Recruitment handbook*. Aldershot: Gower.

JENN, N.G. (2005) *Headhunters and how to use them*. London: *The Economist*/Profile Books.

JENNER, S. and TAYLOR, S. (2000) *Recruiting, developing and retaining graduate talent*. London: FT/ Prentice Hall.

JOHNSON, G. and BROWN, J. (2004) Workforce planning not a common practice, IPMA-HR study finds. *Public Personnel Management*, Vol. 33.4, 379–388.

JOHNSON, P. (2009) HRM in changing organizational contexts, in D. COLLINGS and G. WOOD (eds.) *Human resource management: A critical approach*. London: Routledge.

JOHNSON, R. (2001) Escape from the past. *People Management*. 11 January.

JOHNSON, R. (2007) Sharing the load. *People Management*. 9 August. 40–42.

JOHNSON, R. (2007) An idea past its sell-by date? *People Management*. 1 November. 26–39.

KACMAR, M., ANDREWS, M., VAN ROOY, D., STEILBERG, C. and CERRONE, S. (2006) Sure everyone can be replaced … but at what cost? Turnover as a predictor of unit-level performance. *Academy of Management Journal*. Vol. 49, No. 1. 133–144.

KAKABADSE, A. and KAKABADSE, N. (2002) *Smart sourcing: International best practice*. Basingstoke: Palgrave.

KANDOLA, B. (2009) Under the skin. *People Management*. 30 July. 26–28.

KANDOLA, B., STAIRS, M. and SANDFORD-SMITH, R. (2000) Slim picking. *People Management*. 28 December.

KELLY, C. (2009) UK enjoying biggest baby boom in history statistics show. *Immigration Matters*. www.immigrationmatters.co.uk.

KERSLEY, B., ALPIN, C., FORTH, J., BRYSON, A., BEWLEY, H, DIX, G. and OXENBRIDGE, S. (2006) *Inside the workplace: Findings from the 2004 Workplace Employment Relations Survey*. Abingdon: Routledge.

KETTLEY, P. and KERRIN, M. (2003) *E-recruitment: Is it delivering?* Brighton: Institute of Employment Studies.

KINNIE, N. and SWART, J. (2006) The alchemists. *People Management*. 6 April. 42–45.

KIRNAN, J., FARLEY, J. and GEISINGER, K. (1989) The relationship between recruiting source, applicant quality and hire performance: An analysis by sex, ethnicity and age. *Personnel Psychology*. Vol. 42.

KIRTON, B. and Greene, A-M. (2010) *The dynamics of managing diversity: A critical approach*. Third edition. London. Butterworth-Heinemann.

KISPAL-VITAI, Z. and WOOD, G. (2009) HR planning, in D. COLLINGS and G. WOOD (eds.) *Human resource management: A critical approach*. London: Routledge.

KLEIN, N. (2000) *No logo: No space, no choice, no jobs, taking aim at the brand bullies*. London: Flamingo.

KNIGHT, K.G. and LATREILLE, P.L. (2000) Discipline, dismissals and complaints to industrial tribunals. *British Journal of Industrial Relations*. Vol. 38, No. 4. 533.

KODZ, J., HARPER, H. and DENCH, S. (2002) Work-life balance: Beyond the rhetoric. *Institute for Employment Studies Report*. No. 384. Brighton: IES.

KOSSEK, E.E. and PICHLER, S. (2007) EEO and the management of diversity, in P. BOXALL, J. PURCELL and P. WRIGHT (eds.) *The Oxford handbook of human resource management*. Oxford: Oxford University Press

LABOUR MARKET TRENDS (2002) Labour market spotlight. *Labour Market Trends*. August.

LAHEY, K., KIM, D. and NEWMAN, M. (2006) Full retirement? An examination of factors that influence the decision to return to work. *Financial Services Review*. Vol. 15, No. 1. 1–19.

LAMB, J. (2000) Move to online tests threatens quality of recruitment process. *People Management*. 20 July.

LARKAN, K. (2007) The talent war: How to find and retain the best people for your company. London: *The Times*.

LAROCHE, L. and RUTHERFORD, D. (2007) *Recruiting, retaining and promoting culturally different employees*. London: Elsevier.

LAUDON, K. and STARBUCK, W. (1997) Organizational information and knowledge, in A. SORGE and M. WARNER (eds.) *The IEBM handbook of organizational behaviour*. London: Thomson Learning.

LAWLER, E. (2008) Why are we losing all our good people? *Harvard Business Review*. Vol. 86, No. 6. June. 41–51.

LEA, R. (2001) *The work-life balance and all that: The re-regulation of the labour market*. London: Institute of Directors.

LEAMAN, A. and BORDASS, B. (2000) Productivity in buildings: The 'killer' variables, in D. CLEMENTS-CROOME (ed.) *Creating the Productive Workplace*. London: E & FN Spon.

LEE, T. and MITCHELL, T. (1994) An alternative approach: the unfolding model of employee turnover. *Academy of Management Review*. Vol. 19, No. 1.

LEE, T., MITCHELL, T., HALTON, B., McDANIEL, L. and HILL, J. (1999) The unfolding model of voluntary turnover: A replication and extension. *Academy of Management Journal*. Vol. 42, No. 4.

LEFOWITZ, J. and KATZ, M.L. (1969) Validity of exit interviews. *Personnel Psychology*. Vol. 22.

LEITCH, S. (2006) *Prosperity for all in the global economy – world class skills. The Final Report of the Leitch Review of Skills*. London: HM Treasury.

LENGNICK-HALL, C. and LENGNICK-HALL, M. (1988) Strategic human resource management: A review of the literature and a proposed typology. *Academy of Management Review*. Vol. 13, No. 3. 454–470.

LEVIN, R. and ROSSE, J. (2001) *Talent flow: A strategic approach to keeping good employees, helping them grow and letting them go*. San Francisco: Jossey Bass.

LEWIS, D. and SARGEANT, M. (2009) *Essentials of employment law*. Tenth edition. London: CIPD.

LEWIS, P. (1993) *The successful management of redundancy*. Oxford: Blackwell.

LEWIS, R.D. (1996) *When cultures collide: Managing successfully across cultures*. London: Nicholas Brealey.

LEWIS, S. and ROPER, I. (2008) Flexible working arrangements: From work-life to gender equality policies, in S. CARTWRIGHT and C. COOPER (eds.) *The Oxford handbook of personnel psychology*. Oxford: Oxford University Press.

LIEVENS, F. (2007) Employer branding in the Belgian army: The importance of instrumental and symbolic beliefs for potential applicants and military employees. *Human Resources Management*. Vol. 46, No. 1. 51–69.

LIEVENS, F. and CHAPMAN, D. (2010) Recruitment and selection, in A. WILKINSON, N. BACON, T. REDMAN and S. SNELL (eds.) *The Sage handbook of human resource management*. London: Sage.

LIEVENS, F., VAN HOYE, G. and ANSEEL, F. (2007) Organizational identity and employer image. Towards a unifying framework. *British Journal of Management*. No. 18. s45–59.

LIFF, S. (2000) Manpower or human resource planning – What's in a name? in S. BACH and K. SISSON (eds.) *Personnel management; A comprehensive guide to theory and practice*. Third edition. Oxford: Blackwell.

LINDSAY, C. and McCAULAY, C. (2004) Growth in self-employment in the UK. *Labour Market Trends*. October 2004. 399–404.

LOCKTON, D. (2008) *Employment law*. Sixth edition. London: Macmillan.

LOCKYER, C. and SCHOLARIOS, D. (2004) Selecting hotel staff: Why best practice does not always work. *International Journal of Contemporary Hospitality Management*. Vol. 16, No. 2. 125–135.

LONG, P. (1981) *Retirement: Planned liberation?* London: IPM.

LONGHI, S. and PLATT, L. (2008) *Pay gaps across equality groups*. Manchester: Equality and Human Rights Commission.

LOVERIDGE, R. and MOK, A. (1979) *Theories of labour market segmentation: A critique*. The Hague: Martinus Nijhoff.

LUNN, T. (1989) In pursuit of talent. *International Journal of Hospitality Management*. 89–96.

MACAFEE, M. (2007) How to conduct exit interviews. *People Management*. 12 July. 42–43.

MAERTZ, C.P. and CAMPION, M.A. (2001) 25 years of voluntary turnover research: A review and critique, in I. ROBERTSON and C. COOPER (eds.) *Personnel psychology and HRM*. Chichester: Wiley.

MAKIN, P., COOPER, C. and COX, C. (1996) *Organizations and the psychological contract*. Leicester: BPS.

MANOCHA, R. (2002) Cut out for the role. *People Management*. 2 May.

MANOCHA, R. (2004) Bonding agents. *People Management*. 11 November.

MARCHINGTON, M. and WILKINSON, A. (2002) *People management and development: Human resource management at work*. Second edition. London: CIPD.

MARCHINGTON, M. and WILKINSON, A. (2008) *Human resource management at work*. Fourth edition. London: CIPD.

MARLOW, S. (2002) Regulating labour management in small firms. *Human Resource Management Journal*. Vol. 12, No. 3. 25–44.

MARSHALL, V. and TAYLOR, P. (2005) Restructuring the lifecourse, in M.L. JOHNSON (ed.) *The Cambridge handbook of age and ageing*. Cambridge: Cambridge University Press.

MARTIN, G. (2009) Driving corporate reputations from the inside: A strategic role and strategic dilemmas for HR? *Asia Pacific Journal of Human Resources*. Vol. 47, No. 2. 219–235.

MARTIN, G. and BEAUMONT, P. (2003) *Branding and people management: What's in a name?* London: CIPD.

MARTIN, G., BEAUMONT, P., DOIG, R. and PATE, J. (2004) Branding: A new performance discourse for HR?. *European Management Journal*. Vol. 23, No. 1. 76–88.

MARTINDALE, N. (2008) Talent management in Coca-Cola: The fizz from within. *Personnel Today*. 5 February.

McBEATH, G. (1992) *The handbook of human resource planning: Practical manpower analysis techniques for HR professionals*. Oxford: Blackwell.

McDONALD, L. (1995) *Hired, fired or sick and tired?* London: Nicholas Brearley.

McGREGOR, A. and SPROULL, A. (1992) Employers and the flexible workforce. *Employment Gazette*. May.

McORMOND, T. (2004) Changes in working trends over the past decade. *Labour Market Trends*. January. 25–35.

MEIER, K. and HICKLIN, A. (2007) Employee turnover and organizational performance: Testing a hypothesis from classical public administration. *Journal of Public Administration Research*. No. 18. 573–590.

MESTRE, M., STAINER, A. and STAINER, L. (1997) Employee orientation – the Japanese approach. *Employee Relations*. Vol. 19, No. 5. 443–458.

MICHAELS, E., HANDFIELD-JONES, H. and AXELROD, B. (2001) *The war for talent*. Boston: Harvard Business School Press.

MICKLETHWAIT, J. and WOOLDRIDGE, A. (1996) *The witch doctors*. London: Heinemann.

MICKLETHWAIT, J. and WOOLDRIDGE, A. (2000) A future perfect: The challenge and hidden promise of globalisation. London: Heinemann.

MILES, S.J. and MANGOLD, G. (2004) A conceptualization of the employee branding process. *Journal of Relationship Marketing*. Vol. 3, No. 2/3. 65–87.

MILES, R.E. and SNOW, C.C. (1978) *Organization strategy, structure and process*. New York: McGraw Hill.

MILLMORE, M. (2003) Just how extensive is the practice of strategic recruitment and selection? *Irish Journal of Management*. Vol. 24, No. 1. 87–108.

MILLMORE, M., LEWIS, P., SAUNDERS, M., THORNHILL, A. and MORROW, T. (2007) *Strategic human resource management*: Contemporary issues. Harlow: FT/Prentice Hall.

MILSOM, J. (2009) Key trends and issues in employers' use of behavioural competencies. *IRS Employment Review*. No. 918, March.

MINTZBERG, H. (1976) Planning on the left-side and managing on the right. *Harvard Business Review*. July–August.

MINTZBERG, H. (1994) *The rise and fall of strategic planning*. New York: Prentice Hall.

MOBLEY, W. (1977) Intermediate linkages in the relationship between job satisfaction and employee turnover, in R. STEERS and L. PORTER (eds.) *Motivation and work behaviour*. New York: McGraw-Hill.

MOBLEY, W. (1982) *Employee turnover: Causes, consequences and control*. Reading MA: Addison-Wesley.

MOEN, P. (2007) Not so big Jobs and retirements: What workers (and retirees) really want. *Generations*. Vol. 31, No. 1. 31–36.

MOLONEY, K. (2000) History repeating. *People Management*. 6 July.

MOLONEY, K. (2002) Lines of defence. *People Management*. 11 July.

MORAN, M. (2003) *The British regulatory state*. Oxford: Oxford University Press.

MORGESON, F.P., CAMPION, M.A., DIPBOYE, R.L. and HOLLENBECK, J.R. (2007) Reconsidering the use of personality tests in personnel selection contexts. *Personnel Psychology*. Vol. 60, No. 3. 683–730.

MORGAN, J. (2009) No ladder at Cumbria, not even for laureates. *Times Higher Education Supplement*. 17 December.

MOROKO, L. and UNCLES, M. (2008) Characteristics of successful employer brands. *Journal of Brand Management*. Vol. 16, No. 3. 160–175.

MORRELL, K., LOAN-CLARK, J. and WILKINSON, A. (2001) Unweaving leaving: The use of models in the management of employee turnover. *International Journal of Management Reviews*. Vol. 3, No. 3.

MOWDAY, R.T. (1996) Equity theory predictions of behaviour in organisations, in R. STEERS, L. PORTER and G. BIGLEY (eds.) *Motivation and leadership at work*. Sixth edition. New York: McGraw Hill.

MOYNAGH, M. and WORSLEY, R. (2005) *Working in the twenty-first century*. Leeds: ESRC/The Tomorrow Project.

MOYNAGH, M. and WORSLEY, R. (2009) *Changing lives, changing business*. London: A & C Black

MUNRO FRASER, J. (1979) *Employment interviewing*. Plymouth: MacDonald & Evans.

MURPHY, N. (2007a) Interviewers' roles, responsibilities and training. *IRS Employment Review*. No. 875. June.

MURPHY, N. (2007b) Question styles and formats of job interviewing. IRS *Employment Review* No. 875. June.

MURPHY, N. (2008a) Employers' use of job boards in online recruitment: An IRS survey. *IRS Employment Review*. No. 899. May.

MURPHY, N. (2008b) How employer branding can improve recruitment. *IRS Employment Review*. No. 903. August.

MURPHY, N (2008c) Trends in recruitment methods in 2006 & 2007 (2) Applications. IRS *Employment Review*. No. 893. March.

MURPHY, N (2008d) Trends in recruitment methods in 2006 & 2007 (2) Selection. IRS *Employment Review*. No. 893. March.

MURPHY, N. (2009a) Survey: Succession planning in practice. *IRS Employment Review*. No. 917. March.

MURPHY, N. (2009b) Survey: Managing the survivor syndrome during and after redundancies. *Employment Review*. No. 921. May.

NATIONAL STATISTICS (2006) *Labour market review*. Basingstoke: Palgrave Macmillan.

NATIONAL STATISTICS (2009) Internet Access. www.statistics.gov.uk.

NATIONAL STATISTICS (2010) *Economic & Labour Market Review*, January.

NEIL, A. (1996). *Full disclosure*. London: Macmillan.

NEWELL, S. (2005) Recruitment and selection, in S. BACH (ed.) *Managing human resources: Personnel management in transition*. Fourth edition. Oxford: Blackwell.

NEWSPAPER SOCIETY (2005) *Recruitment choice: A practical guide to the recruitment advertising market*. London: The Newspaper Society.

NKOMO, S.M. (1987) Human resource planning and organization performance: An exploratory analysis. *Strategic management Journal*. Vol. 8. 387–392.

NOLAN, P. (2004) *Back to the future of work*. Leeds: ESRC.

NONAKA, I. and TAKEUCHI, H. (1995) *The knowledge creating company*. New York: Oxford University Press.

ODIORNE, G. (1984) *Strategic management of human resources*. San Francisco: Jossey Bass.

ONREC (2009) *Internet the only choice for an increasing number of jobseekers*. www.onrec.com

ONS (2009) *Pension trends*. London: Office of National Statistics.

O'REILLY, N. (1997) Promotion system too complex. *Personnel Today*. March.

ORLITZKY, M. (2007) Recruitment strategy, in P. BOXALL, J. PURCELL and P. WRIGHT (eds.) *The Oxford handbook of human resource management*. Oxford: Oxford University Press.

OSBORNE-JONES, T. (2004) Managing human talent, in D. REES and R. McBAIN (eds.) *People management: Challenge and opportunities*. Basingstoke: Palgrave.

OVERELL, S. (2006) Fast forward. *People Management*. 9 February. 26–31.

PARKER, S. and OHLY, S. (2010) Extending the reach of job design theory: Going beyond the job characteristics model, in A. WILKINSON, N. BACON, T. REDMAN and S. SNELL (eds.) *The Sage handbook of human resource management*. London: Sage

PARKER, S. and WALL, T. (1998) *Job and work design*. London: Sage.

PARRY, E. and TYSON, S. (2008) An analysis of the use and success of online recruitment methods in the UK. *Human Resource Management Journal*. Vol. 18, No. 3. 257–274.

PEARCE, F. (2009) *Peoplequake*. London: Transworld.

PEARN, M. and KANDOLA, R. (1993) *Job analysis: A manager's guide*. Second edition. London: IPM.

PFEFFER, J. (1994) *Competitive advantage through people*. Boston: Harvard University Press.

PFEFFER, J. and SUTTON, R. (2006) The real brain teaser. *People Management*. 20 April. 28–30.

PHILLIPS, L. (2007) Games of skill. *People Management*. 31 May. 24–29.

PICKARD, J. (2001) When push comes to shove. *People Management*. 22 November.

PICKARD, J. (2004) Should I stay or should I go? *People Management*. 25 March.

PICKARD, J. (2007) Spring in its step. *People Management Guide to HR Outsourcing*. February.

PICKARD, J. (2009) Heavy interest. *People Management*. 3 December. 18.

POCOCK, B. (2008) Equality at work, in P. BLYTON, N. BACON, J. FIORITO and E. HEERY (eds.) *The Sage handbook of industrial relations*. London: Sage.

POELMANS, S., CHINCILLA, N. and CARDONA, P. (2003) The adoption of family-friendly HRM policies: Competing for scarce resources in the labour market. *International Journal of Manpower*. Vol. 24, No. 2. 128–147.

POLLERT, A. (1987) The flexible firm: A model in search of a reality (or a policy in search of a practice?). *Warwick Papers in Industrial Relations*. No. 19. University of Warwick.

POLLERT, A. (1988) The flexible firm: Fixation or fact? *Work, Employment and Society*. 2 March.

POLLOCK, L. and COOPER, C. (2000) Teenage picks. *People Management*. 24 August.

PORTER, M. (1985) *Competitive advantage: Creating and sustaining superior performance*. New York: Free Press.

PRICE, J. and MUELLER, C. (1986) *Absenteeism and turnover of hospital employees*. Greenwich, Connecticut: JAI Press.

PURCELL, J. (1989) The impact of corporate strategy on human resource management, in J. STOREY (ed.) *New perspectives on human resource management*. London: Routledge.

PWC (2007) *Managing tomorrow's people: The future of work to 2020*. London: PriceWaterhouseCoopers.

RANKIN, N. (2006) Welcome stranger: Employers' induction arrangements today. *IRS Employment Review*. No. 849. June.

RANKIN, N. (2008a) The IRS graduate recruitment survey 2008/9. *IRS Employment Review*. No. 907. 20 October.

RANKIN, N. (2008b) Survey: Competencies in the workplace. *IRS Employment Review*. 6 October.

RANKIN, N. (2008c) How self-selection can improve recruitment and retention. *IRS Employment Review*. No. 889. 21 January.

RANKIN, N. (2008d) The drivers of staff retention and employee engagement. *IRS Employment Review*. No. 901. July.

RANKIN (2008e) Survey: Getting the most out of age discrimination and equalities law. *Employment Review*. No. 908. November.

RANKIN, N. (2009) Labour turnover rates and costs in the UK in 2008. *IRS Employment Review*. No. 920. May.

REDMAN, T. and WILKINSON, A. (2009) Downsizing, in T. REDMAN and A. WILKINSON (eds.) *Contemporary human resource management: Text and cases*. Third edition. London: FT/Prentice Hall.

REED, A. (2001) *Innovation in human resource management: Tooling up for the talent wars*. London: CIPD.

REILLY, P. (1996) *Human resource planning: An introduction*. Brighton: Institute for Employment Studies.

REILLY, P. (2001) *Flexibility at work*. Aldershot: Gower.

REYNOLDS, P. and BAILEY, M. (1993) *How to design and deliver retirement training*. London: Kogan Page.

REYNOLDS, D.H. and WEINER, J.A. (2009) *Online recruiting and selection*. Chichester: Wiley-Blackwell.

RIDDOCH, V. (2007) Safety net, in *The People Management guide to assessment*. October. 21–24.

RITZER, G. (1996) *The McDonaldization of society: An investigation into the changing character of contemporary social life*. Revised edition. Thousand Oaks, California: Pine Forge.

ROBERTS, G. (2000) *Recruitment and selection: A competency approach*. Second edition. London: CIPD.

ROBERTS, Z. (2001) United Biscuits to halve costs by recruiting online. *People Management*. 30 August.

ROBERTS, Z. (2004) Lords call for unfair dismissal review. *People Management*. 29 July.

ROBERTSON, I. (2001) Undue diligence. *People Management*. 22nd November.

ROBERTSON, I. and MAKIN, P. (1986) Management selection in Britain: A survey and critique. *Journal of Occupational Psychology*. Vol. 61.

ROTHWELL, J. (2000) How to break the news of redundancies. *People Management*. 23 November.

ROTHWELL, S. (1995) Human resource planning, in J. STOREY (ed.) *Human resource management: A critical text*. London: Routledge.

ROTHWELL, W.J. (2005) *Effective succession planning*. Third edition. New York: Amacom.

ROUSSEAU, D. (1995) *Psychological contracts in organizations*. Thousand Oaks, California: Sage.

RYNES, S., BARBER, A. and VARMA, G. (2000) Research on the employment interview: Usefulness for practice and recommendations for future research, in C. COOPER and E. LOCKE (eds.) *Industrial and organizational psychology*. Oxford: Blackwell.

SAKO, M. (2006) Outsourcing and offshoring: Implications for productivity of business services. *Oxford Review of Economic Policy*. Vol. 22, No. 4. 499–512.

SALAMAN, G. (2007) Managers' knowledge and the management of change, in J. STOREY (ed.) *Human resource management: A critical text*. Third edition. London: Thomson.

SALGADO, J.F. (2001) Personnel selection methods, in I. ROBERTSON and C. COOPER (eds.) *Personnel psychology and HRM*. Chichester: Wiley.

SALOVEY, P. and MAYER, J. (1989) Emotional intelligence. *Imagination, Cognition and Personality*. Vol. 9, No. 3.

SAMBROOK, S. (2005) Exploring succession planning in small, growing firms. *Journal of Small Business and Enterprise Development*. Vol. 12, No. 4. 579–594.

SAMUAL, P. (1969) *Labour turnover: Towards a solution*. Institute of Personnel Management.

SCARBROUGH, H., SWAN, J. and PRESTON, J. (1999) *Knowledge management: A literature review*. London: IPD.

SCHEIN, E. (1980) *Organizational psychology*. Englewood Cliffs: Prentice Hall.

SCHMITT, N. and CHAN, D. (1998) *Personnel selection: A theoretical approach*. Thousand Oaks, California: Sage.

SCHREYER, R. and McCARTER, J. (1998) *The employer's guide to recruiting on the internet*. Manassas Park, Virginia: Impact Publications.

SCHULER, R.S. and JACKSON, S.E. (1987) Linking competitive strategies with human resource management. *Academy of Management Executive*. Vol. 1, No. 3. 207–219.

SCHULER, R.S. and JACKSON, S.E. (2007) *Strategic human resource management*. Second Edition. Oxford: Blackwell.

SCHUYLER, M. (2006) Using workforce analytics to make strategic talent decisions, in R.P. GANDOSSY, E. TUCKER and N. VERMA (eds.) *Workforce wake-up call*. Hoboken, New Jersey: John Wiley & Sons.

SEARLE, R.H. (2003) *Selection & recruitment: A critical text*. Milton Keynes: The Open University/ Palgrave.

SENEVIRATNA, C. (2001) Dependant's day. *People Management*. 6 December. 38–40.

SHACKLETON, J.R. (2005) Regulating the labour market in P. BOOTH (ed.) *Towards a liberal utopia?* London: Institute of Economic Affairs. 128–143.

SHEA, G.F. (1985) Induction and orientation, in W.R. TRACEY (ed.) *Human resources management and development handbook*. New York: AMACOM.

SIDDIQUE, C.M. (2004) Job analysis: A strategic human resource management practice. *International Journal of Human Resource Management*. Vol. 15 No. 1.219–244.

SILVER, M. (1983) Forecasting demand for labour using labour productivity trends, in J. EDWARDS *et al* (eds.) *Manpower planning: Strategy and techniques in an organisational context*. London: John Wiley.

SILVESTER, J. and BROWN, A. (1993) Graduate recruitment: Testing the impact. *Selection and Development Review*. Vol. 9, No. 1.

SIMMS, J. (2006) In their shoes. *People Management*. 20 April. 36–38.

SIMMS, J. (2006) Zoom at the top. *People Management Guide to Recruitment Consultancies*. April. 27–28.

SISSON, K. and STOREY, J. (2000) *The realities of human resource management: Managing the employment relationship*. Buckingham: The Open University Press.

SKEATS, J. (1991) *Successful induction: How to get the most from your new employees*. London: Kogan Page.

SKILL NEEDS IN BRITAIN (1993) London: IFF Research

SMEDLEY, T. (2007) Underneath the arches. *People Management*. 26 July. 28–31.

SMETHURST, S. (2004) Onto a winner. *People Management*. 29 January.

SMETHURST, S. (2004) The allure of online. *People Management*. 29 July.

SMETHURST, S. (2005) Faking it. *People Management*. 16 June. 35–36.

SMETHURST, S. (2005) Batteries recharged. *People Management*. 5 May. 24–27.

SMETHURST, S. (2006) The window test. *People Management*. 26 January. 28–30.

SMITH, K. (1996) Managing without traditional strategic planning: the evolving role of top management teams, in P. FLOOD *et al* (eds.) *Managing without Traditional Methods: International innovations in human resource management*. Wokingham: Addison Wesley.

SMITH, M., GREGG, M. and ANDREWS, D. (1989) *Selection and assessment: A new appraisal*. London: Pitman.

SMITH, M. and ROBERTSON, I. (1993) *The theory and practice of systematic personnel selection*. London: Macmillan.

SMITH, M. and SUTHERLAND, V. (1993) *Professional issues in selection and assessment. Vol. 1*. Chichester: John Wiley.

SPARROW, P. (1998) New organisational forms, processes, jobs and psychological contracts: Resolving the HRM issues, in P. SPARROW and M. MARCHINGTON (eds.) *Human resource management: The new agenda*. London: FT/Pitman.

SPARROW, P. and COOPER, C. (2003) *The employment relationship: Key challenges for HR*. London: Butterworth-Heinemann.

SPEECHLY, N. (1994) Uncertainty principles. *Personnel Today*. May.

STAINER, G. (1971) *Manpower planning*. London: Heinemann.

STEEN, M. (1999) Readers don't all agree with HR's suggestions for exit interview etiquette. *InfoWorld*. No. 21. 34.

STEERS, R. and MOWDAY, R. (1981) Employee turnover and post-decision accommodation processes, in L. CUMMINGS and B. STAW (eds.) *Research in organizational behavior*. Greenwich, Connecticut: JAI Press.

STEERS, R., SANCHEZ-RUNDE, C. and NARDON, L. (2010) *Management across cultures: Challenges and strategies*. Cambridge: Cambridge University Press.

STILES, P. (2007) A world of difference. *People Management*. 15 November. 36–40.

STOREY, J. (2001) Looking to the future, in J. STOREY (ed.) *Human resource management: A critical text*. Second edition. London: Thomson Learning.

STOREY, J. and QUINTAS, P. (2001) Knowledge management and HRM, in J. STOREY (ed.) *Human resource management: A critical text*. Second edition. London: Thomson Learning.

STRACHAN, A. (2004) Lights, camera, interaction. *People Management*. 16 September. 44–46.

STREDWICK, J. and ELLIS, S. (2005) *Flexible working*. London: CIPD.

STURGES, J. and GUEST, D. (2004) Working to live or living to work? Work life balance early in the career. *Human Resource Management Journal*. Vol. 14, No. 4. 5–20.

SUFF, R. (2004) A gem of a resourcing strategy. *IRS Employment Review*. No. 809.

SUFF, R. (2006) Building a McReputation to aid recruitment and retention. *IRS Employment Review*. No. 853. 42–44.

SUFF, R. (2008) Background checks in recruitment: Employers' current methods. *IRS Employment Review*. No. 896. April.

SUFF, R. (2009a) The impact of the recession on recruitment: The April 2009 IRS Survey. *IRS Employment Review*. No. 924. June.

SUFF, R. (2009b) Survey: Employers' use of employment agencies and recruitment agencies 2009. *IRS Employment Review*. 921. May.

SUFF, R. (2009c) Leading high performance at British American Tobacco. *IRS Employment Review*. No. 914.

SULLIVAN, J. (2004) Eight elements of a successful employment brand. *ER Daily*. 25 November.

SVENDSEN, L. (2008) *Work*. Stocksfield: Acumen Publishing.

SWART, J. (2007) HRM and knowledge workers, in P. BOXALL, J. PURCELL and P. WRIGHT (eds.) *The Oxford handbook of human resource management*. Oxford: Oxford University Press.

SYEDAIN, H. (2006) Gown and town. *People Management*, 23 March. 38–39.

SYEDAIN, H. (2007) A judicious review. *People Management*. 4 October. 37.

TAYLOR, R. (2002) Britain's world at work – Myths and realities. *ESRC Future of Work Programme Seminar Series*. Leeds University.

TAYLOR, R. (2004) Skills and innovation in modern workplaces. *ESRC Future of Work Programme Seminar Series*. Leeds University.

TAYLOR, S. (2002) *The employee retention handbook*. CIPD.

TAYLOR, S. (2009) Occupational pensions, in G. WHITE and J. DRUKER (eds.) *Reward management: A critical text*. London: Routledge.

TAYLOR, M.S. and COLLINS, C.J. (2000) Organizational recruitment: Enhancing the intersection of research and practice. In C. COOPER and E. LOCKE (eds.) *Industrial and Organizational Psychology*. Oxford: Blackwell.

TAYLOR, S. and EMIR, A. (2009) *Employment law: An introduction*. Second edition. Oxford: Oxford University Press

TAYLOR, S. and TEKLEAB, A. (2004) Taking stock of psychological contract research: assessing progress, addressing troublesome issues and setting research priorities, in J. COYLE-SHAPIRO, L. SHORE, S. TAYLOR and L. TETRICK (eds.) *The employment relationship: Examining psychological and contextual perspectives*. Oxford: Oxford University Press.

TON, Z. and HUCKMAN, R. (2008) Managing the impact of employee turnover on performance: The role of process conformance. *Organization Science*. Vol. 19, No. 1. 56–68.

TOPLIS, J., DULEWICZ, V. and FLETCHER, C. (2005) *Psychological testing: A manager's guide*. Fourth edition. London: CIPD.

TORRINGTON, D., HALL, L. and TAYLOR, S. (2008) Human resource management. Seventh edition. London: FT/Prentice Hall.

TORRINGTON, D., HALL, L., TAYLOR, S. and ATKINSON, C. (2009) *Fundamentals of human resource management: Managing people at work*. Harlow: FT/ Prentice Hall.

TRAPP, R. (2004) Older and wiser. *People Management*. 23 December.

TRAPP, R. (2004) A life's work. *People Management*. 6 May. 26–39.

TRIST, E.L. HIGGIN, G.W., MURRAY, H. and POLLOCK, A.B. (1963) *Organisational choice: Capabilities of groups at the coal face under changing technologies*. London: Tavistock.

TROMPENAARS, F. (1993) *Riding the waves of culture: Understanding cultural diversity in global business*. London: McGraw Hill.

TROMPENAARS, F. and WOOLLIAMS, P. (2002) Model behaviour. *People Management*. 5 December.

TULGAN, B. (2007) Drill inspection. *People Management*. 22 February. 44–45.

TWENGE, J.M. and CAMPBELL, S.M. (2008) Generational differences in psychological traits and their impact on the workplace. *Journal of Managerial Psychology*. Vol. 23, No. 8, 862–877.

UKCES (2010) *Skills for jobs: Today and tomorrow. The national strategic skills audit for England. Volume 1: Key findings*. London: UK Commission for Employment and Skills.

VICKERSTAFF, S., BALDCK, J., COX, J. and KEEN, L. (2004) *Happy retirement? The impact of employers' policies and practices on the process of retirement*. Bristol: Joseph Rowntree Foundation/Policy Press.

WADSWORTH, J. (1989) *Job tenure and inter-firm mobility*. Centre for Economic Performance, London School of Economics. Working Paper. No. 1187.

WALBY, S., ARMSTRONG, J. and HUMPHRIES, L. (2008) *Review of equality statistics*. Manchester: Equality and Human Rights Commission.

WALDON, C. (2002) Questions of trust. *People Management*. 7 March.

WALKER, J. (1992) *Human resource strategy*. New York: McGraw Hill.

WALKER, L. (1996) Instant staff for a temporary future. *People Management*. January.

WALKER, P. (2008) *Employer branding: A no-nonsense approach*. London: CIPD.

WANOUS, J.P. (1992) *Organizational entry*. Reading, Massachusetts: Addison Wesley.

WARD, K., GRIMSHAW, D., RUBERY, J. and BENYON, H. (2001) Dilemmas in the management of temporary work agency staff. *Human Resource Management Journal*. Vol. 11, No. 4. 3–21.

WATKINS, J. (2003) A mini adventure. *People Management*. 6 November.

WATSON, T. (1994) Recruitment and selection, in K. SISSON (ed.) *Personnel management: A comprehensive guide to theory and practice in Britain*. Second edition. Oxford: Blackwell.

WEISINGER, H. (1998) *Emotional Intelligence at work*. San Francisco: Jossey-Bass.

WHALLEY, L. and SMITH, M. (1998) *Deception in selection*. Chichester: Wiley.

WHIDETT, S. and KANDOLA, B. (2000) Fit for the job? *People Management*. 25 May.

WHITE, K. (2004) Year we go, year we go. *People Management*. 17 June.

WHITE, M., HILL, S., MILLS, C. and SMEATON, D. (2004) *Managing to change?: British workplaces and the future of work*. Basingstoke: Palgrave Macmillan.

WHITENACK, A. (2001) Brand marketing basics. www.experience.com.

WILDEN, R., GUDERGAN, S. and LINGS, I. (2004) *Employee-based brand equity*. Paper delivered at the SERVISG research conference in Singapore.

WILKINSON, K. (2004) *An investigation into nurse turnover and the validity of the exit interview questionnaire*. Unpublished MA Dissertation.

WILLEY, B. (2009) *Employment law in context*. Third edition. London: FT/Prentice Hall.

WILLIAMS, C. (2007) *Rethinking the future of work*. Basingstoke: Palgrave Macmillan.

WILLIAMS, H. (2002) Strategic planning for human resources, in J. LEOPOLD (ed.) *Human Resources in Organisations*. London: FT/Prentice Hall.

WILLIAMS, H. (2009) Survey: The trend towards web-based recruitment. *Personnel Today*. 9 June.

WILLIAMS, M. (2000) *The war for talent*. London: CIPD.

WILLIAMSON, P. (2006) Sphere of influence. *People Management*. 12 October. 32–34.

WILTON, N. (2006) Strategic choice and organisational context in HRM in the UK hotel sector. *The Service Industries Journal*. Vol. 28, No.8. 903–919.

WOLF, A. and JENKINS, A. (2006) Explaining greater test use for selection: the role of HR professionals in a world of expanding regulation. *Human Resource Management Journal*. Vol. 16, No. 2. 193–213.

WOLFF, C. (2009a) IRS flexible working survey 2009: Availability, take-up and impact. IRS *Employment Review*. No. 921. May.

WOLFF, C. (2009b) IRS flexible working survey 2009: Handling requests. *IRS Employment Review*. No. 921. May.

WOOLF, C. (2009c) Equality and diversity in the workplace: 2009 IRS survey. *IRS Employment Review*. No. 923. June.

WOLFF, C. (2009d) The use of buddy schemes in the induction of new recruits: the 2009 IRS survey. *IRS Employment Review*. No. 920. May.

WOLFF, C. (2009e) Employee induction: The 2009 IRS survey. *IRS Employment Review*. No. 918. March.

WOLFF, C. (2009f) KPMG avoids redundancies through flexible working. *IRS Employment Review*. No. 924. July.

WOOD, R. and PAYNE, T. (1998) *Competency based recruitment and selection*. Chichester: Wiley.

WOOD, S. and ALBANESE, M. (1995) Can we speak of high commitment management on the shop floor? *Journal of Management Studies*. Vol. 32, No. 2. 1–33.

WOODHAMS, C. and DANIELI, A. (2000) Disability and diversity: A difference too far? *Personnel Review*. Vol. 29, No. 3. 402–416.

WOODRUFFE, C. (1993) *Assessment centres: Identifying and developing competence*. Second edition. London: IPD.

WOODRUFFE, C. (1999) *Winning the talent war*. Chichester: Wiley.

WOODRUFFE, C. (2001) Promotional intelligence. *People Management*. 11 January.

WOODRUFFE, C. (2002) Intelligence test. *People Management*. 16 May.

YEW, J. (2005) *Dismissals: Law and practice*. London: The Law Society.

ZARANDONA, J.L. and CAMUSO, M.A. (1985) A study of exit interviews: Does the last word count? *Personnel*. Vol. 62, No. 3.

ZEMKE, R, RAINES, C. and FILIPCZAK, B. (2000) *Generations at Work*. New York: Amacom.

Cases cited

Birmingham City Council v Wetherill and others [2007] IRLR 781

Carmichael v National Power [1999] ICR 1226

Durrant v Financial Services Authority – cited in chapter 2

Grainger PLC and others v Nicholson – cited in chapter 4

Hussein v Saints Complete House Furnishers [1979] – cited in chapter 6

Iceland Foods v Jones [1983] – cited in chapter 17

James v Eastleigh Borough Council [1990] – cited in chapter 4

Mahmoud v Bank of Credit and Commerce International [1997] – cited in chapter 12

Murray v Foyle Meats [1999] – cited in chapter 18

Northern Joint Police Board v Power [1997] – cited in chapter 6

O'Kelly and others v Trusthouse Forte [1983] ICR 728

Polkey v Deyton Services Ltd [1987] – cited in chapter 17

Rolls Royce v Unite [2009] – cited in chapter 18

Whitbread v Hall [2001] – cited in chapter 17

Index